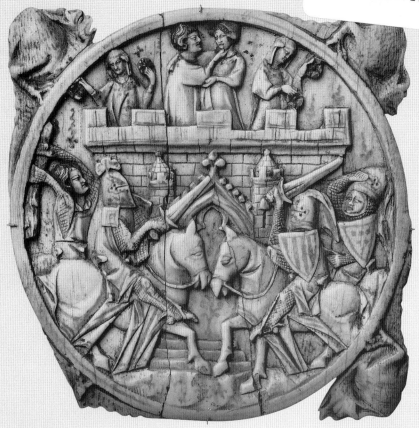

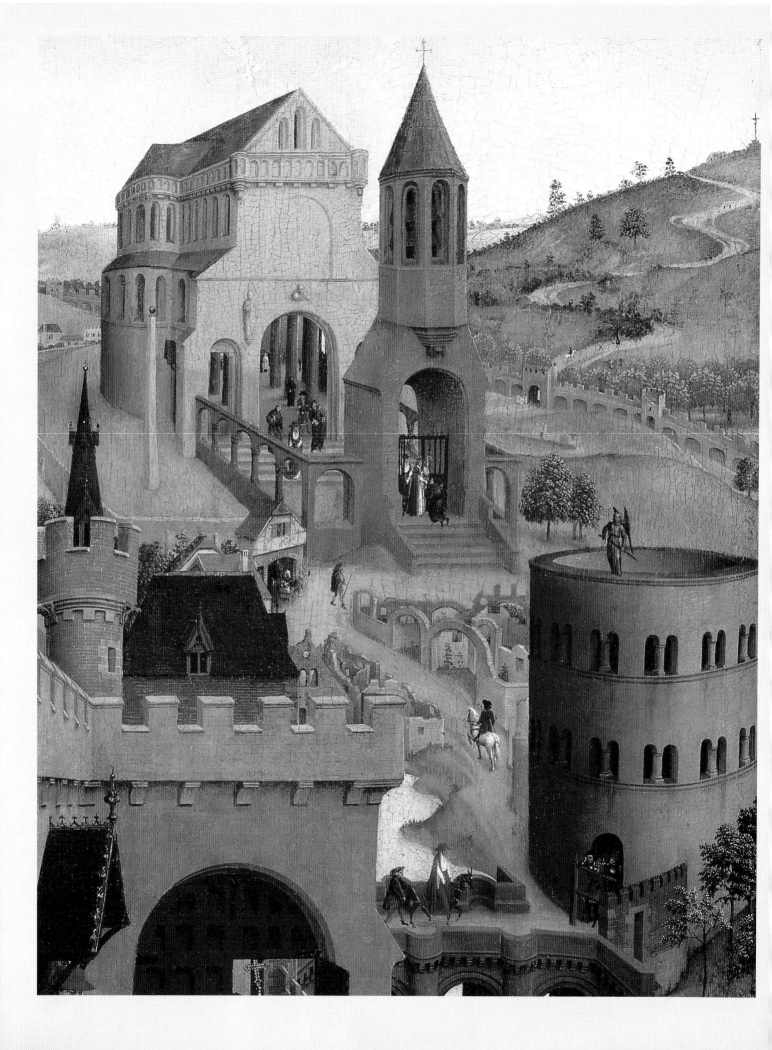

Edited by Robert Bartlett

THE
MEDIEVAL
WORLD
COMPLETE

with over 800 illustrations

Half title page: ivory mirror-back showing the Siege of the
Castle of Love. French, 14th century.

Frontispiece: detail from *The Dream of Pope Sergius*. Workshop
of Rogier van der Weyden, *c.* 1440.

First published in the United Kingdom in 2001 as *Medieval Panorama*
by Thames & Hudson Ltd, 181A High Holborn, London WC1V 7QX

First paperback edition published in 2010 as *The Medieval World Complete*

First published in the United States of America in 2001 in hardcover
as *Medieval Panorama* by Getty Publications.

Paperback edition first published in the United States of America in 2014
by Thames & Hudson Inc., 500 Fifth Avenue, New York, New York 10110

Reprinted 2022

Introduction and Chapter Introductions:
Text © 2001 Robert Bartlett
Biographical Dictionary: Julie Kerr
Texts on picture-spreads: Ian Sutton
Design: Ian Mackenzie-Kerr
Jacket design: Shalom Schotten
Picture Research: Georgina Bruckner
Maps: Draughtsman Maps
Editorial: Jenny Wilson
Editorial Assistant: Kate Lamb
Production: Sheila McKenzie

British Library Cataloguing-in-Publication Data
A catalogue record for this book is available from the British Library

Library of Congress Control Number 2014932782

ISBN 978-0-500-28333-2

Printed and bound in China by Everbest Printing Co. Ltd

Be the first to know about our new releases,
exclusive content and author events by visiting
thamesandhudson.com
thamesandhudsonusa.com
thamesandhudson.com.au

FSC
www.fsc.org
MIX
From responsible
sources
FSC® C124385

Contents

Introduction

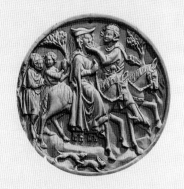

Perspectives on the Medieval World

Renaissance to Enlightenment · The Romantic Revolution
The Middle Ages and the Nation · The Controversial Middle Ages
The Twentieth Century

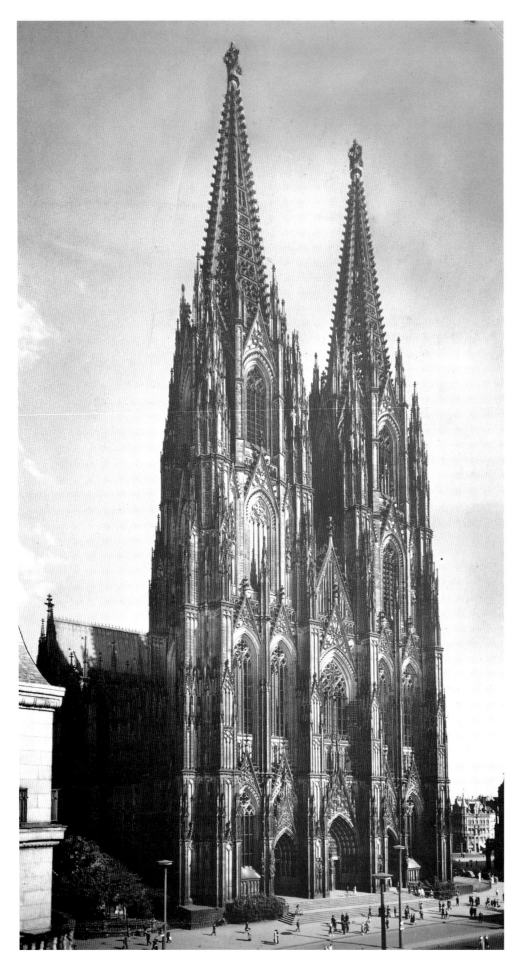

Cologne Cathedral was begun in 1248. By the end of the 13th century the choir had been built and one of the west towers begun. After that, for various reasons, work stopped and it remained a fragment for 500 years, while Gothic architecture sank lower and lower in esteem. But by the 1820s the Romantic movement had brought the Middle Ages back into favour, and for the first time there was the motivation to complete the building. By a happy chance the original drawings for the west front, of about 1300, survived and work started again in 1824. It was finally finished in 1880. Of what we see here, only the lowest storey of the right-hand tower is old; the rest is a 19th-century cathedral that is yet authentically medieval.

E VERY CENTURY creates its own Middle Ages. The Middle Ages of the eighteenth-century Enlightenment – brutal, superstitious, sordid – was utterly different from the Middle Ages of the Romantics – spiritual, chivalrous, beautiful. The Romantic Middle Ages has largely survived in the form of films like *El Cid*. Can we ever know the 'real' Middle Ages? In this book we present history through representations created by men and women of that time, and through pictures of the buildings and artefacts they produced. It is the visual equivalent of a collection of written sources, texts from the past expressing the thoughts and feeling of medieval people. Yet even this can never be wholly objective. Those medieval men and women themselves had their own picture of the world in which they lived, and this conditioned the way they represented it. The choice that scholars make today from that material is similarly conditioned by the picture that we intend to convey. This Introduction explores the different ways that the medieval period has been regarded and imagined over the years since the term was first used, and shows that our modern view of the Middle Ages is itself the product of many centuries of development and debate.

Renaissance to Enlightenment

Of course no one in the Middle Ages knew they were living in the Middle Ages. The term is a retrospective label, applied by subsequent generations who felt they had emerged from that 'middle' period to a new one. The condescending tag was first used by the humanist scholars of the Renaissance, who believed that they shared common cultural assumptions not with their medieval predecessors but with the educated patricians of ancient Rome. Hence their threefold periodization of history: the ancient world, the Middle Ages, themselves. It was not long before these humanists were using another self-congratulatory term for their own period: it was the age of 'rebirth' – Renaissance.

Originally the terms 'Middle Ages' and 'Renaissance', as used by these humanists, had a narrowly cultural meaning, referring to the absence or presence of pure classical Latin and Roman inspiration in the high culture of educated Western Europeans. Italian scholars of the fourteenth and fifteenth centuries focused more intensely than ever before upon the literature of pagan Rome and Greece, sought out lost texts, changed their handwriting to imitate what they thought was classical script, produced buildings, sculptures and paintings in a classical style. In doing so they also created the Middle Ages – everything that lay between the classicism of ancient Rome and that of their own day. In the formulation of such men as Leonardo Bruni, Chancellor of Florence (d. 1444), Latin literature reached perfection under Cicero, declined with the Roman Empire and the invasions of Goths and other barbarians, then made halting steps to recovery until the time of Petrarch (d. 1374), who 'restored to light the ancient elegance of style which was lost and dead'.

Naturally, a term that was invented as part of a conscious ideological campaign to foster one cultural style and decry another cannot be regarded as a neutral term of historical analysis. 'The Middle Ages' thus belongs to the group of historical labels like 'Dark Ages', 'Reformation' and 'Enlightenment' which were invented to express approval or disapproval rather than attempt description. One of the reasons the phrase 'Middle Ages' stuck was that the humanists did not

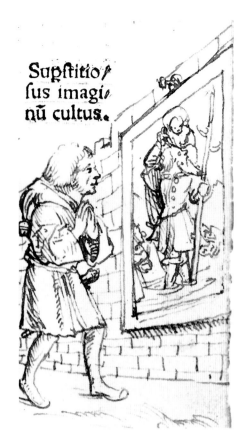

Supstitio∫
∫us imagi∕
nũ cultus.

Erasmus remained faithful to the Catholic Church but ridiculed its superstitions. One of Holbein's drawings in the margin of his 'Praise of Folly' shows a fool praying before an image of St Christopher.

fade away as a passing cultural fad of the fourteenth and fifteenth centuries but managed to capture the central institutions of higher education and make their programme the core of elite culture down to the twentieth century – hence its strong classical bias. Educated Europeans of 1900 knew about Plato and Cicero and might even have been forced to imitate their style; only a minority of them (and those usually of one denominational tradition) had encountered Abelard or Aquinas. The ancient Greeks and Romans were more like 'us' – the moderns – than were the oddities of the medieval period. At the heart of the idea of 'the Middle Ages' is 'the Other'.

The picture that the Renaissance humanists created of their medieval predecessors – men enmired in crude Latin and logic-chopping – was both reinforced and redrawn by the Protestant reformers who came fast upon their heels. Protestants agreed with humanists that there had been a golden age, although for them it was the time of the primitive Church rather than the heyday of classical Latin literature, and they also saw the thousand years before their own time as a trough or depression from which they wished to climb. For them, however, it was the tyranny of popes, bishops and monks that they aimed to end, along with their 'superstitions' – reverence for saints and relics, belief in Purgatory, prayers for the dead, the paraphernalia of a celibate priestcraft. The medieval period was regarded not only as an age of barbarous Latin and clumsy art but also as a time of papistry and credulous beliefs.

After the Reformation a third of Europe was divorced from its Catholic past. Travellers from England, Holland, Scandinavia and the other Protestant countries, coming to the Catholic south, entered a world which still seemed bogged down in the superstitious practices of the papistical yesterday, which Protestants found repulsive or puerile. 'I could not contain myself from laughing,' wrote the Scottish Presbyterian, Lord Fountainhall, observing the reverence displayed to the relics of Saints Benedict and Martin at the French monastery of Marmoutier in the middle of the seventeenth century. For Protestants the world of proud prelates, celibate and scheming priests and monks and silly devotions had both a geographical and a chronological location, in the Catholic parts of Europe and in the medieval past. One of the very first uses of the term 'Middle Ages' in English is in an anti-Catholic allusion by John Selden, which dates to 1618, referring to the medieval biographies of the popes. He asserted that 'those kinds of acts and legends of popes and others are indeed usually stuffed with falsehoods, as being bred in the Middle Ages among idle monks'.

An indication of the way Protestantism shaped views of the medieval past is provided by the Tudor dramas on the subject of King John of England (1199–1216). At the present day the most common popular image of John is of a tyrant who was forced to grant the important constitutional liberties expressed in Magna Carta. Priorities among sixteenth-century English Protestants were different. It was the King's opposition to papal authority that caught their interest. John Bale, author of the innovative historical drama *King Johan* in the 1530s – the decade of the English Reformation – presents the medieval monarch as 'a faithful Moses' who 'withstood proud Pharaoh [the pope] for his poor Israel'. Bale blends monarchism and anti-papalism: '... give to your king his due supremacy/And exile the pope this land for evermore'. Bale, who had been a Carmelite friar before becoming a radical Protestant, thus picked his way through the Middle Ages guided by the simple twin yardsticks of nationalism and anti-

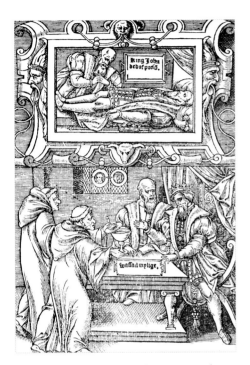

King John's dispute with the papacy made him a proto-Protestant in the eyes of 16th-century reformers. Foxe's 'Book of Martyrs' retells the story that he was poisoned by a monk.

Catholicism. His example was followed later in the century, in the anonymous *Troublesome Reign of John, King of England* (1591), which likewise presents a heroic picture of the King: 'For Christ's true faith endured he many a storm/And set himself against the Man of Rome.' A few years later this mixture of xenophobia, anti-papalism and English pride found its most effective voice in Shakespeare's *King John*: 'Tell him this tale; and from the mouth of England/Add this much more, that no Italian priest/Shall tithe or toll in our dominions.'

During the years 1500 to 1800 the Middle Ages were thus usually viewed negatively, either because they failed to meet humanist and classicist standards and hence were barbaric or because they were an abomination in Protestant judgment, or, of course, on both grounds. A case in point is the poet John Milton, who not only contrasted 'the old and elegant humanity of Greece' with the 'barbaric pride of a Hunnish and Norwegian stateliness [i.e. arrogance]' but also railed against the usurpation of political power by popes and bishops in the centuries after 'Constantine's lavish superstition', when Church and State first became entwined. He both rejoiced that 'we are not yet Goths and Jutlanders' and deplored the medieval intrusion of bishops into political affairs, as in John's reign, because it undermined the nation and monarchy.

There were some exceptions to this generally hostile and dismissive attitude. The scholars who first worked out the theory of feudalism, for instance, thought that this system, which was in their view characteristic of the Middle Ages, had good as well as bad points. The French legal theorist François Hotman, a Protestant who published his main work, the *Francogallia*, in 1573, and his followers like the Scot Thomas Craig and the Englishman Henry Spelman, whose works appeared in the following century, developed the analysis of feudal law to such a point that the contours can already be seen of the idea, which was to come to full growth in the Enlightenment, that 'feudalism' was a stage of society. Stemming from the irruption of the Germanic tribes ('Goths') into the Roman Empire and elaborated in the barbarian kingdoms of the West, feudalism could be seen as a natural growth, a form of society adapted to its time, with the advantage that liberty and property were widely diffused. Following in this path, eighteenth-century French theorists like Boulainvilliers and Montesquieu saw the medieval period as a time of 'feudal government' or 'Gothic government', when a Germanic nobility with great local power counterbalanced any tendency towards royal absolutism. The Middle Ages could thus be pictured not as a time of cultural backwardness or priestly dominance but of Germanic freedom, even if only for the few.

A yet more positive appreciation of the medieval past was attained by the scholars who undertook serious research into the period. It is not simply that there continued to be an interest in the epoch, inspired by national or denominational loyalties, but that entirely new historical methods were devised in order to investigate the Middle Ages. Two great landmarks are the *Glossary to the Writers of Middle Latin* of Charles Du Fresne Ducange and the treatise on 'diplomatic' by the Benedictine Jean Mabillon, both published in France within a few years of each other (1678, 1681). Ducange, who was a lawyer, a bureaucrat and the father of ten children as well as a pioneer of historical and philological scholarship, recognized not only that the Latin of the Middle Ages was different from that of the ancient Romans but also that the new terms developed in the

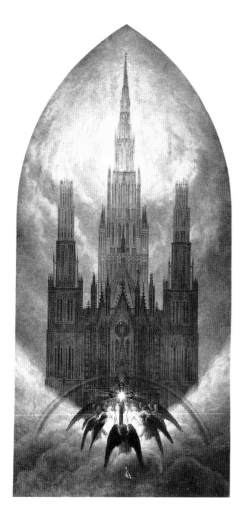

Romanticism made the Middle Ages into an ideal of beauty and sublime poetry. In Caspar David Friedrich's painting 'The Cathedral' a fantasized Gothic cathedral is literally lifted out of this world by angels.

medieval period could form an important gateway to understanding the customs and everyday social life of the period. Hence the entries in his glossary for such terms as 'fief' or 'trial by ordeal' are actually essays on distinctive institutions or practices of the Middle Ages. Mabillon likewise analyzed the linguistic and shed light on the historical reality. The science of 'diplomatic', of which he was in essence the founder, makes it possible to distinguish genuine and forged documents and to date writings by their formal features. All documents give some intrinsic signs of their origin. For example, if we know, as we do, that Henry II of England (1154–89) used the title 'king *by grace of God*' only after 1171, then we can date his documents accordingly and look with suspicion on any that seem to be earlier but use that title. Mabillon established the value of criteria of this type.

Interest in the Middle Ages, scholarly work upon the period and sometimes sympathy for some aspects of it could thus be found in the seventeenth and eighteenth centuries. This all remained a subordinate strand, however. More common was lack of interest or contempt. The Middle Ages lay in shadow on the far side of a fissure created by Renaissance art and letters or religious reformation or new inventions, such as printing and gunpowder, or the discovery of the New World. Disdain about the medieval past was especially forthright amongst the critical and rationalist thinkers of the Enlightenment. For them the Middle Ages epitomized the barbaric, priest-ridden, hierarchical world that they were attempting to transform. They referred to 'these dark times', 'the centuries of ignorance', 'the uncouth centuries'.

Voltaire, the most famous of the French rationalist philosophers of the eighteenth century, was a characteristically outspoken proponent of such views. His *Essay on the Customs and Spirit of Nations*, first published in the 1750s, dedicates over a hundred chapters to the medieval period. Its failure, in Voltaire's view, was partly political. It was an age of ferocity and anarchy when Europe 'was divided among a countless number of petty tyrants'. The centuries after the collapse of the Carolingian Empire were an especially dire epoch of 'confusion, tyranny, barbarism and poverty'. 'Picture to yourself a wilderness,' he wrote, 'where wolves, tigers and foxes slaughter straggling timid cattle – that is the portrait of Europe over the course of many centuries.' For Voltaire 'feudal government' had no redeeming features, being simply a recipe for civil war.

The brutal anarchy of the Middle Ages was linked with its ignorance and the foolishness of its beliefs. Early medieval law was 'the jurisprudence of ferocity and superstition'. When one considered the 'ridiculous customs' found in the religion of the medieval West, 'one would believe one was looking at a portrait of Negroes and Hottentots'. Even the sophisticated thinking of the later medieval scholastics produced merely 'systems of absurdity'. Ignorance and superstition were not attacked but fostered by the Catholic Church: 'in all the disputes which have incited Christians against each other since the birth of the Church, Rome has always come down in favour of the opinion that subjected the human spirit most fully and crushed reason most completely'.

The Crusades epitomized both the fanaticism and the savagery of the time. Voltaire attempted a balance sheet of the vast losses of men and money that these wars represented. St Louis (Louis IX, d. 1270), for whom the French philosopher had some respect, had been blinded and led astray by the crusading urge. An especially severe judgment was reserved for the Fourth Crusade, when Westerners had attacked not Muslims but the Greek Christians of Byzantium:

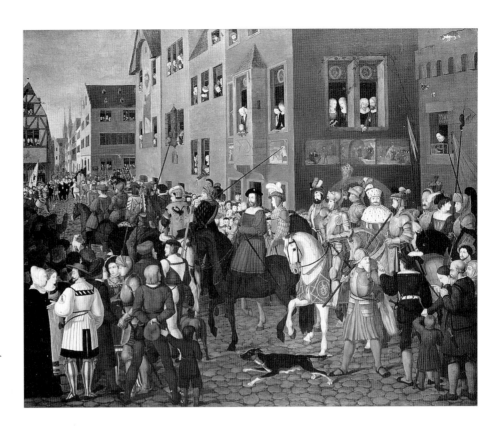

Franz Pforr: 'The Entry of Emperor Rudolf of Habsburg into Basle in 1273', 1808–10. This not only represents a medieval event but is painted in a (much later) medieval style.

'the only fruit of the Christians in their barbarous crusades was to exterminate other Christians'. Again the lack of discipline consequent upon 'feudal government' was invoked, to account for the crusaders' failures: 'leaders without experience or skill led disorderly multitudes into unknown countries'.

The Romantic Revolution

Remarkably, this crescendo of denunciation of 'those uncouth times that one calls the Middle Ages', as Voltaire put it, was soon to be followed by a revolutionary change in attitudes to the medieval past – a change to which we are the heirs. The term 'Middle Ages' may have been invented by the Renaissance humanists but the image of the medieval world we have today is a creation of the Romantics of the late eighteenth and nineteenth centuries. The Romantic movement was indeed defined by one of its participants, the poet Heinrich Heine, as 'nothing but the reawakening of the poetry of the Middle Ages, as it manifested itself in songs, pictures and works of art, in art and life'. In contrast to the formalism, classicism and rationalism associated with the eighteenth century, the Romantics stressed emotion and mystery, local colour and popular speech, the simple and the natural. Whether they were right to link these things with the Middle Ages or not, they did so, and, in doing so, gave birth to the image of the age that still predominates.

The Romantics not only studied the Middle Ages but also sought to recreate it, in literature, art and architecture. They took up medieval themes and topics and revived medieval forms. Painters like the German Nazarenes (1809) or the English Pre-Raphaelites (1848) looked for inspiration beyond the great masters of the High Renaissance, with their rich colour, heightened light-and-shade and often stormy drama, to the luminescence and clarity of the painters of the fourteenth and fifteenth centuries. The Nazarenes even decamped to Rome, there living in a quasi-monastic community and creating religious and historical paintings, including some in the fresco technique of the late medieval Italian artists they so admired. A composition by one of the

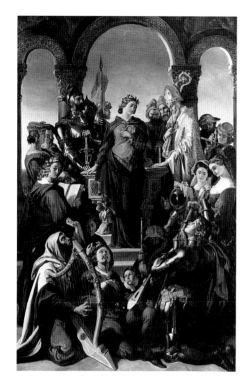

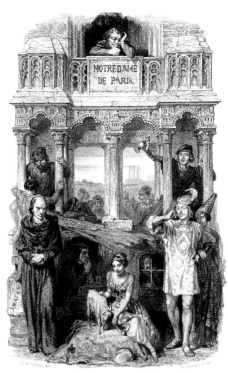

The Romantic Middle Ages in art and literature. Far left: Daniel Maclise's highly self-conscious 'Spirit of Chivalry' of 1845 – poetry, music, religion and knighthood unite in the veneration of woman. Left: frontispiece of Victor Hugo's 'Notre-Dame de Paris', first published in 1831, a darker but hardly more realistic side of medieval life.

Nazarenes, Franz Pforr, of *The Entry of Emperor Rudolf of Habsburg into Basle in 1273* exemplifies the large-scale historical painting that was to be one of the main means of transmitting the romantic image of the medieval period.

Equally significant in forming the modern picture of the Middle Ages was the historical novel, a genre virtually invented by the Romantics. Its pre-eminent practitioner, Sir Walter Scott, established the tone for all subsequent fiction set in the medieval period in novels such as *Ivanhoe* (1819) and *Quentin Durward* (1823). It was a world where knights, some loyal, others treacherous, and fair maidens undertook bold action in archaic language. The setting was as vivid as possible, the moral dilemmas often acute and an attempt was made to give the characters comprehensible, if often extreme, motives and emotions. Scott could be critical of feudal tyranny and the contradictions of chivalry but also allowed a certain idealization of the medieval code. In the opening remarks prefaced to *Quentin Durward*, he writes:

> The scene of this romance is laid in the fifteenth century, when the feudal system, which had been the sinews and nerves of national defence, and the spirit of chivalry, by which, as by a vivifying soul, that system was animated, began to be innovated upon and abandoned by those grosser characters, who centred their sum of happiness in procuring the personal objects on which they had fixed their own exclusive attachment.

Modern egotism thus replaced medieval chivalry.

Scott's powerful picture of the Middle Ages generated a fashion, indeed a craze. *Ivanhoe* was an immediate best seller and was frequently adapted for the stage, on one occasion four different versions running simultaneously in London theatres. Nine operas were based on the novel, from that of 1826, with music by Rossini, to the 1891 *Ivanhoe* of Arthur Sullivan (of Gilbert and Sullivan). Scenes from the book were amongst the most popular subjects of Victorian narrative painting, including a fresco in the rebuilt House of Lords of *The Spirit of Chivalry* by Daniel Maclise, a friend of Dickens and Disraeli, and painter of historical and

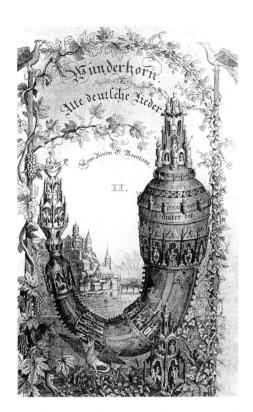

'Des Knaben Wunderhorn' ('The Boy's Magic Horn'), published in 1808, was a collection of old German ballads and folk poems collected by Achim von Arnim and Clemens Brentano.

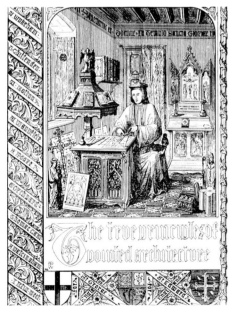

Pugin's 'True Principles of Pointed Architecture' (1841) was a passionate plea for a return to medieval values, religious, social and artistic.

Arthurian scenes. Nor was Scott's influence limited to Britain. His novels were influential both on the European continent and amongst English speakers worldwide. Victor Hugo, whose *Notre-Dame de Paris* of 1831 is set in the same historical time and place as Scott's *Quentin Durward* (the France of Louis XI), recognized his debt to the Scottish novelist.

Scott was not only the great shaper of the historical novel but also a champion of the study and imitation of ancient ballad form. This was another concern of the Romantic movement, with its interest in the folkloric and the popular, and was taken to be a direct link with the medieval past. Thomas Percy's *Reliques of Ancient English Poetry* (1765) had made a large body of historical and romantic ballads available to the reading public and poets such as Wordsworth, Coleridge and Scott emulated their form and subject matter. At the same period the German poets Achim von Arnim and Clemens Brentano collected folk poetry for publication in *Des Knaben Wunderhorn* (*The Boy's Magic Horn*), 1806–08. A few years later came the prose equivalent, the *Children's and Household Tales* of the Brothers Grimm. The work of these two German polymaths shows how closely linked were interest in the medieval period, in the culture and spirit of the people and in language. Apart from their famous collection of folktales, they published studies and editions of Germanic epics, works on ancient Germanic law and mythology, and they initiated the mammoth German dictionary that was only finally completed in 1960.

The most obvious witness to the impact of the Romantic medieval revival is the vast amount of pseudo-medieval architecture built in the nineteenth and twentieth centuries, beginning with the so-called Gothic Revival. From the Renaissance to the age of the Romantics the word 'Gothic' had been used to indicate the barbarity of the Middle Ages. The Goths had sacked Rome in 410 and served as a symbol of everything non-Roman, non-classical, coarse and ignorant. The script of medieval manuscripts was 'Gothic', the architecture and sculpture 'Gothic', and even, as we have seen, the organization of medieval society 'Gothic government'. The seventeenth-century dramatist Molière wrote of 'the insipid tastelessness of Gothic ornamentation', which was a product of 'ignorant centuries', while his contemporary, the architect Christopher Wren, wished to rebuild St Paul's Cathedral in London 'after a good Roman manner' rather than according to 'the Gothic rudeness of the old design'. 'Gothic architecture' was thus the coarse and tasteless architecture of the Gothic age.

The word 'Gothic' was reclaimed in the Romantic period just as the Middle Ages were revindicated. It ceased to be a general label meaning 'barbarous and medieval'. Gradually a distinction was drawn between the round arch style of the earlier Middle Ages (eventually christened Romanesque) and the pointed arch Gothic (in a narrower sense) that arose in the twelfth century. Early in the nineteenth century studies appeared in which Gothic architecture or 'the pointed arch style' was discussed objectively and even with appreciation. 'Gothic architecture has beauties of its own,' wrote the French nobleman-scholar Alexandre de Laborde in 1816. Engravings of medieval ecclesiastical buildings became popular, while appreciations and studies of the great cathedrals were published. The completion of Cologne Cathedral in the Gothic style (discussed in Chapter 4 of this book) marked a new stage in bringing the medieval into the modern world.

One of the chief figures of the Gothic revival was A. W. N. Pugin, whose manifestoes, such as *The True Principles of Pointed Architecture* of 1841, boldly

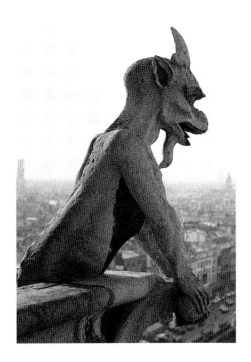

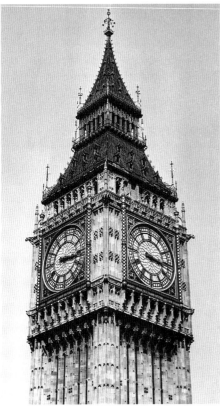

asserted the superiority of the Gothic style and its essentially Christian nature. 'The pointed arch was produced by the Catholic faith,' he claimed. Although he died young, Pugin's astonishing energy enabled him to produce numerous important neo-Gothic buildings, such as the Catholic cathedrals at Birmingham and Southwark, the chapel at Alton Towers and churches throughout the British Isles. He was entrusted by Charles Barry with the decoration and ornamentation of the new British Houses of Parliament constructed in the 1840s and hence was able to leave a conspicuous monument of Victorian Gothic in the heart of imperial London.

At the same time that Pugin was working on this landmark, the French architectural restorer Viollet-le-Duc (1814–79) was preparing to begin one of the most dramatic examples of historical reconstruction of a medieval site: the walled city of Carcassonne. Its twin circuits of walls, bristling with crenellations, its circular towers capped with conical slate roofs, its heavily fortified gates, all convey the most immediate and arresting image of the archetypal medieval city. The nineteenth century created the Middle Ages not only in the mind but often also in material reality. Viollet-le-Duc's restorations, which included Notre-Dame and the Sainte Chapelle in Paris as well as Carcassonne, epitomize the often controversial rebuilding that produced many of the 'medieval' edifices we see today.

By the middle of the nineteenth century, the medieval revival had fundamentally refashioned European art, literature and architecture. To interpret a movement as diverse and fundamental as this is not easy, but it is possible to make some sense of it by placing it in its wider historical context. The Romantic revolution in sensibility and culture, which included as a vital element this new evaluation of the Middle Ages, coincided with two other revolutions, political and economic. In 1789 the French Revolution began a period of radical political change in which 'liberty, equality, fraternity' were watchwords. In a slower rhythm, but yet more irresistibly, the very shape of the Western economy and society was transformed by industrialization.

It might seem at first sight that Romantic medievalism and democratic revolution were opposites. The revolutionaries certainly thought the bad old regime was a feudal regime. In 1789 the French National Assembly decreed the 'abolition of the feudal system' and even the Napoleonic constitution of 1802 was avowedly against 'any undertaking that tends to re-establish the feudal regime'. It is certainly the case that some of the pioneer champions of chivalric values and Gothic style, like Chateaubriand, were victims of the Revolution and supporters of the restored Bourbon monarchy. This is far from the whole story, however. When Romantics idealized the popular, they were often thinking of language – 'the language of conversation in the middle and lower classes of society', as Wordsworth put it – but they might also attribute to 'the People' qualities and virtues that could lead to avowedly democratic political beliefs. This liberal and radical strand in Romanticism produced its own Middle Ages, as we shall see.

If it is the case that Romanticism created the Middle Ages, it is also probable that the Industrial Revolution generated Romanticism. Industrialization was one of the deepest breaks with the past that Europeans had ever encountered, representing a far more profound rupture than even the most important political changes, such as the fall of the Roman Empire, or religious changes, such as the Reformation. Every aspect of life was affected. Human productivity was revolutionized, human demography assumed unprecedented shapes and the

Nineteenth-century architects worked in a medieval idiom but produced works that are clearly of their own time. Above: Viollet-le-Duc's re-creation of a Gothic gargoyle on one of the towers of Notre-Dame, Paris. Below: Barry and Pugin's fantasy of a medieval clock tower, had such a thing existed: Big Ben on the Houses of Parliament.

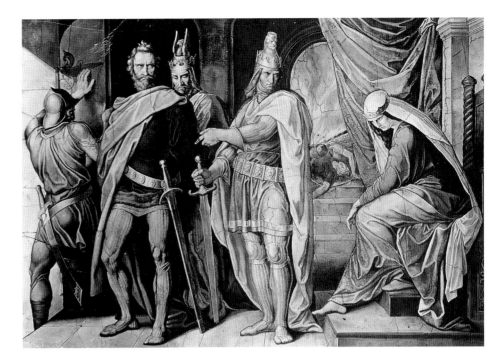

Romanticism was part of the search for national identity, and thus encouraged interest in ancient myths and sagas. For the Munich Residenz, Ludwig Schnorr von Carolsfeld went to the German national epic, the 'Nibelungenlied'. Here Siegfried's murderer Hagen is led away captive in the presence of Krimhilde.

scale, speed and scope of human activity were transformed. Reflective men and women were aware of this and looked back on the world they had left with a variety of responses: some were triumphant at leaving that world, others wistful or frightened. Whatever had been the strength of the Enlightenment sense of distance from medieval barbarity, members of industrial societies had to have a most profound feeling of the distance and difference of the pre-industrial past. This past was Europe's Middle Ages, together with the uncertain appendage of the sixteenth and seventeenth centuries (where many Romantic historical novels were in fact set). The periodization that had been defined in cultural and religious terms by the humanists and reformers of the fifteenth and sixteenth centuries was now deeply reinforced by the great transformation that created industrial society. The medieval was on the far side of a barrier in time.

The Middle Ages and the Nation

While Romanticism was a Europe-wide movement, it was also intensely nationalist. The search for the popular was always the search for one's own people. The theorist Johann Gottfried von Herder, who was important in the evolution of the Romantic movement, had posited the existence of nations, defined as communities of common language, each with its own spirit. The early and popular songs and poetry of a nation expressed and indeed might be said to have created the national spirit. Herder's ideas, and his interest in collecting old poetry and folktales, became central parts of Romantic historicism. The major French historian of this school, Jules Michelet (1798–1874), asserted that 'the history of France begins with the French language. Language is the principal sign of a nationality' and claimed that traditional tales, such as those of the Swiss hero William Tell, 'are the true national history of a people, such as its genius had led it to conceive'.

A new appreciation of medieval vernacular literature was one consequence of this stress on the nation's linguistic treasures. In France the pioneering work of the eighteenth-century scholar Jean-Baptiste de la Curne de Sainte-Palaye, who had worked on editing 'our ancient French authors', was continued by the Romantics, who turned to medieval literature in pursuit of the voice of the

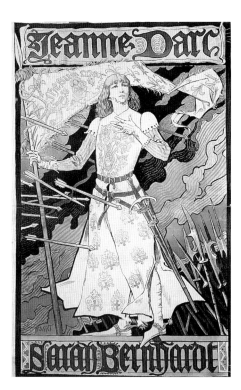

Every nation chose its heroes and heroines from the Middle Ages. Joan of Arc became identified with the glory of France. On a theatre poster of 1894, and in the person of Sarah Bernhardt, she withstands a lethal shower of cross-bow bolts and pikes.

people and the nation. A large selection of troubadour poetry was published by the scholar François-Juste-Marie Raynouard between 1816 and 1821, just as Scott's historical novels were coming into fashion, and the first edition of the Old French epic *The Song of Roland* appeared in 1837. In the same period the scholars of other nations turned their attention to their own 'national epics'. The first edition of *Beowulf* appeared in 1815, while the German Romantics were fascinated by the medieval German epic, the *Nibelungenlied,* hailing it as 'the German *Iliad*' and 'the foundation of our poetry'. During the so-called 'War of Liberation' against Napoleon, a pocket-sized translation into modern German was published for the use of German soldiers on campaign.

Nationalist fervour could be a genuine spur to learning. One of the great achievements of nineteenth-century Romantic and nationalist scholarship was the project of editing texts: the very words of those who lived in the Middle Ages were now to be available in all major libraries and were henceforth to be the foundation on which the picture of the past was to be based. The great prototype of such national collections of printed texts was the Monumenta Germaniae Historica, founded in 1819 in the aftermath of the Napoleonic wars, with the motto 'Holy love of the fatherland gives spirit'. The Society for the History of France began publishing sources for French history in 1835 and much of its work concerned the Middle Ages. Later in the century knowledge of medieval vernacular literature was extended by the publications of such organizations as The Early English Text Society, created by the Romantic progressive F. J. Furnivall in 1864, or the Society for Ancient French Texts, which began publishing in 1875.

While these projects established new standards of scholarship, they were not without a political edge. The French were particularly irked by the German supremacy in linguistic and philological studies, even including the study of medieval French. Launching a new French journal devoted to the study of the Romance languages and literatures in the year after the defeat of France by the Germans in 1870–71, the editors explained that they had taken the decision to launch the new periodical because 'it seemed to us that the centre of Romance studies ought to be in France rather than Germany'. Writers on Gothic architecture were equally embroiled with nationalist partiality. In the first half of the nineteenth century Germans, French and English all claimed it for their own, the English boldly coining the term 'Early English' for the first century of Gothic architecture in their country. In his preface to the 1832 edition of *Notre-Dame de Paris*, Victor Hugo appealed, 'Let us inspire in the nation, if it is possible, love for the national architecture.'

An extraordinary instance of nineteenth-century nationalist medievalism is the lecture delivered by the literary scholar Gaston Paris to the Collège de France in December 1870. At that time the French capital was surrounded by German armies and in the third month of a desperate siege. Gaston Paris' topic was '*The Song of Roland* and French Nationality'. He did not fail to mention 'the ring of steel that the armies of Germany place around us' and noted that many of his listeners from earlier years might now well be found among the enemy. He explicitly decried mixing patriotism and scholarship but the heroine of his talk was France. *The Song of Roland* dated to a time (around 1100) when France 'became fully conscious of herself'. National life and national consciousness sprang from an organically connected community and expressed themselves in love: 'a nation does not really exist except when she loves and is loved'. Literature is the expression, even the creator, of national life. *The Song of Roland* belongs to the epoch when the French nation blossomed under feudalism and expressed its two great traits: unity and expansionism. 'Yes, gentlemen,' proclaimed Gaston Paris, 'eight centuries ago, when no other nation in Europe had become truly conscious of itself, when many of them, such as England, still awaited the basic elements for their formation, the French fatherland was founded: national sentiment existed in its most intimate, noble and tender form.'

Here, in an extreme form and in time of crisis, the post-Romantic nationalist use of the Middle Ages is fully expressed. By this period, the later nineteenth century, it could be found everywhere. Pseudo-medieval political rituals and symbols were the routine stock of the monarchical states of the time. The Prussian kings and German emperors played on the image of the Teutonic Knights as military champions of Western civilization, dressing up in medieval costumes and rebuilding the great medieval castle of the Order at Marienburg. Mad King Ludwig II of Bavaria, who reigned from 1864 to 1886, wanted his fairy-tale castle of Neuschwanstein built 'in the genuine style of the old German knights' castles'. He created a dream-like *château* that was to shape the perception of generations and to serve as a model for Walt Disney. The king had it decorated with paintings of scenes from Wagner's operas, another major force in the dissemination of a popular image of the medieval period. In Victorian Britain the iconography of a chivalric past – partly English and partly Arthurian, with a dash of Scotch – gave a distinctive flavour to court-life and aristocratic culture. At Windsor and Balmoral medieval survival and medieval revival rubbed shoulders.

Some nineteenth-century nationalist historians could look back with complacency on the medieval origins of their own nation-states. The English had an unparalleled vision of continuity from Anglo-Saxon gatherings of wise men under kings like Alfred, with good legislative and nautical credentials, through the parliaments of Simon de Montfort and Edward I, down to the British constitution of their own day. In the first volume of his *Constitutional History of England*, Bishop Stubbs, the giant among Victorian medievalists, 'traced the process of events by which the English nation reached that point of

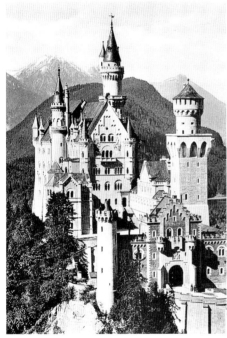

King Ludwig II of Bavaria's infatuation with the Middle Ages led him to subsidize the operas of Richard Wagner and to build his fantasy castle of Neuschwanstein (1868) – in fact a highly imaginative exercise in Neo-Romanesque that still haunts stage-designers and film-makers.

Art and politics merge in the murals painted by Herman Wislicenus in the restored palace of Goslar, giving historical precedent for the German Empire after 1871. This is the return of Henry III in 1047.

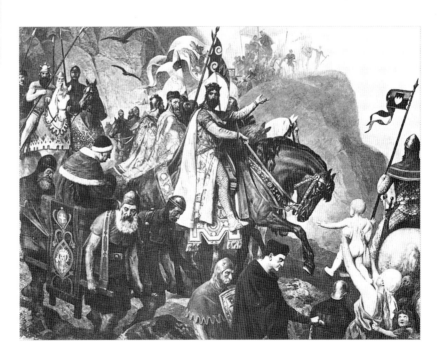

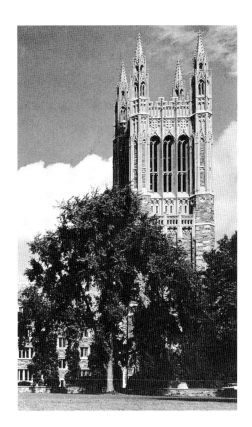

In the USA English Gothic was considered especially suitable for churches and universities. Ralph Adams Cram's Graduate College at Princeton would not be out of place at Oxford.

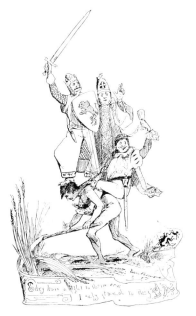

Mark Twain took a less romantic view of the Middle Ages. In 'A Connecticut Yankee in King Arthur's Court' he satirizes knight, bishop and jester all riding on the back of the peasant.

conscious unity and identity which made it necessary for it to act as a self-governing and political body'. The point was Magna Carta of 1215 and thereafter 'the continuity of life and the continuity of national purpose never fails'.

Other states had other pasts and sometimes an effort was needed to construct the unity, identity and continuity that Stubbs (and Gaston Paris) took as characteristic of the national story. The cycle of wall paintings in the restored medieval imperial palace at Goslar by Herman Wislicenus, painted in the period after the proclamation of the German Empire in 1871, claims implicitly that the new *Reich* is the heir to the old – that of Barbarossa and Charlemagne. A 'German' Charlemagne could be invoked against a 'French' Charlemagne, for both nations were eager to claim this brutal and self-righteous Frankish war-leader as their own (he has now been chosen as a symbolic figure for the present-day European Union). The Frankish period has always presented French and German historians with problems of identity, since the Frankish realms covered large parts of modern France and Germany but cannot be simply equated with either. Even in the 1990s an American book on the early Frankish Empire, which originally bore the title *Before France and Germany*, appeared in French translation as *The Birth of France*!

All the European nations of the nineteenth and twentieth centuries sought national origins in the medieval period. For nationalists it is axiomatic that nations are ancient primordial units. Ideally they should have states equally old and hence the appearance of books with titles such as *The German State of the Middle Ages* by the Prussian conservative Georg von Below, published in the year that the First World War began, or the boldly tendentious work by Alice Stopford Green, *The Irish State to 1014*, published in 1925 in the aftermath of the end of British rule in most of Ireland. Professional historians have debated the degree to which anything like national consciousness can be discerned in the medieval period, but popular imagination is less fastidious and often finds in the struggles of the past the mirror of national conflicts of today.

The medieval world came to form an element of national culture in a host of different ways. One of the more unusual stories is that of the USA, which had no Middle Ages of its own and hence a less pressing need for a medieval genealogy. Here the emblems and language of the state were classical, the Enlightenment heritage was strong and Romanticism was late and weak. Mark Twain's *A Connecticut Yankee in King Arthur's Court* (1889) crudely parodied the aristocratic vices, clerical domination and technical backwardness of the Middle Ages. Yet gradually a sympathetic and informed picture of the period emerged, at first among a Europhile patrician elite. Henry Adams' *Mont-Saint-Michel and Chartres* (1904) is a remarkable instance of a learned yet entertaining stroll through the culture of high medieval France, with diagrams from Viollet-le-Duc, imaginary conversations with Abelard and snippets from both the Latin and vernacular literature. In the 1913 reissue the enthusiastic editor declared that Adams' book was 'a revelation of that greatest epoch of Christian civilization'. He expressed his admiration for the way it captured the 'unity and dynamic force' of that 'rounded and complete civilization' with its 'youthful ardour and abounding action, its childlike simplicity and frankness'. He looked forward to the 'prospect of another thirteenth century in the times that are to come'.

One way in which that improbable aspiration was realized was in college architecture, for, while the Gothic revival came to America late, it came to the academic world with force. A major protagonist was Ralph Adams Cram

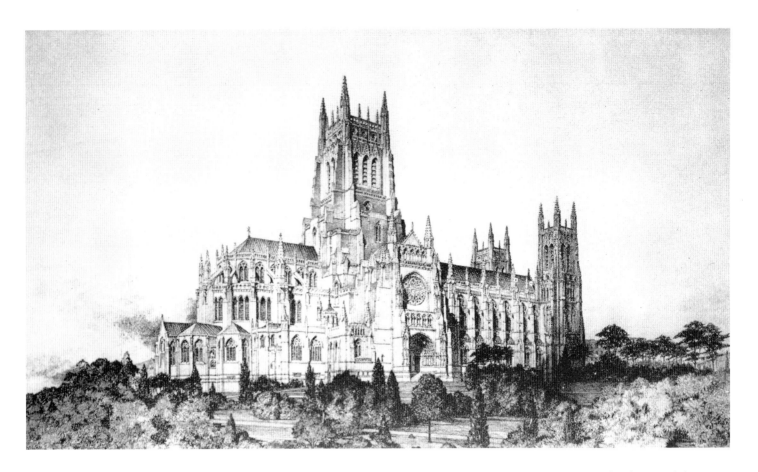

Ralph Adams Cram's most ambitious work in English Gothic was his design for the Cathedral of St John the Divine in New York of 1911, which has been much altered in the actual building.

(1863–1942), an enthusiast in youth for Wagner, the Pre-Raphaelites and the Victorian medievalism of Ruskin and Morris, and architect of major examples of American Gothic such as the Cathedral of St John the Divine in New York. He appropriated the Gothic past with authority: Gothic was 'the style hewn out and perfected by our own ancestors and become ours by uncontested inheritance'. His special field was the building of the new and expanding colleges of the United States. At Princeton he left a deep imprint, notably in the Graduate College with its huge tower modelled on late medieval English Gothic. Cram was but one of many practitioners of 'Collegiate Gothic' and the popularity of the style as appropriate for academic building explains why even in the most modern society in the world scholarly research often goes on within Gothic doors and windows.

The Controversial Middle Ages

The Middle Ages of the Romantics captured the public imagination and has never lost it. This does not mean that there has been general agreement about all details or emphases when interpreting the period. Quite the contrary: the Middle Ages have been fought over in the nineteenth and twentieth centuries with a vigour that would not disgrace the Knights of the Round Table. Controversies have been generated especially by the clash of religious denominations and by class politics.

One thing that most clearly sets the Middle Ages apart from earlier and later periods of European history is the existence of a powerful unified Church. In the centuries between the ending of pagan persecution in the later Roman Empire and the schisms of the Reformation, the Christian faith formed part of the identity of most Europeans and it was a faith that was embodied in concrete institutional form. Among moderns, attitudes to the Church have thus naturally shaped attitudes to the medieval period. For some it was 'An Age of Faith', when

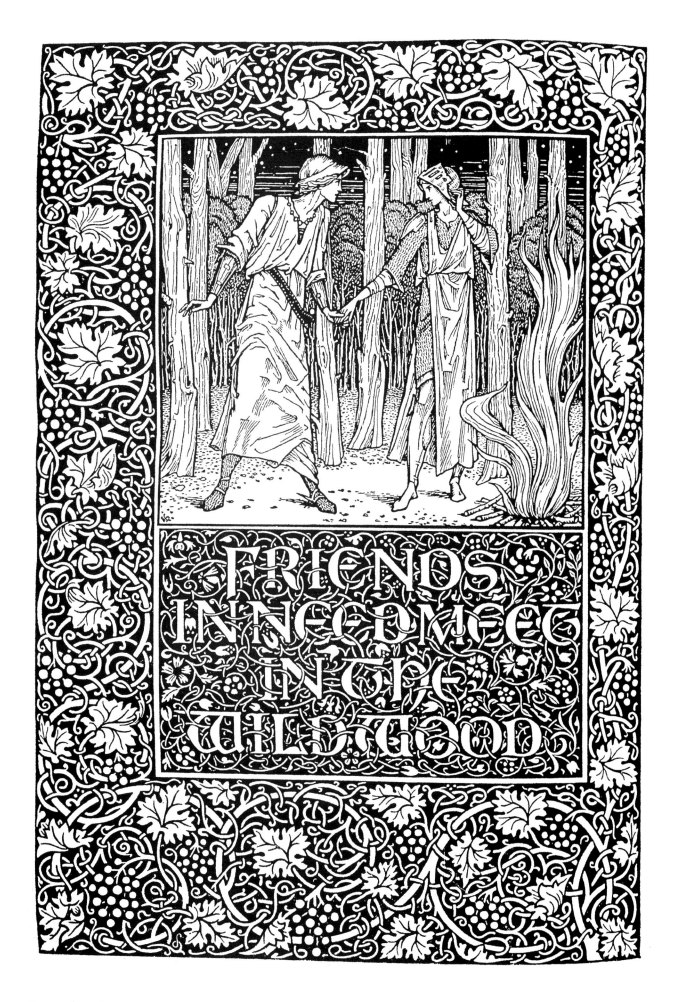

FRIENDS INNEED MEET IN THE WILDWOOD

a common Christianity provided people with solidarity, charity and purpose. For others it was a regime of 'Superstition and Force', the cradle of 'A Persecuting Society'.

The institutions of the Roman Catholic Church had a special relationship with the medieval past. Despite the changes which took place during the Catholic reformation of the sixteenth century, there were deep continuities in practice, in place and in structures. Modern popes preside in the church above the tomb of St Peter and see themselves as his successor, and the line goes unbroken back through all the centuries of the Middle Ages. Benedictine monks follow the same Rule as the thousands of black monks of medieval Europe. If modern nations have often struggled to claim a medieval past, the Church could presume it. One consequence was a long tradition of outstanding scholarly work, especially in the history of religion, where the expertise and commitment of the religious orders were buttressed by their long perspectives. The *Acta Sanctorum* ('Deeds of the Saints'), edited by the Bollandist branch of the Jesuits and containing Lives of ancient and medieval saints, must have one of the longest publishing records in history. The first volume appeared in 1643 and work on the last few continues today.

For some nineteenth- and twentieth-century thinkers the main appeal of the Middle Ages was that they were an essentially Christian period, even, as we have seen, the 'greatest epoch of Christian civilization'. Interest in the medieval period and adherence to Catholicism often went together. Among notable converts were Johann Friedrich Overbeck, one of the founders of the Nazarene movement, and Pugin, the champion of the Gothic revival. The faith and the Christian unity of the Middle Ages could be contrasted with the self-seeking materialism of the modern world. One of the more eloquent proponents of a Catholic history of the medieval period was Christopher Dawson, who published his study of the Dark Ages, *The Making of Europe*, in 1932. He went so far as to assert that only a Catholic could appreciate the period properly: 'to the Catholic they are not dark ages so much as ages of dawn ... if we do not realise this point of view we are cut off from the European past by a spiritual barrier'. He saw modern Europeans ('us') as inheritors: 'The world of the early Middle Ages is the world from which we have come.' In the face of the political and economic disasters of the twentieth century, it was possible to turn to the European unity that the Catholic Middle Ages represented. 'The ultimate foundation of our culture is not the national state but the European unity ... We must rewrite our history from the European point of view.'

Protestant, anti-clerical and sceptical thinkers might dispute this image of organic unity. Some sought out their own spiritual ancestors in the heretics of the Middle Ages, casting them as harbingers of Reformation or pioneers of European dissent. Others might express their views through what they put in and what they left out of the picture, like the Protestant editors who omitted the miracle accounts from medieval texts, perhaps with a laconic comment, 'the miracles that follow I have omitted, since they will cause distaste rather than carry conviction'. Between 1866 and his death in 1909 the American scholar Henry Charles Lea published a series of well-researched studies of what he saw as the more brutal or irrational consequences of the domination of the Church – trial by ordeal, torture, the inquisition, the celibacy of the priesthood. He claimed objectivity but was also quite explicit that organized Christianity had been responsible for much cruelty. A robust unfriendliness towards the

For William Morris, the Middle Ages were a sort of Utopia where the Christian virtues of Faith and Charity prevailed and the craftsman was happy in his work. He tried to practice what he preached, though his own graphic style and that of his Pre-Raphaelite friends hovered between the Middle Ages and the early Renaissance. This page from 'The Well at the World's End' is by Edward Burne-Jones.

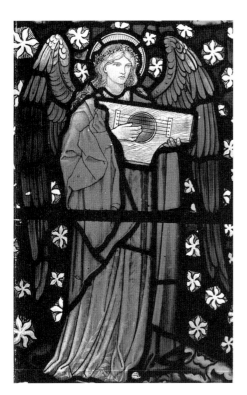

William Morris revived stained-glass as an art form, but the products of his workshop are not slavish imitations of medieval work. This dulcimer-playing angel is in the church of Cattistock, Dorset.

medieval Church can also be found in some of Lea's heirs among the pragmatic and anti-clerical historians of the twentieth century. One English historian, analyzing the world-renouncing rhetoric of an Anglo-Saxon charter in a book still in print, commented: 'We have, of course, to take the attitude of the church into account. It is this contempt for the transitory world which discouraged rational thought, political effort, and planning for the generations to come. It is what explains the Middle Ages.' Voltaire could not have put it better.

The French Revolution had abolished 'feudalism', and the left-wing tradition that it helped to form continued to characterize the medieval past as a time of shackled freedom. This did not stop socialists and others of the left from studying and commenting on the medieval period, often with decisive influence. By far the most important was Karl Marx himself, whose analysis of capitalism involved him in a theory of history. The Marxist theory of history reinforced the idea that there were three great historical periods but instead of using culture or religion as the yardstick Marxism divided human history into successive economic systems: slavery, feudalism, capitalism. An opposition between an exploiting and an exploited class characterized each: slaves and masters, peasants and lords, proletarians and bourgeois capitalists. The origins of a new economic system lay in the contradictions within the preceding one. Hence, for Marxist historians, writing the history of the Middle Ages meant tracing the replacement of the slave system of antiquity with feudalism and then, eventually, the growth within feudalism of the germs of the new bourgeois system that was to replace it.

The exact chronology of these processes could be a matter of debate. Especially complex was the question of the place of the centuries situated between the traditional end of the Middle Ages around 1500 and the emergence of industrial society around 1800. When did the bourgeoisie triumph? Could the British civil wars of the mid-seventeenth century be seen as the clash of feudalism and capitalism? How did the French Revolution fit in? These have long been among the central debates of Marxists and their critics. More recently professional Marxist historians have addressed the other end of the period. When did the ancient world end? Was there a transitional crisis, from slavery to feudalism, just as there was from feudalism to capitalism? These questions have always been debated within the hard casing of the prior assumptions of the theory, and often with the ferocity of small sects, but have produced studies, especially of the peasantry and of economic life, that have been illuminating and influential beyond the bounds of those committed to the theory.

William Morris (1834–96) was a noted example of someone who combined socialism with the romantic vision of the Middle Ages. One influence on him was John Ruskin, especially his idealization of the medieval guild as a cooperative rather than competitive organization of labour. A great admirer also of the Pre-Raphaelites, Morris founded a firm that produced stained-glass, textiles and wallpaper with designs modelled on those of the Middle Ages. His publications included medieval-style ballads and romances, such as *The Defence of Guenevere* and *The Well at the World's End*, as well as translations of medieval works, especially Norse sagas and poems. He was also an active propagandist for socialism. The fit between the pseudo-archaic Arthurian material he wrote and pamphlets such as *Chants for Socialists* or *Socialism: Its Growth and Outcome* may not always be obvious, but an important part was played by his belief that modern industrial society had dehumanized work. 'The Voice of Toil' calls out against the modern world:

Where fast and faster our iron master,
The thing we made, for ever drives,
Bids us grind treasure and fashion pleasure
For other hopes and other lives.

The Middle Ages was a time when 'Art' – the useful and beautiful product of human hands – was cherished. That was no longer true of the modern age. The proletariat is compared, initially surprisingly, to the barbarians who brought down Rome. There would be disruption no doubt, but great virtues would be reawakened, perhaps like those the northern barbarians brought to the effete ancient world: 'hatred of lies, scorn of riches, contempt of death, faith in the fair fame won by steadfast endurance, honourable love of women'. Somehow Morris wove together the heroic Middle Ages, the chivalric Middle Ages, the Middle Ages of idyllic community and the Middle Ages of the Common Man to support a late-nineteenth-century socialism.

The Twentieth Century

In the twentieth century two very different forces were important in shaping the picture of the medieval past. The first was the growth of academic study of the period in universities. Medieval history and culture have been studied by thousands of undergraduates in history and literature departments and have generated hundreds of textbooks, surveys and monographs. At the same time a more effective and less manageable force has presented its own Middle Ages: the cinema.

Over the course of the late nineteenth and early twentieth centuries 'History', 'Literature' and, eventually, 'Art History' became professions and fields of study. Professorial chairs were established and multiplied, courses, degrees and departments organized. Learned journals proliferated. Professional bodies committed to the study of the Middle Ages appeared, such as the Medieval Academy of America, formed in 1925. As a result of this major development in organization and funding, the Middle Ages were now partly in the hands of professional academics, who sought to impart their picture of the period to the young middle-class people they educated. The views of the academics, even if not always fully grasped, helped create whatever image of the period their students would hold, and these views have been subject to change.

Academic history has gone through three great waves – the first, in the early twentieth century, emphasizing political and constitutional history and functioning as a training for civil servants and imperial administrators, the second placing more weight on economic and social history, as the ideological debates of the middle decades of the century had their influence, and the third arising from the consumerism, hedonism and feminism of the present, which has made cultural history a natural focus. Obviously one can find contrary examples at all times, but the trends are clear. Student generations grounded in the slog of studying the great documents of their nation's constitutional history contrast with those excitedly debating the Marxist interpretation of the Middle Ages or the value of the French Marxist-influenced *Annales* school or with modern undergraduates in courses on gender or the body in the Middle Ages. Changes in the sociology and educational background of the student body have been accompanied by changes in the very picture of the Middle Ages being taught.

It was not only the waves of internal fashion that shaped medieval studies in the twentieth century. The new discipline was also sadly subservient to the

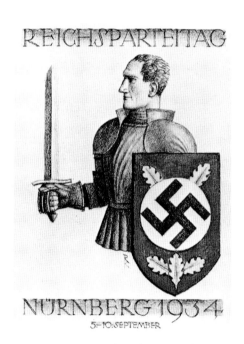

The Nazis could still use the Germanic Middle Ages to appeal to patriotic fervour: a knight with a swastika shield.

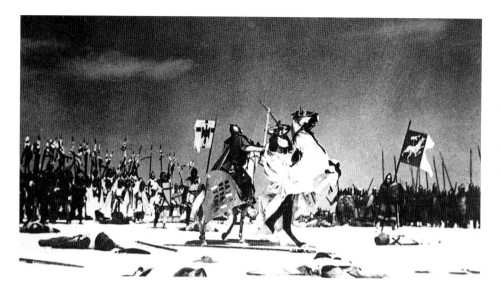

The coming of the cinema brought new life to the Romantic Middle Ages. Eisenstein's 'Alexander Nevsky' (1939) dramatized the battle between medieval Russia and the Teutonic Knights, soon to be re-enacted in earnest.

prevalent political regimes. In 1937 the chief German historical periodical devoted to the Middle Ages changed its name from *Neues Archiv* ('New Archive' or 'New Record') to *Deutsches Archiv* ('German Archive') and its typeface from roman print to the pseudo-medieval *Fraktur* or Gothic. The first article of the new journal was entitled 'The German Middle Ages' and its first sentence reads: 'It lies at the very heart of National Socialism that the claim of its world-view to be universal has also seized hold of German scholarship in its full extent – and will keep hold of it for the whole future'. This acceptance by German scholars of the embrace of Nazism is obviously not the whole story, as witness the permanent enrichment of English and American universities by German émigrés, but it is part of it.

In Communist countries authors were expected to include Marx and Engels in their bibliographies and to structure their thinking according to the nineteenth-century theory of social evolution that these founders of Communism had espoused. This did not always lead to poor empirical scholarship, and one of the pioneering studies of the medieval English peasantry was produced by the impeccably orthodox Marxist E. A. Kosminsky. His *Studies in the Agrarian History of England in the Thirteenth Century* appeared in English translation in 1956, with a preface by the author which proclaimed, 'My work has been written on the basis of Marxist-Leninist method', and included a footnote citing with respect the last work of Joseph Stalin. The book itself is a major empirical study of patterns of landholding in the medieval period. The rigidities of Marxism have proved less of a poison to true historical work than the racism of the Nazis.

Between the year 1900 and the present, then, a large academic and university sector grew up, devoted to explicating and representing the Middle Ages to a fair-sized public. This is important, but overwhelmingly more important as a conveyer of images has been the screen. Very soon after the birth of the cinema, films with medieval subjects were being made. Joan of Arc was on celluloid by 1900 and the first Robin Hood movie dates to 1908. Just as present Western images of the Roman Empire or the Wild West are ninety per cent cinema and ten per cent knowledge, so too the Middle Ages, if people consider them at all, are likely to be a Middle Ages drawn from the screen.

Examples of strong cinematic images of the Middle Ages can of course be found in European cinema: Lang's expressionist rendering of the old Germanic

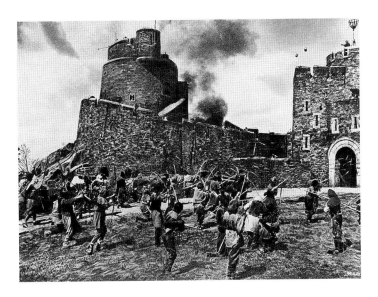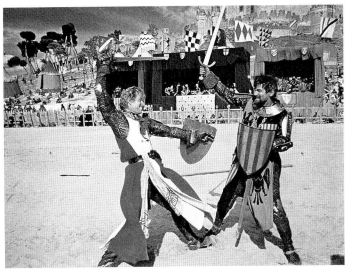

Two spectacular productions which did much to mould the popular image of the Middle Ages were 'Ivanhoe' (left) of 1952 and 'El Cid' (right) of 1961.

tales of the *Nibelungenlied* (1924), Eisenstein's classic nationalist battle epic *Alexander Nevsky* (1938) or Bergman's gloomy and evocative picture of soul-searching and death in the later Middle Ages, *The Seventh Seal* (1957). French cinema has produced several memorable interpretations of Joan of Arc. It has been Hollywood, however, that has dominated this genre, producing filmed versions of historical events, of the legends of the Middle Ages and of fiction set in the medieval period. The historical novels of the Romantics, which had themselves done so much to create the vivid and picturesque Middle Ages, were translated to the screen. Adapting one of Scott's most influential medieval romances, MGM produced their *Ivanhoe* of 1952, complete with a specially constructed castle that had been allowed to age for a year before shooting commenced. In 1958 the same book generated a TV series. Victor Hugo's *Notre-Dame de Paris* was filmed seven times, first in France in 1906, and ninety years later in the Disney version of 1996.

Hollywood epics such as *El Cid* (1961) have had as strong an influence on the popular image of the Middle Ages as anything written by historians. In this film a loyal and towering Charlton Heston wends his way through a wicked world of squabbling dynasts and terrifying invaders. In keeping with the conventional eirenic apologia to be found in war films of the period, he is portrayed neither as he was in reality, as a kind of successful mercenary leader, nor as a champion of Christian against Muslim. He is instead a loyal son of 'Spain', a multicultural Spain that can include urbane local Muslims. The common enemies are the black-clad fundamentalist invaders from Morocco. He fights an elaborate tournament before the walled city of Calahorra, shows both courage and pity in his battles and dies in the defence of Valencia against the African besiegers. Love interest is provided by Sophia Loren, as the Cid's wife, Chimene, whose emotions are complicated by the fact that El Cid has killed her father (a romantic twist already explored in the French classical drama of the seventeenth century and not, as one might expect, an invention of Hollywood).

Like the great historical paintings of the nineteenth century or the operatic works of Wagner and others, films on medieval topics present vivid, forceful and unforgettable images to an audience far greater than the number exposed to the conclusions of academic study. Indeed the Hollywood historical epic is seamlessly continuous with the historical paintings and operas of the earlier

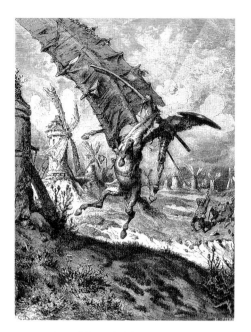

One sign of the end of the Middle Ages was the appearance of books mocking the medieval ideal of chivalry, of which the earliest was Cervantes' 'Don Quixote' (1605–10). A 19th-century illustration by Doré shows the Don tilting at windmills, believing them to be giants.

period. It belongs to the same late Romantic culture, as is clear not only from its theme music but also from its idealized heroism, simplified portrayals of masculinity and femininity and earnest and uplifting tone. Reinforced by the stream of pseudo-medievalist fantasy, such as the works of Tolkien, and finding new expression in computer games, the romantic Middle Ages has been transmitted through electronic form to become a widely diffused common image of modern culture.

This survey has sought to show that there have been many different representations of the Middle Ages. While these representations are obviously subjective, they are not completely illusory. Each is clearly shaped by the concerns and culture of its own day but it is nonetheless likely that any powerful image of the medieval past will contain an ingredient of truth. The Renaissance humanists were right to point out that medieval Latin was unlike that written by Cicero and that scholasticism placed a priority on elaborate logical distinctions. The Protestant Reformers could rail against a medieval Church that truly was hieratic, authoritarian and repressive. Romantics who painted a medieval world in which love and honour were pursued by gallant knights were not telling the whole story, but the aristocratic culture of the Middle Ages really did enshrine such ideals. Neither Marxists seeking class conflict between lords and peasants nor nostalgic conservatives emphasizing the medieval spirit of community need invent their material – the life of the Middle Ages can produce large amounts of support for both positions. Even parodies of the Middle Ages – and there is a long history of these, from Cervantes' burlesque of chivalry, *Don Quixote*, to the anarchic absurdism of *Monty Python and the Holy Grail* – usually make their point from distortion rather than pure invention. A thousand years of European history and culture is a kaleidoscope big enough to shake up into many different pictures.

Samuel Daniel (1562–1619) was a poet of the Elizabethan and Jacobean period who had a precocious sympathy with the Middle Ages, recognizing the debt that his own time owed to the law and culture of that earlier epoch and unwilling to dismiss out of hand any long age of human history. 'Is it not a most apparent ignorance,' he wrote, 'both of the succession of learning in Europe and the general course of things, to say that all lay pitifully deformed in those lack-learning times from the declining of the Roman Empire till the light of the Latin tongue was revived?' He had an explanation for this condescending attitude:

> It is but the clouds gathered about our own judgement that makes us think all other ages wrapped in mists, and the great distance betwixt us that causes us to imagine men so far off to be so little in respect of our selves. We must not look upon the immense course of times past as men overlook spacious and wide countries from off high mountains and are never the near to judge of the true nature of the soil or the particular site and face of those territories they see.

This book is avowedly a 'Panorama' of the Middle Ages, a sweeping view of a huge terrain. It would be a very happy result if reading it and looking at it led readers to the desire to know more about 'the true nature of the soil or the particular site and face of those territories they see'.

Opposite: a man sowing, by the Master of the Brussels Initials. From an Italian missal, between 1389 and 1404.

A Medieval Panorama

1
Prologue: What Made the Middle Ages?

IN THE YEAR 400 the Mediterranean lands and the countries around them, from Morocco to Syria and from Egypt to Britain, formed one state – the Roman Empire – that had Latin as its official language of government and Christianity as its official religion. By the year 800 this Christian and Roman unity had been shattered, first, in the fifth century, by Germanic warriors and their followers, who settled in Western Europe and North Africa, establishing their own kingdoms, and second, in the seventh century, by the dramatic expansion of Islam. In the century after the death of Muhammad (632) Muslims created by conquest an empire that extended from the borders of China to the borders of France. Much of the old Christian Roman Empire (Syria and Palestine, Egypt and North Africa, most of Spain) became part of the new Arab-dominated caliphate. The surviving, eastern section of the Roman Empire, known to historians as Byzantium, was limited to those parts of Asia Minor and south-east Europe closest to the imperial capital, Constantinople (modern Istanbul). By this time Greek, the language of most of its inhabitants, had also become its language of government.

This tripartite division of Europe and the Mediterranean into western Christian, eastern Christian and Muslim parts has had a deep and long-term effect on the region's culture and history. Hostilities and misunderstandings between Muslims and Christians became a permanent feature of Mediterranean history, marked most spectacularly by the crusades that began in 1095 and by the capture of Constantinople by the Ottoman Turks in 1453. Eastern (Orthodox) and western (Catholic) Christians drifted ever further apart. In 1204 a Catholic army from Western Europe even stormed and sacked Constantinople, the capital of the Orthodox world. These tensions have been enduring. The protagonists in the Bosnian war of 1992–95 were, in effect, representatives of those three main traditions.

In Western, Catholic Europe (which is the main focus of this book) the mark and memory of the Roman past lasted throughout the medieval period. As in the ancient world, the language of government, law and learned literature was Latin, only slowly replaced by the local vernacular languages in the later centuries of the Middle Ages. When a particularly powerful ruler arose, with some kind of hegemony in the Christian West, he signified his pretensions by being crowned in Rome and adopting the title 'Emperor', as Charlemagne did in 800 and Otto I of Germany in 962. In the eleventh and twelfth centuries the study of Roman Law, as codified in the later Roman period by the Emperor Justinian, became a central part of the training of the new university-educated lawyers. The Catholic Church, famously described by Gibbon as 'the ghost of the Roman Empire sitting crowned on the grave thereof', naturally continued many Roman habits, in its language (Latin), the dress of its priests and its theology, shaped by the Church Fathers, such as Augustine, Jerome and Ambrose, citizens of the Roman Empire of the fourth and fifth centuries whose works laid the foundations of Western Christian thinking through the centuries.

What are termed 'classics' in the present day were 'classics' of the Middle Ages too – not the Greek authors, such as Homer and the Athenian dramatists, whose language was generally unintelligible to medieval Westerners, but the Latin writers of Rome, both pagan and Christian. The works of the scurrilous poet Ovid

The Emperor Theodosius I (379–95) flanked by his sons Valentinian and Arcadius, and by his German bodyguard: a silver dish of the 5th century AD. In the crucial decades after Constantine, classical Roman civilization and Christianity fruitfully co-existed, and it was during this time that most of the fundamental doctrines of the Catholic Church were worked out.

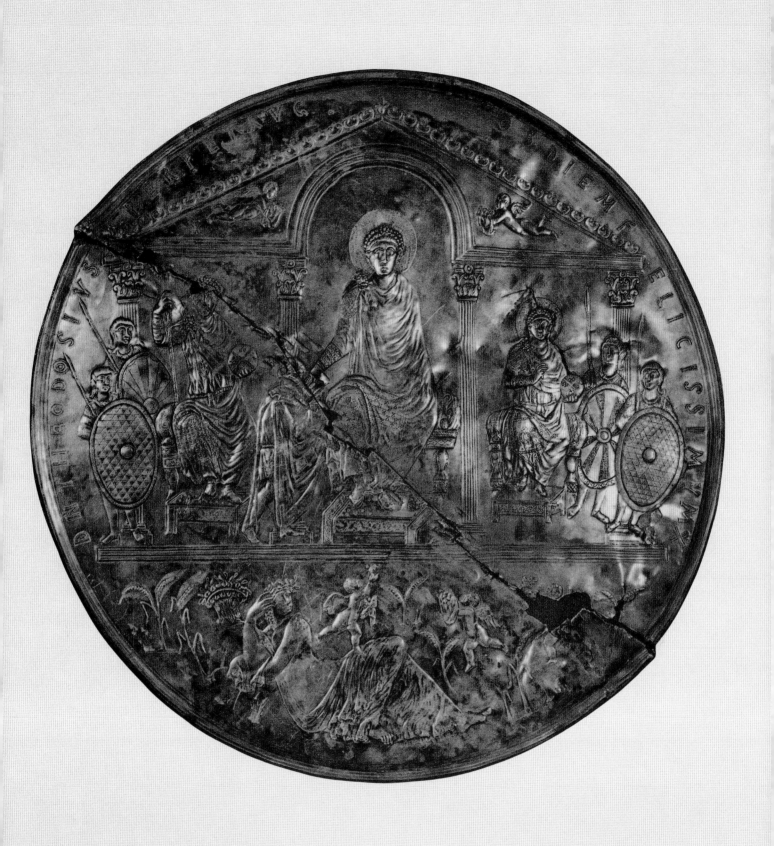

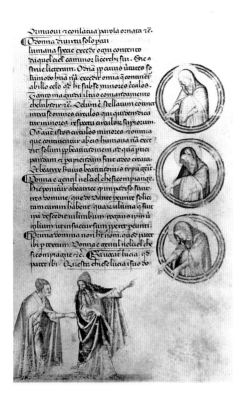

Symbolic of classical civilization's role as mentor to the Middle Ages is the fact that Dante's guide through Hell and Purgatory is the Roman poet Virgil, whose works were seen as an unconscious prophecy of the Christian age. This miniature is from a 14th-century commentary on Dante's 'Divine Comedy'.

were laboriously copied out by Benedictine monks, ancient historians like Sallust and Tacitus provided models and often phrases for medieval chroniclers, while Virgil, poet of imperial Rome in its infancy, provided one of the basic components of elite literary education even down to the present century. His *Aeneid* (or at least its early books) was studied by schoolboys, his praise of the Emperor Augustus reinterpreted as Christian prophecy and he was chosen by the great Italian poet Dante as his guide through hell and purgatory in his own epic, the *Divine Comedy*. Throughout the medieval period rulers, churchmen, writers and artists looked back to the ancient world, sometimes dreaming of reviving it, sometimes imagining they had. The Italian Renaissance was simply one of the more far-reaching of these dreams.

Imperial Rome and the Christian religion were born in more or less the same generation, as medieval thinkers often pointed out, but it was a long and bloody road before the two accepted each other. Persecution of Christians by the Roman state continued over hundreds of years, giving the Christians their first saints in the martyrs who died for their religion and whose tombs were venerated as especially holy spots. Eventually, after a fierce bout of persecution in the very early years of the fourth century, the situation was suddenly, dramatically and permanently changed by the conversion of the Emperor Constantine (d. 337). He favoured the Church, presided over the Council of Nicaea (325) that laid down the basic Christian ('Nicene') Creed and founded the city of Constantinople, named after him, as a new Christian Rome. This autocratic but pious emperor provided one of the great role models for medieval Christian kingship.

It was not the only one, however. Alongside the Roman and Christian roots of the Middle Ages, there are Germanic foundations too, laid by the invaders who replaced the Empire in Western Europe and established their own kingdoms: Franks in the area of modern France and Western Germany, Goths in Spain and Italy, Anglo-Saxons in Britain. Their war-leaders did not expect to read Virgil or wear a toga. Germanic kingship borrowed much from Rome, but had traditions and symbols of its own. Alongside their new assumptions about political power, the invaders brought new judicial practices, like the duel, new words, like 'war' (*guerre, guerra*), and new names, such as Ludwig/Louis/Luis. Even in areas like Italy, where the Roman heritage was particularly strong, the presence of a ruling class of Germanic origin gave a new seasoning to the culture.

Some of the Germanic kingdoms of the early Middle Ages endured and became the basis of modern states, but others were destroyed by their enemies. The Gothic realm in Italy was annihilated by a renascent Roman Empire under Justinian, but the victors then had to confront a new Germanic invasion, that of the Lombards, who established their own kingdom in the north of the peninsula (Lombardy). In 711 the Goths in Spain were faced by a Muslim army, led across the straits of Gibraltar by the Berber general who gave them their name, Tariq ibn Zayyad (Gibraltar=Jebel Tariq, 'Tariq's Mountain'). The Gothic army was defeated, the Gothic king disappeared, and Tariq marched on and occupied Toledo, capital of the kingdom. Within a few years most of the Iberian peninsula was under Muslim rule and parts of it would continue to be so for the whole of the Middle Ages, down to the Christian conquest of Granada in 1492.

The most successful of the Germanic kingdoms was that of the Franks, which extended from the Rhine to the Atlantic and from the English Channel to the Mediterranean. Its first Christian ruler, Clovis (a form of the name 'Louis'), was a vigorous war-leader but he also established a cooperative relationship with the

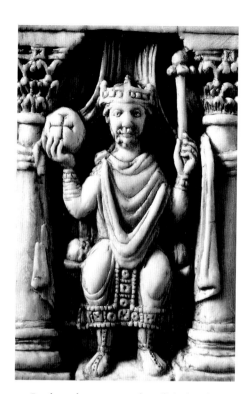

By about the year 1000 the political and religious outline of medieval Europe had taken shape. The Ottonian dynasty identified its empire, inherited from Charlemagne, as both Christian and classical, Holy as well as Roman. This detail of an ivory situla shows Otto III, c. 1000.

Christian Church – he was indeed later dubbed 'a new Constantine'. This alliance of Frankish military power and ecclesiastical leadership was to be continuously important in following centuries. It came to especial prominence under the family that replaced Clovis' dynasty in the eighth century, the Carolingians. The most remarkable member of this Frankish clan was Charlemagne ('Charles the Great'), who came to the throne in 768, annexed Lombardy and Bavaria, pushed back the Muslims in Spain, conquered and converted the pagan Saxons in a series of long and brutal campaigns and, on Christmas Day 800, was crowned emperor in Rome. By that date his dominions were virtually coterminous with Christian Western Europe, so his new title was not entirely preposterous, even though the rulers in Constantinople might object that the position of Christian emperor was not in fact vacant.

Charlemagne's empire was the direct foundation of most of the various societies to be found in Western Europe over the following centuries. It combined a Roman, a Christian and a Germanic past. It asserted a separate identity against both Byzantium and Islam. Some of its legal and political institutions, such as counties and fiefs, were important elements in all later kingdoms. The books that were copied out in the Carolingian period, including Latin classics and works of the Church Fathers, formed the basis of all later libraries and the script that Carolingian scribes developed ('Caroline minuscule') diffused gradually throughout Western Europe (it is the basis of modern printed type). Charlemagne and his dynasty were not simply successful warrior kings, but also anointed Christian kings with a mission. They were concerned that Church doctrine and liturgy should be uniform and correct, they legislated on religious practices, they backed the Church and expected its backing in return.

Carolingian culture and institutions thus formed an important common inheritance in Western and Central Europe (hence the usefulness of Charlemagne as a symbol in the present European Community). The political unity of Charlemagne's empire, however, did not last. His grandsons divided it up between themselves and soon the eastern, western and southern parts – the embryonic forms of France, Germany and Italy – went down separate political paths. These units themselves then began to fragment. At the same time a new wave of Germanic assaults began, originating from Scandinavia, where the native pagan peoples had developed seafaring and shipbuilding techniques that gave them the freedom of the seas and major rivers throughout Europe and beyond. Viking raids began during Charlemagne's lifetime and for the next three centuries Scandinavian fleets shook and shaped European life. They sailed west to North America, south into the Mediterranean, east into Russia and beyond. Settlements and colonies were established throughout Britain and Ireland and in northern France (Normandy, 'land of the Northmen'). While the coastal regions were vulnerable to Vikings, the central parts of Christian Europe faced the raids of the pagan nomadic Magyars. It was only after these northern and eastern raiders converted to Christianity and formed settled kingdoms of their own, around the year 1000, that Catholic Europe could begin a development freed from major external threats.

What Made the Middle Ages? 33

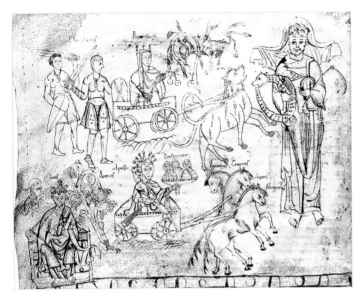

1. Classical gods, as imagined by an artist of around 1100. Top left, Cybele in a chariot with tiny drums and sacred tree; top right, Saturn with a veil looking rather like a halo; lower left, Jupiter with raven and oak tree; and Apollo in his chariot holding the Three Graces in his hand.

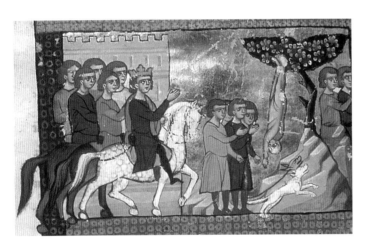

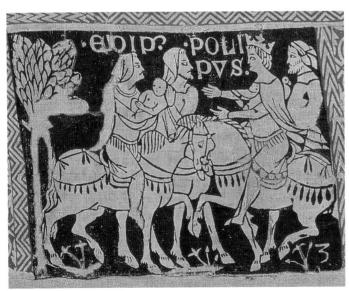

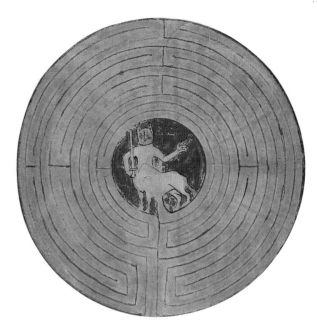

5. The Minotaur in the centre of the Labyrinth, from a French manuscript of about 1120.

Reading the classics

Most of the heritage of classical literature was available to medieval readers. True, Greek was forgotten, but Latin writers drew upon the same repertoire of myth and legend as Homer and the Greek dramatists. A few Roman authors – Catullus was one – disappeared and had to be rediscovered at the Renaissance. But the classical myths and stories were part of normal educated discourse and allusions to them were widely understood. They were visualized, however, almost entirely in medieval terms and interpreted in ways that would have surprised their creators.

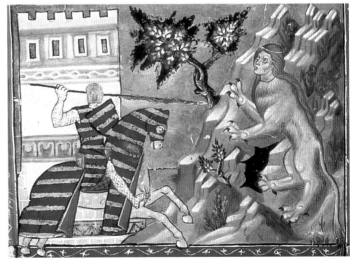

2, 3, 4. Three episodes from the story of Oedipus. Above left: as a baby he is exposed on a mountain, bound by the ankles and, above, he fights the Sphinx, both from a manuscript of *c.* 1286. Left: he is brought as a baby to Polybius, King of Corinth; 14th-century printed wall hanging.

Medieval theatre 228-229　　Classicism reborn 262-263

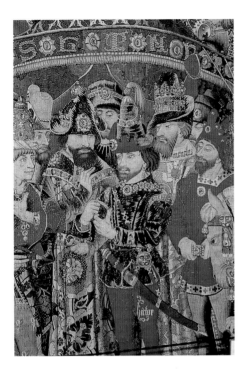

6. Detail of a Tournais tapestry illustrating the Trojan War. Hector is in the centre, Menelaus behind him; 15th century.

7. The three goddesses Venus, Juno and Pallas Athene approach the sleeping Paris; French, 15th century.

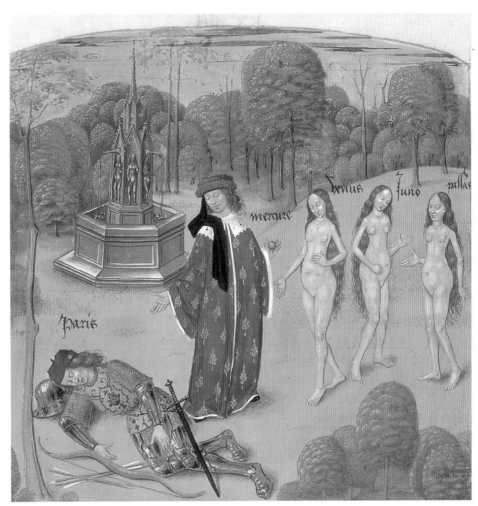

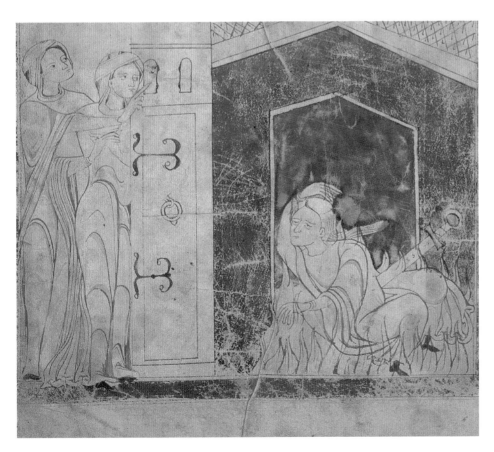

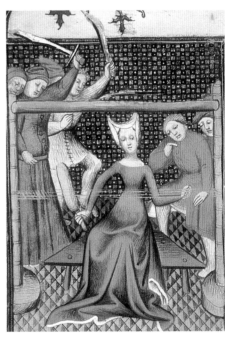

9. Penelope at her loom, surrounded by her increasingly exasperated suitors; from a 14th-century manuscript.

8. Left: the death of Dido, from a German retelling of the *Aeneid*, 1210–20.

What Made the Middle Ages?　　35

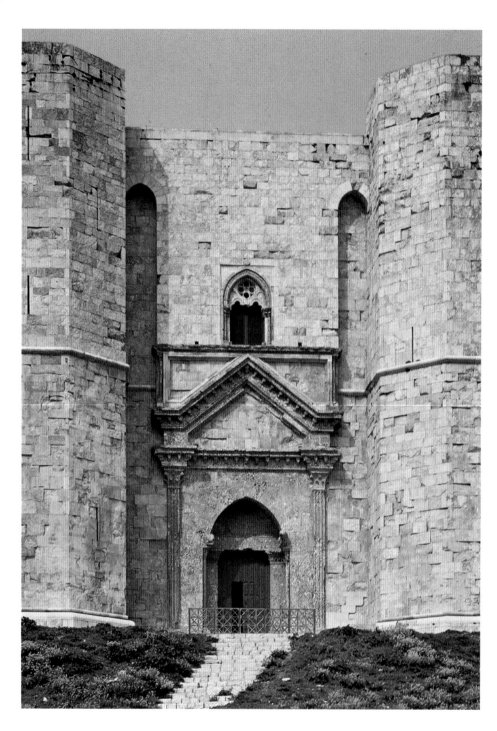

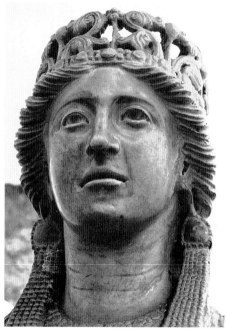

1. Left: the classical entrance to Frederick II's otherwise purely Gothic Castel del Monte, Apulia (1240).

2. The very Roman head of 'Ecclesia', from the pulpit of Ravallo Cathedral, Italy; 13th century.

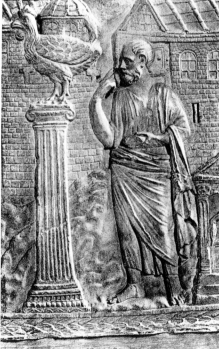

3. St Peter and the cock, a relief from the 'Sarcophagus of St Peter', Rome; 4th century.

Classical revivals

Just as the Latin classics never ceased to be read, so Roman architecture and sculpture were ever-present in the Christian Middle Ages. In the early centuries, the classical style was the natural convention of the time (3). Later, as at the court of the Emperor Frederick II (1, 2), revived classicism could be a deliberate ideological statement. Elsewhere as in 12th- and 13th-century Italy (7) and France (4, 5, 6), one finds architects and sculptors copying features from ancient Rome without any definite programme, to confer the authority of a culture still widely revered, or simply because examples of it were still all around then.

Charlemagne: Rome reborn 52-53

Italy and the Roman tradition 150-151

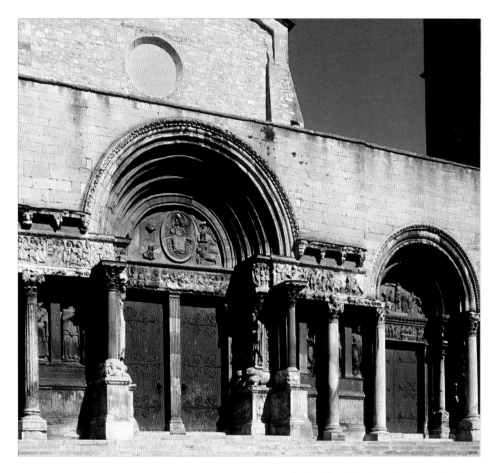

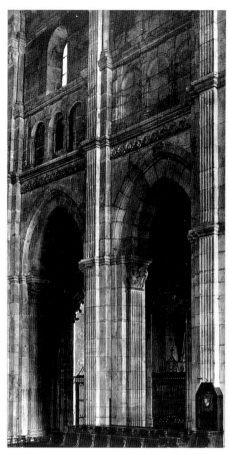

4. The façade of the church of St-Gilles-du-Gard, Provence (mid-12th century) bears witness to the presence of Roman temples in the vicinity.

5. At Autun Cathedral, in Burgundy (*c.* 1120) classical fluted pilasters appear in the piers of a Romanesque arcade.

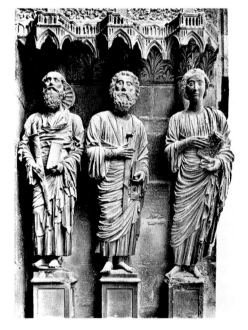

6. Apostles wearing togas modelled on Roman drapery, from the north transept of Rheims Cathedral, *c.* 1230.

7. The Adoration of the Magi, from the pulpit of Pisa Baptistery, *c.* 1260, by Nicola Pisano, no doubt imitated from sarcophaguses in the nearby Campo Santo, with the Virgin like a Roman matron.

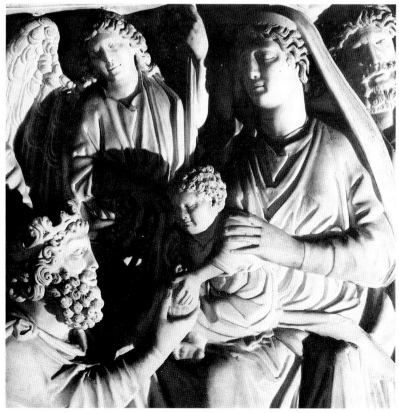

What Made the Middle Ages? 37

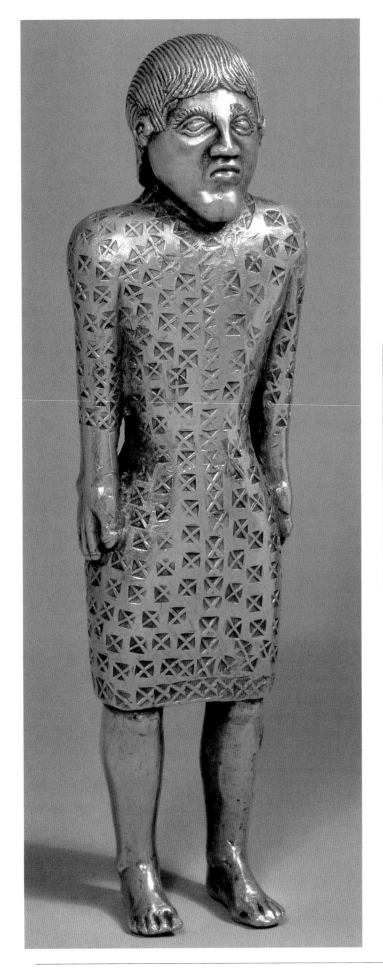

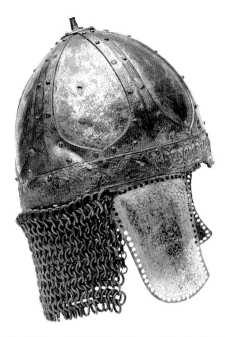

1. Gold figurine of a warrior, probably Frankish, found in France; late 4th-early 5th century.

2. Frankish helmet from Germany; *c.* 600.

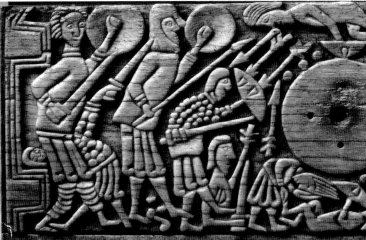

3. Egil the archer defending his home, an episode from Anglo-Saxon history on a whalebone casket; 7th century.

Germanic invaders

'Invaders' is a misleading term. The 4th and 5th centuries were years of large-scale migration by nomadic peoples in Eastern Europe and the steppes, the causes of which are still obscure. When these peoples came up against the frontiers of Rome they were at first peacefully absorbed and used as buffers against succeeding waves. But as Roman military control weakened (for reasons equally obscure) they established independent states which finally took over the Empire altogether. It was from these states that the nations of medieval (and modern) Europe descended. The Franks (1, 2) began to occupy what is now France in the 5th century. At the same time Visigoths and Ostrogoths (6, 8) invaded Italy, the latter settling there, the former moving on to Spain. The Lombards (4, 5) entered Italy in 568, while the Angles and Saxons (3) too arrived in England in the 4th and 5th centuries. Culturally, distinctions between these tribes are hard to draw, particularly in their luxury goods (6, 7, 8), which share a common style.

The assault on Christian Europe 54-55

From barbarians to nation-states 266-267

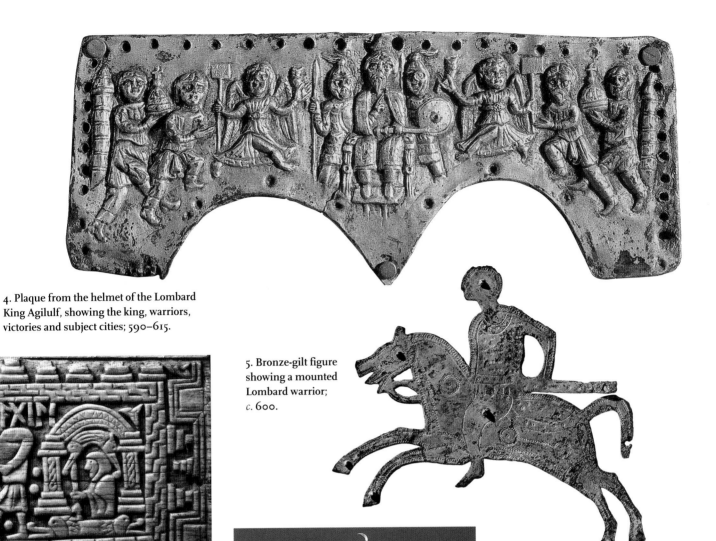

4. Plaque from the helmet of the Lombard King Agilulf, showing the king, warriors, victories and subject cities; 590–615.

5. Bronze-gilt figure showing a mounted Lombard warrior; *c.* 600.

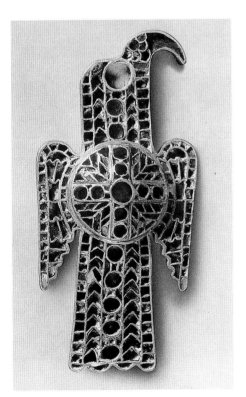

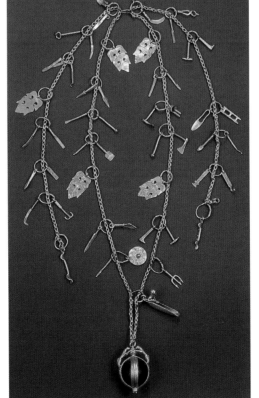

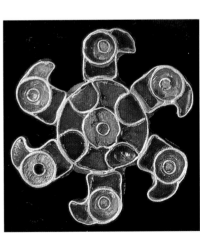

6, 7, 8. Three pieces of Germanic jewelry found in graves. Far left: eagle brooch with garnets, probably Ostrogothic but of a type found in many Germanic areas. Centre: gold chain with tools relating to various trades, from Transylvania; 4th-5th century. Above: Ostrogothic fibula of eagles' heads.

What Made the Middle Ages? 39

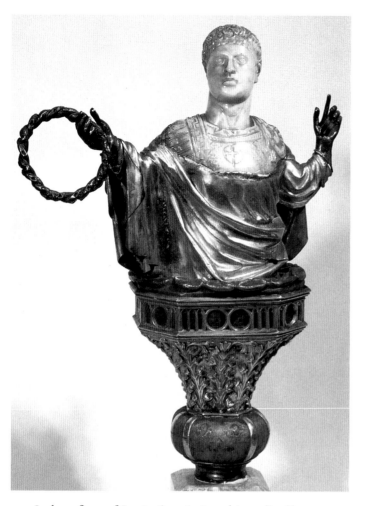

From Constantine to Justinian

The Emperor Constantine (1) made two of the most momentous decisions in world history: to make Christianity the official religion of the Roman Empire and to move the capital from Rome to Constantinople. As a consequence of the first, Christians could come out of hiding, build the first churches (2) and organize a power-structure of pope, bishops and priests. The second led to the eventual division of the Empire into a Greek East and a Latin West and to the creation of Byzantine civilization, which was to be a constant background and stimulus to the European Middle Ages. Constantinople was founded in 330. Under Theodosius (370–95) the two halves of the Empire were separated administratively. In 476 the Western Empire came to an end. In 536–40 Justinian attempted to reconquer it but this could not be sustained. The great church of Hagia Sophia (4) remains his lasting monument.

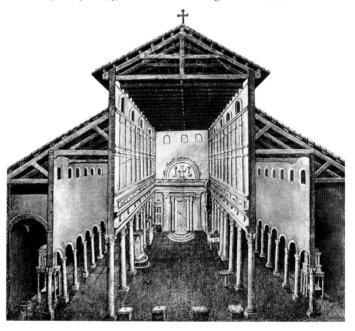

1. Sardonyx figure of Constantine art set on a late-medieval base.

2. Right: the interior of the first St Peter's, Rome, early 4th century: one of several huge churches built as part of Constantine's ambitious building programme.

3. Below: a relic casket is carried in procession to the door of a still-unfinished church, where the emperor (possibly Theodosius) hands a candle to the patriarch who holds a cross; 5th or 6th century.

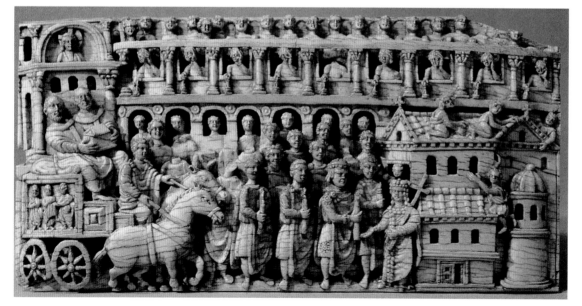

4. Opposite: the church of Hagia Sophia (Holy Wisdom) in Constantinople (Istanbul), begun 532; the unique and unsurpassed masterpiece of Justinian's reign.

The politics of conversion
42-43

The Church in a new age
264-265

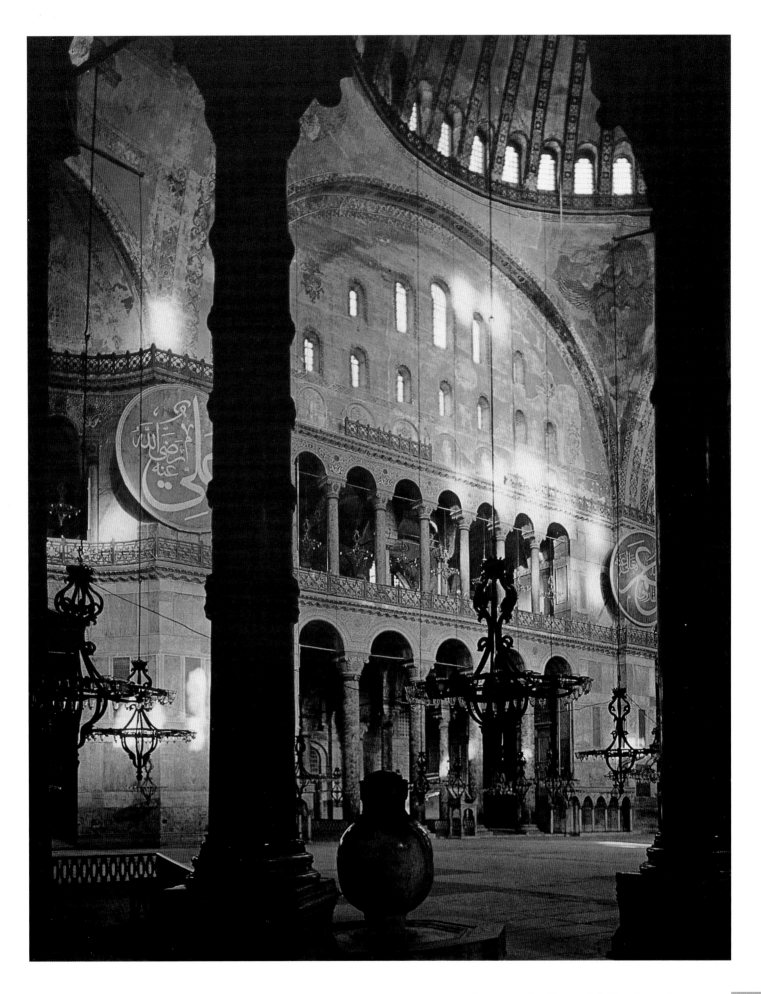

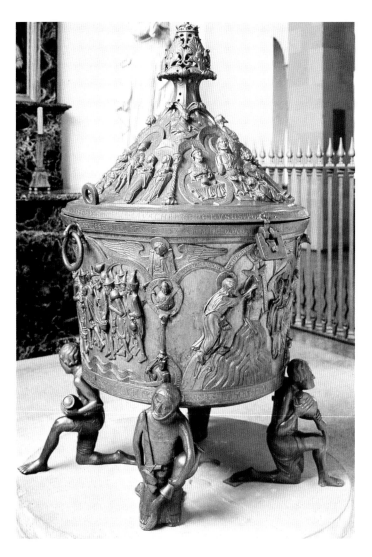

1. Left: bronze font in the Cathedral of Hildesheim, Germany; *c.* 1225. The kneeling figures represent the four rivers of Paradise. The bowl includes a relief of Christ's baptism.

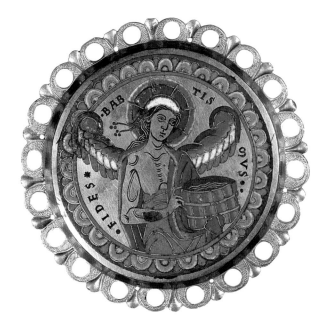

2. Allegory of the Faith in Baptism: a Mosan enamel medallion of the mid-12th century.

The politics of conversion

Christianity spread slowly and sporadically among the Celtic and Germanic peoples, depending on many factors of which personal conviction was perhaps the least important. The decision to convert was the ruler's, and it involved accepting not just the doctrines of the Church, but also other far-reaching changes – social (new legal and moral codes), administrative (the whole ecclesiastical and monastic hierarchy) and cultural (the acquisition of literacy and Latin education). The Franks were largely Christian a generation after the end of the Roman Empire. The Irish were converted from Britain and Gaul, where St Patrick had studied, and in their turn sent missions to Germany (4, 6). Scandinavia (3) and Eastern Europe (5, 7) came last. Entry into Christianity was symbolized by the sacrament of baptism (2). Thereafter the font (1) stood near the entrance of every church.

3. The Danish King Harold Bluetooth was converted and baptized about 980 by a missionary called Poppo, an event commemorated in a gold plaque of the Tamdrup altar, *c.* 1200.

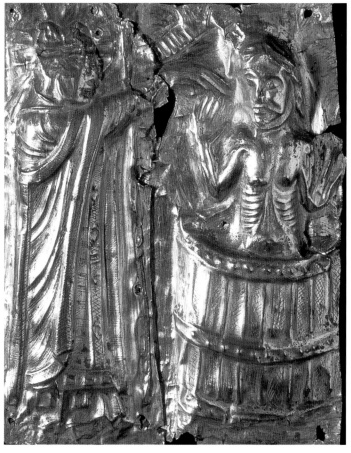

From Constantine to Justinian 40-41

Picturing the new faith 44-45

6. St Boniface, born in England about 675, became Archbishop of Mainz, in Germany, and a missionary in the Netherlands. An 11th-century manuscript records his success in baptizing converts and his eventual martyrdom in Friesland, aged nearly eighty.

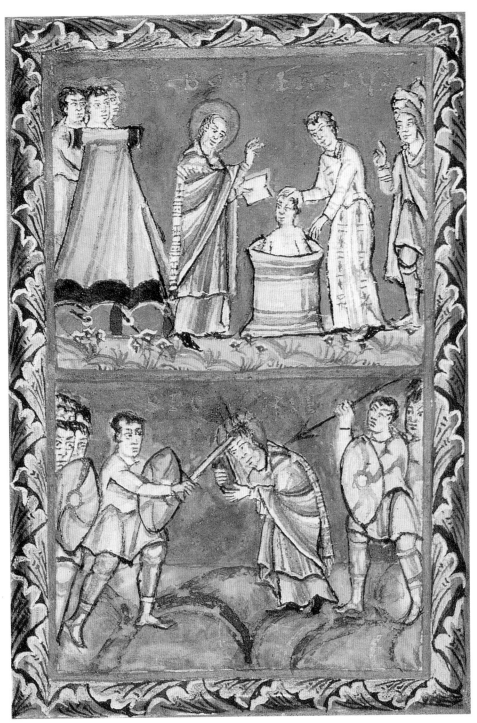

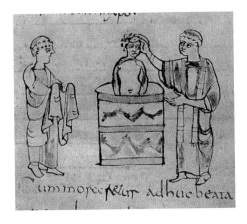

4. Representation of a baptism, from a German manuscript of the early 9th century.

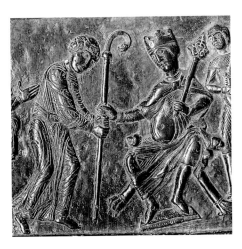

5, 7. The 10th-century St Adalbert of Prague receives his bishop's staff from the Emperor Otto III (above) and baptizes heathen Prussians (right): two details from the bronze doors of Gniezno Cathedral, Poland, 1170.

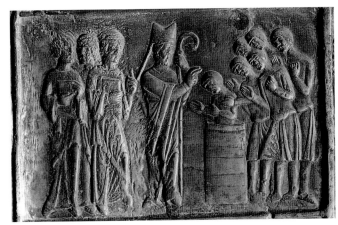

What Made the Middle Ages?   43

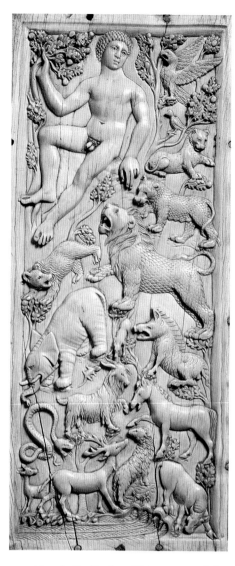

1. Adam in the Garden of Eden surrounded by the animals; ivory relief, 380–400.

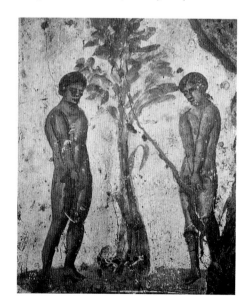

2. Adam, Eve and the Serpent, from the Catacomb of Peter and Marcellinus, Rome; late 3rd century.

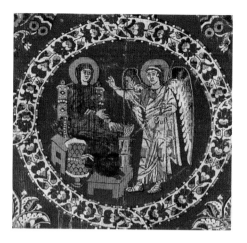

3. The Annunciation; Byzantine silk, 7th century.

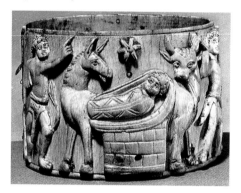

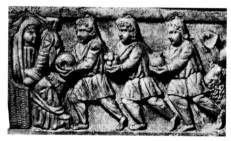

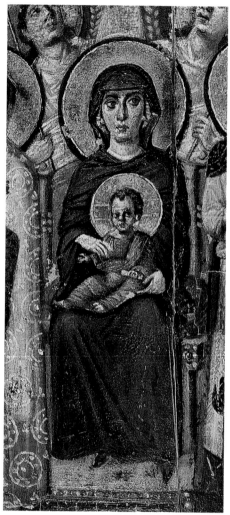

6. The Madonna and Child, one of the earliest representations, from St Catherine's Monastery, Mount Sinai; 5th century.

4. Above left: Nativity, from an ivory pyxis; 5th or 6th century.

5. Left: Adoration of the Magi, from the Sarcophagus of Aurelius; 4th century.

Picturing the new faith

When Christianity was adopted as the official religion of the Roman Empire a whole repertoire of images – that of pagan mythology – became obsolete and a new one – the life of Christ – had to be invented. For these subjects there was no precedent in art. Yet the scenes that these first Christian painters and sculptors composed established conventions that would be followed for a thousand years. They created Christian art. Certain Old Testament scenes were also popular, especially the Garden of Eden and the Fall, since this was the beginning of original sin from which Christ had redeemed mankind.

The image of salvation 46-47

The many faces of Christ 74-75

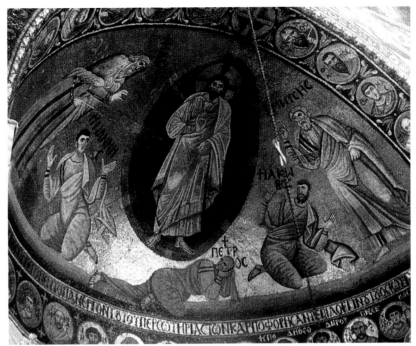

9. The Transfiguration; mosaic at St Catherine's, Mount Sinai, 550.

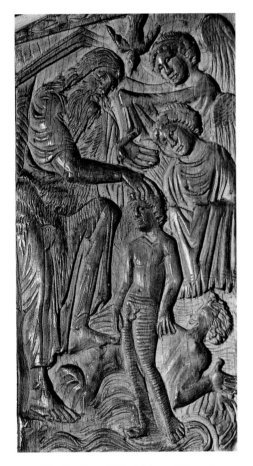

7. The Baptism of Christ; ivory, 6th century. Note the river god bottom right, a vestige of the pagan past.

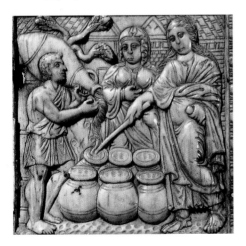

8. Changing water into wine at the Marriage at Cana; ivory plaque from Palermo, Sicily, 450–60.

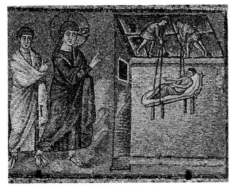

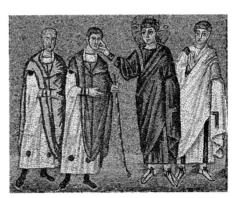

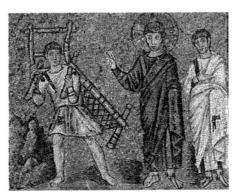

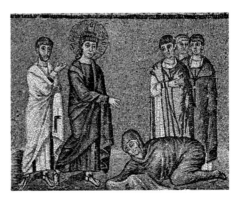

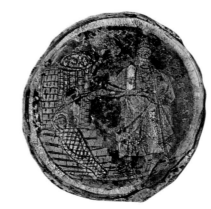

10. Mosaic panels in the church of S. Apollinare Nuovo, Ravenna, 520–26, showing Christ's healing miracles. Top left to bottom right: healing of the paralytic; healing of the blind man; 'Take up thy bed and walk'; woman with the issue of blood.

11. The raising of Lazarus; gold painted glass, 4th century.

What Made the Middle Ages? 45

The image of salvation

It was Christ's death on the cross to atone for the sins of mankind that formed the core of the Christian message. The story of the Passion, from the Entry into Jerusalem to the Ascension, therefore figures prominently in images. But, curiously, representations of the Crucifixion itself (3) are virtually unknown before the 5th century. In other scenes some conventions have changed with the centuries, such as the depiction of the Last Supper (2) as a Roman feast with the guests reclining on couches, or the tomb of Christ as a Roman mausoleum (4, 5). But many other small details, like the man climbing the tree to see Christ entering Jerusalem (1) remained remarkably consistent.

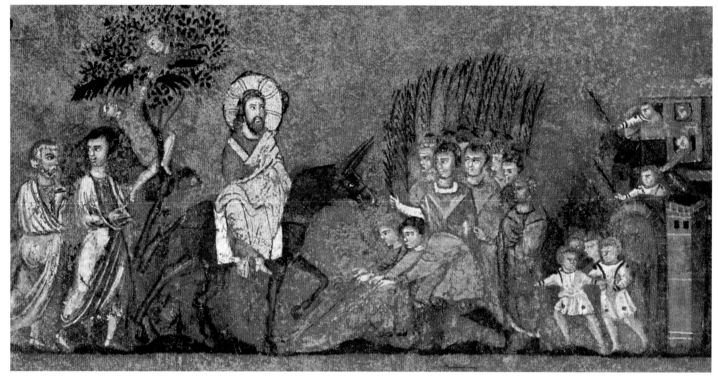

1. Christ's entry into Jerusalem, from the Rossano Gospels; 6th century.

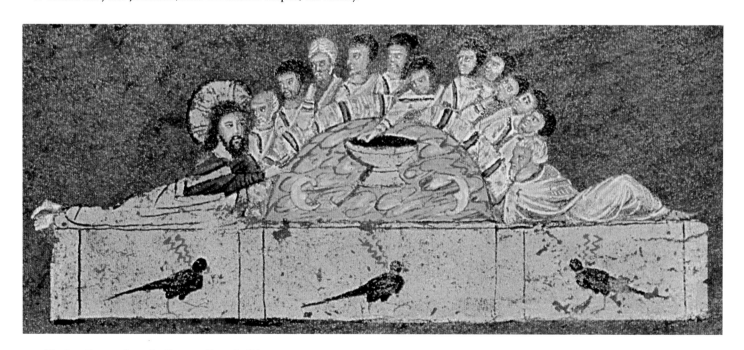

2. The Last Supper, from the Rossano Gospels; 6th century.

The many faces of Christ
74-75

Joys and sorrows of Mary
76-77

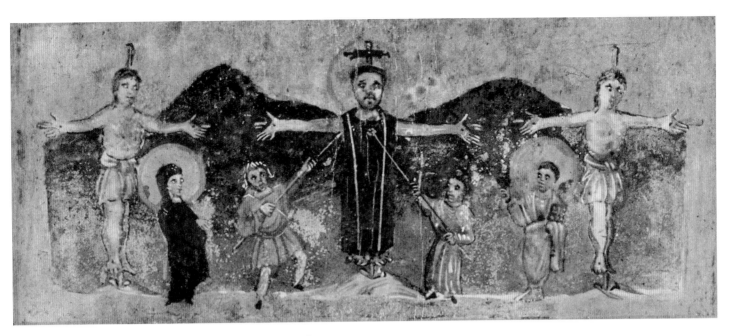

3. The Crucifixion; painting on a wooden reliquary, *c.* 580–600.

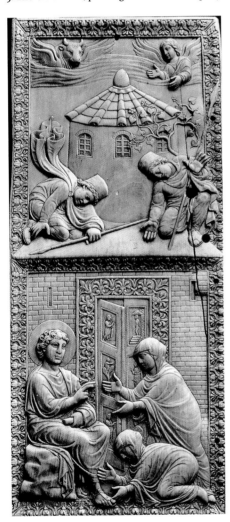

4. The Angel greeting the Marys (only two here) at the empty tomb, represented as a classical mausoleum; from an ivory diptych, 380–400.

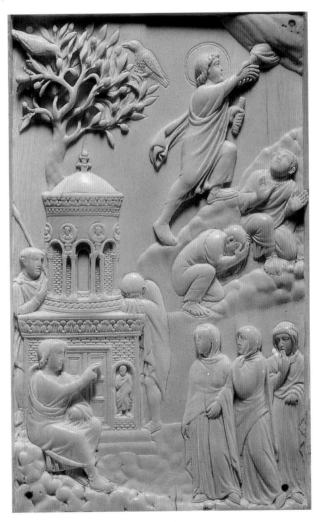

5. Ascension of Christ, with the (three) Marys at the tomb, again shown as a mausoleum; ivory plaque, *c.* 400.

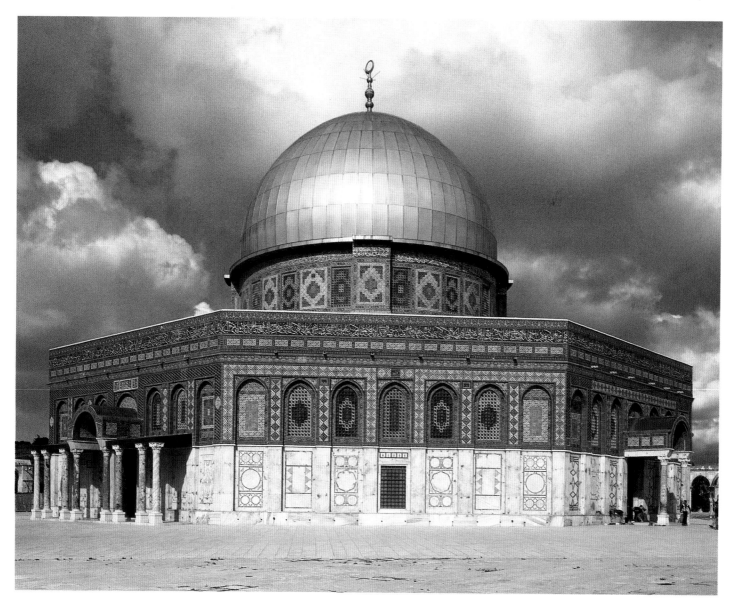

1. The Dome of the Rock from the south west. A domed octagon, this first of Islamic holy places marks the site of Muhammad's Night Journey to Heaven. The marble plaques and coloured tiles date from the 16th century, much renewed in the 20th.

The rise of Islam

At a time when the Christian Church was still struggling to formulate its doctrine and establish its dominance over what had been the Roman Empire, it faced a rival that threatened its very existence: Islam. Unlike Christianity, Islam's triumph was a matter of decades rather than centuries. Muhammad died in 632. By 720 his followers controlled Arabia, the Levant, the whole southern shore of the Mediterranean and most of Spain. The two outstanding monuments of this early phase of Islam are the Dome of the Rock in Jerusalem (691) (1) and the Great Mosque of Damascus (706–15) (3, 4).

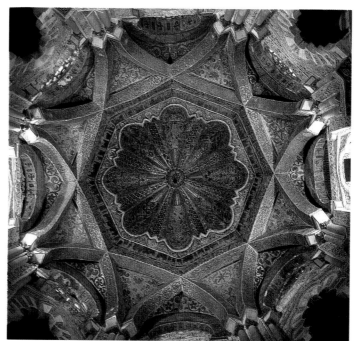

2. The ceiling of the *mihrab* antechamber of the Mosque of Cordoba, 965, the most splendid monument of early Muslim Spain.

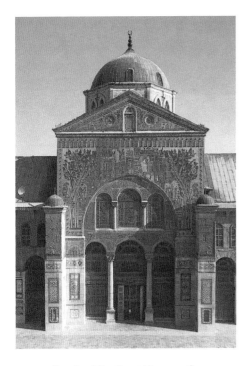

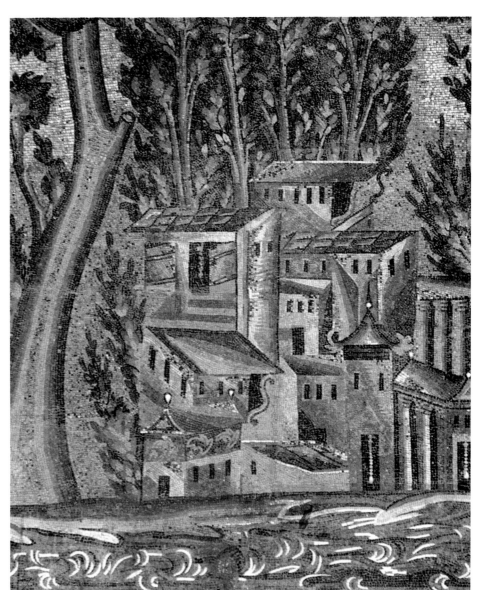

3, 4. Façade of the Great Mosque of Damascus and (right) a detail of the courtyard mosaics.

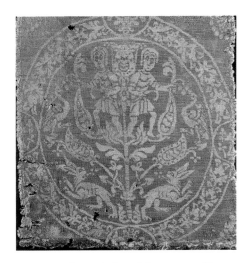

5. Part of a textile from 8th-century Syria or Egypt showing bird-catchers in a garden.

6. Right: ivory casket from Cordoba, *c.* 970; a nobleman riding on an elephant.

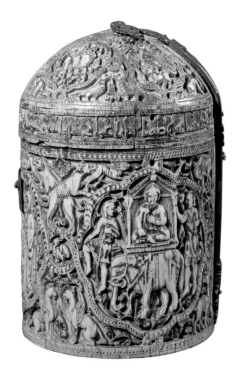

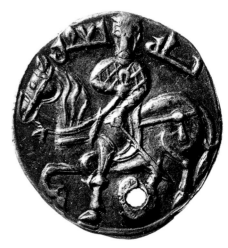

7. Silver *dihram* showing the Abbasid Caliph al-Muqtadir, 908–32.

What Made the Middle Ages?   49

The parting of the ways

By the 9th century the old unity of Mediterranean culture had permanently split into three: the Latin West, the Byzantine East and Islam. Language, architecture and religion are three obvious aspects of this division. Greek (2) and Latin (1), once closely linked, now went separate ways, while Arabic (3), previously confined to the fringe, spread rapidly through the Middle East, North Africa and Spain. In architecture, all three regions looked to classical Rome but evolved their own characteristic details, such as the capitals of columns (4, 5, 6). The contrasts are most marked in religious observance. In the West everything centres upon the altar (8), where the bread and wine are consecrated. In the Byzantine church and its offspring, the Russian and Greek Orthodox churches, this consecration takes place behind a screen of images, the iconostasis (7). In Islam there are no sacraments: the congregation simply turns in the direction of Mecca, indicated by the *mihrab* niche (9).

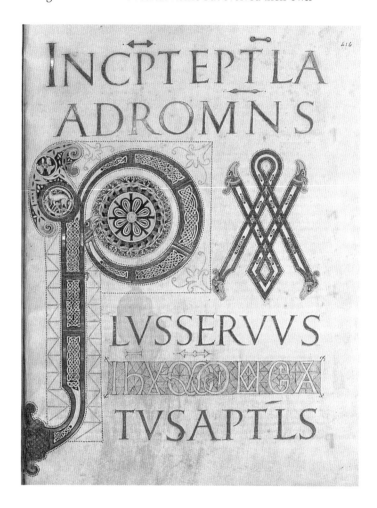

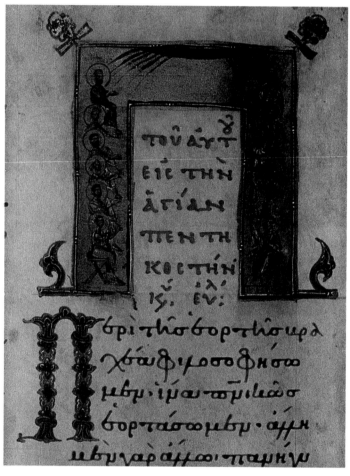

1. Detail from the Bible of Charles the Bald, 840s. Carolingian scribes added highly individual decorations to their classical alphabet.

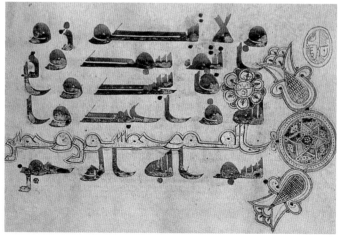

2. Illustrated initial *Pi* from a Byzantine manuscript of about 1100. It portrays Pentecost, the outpouring of the Holy Spirit on the assembly.

3. A verse from the Quran, written in 'black Kufic'. Arabic was the newest of the written languages. Up to the 7th century there were several variant forms. Standardization is due mainly to the Quran, a text whose sanctity extended to the script itself.

From Constantine to Justinian 40-41

The rise of Islam 48-49

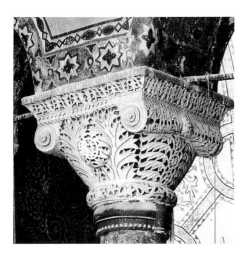

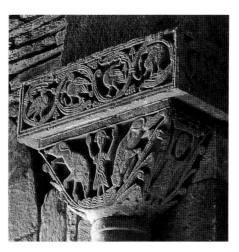

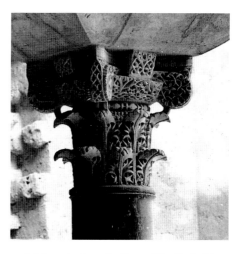

4. Byzantine capital from the church of Hagia Sophia, Constantinople, *c.* 535, still close to the ancient Corinthian order.

5. Romanesque masons experimented with figure sculpture: at S. Pedro de la Nave, Spain, 691, a scene of the Sacrifice of Isaac.

6. Islam also kept the form of the Corinthian capital, but covered it with abstract pattern; from Cordoba, 10th century.

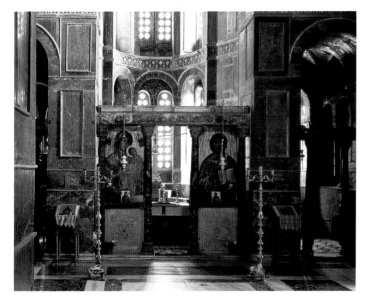

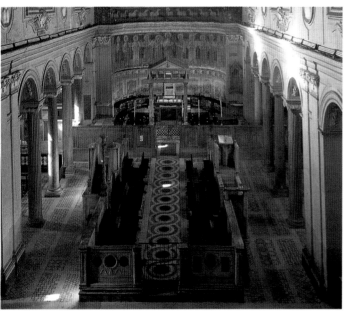

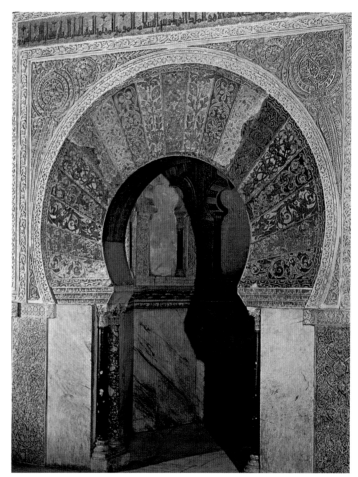

9. The *mihrab* of the Great Mosque at Cordoba (8th century) – an empty niche marking the direction of Mecca.

7. Above left: the iconostasis of the church of Hosios Lukas, Greece (*c.* 1020), an early stage in the development of the image-screen.

8. Left: chancel and altar of S. Clemente, Rome, preserved from an earlier 6th-century church.

Charlemagne: Rome reborn

A new Christian empire – Rome ruled by Christ – was a vision that was to haunt the whole European Middle Ages. Charlemagne's achievement in uniting large parts of Germany, France and Italy seemed to bring the dream closer, and he was crowned 'Emperor' by the Pope in 800. Charlemagne very deliberately utilized Roman imagery. His palace chapel at Aachen (1, 2, 5) was modelled on Justinian's imperial church of S. Vitale at Ravenna. His legal code, encouragement of scholarship and patronage of the arts (6) all made explicit allusion to the classical world. That this was also a *Christian* world was just as important, and in 1165 he was actually canonized (3, 4, 7). In the late 10th century he could be seen as the founder of what was then called the *Holy* Roman Empire.

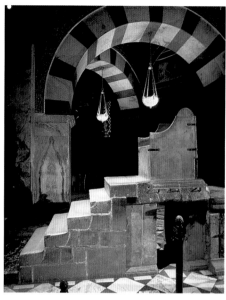

1, 2. Charlemagne's chapel at Aachen, *c.* 790 (left), formed part of his now destroyed palace. The throne stands on the upper gallery facing the altar.

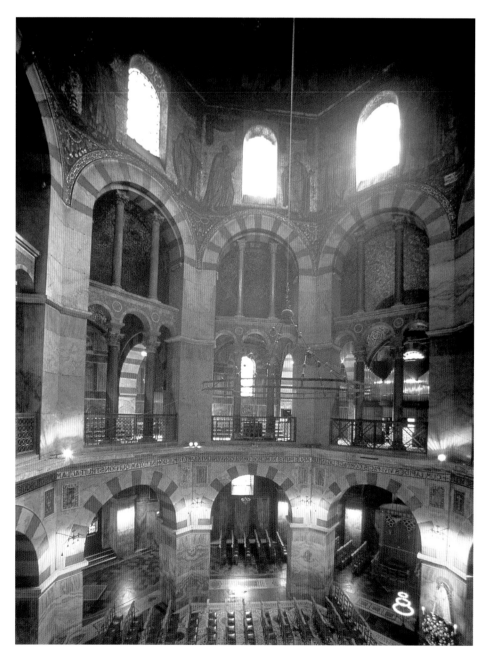

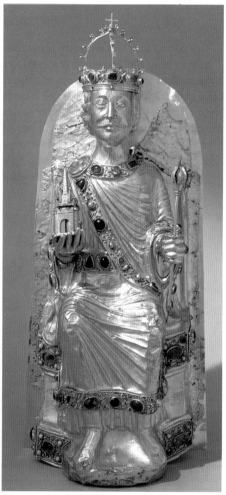

3. When Charlemagne died he was buried in a Roman sarcophagus. In 1215 his bones were re-interred in an ornate Gothic shrine including the figure of the emperor.

Empire and Papacy 96-97   Reconquest: the end of Muslim Spain 242-243

6. St Mark from the Gospel Book of Godescalc, painted probably at Aachen, 781–83.

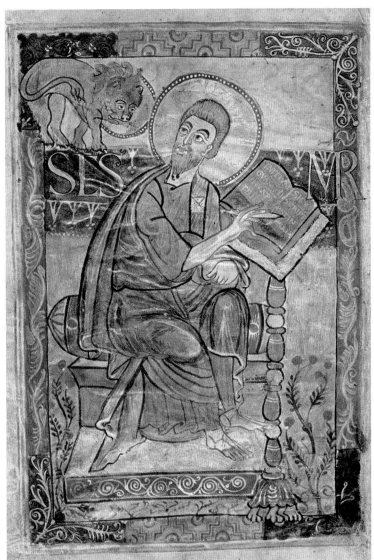

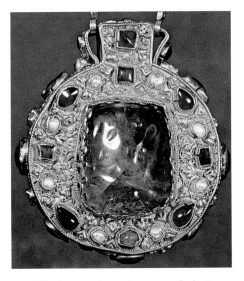

4. Charlemagne's amulet was made during his lifetime. It holds fragments of the True Cross.

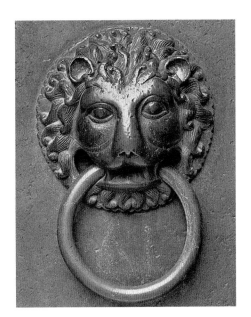

5. The lion-head door-handle of the palace chapel clearly follows a classical model.

7. Right: Charlemagne dedicates his chapel to the Virgin, a panel from the Gothic shrine of 1215.

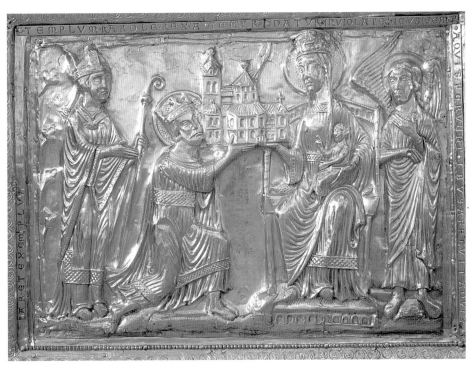

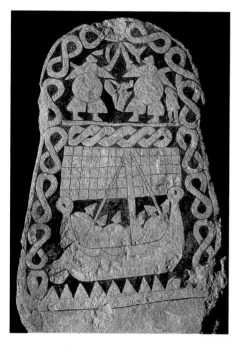

1. A pre-Christian (*c.* 7th century) Viking memorial stone from Gotland, Sweden, showing a mounted warrior, to whom a woman offers drink, and a ship sailed by two bearded men.

The assault on Christian Europe

A second wave of invaders struck Europe during the 8th and 9th centuries, after the Roman Empire had disintegrated but before the Christian kingdoms had attained real stability. The Vikings (**1, 2, 3**), whose original home was Scandinavia, first raided and then settled northern Britain and France (their descendants, the Normans, later conquered England and southern Italy). The Magyars (**6**), from the steppes of Eastern Europe, ravaged Italy in the late 9th century before settling in Hungary. The Saracens (**4**) also threatened Italy – even Rome itself in 846 – but only in Spain was Muslim conquest permanent.

2. The Gokstad ship, one of several Viking ships recovered from burials in Norway; 9th century.

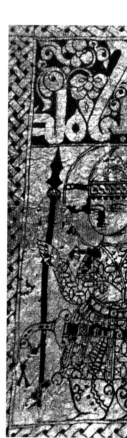

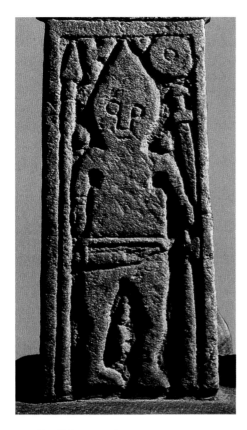

3. Detail from a 10th-century stone cross showing an armed Viking settler in northern England.

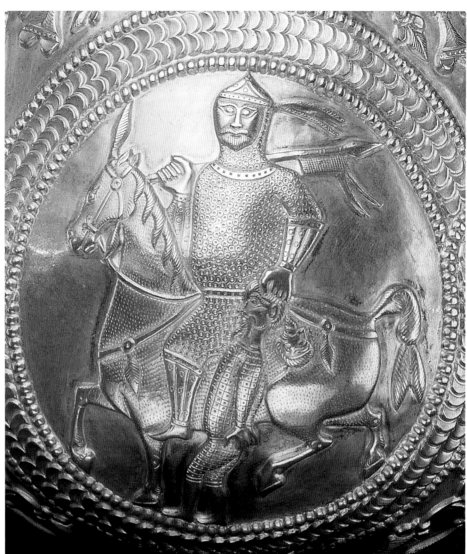

5. Medallion from an Avar jug of the 7th century: a nomad prince in armour.

4. Left: Saracen warriors; a drawing from Fatimid Egypt, 11th century.

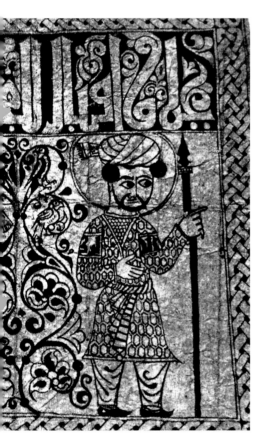

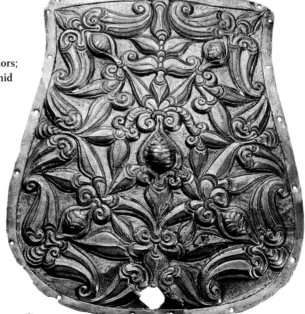

6. Magyar *sabretache*, or military purse; early 9th century.

2

Salvation of the Soul

THE TERM 'THE CHURCH' usually conjures up images of a specifically clerical or monastic community, from the pope to the parish priest, from cardinals and inquisitors to simple monks, friars and nuns. In the Middle Ages the word could also be used in a broader sense. The simplest and most direct translation of the word 'society' in medieval Europe would be 'the Church'. Everybody apart from the tiny Jewish and Muslim minorities would be baptized. Their marriage and burial would also usually take place under the auspices of the clergy. 'Christian' was the label that all these people, from whatever region – Bavaria, Scotland, Connacht, Sicily – could apply to themselves. Of course there were ethnic and class identities, but over them all was the fact that these scattered populations saw themselves as part of a larger Christendom.

Amongst this Christian population some had undertaken a more complete commitment to the religious life. Priests, deacons and other clerics promised chastity and bore the external marks of the tonsure and clerical dress, while those who entered the monastic orders abandoned not only sexual and family life but also private property and their own will. The idea of Christian monasticism, that is, of communities living a life of chastity and poverty in obedience to a superior, arose in the deserts of Egypt in the late Roman period, spread to Western Europe and there was given its distinctive Western form by St Benedict of Nursia in the sixth century. His *Rule*, the foundation stone of Benedictine monasticism, was the basic code of almost all western monasteries by the year 1000.

The life of a Benedictine monk or nun centred on the cycle of church services. The prayers, chants and psalms of the Divine Office and the celebration of Mass required hours each day, from dawn to night. The year was shaped by the liturgical rhythm, with its high points at Easter, Christmas and Pentecost. At least a basic literacy was necessary for these activities and, in the early Middle Ages, the production and preservation of books was almost exclusively the work of the monasteries. Since many monks and nuns entered the monastery as children and were bound by a vow of stability to remain there, it was possible for them to spend virtually their entire lives within one community – 'a cloistered life' in the literal sense.

By the eleventh century the Benedictine monasteries of Western Europe had become rich, profiting from the willingness of kings and great aristocrats to give them lands in return for their prayers. The liturgy became ever more elaborate. Abbots of the greater monasteries, such as Cluny in Burgundy, the most famous abbey of its time, were figures of international importance. It is not surprising that this provoked a reaction, or movement of reform, as its protagonists viewed it. The monastic life, they argued, was meant to be simpler and more austere. Monks should work with their hands and not be landlords. The elaborate decoration and carvings of the old Benedictine churches were distracting. 'Back to the desert' was the watchword of the reformers.

The Cistercians were the most successful of the reformed Benedictines. Founded at Cîteaux (not far from Cluny) in 1098, the order numbered over 500 abbeys by the year 1200, in large part because of the charismatic leadership of St Bernard of Clairvaux, who, although in rank only an abbot, became a dominating figure in the ecclesiastical politics of the years between the 1120s and his death in

To expound the entire scheme of Christian justice, two Benedictine nuns in the late 11th century commissioned this painting from the artists 'Nicolaus' and 'Johannes'. At the top, God the Father presides with angels and seraphim; in the next row, Christ with angels and the twelve Apostles. The next row features St Paul and St Stephen and three of the Works of Mercy – feeding the hungry, visiting the prisoner and clothing the naked. The next row shows the resurrection; on the left those whose bodies have been eaten by wild animals and fishes and have to be reconstituted, on the right those buried in graves. The panel at the bottom shows the Virgin with angels and the two nuns who commissioned the work, and on the right the damned are cast into Hell.

+ REGNVM PERCIPITE BENEDICTI QVIO VENITE · VOBIS PARATVM PER SECLA CVNCTA DONATVM ·

+ OFFERET VT PAVLVS EVERIT QDOVISQ LVCRATVS QD MARTYR STEPHANVS CLAMAT GREX IST E PVSILLV MEQ PAVISTI POT P SEPE DEDISTI VEL SIMVL IN DVTO REPARASTI CORPORE N VD

OMEGENVS VOLVCRV VEL REPTILIS ATQ FERARV REDDVNT HVMANA PISCES QVOQ MENBRA VORATA
LANGOR ET VBAESS RGVNT DE PVLVEREE RRE NICOLAVS IOHS PICTO

VSTIS EST ES PARADISI RDIS HOS BLISIRA

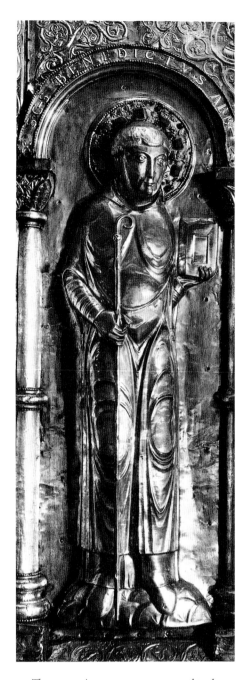

The monastic movement was central to the development of medieval Christianity, and its crucial figure was St Benedict of Nursia, whose Rule, first formulated in the 6th century, was adopted by virtually all monasteries and underlay even the later reformed orders. He is shown holding a copy of his Rule and an abbot's staff in this bronze relief of the 11th century.

1153. He encouraged the crusading movement, assailed those whom he suspected of heresy, and preached and wrote with passion and eloquence of the mystical path to God. Everywhere Cistercian monasteries sprang up, marked by their simple, uniform plan, their austerity of style and the fact that, initially at least, their lands were worked by monks and lay brothers rather than by peasant tenants.

The Cistercians, and other reformed orders of the twelfth century, while representing a new adaptation of the ancient tradition of Christian monasticism, still preserved many of its established features. The friars of the early thirteenth century were more revolutionary in their basic approach to the full-time religious vocation. The model of St Francis, the founder and inspiration of the friars, pointed to a life of wandering, preaching and begging from door to door (hence the friars are also termed 'mendicants' or beggars). Just as the Cistercians had aroused the religious enthusiasm of Europe in the twelfth century, so the Franciscans and Dominicans dominated the thirteenth, establishing themselves across the whole of Catholic Christendom, forming an intellectual elite that elaborated a Christian form of philosophy ('scholasticism') and through their preaching bringing Christian doctrine and practice to the laity in a way never before attempted.

Over the course of its long history the Christian religion has often veered between stressing belief in a set of doctrines and concentrating on rituals and practices. Medieval Christianity was certainly based on a set of doctrines, and those who dissented from those doctrines were persecuted and sometimes executed, but the heart of the religion was not creed but a range of ritual and devotional customs. The Christian life was framed by the sacraments of baptism, confirmation, marriage and anointing of the dead, and found regular expression in the sacraments of mass and penance. The fate of the soul after death could be affected by the prayers and charity of the living. Good deeds, such as alms-giving, brought merit. So did punishment of the flesh: fasting and flagellation were ways of lessening the future pains of purgatory by inflicting them here and now.

The Christian could seek the aid of supernatural power in many ways, from the saints, from the angels, from Mary, mother of God, and from Christ himself, as the baby in his mother's arms, as the tortured figure on the crucifix or in the form of the Eucharist, which was viewed as Christ's body and had, from 1264, its own annual feast day, Corpus Christi ('the body of Christ'). The whole of Western Europe was filled with shrines where local saints could be invoked for help, especially for their healing powers. Some of these shrines became centres of international pilgrimage. Santiago de Compostela, where the bones of St James were supposedly discovered in the ninth century, drew pilgrims from all over Western Christendom and their route across northern Spain – 'the French trail' as it was called – was marked by new bridges, hostels and churches, and towns flourishing from their traffic (its significance is illustrated by the fact that in modern Spanish the Milky Way is termed 'the Santiago trail').

Especially in the later Middle Ages, mystics and visionaries were important in the Christian religious life. The Low Countries and the Rhineland produced remarkable figures, including Meister Eckhart, his followers Johann Tauler and Heinrich Suso, and the Fleming, Jan van Ruysbroeck, whose *Adornment of the Spiritual Marriage* culminated in a lyrical account of the mystic's goal: 'rapturous meeting', 'eternal rest in the fruitive embrace of an outpouring Love', 'the dark silence in which all lovers lose themselves'. Women had been important in

Christian mysticism since the time of Hildegard of Bingen (d. 1179) and they continued to be so throughout the following centuries, with such figures as Catherine of Siena and the English mystics Juliana of Norwich and Margery Kempe pursuing ecstatic rapture and visionary experiences.

The medieval Church was not a democratic or liberal institution but a hierarchical and authoritarian one. Those who dissented from official doctrine were not tolerated. Apart from in the exceptional case of the Jews (and Muslims in some parts of Spain), the Church authorities regarded difference in belief as an evil to be rooted out. Theologians had to be careful to avoid unorthodox theories or, like Peter Abelard in the twelfth century and John Wycliffe in the fourteenth, they might find themselves the target of accusations of heresy. Abelard's books were burned, but, as the poet Heine remarked, 'where they begin by burning books, they end by burning men'. As the Church came to feel that the challenge of heresy was growing in strength, so it devised more thorough and more brutal forms of inquisition and repression. The forcing house for these new policies was southern France, where the heretical groups known as Cathars became so numerous that Pope Innocent III launched a crusade against them in 1209, while in the 1230s Pope Gregory IX followed this up by establishing the inquisition to hunt out heretics.

Catharism was eventually exterminated, after hundreds of its followers had been burned, but other heretical movements arose, challenging the authority of the Church hierarchy and advocating alternative doctrines and structures. The Waldensians believed that ordinary lay people, including women, had the right to preach; the Spiritual Franciscans clashed with the papacy because of their extreme commitment to the ideal of poverty; the Lollards, who took up some of Wycliffe's ideas, cited Scripture to attack the authority and property of the Church, rejected pilgrimage, prayers to the dead and reverence for images and argued that every righteous layman was a true priest. The most successful of the heretical movements of the later Middle Ages was that of the Hussites, who actually seized control of Bohemia for seventeen years (1419–36), defeating crusading armies that were sent against them and threatening to spread their beliefs through force into the neighbouring territories. They had a radical and a moderate wing, the former advocating complete disendowment of the Church and socially revolutionary principles. Not unnaturally, the Hussites have been seen as precursors of the Reformation a century later that destroyed medieval Christendom for good.

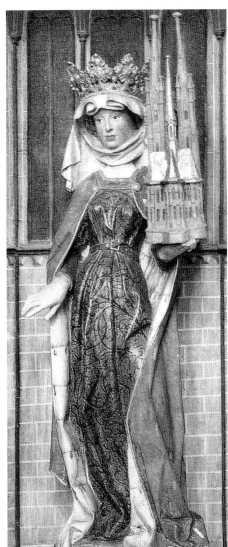

Female saints became increasingly popular in the later Middle Ages. St Elizabeth (1207–31), shown here holding a model of her church at Marburg, suffered persecution because of the lavishness of her almsgiving.

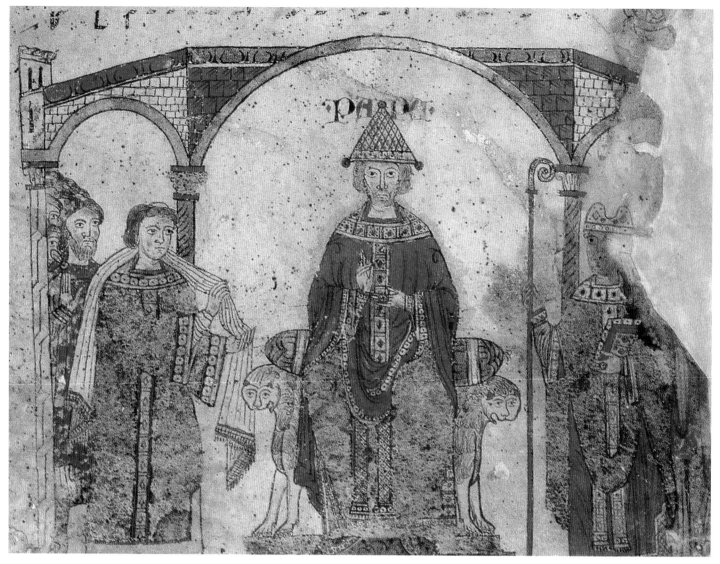

1. Pope, with bishop (right) and clergy (left); Montecassino, c. 1087.
All the details on these pages are from Exultet Rolls of southern Italy.

The hierarchy of the Church

The medieval Church was for hundreds of years the most centralized and absolute institution in Europe. Its authority was entirely spiritual, but despite some serious clashes with emperors and other secular rulers, it was generally accepted and obeyed. The pope, after all, was the vicar of Christ and held the keys of Heaven and Hell. Within the Church, authority was rarely challenged, the most notable exception being the Great Schism of 1378–1417 when there were two rival factions, each electing its own popes. Normally any dispute was referred from rank to rank – deacon (**2**), priest (**5**), bishop (**3**, **4**) – until it reached the pope (**1**), whose decision was final. There was no machinery for disagreement. The rejection of authority was heresy, to be dealt with by excommunication and punishment.

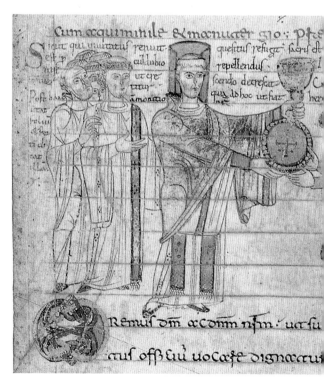

2. Ordination of subdeacons: the empty paten and chalice conferred by the bishop; pitcher, basin and towel conferred by the archdeacon; Pontifical, Benevento, c. 970.

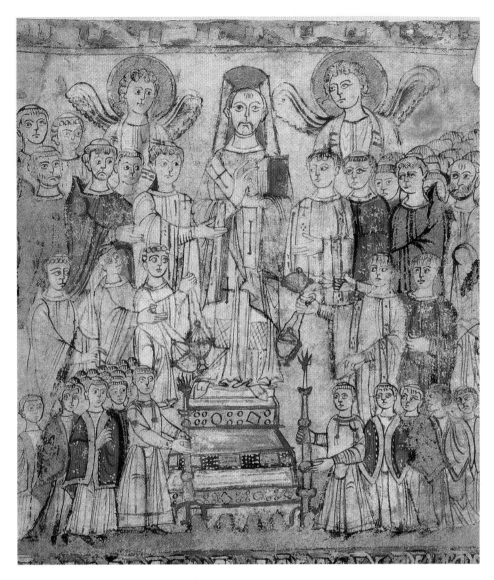

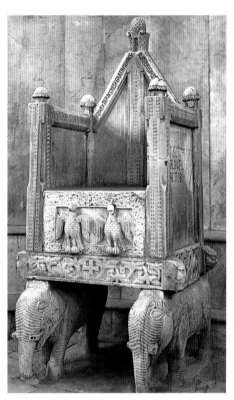

3. Bishop and clergy (with two angels in unseen attendance); Benevento, 981–87.

4. Bishop's throne at Canosa di Puglia, south Italy; 1089.

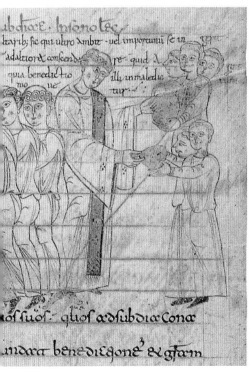

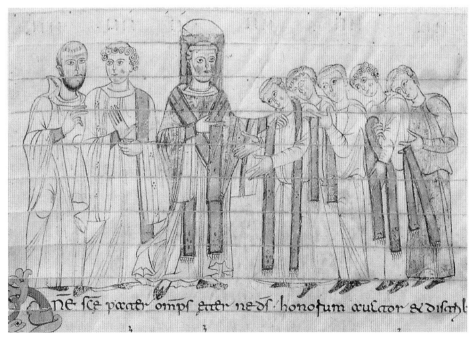

5. Ordination of priests: investing with the stole; Pontifical, Benevento, c. 970.

The seven sacraments

The medieval Church, like the Catholic Church today, defined seven specific occasions when (except in very unusual circumstances) the presence of a priest was required as an instrument of God's grace. They were Baptism (6, 8), symbol of entry into the Christian community; Confirmation (4), the conscious renewal of that commitment; Confession and Penance (5), the expression of the Church's power to forgive sins; Holy Communion, or the Eucharist (2), the central rite of the Church, when the bread and wine become Christ's body and blood; Ordination (7), the conferring of priestly powers; Marriage (3), the foundation of the family and legitimate offspring; and Extreme Unction (9), the preparation of the soul for its passage to Heaven. This English stained-glass series of the Seven Sacraments is from Doddiscombsleigh, Devon, *c.* 1500.

2. The Eucharist, or Holy Communion: Early Christians took part in a communal meal (*agape*), which later theologians, following St Paul, linked with the Last Supper, identifying the bread and wine with the body and blood of Christ.

3. Marriage was long regarded as a civil contract, and it was some time before the presence of a priest became accepted as necessary.

4. Confirmation followed baptism and preceded the Eucharist.

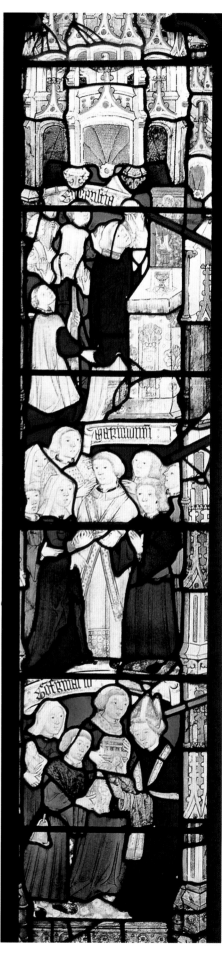

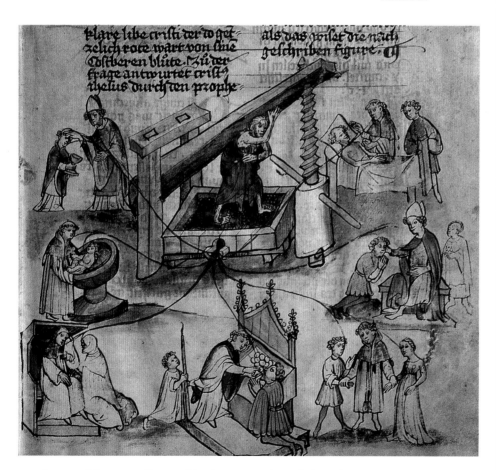

1. German 16th-century allegory of the Sacraments. From Christ's wine-press, the wine (his blood) flows to each of the seven sacramental occasions.

5. Confession and Penance were fundamental to the Church's claim to absolve sins. Like other sacraments, the full doctrine of the priestly powers took years of argument to finalize. The idea of secret confessions goes back to the 5th century.

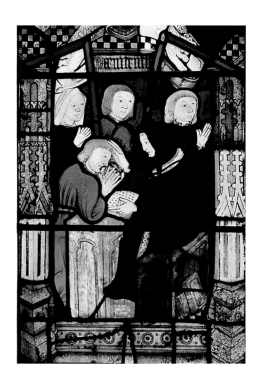

6. A Seven Sacrament font at Walsoken, England; 15th century. In the centre, Extreme Unction and to the right, Marriage.

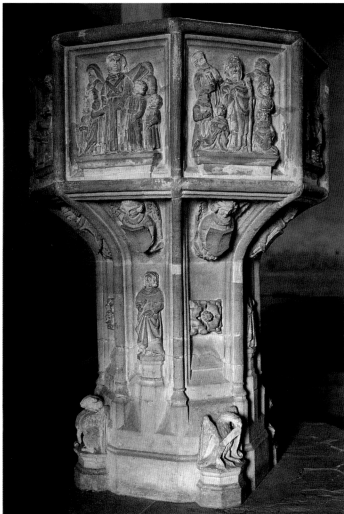

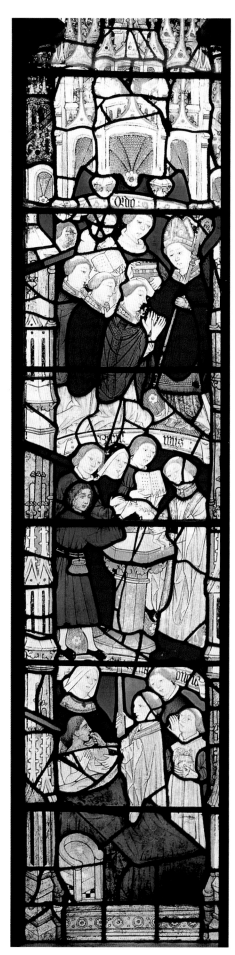

7. Ordination grew with the organization of an ecclesiastical hierarchy. Early Christian writers stressed the continuity with the Old Testament priesthood. Like Confirmation, Ordination required the presence of a bishop.

8. Baptism is probably the oldest sacrament, a ritual cleansing of sins and entering upon a new life. But the issue of whether it should be performed in infancy or adult-hood long remained controversial.

9. Extreme Unction was traced back to the practice of the Apostles, who anointed the sick and forgave them their sins as a preparation for death. The Latin term, *viaticum,* meant 'provision for a journey'.

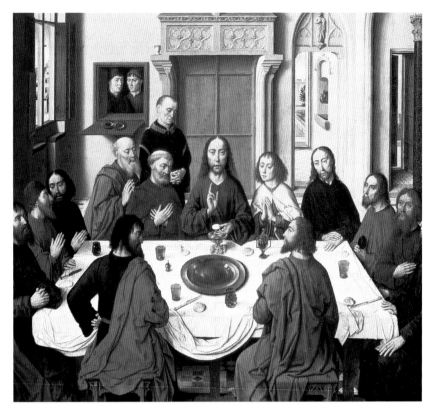

1. The Last Supper, by Dirk Bouts (detail), *c.* 1465.

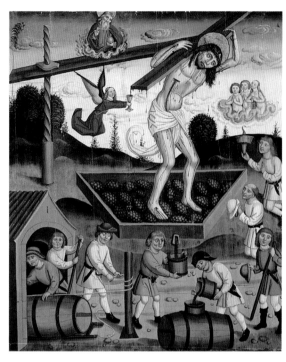

2. The Wine-Press of the Lord; Bavarian altarpiece, *c.* 1500.

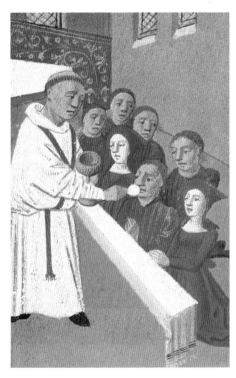

3. Priest administering the Eucharist
to the laity; French, 15th century.

4. Mass of St Gregory, by Bernt Notke,
Åarhus Cathedral, Denmark, 1479.

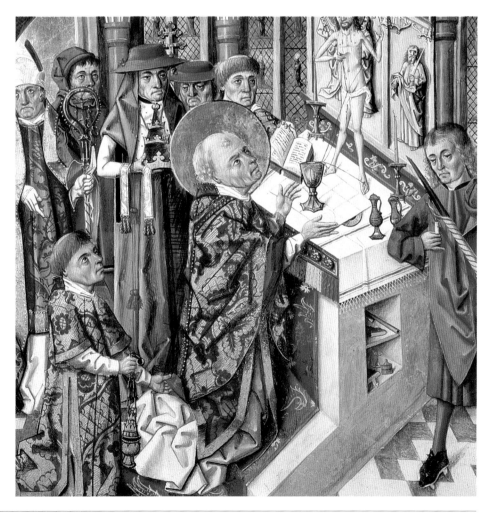

The seven sacraments
62-63

The many faces of Christ
74-75

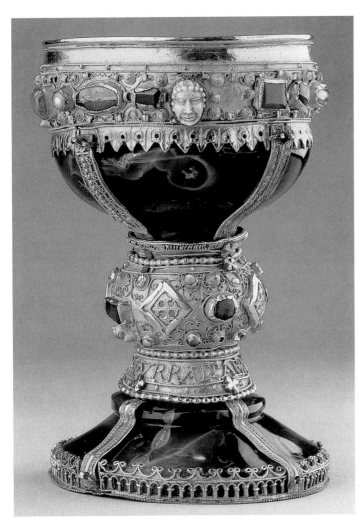

5. Chalice of Urrace, León, Spain; 11th century.

The Eucharist

The Eucharist, or Holy Communion, was the central mystery of the Christian liturgy, the daily miracle when, at the priest's words of consecration (6), the bread and wine actually become the body and blood of Christ, to be taken into the mouths of the faithful (3). It was a rite supposedly initiated by Jesus himself at the Last Supper (1). For the intellectual it was argued (by St Thomas Aquinas) that while the 'accidents' of bread and wine (appearance, taste, etc.) remained the same, the 'substance' (their essential identity) was changed. For the unphilosophical it was conveyed through images, such as the metaphor of the wine-press (2) and by legends such as the Mass of St Gregory (4), when Christ manifested himself on the altar, to prove his 'real presence' in the chalice. Chalices (5) were themselves semi-sacred objects.

6. Priest at the altar; Ottonian ivory book-cover, 10th century.

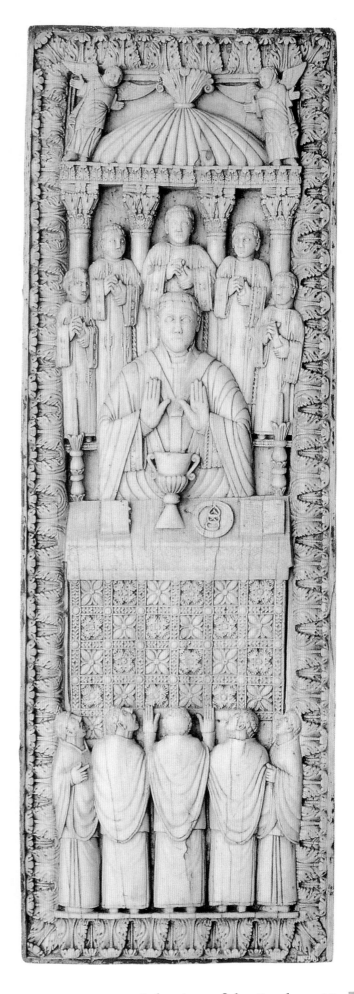

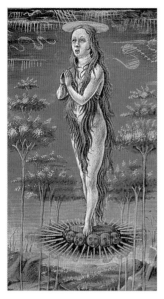

1. St Mary Magdalene penitent; by Taddeo Crivelli, c. 1469.

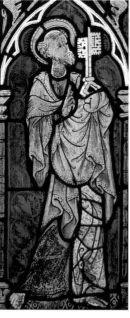

2. St Peter with the keys of Heaven and Hell; English stained glass, c. 1320.

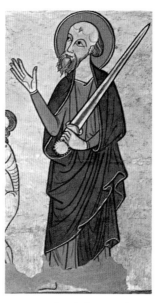

3. St Paul with the sword; Catalan, 13th century.

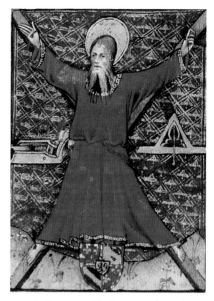

4. St Andrew, crucified on an x-shaped cross; French, 1406–15.

The fellowship of the saints

Saints were Christians (primarily the apostles, evangelists and martyrs) who by their conspicuously holy lives were guaranteed a place in heaven. In early times they were accepted on the basis of legend; later the process of canonization was formalized and controlled (as it is today) by the papal court. To ordinary men and women the saints were familiar presences – protectors, supporters and friends. 'Patron saint' was no mere form of words. Petitioning favours from a saint was very like petitioning an earthly lord: gifts were offered, vows made, bargains struck. (Saints could be difficult; failure to keep one's promises often had unpleasant consequences.) Images of the most popular saints were everywhere, each easily identified by his or her attributes – St Peter by his keys (**2**), St Paul by his sword (**3**), St Barbara by her tower (**10**) and so on. Sometimes the images themselves came to be accorded veneration, leading at the end of the Middle Ages to accusations of idolatry.

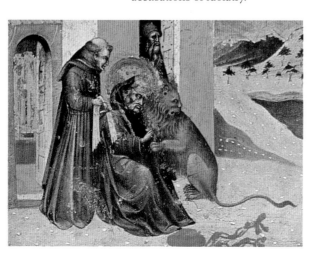

5. St Luke, by Simone Martini, c. 1330.

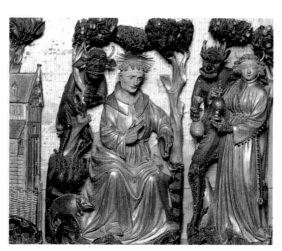

6. St Jerome with his companion the lion; Sienese, 1436.

7. St Antony, tempted by evil spirits; Spanish, 1390–99.

The unseen power of relics 68-69

Shrines and miracles 70-71

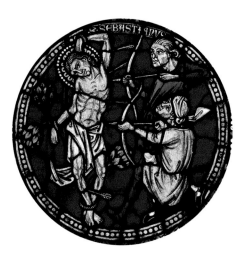

8. St Sebastian, shot with arrows; Freiburg Cathedral, 13th century.

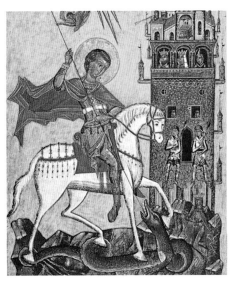

9. St George slaying the dragon; Russian, 15th century.

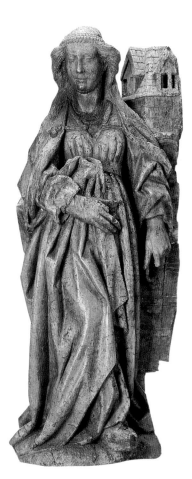

10. St Barbara holding the tower in which she was imprisoned; Flemish, c. 1435.

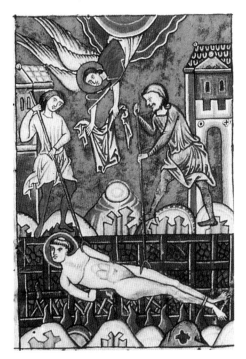

11. St Lawrence, martyred on a gridiron; South German, 13th century.

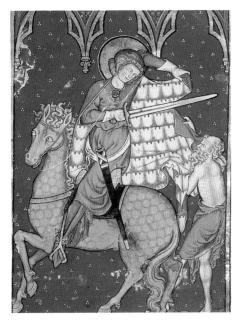

12. St Martin sharing his cloak with a beggar; French, c. 1290.

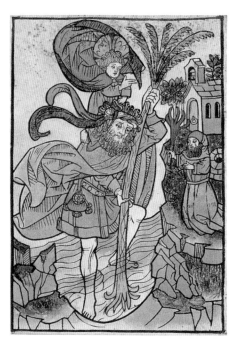

15. St Christopher bearing the Christ-child on his shoulders; German woodcut, 15th century.

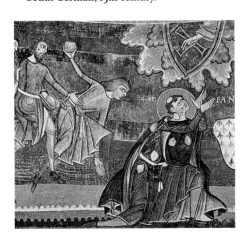

13. St Stephen, stoned to death; wall-painting, South Tyrol, 1163–80.

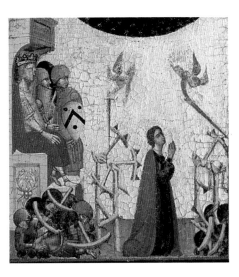

14. Left: St Catherine of Alexandria, the wheel on which she was being tortured miraculously shattered; by Donato and Gregorio d'Arezzo, c. 1330.

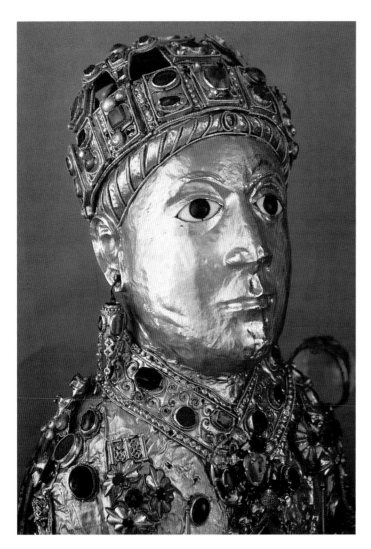

1. Reliquary of Ste Foy, Conques, *c.* 985; made of gold with precious stones added over many years.

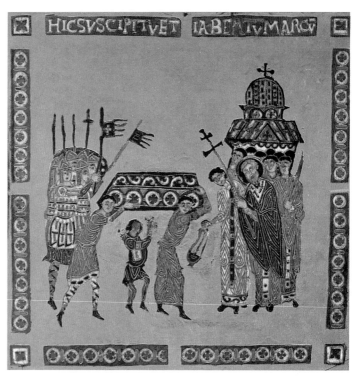

2. Bringing the body of St Mark to Venice after it had been stolen from Alexandria; enamel plaque from the Pala d'Oro, Venice, 13th century.

The unseen power of relics

Saints were more powerful dead than alive. In Heaven they could petition Christ to intercede with the Father on behalf of their devotees. Their bodies, or parts of their bodies, or objects associated with them, were reverently preserved, and the closer one came to them the better were one's chances of being heard. The cult of relics was thus a major preoccupation of both clergy and laity, and there was keen competition to acquire those with most fame and prestige. Some churches accumulated whole treasuries of relics, which attracted worshippers, who in their turn enriched the church with their offerings. The most prized relics were those associated with Christ himself (5), followed by those of major figures such as St Mark (2) and St Thomas Becket (3). But there were also obscure saints whose reputation seems more or less fortuitous, such as Ste Foy of Conques (1), a little girl of twelve martyred in 303.

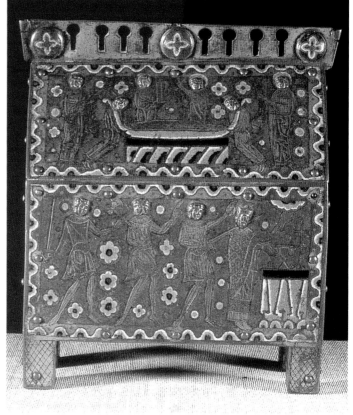

3. A Limoges enamel reliquary of St Thomas Becket, with a scene showing his martyrdom; 12th century.

Shrines and miracles 70-71   The pilgrimage 72-73

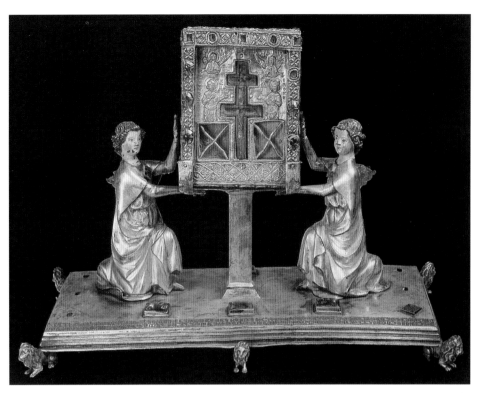

5. Reliquary containing a fragment of the True Cross, supported by the archangels Michael and Gabriel. Within the frame are figures of Constantine and Helena, who discovered the Cross in Jerusalem; *c.* 1340–60.

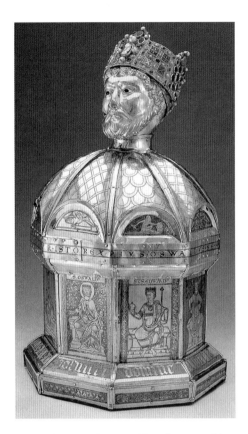

4. Reliquary of St Oswald, a 7th-century king of Northumbria; 1170–80, head and crown after 1185. He was revered in Germany, where this reliquary was commissioned probably by Henry the Lion, Duke of Saxony, who had married an English princess, Matilda.

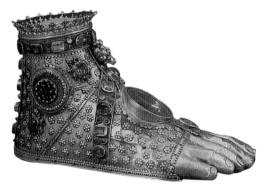

6. Foot reliquary of one of the Holy Innocents; German, *c.* 1450.

7. The arm reliquary of St John the Baptist, in Zara Cathedral; 15th century. One of many reliquaries modelled on the part of the body that it contained.

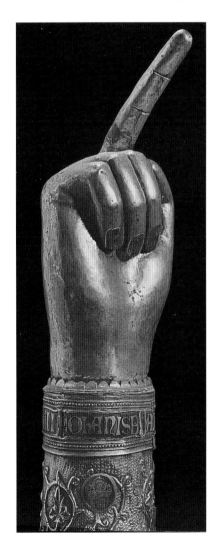

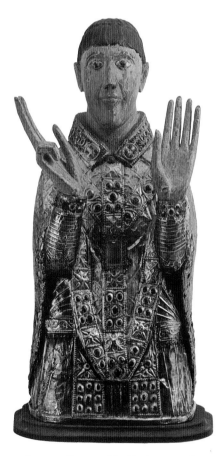

8. Bust reliquary of St Césaire, an early bishop of Arles; late 12th century.

Shrines and miracles

Access to the bodies of saints was made easier by placing them in shrines round which the faithful could file in an orderly manner – either in a crypt or (in abbeys and cathedrals) normally behind the high altar. These shrines were sometimes extremely magnificent and costly, so that a constant watch was kept over them (3). Often they were constructed in such a way that the worshippers could literally crawl inside and touch the coffin (1). Their prayers were usually for a cure for illness, and in this respect saints' bones seem to have been as effective as most other forms of alternative medicine (6). Many shrines were adorned with the crutches left behind by the lame and the crippled, now restored to health.

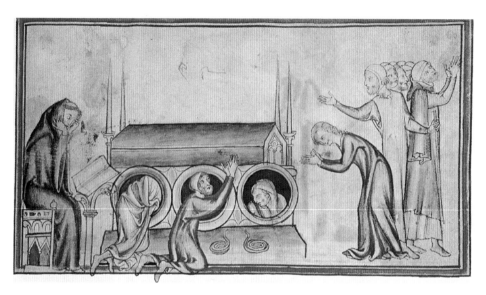

1. Pilgrims at the shrine of St Edward the Confessor, Westminster, 13th century. Holes at the sides enable them to creep close to the saint's body.

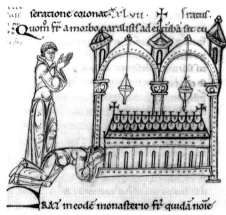

2. Monks praying at the shrine of St Cuthbert, Durham; from a manuscript of Bede's Life of St Cuthbert, 12th century.

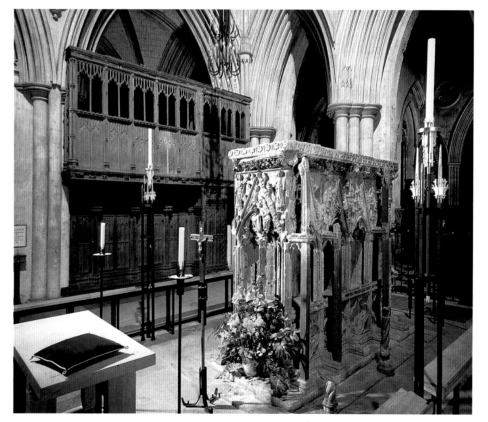

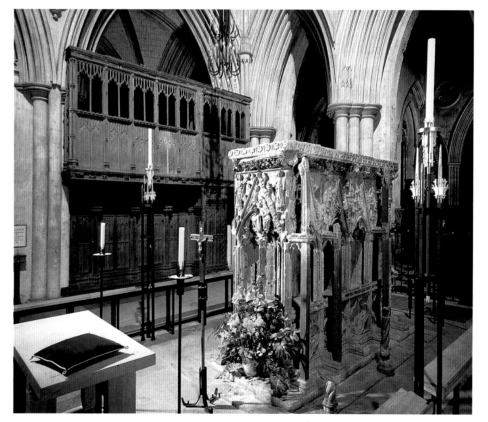

4. Prayers at the shrine of St Edmund, Bury St Edmunds, England; 15th century.

3. Left: the shrine of St Alban, St Alban's Cathedral, England; 13th century. From the watching chamber behind, a monk could stand guard. The shrine was smashed at the Reformation but reconstructed in the 19th century from 2,000 fragments.

The pilgrimage 72-73

Joys and sorrows of Mary 76-77

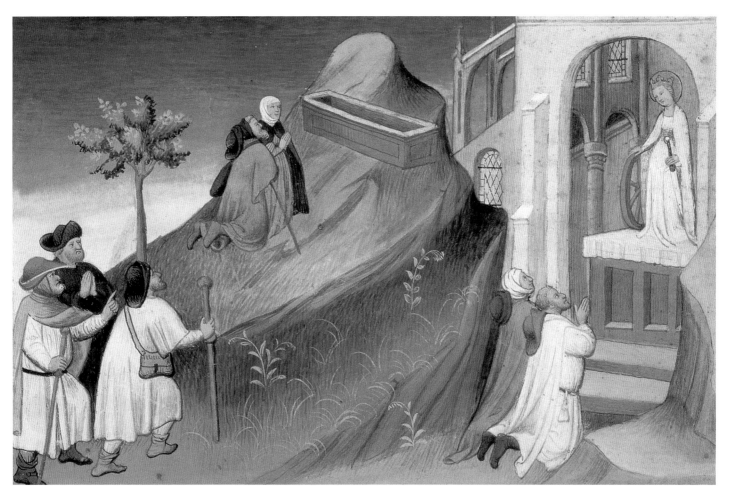

5. Pilgrims at the shrine of St Catherine of Alexandria at her monastery on Mount Sinai, a remote outpost to which only the most resolute penetrated.

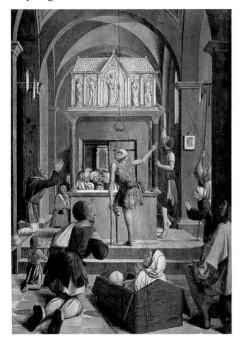

6. The sick come to pray at an Italian shrine; early 15th century. In the foreground, a man lies on an improvised litter very like a coffin.

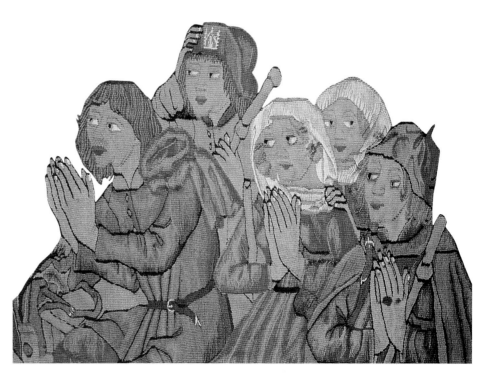

7. Detail of a 14th-century Rhineland tapestry showing worshippers praying before the shrine of St Adolphus.

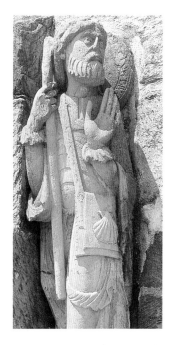

1. St James (Santiago) of Compostela, shown as a pilgrim with staff and scallop shell.

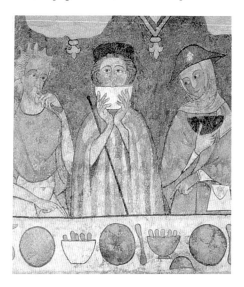

2. Spanish fresco showing pilgrims receiving hospitality on the road to Compostela; 13th century.

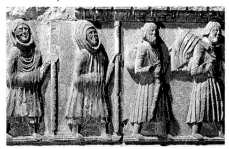

3. Pilgrims in winter clothes bound for Compostela from Italy; a relief at Fidenza Cathedral.

5. Right: pilgrims at an inn; a 15th-century English manuscript.

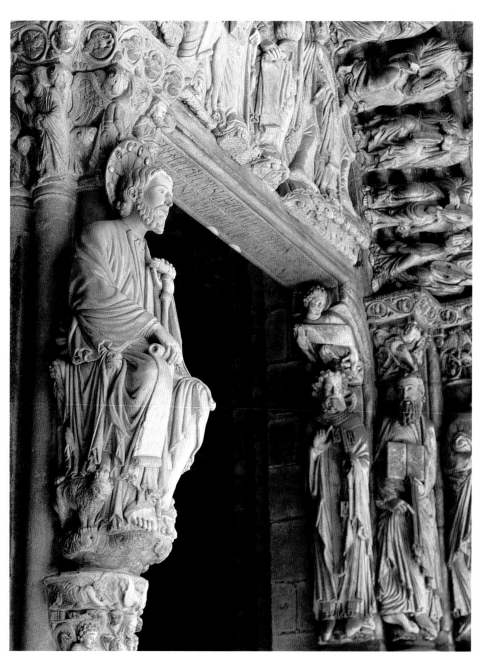

4. The Portico della Gloria, the magnificent 12th-century entrance portal to the church of Santiago de Compostela, the final goal of the long pilgrimage.

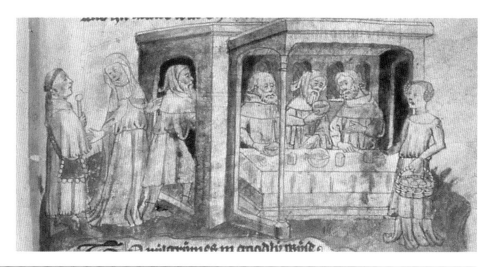

Shrines and miracles 70-71   Travel by land and sea 176-177

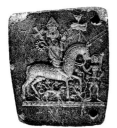
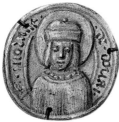

6, 7. Two pilgrim badges, mass-produced from moulds.

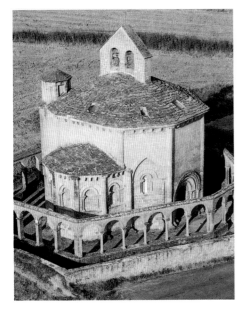

8. A 12th-century chapel at Eunate in Navarre on the road to Compostela which includes a cemetery for pilgrims who died on the way.

10. Right: the 12th-century church at Conques, in central France, was a stopping-place on the road to Compostela containing the relics of Ste Foy.

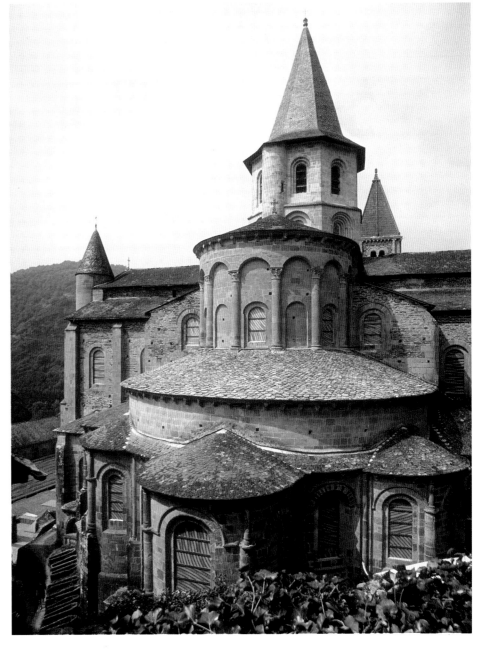

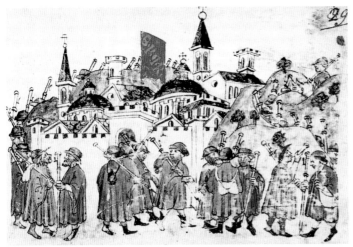

9. Pilgrims arriving in Rome for the Jubilee of 1300; from a 15th-century Italian chronicle.

The pilgrimage

The three most popular shrines in the Middle Ages were Compostela (1, 4), at the northwest tip of Spain, Rome and Jerusalem. All three involved long, uncomfortable and often dangerous journeys (8). Why were they undertaken in such numbers? Pilgrimage was certainly a good spiritual investment; one accumulated merit by worshipping before the relics of saints, and there were numerous less important shrines to be visited along the way, such as that of Ste Foy at Conques (10). But clearly there was an element of pleasure in the mere journey, the camaraderie of the road and the adventure of seeing foreign lands (2, 3, 5). At each shrine pilgrims could acquire badges (6, 7) as evidence of their pious enterprises.

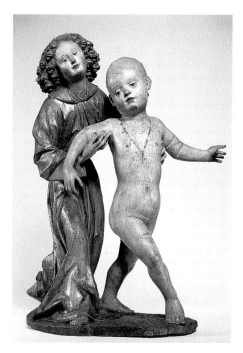

1. The infant Jesus with an angel; coloured wood sculpture from Bavaria, *c.* 1480.

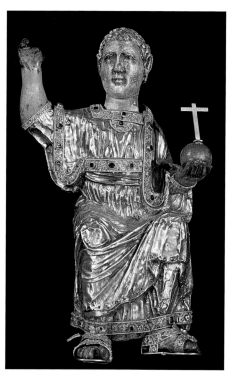

2. Jesus as a boy in royal robes; Spanish, 13th century.

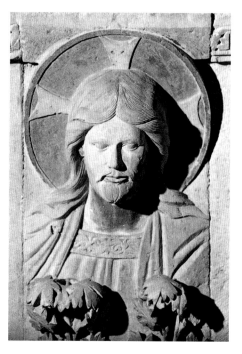

3. Head of Christ, in Todi Cathedral, Italy; 13th century.

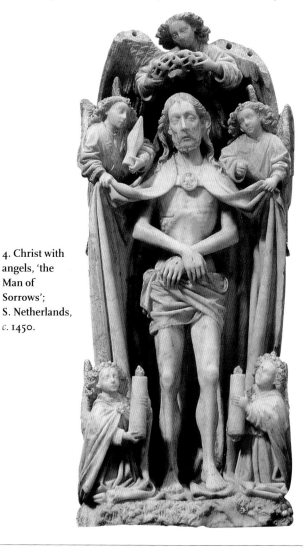

4. Christ with angels, 'the Man of Sorrows'; S. Netherlands, *c.* 1450.

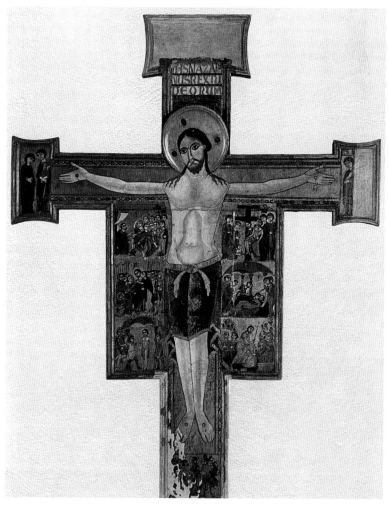

5. Christ on the cross; Italian, early 12th century.

Picturing the new faith
44-45

The image of salvation
46-47

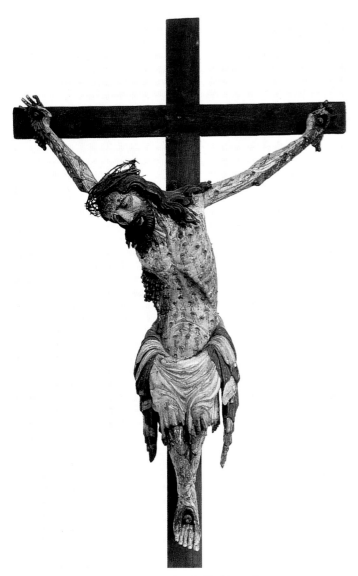

6. Christ on the cross; German, first half of the 14th century.

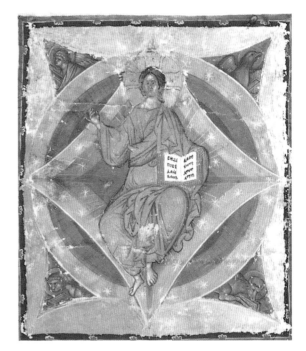

7. Christ in glory; Russian, early 15th century.

The many faces of Christ

The figure of Christ was central to every aspect of medieval life and thought, and no single image could encompass all the meanings that he embodied. Christ was both human and divine. Even as a child he could be seen either as a vulnerable and appealing infant (1) or as a celestial prince (2). His death on the cross was the turning-point of human history (5, 6), but his suffering was ambivalent, at once a defeat and a triumph. The resurrected Christ could also evoke varying responses: from the stern and awful judge, ruler of the universe (7) to the gentle saviour leading mankind to everlasting bliss (8). Emphasis could change with time. In the 12th century the crucified Christ was a calm, almost abstract icon of sacrifice (5); later, partly through the influence of popular preachers like St Francis, it was the all-too-human agony of a real tortured body that was stressed (6).

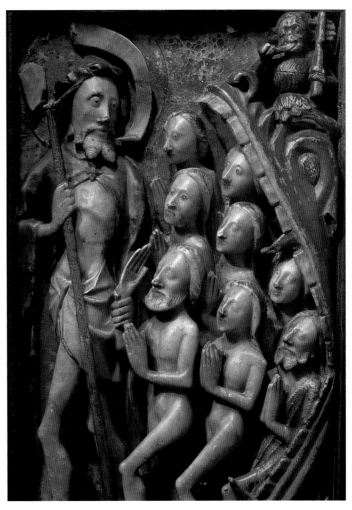

8. Christ leading souls out of Hell; English alabaster, 15th century.

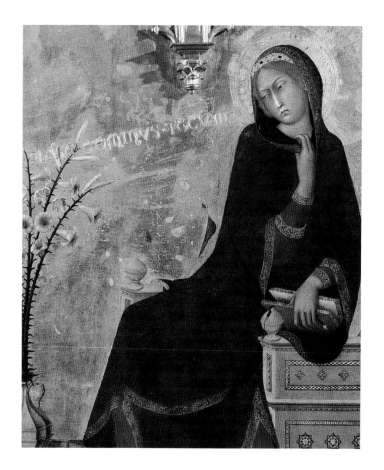

Joys and sorrows of Mary

The cult of the Virgin Mary proliferated throughout the Middle Ages until in the popular mind (though not, of course, in official doctrine) she almost became a fourth person of the Trinity. At once the most merciful and the most powerful of the heavenly hierarchy, she was happy to perform miracles for her devotees, and wonder-working images of her far outnumber those of any other saint. Her sad life-story – modest and shrinking as a young girl (**1**), tender and loving as a mother (**2, 3, 4**), grief-stricken at the death of her son (**6**) – was one that she shared with most of her worshippers. But at the same time she was Queen of Heaven (**5**) and divine protectress of mankind (**7**). Artistic conventions went hand in hand with emotional attitudes. Early representations of her are remote and hieratic (**2**). Later she is shown as human and playful (**3, 4**) or contorted with the agony of loss (**6**).

1. Simone Martini: The Annunciation, 1333. Mary draws back timidly from the apparition of the angel Gabriel.

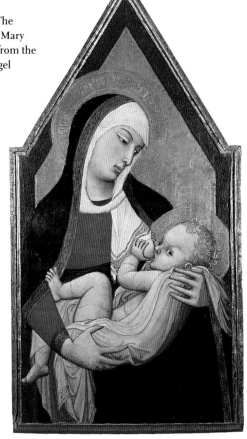

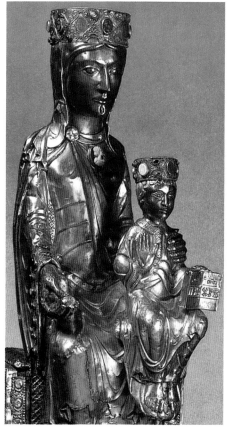

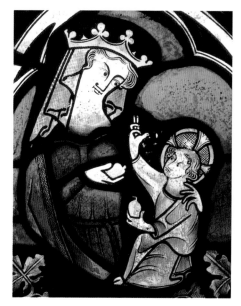

3. Madonna and Child, from an English stained-glass window; 1330–40.

2. Left: Madonna and Child Enthroned. A French 12th-century image in silver, set with precious stones like a reliquary.

4. Ambrogio Lorenzetti: Nursing Madonna, mid-14th century.

Picturing the new faith 44-45

Women: weakness and strength 164-165

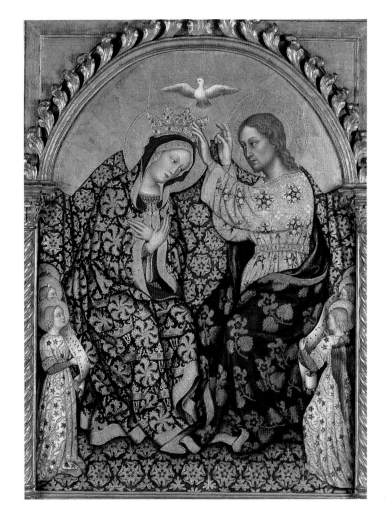

5. Gentile da Fabriano: Coronation of the Virgin, c. 1420.

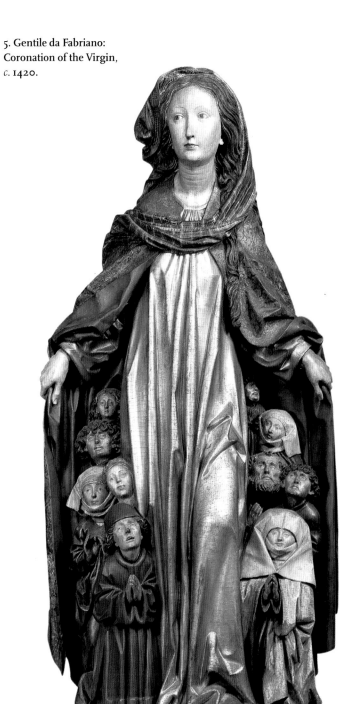

7. Michel Erhart of Swabia: the Virgin of Mercy, c. 1480. The human race seeks shelter under her protective cloak.

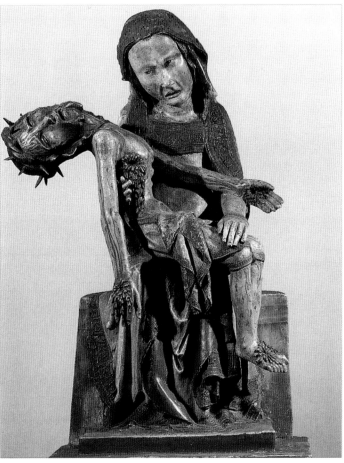

6. The Virgin with the dead Christ on her lap; German woodcarving from the Rhineland, c. 1300.

Salvation of the Soul　77

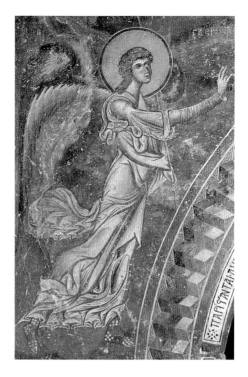

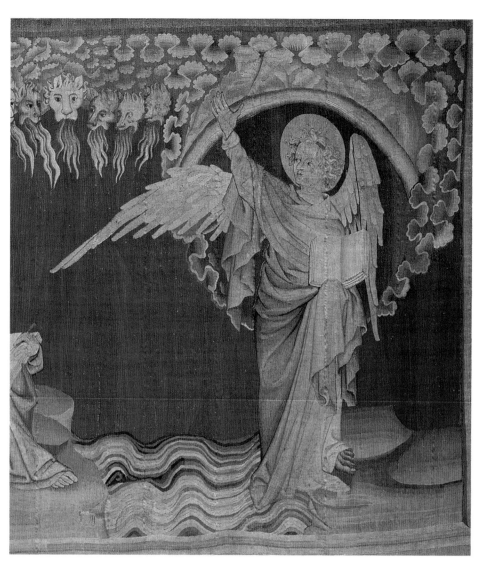

1. Gabriel, the Angel of the Annunciation; a wall-painting at Kurbinovo, Macedonia, 1191.

2. Right: 'And I saw another angel, a strong one, coming down from heaven, clothed in a cloud, and the rainbow was over his head, and his face was like the sun, and his feet like pillars of fire. And he had in his hand a little open book, and he set his right foot upon the sea and his left upon the earth.' From the Angers Tapestry of the Apocalypse, *c.* 1379.

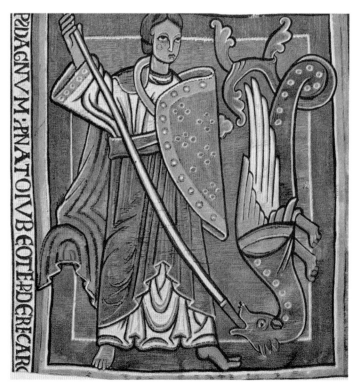

Angels of light

These heavenly messengers had a complex Romano-Hebrew ancestry. As Christian theology developed, their degrees and special tasks were more and more precisely defined. To most people they were as familiar as the saints and the object of similar devotion. Gabriel (**1**), the gentle archangel, was charged with announcing Mary's forthcoming motherhood to her. Michael (**3**), the warrior, commanded the heavenly host in its battle with Satan. The lower ranks of angels served God's purposes through the universe, making music (**5**), presiding over the end of the world (**2**) and welcoming the saved into Paradise (**6**).

3. St Michael defeats Satan, the dragon; detail from a tapestry in Halberstadt Cathedral, *c.* 1156–90.

The powers of darkness 80-81

Mystical visions 88-89

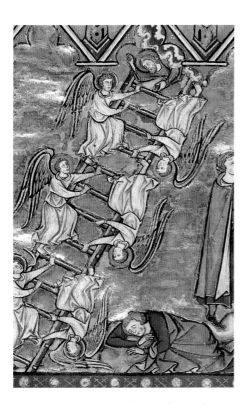

4. Jacob's Dream, angels ascending and descending a ladder; French, *c.* 1250.

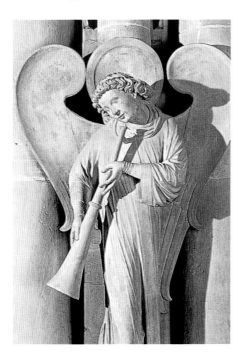

5. Angel musicians in Strasbourg Cathedral, 13th century.

6. Hans Memling: detail from the Last Judgment, *c.* 1470. Angels clothe the naked bodies of the saved as they enter Paradise. This painting makes very clear how the great Gothic cathedrals were seen as images of the Heavenly Jerusalem.

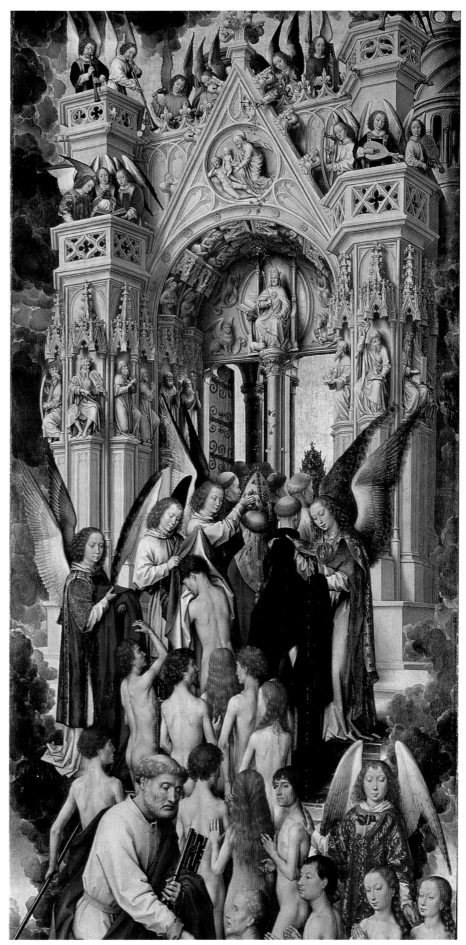

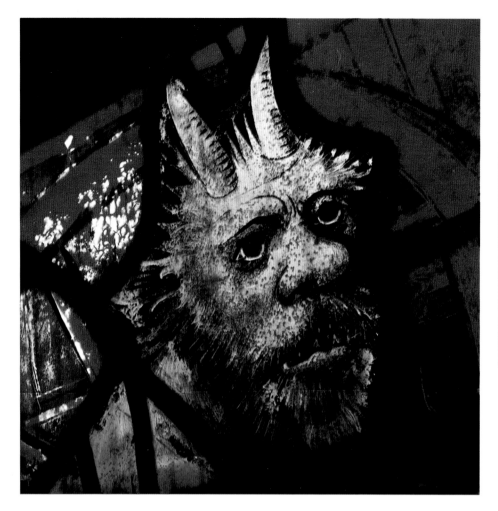

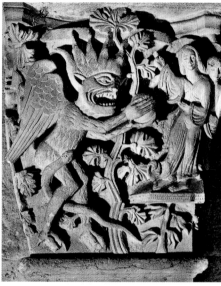

2. Satan tempting Christ, a capital from Autun Cathedral, France; 12th century.

1. Left: devil, from a stained-glass window at Fairford, England, c. 1500.

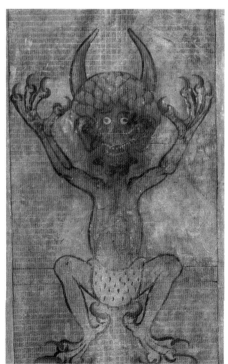

3. The lighter side of Hell: a devil from a Bohemian manuscript, 1204–30.

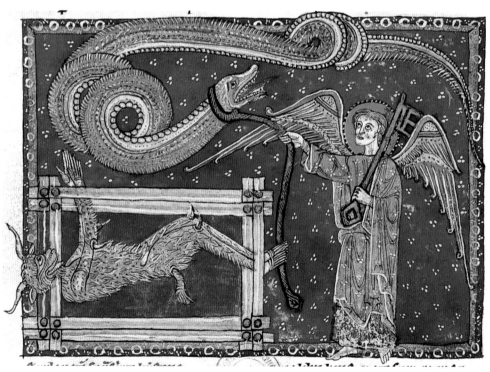

4. 'And I saw an angel coming down from heaven, having the key of the abyss and a great chain in his hand. And he laid hold on the dragon, the ancient serpent, who is the devil and Satan, and bound him for a thousand years.' From a Spanish commentary on the Apocalypse by Beatus of Liebana; early 13th century.

Angels of light 78-79

Buildings in the mind 144-145

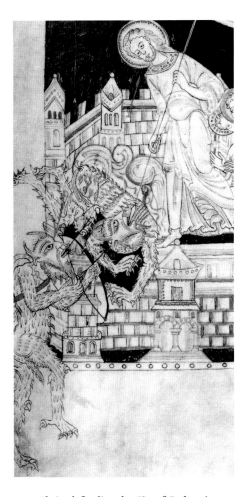

5. Christ defending the City of God against Satan, an English manuscript of the Apocalypse; 12th century.

6. At the Last Judgment the trumpet shall sound, the dead will awaken and the wicked will be cast down into everlasting torment – a terrifying vision that must have been present in all too literal terms to the medieval imagination. This spine-chilling picture is from the *Très Riches Heures* of the Duc de Berry; mid-15th century.

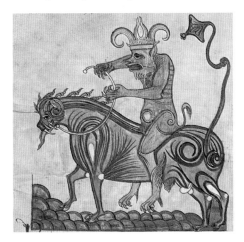

7. Satan as Antichrist riding on the back of the monster Behemoth; Northern French, early 12th century.

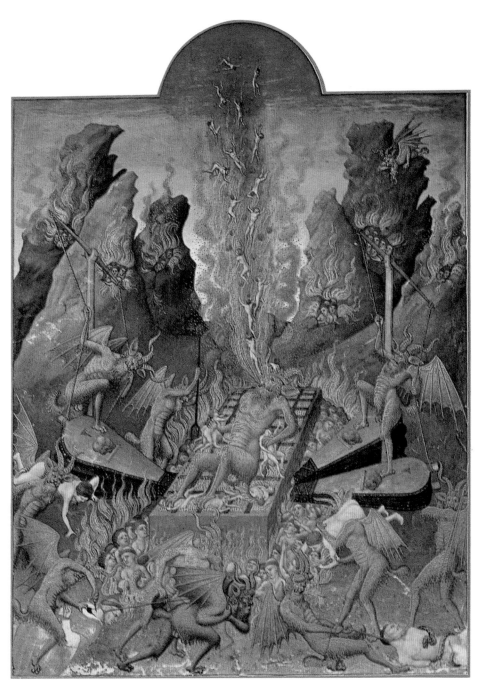

The powers of darkness

Satan and his devils were originally angels who had rebelled against God. They were defeated in a great battle in Heaven (5), cast into Hell and made the agents of God's punishment of the wicked. The idea of Hell, only adumbrated in the Gospels, was developed in apocalyptic literature (4) and took a firm hold on the medieval mind. Sermons dwelt vividly on its pains, and it was widely represented in sculpture (2), stained glass (1) and painting (3, 6). After a thousand years, it was believed, Satan would be set free and allowed to roam the earth in the form of Antichrist (7), and this would herald the end of the world.

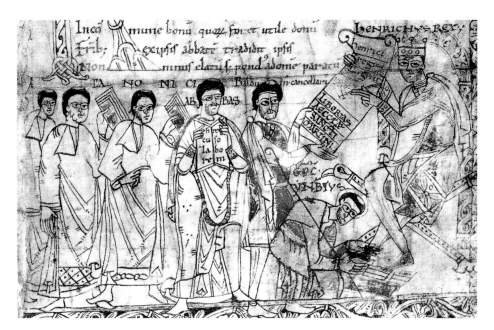

1. Henri I of France grants a charter to the monastery of St Martin des Champs, Paris; 11th century.

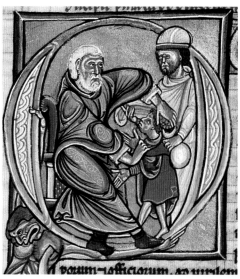

2. A child enters a monastery: behind him is his father holding money for an endowment; *c.* 1170–80.

3. A novice, having taken his vows, receives the monk's habit; 13th century.

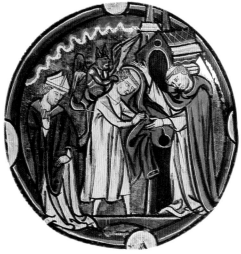

The monasteries: bastions of learning

The urge to withdraw from the world and dedicate one's life to God was widespread in early Christianity. It took many forms, from the deserts of Egypt to the Atlantic coast of Ireland, most of them based on the solitary life of prayer and fasting. Western monasticism, founded by St Benedict of Nursia about 530, was, on the contrary, essentially communal. Often richly endowed and protected (1), monasteries were places of peace and order in a disturbed society, organized round a routine of liturgy, work (8), study and regular meetings (5, 6, 7), in which a man could spend his whole life (2, 3, 9). It was in the monasteries that classical learning, literature, music and art survived for several crucial centuries. In the process they became less a refuge from the world and more a power within it.

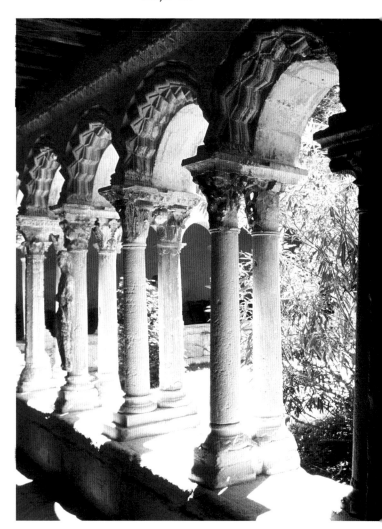

4. The cloister of Aix-en-Provence, France; 12th century. The cloister was the heart of the community, connecting the church with the monastery.

Brothers and sisters of poverty 86-87

Military monks: Hospitallers, Templars and Teutonic Knights 248-249

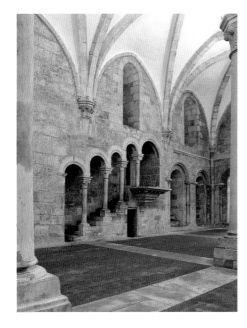

5. The refectory at Alcobaça, Portugal. During meals a monk read from the raised pulpit; late 12th century.

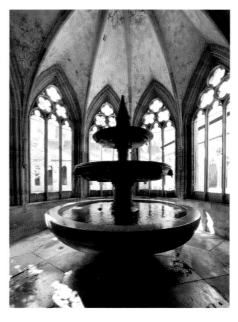

6. Outside the refectory stood the 'lavatorium' or washing place, often a fountain; Maulbronn, Germany, 13th century.

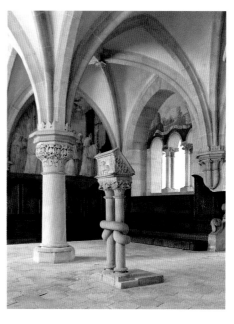

7. Administrative questions were settled in the chapter house, where the abbot presided; Osek, Bohemia, c. 1100.

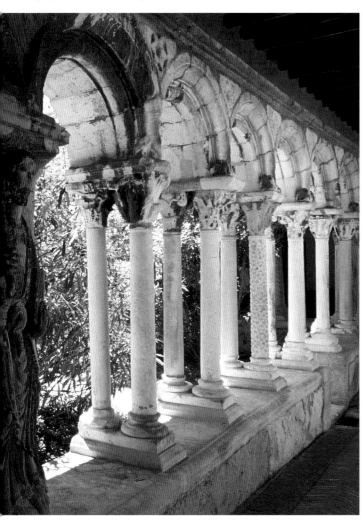

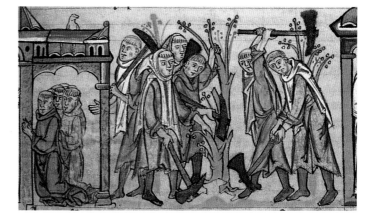

8. Cistercian monks at prayer and at work in the fields; 12th century.

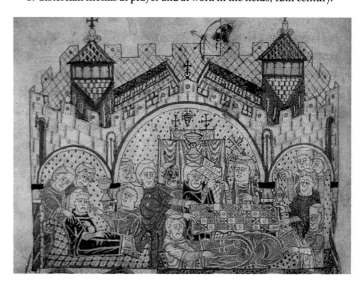

9. Death and funeral of a monk, from a Northern French manuscript of the late 11th century.

In the scriptorium

In the early Middle Ages monasteries were virtually the only source of literacy and of books. The copying of manuscripts, a highly specialized skill, was rewarded with appropriate esteem, and a number of scribes are known by name (2). The detailed organization of a monastic scriptorium is still imperfectly known, but illustrations show desks and writing materials (1, 3) and the preparation of the parchment (4). To copy a whole book counted as a work of merit (5) and the Bible was itself a sacred object (6).

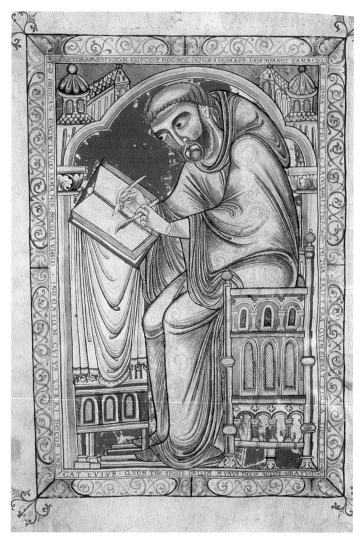

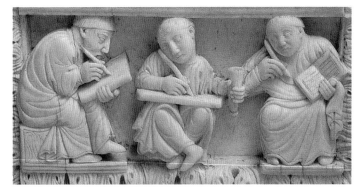

1. Three scribes at work; a German ivory relief, 9th-10th century.

2. The English scribe Eadwine of Canterbury, *c.* 1150. He writes with his right hand and holds the page down with the other. The inscription round the border begins: 'I am the prince of writers; neither my fame nor my praise will die quickly...'

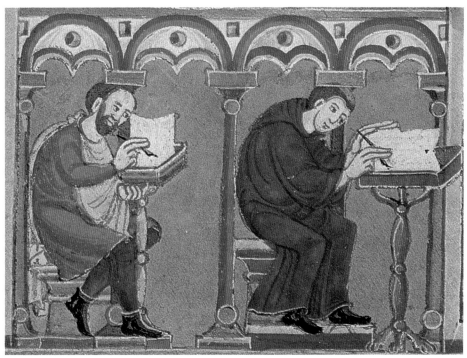

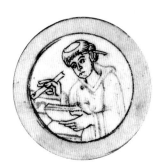

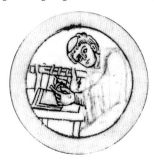

4. Two details from a German manuscript of the early 12th century, showing a scribe ruling up a page (note the pen behind the ear) and sewing the gatherings together to form a codex.

3. Two scribes in the scriptorium of Echtemach; the scriptorium often occupied a sheltered part of the cloister; German, *c.* 1040.

Marginal art 156-157   Music at court 124-125

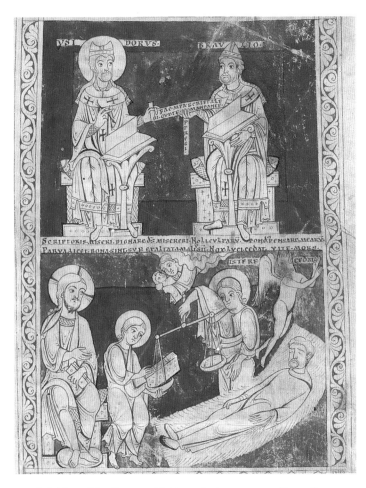

5. St Isidore of Seville wrote his Etymologies, a compendium of contemporary knowledge, in the 7th century. In this 12th-century picture, the copyist's work, after his death, outweighs his sins in St Michael's scale.

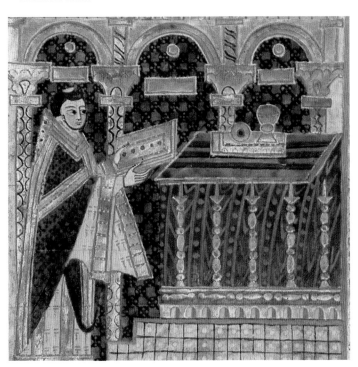

6. Bishop Bernward of Hildesheim reverently places his copy of the Gospels on the altar of his church of St Michael; early 11th century.

In the choir

Music was re-invented in the Middle Ages, and the key figure in this process was the Benedictine monk Guido of Arezzo. *c.* 990–1050. It is to him that we owe the six-note scale, later extended to seven (do, re, me, fa, so, la, ti, do) and the four-line stave. The 'Guidonian Hand' (7) represented the scale in diagramatic or mnemonic form, to which the singing master could point when teaching.

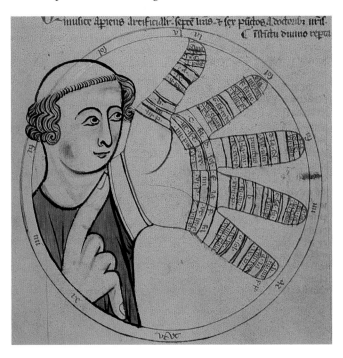

7. The 'Hand' of Guido of Arezzo, author of the first textbook on musical theory; a manuscript of 1274.

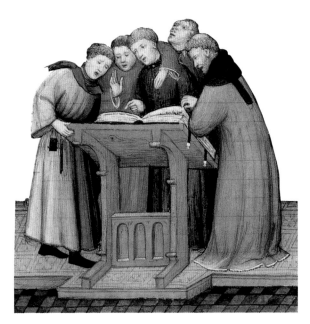

8. A choir master directs chanting choristers by using hand gestures; French, late 14th century.

Brothers and sisters of poverty

The Franciscan and Dominican orders, like the Cistercians, began as movements of reform. Repelled by the worldliness and luxury of both the monasteries and the clergy, Francis of Assisi (2), around 1200, determined to follow Christ literally, to renounce all possessions and exist only on charity. Narrowly escaping papal censure, he was eventually permitted to found his own order of friars and after his death was canonized as a saint. He was also a poet and a mystic, and a whole corpus of legends grew up around his appealing personality – his love of nature, his marriage to 'Lady Poverty' (4), his preaching, when humans would not listen, to birds, who would (1), and the austerity of his life (3). He attracted followers throughout Europe, communities of brothers and sisters (5, 6) living and preaching in the world, not in enclosed convents. Very different was the character of St Dominic. As a Spaniard and an intellectual, he saw his mission as a crusade against error and heresy (7). Both Franciscans and Dominicans were mendicants and preachers, their churches (8) wide and spacious to accommodate the largest possible congregations.

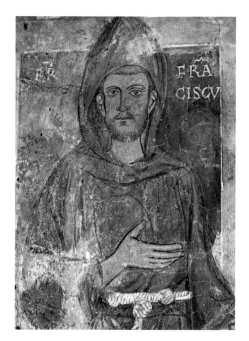

2. The earliest portrait of St Francis; a fresco at Subiaco, 13th century.

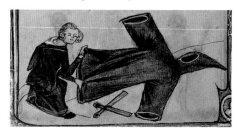

3. St Francis making his own habit from coarse brown cloth; an English miniature, c. 1325.

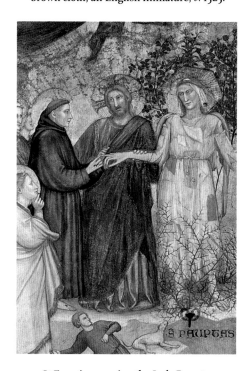

4. St Francis marrying the Lady Poverty; fresco in the Lower Church of S. Francesco, Assisi, 14th century.

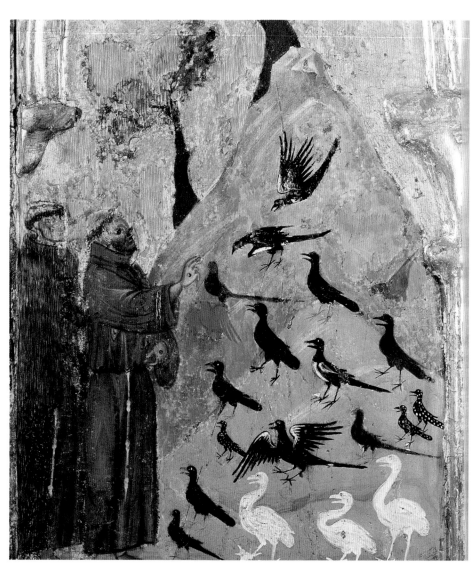

1. St Francis preaching to the birds, by Guido di Graziano; 13th century.

The monasteries: bastions of learning 82-83

The Church in a new age 264-265

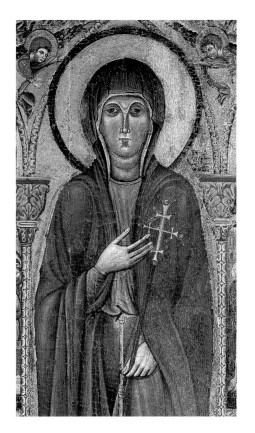

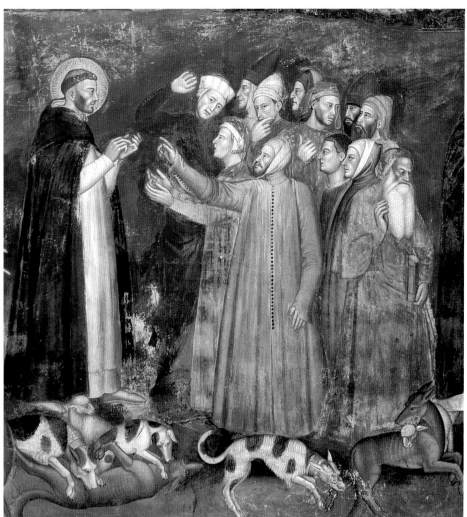

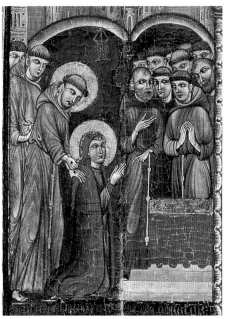

5, 6. St Clare, friend and companion of Francis and founder of the order of Poor Clares: an altarpiece with her portrait (top) and a detail showing her with St Francis consecrating her life to her order, in the church of S. Chiara, Assisi, *c.* 1280.

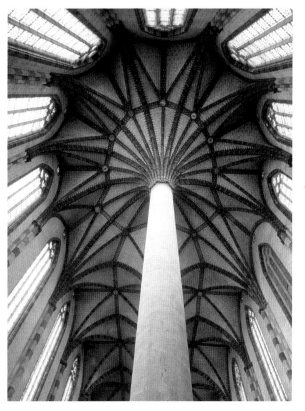

7. St Dominic disputing with heretics, counting off his arguments on his fingers; below, the 'dogs of the Lord' (a pun: *domini canes*) rescue sheep from the wolves; fresco by Andrea da Firenze in Florence, early 14th century.

8. Interior of the Dominican church of Toulouse, 1260–92.

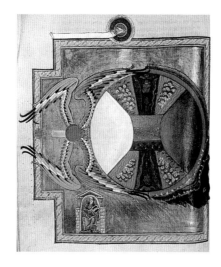

1. Hildegard's vision of the Jaws of Hell and the Place of Purification. The four-winged creature on the left signifies the Zeal of God. Underneath is the miniature figure of the author.

Mystical visions

The tradition of Christian mysticism went back to St John the Divine, whose visions make up the Book of Revelations. Although mystical experience – a private revelation from God – was to a degree incompatible with the dogmatic structure of Catholic belief, the visionaries, once accepted, were among the most popular of saints: St Catherine of Siena (6), who dreamed that she married the infant Jesus, St Francis (7), whose identification with Christ was so intense that the wounds (*stigmata*) appeared on his body, and many more. Few, however, left any visual record of their visions, and this is what makes the works of Hildegard of Bingen (1, 4, 5) so exceptional. Born in 1098, she became mother superior of the Benedictine convent of Bingen, on the Rhine, from where she corresponded with popes and emperors, wrote, painted and composed music. In spite of her explanations, her extraordinary visions, after the manner of mystics, are still hard to understand fully.

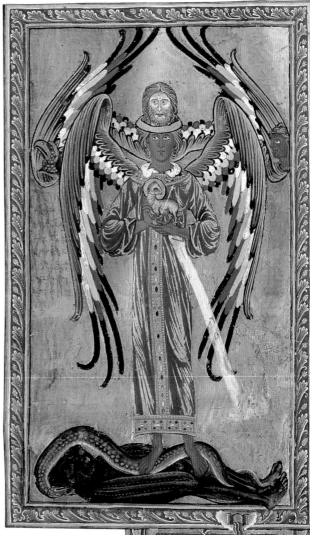

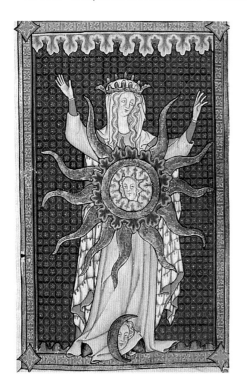

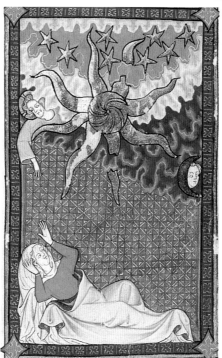

2, 3. Two pages from a German 13th–14th-century illuminated manuscript of the *Song of Songs*, finding mystical meanings in this lyrically erotic poem.

4. Illustration from Hildegard's First Vision, described as 'the fiery life-force'. 'I looked upon a human figure ... with a face of such beauty and clarity.... Above it was a second head.... It was attired in clothing that gleamed like the sun. In its hands it held a lamb which was as bright as the shining day. Wings grew out of its neck, with an eagle's head on one side and a man's on the other. The figurine trampled on a monster which was poisonous and black. The figure spoke: I am the highest fiery power. I have kindled all living sparks and extinguished nothing mortal.' Underneath is a portrait of Hildegard with a companion, dictating her Vision to a scribe.

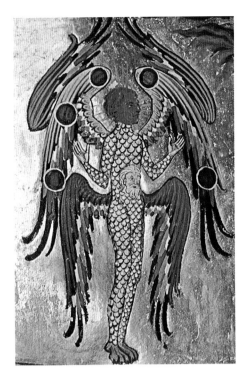

5. Detail from Hildegard's Ninth Vision, the personification of God's power.

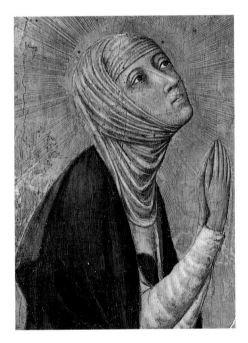

6. St Catherine of Siena in a mystical trance, by Lorenzo di Pietro; 15th century.

7. St Francis receives the stigmata; Italian, 14th century.

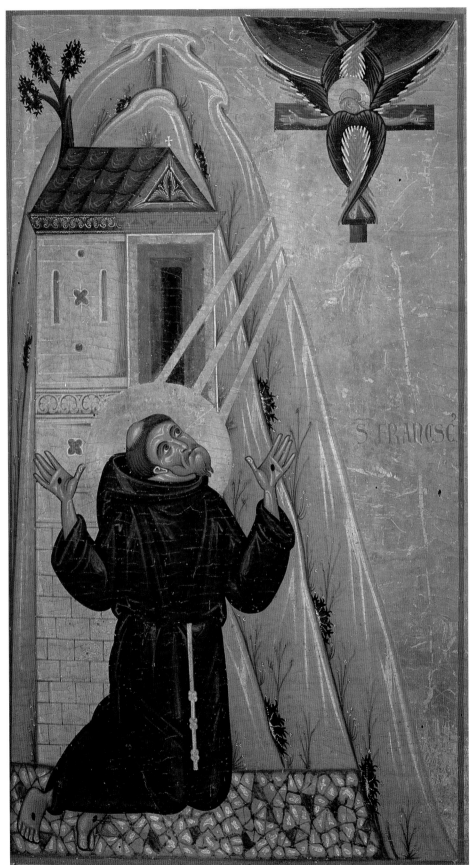

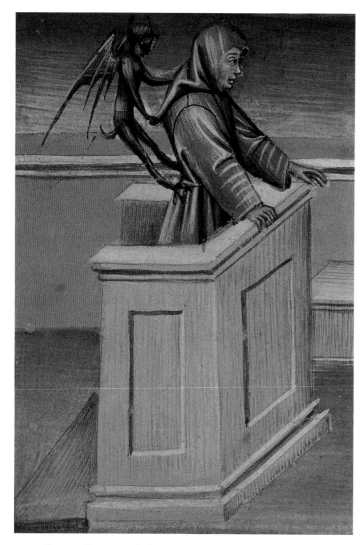

1. Allegory of heresy, with the Devil at the preacher's ear: Giovanni di Paolo's illustration to a verse in Dante's Paradiso, where Beatrice speaks of preachers who do not follow orthodox doctrine.

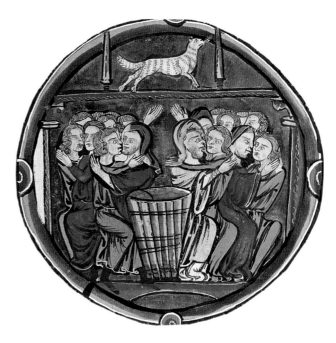

2. Anti-Cathar propaganda, c. 1230: Cathars wearing long blue gowns seduce the faithful. The Cathars, who believed that everything to do with the body belonged to the Devil, were thought to promote loose sexual morality.

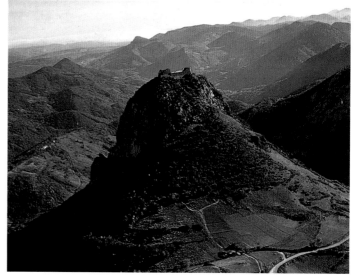

4. Montségur, in the Pyrenees, scene of the Albigensians' last stand in 1244.

5. After the defeat of the Albigensians, the Catholic Inquisition, led by the Dominicans, ruthlessly hunted down those who survived and handed them over to be burnt; here, the execution of Raimond de la Coste, early 14th century.

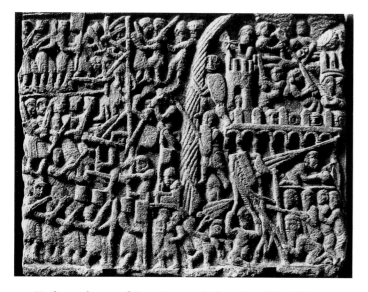

3. Toulouse, the seat of Count Raymond, champion of the Albigensian cause, was besieged several times. In this contemporary relief the attackers are on the left, the defenders on the right, working a great catapult.

The hierarchy of the Church 60-61   The Church in a new age 264-265

The fate of heresy

Faced with differences of opinion, the Church could maintain the purity and authority of its doctrine only by ruling that one was true and the other false (1). The losers were pronounced heretics and excommunicated, a practice that went back to the very earliest Christian councils (Nicaea, 325). In the Middle Ages the most serious heretics were the Albigensians, or Cathars, in the 13th century, the Waldensians (6) in the 12th-14th centuries, and the Hussites in the 15th. The former were the most radical; they believed that the world was a battleground between God and the Devil, and that everything material belonged to the Devil and was inherently evil. The Hussites, followers of John Huss (7), were proto-Protestants who denied the supremacy of the pope and the necessity of priests for the sacraments and believed that the laity should take communion in the wine as well as the bread. The Albigensians were crushed in a bitter war (3) which ended at Montségur in 1244 (4). The Hussites suffered a major setback when Huss was burned in 1415 (8), but his movement survived and found a new voice in Luther.

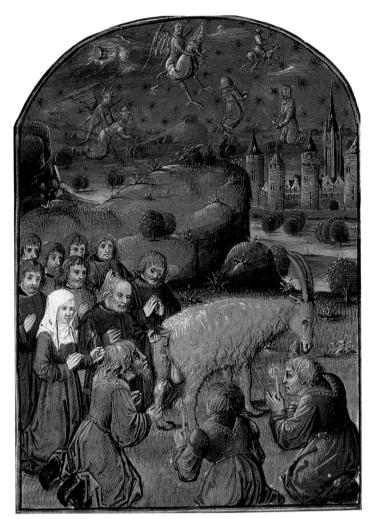

6. Heretics stimulated sometimes hysterical opposition from Catholics, who attributed to them fantastic and bizarre practices. Here Waldensians are seen worshipping Satan in the form of a goat. In fact their main offence was to allow ordinary lay people, including women, to preach. Condemned by the Church from the 12th century, they survived and were eventually absorbed into Protestantism.

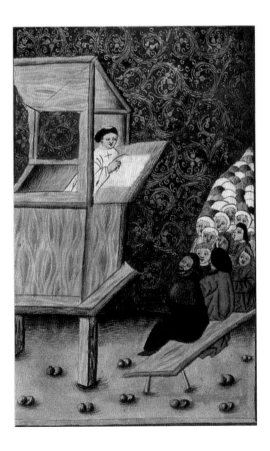

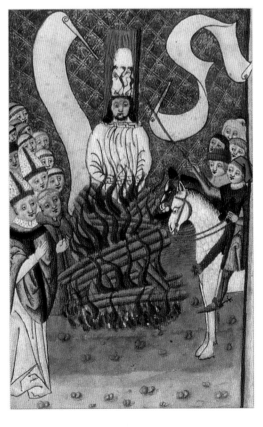

7. Far left: John Huss in the pulpit of the Bethlehem Chapel, Prague, where he first proclaimed his critical views on the papacy; illustration of *c.* 1500.

8. Left: lured to the Council of Constance by a false promise of safe conduct, Huss was tried, condemned and executed in 1415; from a near-contemporary chronicle.

3

Earthly Powers

DESPITE the predominance of a common Christian culture, medieval Europe was divided into various competing states. Many were kingdoms, where political power centred upon a ruling family, whose members looked upon the highest authority as an inheritance and regarded the kingdom as their own private property. Much of the continual political conflict and incessant warfare of the Middle Ages was engendered by quarrels within and between these ruling families: the Hundred Years' War between the Plantagenet kings of England and the Valois kings of France (1337–1453) is a particularly prolonged and wide-ranging instance of such a dynastic contest, but there are many others. New families making their way to power, like the Habsburgs, who began as local counts but eventually monopolized the position of Holy Roman Emperor, rose by defeating rival families. Medieval political history is family history.

Medieval states had far smaller resources than those of the present but this did not stop them making great claims. The Holy Roman Empire, consisting basically of modern Germany and northern Italy, saw itself as the literal successor to the Roman Empire of ancient times. Its ruler from 1198 to 1208 was styled 'Philip II' rather than simply 'Philip' because there had been a Roman emperor called Philip in the third century, almost a thousand years before. These exalted pretensions could be a source of weakness as well as strength. Because the emperor was seen as the head of Christendom – as, in some sense, an office-holder rather than a simple dynastic ruler – his succession came to be governed by rather different rules from those of other kings. He could only be formally entitled emperor after he had been crowned by the pope and, while most European kingdoms established clear rules of hereditary succession, the Empire went in the other direction: the emperor was elected by the chief princes of the Empire (who were hence termed 'Electors'). While England, France, Castile and the other dozen or so kingdoms of Catholic Europe were ruled by hereditary dynasties, successive rulers of the Holy Roman Empire could, and did, come from different and rival dynasties, especially in the later Middle Ages (the eight rulers between 1273 and 1410 were from four different families).

The fortunes of the empire and the papacy were intertwined not only because popes crowned emperors but also because their territorial interests clashed. Medieval popes claimed the lordship of Rome and a great swathe of central Italy, the 'Papal States'. Some enforced these claims more effectively than others, but all were wary of emperors who sought to exercise real authority south of the Alps. On occasion conflicts between popes and emperors became deep, long and violent, fuelled by the ideological intransigence of both parties. The first of these clashes, under Pope Gregory VII (1073–85), has even been seen as the prototype of all later European revolutions. These contests were certainly waged with an unusual ferocity and intensity. In the thirteenth century the popes pursued their vendetta against the emperors of the Hohenstaufen family until the dynasty had not only been deprived of its thrones (the Hohenstaufen ruled the kingdom of Sicily as well as the Empire) but had been completely exterminated.

In these disputes between emperor and pope, the latter had valuable allies – allies representing a kind of political organization quite different from the dynastic monarchies that otherwise dominated Europe. These were the Italian cities. Over the course of the eleventh and twelfth centuries, urban communities

Earthly power is transitory and precarious, a truth expressed by the symbol of Fortune's wheel. A king sits enthroned at the top, but he can easily descend (on the right) to the depths, just as the humble can rise. At the centre sits Fortune, or Luck, impassively turning her wheel. From a manuscript of Lydgate's 'Troy Book', 15th century.

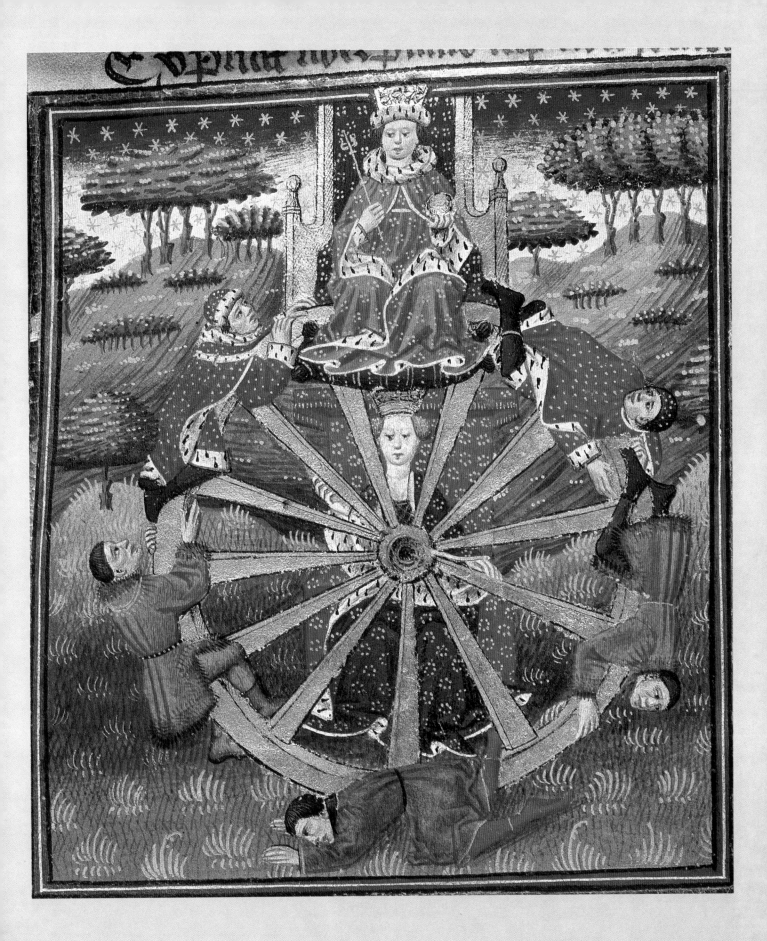

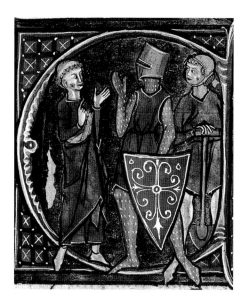

Those who pray, those who fight and those who work: the three estates of medieval social theory; a Franco-Flemish manuscript of the late 13th century.

throughout Europe became more numerous, larger and richer. The most numerous, largest and richest were to be found in Italy. By 1100 some of them, and by 1200 many of them, aspired to effective political autonomy. They formed leagues such as the Lombard League, victor over its nominal suzerain the Emperor Frederick Barbarossa at the battle of Legnano (1176); they established the organs of self-government, such as consuls and councils, and began to levy taxes and wage war; they extended their authority into the surrounding countryside, forming city-states. Similar developments took place elsewhere in Europe, especially in the Rhineland and the Low Countries, but it was in Italy that the independent or semi-independent city state of the Middle Ages reached its furthest development, as is evident from the surviving architectural remains of great public and communal buildings in places like Venice, Florence and Siena.

Law, war and the money to pay for them were the three main concerns of government in the Middle Ages. Rulers, whether dynastic princes or city regimes, expected to execute justice, decide disputes in their lawcourts, fight their rivals and tax their subjects to pay for all this. Over the course of the medieval period many states developed ever more effective methods of taxation and bureaucracies that took for granted the use of writing in government and administration. As states became more intrusive, they found it necessary to allow their subjects, or at least the more powerful amongst them, a voice in political decisions, and from the twelfth and thirteenth centuries representative institutions arose, some of which, such as the Parliaments of the British Isles, were to have a long future and form the root of similar institutions throughout the world.

Political participation was, however, strictly limited. One model of society that was common in the Middle Ages was that of the three estates or orders: the clergy, who prayed; the knights, who fought; the peasants, who laboured. It was a simplistic picture, but there was some truth in it. A large rural population supported by its labours a small clerical and lay aristocracy above it. This aristocracy led a life that was marked out by its power, wealth and style, a style that became ever more elaborate and ceremonial over the course of the medieval period. The twelfth century saw the beginning of the tournament, heraldry and Arthurian romance. The princely courts, as well as centres of political power, were theatres where rulers and aristocrats staged a drama of display and fantasy. The Order of the Golden Fleece, instituted by the dukes of Burgundy in 1430 and one of the most magnificent of the princely orders of chivalry, had as its avowed purpose 'to bring glory and high renown to the good'.

The glamour of Arthurian romance and the glitter of court life should not disguise the fact that the aristocracy of medieval Europe was trained above all to fight with sword and lance. Nobles formed the commanders and heavy cavalry of most armies in this period. They had the training and military resources to put at the disposal of princes and rulers, but also to oppose them quite effectively. 'Chivalry', a set of ideals and conventions about how knights should treat one another (and how they should behave towards ladies), ensured that slaughter among members of the upper class was regulated. It was more usual for defeated noble opponents to be ransomed than executed. After the battle of Poitiers in 1356 the victorious Black Prince served the captive king of France at supper on bended knee. This did not meant that the Prince was unwilling to order the massacre of unarmed civilians of the lower classes, as at Limoges some years later. 'There is no man so hard hearted,' wrote one contemporary, 'that, if he had been in Limoges on that day, and had remembered God, he would not have wept bitterly at the fearful slaughter which took place.'

Medieval warfare consisted primarily of low intensity operations, such as ravaging one's enemy's lands or besieging his castles. Decisive battles did occasionally occur, for example at Hastings (1066), when the Normans conquered England, Benevento (1266), Tagliacozzo (1268), when Charles of Anjou, at the invitation of the papacy, conquered the Kingdom of Sicily and destroyed the Hohenstaufen dynasty, and Agincourt (1415), where a remarkable victory by Henry V of England ensured that France would be torn by the Hundred Years' War for another forty years, but these were exceptional. The dense network of fortifications that covered Europe meant that military operations turned on time-consuming blockades or dangerous assaults of strong points. Castles of a simple timber and earthwork construction had spread everywhere in the tenth and eleventh centuries and in the following period they became larger, stronger and more elaborate. The huge, expensive stone castles of the thirteenth and fourteenth centuries, with their rows of cylindrical towers and complex concentric walls, were instruments and symbols of princely and aristocratic power, dominating their surroundings, often giving their names to the families that possessed them (the 'de' and 'von' of French and German noble surnames are often followed by the name of a castle – this is where they were 'of').

Castles were not, of course, invulnerable. There were techniques available to the attacker, from simply setting timber and thatch on fire, to undermining the walls through tunnelling, to bombardment by giant throwing machines such as the mangonel and trebuchet. In the later Middle Ages a new weapon came to hand. Gunpowder was used in Western European warfare from the 1320s and is reported at the battle of Crécy in 1346 but it was of very marginal importance for the following century. During the fifteenth century handgunners and artillery acquired increasing effectiveness and an ambitious and up-to-date ruler like Charles the Bold of Burgundy (1467–77) would take hundreds of artillery pieces and thousands of handgunners on his campaigns. The value of artillery in demolishing castles was particularly evident. The advantage now lay with those who had the resources to support an artillery train – kings and princes rather than local aristocrats in their castles.

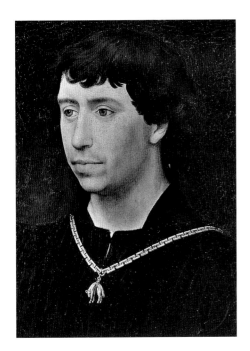

Charles the Bold, Duke of Burgundy, wears the Order of the Golden Fleece, one of the primary orders of knighthood instituted as a mark of prestige and honour.

A giant crossbow, one of the siege machines of the 14th century that were brought to bear against castles prior to the use of gunpowder.

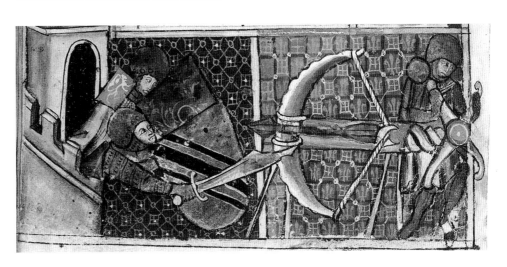

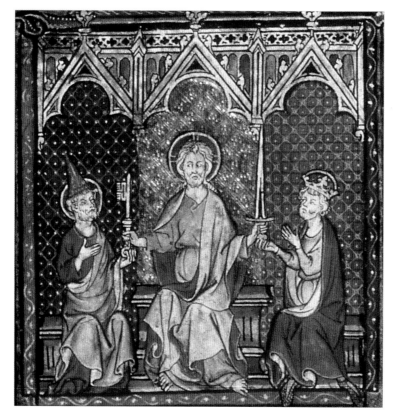

1. Christ giving the key to the pope and the sword to the emperor; a 12th-century manuscript of Gratian's textbook of canon law.

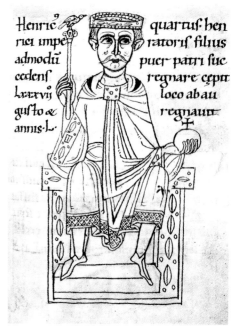

2. The Emperor Henry IV (1050–1106). It was during his reign that the Investiture Contest, the dispute over who had the right to appoint bishops, came to a head. Henry was forced to concede to Pope Gregory VII.

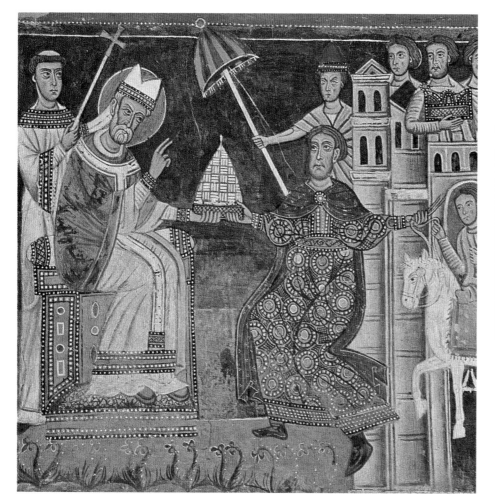

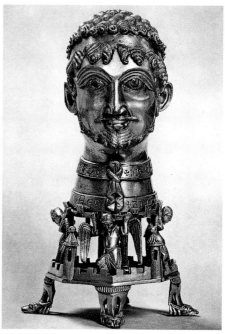

4. Frederick Barbarossa (1123–90), a powerful Hohenstaufen emperor. Like Henry IV he came into conflict with the papacy and invaded Italy five times; a gilded reliquary, late 12th century.

3. Left: Constantine bestowing temporal authority on Pope Sylvester, 'the Donation of Constantine'; fresco in the church of Quattro Santi Coronati, Rome, 12th century.

Charlemagne: Rome reborn 52-53   The three estates 100-101

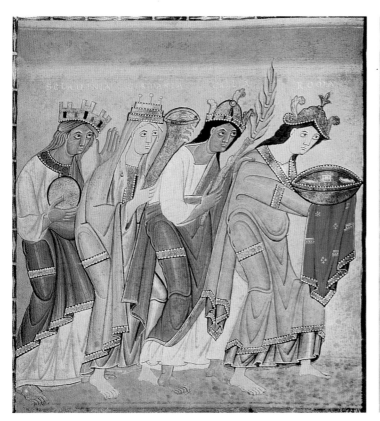

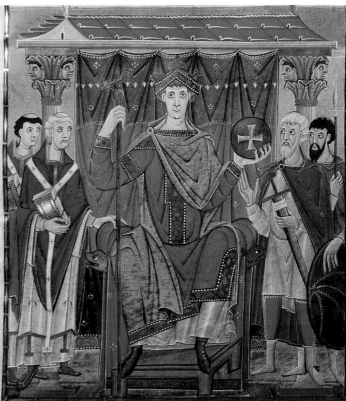

5, 6. Otto III enthroned with members of his court, and on the left personifications of the four chief provinces of the Empire paying homage: Slavinia (the country of the Slavs), Germany, Gaul and Rome.

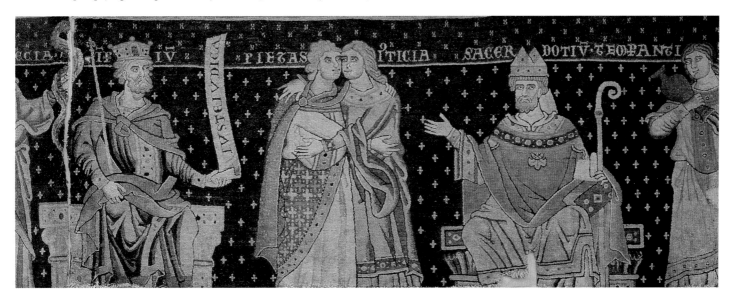

7. The Concord of Church and State; German tapestry, late 12th century.

Empire and Papacy

The Emperor and the Pope were the twin peaks of medieval authority, one secular, the other spiritual (1). In both cases theoretical justification rested on dubious history. The Empire was seen as the heir of Rome, now legitimized ('Holy' as well as 'Roman') by the sanction of Christ – a claim that went back to Charlemagne but was formalized by Otto I, in 962, and his successors (5, 6). The imperial title, however, was not hereditary but elective, though it tended to be hijacked by certain ruling dynasties such as the Hohenstaufen (4). The papal claim rested

upon Christ's charge to Peter, who was reckoned to be the first Bishop of Rome: 'Upon this rock I shall build my Church.' The pope's secular authority within the papal states was based on a document supposedly recording a gift from Constantine (3), later proved to be a forgery. Medieval political theory saw the sharing of powers between Church and State as a perfect harmony (7). In practice there was continual discord. Until the 11th century the pope was generally subordinate to the emperor, but after the Investiture Contest (2) the Church attained at least equality.

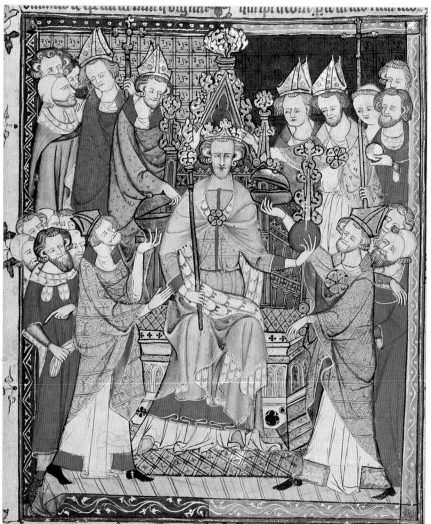

1. The coronation ceremony; probably French, early 14th century.

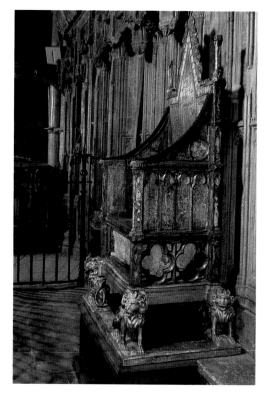

2. English coronation chair in Westminster Abbey, *c.* 1300.

Kingship

Kings were not chosen by their subjects; they were appointed by God. The doctrine of divine right, which goes back to the kings of the Old Testament, was progressively refined throughout the Middle Ages. Legitimacy rested on dynastic succession but had to be confirmed by the Church. Rebellion was sacrilege, but a king who failed to keep his coronation oath could be deposed. Coronation (1), which involved anointment with holy oil, was a consecration, and kingship a form of priesthood. These concepts were reinforced through powerful symbols – the throne (2), the crown (3, 5), the orb (7) and sceptre (4). Although it might not provide the best man for the job, hereditary kingship provided an image of stability buttressed by psychological and religious sanctions that in practice were difficult to challenge or ignore.

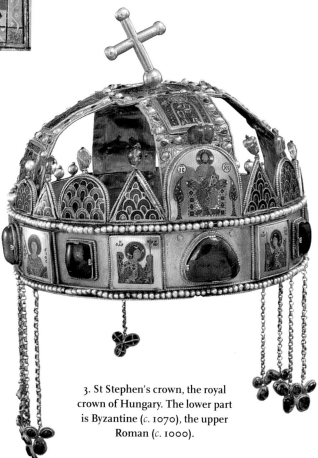

3. St Stephen's crown, the royal crown of Hungary. The lower part is Byzantine (*c.* 1070), the upper Roman (*c.* 1000).

The three estates 100-101   Kings and Parliaments 102-103

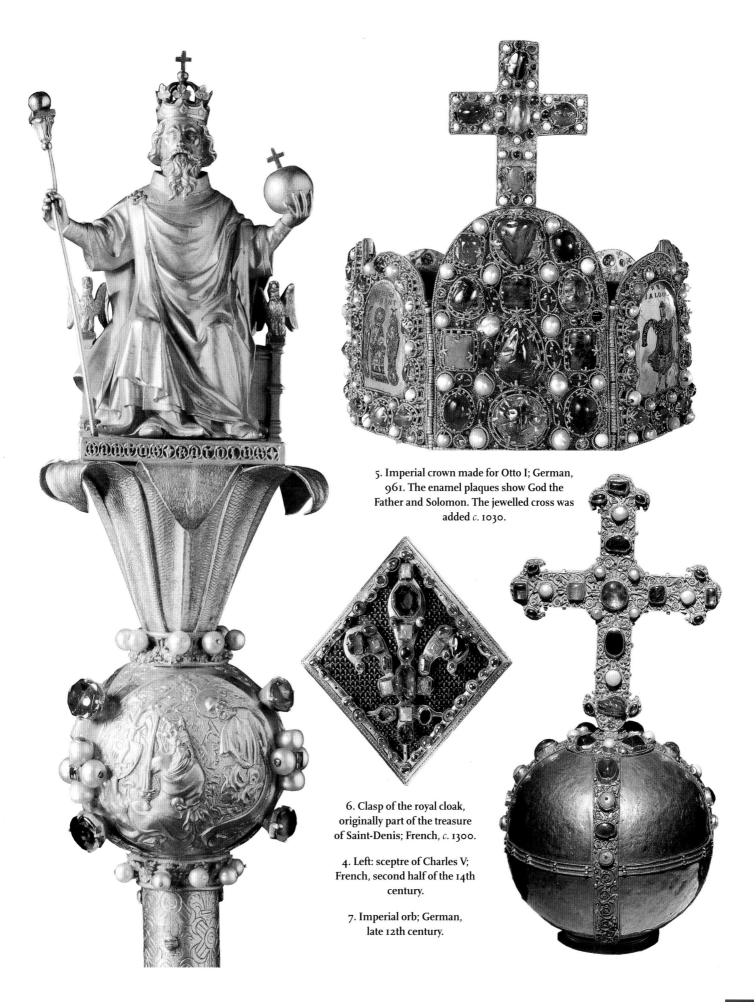

5. Imperial crown made for Otto I; German, 961. The enamel plaques show God the Father and Solomon. The jewelled cross was added *c.* 1030.

6. Clasp of the royal cloak, originally part of the treasure of Saint-Denis; French, *c.* 1300.

4. Left: sceptre of Charles V; French, second half of the 14th century.

7. Imperial orb; German, late 12th century.

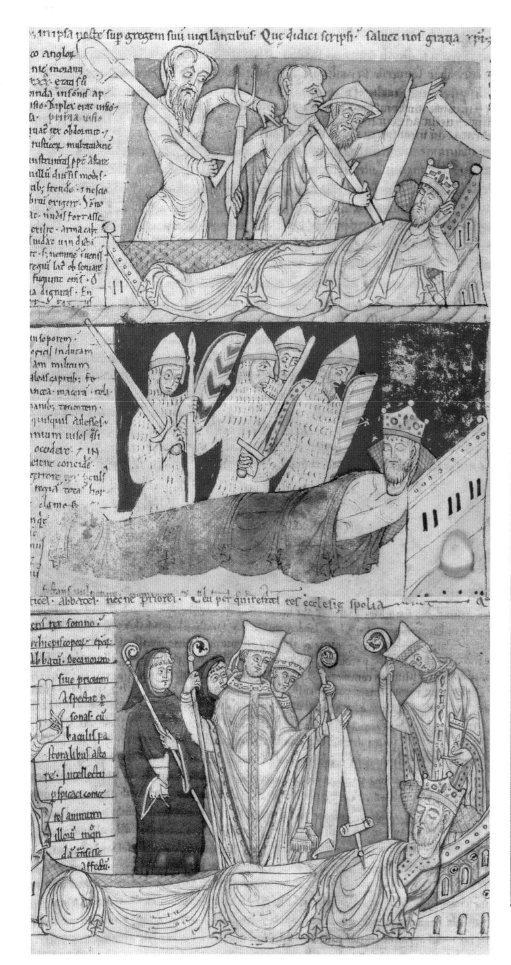

1. King Henry I's dream, from the Chronicle of John of Worcester; English, *c.* 1130–40.

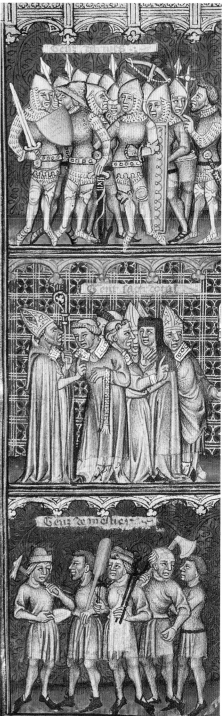

2. Nobility, clergy and peasants; from a 14th-century French manuscript of Aristotle's *Politics*.

Kings and Parliaments
102-103

The craftsman's skill 174-175

The three estates

The idea of dividing society into three classes – those who fought, those who prayed and those who worked (2, 3) – goes back at least to the 9th century. By the 12th century it had already become slightly anachronistic through the emergence of a 'middle' class between the nobles and the peasants: lawyers, doctors, merchants and so on. But the 'three estates' was a convenient model, long perpetuated in the division of parliaments into lords temporal, lords spiritual and commoners. The most vivid of all representations of this model is King Henry I of England's dream (1), as recorded by John of Worcester. The king dreamed that all three estates united against him: the peasants with scythes and pitchforks 'gnashing their teeth', the knights 'looking as if they wanted to kill him', and the bishops and abbots seeming 'to want to attack him with the points of their croziers'.

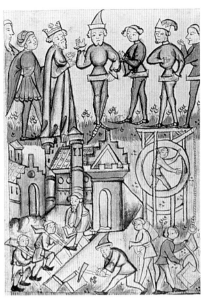

3. Class division within the town; South German, 14th century.

4. Two classes in harmony, in an Italian 15th-century fresco at Castello del Buonconsiglio, Trento. Labourers toil at the land, harrowing, sowing and ploughing, while well-dressed ladies enjoy the countryside.

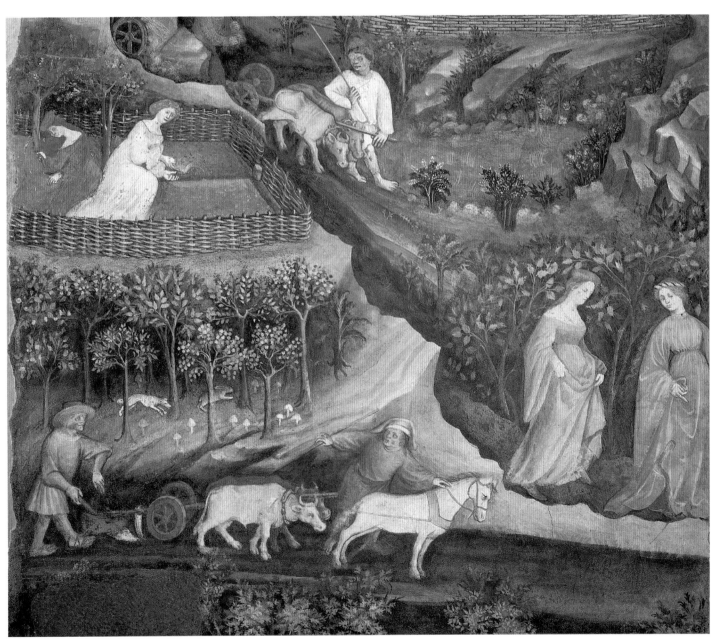

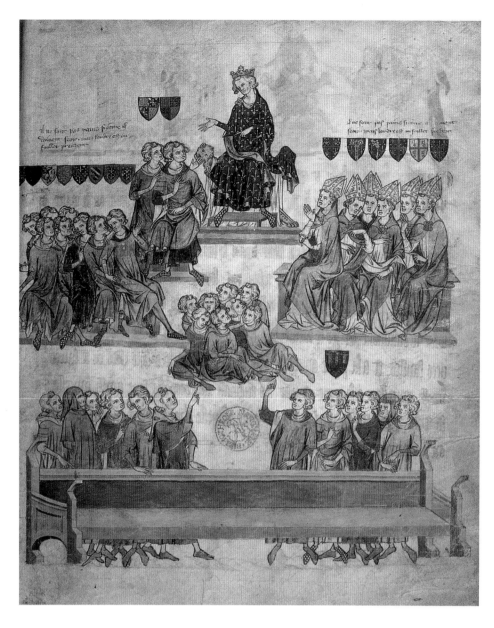

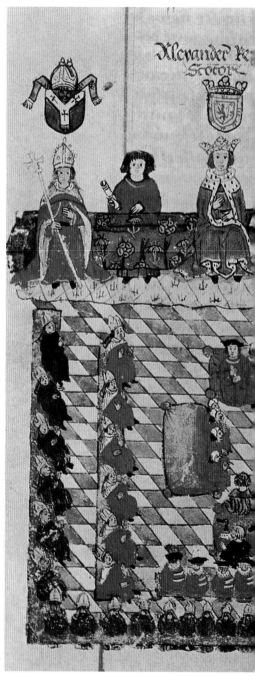

1. France: Philip IV and his councillors; early 14th century.

Kings and Parliaments

Kings did not rule alone. Inevitably they were guided by the advice of their leading subjects. This led gradually to the granting of limited rights in the making of laws, particularly those relating to taxation, to assemblies of lords, bishops and commoners. These assemblies were the origin of modern parliaments, but it would be a mistake to see them too literally in these terms. Only rarely could they oppose the will of the king, and it was entirely at the king's discretion whether to call a parliament at all. Constitutionally he alone exercised power, though that power could be delegated. In this respect the Renaissance brought no change. Indeed, it could reasonably be said that politically the Middle Ages lasted in England until the 17th century, in other European monarchies until the 18th or 19th, and in Russia until the 20th.

2. England: Edward I and his Parliament, an anachronistic illustration painted in Tudor times. The lords spiritual are on the left, the lords temporal on the right. The King of Scotland and Prince of Wales are also shown as being present, though they never were.

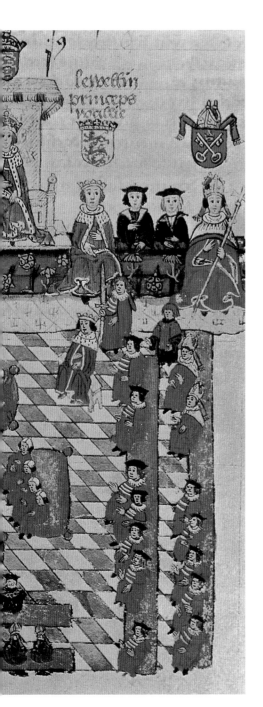

3. Spain: James II of Aragon with the Cortes of Barcelona; *c.* 1300.

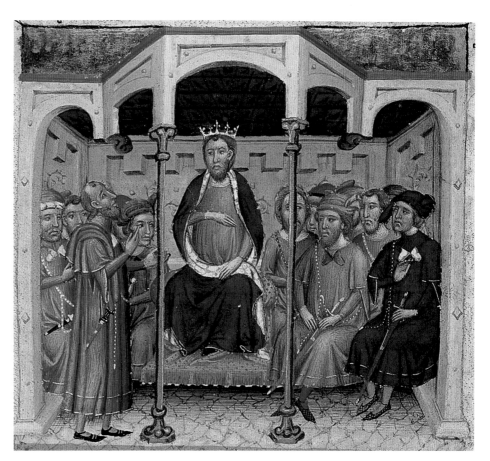

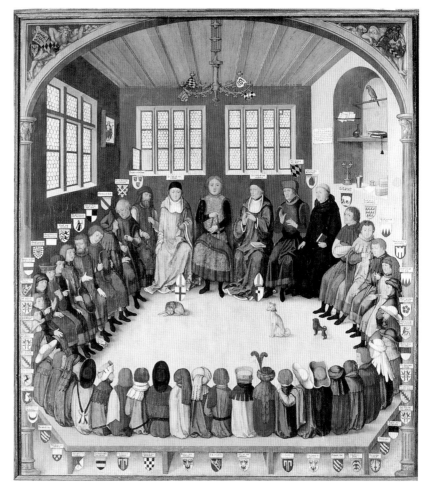

4. Germany: Duke Eberhard of Württemberg with his councillors; a 16th-century copy of an original of about 1400.

Italy: the land without kings

Italy was as unified linguistically and culturally as England and France, but unlike those countries it never coalesced into a single state under a monarchy. Instead, it developed into a large number of separate city-states calling themselves republics, governed according to a wide variety of constitutions and frequently in conflict with one another. The smaller states, such as Gubbio (**3**) fluctuated between periods of independence and domination by more powerful neighbours (it was swallowed at different times by the duchy of Urbino and the Papal States). But the leading cities, including Venice (**1**), Florence (**4**), Siena (**2**, **5**) and Genoa (**6**), remained autonomous throughout the Middle Ages, jealous of their freedom and proud of their civic virtues. The great allegorical fresco painted by Ambrogio Lorenzetti about 1340 in the Palazzo Pubblico of Siena (**2**) expressed an ideology that would have been generally endorsed by the others. The central figure represents the *commune* of Siena. Above his head hover Faith, Hope and Charity. Peace, Fortitude and Prudence sit beside him on the left, Magnanimity, Temperance and Justice (who holds a severed head and a crown – punishment and reward) on the right. In the foreground are citizens of Siena and warriors guarding a group of prisoners, and at the feet of Siena are Romulus and Remus.

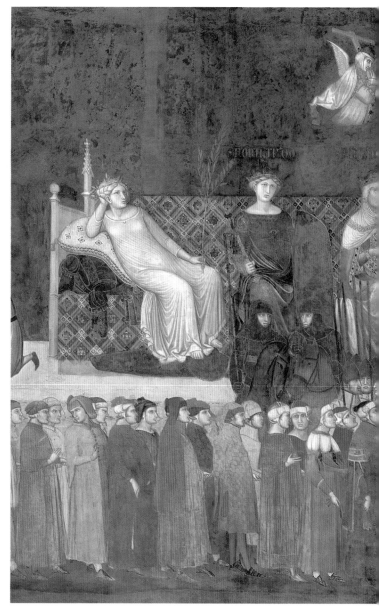

2. Right: Ambrogio Lorenzetti's Allegory of Good Government; fresco in the Palazzo Pubblico, Siena, *c.* 1340.

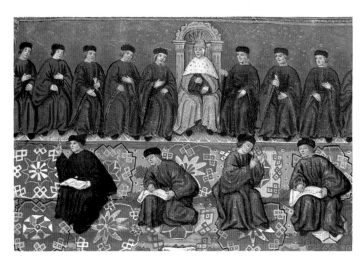

1. The Doge of Venice, with councillors and secretaries; French, late 15th century. Venice was an oligarchy, with the doge elected from about two hundred top families.

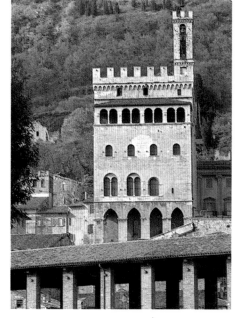

3. Gubbio: the Palace of the Consuls, built 1332–46, when Gubbio was a self-governing city. In the foreground is the loggia of the weavers.

Kingship 98-99

Italy and the Roman tradition 150-151

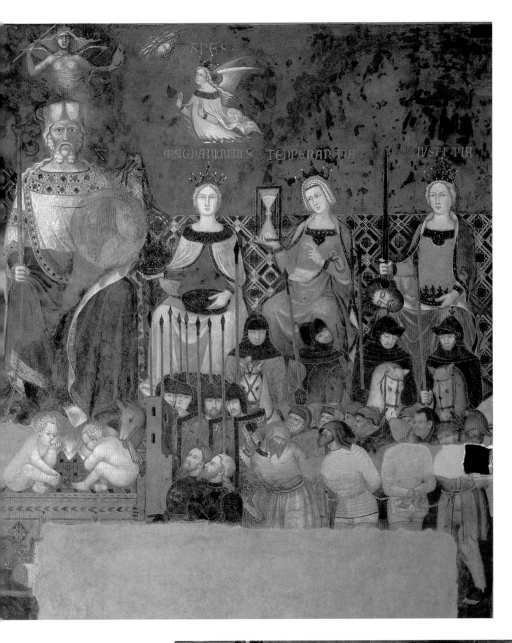

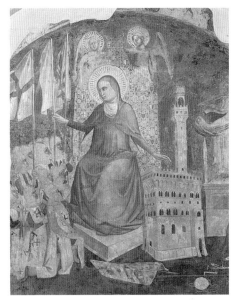

4. Florence: allegory showing St Anne handing flags of freedom to Florentine militia, with the Palazzo Vecchio in the background; 14th century.

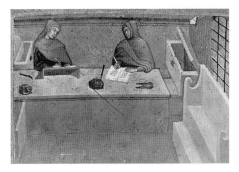

5. Sienese state treasurer with his secretary; 1388.

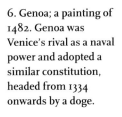

6. Genoa; a painting of 1482. Genoa was Venice's rival as a naval power and adopted a similar constitution, headed from 1334 onwards by a doge.

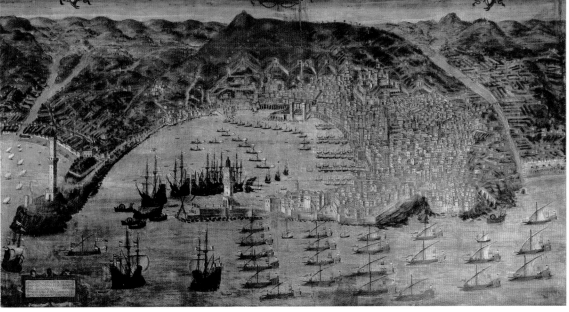

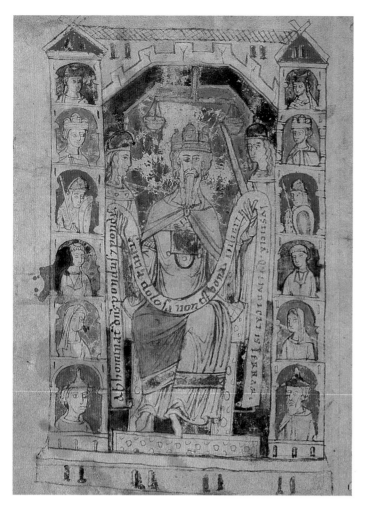

1. King Solomon as judge; German, 12th century. At the top, the scales of justice. Around him, quotations from Proverbs and Wisdom: 'Love justice ye who judge the earth.'

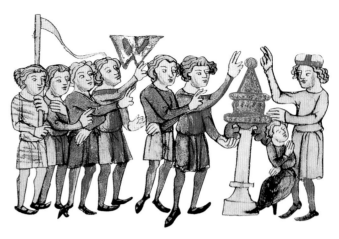

2. An accused man cowers before the judge, a count. On the left, six witnesses swear to his guilt; from the *Sachsenspiegel*, 13th century.

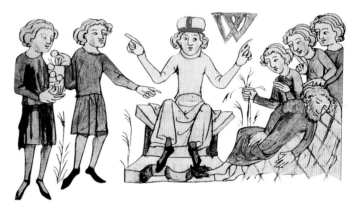

3. A dispute has arisen between the heir of an estate (his dead father lies on the ground) and a man who claims to have bought it. The judge is a duke; from the *Sachsenspiegel* of Eike von Repgow, 13th century.

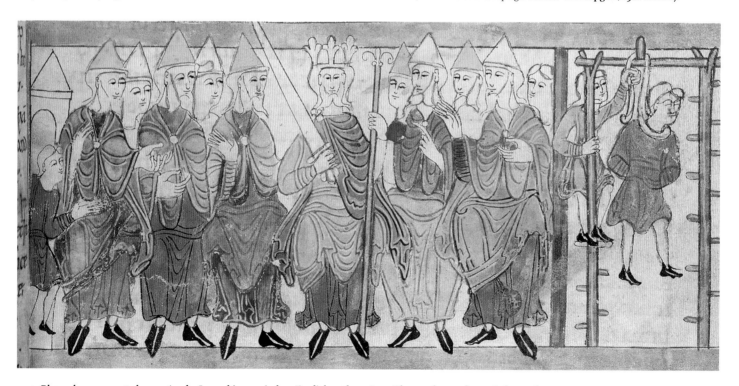

4. Pharaoh, represented as an Anglo-Saxon king, as judge; English, 11th century. The condemned man is hanged.

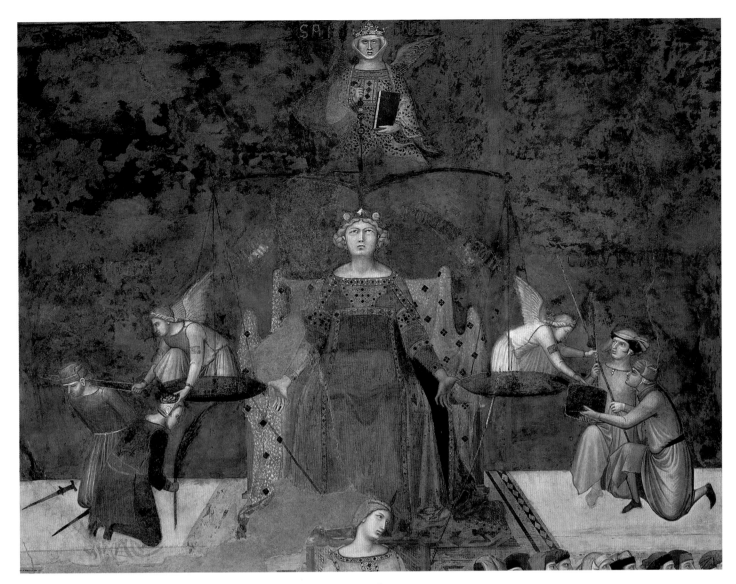

5. Allegory of Justice by Ambrogio Lorenzetti, c. 1340. At the top the crowned figure of Wisdom holds scales from which hang two pans which Justice, enthroned, keeps level with her thumbs. On the left an angel cuts off the head of a murderer and crowns a victorious warrior. On the right another angel gives money, a lance and a staff of office to two citizens, signifying distributive justice.

Justice and the law

The task of reconciling Roman law as codified by Justinian, the laws of the barbarian peoples (4) and Christian ethics (1, 5) was indeed just as difficult as might be supposed. In the 12th century, the publication of Gratian's *Decretum* was a milestone but affected canon law only. Secular law meant most importantly the king's law; serious offences were tried by the king's judges in the king's courts. Cases brought by ordinary litigants in towns or villages would be tried in urban and manorial courts, which worked by way of a dense mass of customary law, often confined to specific localities (2, 3). Lawyers were in demand largely to draw up documents in proper form (6). Criminal and civil law had separate courts, but it was usually left to the aggrieved party to bring the prosecution.

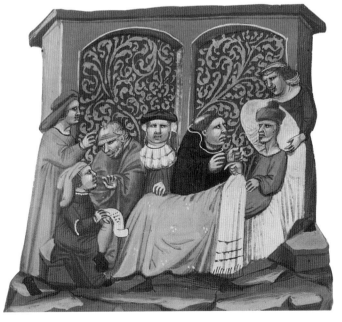

6. A dying man dictates his will to a lawyer at the foot of his bed; Italian, early 14th century.

The order of knighthood

Knights were originally simply armoured cavalrymen, feudal landowners bound to the service of their overlord. In time they evolved into professional soldiers, not necessarily with a stake in the land but commissioned directly by the king, for whom fighting was a career. But the knightly code was one of high chivalric ideals involving elaborate rituals (5, 6, 7) and expressed through heraldry and pageantry (1, 3, 4). At the end of the Middle Ages, the orders of knighthood, dedicated to the Christian virtues, could lose their military associations altogether and become symbols of rank and status (2).

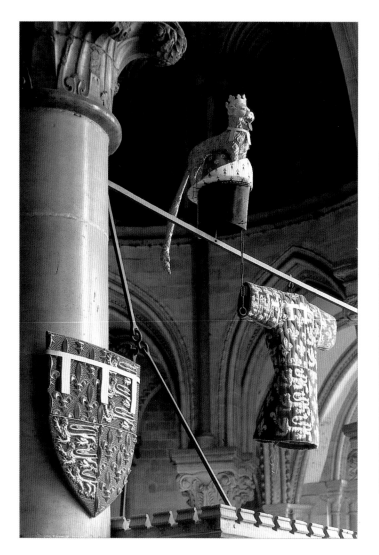

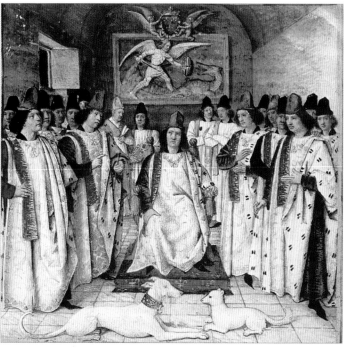

2. Louis XI of France presiding over the Order of St Michael; a painting attributed to Jean Fouquet, *c.* 1468.

1. The armour of the Black Prince hanging over his tomb in Canterbury Cathedral, *c.* 1380.

3. Tomb of the Black Prince, Canterbury Cathedral, *c.* 1380.

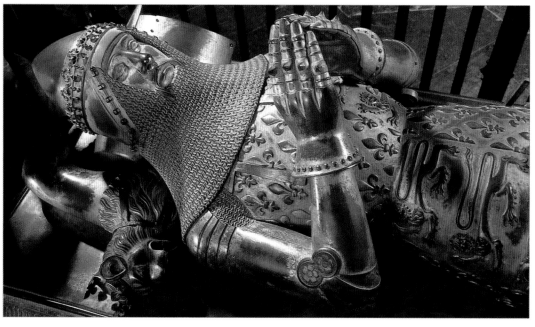

Tournaments: playing at war 116-117

Arthurian romance 226-227

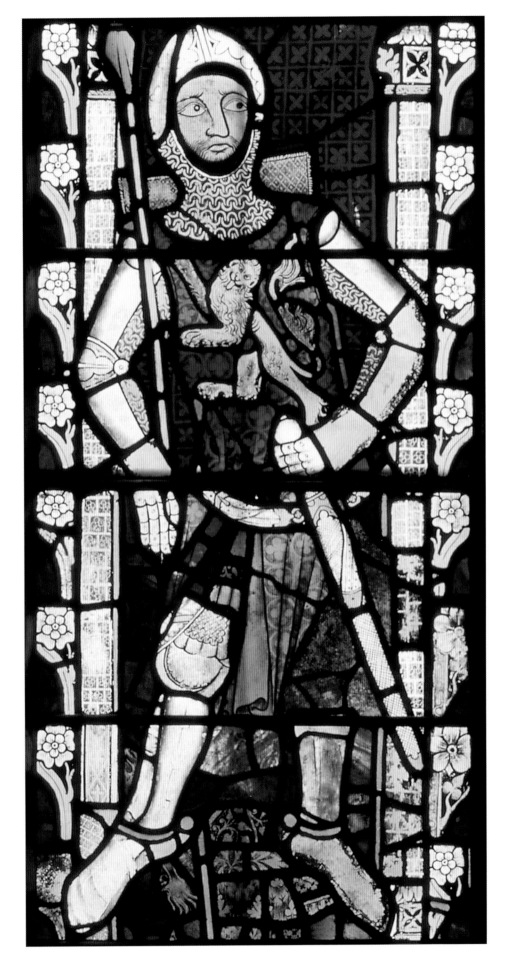

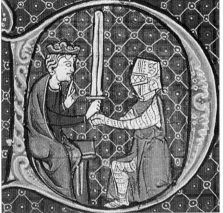

5. The knight receives his sword from the king; late 14th century.

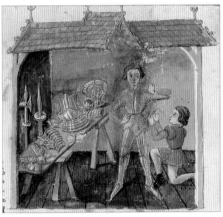

6. Arming the knight, showing his accoutrements assembled on a table; English, mid-15th century.

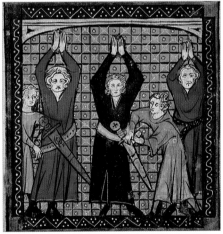

7. Three new knights are girt with their swords; French, 14th century.

4. Left: Robert Fitzhamon in armour, a stained-glass window in Tewkesbury Abbey, England, c. 1340.

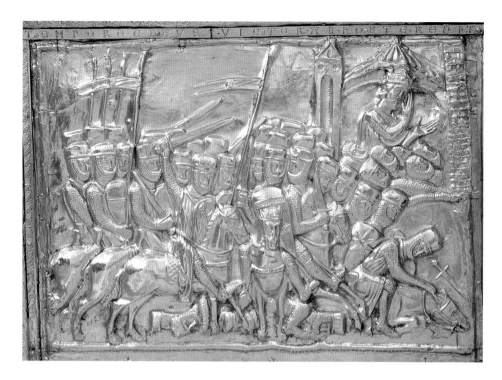

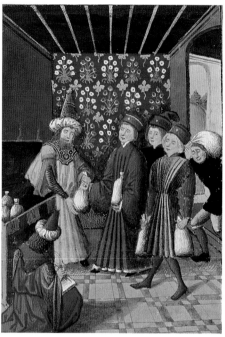

1. Charlemagne as a 13th-century knight (with the eagle shield) leading his troops to victory against the Saracens; a relief from the shrine of Charlemagne, 1215.

2. Ransom is paid to the Turkish sultan for the release of the Count of Nevers; French, 15th century.

War: the heroic image

For the knight and the feudal gentry, war was a heroic enterprise in which a man could win glory and reputation. The cult of chivalry sanctified war as long as it was just. War against heathens (1) was not subject to the same humane rules as war against fellow Christians, though this probably made little difference to the fate of the common soldier. The fact that in the event of defeat a member of the nobility was more likely to be ransomed (2) than killed, no doubt helped war to retain its glamour. In Italy, moreover, armies consisted largely of mercenaries (even the generals were paid professionals) who were not motivated to fight to the death. The result was that the representation of war in medieval art nearly always has an air of unreality, even when weapons, armour and tactics are depicted accurately. The outcome of a war more often depended upon besieging a castle (3, 5) than fighting a pitched battle, which was generally avoided.

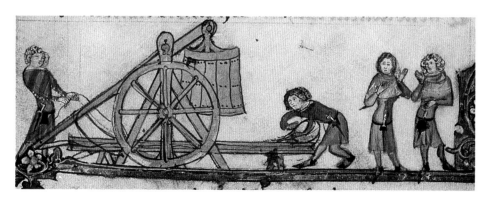

3. A 14th-century siege engine, from a Flemish manuscript.

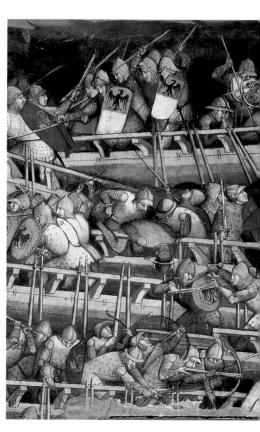

4. Venetian galley fighting the troops of Frederick Barbarossa; fresco by Spinello Aretino, *c.* 1400. Venice and Genoa, virtually impregnable from the land, relied on their navies for defence.

The order of knighthood 108-109

War: the grim reality 112-113

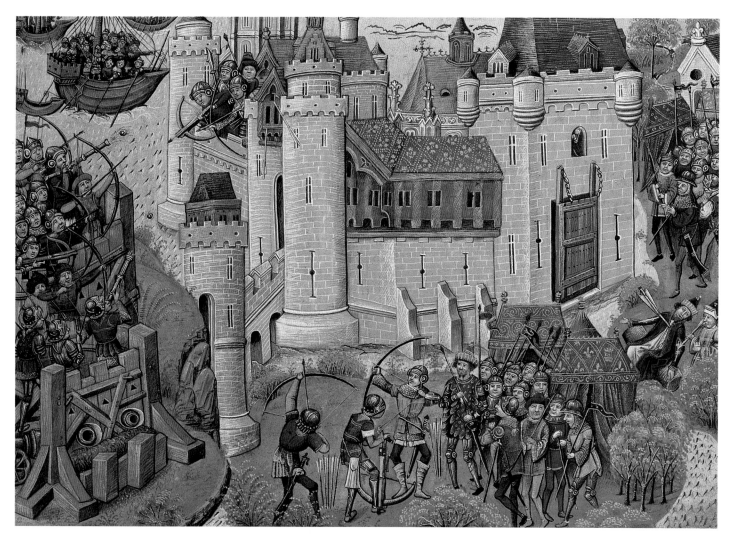

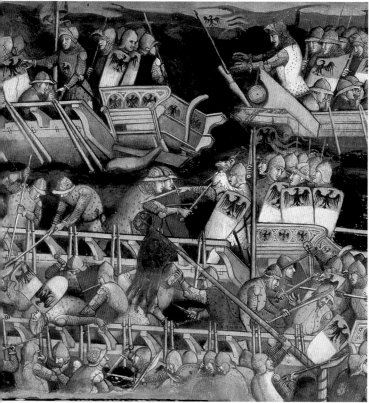

5. The siege of Mortagne, near Bordeaux, in 1377. The castle was held by the English and besieged by the French under a Welshman in the French service, Owen of Wales, who was treacherously killed (far right) by an arrow. This miniature reflects conditions in the late 15th century, when it was painted, rather than the 14th. On the left are a pair of cannon and just above them two men are firing primitive muskets. Crossbows are also shown (one being loaded in the foreground), but the main reliance is on the longbow; note the supply of arrows stuck into the ground. The castle held out for over six months.

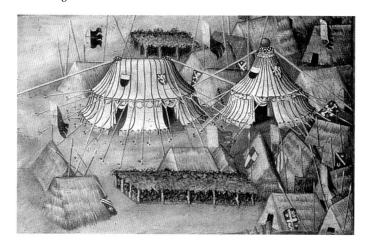

6. An encampment of Italian mercenaries during one of the petty wars between cities; fresco by Simone Martini, 1328.

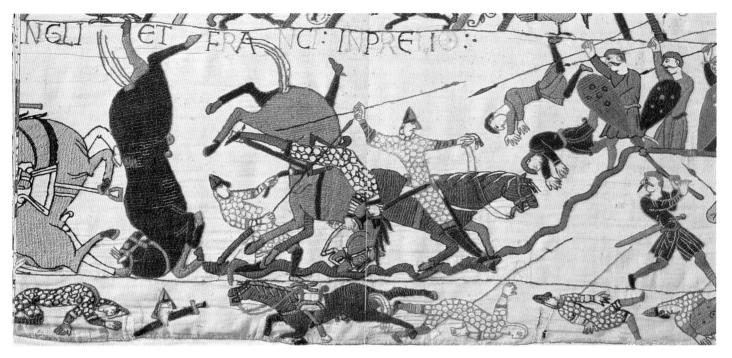

1. Detail from the Bayeux Tapestry; English or French, late 11th century.

2. 'And Joshua drew not his hand back until he had utterly destroyed all the inhabitants of Ai. And the King of Ai he hanged on a tree until eventide.' An episode from the Book of Joshua depicted in contemporary terms with gruesome realism in a French Bible of about 1250.

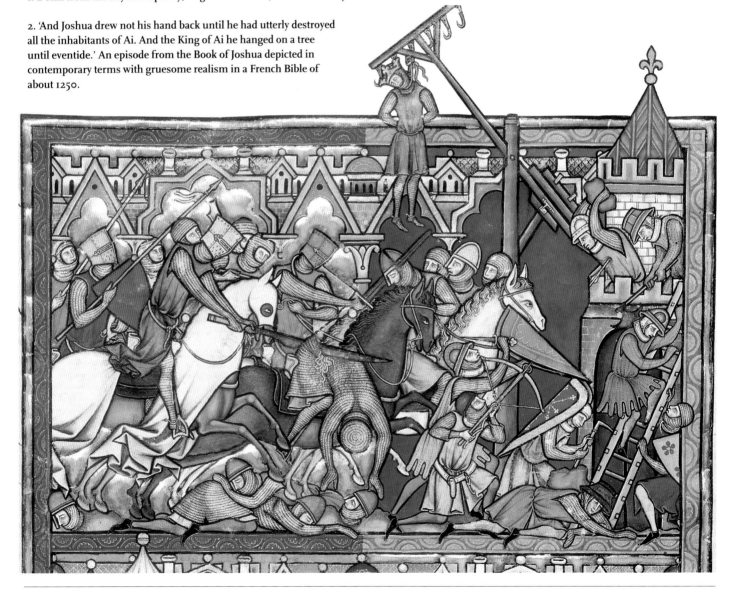

War: the heroic image 110-111

A good death 188-189

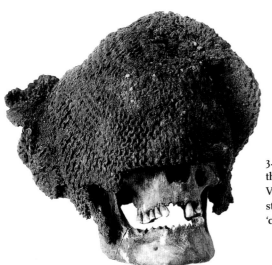

3. A skull from the battlefield of Visby, Sweden, still covered by its 'coif' of mail; 1361.

War: the grim reality

Exceptionally, medieval artists would sometimes convey the full horror of war. Among the most vivid examples is one of the earliest: the Bayeux Tapestry, made in the years after the Norman conquest of England (**1**). Here the Battle of Hastings (fought before the age of chivalry) is depicted in harrowing detail – dismembered corpses, crushed bodies and injured horses. Some later manuscript illuminations are equally realistic (**2**). Nothing, however, is so evocative as the evidence revealed by the excavation of an actual battlefield on the island of Gotland in Sweden. Here, in 1905, a series of burial pits were discovered containing the bodies of those killed at Visby in 1361 when King Waldemar of Denmark attacked and plundered the town. Bodies were hurriedly buried where they fell, some still wearing their armour (**3, 4**). It was during this period, roughly 1350 to 1480, that armour was at its heaviest, coats of mail at their strongest and visored helmets at their most aggressively sinister (**5**). None of this saved the men of Visby.

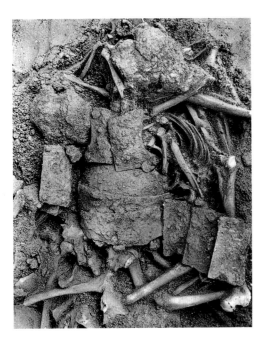

4. Rusting armour lying with fragments of skeleton where they were thrown after the fight at Visby; 1361.

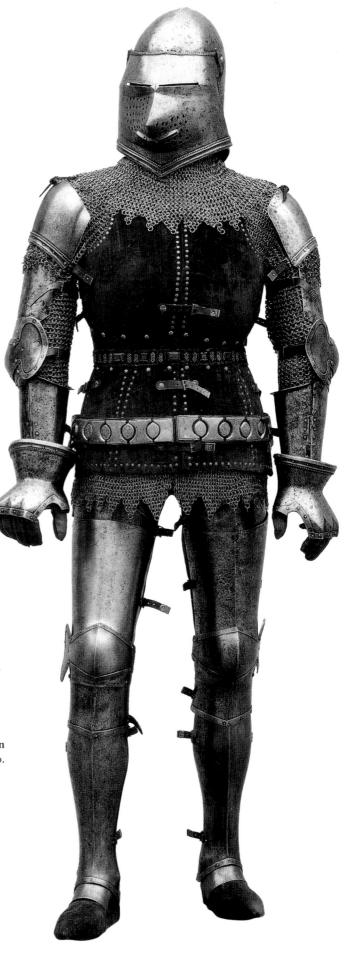

5. Suit of Italian armour, c. 1400.

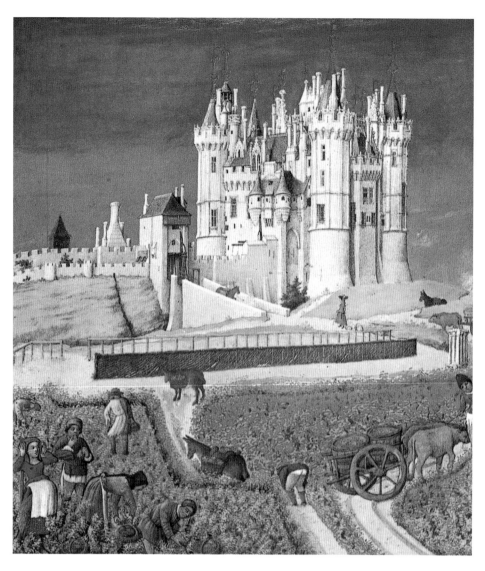

1. Left: Saumur, France, from the *Très Riches Heures* of the Duc de Berry.

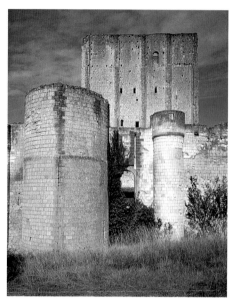

2. Loches, France: an early citadel combining castle, palace and church.

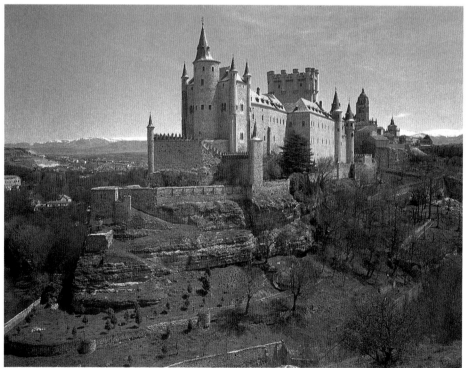

3, 4. Above: Onate. Left: Segovia. Two castles in Castile, vestiges of the long struggle between Christians and Muslims in Spain.

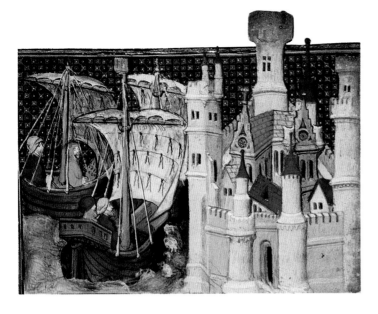

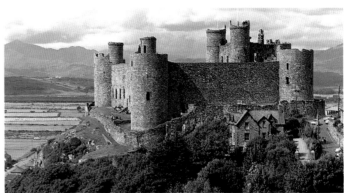

5. Left: Conway Castle, Wales, in a 15th-century miniature showing the arrival of the Earl of Salisbury.

6. Harlech Castle, Wales, built by Edward I to subjugate the Welsh.

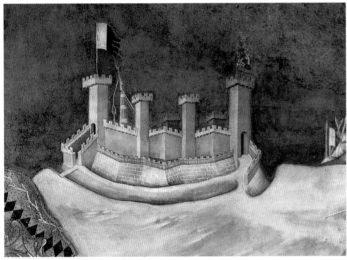

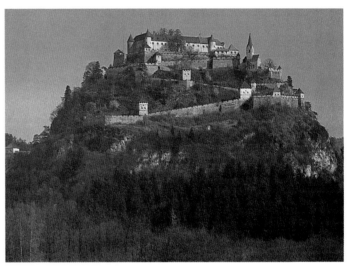

7. Hill fort near Siena, Italy: detail from a fresco by Simone Martini, mid-14th century. Here the castle is being besieged – there is a catapult behind.

8. Hochosterwitz, Austria: a fortified house defended by lines of castellated walls running down the hill.

Castles: the indispensable weapon

An impregnable castle was the nuclear deterrent of the Middle Ages. It represented secure possession; attempts to reduce it by assault or siege were long, costly and uncertain, and the majority of castles were never put to the test. Militarily they were continuously evolving, from the primitive motte and bailey (a fortified tower on a mound surrounded by a wall) to the later more sophisticated system of concentric curtain walls – until the development of gunpowder in the 16th century made them obsolete. The romantic air that to modern eyes surrounds castles was not entirely alien to the Middle Ages. For poets and painters they had strong symbolic overtones; allegorical castles occur in romances, and even real castles (1, 5) are given an almost fairy-tale glamour.

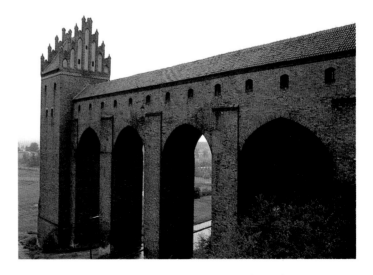

9. Kwidzin, Poland: a castle of the Teutonic Knights with its characteristic 'lavatory tower'.

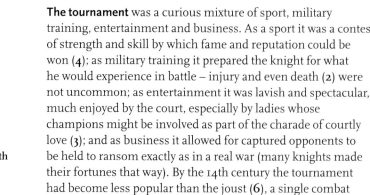

1. Italian ceremonial dragon helmet; early 15th century.

Tournaments: playing at war

The tournament was a curious mixture of sport, military training, entertainment and business. As a sport it was a contest of strength and skill by which fame and reputation could be won (4); as military training it prepared the knight for what he would experience in battle – injury and even death (2) were not uncommon; as entertainment it was lavish and spectacular, much enjoyed by the court, especially by ladies whose champions might be involved as part of the charade of courtly love (3); and as business it allowed for captured opponents to be held to ransom exactly as in a real war (many knights made their fortunes that way). By the 14th century the tournament had become less popular than the joust (6), a single combat between mounted knights armed with lances.

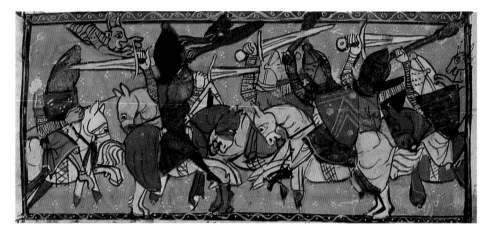

2. The mêlée was a mock battle which sometimes claimed lives – deaths which the church regarded as sinful. Here a devil claims the soul of the dead man; 14th century.

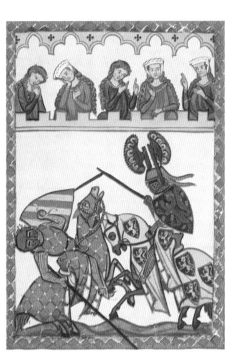

3. The victory of Sir Walter von Klingen, watched by ladies; German, early 14th century.

4. Tournament scene, from Froissart's *Chronicles*; 15th century.

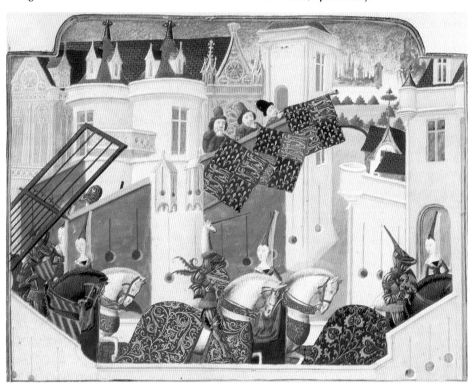

War: the heroic image
110-111

Courtly love: sex and
sublimation 224-225

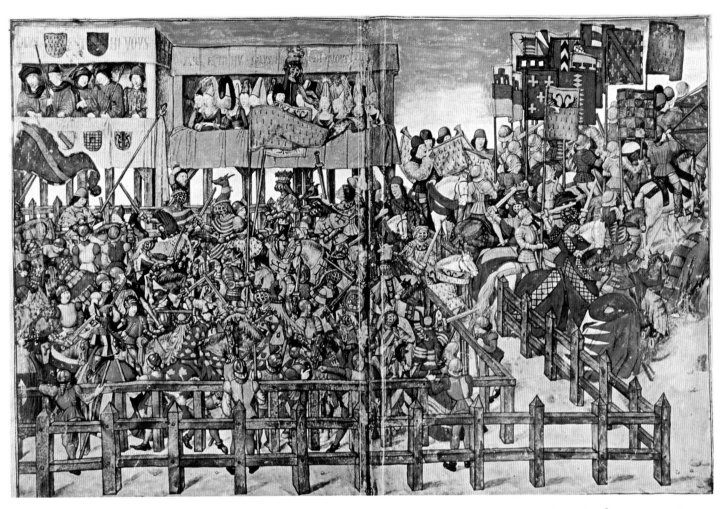

5. Preparation for a tournament; massed horsemen about to do battle. From King René of Anjou's *Livre des Tournois*, 1460–65.

6. Sir Geoffrey Luttrell in full jousting armour, being seen off by his wife and daughter-in-law. From the Luttrell Psalter, English, 1335–40.

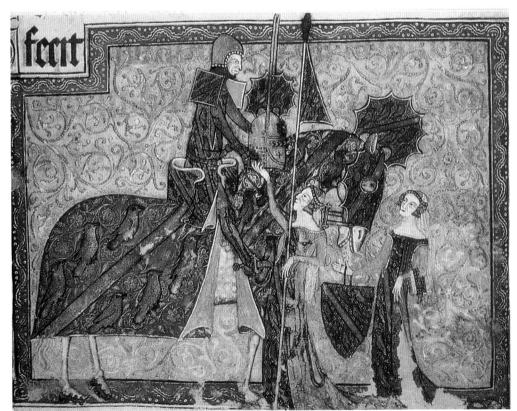

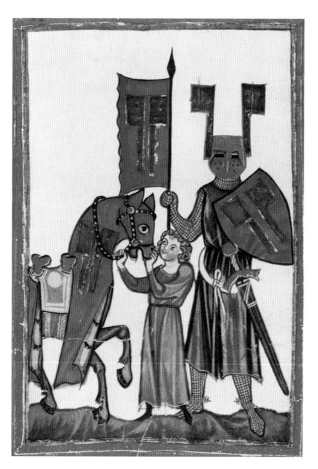

The language of heraldry

Armorial bearings – symbols identifying individuals and families, and by extension institutions and nations (5, 6) – began as military insignia to be displayed on shields (3). The complete ensemble would include a crest worn above the helmet (1), supporters of human or animal figures on each side (5) and a motto. Arms were the privilege of the nobility, granted only by the king and regulated by an officer of his household known as the 'King of Arms' (4). Through a complex system of combining, or 'quartering', family arms, whole dynastic histories could be expressed (6). Heraldry seems to have begun in the 12th century and reached its climax in the 16th, appearing not only on armour but also on seals, tombs (7), memorials, decoration (2) and documents.

1. The poet Wolfram von Eschenbach, displaying his arms (two axes) on his horse, banner, shield and helmet; German, 1304.

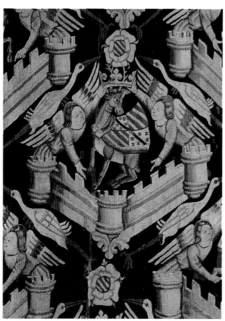

2. Detail of a tapestry showing the arms of the cities of Beaufort, Tarenne and Comminges, each supported by angels; Franco-Flemish, late 14th century.

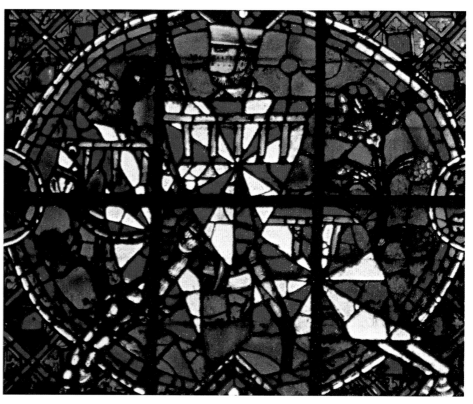

3. A nobleman represented in the stained-glass window that he donated to Chartres Cathedral in the early 13th century. His arms identify him as belonging to the family of Beaumont-sur-Oise.

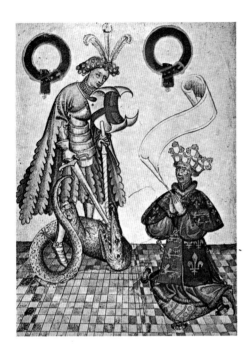

4. William Bruges, first Garter King of Arms (i.e. of the English Order of the Garter) kneeling before the patron of the order, St George. He wears the royal arms of England and France; English, c. 1430.

6. Right: knight dressed in the arms of Castile (castles) and León (lions).

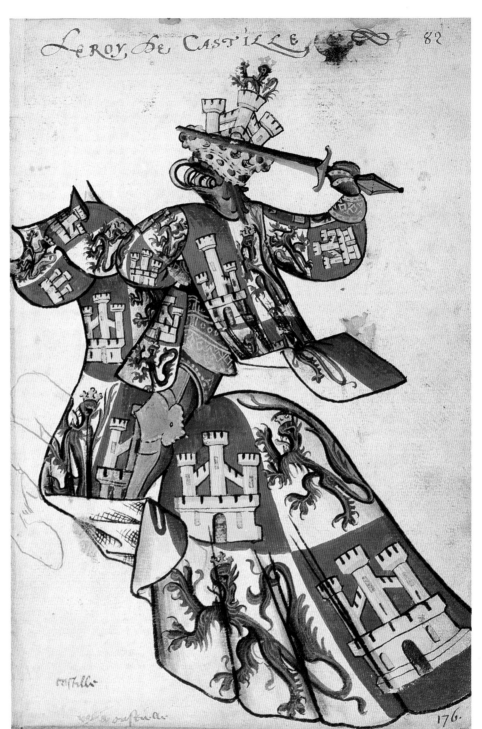

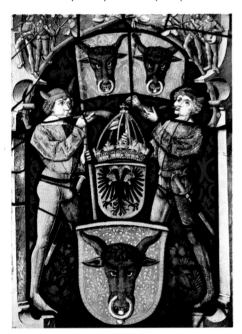

5. Stained glass showing the arms of the Swiss canton of Uri, by the Zurich glass-painter Lukas Zeiner, c. 1500.

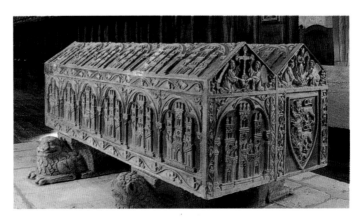

7. Tomb of Alfonso VIII of Castile and his queen in the monastery of Las Huelgas which they founded near Burgos, Spain, c. 1214, again combining the arms of Castile and León.

The hunt

Hunting as a pastime of the ruling class goes back to the early civilizations of Mesopotamia, but seems not to have been a particular passion of the Greeks and Romans, nor of the 'barbarian' nations who replaced them. But by the time of Charlemagne hunting had become the sport of kings. The English and French royal families were devoted to it (2) often at the expense of serious business. It was even widely popular among clergy and monks. The golden age of hunting was the 14th century when many of the classic treatises were produced (5, 6). Large estates were set aside as game parks, and strict regulations protected the animals, keeping the hunt as an aristocratic privilege. The favourite quarry were wild boars (5) and stags (1, 2). Fox-hunting was not a sport of the higher aristocracy. A more specialized sport was falconry (4, 7), a special interest of the Emperor Frederick II (3).

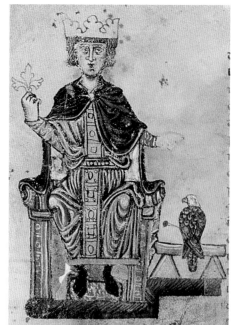

3. The Emperor Frederick II with his falcon; an illustration from his book on *The Art of Hunting with Birds* ('De Arte Venandi cum Avibus'), late 13th century.

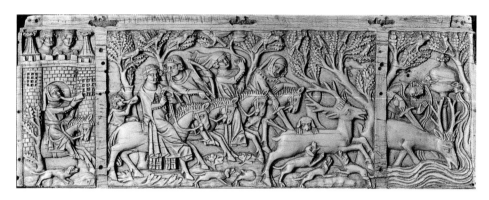

1. Ivory panel showing a royal stag-hunt; the king carries a falcon; French, first half of the 14th century.

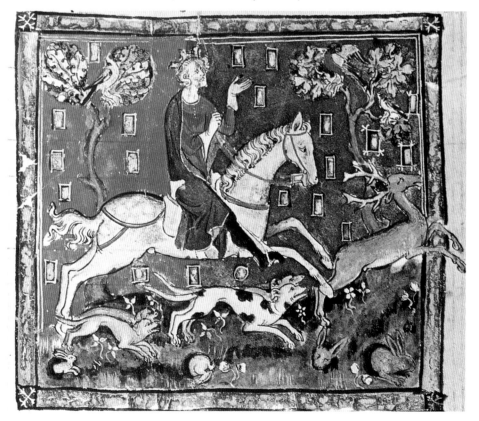

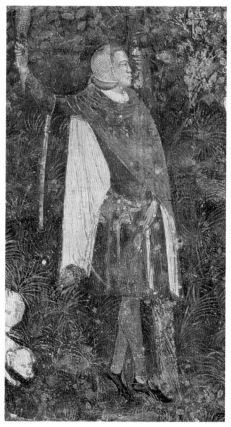

4. Falconer, fresco in the papal palace of Avignon; 14th century.

2. Left: King John of England hunting; English, 15th century.

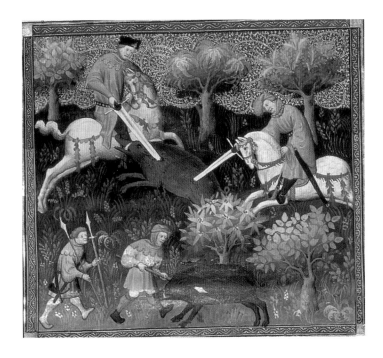

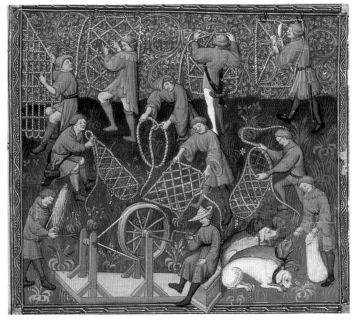

5, 6. Hunting the wild boar and how to make snares and nets, from one of the most famous hunting books, by Gaston Phebus, painted in Burgundy about 1407.

8. The end of the hunt. Two greyhounds receive their reward after the killing of the deer; Flemish tapestry, 15th century.

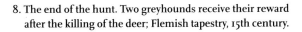

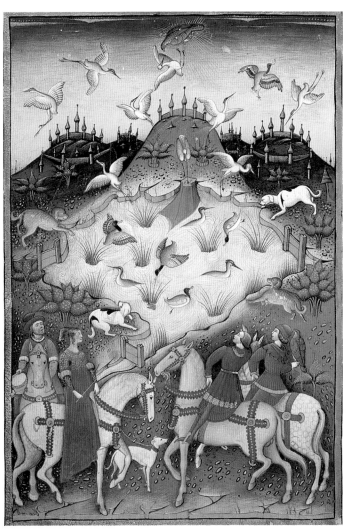

7. A mixed party including ladies hunting birds with falcon and dogs on a river; French or Italian, 15th century.

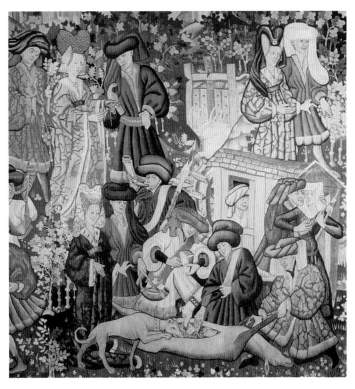

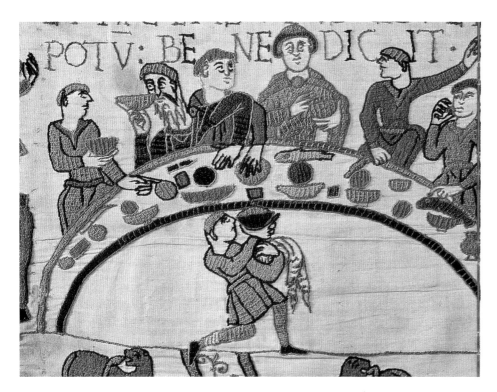

1. Bishop Odo blesses the feast given by William of Normandy before setting out for Hastings in 1066. From the Bayeux Tapestry, late 11th century.

The feast

To mark great formal occasions with a banquet has been characteristic of all times and cultures, but arguably the Middle Ages took this to its extreme. Nowhere was consumption more conspicuous or ceremony more elaborate. A large proportion of medieval illuminations depict feasts and feasting (1, 7), emphasizing the attention given to the preparation of food (4), the precious vessels and plates on which it was served (2, 3, 5, 8) and the social code that governed its rituals (6, 7).

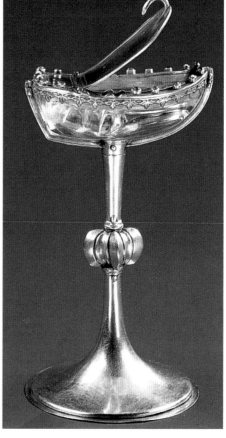

2. Salt-cellar, gold with rock crystal, emeralds and pearls; French, mid-13th century.

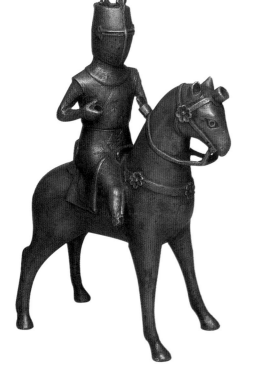

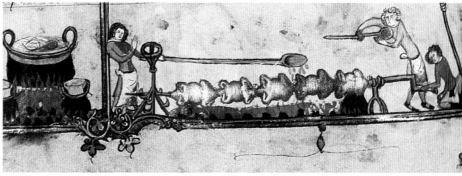

4. Flemish manuscript: scenes showing the preparation of food; 1450.

3. Left: aquamanile (water jug), filled through the helmet and poured through the forehead of the horse; English, late 13th century.

The family at home 170-171   Pleasures of the table 184-185

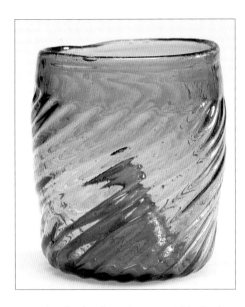

5. Glass beaker from the Lower Rhineland; 1400–50.

6. Feast in honour of the bride; French, early 14th century.

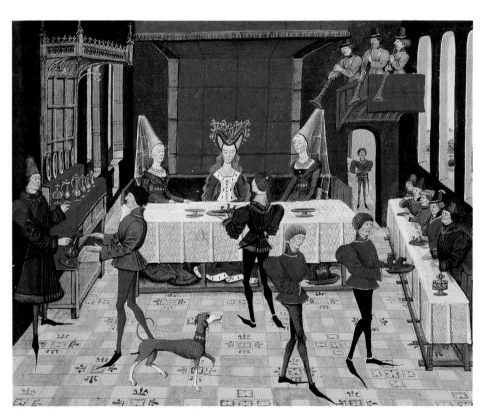

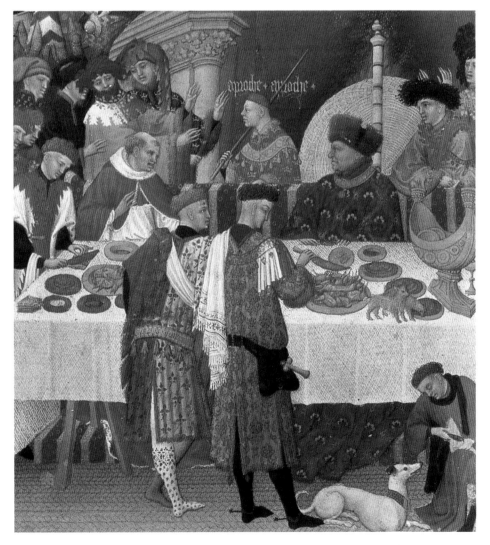

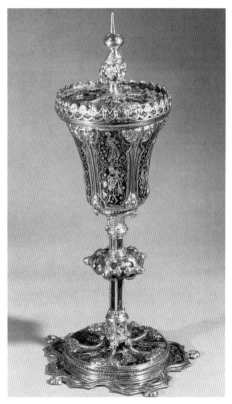

8. Beaker of rock crystal, with gold, diamonds, rubies and pearls, belonging to Duke Philip the Good of Burgundy; Burgundian, mid-15th century.

7. Left: Feast of the Duc de Berry: 'January' from the *Très Riches Heures*. Miniature, by the Limbourg brothers, 1413–16.

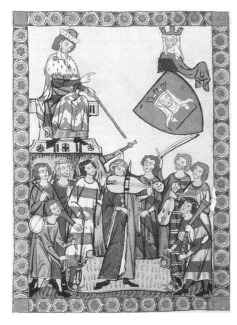

1. The troubadours or (in German) Minnesänger, carried courtly love-songs through the noble households of Europe. Here Henry of Meissen (known as 'Henry of the Love of Women') is accompanied by an ensemble of instruments; German, 1304.

2. Miniature showing dancers in a garden, with music by Guillaume Machaut beneath; c. 1400.

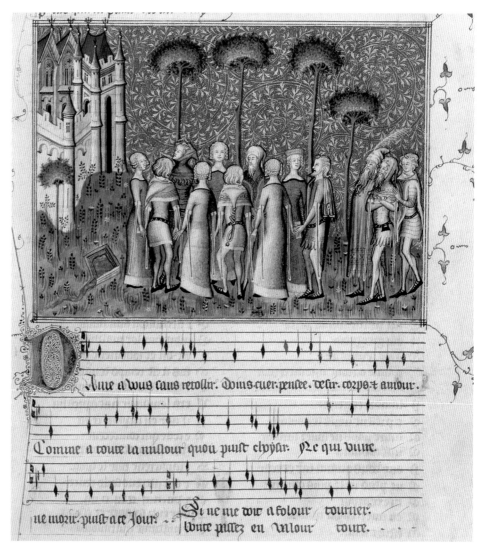

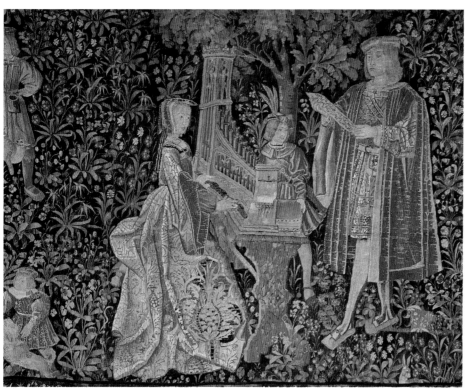

3. A ballad accompanied by the organ; tapestry from the Low Countries, c. 1420.

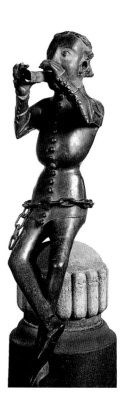

4. Bronze figure from a fountain in the shape of a piper; German, c. 1380.

Music at court

European music reached new heights in the Middle Ages, because of the invention of a standard system for writing it down. From the simple plainchant of the monastery grew a second line of harmony – *organum* – and from there came complex music involving several independent voices (polyphony). As with the written word, music notation was largely in the control of the Church, and secular music continued to be based upon improvisation around familiar themes. This was the age of the minstrel and travelling musician (1, 4), who performed without written music. Even when notated music is shown (2, 7) it is usually only one line. Once the system of music notation became universal, it paved the way for the highly sophisticated polyphony of the Renaissance and for the increase in variety of instrument types, as composers expressed their art by trying different combinations of ensembles (6). These groups of brass, wind, and stringed instruments would be the cornerstone for the creation of the modern orchestra.

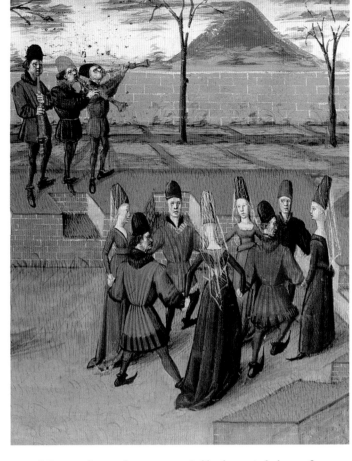

6. Dancers in a garden, accompanied by three wind-players; from the Romance of the Rose, 15th century.

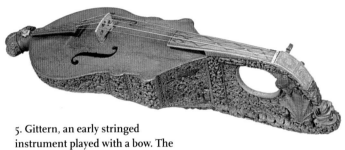

5. Gittern, an early stringed instrument played with a bow. The sides are carved with foliage and the Labours of the Months; English, 14th century.

7. A heart-shaped page for a collection of love-songs; French, *c.* 1475.

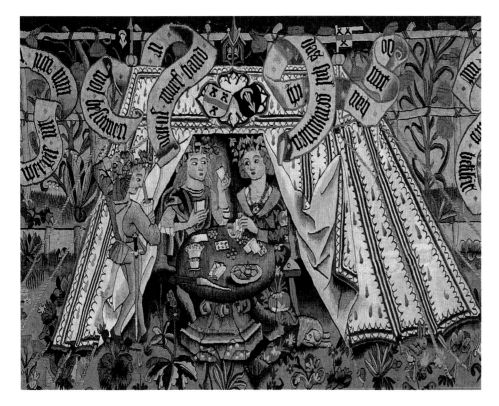

1. Left: detail from a German 15th-century tapestry showing a game of cards.

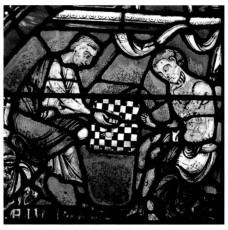

3. The Prodigal Son loses most of his clothes gambling. It is not clear how the chessboard relates to the dice; a stained-glass window in Chartres Cathedral, 13th century.

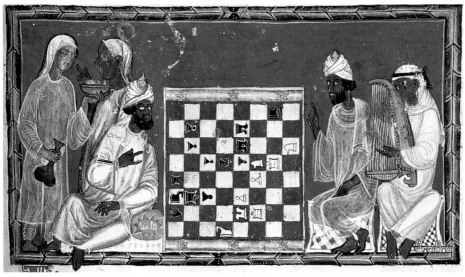

2. Chess in Muslim Spain, accompanied by a harp-player and attended by a Christian servant; from *The Book of Games* by Alfonso the Wise, 1282.

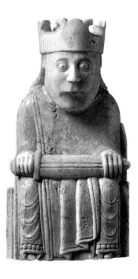

4. Queen, from a walrus-ivory chess-set from the Isle of Lewis, Hebrides; mid-12th century.

Games of skill and chance

Chess, playing-cards and dice have long histories. Chess probably originated in India, reaching Europe via Persia and Muslim Spain (2) – 'check mate' derives from the Arabic '*shah mat*', 'the king is dead'. The first reference to chess in Italy dates from 1061 (a priest was disciplined by his bishop for playing it). Thereafter it gained rapidly in popularity. There are numerous illustrations, and even surviving chessmen (4, 8). Draughts, or chequers, is a simpler game using the same board (5). Playing-cards also originated in the East. They appear in Europe in the 13th century, introduced either through Spain or by Crusaders (1, 6). Besides the pack that we know today, there were many others, including the tarot, and the number of games played with them is almost infinite. Dice, on the contrary, have hardly varied from ancient Egypt. They were immensely popular in Rome, and from there passed to the new nations of medieval Europe (3, 7). In gambling, two or three dice were commonly used.

Tournaments: playing at war 116-117

Mimes, minstrels and jongleurs 230-231

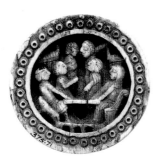

5. Draughtsman of walrus-ivory, showing a man and woman playing draughts; English, 12th century.

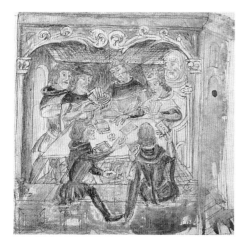

6. One of the earliest representations of a card-game, from a French, late-14th-century Romance. There are four players and three onlookers.

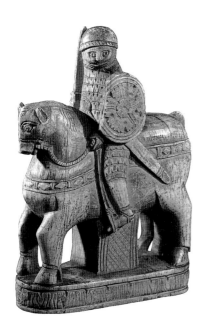

8. Knight, from a chess-set from southern Italy; 11th century.

9. Detail from a German 15th-century tapestry showing various games including blind-man's-buff.

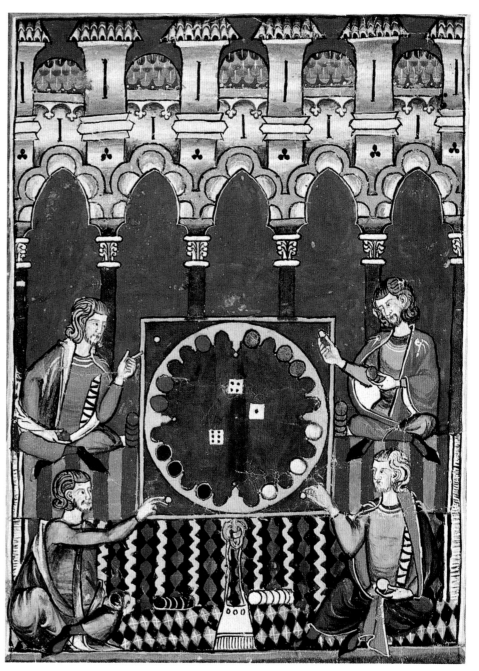

7. Gaming table with dice, from *The Book of Games* by Alfonso the Wise, 1282.

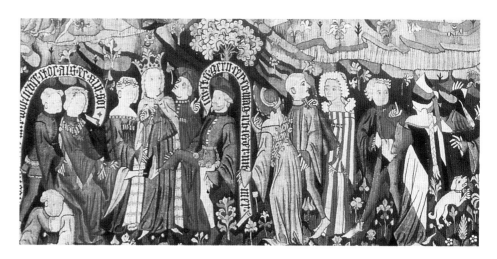

4

The Legacy of Medieval Art

THE MOST VISIBLE SURVIVAL from the medieval period is the art and architecture that remains: the elaborate and beautiful painted miniatures in manuscript books, the great churches, the tapestries, carvings and other small works of art. Much of this is ecclesiastical, for the Church was not only a wealthy patron but also the great reservoir of symbols, with a message it continually communicated in word and image. It is the great churches – cathedrals, monasteries and collegiate churches – that give the best impression of at least one type of medieval physical environment. The castles are mostly in ruins, the peasant huts long disappeared, but many cloisters, towers, crypts and naves of medieval churches are now as the masons left them.

From the early Middle Ages virtually all surviving art and architecture is monastic but gradually the picture diversifies. The cathedrals of Europe, which numbered around 800, were mostly located in towns and often had as benefactors the local citizens alongside the bishop and cathedral clergy. Parish churches of great size and beauty were erected, some, like the so-called wool churches of late-medieval England, built with the profits of pious merchants. In Italy and elsewhere civic buildings were created, while all over Europe princes raised their castles and palaces – a particularly elaborate example is Karlstejn (Karlstein) Castle outside Prague, built for the Holy Roman Emperor Charles IV (1347–78). Slowly the ecclesiastical monopoly of art (as well as of learning) diminished.

The predominant architectural style of the eleventh and twelfth centuries is that subsequently labelled Romanesque, characterized by its round arches and massive masonry. Majestic Benedictine churches, like Durham in the north of England and Vézelay in Burgundy, and huge cathedrals, such as Speyer or Santiago de Compostela, are impressive representatives of this style. In the first half of the twelfth century new developments led to the emergence of a different fashion, Gothic. The abbey church of Saint-Denis, built by Abbot Suger (1122–51), is conventionally reckoned the first building in this style. Its eastern end has the open, light and airy quality seen as characteristic of Gothic architecture. Over the course of the years 1150 to 1250 Gothic disseminated from the north of France to every part of Catholic Europe, so that its distinctive features formed a common international architectural language. Sometimes this involved French masons working abroad, such as William of Sens, who was responsible for the first stage of the rebuilding of the choir of Canterbury Cathedral in 1175–78, the earliest Gothic construction in England, or Stephen of Bonneuil, master mason, whose contract to work on the cathedral of Uppsala in Sweden was drawn up in 1287.

The pointed arches, ribbed vaults and flying buttresses of the Gothic style were devices for transferring thrust from the roof and walls to the ground. Because they did this in a systematic and efficient way, the walls of Gothic buildings could be less massive and the interiors lighter than their Romanesque predecessors. Some great Gothic churches resemble a framework of stone, with the interstices filled with glass and tracery. The effects can be seen in Chartres, with its elaborate programme of stained-glass images, or in the huge rose windows of the so-called rayonnant style of the thirteenth century, or in the Sainte Chapelle in Paris, a glass box of a building created by St Louis to house his relic collection in a flood of coloured light. The upward thrust so characteristic of

The art of stained glass and the form of the rose window were both inventions of the Middle Ages. The spectacular north rose of Notre-Dame, Paris (c. 1268), contains the Virgin and Child in the centre. The three outer rings show Old Testament prophets and kings. It has been calculated that the window contains 50,000 separate pieces of glass.

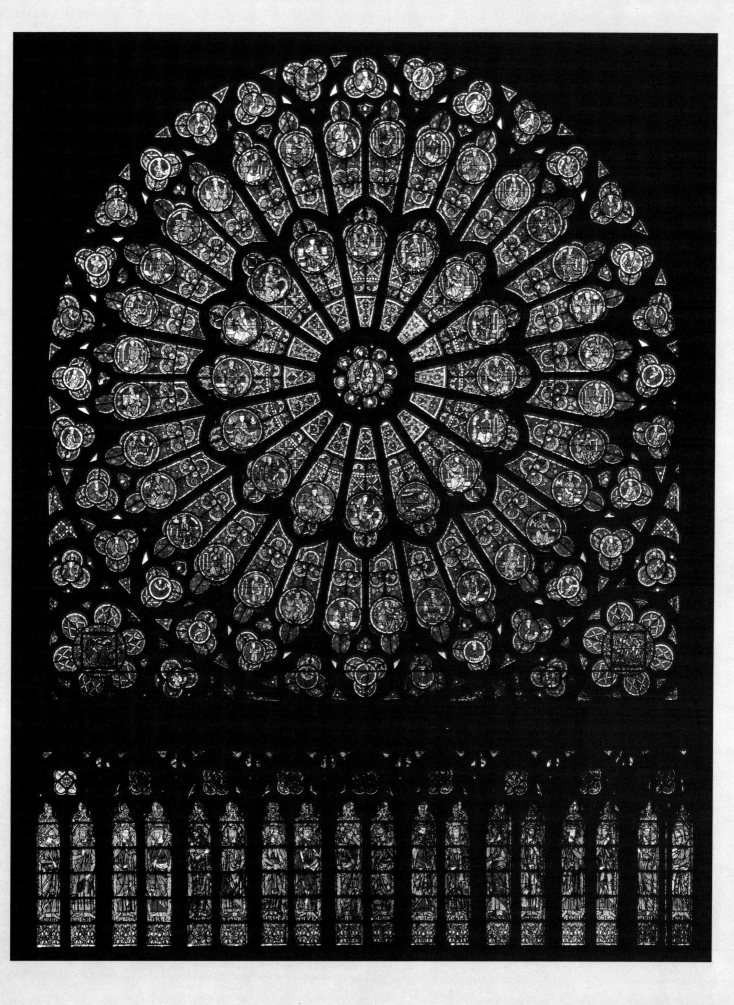

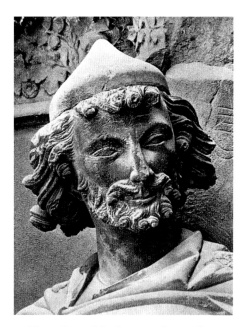

The sculptor of the figures on the west front of Rheims Cathedral (c. 1260) achieved a particularly elegant, slightly worldly charm. His speciality was the 'Rheims smile' ('le sourire de Reims'), seen here on the face of St Joseph.

Gothic architecture is a matter partly of many recurring vertical lines and partly of a literal attempt to go higher and higher. The highest Gothic vault ever built was that of the cathedral choir at Beauvais, which reached an astonishing 158 ft (48 m). The collapse of this structure in 1284, even though it was subsequently reconstructed with additional supports, shows that the limits of aspiration were being reached.

The construction of one of the great churches of the Middle Ages was a long and expensive process. At Winchester Cathedral the earliest visible work dates from the reign of William the Conqueror (1066–87), but there are substantial examples of building from every one of the succeeding centuries down to the time of the Tudors, when important work was done on the very eve of the Reformation. In such a building the distinctive variations in style, from Romanesque through all the varieties of Gothic, are clear. The most astonishing building saga is that of Cologne. Construction of a huge new Gothic cathedral began in 1248. The choir (eastern end) was 150 ft (almost 46 m) high, one of the tallest in Europe. It was eventually consecrated in 1322. Work on the rest of the church progressed slowly and finally ground to a halt in the later Middle Ages, with the west end incomplete. Amazingly, the medieval plans for the west end were preserved and, in the early nineteenth century, a German enthusiast for Gothic art and architecture rediscovered them. Construction at Cologne Cathedral then resumed on the basis of these plans. The building was completed in 1880, 632 years after it had been started!

Medieval churches were not only impressive and often beautiful buildings in their own right but they also formed the setting for representative images and abstract designs in many media: carving and sculpture, painting, stained glass. Especially remarkable is the tradition of human figures, some life-size or near life-size, sculpted in stone on the walls and arches of the great churches. At Moissac in the south of France the Romanesque cloister has, alongside the many carved capitals with biblical scenes, a sequence of saints carved on the corner piers, tall, powerful, stylized figures that convey solemn and patriarchal authority. In the portal of the adjoining church the tympanum (the semi-circular area below the arch), which is over 18 ft (some 5 1/2 m) wide, represents Christ in majesty, surrounded by the emblems of the evangelists (the man of Matthew, lion of Mark, bull of Luke and eagle of John) and the twenty-four elders mentioned in the Book of Revelation.

Such portals, with sculptured messages confronting those who entered the building, were developed to a new level of elaboration in the Gothic cathedrals. The west façade, which was the public face of the great church, often had three portals, each elaborately carved and surrounded by sculpture, while the portals of the north and south transepts were often similarly rich in carving. Famous examples are Chartres, Rheims and Amiens, where the new naturalism of the Gothic style attained some of its most remarkable results: the six transept portals at Chartres tell the story of the life of the Virgin Mary and the Last Judgement and the jambs are formed of rows of life-like figures, some in seeming conversation with each other; Rheims, the coronation church of the kings of France, possesses sculpted figures of the encounter of the Virgin Mary and St Elizabeth (mother of John the Baptist), clearly inspired by the art of ancient Rome, as well as a famously debonair St Joseph; while the west front of Amiens, completed in the relatively short period 1225–40, is one of the most unified and imposing Gothic façades still surviving.

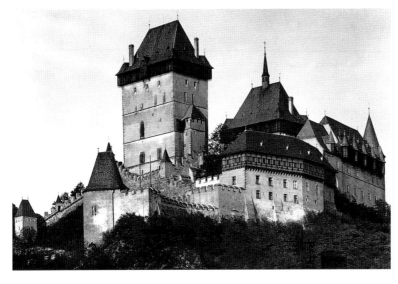

Karlstein Castle, outside Prague, was built for the Emperor Charles IV between 1347 and 1355. Designed as a royal residence, not as a fortress, it still preserves its imperial apartments, notably the Chapel of the Holy Rood, with paintings by Master Theodoric and walls inlaid with precious stone.

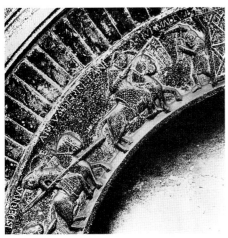

The earliest allusion to King Arthur is not in a literary text but in a sculptural relief running round the arch of the north door of Modena Cathedral. It is by a follower of Wiligelmo, c. 1100.

Church carvings were not limited to the main Christian themes of creation, salvation and damnation. In nooks and crannies, on the underside of choir-stalls and occasionally in more public positions, medieval sculptors produced a wide variety of secular, everyday and sometimes grotesque or obscene images. The earliest depiction of King Arthur is on an arch at Modena Cathedral that was carved around 1100, long before the date of any surviving Arthurian romances. The capitals of Canterbury Cathedral's crypt show jugglers, dragons in battle and a goat playing a pipe, while high in the choir of Lincoln Cathedral stands the phallic figure of the 'Lincoln Imp'.

A similar interplay between the central doctrinal image and the playfulness of the margins can be seen in the manuscript painting of the medieval period. There are the large illustrated Bibles and Psalters of both the Romanesque and Gothic periods, like the twelfth-century Winchester Bible or the Psalter produced for St Louis, with their full-page biblical scenes, but there are also, especially in the later centuries of the Middle Ages, the margins of the great illustrated books full of apparently irrelevant birds and beasts and drolleries of all kinds. Alongside the heavy volumes employed in the liturgy of the Church there appear Books of Hours, prayer-books for the use of lay aristocrats, and many purely secular illustrated texts, including the illuminated romances and histories produced in the fourteenth and fifteenth centuries. By the end of the Middle Ages painted books had become more diverse and more secular, serving as private recreation as well as sacred icon.

Unlike artists of the modern period, those of the Middle Ages were generally anonymous. It is only exceptionally that a stray piece of information allows painters and architects to be identified. It was unusual for them to sign their work, though there are cases like the Romanesque sculptor Gislebertus, so proud of the figures he created at Autun in the 1120s (including an elegiac naked Eve) that he carved his name on the tympanum of the portal. A similar lack of reticence was displayed by Nicola Pisano and his son Giovanni, working in northern Italy in the second half of the thirteenth century: 'In the year 1260 Nicola Pisano carved this noble work' reads the inscription on the pulpit in the Pisa Baptistery. 'May so greatly gifted a hand be praised as it deserves.' More usually, masons and painters were viewed as craftsmen, members of guilds who had to demonstrate their competence and who worked in teams or workshops. It was not the individual creative genius that mattered, but the end results.

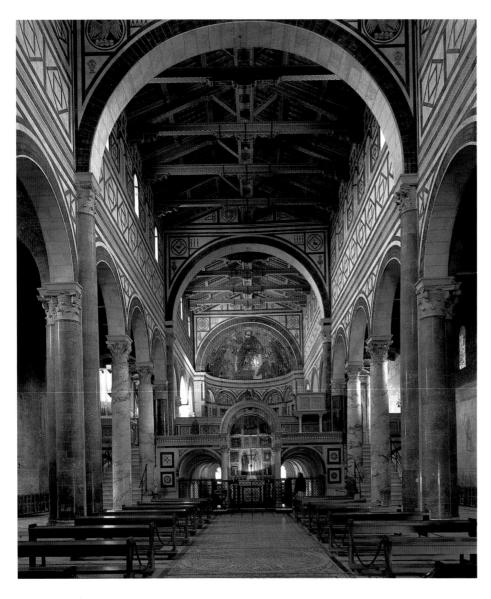

1. Italy remained closest to the classical language of architecture. S. Miniato al Monte, Florence, uses Corinthian columns and marble veneer; mid-11th century.

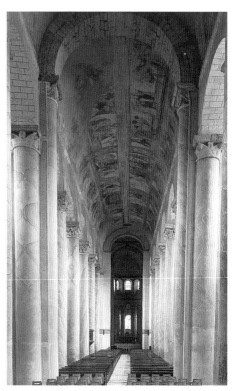

2. France: at St Savin-sur-Gartempe the arcade is painted to resemble marble and the vault covered with an ambitious cycle of frescoes illustrating the Old Testament; 11th century.

Architecture: the Romanesque prelude

It is its buildings that keep the Middle Ages most conspicuously alive and that are, for most Europeans, its most immediate legacy. Nor is this inappropriate. Architecture was the dominant art; not only did it achieve feats of aesthetic and structural imagination that have never been surpassed but it was the setting for a large proportion of sculpture, painting and stained glass, while its forms were reflected everywhere in furniture, metalwork and even manuscript illumination. By about the year 1000 a definable style had emerged which, because of its ultimate dependence on Roman models, has come to be called Romanesque. It used round arches, classical columns and capitals, and vaulting in stone or brick. Major churches followed the basilican form of Roman law-courts rather than temples; a central vessel (the nave) defined by arcades flanked by aisles and supporting an upper wall with windows (the clearstorey). Though sharing the same basic components, the architecture of each region displays characteristic features of its own.

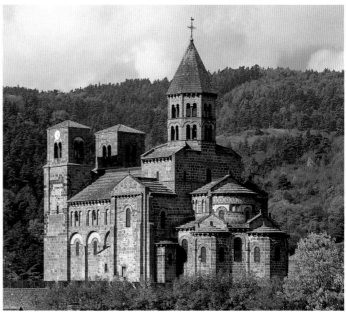

3. France: St Nectaire is a typical church of the Auvergne, with an octagonal crossing tower and a round apse with radiating chapels; *c.* 1080.

Classical revivals 36-37　　The monasteries: bastions of learning 82-83

6. Germany: the abbey church of Maria Laach exemplifies a particular German form of Romanesque with apses and round towers at both east and west ends; mid-12th century.

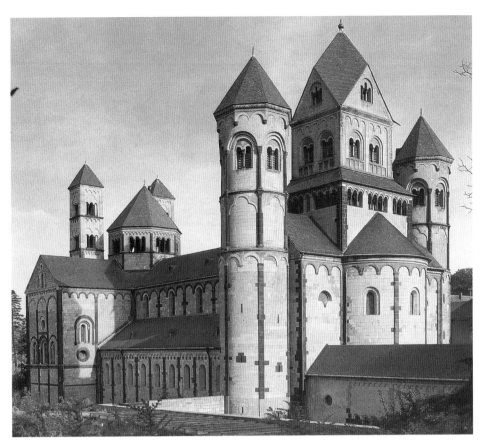

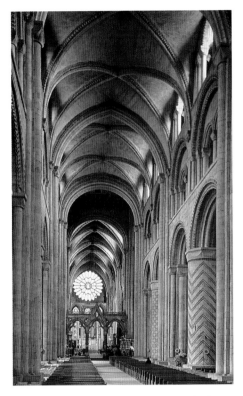

4. England: Durham Cathedral has thick circular piers with incised (and originally painted) patterns and one of the earliest rib-vaults in Europe; early 12th century.

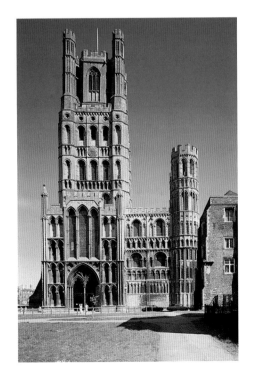

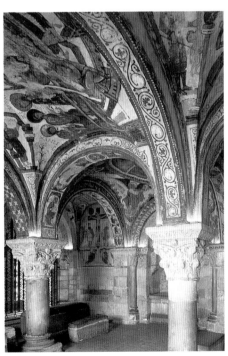

7. Spain: the Pantheon of the Kings at León, with re-used Roman capitals and lavish painted decoration; c. 1063–1100.

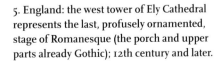

5. England: the west tower of Ely Cathedral represents the last, profusely ornamented, stage of Romanesque (the porch and upper parts already Gothic); 12th century and later.

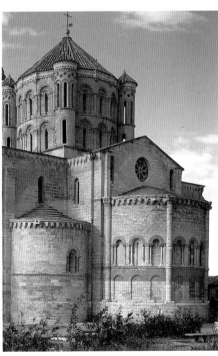

8. Spain: the cathedral of Toro. The crossing tower is a Spanish speciality – an octagon of repeated arches with four tourelles at the corners; 1160.

The Legacy of Medieval Art 133

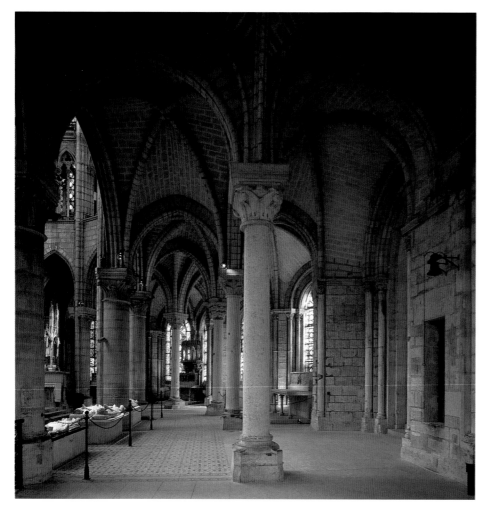

1. The east end of the abbey church of Saint-Denis (1140–44). The technique of Gothic architecture allows spaces to flow freely into one another instead of being compartmentalized.

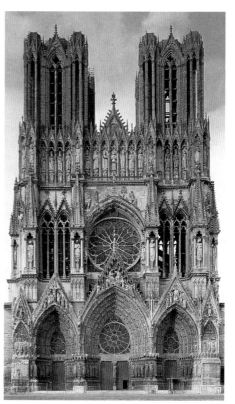

4. The west front of Laon Cathedral (*c.* 1200) retains a certain Romanesque solidity and depth.

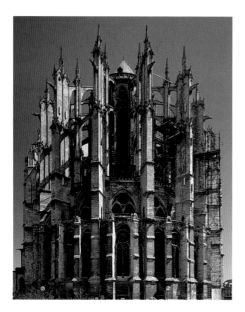

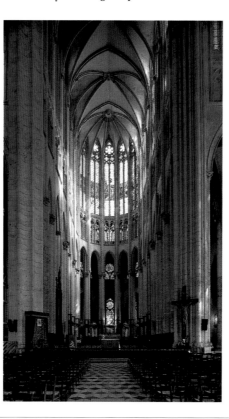

2, 3. Beauvais Cathedral (begun 1225), of which only the choir and crossing were ever built, was the highest of all Gothic churches. The vault in fact collapsed in 1284 and had to be rebuilt, supported by a dense cluster of flying buttresses.

5. Above: at Rheims Cathedral (after 1254) everything is subordinated to aesthetic unity and upward movement, including window tracery and sculpture.

The flowering of Gothic

Gothic architecture was both a structural innovation and a spiritual opportunity. (It has nothing to do with the Goths; the word is a post-Renaissance misnomer.) Pointed arches meant that arches of different span could reach the same height; rib-vaults (3, 6) meant that the thrust could be conducted to specific points along a wall; and precise buttressing including the flying buttress (2) meant that these thrusts could be transmitted securely to the ground. All this was merely engineering. But by transforming the structure into a skeleton in which opposing forces were held in equilibrium, solid walls could be replaced by slender shafts, windows filled with stained glass could occupy all the surface between the shafts, and the whole building could be given a new vertical emphasis expressive of heightened religious emotion. Beginning with Saint-Denis near Paris (1), under the powerful Abbot Suger, the Gothic style was taken up between 1150 and 1250 in the rest of France (2, 3, 4, 5), England (6, 7, 8), Spain and Germany.

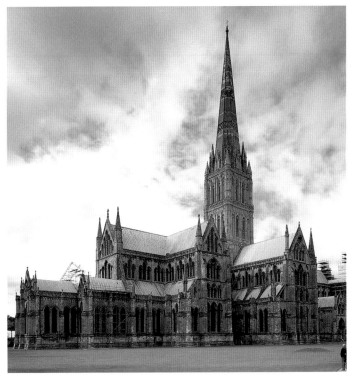

7. The plan of Salisbury Cathedral (begun 1220) is characteristically expansive, in contrast to the compact outline of a French cathedral.

6. Left: the nave of Lincoln Cathedral (c. 1220–40): English architects consistently favoured greater complexity. At Lincoln seven vault-ribs spring from one point instead of three, as was normal in France.

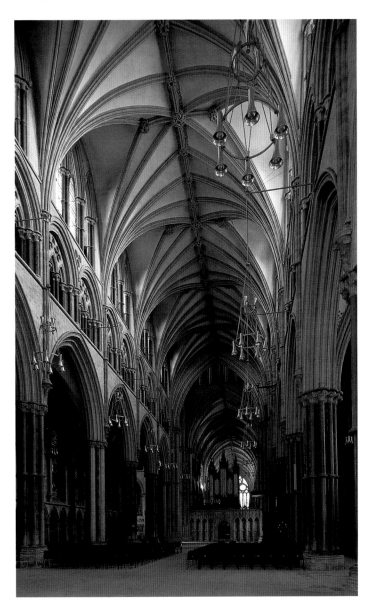

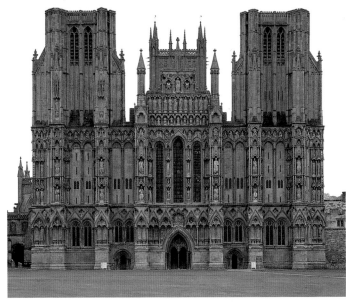

8. The west front of Wells Cathedral (begun c. 1230), wider than the nave behind it, is a screen for sculpture rather than the ceremonial statement of Laon or Rheims, and the single entrance portal quite insignificant. Originally all these façades would have been brightly coloured, the figures painted naturalistically and the background in vivid reds and blues.

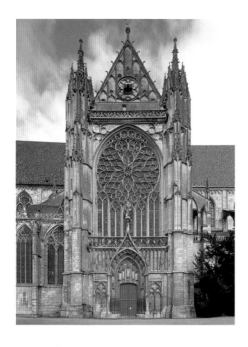

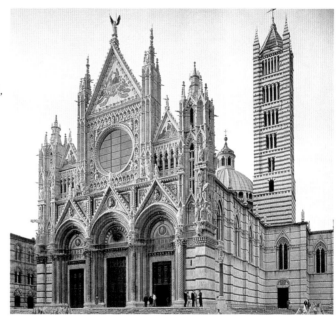

1. The south transept of Sens Cathedral (1490–1512), with its huge Flamboyant window.

2. Siena Cathedral (14th century), still classical in its proportions and even retaining the round arch.

Gothic: the last phase

During the 14th and 15th centuries Gothic architecture ceased to be international and split into definable regional styles. In France this is characterized by its curvilinear, flame-like window tracery – hence the name Flamboyant (1). Italy (2) never conformed to the verticality of northern Gothic, except at Milan, whose cathedral (5) is eccentric in any context. Spain and Portugal experimented with vast scale (3) and bizarre decorative forms (4). In England the first Gothic style (Early English) was succeeded by Decorated (8) and Perpendicular (9), while Germany and Central Europe indulged in amazingly complex vaulting patterns (6, 7). It is hard to imagine how these great churches must have impressed ordinary laymen and women. In grandeur, in richness and in symbolic power they had no parallel in the secular world. Intentionally, for the population at large, they were images of the New Jerusalem, a foretaste of Heaven.

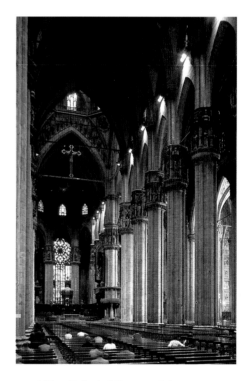

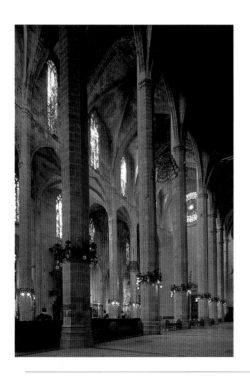

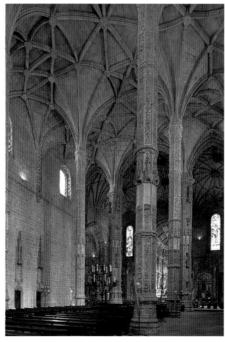

5. Milan Cathedral (begun 1387); mysteriously dark in spite of its size and with a ring of life-sized statues in place of capitals.

3. Far left: the cathedral of Palma, Mallorca (14th century); piers and walls are reduced to a masonic minimum.

4. Left: the monastery church of Belem, near Lisbon (1501–19), in the exotic style known as Manueline.

The flowering of Gothic
134-135

The legacy of sculpture
148-149

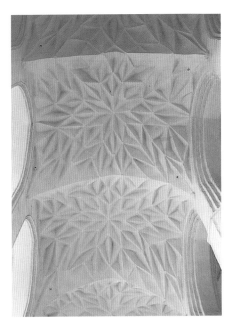

6. Danzig (Gdansk), now in Poland (late 15th century), employs a 'cellular' vault that has no structural rationale and is made of plaster, not stone.

7. At Annaberg, in south Germany (1525) the vault blossoms into flower-like patterns. This is a typical Central European hall-church, the aisles equal in height to the nave.

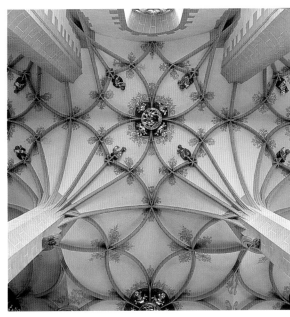

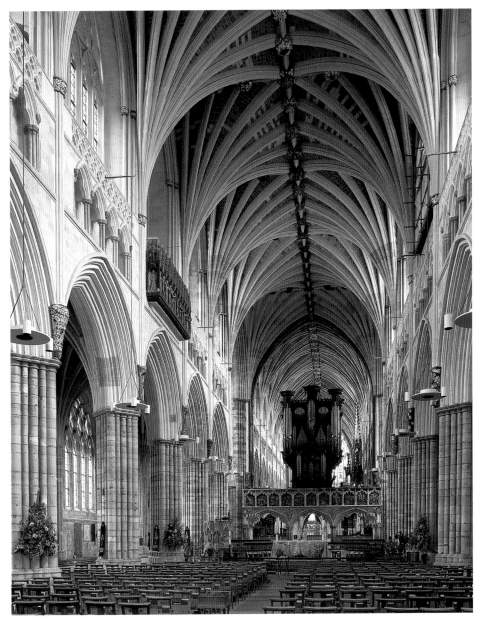

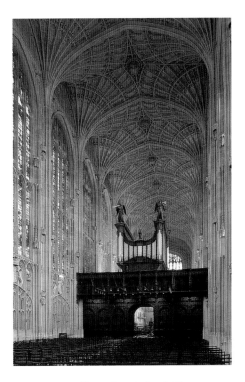

9. King's College Chapel, Cambridge (1466–1515), represents the Perpendicular style at its most lavish, with vast windows divided by grid-like mullions and that uniquely English speciality, the fan-vault.

8. Exeter Cathedral nave (c. 1310) exemplifies the English Decorated style, the piers formed of thick clusters of shafts, the vaulting-ribs multiplied so that eleven spring from one point.

The Legacy of Medieval Art   137

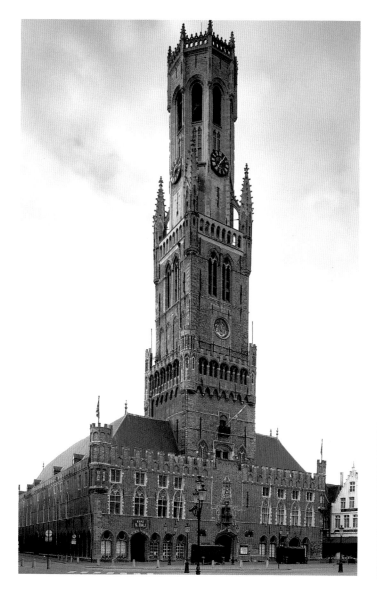

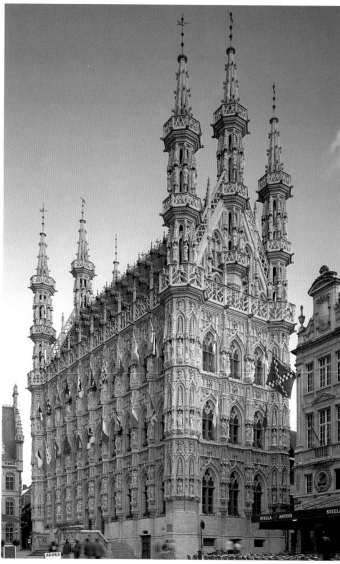

1. The Cloth Hall of Bruges, Belgium, its immensely tall belfry (completed 1486) dwarfing the surrounding buildings.

2. The Town Hall of Louvain, Belgium (1448–63), a superb display of decorative sculpture.

3, 4. Two ingenious Gothic staircases – in the Albrechtsburg, the ducal palace of Meissen, Germany (c. 1470), and Maximilian I's castle at Graz, Austria (c. 1500), where two spirals interweave.

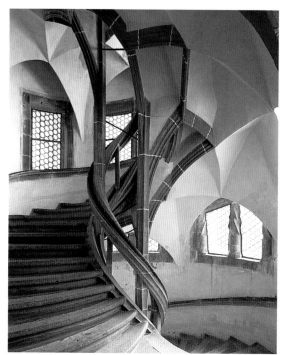

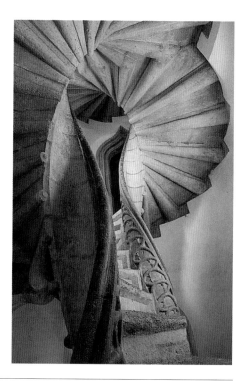

Castles: the indispensable weapon 114-115

The city as work of art 142-143

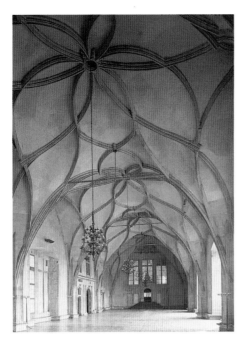

5. The Vladislav Hall, Prague Castle, one of the Imperial capitals. This comes at the very end of the medieval period (1493–1515) and the architect, Benedikt Ried, created a fantasy on Gothic vaulting, with ribs meandering and abruptly stopping short in apparent mockery of any functional purpose.

Royal splendour, civic pride

Secular building never matched religious. The magnificence routinely accorded to God was beyond the capacity of kings. It is a measure of medieval priorities to compare cathedrals and palaces. While nearly all cathedrals, for instance, were given stone vaults, virtually no royal halls were: Prague (5) is the exception. Even the most splendid of all – Richard II's Westminster (6) – has a wooden roof. They are, on the whole, less well preserved than ecclesiastical buildings (most have perished altogether), and interest often centres on the details (3, 4) rather than the whole. More prominent in the urban scene are the buildings erected by civic and commercial bodies in Italy, Flanders (1, 2) and the Netherlands, which often dominate their cities, providing a symbolic accent to balance that of the church.

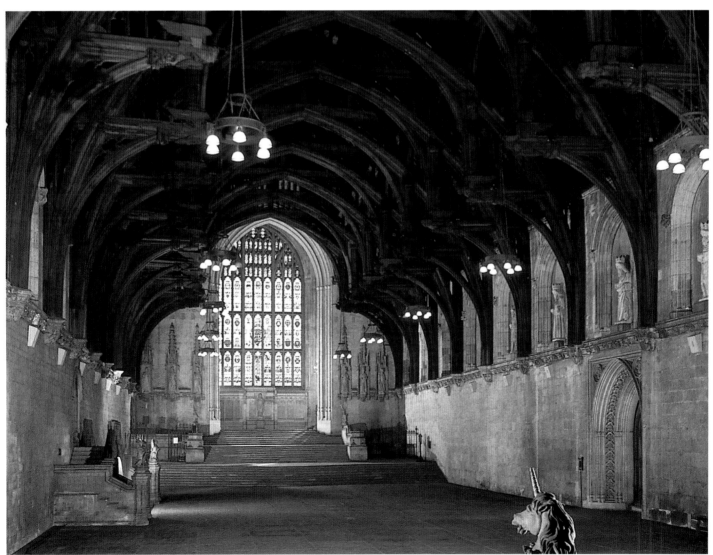

6. Westminster Hall, London, almost the only vestige of the old royal Palace of Westminster. Dating originally from Norman times, it was given its magnificent hammer-beam roof by Richard II's carpenter, Hugh Herland, from 1394 to 1401.

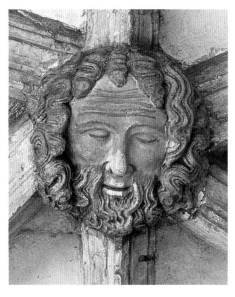

1. Henry Yevele, architect of the nave of Canterbury Cathedral; late 14th century.

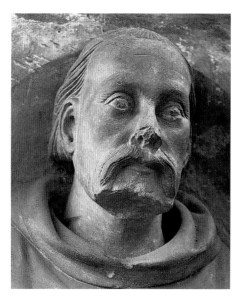

2. Peter Parler, master-builder of Prague Cathedral; c. 1380.

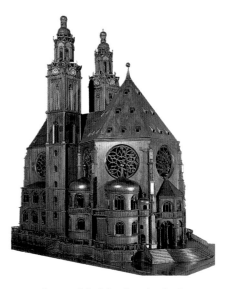

3. Wooden model of the church of Schöne Maria, Regensburg, designed by Hans Hieber; c. 1520.

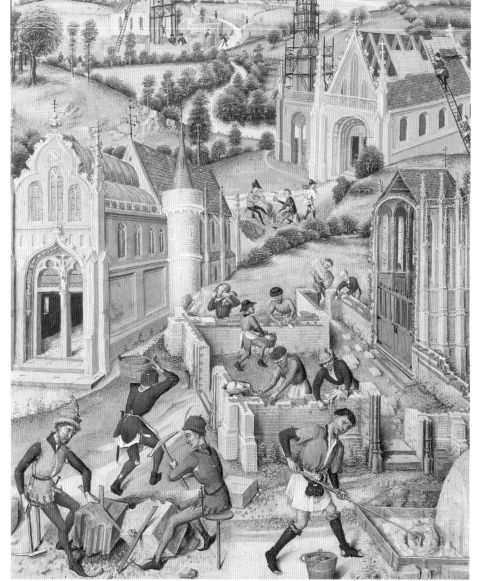

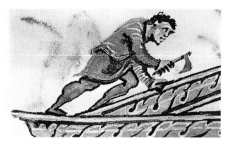

5. Roofer at work; detail from a Carolingian Gospel Book, 9th century.

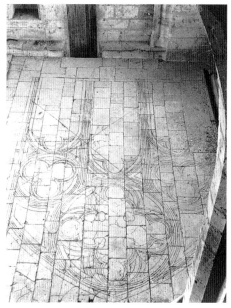

6. Full-scale drawing of a window on the tracing-floor of Bourges Cathedral, France; probably 13th century.

4. Miniature showing the building of twelve churches in honour of the Apostles by Girart de Roussillon; France, 1448.

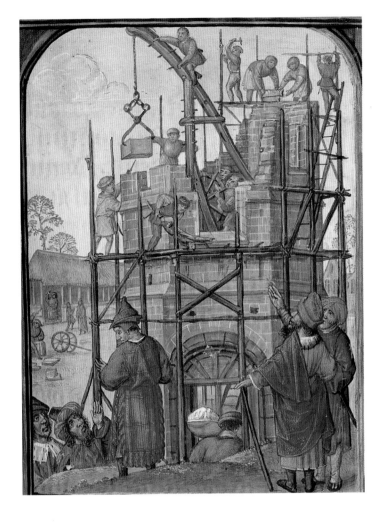

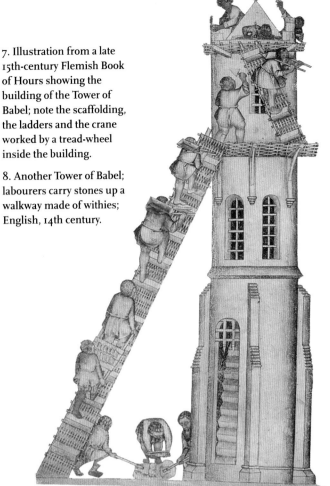

7. Illustration from a late 15th-century Flemish Book of Hours showing the building of the Tower of Babel; note the scaffolding, the ladders and the crane worked by a tread-wheel inside the building.

8. Another Tower of Babel; labourers carry stones up a walkway made of withies; English, 14th century.

Architects and builders

Most cities of the Middle Ages must have seemed like giant building-sites. Work was almost continuous on town walls and fortifications; great houses and civic buildings were being demolished and remodelled according to new fashions; while large churches and cathedrals took decades, sometimes centuries, to complete, and after that were subject to repeated additions and alterations. The building trade was therefore a major industry. At its head were the architects, or master-builders, who personally oversaw operations. They were eminent men and many of their names are known (1, 2). Under them were teams of masons, carpenters (9), roofers (5), stone-cutters and labourers organized into guilds to which entry was strictly limited. There are many illustrations showing buildings under construction, with vivid pictures of scaffolding, ladders (8), and cranes (7). One of them (4) shows the chancel of a church already built so that it can be used for Mass, as was normal, followed by the transepts, built of brick with stone facing. Some kind of drawn plan must have been used from the beginning, though none survive until the later Middle Ages, and there were wooden models (3) to show to patrons. Details such as window tracery were drawn out full-size on the ground (6).

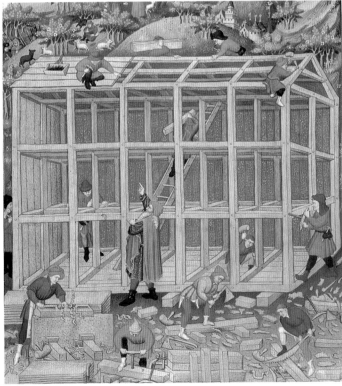

9. Medieval carpentry: Noah building the Ark, featuring tools that include a plane, a drill, an axe and a saw; French, c. 1423.

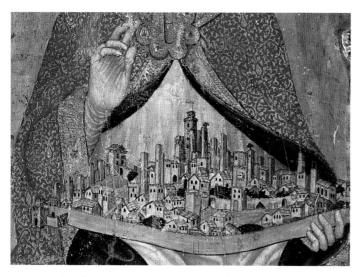
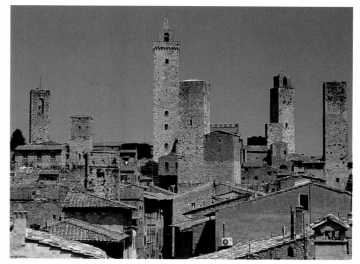

1, 2. Model of San Gimignano, Italy, held by the saint himself in a painting by Taddeo di Bartolo, *c.* 1400, and the city today.

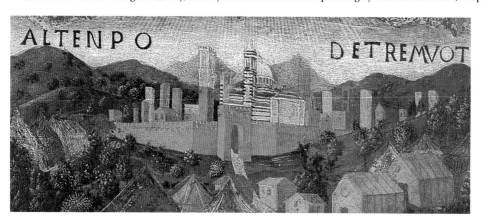

ALTENPO DETREMVOT

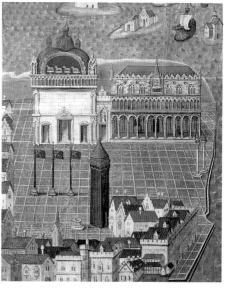

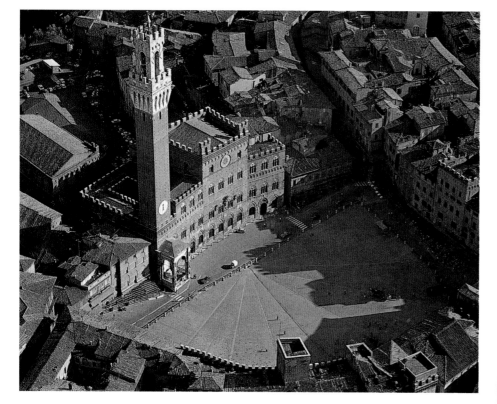

5, 6. St Mark's and the Ducal Palace, Venice, from a French manuscript of the 15th century and (below) as it really is.

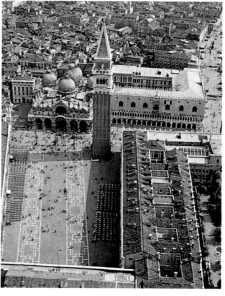

3, 4. Siena depicted in 1467 by Francesco di Giorgio Martini, and the Piazza del Campo today; the Palazzo Pubblico, built 1289–1305.

Italy: the land without kings 104-105

Royal splendour, civic pride 138-139

The city as work of art

It is still possible to enjoy the visual qualities of medieval cities, though not to experience them as living environments. Many retain their circuits of walls, town halls and public spaces. Although normally growing by unplanned accretion (not always: some were consciously designed), these cities were evidently loved and admired and depicted in detail, though not always accurately. Such pictures are part topographical record – there are always familiar landmarks still recognizable today – and part symbolic image. Buildings are reduced to conventional stereotypes: the towers of San Gimignano (**1**, **2**), the Palazzo Pubblico and Cathedral of Siena (**3**, **4**), the Campanile and Doge's Palace of Venice (**5**, **6**) and the double walls of the citadel of Carcassonne (**7**). It was this tendency to find the universal in the particular (man as microcosm, the animal world as a structure of moral lessons) that, as we shall see, made it so easy to translate architecture itself into an allegorical language.

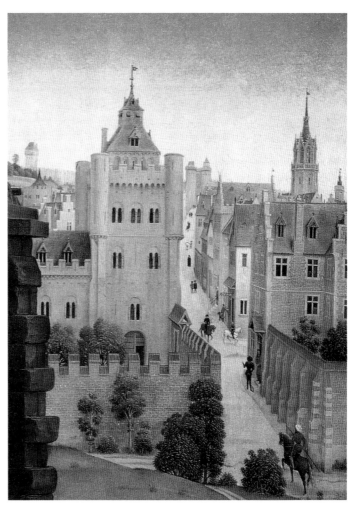

8. Rogier van der Weyden: detail from the Bladelin Altarpiece; after 1456.

7. The citadel of Carcassonne, France, in its present (restored) state. The walls, greatly enlarged in the Middle Ages, go back to Merovingian times.

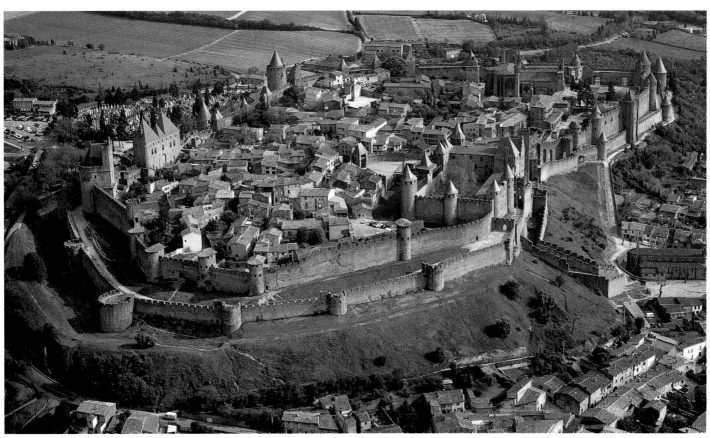

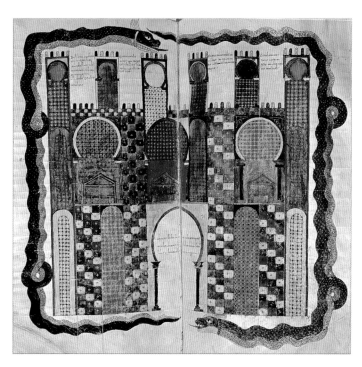

1. Candelabrum representing the gates of the New Jerusalem; from Hildesheim Cathedral, mid-11th century.

Buildings in the mind

Architecture haunted the medieval imagination. Heaven was seen as a city or a cathedral (1, 2). Hell was a fiery dungeon (3). In origin this probably goes back to St John's apocalyptic visions and their imagery of the New Jerusalem. But by the 14th century such visual archetypes had become universal. 'Micro-architecture' proliferated on altars, tombs, chantries, niches for statues and church portals. Reliquaries sprouted spires and domes (4); choir-stalls generated a fantastic skyline of crockets and gables. Furniture, both sacred and secular, revelled in displays of tracery like cathedral windows. Among the most elaborate examples of symbolic architecture is a Flemish allegory of the Fountain of Grace (5). Christ, the source of grace, sits enthroned in the centre under a Gothic canopy flanked by the Virgin and St John. Musical angels play in a Paradise Garden, while in the foreground the Water of Life nourishes the hierarchy of the Church on the left, while opposite them the Jews, led by Synagogue (his staff broken) reject Christ's saving Grace.

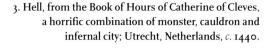

2. The Heavenly Jerusalem as a city of towers and Moorish arches, from Beatus of Liebana's commentary on the Apocalypse; Spanish, 975.

3. Hell, from the Book of Hours of Catherine of Cleves, a horrific combination of monster, cauldron and infernal city; Utrecht, Netherlands, c. 1440.

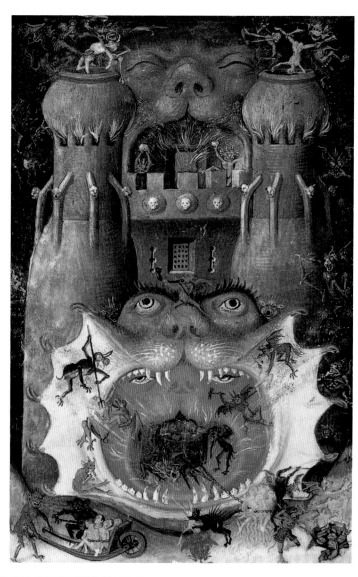

Angels of light 78-79   Mystical visions 88-89

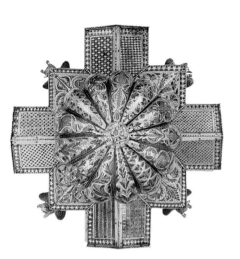

4. German reliquary in the form of a cruciform domed church, seen from above; Cologne, *c.* 1175–80.

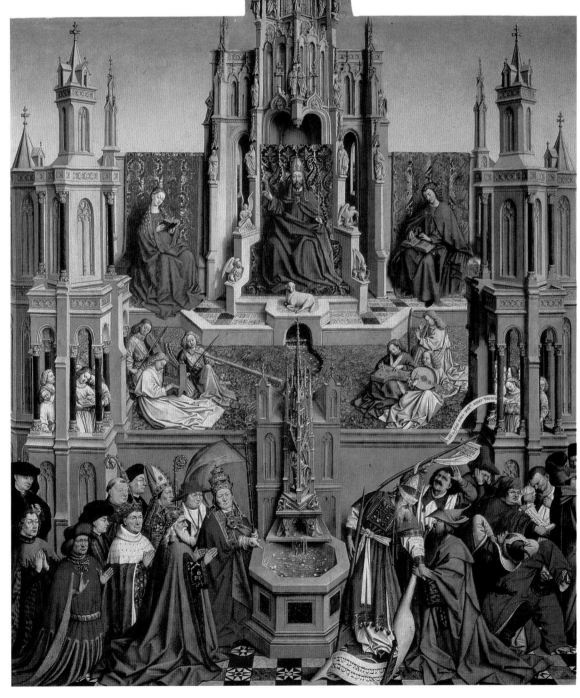

5. The Fountain of Grace, by a Flemish artist of about 1450.

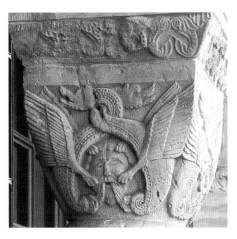

1. Capital in the abbey church of St Simon and Juda, Goslar, Germany; mid-12th century.

3. Right: portal of the abbey church of St Pierre, Moissac, France, 1120–35. The tympanum shows Christ with the symbols of the Evangelists, surrounded by the twenty-four Elders of the Apocalypse.

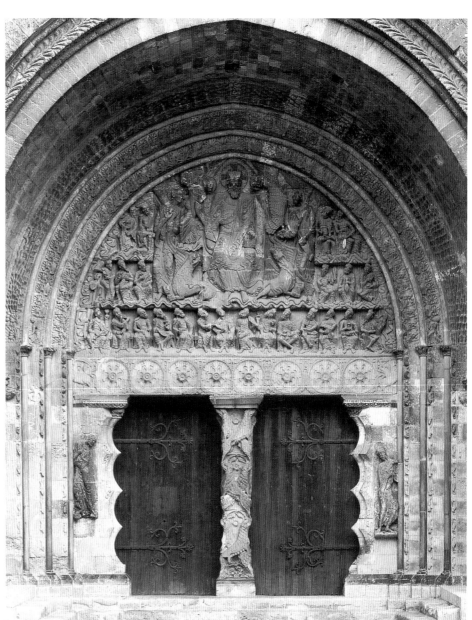

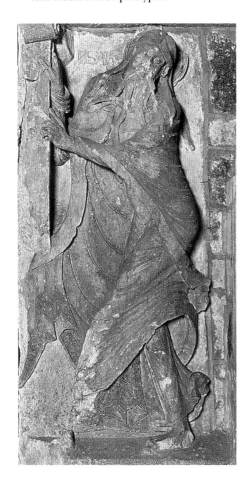

2. Isaiah, from the church of Ste Marie, Souillac, France; 1120–35.

4. Eve plucking the apple, from the church of St Lazare, Autun, France; c. 1130.

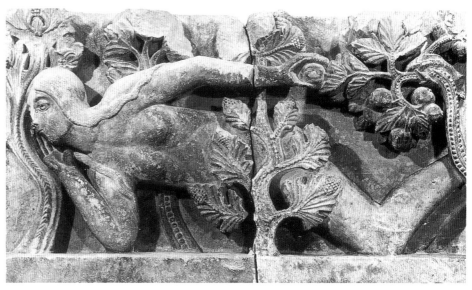

The legacy of sculpture 148-149

Italy and the Roman tradition 150-151

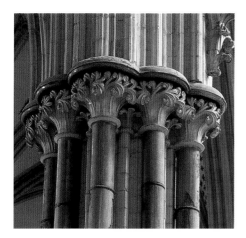

5. Foliage capitals in Lincoln Cathedral, England; early 13th century.

7. Right: portal of Sta Maria la Mayor, Toro, Spain; late 13th century. In the tympanum, the Coronation of the Virgin.

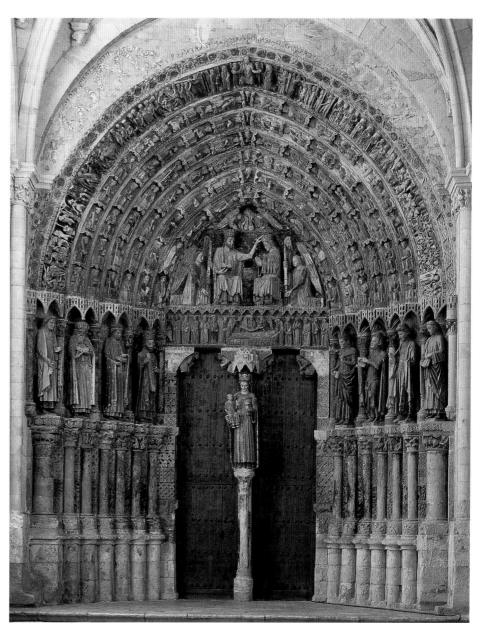

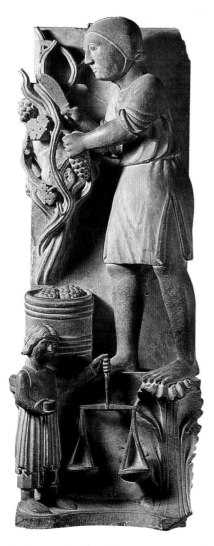

6. The grape harvest, illustrating the month of September; sculpture by Benedetto Antelami, in the Baptistery at Parma, late 12th century.

Sculpture reborn

Between the end of the Roman Empire and the early 11th century there was virtually no figure sculpture in Europe. The art had to be re-invented. It began tentatively in the form of small low reliefs, developing slowly into life-size sculpture in the round (6). In Southern France this came to be concentrated round the main portals of churches, the tympanum above the door being filled with elaborate relief scenes and the door itself flanked by standing saints. It was an age of bold experiment, with dynamic figures in violent motion (2) or dramatically sensuous poses (4). At Moissac (3) St Peter and St Paul face each other across a central pillar of interlaced beasts. The strange cusps show Islamic influence. In the 12th century this scheme was developed in Northern France and from there made its way to the rest of Europe, the standing saints now less agitated and a graceful Virgin and Child against the central post, or *trumeau*. The west portal of Toro, in Spain (7), conforms to the Northern French arrangement with rows of 'column-figures' on each side, still with many traces of original colour. Decorative carving on capitals followed the same evolution, the often bizarre hybrid animal forms (1) giving way to a refined and graceful naturalism (5).

2. Doubting Thomas, S. Domingo de Silos, Spain; early 12th century.

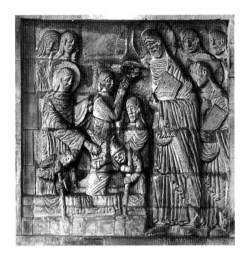

1. The raising of Lazarus, Chichester Cathedral; c. 1140.

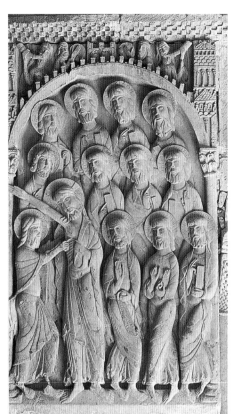

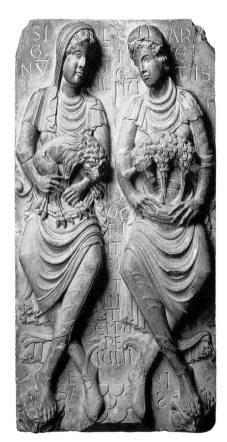

3. Ekkehard and Uta, Naumburg Cathedral, Germany; c. 1250.

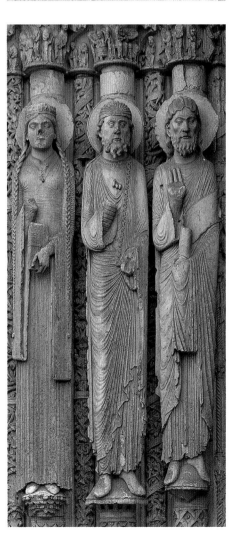

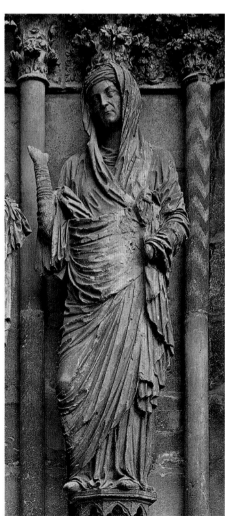

4. Relief of two women from the church of St Sernin, Toulouse, c. 1115–20.

5. The Queen of Sheba and Solomon, Chartres Cathedral; c. 1145–55.

6. St Elizabeth, Rheims Cathedral; 1260–74.

Sculpture reborn 146-147   Italy and the Roman tradition 150-151

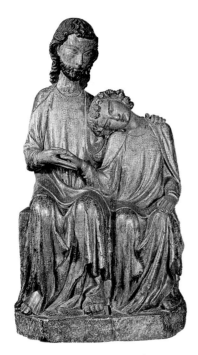

7. Christ and St John. Limewood; German, c. 1340.

9. Right: The Death of the Virgin, altarpiece of St Mary's, Cracow, Poland, by Viet Stoss; 1477–89.

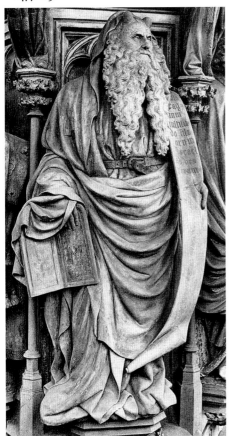

8. Moses, by Claus Sluter, Dijon; 1296–1405.

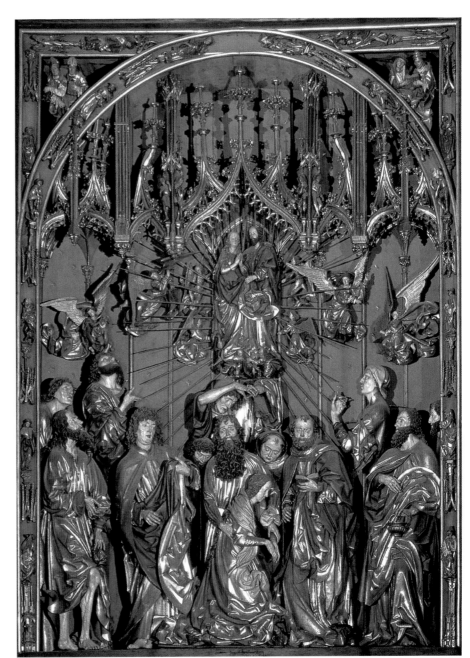

From the technically primitive but emotionally powerful works of early Romanesque to the totally assured achievements of late Gothic, medieval sculpture is an aesthetic world of its own. The early style excelled at story-telling: the raising of the already shrouded Lazarus (1), or the physical obsessiveness of Doubting Thomas (2). Later sculpture, by contrast, increasingly made its central theme the heroic human body, not nude as in classical art, but clothed. This entailed a concentration on drapery, something that can be followed very clearly in France, beginning with the abstract incised lines of Toulouse (4) and the shallow parallel grooves of Chartres (5) to the rich, majestic folds of Rheims (6) and finally to the broad, baggy textures of Claus Sluter at Dijon (8). German (3, 7) sculptors learnt much from France, never losing sight of either the naturalistic or the ideal. Finally, the very latest German sculpture in wood (9) united extreme technical virtuosity with intense feeling.

The legacy of sculpture

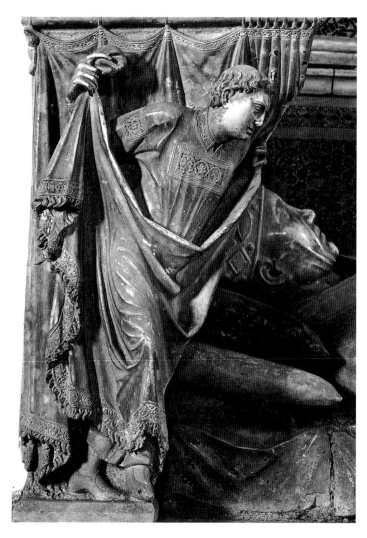

1. Detail of an angel from Arnolfo di Cambio's tomb of Cardinal de Braye in S. Domenico, Orvieto; after 1282.

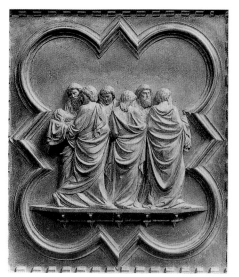

2. Andrea Pisano: panel from the bronze doors of the Baptistery, Florence (originally east door, now south). John the Baptist's disciples carry his body to burial; 1336.

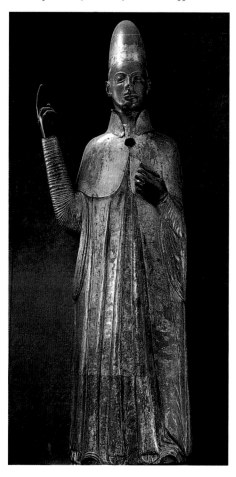

Italy and the Roman tradition

Italian sculptors remained closer to the classical style than did those of northern Europe – so close, indeed, that their works can easily be interpreted as forward- rather than backward-looking, as the dawn of the Renaissance rather than the sunset of the Antique world. At their best, they can magically combine the attributes of both. The early bronze doors of Florence Baptistery by Andrea Pisano feature toga-clad figures within archetypically Gothic quatrefoils (2). Much depended on patronage. When the Consiglio del Popolo of Bologna commissioned an over-life-size statue of Pope Boniface VIII in 1300, there was no classical precedent and the result is unmistakably medieval (3). Yet a decade or so earlier Nicola Pisano (no relative of Andrea), his son Giovanni and his assistant Arnolfo di Cambio were taking up Roman motifs (Pisa was rich in antique sarcophagi of the highest quality) and endowing them with Gothic energy. Arnolfo created a new type of tomb monument in which angels draw aside curtains to reveal the dead man (1). Giovanni Pisano was the most versatile of all. His pulpit in Pisa Cathedral (4) clearly belongs to his father's Roman manner, yet is so Gothic in feeling that historians have had to postulate an unrecorded visit to France.

3. Manno Bandini da Siena: statue of Pope Boniface VIII; 1300.

4. Giovanni Pisano: pulpit in Pisa Cathedral; 1310. The four large figures in the centre are the Theological Virtues. The two curved panels facing us show the Adoration of the Magi and the Presentation in the Temple.

Classical revivals 36-37   Classicism reborn 262-263

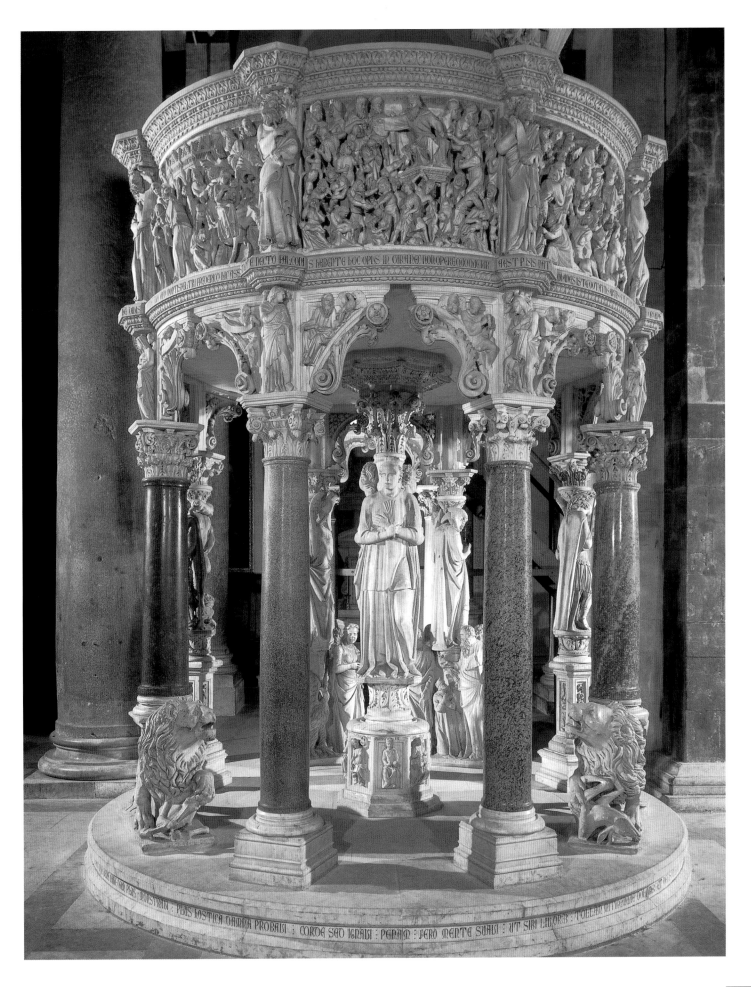

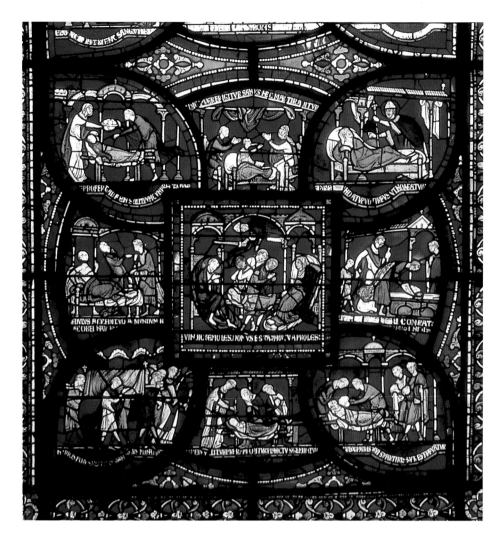

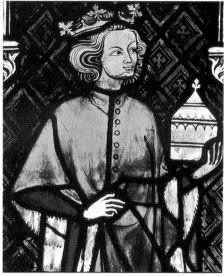

2. One of the three Magi, from a window at Königsfelden, Germany; 1325–30.

1. Left: detail of window in Trinity Chapel, Canterbury Cathedral; 13th century.

Painting in light

Colour and light, for which the art of stained glass is the perfect expression, were attributes of divinity. The subject was expounded in medieval mystical texts, and that these texts were known to architects and patrons is clear from Abbot Suger's account of the building of Saint-Denis. The emotional impact of a great church complete with all its original glass is something that can be experienced today in only a few places. One of these is León (4), where the whole 13th–14th-century ensemble survives – a glowing, magical, calculatedly spiritual effect. Looked at in detail, the message was reinforced, with large authoritarian figures of saints and prophets in the high windows and small narrative scenes in the lower. The nine panels of the Canterbury window shown here (1) tell the story of one of St Thomas Becket's miracles. It starts at the bottom, left to right, then goes to the upper row, and finally to the row between them. Plague has come to the house of Sir Jordan Fitzeisulf. A nurse has died and is buried; the 10-year-old son dies; pilgrims arrive and Sir Jordan pours water from Becket's tomb into the boy's mouth. He puts coins in the boy's hands, to be paid as a votive offering; the child is restored and sits up; St Thomas appears to a leper, telling him to warn Sir Jordan not to forget his vow. The leper delivers the message to Sir Jordan and his wife; Sir Jordan fails to give the money and a second son dies; he then performs his vow and pours gold and silver on Becket's tomb.

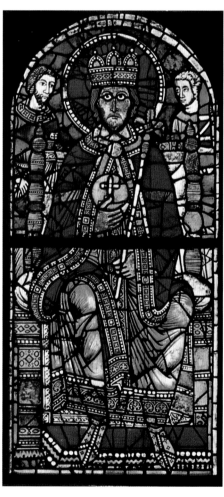

3. Charlemagne, in Strasbourg Cathedral; c. 1200.

Artist-craftsmen 154-155   The Labours of the Months 182-183

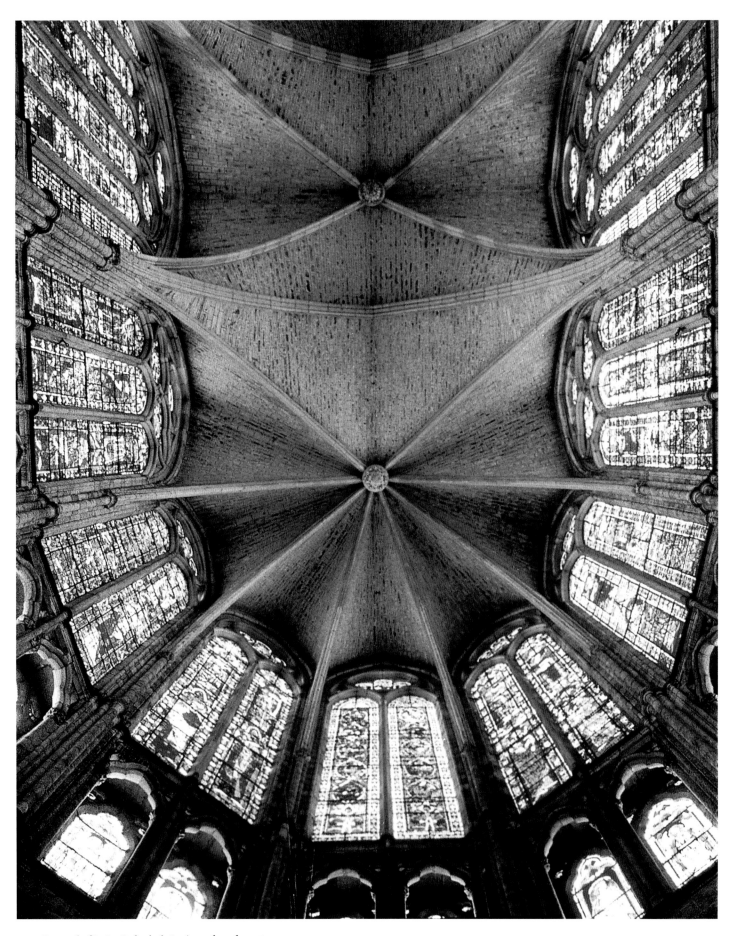

4. East end of León Cathedral, Spain; 13th-14th century.

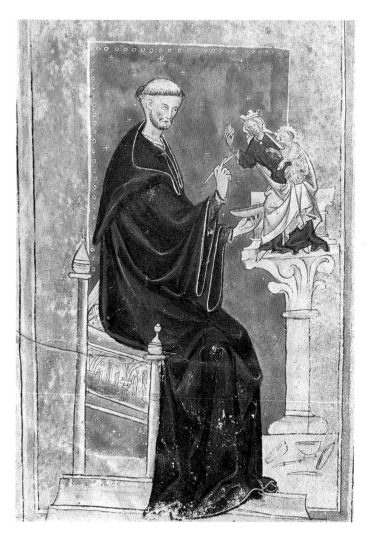

1. Benedictine monk colouring an image of the Virgin; English, *c.* 1260.

Artist-craftsmen

In the Middle Ages no distinction was made between artists and craftsmen. Painters (1, 2, 3, 4, 6), sculptors (5, 7), stained-glass artists, jewellers, metal-workers and goldsmiths were all men, or occasionally women (3), with particular skills who executed work commissioned from them, usually specified in considerable detail. All art had a use and a purpose, either religious (altarpieces, devotional images or scenes from sacred history) or secular (the commemoration of great families or the decoration of interiors and objects). The idea of the artist as a specially gifted genius whose main function was to express his own vision of the world would have been quite incomprehensible. Artists were nevertheless highly esteemed; many are known by name, and some proudly signed their works (4), hoping to be remembered by posterity. The fact that they were working in precious materials no doubt added to their prestige. In the early Middle Ages artists were likely to be monks (1), but by the 14th century they were lay professionals organized into guilds. Some were affiliated to royal courts and enjoyed an aristocratic lifestyle.

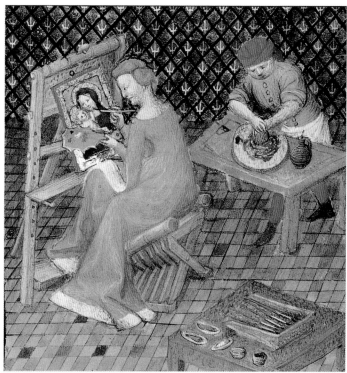

3. A female artist paints the Virgin and Child while a (male) assistant mixes her paints; Italian, 1402.

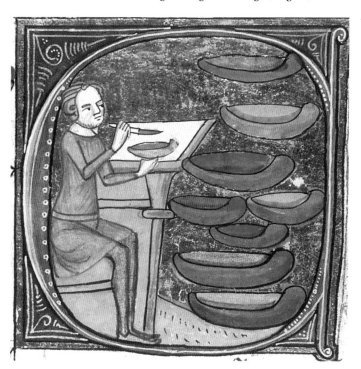

2. A painter or his assistant with dishes of colour; from an English encyclopedic work, *c.* 1350.

Architects and builders 140-141

The craftsman's skill 174-175

6. A 15th-century illustration of one of Cicero's works showing the Greek painter Zeuxis, who was said to have taken the best features of several women to create the ideal beauty.

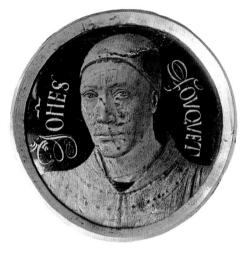

4. Jean Fouquet, one of the most outstanding painters of 15th-century France; a self-portrait of 1452.

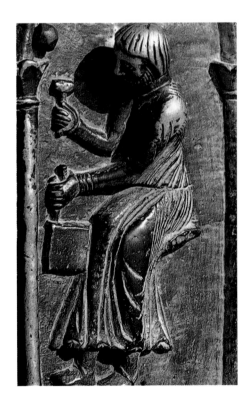

5. Sculptor, detail from the bronze doors of San Zeno, Verona; 11th century.

7. Sculptor at work on tomb, part of a miniature by Jean Colombe illustrating the history of Troy; after 1490.

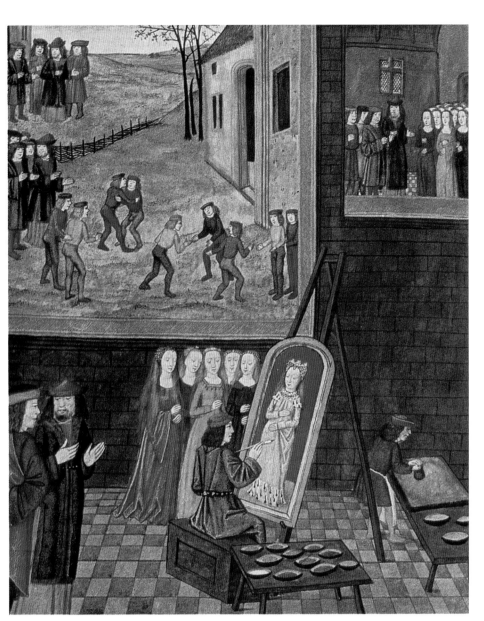

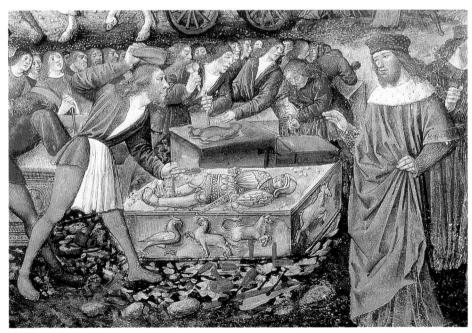

Marginal art

After the profound and moving works of religious art that characterize the Middle Ages, it comes as a puzzling surprise to encounter the vast amount of bizarre, grotesque and often apparently subversive imagery that leaps out at us from the margins of devotional manuscripts, the capitals of churches and cloisters and the undersides of choir-stalls. Bernard of Clairvaux's condemnation is well known: 'To what purpose are those unclean apes, those fierce lions, those monstrous creatures, those half-men…? Many bodies are there seen under one head, or again many heads to a single body. Here is a four-footed beast with a serpent's tail; there, a fish with a beast's head…. For God's sake, if men are not ashamed of these follies, why at least do they not shrink from the expense?' St Bernard's questions are still unanswered, in spite of much scholarly effort. Are these images simply light-hearted *jeux d'esprit* that mean nothing? An escape from too rigid constraints? Expressions of the unconscious? Evidence of scepticism? Or on the contrary, proof that religious belief was so strong that it could laugh at itself?

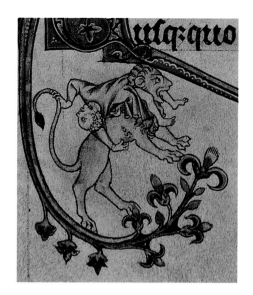

1. Lion carrying off a man, from an English Psalter; *c.* 1280.

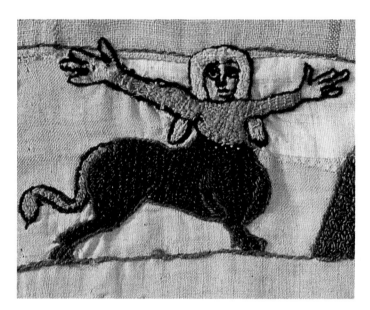

2. Centaur from the border of the Bayeux Tapestry, late 11th century.

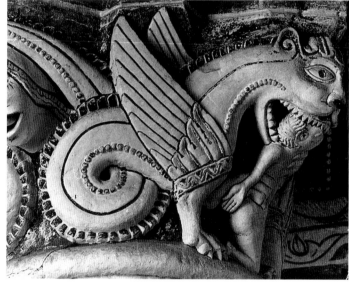

3. Dragon eating a man, a 12th-century capital from the church of St Pierre, Chauvigny, France.

4. Marginal painting from a French missal of 1323 showing monkeys, one of them displaying his backside to a scribe. This may have been suggested by a word-division some lines above, where *culpa* (sin) has been broken at *cul-* (meaning bum).

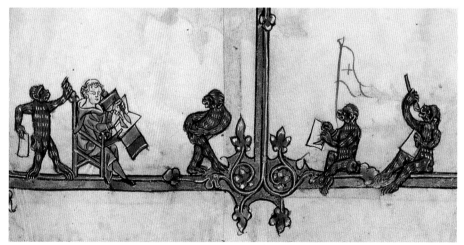

The Bestiaries 220-221   Beyond the known world 256-257

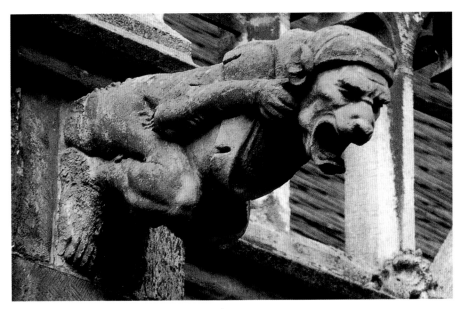

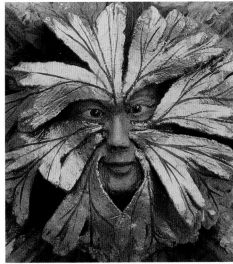

6. Foliate head ('Green Man'), vault boss in the east cloister of Norwich Cathedral; 14th century.

5. Gargoyle in the form of a dog-faced man, Utrecht Cathedral, Holland.

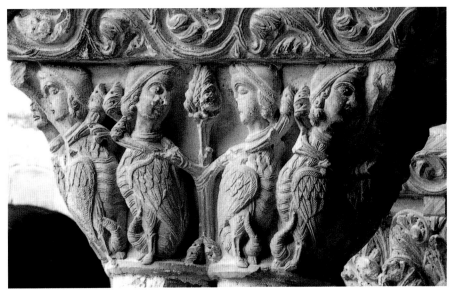

7. Harpies – birds with women's heads – from the cloister of S. Domingo de Silos, Spain; 12th century.

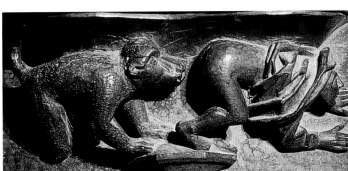

8. Man with exposed backside followed by a bear, misericord from the Cathedral of Zamora, Spain; 12th century.

9, 10. A hybrid monster, dragon on wheels and two-headed *gryllus*, apparently on stilts, from the Luttrell Psalter; English, 1335–40.

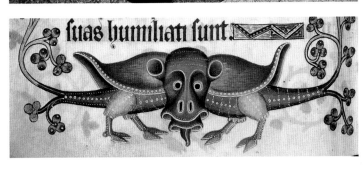

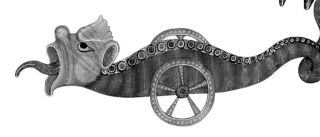

5

Everyday Life

BECAUSE contraception was extremely rudimentary in the medieval period, women tended to have many children; because medicine and sanitation were equally rudimentary, these children were unhealthy and short-lived. This regime of high fertility and high mortality produced families of moderate size, typically consisting of a married couple with two or three children. This was not the result of planning but of savage attrition: half of all children died before they were seven. The medieval world was full of children – almost half the population was younger than fourteen – but it was only the lucky ones who reached adulthood. Life expectancy at birth was around 30 years in the more fortunate periods and places of medieval Europe, a mere 20 in the ill-starred ones.

The demographic history of the Middle Ages is cut by a great fault-line in the mid-fourteenth century. Up until that time, despite the high levels of mortality, population had been growing slowly but continuously. Woodland was cleared and marshes were drained to establish new farms, while towns grew in size and number. Then, however, the Black Death – a pandemic of bubonic plague and associated diseases that hit Europe in the years 1347 to 1350 – killed between a third and a half of the population. The plague returned regularly in subsequent decades, becoming a feature of European life, albeit on a gradually decreasing scale, until the end of the seventeenth century. The insanitary and crowded towns, the death-traps of the Middle Ages, were particularly hard hit. As a result, the population of Europe in 1500 was substantially smaller than that of 1300 and individual life expectancy had contracted.

Women tended to marry earlier than men. In late medieval Tuscany women married at around 19, men almost ten years later, although this age gap may be unusually great. The poet Dante, born in Florence in 1265, married by the time he was 20, and this may be more typical. Because of the high mortality marriages were often broken by death and remarriage was common. Hence the relationship between step-parents and step-children, and between half-siblings, was a normal feature of medieval family life (and therefore of fairy tales).

Women who survived childbirth and outlived their husband or husbands might find themselves in the potentially most independent position a woman could expect – that of the widow with property. Pressure to remarry was great (English aristocratic widows often paid the king large sums to be allowed to remain unmarried) but, if they resisted it, widows of all social classes had an autonomy that was usually denied to women. The ideals of courtly love elaborated by the poets of the twelfth century elevated 'the lady', whom the troubadours often addressed as 'my lord' (*midonz*), but the reality was that female family members were almost always subject to the authority of male family members.

Despite the growth in the size and number of towns in the medieval period, the majority of the population continued to live in the countryside. Even in highly urbanized areas, like in later medieval Italy, the proportion of town-dwellers never exceeded 25 per cent, while in the rest of Europe 10 per cent was more common. Most people were rural smallholders, living on and working the land. Their fortunes were determined by two things, how much land they had and how free they were. Some were without land of their own or had only a cottage garden and these constituted a rural proletariat, working for others.

The fantastic clock on the Old Town Hall of Prague was made about 1410 by Magister Hanus, the university astronomer. Its mechanism was renewed in the 16th century, and its face has been much restored in later times. The big outer ring, with Arabic numbers, relates to the Bohemian 24-hour day (which began at sunset), and the face with Roman numerals to the motions of the stars and planets. The smaller ring shows the position of the sun and moon in the Zodiac. At the top, at each hour, the mechanical figures of the Apostles, Death and allegorical Virtues process out of one opening and into another.

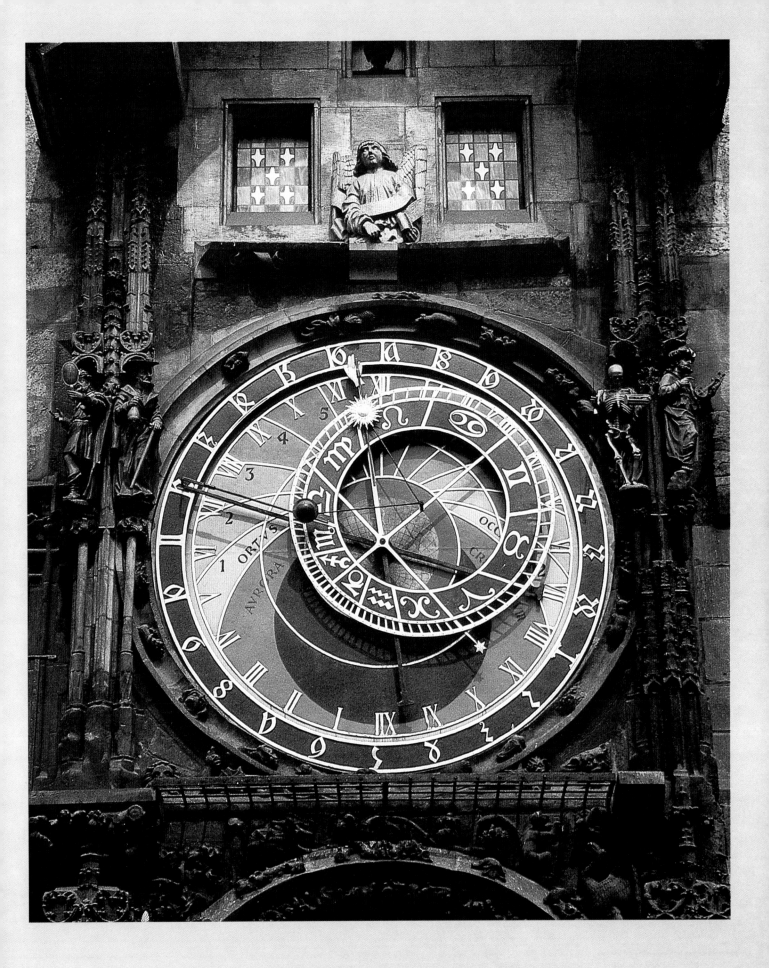

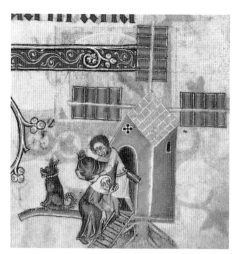

The windmill was among the most useful inventions of medieval technology. But for the peasants its advantages were somewhat diminished by their being obliged to take their corn to the landlord's mill and pay a commission. An English 14th-century illustration.

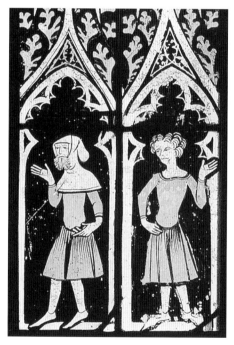

Two of the rare representations of peasants in medieval stained glass, from Ely Cathedral, c. 1340–49.

Rich peasants, by contrast, would need to employ labour and could go beyond self-sufficiency to profit from the market. Degrees of freedom were also crucial. Most peasants had a lord, but this could mean simply a landlord, to whom rent was due, or it could signify a seigneur with extensive rights over his serfs. At its most burdensome, serfdom meant that unfree peasants could not leave their village, had to work half the week on their lord's farm, provide him with produce and cash, seek his consent for marriage and receive justice at the court he or his ministers operated. It is not surprising that in times of economic or political crisis, large-scale peasant rebellions broke out, such as the French Jacquerie of 1358, the English rising of 1381 or the so-called remensas wars in Catalonia in the 1460s and 1470s.

The rural population faced an annual round of heavy labour, whether in the clay fields of the English Midlands, producing barley for bread and beer, or in the olive groves and vineyards of Tuscany. Diet and climate varied from region to region but the endless toil required to produce food did not. Mechanization of agricultural tasks was very limited, the only large machine being the mill, which harnessed the power of water and wind to grind grain. Watermills had existed in Europe since Roman times, but windmills were an important technological invention of the medieval period, first appearing in the twelfth century in England and France and quickly spreading. Most tasks, however – ploughing, sowing, weeding, harvesting and threshing – relied on the muscle-power either of humans alone or of humans and oxen, gradually supplemented over time by draught horses. In the Middle Ages all communities were frighteningly vulnerable to the natural environment and a bad harvest meant hunger and death, while a series of them, as in the Great Famine of 1315–17, could decimate the population.

Medieval towns were small by modern standards. Even the largest, such as Venice, Florence, Milan and Paris, did not exceed 100,000 in population, while most had only a few thousand inhabitants. This did not mean that these small towns were simply villages with pretensions, for they usually enjoyed a separate legal status and they fulfilled special functions. They were the centre of manufacture and exchange. Although many villages would have a smith (making the surname Smith/Schmidt/Fevre, etc. one of the most common across Europe), a variety of artisans at work, producing such necessities as shoes, clothing, furniture, pottery and leather goods, would be found only in urban settings. The professionals – lawyers, doctors, schoolteachers – were town-dwellers, and financiers and merchants were also based in cities and towns. Although many villages did have markets, the weekly market was an essential feature of the town and every town had a hinterland for which it served as a central place with trading and other functions. Both merchants and craftsmen were organized in guilds, associations with a variety of purposes, both economic and non-economic. Guildsmen drank together, prayed together and provided a proper funeral for dead members. They also made rules about who could practise a trade and what the standards and regulations governing it should be.

Traffic and transport that grew increasingly intense tied the urban network together. Much of this was water-borne, because water travel was far cheaper than land travel, and the Italian merchants in the Mediterranean and the Hanseatic traders of the north created maritime trade routes that ran from Egypt and the Black Sea to Britain and Russia. In 1277–78 the Genoese sailed directly to northern Europe for the first time and from 1325 the Venetians sent annual

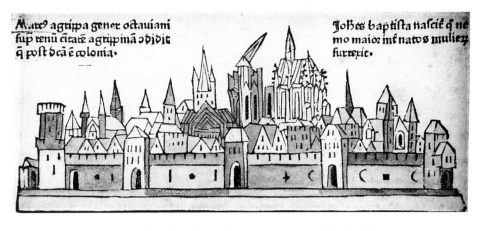

Cologne as it looked throughout the Middle Ages. The high choir of the unfinished cathedral looms over the city. To its left is the base of the south-west tower on which stands a wooden crane.

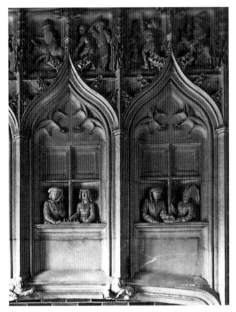

Jacques Coeur was a successful French merchant and financier with interests in textiles, paper-making and mining. In 1451 his enormous wealth roused the jealousy of Charles VII and he was stripped of his possessions. His luxurious house at Bourges survives, full of amusing conceits like these fictive onlookers peering from windows over a fireplace.

convoys to Flanders and England. Land travel was more limited, but even so long-distance routes did exist, both for merchants and for other travellers, like the pilgrims who followed the road of Santiago or the litigants and diplomats making their laborious way to Rome and back. Improved communications, especially through the provision of bridges and accommodation for travellers, made these journeys slightly less arduous over the course of the medieval centuries, but the rate of travel was slow.

The human environment of the Middle Ages would strike the modern observer as quieter and smellier than that of the present day, constructed with more irregular forms and more natural materials. The wood and thatch of most dwellings, or the stone buildings in the regions where it was found, would blend with the surroundings and age organically, creating villages and towns that looked as if they had grown from the earth rather than been imposed on it. The absence of much mechanical noise would be countered by the sounds of humans and animals, while the lack of any effective waste-disposal system would immediately announce itself to the nose. Privacy in the small houses of the period, which peasant families often shared with their cattle, was hard to obtain.

Death was an everyday part of life. In a largish village of a hundred households or so a funeral would take place on average every 18 days. Christians did not take anything with them to the afterlife, not even their clothes, although the bishop was allowed his robes and the priest his chalice. The dead were laid in the ground in shrouds or coffins, their resting-places (unlike those of the ancient world or of Islamic society) intermingled with the dwellings of the living. It was important that the naked dead in the churchyards be given the chance of a smooth journey and this was the purpose of the hundreds of masses said and sung for the dead, easing their way through Purgatory. The rich could afford memorials, although even these emphasized mortality and the decay of the flesh as much as the earthly status of the commemorated, but for the multitude of the poor there was only the bare earth and the charnel house. After their twenty or thirty years perhaps the main thing that death offered was 'the beginning of rest, the end of labors'.

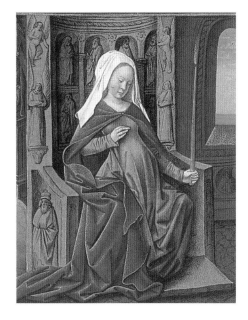

1. A pregnant woman lights a candle and prays for a safe delivery; French, 15th century.

2. Birth by caesarean section, a dangerous operation, rarely used. In this case the woman has died during labour; French, 15th century.

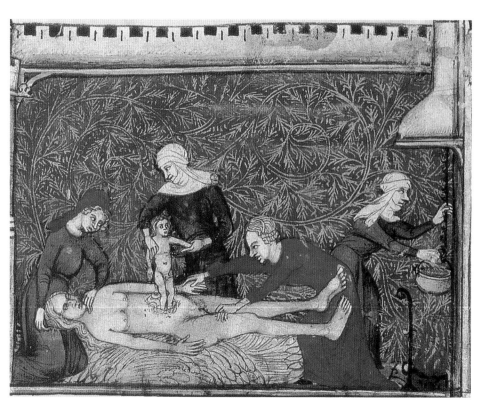

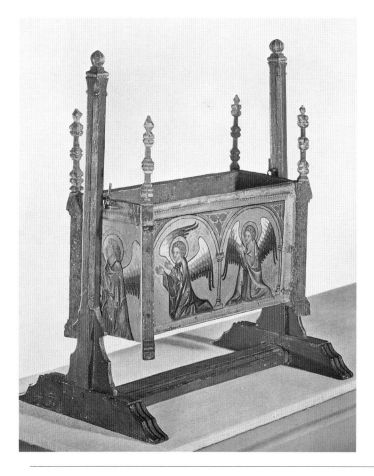

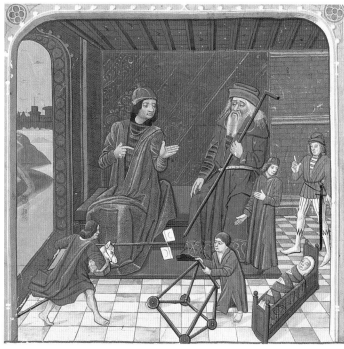

4. Three children of a rich family, one swaddled in a cradle, one learning to walk with a frame on wheels and the third galloping on a hobby-horse; French, 15th century.

3. German cradle, decorated with angels worshipping the newborn Jesus; 1320.

Women: weakness and strength 164-165

Sex and sexuality 166-167

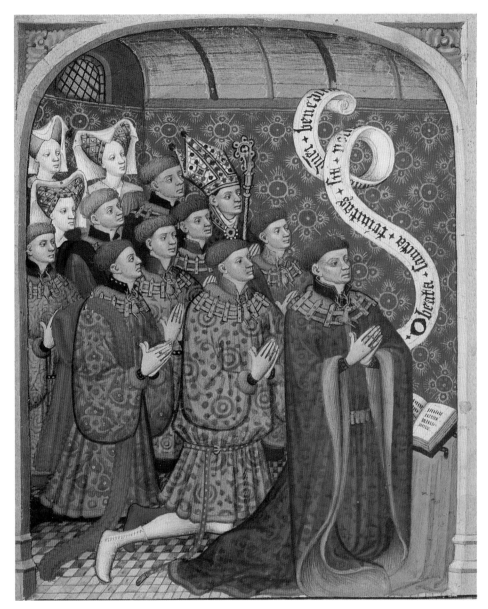

5. Ralph Nevill, Earl of Westmoreland, with the twelve children of his second marriage, one of whom is already a bishop; French, 15th century.

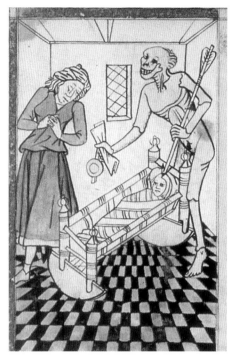

6. Death comes for the child; a French woodcut from a 15th-century Dance of Death series.

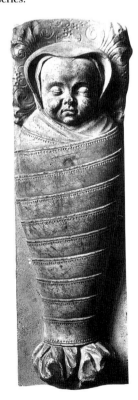

7. Funerary effigy of a swaddled infant; Italian, 15th century.

The world of childhood

Childhood was brief in the Middle Ages: by fifteen boys and girls were ready to take their place in the adult world. It was also hazardous. A family would expect to lose anything up to half their offspring before they grew up (**6, 7**). Parents must have been reconciled to this, but the idea that they loved their children less than parents do today is not supported by the evidence (**4**). For both rich and poor, large families were an economic advantage (**5**). Women spent half their lives pregnant (**1**) and facing the considerable risks of childbirth (**2**).

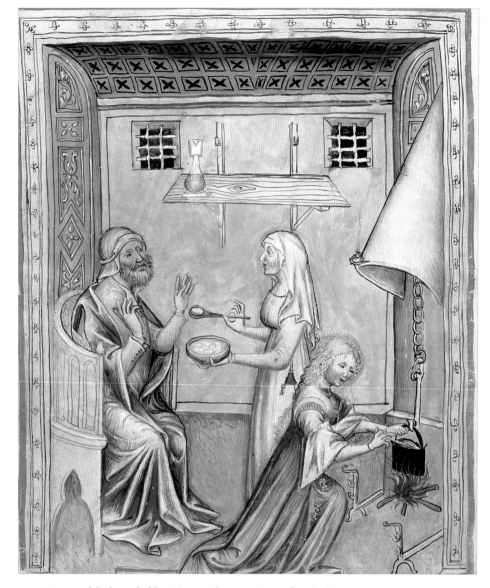

1. Women of the household minister to the master's comfort; Italian, 1390–1400.

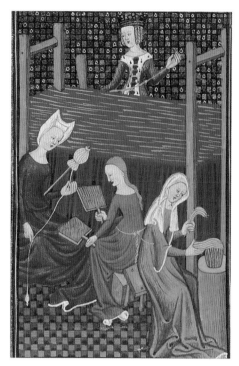

2. Women winding wool, spinning and weaving; Italian, early 15th century.

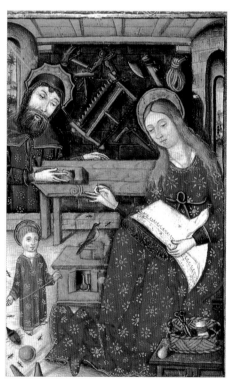

4. The husband at his carpenter's bench, the wife working at embroidery, the child playing on the floor: a normal (Holy) family at home; Spanish, late 15th century.

3. Poor Clares – female equivalents of the Franciscans – in choir; French, c. 1430.

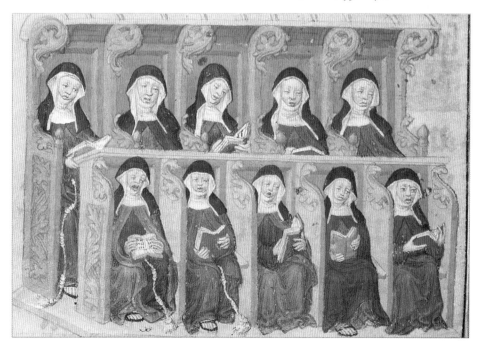

The world of childhood 162-163

Courtly love: sex and sublimation 224-225

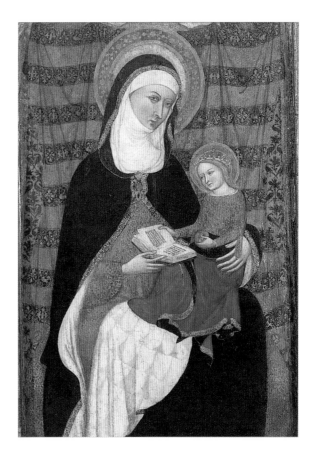

5. The Virgin with St Anne; Portuguese, 1353.
St Anne is often shown teaching her daughter to
read, which must reflect contemporary practice.

Women: weakness and strength

Most medieval women existed only as the mothers, wives and
daughters of men, with few legal rights or opportunities of their
own. Their status was determined by male attitudes, and these
were strangely inconsistent. Women were at the same time the
source of sin (Eve) and the embodiment of purity (the Virgin
Mary). In the home, they were often little better than serfs, yet
in the conventions of courtly love were semi-divine beings to be
revered. Amid all this male stereotyping it is hard to make
contact with women as they really were. Those whom we know
best are exceptions rather than the rule – women who escaped
the drudgery of marriage (1), motherhood (5) and manual
labour (2, 7) to make an impact in their own right. As members
of religious communities (3, 6) or occasionally as widows with
independent means, like Chaucer's Wife of Bath, they could
enjoy power and exercise their creative talents. And a limited
number were able to enter the professions, practise trade and
manage businesses.

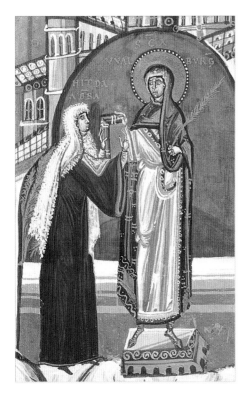

6. The Abbess Hilda offers her Gospel Book
(of which this is one miniature) to her
patron, St Walburga; German, c. 1020.

7. Women in the fields, milking cows and
collecting eggs: wall-painting from Castel del
Buonconsiglio, Trento; Italian, 15th century.

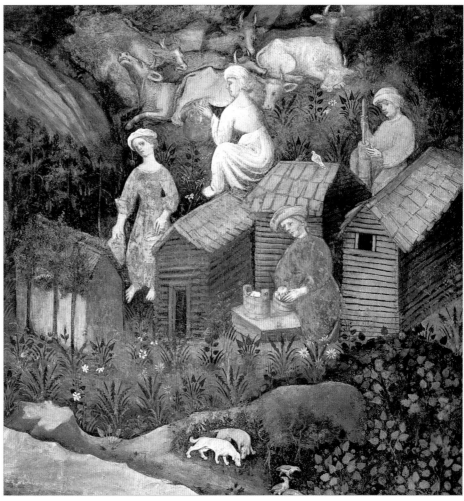

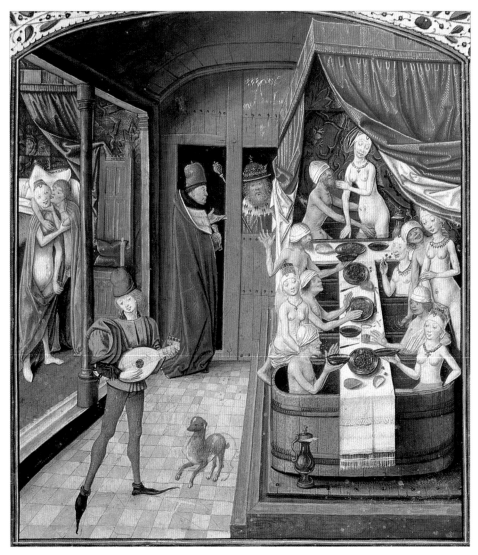

1. Sexual licence in a public bath; German, *c.* 1470.

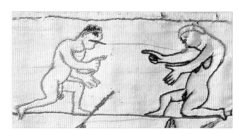

2. An unexplained erotic scene on the border of the Bayeux Tapestry; English or Norman, late 11th century.

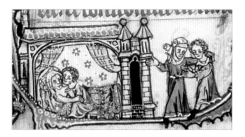

3. Young man entering a brothel; marginal illustration from a Flemish Book of Hours, *c.* 1320–30.

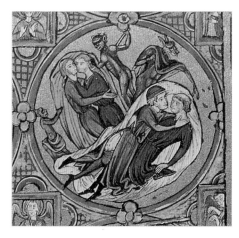

4. Forbidden love: male and female homosexuality encouraged by devils, from a *Bible Moralisée*; French, *c.* 1220.

7. Opposite: the bath-house, by a German artist of about 1480, proving that cleanliness was not always next to godliness.

Sex and sexuality

Happy sexual union – the proper ending for all love stories from the Renaissance onwards – plays curiously little part in medieval art and literature. In the conventions of courtly love, the lover placed his lady on a plane above mere physical passion (though this was not invariably the case, either in fiction or in life). To the Church, sexual desire was a sin (*luxuria*), tolerated, within marriage, only as a means of producing children (5). And to the popular mind sex seems to have been chiefly comic, an irrational urge that led men and women into laughable indignities (2, 3, 6). In the later Middle Ages realistic scenes in bath-houses, which often functioned as brothels (1, 7), provided opportunities for erotic invention, but they are more satirical than pornographic. It is rare to find any allusion to homosexuality (4).

The discipline of marriage 168-169

Courtly love: sex and sublimation 224-225

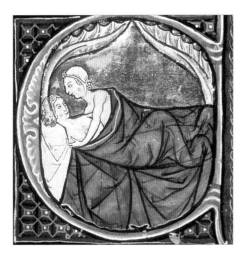

5. Sexual intercourse, portrayed in Aldobrandino of Siena's *Régime du Corps*, a book of advice on hygienic matters including the best time for conception; French, *c.* 1285.

6. Aristotle was said to have been subjugated by his shrewish wife Phyllis, a comic inversion of the right hierarchy of the sexes; a Netherlandish acquamanile, *c.* 1400.

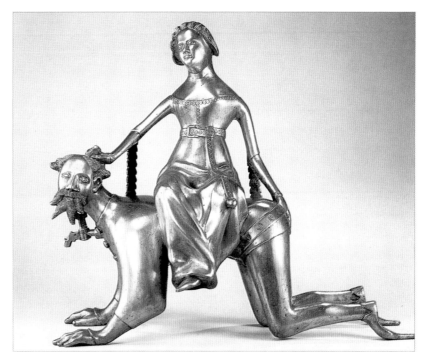

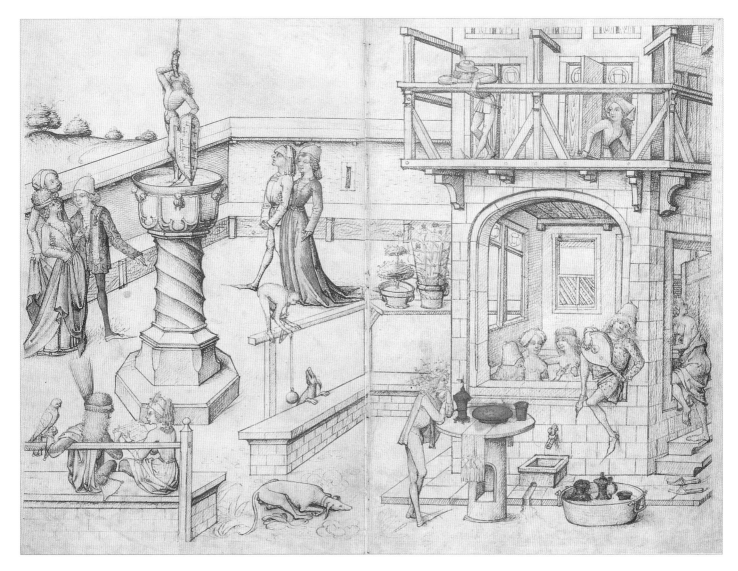

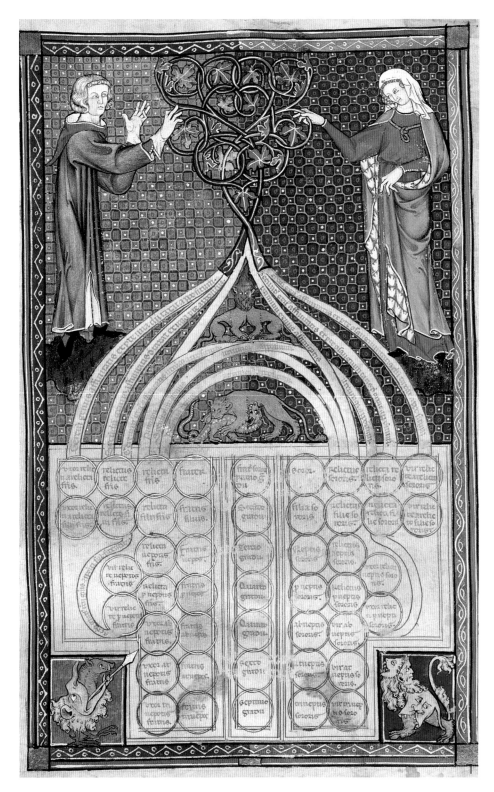

1. Table of consanguinity, showing the degrees of kinship between which marriage was forbidden. Besides the prohibitions which still exist, medieval canon law extended, until 1215, as far as sixth cousins, and relatives through marriage counted as blood-family. Infringement of these rules was theoretically incest (Henry VIII's divorce turned on such a technical point), though it is uncertain how far they were generally applied; German, *c.* 1300.

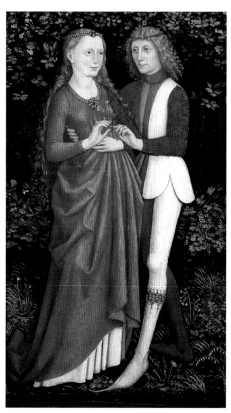

2. Bridal pair; German, *c.* 1470. The happy appearance of this scene is belied by the picture on its reverse side, which shows the lovers as rotting corpses. All is vanity.

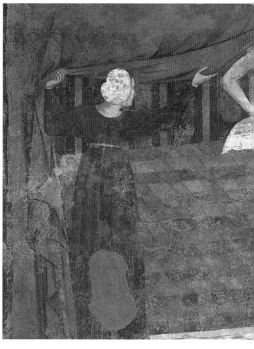

3. The wedding night; Italian, 14th century.

The seven sacraments
62-63

Sex and sexuality 166-167

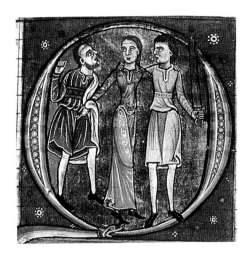

4. The legal complexities of marriage were analysed by Gratian in his digest of canon law, the *Decretum*; illuminated initial, French, 14th century. Is a lady whose betrothed has taken religious vows committing bigamy if she marries someone else?

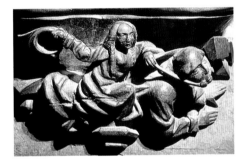

5. Marital failure – a shrewish wife beats her husband; misericord from Zamora, Spain, 15th century.

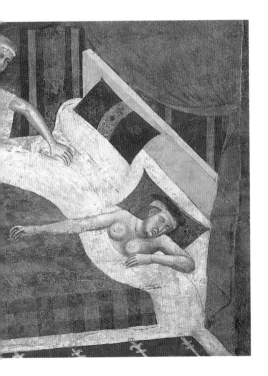

The discipline of marriage

Marriage was a contract and a sacrament. As a contract it regulated property and status. The higher the social scale, the more important this aspect became and among the ruling class dynastic marriage (6) was a key element of diplomacy. As a sacrament marriage took away the sin of lust, but was second-best to celibacy. Such, at least, was the theory. In practice, companionship, common purpose and mutual respect in marriage seems to have been as widespread as at any other time (2). That it was not a relationship of equality was accepted by both sexes as God's will (as in the marriage service it still is). Henpecked husbands were objects of contempt (5).

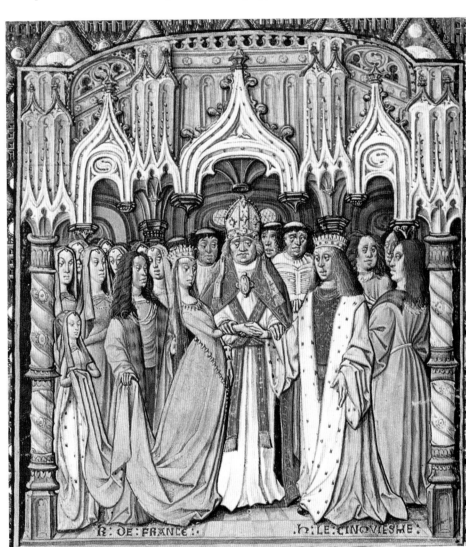

6. Dynastic marriage: Henry V of England marries Catherine, daughter of the King of France, thus consolidating his conquest of the kingdom; English, 15th century.

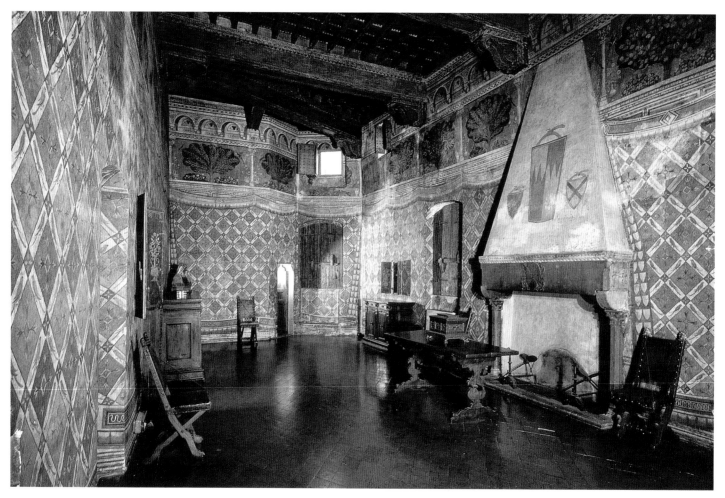

1. A 14th-century dining room in the Palazzo Davanzati, Florence, painted with imitation tapestry. It is called the Parrot Room after the parrots in the frames around the lozenges. Above this are panels showing trees. Characteristic of the time are the extremely small windows.

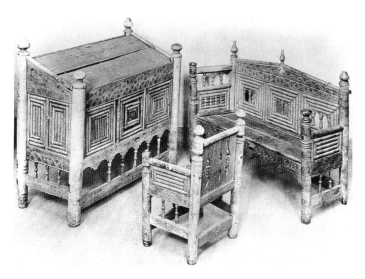

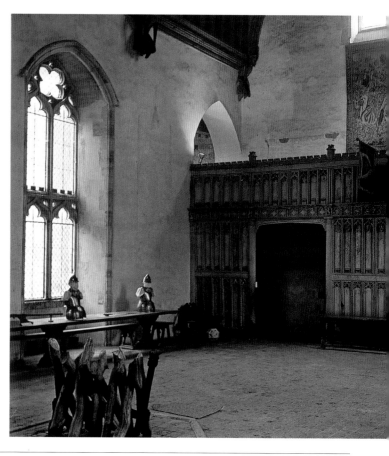

2. Desk, bench and chair in carved and turned wood, preserved in a church in Gotland, Sweden; *c.* 1200.

3. The great hall of Penshurst Place, England; *c.* 1340.

6. Far right: bedchamber in Burg Eltz, Germany; 14th century.

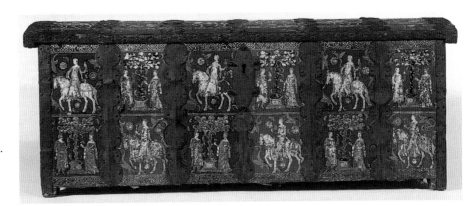

4. Italian chest decorated with painted figures modelled in gesso; Tuscan, *c.* 1350.

5. Spanish chair panelled and carved in walnut; 14th-15th century.

The family at home

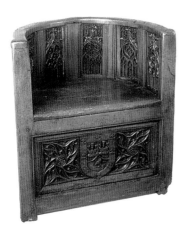

In the early Middle Ages furniture was sparse, and even by the end of the period most rooms would seem to us relatively empty. The rich were constantly on the move, so chairs, tables, buffets, and even beds were made so that they could be dismantled and transported. They could, nevertheless, be elaborately decorated (**4, 5**). Romanesque furniture (**2**) was mostly turned on a lathe; Gothic used painting and carving often derived from architecture. Fixtures such as fireplaces and wall-frescoes often remain, but it is almost unknown for a medieval room to survive intact with its furniture. Of those shown here, the 14th-century hall of Penshurst (**3**) is the least altered, retaining its original timber roof, tiled floor, dais and central hearth; the screen dates from 1552. Both the Palazzo Davanzati in Florence (**1**) and Burg Eltz in Germany (**6**) have suffered changes and been carefully restored in modern times. Palazzo Davanzati remained a private dwelling until 1956 and keeps its early wall decoration. Eltz, once the seat of the Archbishop-Electors of Trier, is one of Germany's most picturesque castles, perched on a crag above the Moselle, its interiors preserving many medieval features.

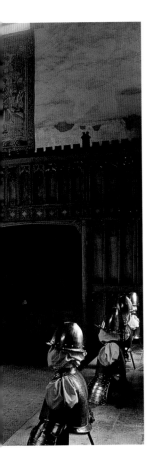

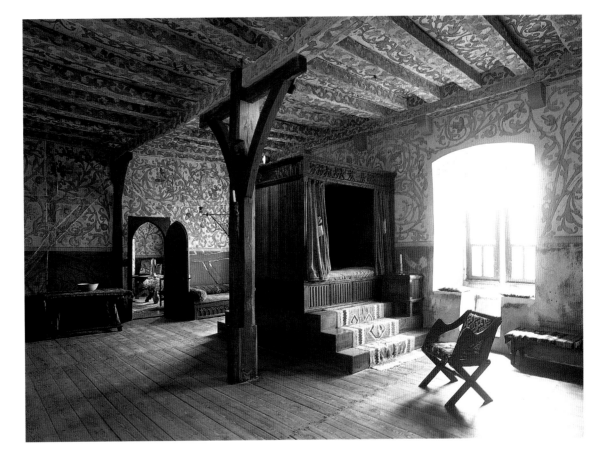

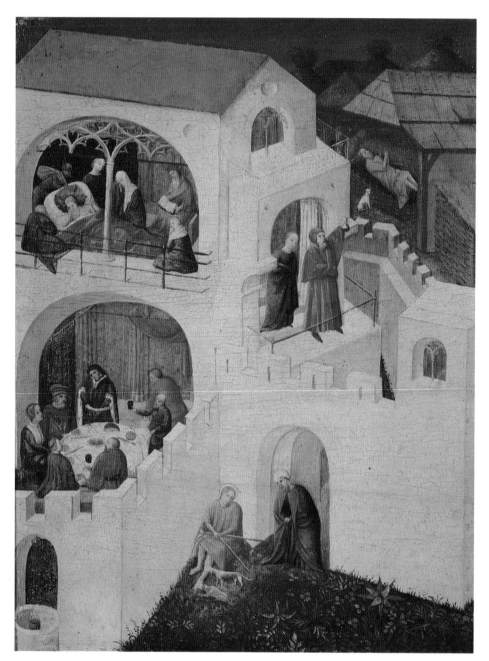

1. The parable of *Dives and Lazarus*; French painting on panel, *c.* 1420.

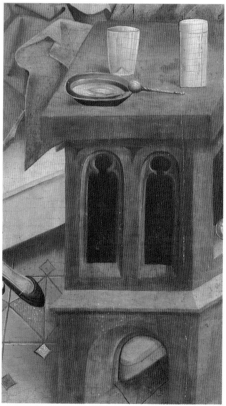

3. Detail from an Italian *Birth of the Virgin*. Note the panelled bed and matching bench alongside it; Sienese, *c.* 1340.

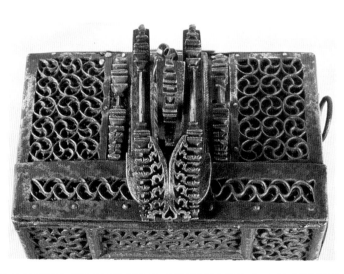

2. Ornamental box for keeping a prayer book; French, 15th century.

4. Detail from a German *Birth of the Virgin* showing a Gothic side-table with a glass, a wooden container, a pewter dish and spoon and slippers on the floor; *c.* 1494.

The feast 122-123   The family at home 170-171

Glimpses of domesticity

Better than any actual surviving room, the backgrounds of medieval paintings can often give us a vivid impression of domestic life in its setting. The pictures may be of biblical subjects but they are set in authentic contemporary surroundings with furnishings often meticulously represented (3, 4, 5, 6). One of the most intriguing is a panel of the story of *Dives and Lazarus* (1) where we see the whole house cut away like a diagram. Downstairs the rich Dives is feasting with his friends. Upstairs he is dying in bed, with a devil waiting to take away his soul. Outside, the poor man Lazarus sits at the door, the dogs licking his sores. Paintings of the *Birth of the Virgin* (3) commonly show the bed with its furnishings. In the *Annunciation* she is often seen at a table (5), while saints have their household objects around them (6).

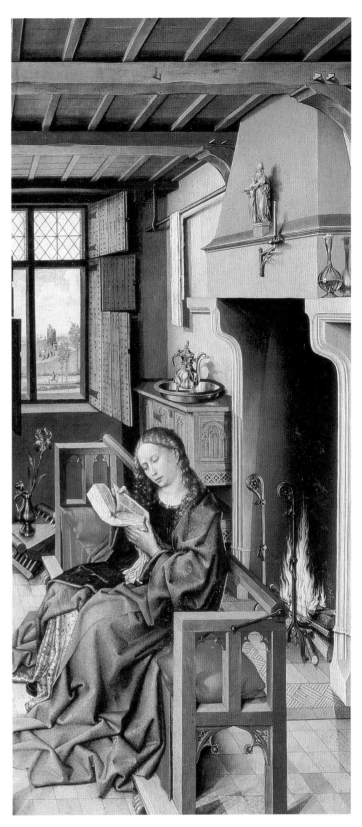

6. Robert Campin's *St Barbara* sits in a well-furnished room on a Gothic settle with an elaborate pitcher and dish on a sideboard at the back. Through the window we see the tower in which she will be imprisoned being built; Netherlandish, 1438.

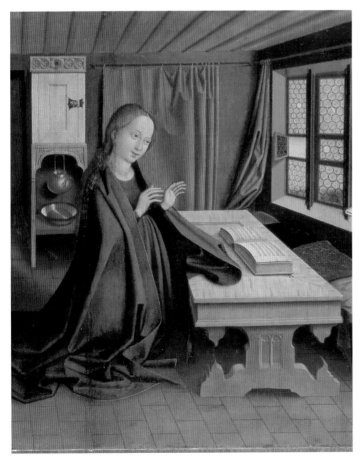

5. Detail from an *Annunciation*: a splendid Gothic table, a window with small round panes and pewter dishes in a cupboard behind; German, 1460–70.

The craftsman's skill

One of the ways in which medieval society changed over the centuries was the rise of a class of skilled artisans occupying a middle rank between the peasant farmer and the nobility. Increase in the size of towns led to increasing division of labour and increasing power for the craftsman. By the 15th century they were tightly organized into guilds with strict codes regulating entry and practice. In the great monarchies – England, France – they were forces with which governments had to reckon. In the free cities of Germany and Italy they were often virtually the government themselves.

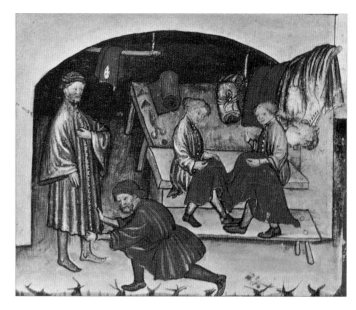

1. The tailor measures a customer while two assistants cut the woollen cloth; Italian, 14th century.

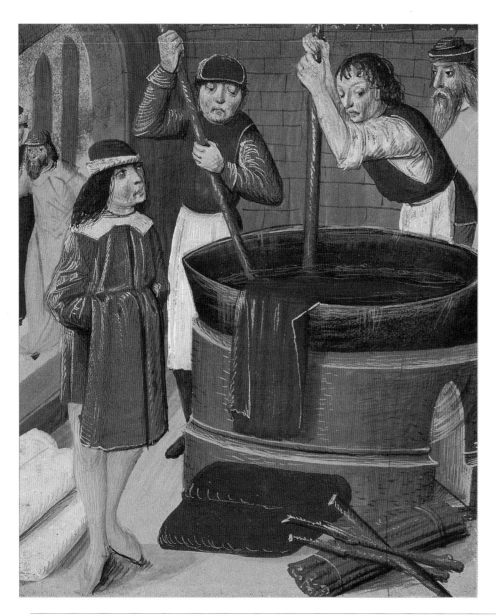

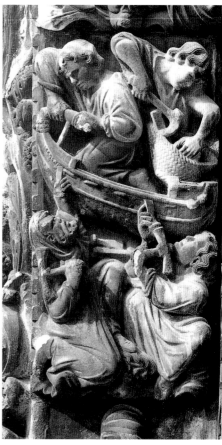

3. Shipbuilders: a relief on the façade of St Mark's, Venice, showing the use of a two-handed auger, adze, hammer and chisels; 13th century.

2. Dyeing in a large cauldron over a fire; Flemish, 1482.

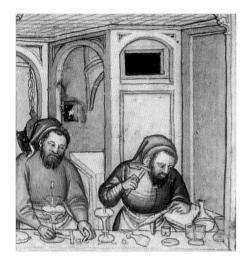

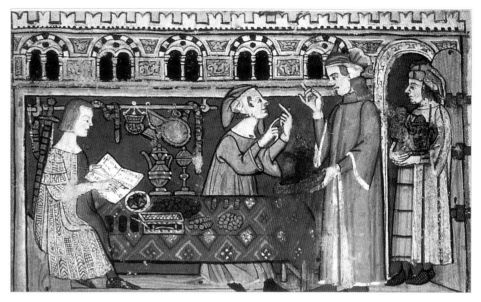

4, 5. Two scenes of 14th-century Italian goldsmiths at work. In one (above) they are making candlesticks, using a miniature anvil. In the other (right) an item is being sold, while an assistant makes a note of the price; there is a pile of cash on the table.

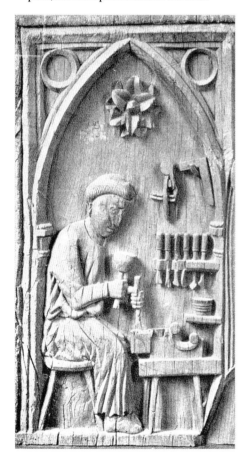

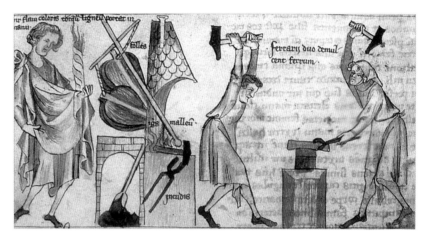

7. Blacksmiths: note their leather aprons, the furnace and bellows and the large pairs of tongs; Netherlandish, 14th century.

6. A carpenter using mallet and chisel, with other tools in a rack behind him; German, 1284.

8. Glass-blowing: the glass, having been heated in the furnace which a boy is stoking on the right, is then blown and spun. Behind the furnace the master inspects the finished pots; Bohemian, early 15th century.

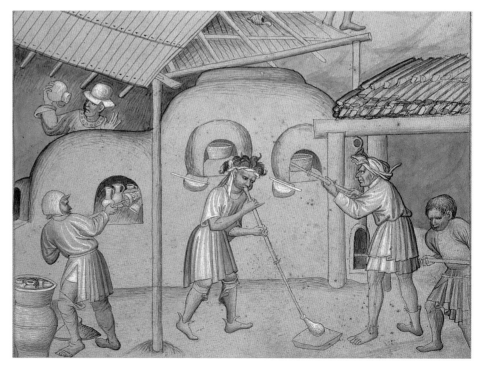

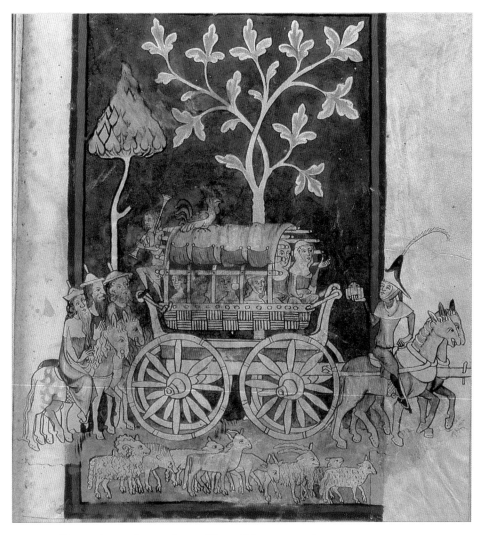

1. Travelling carriage, using an advanced form of slung suspension; German, 14th century.

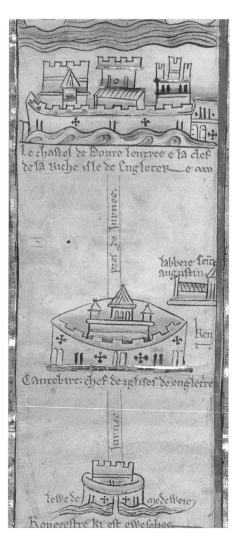

2. Part of Matthew Paris's Itinerary from London to Apulia; English, c. 1250.

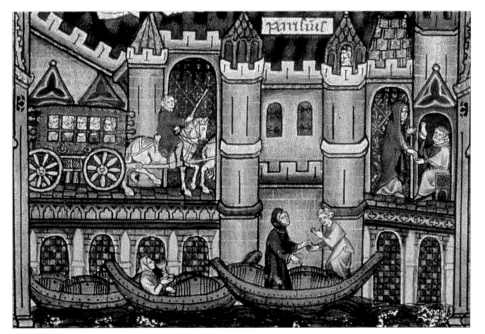

3. Covered waggon and wine-barges in Paris; French, 14th century.

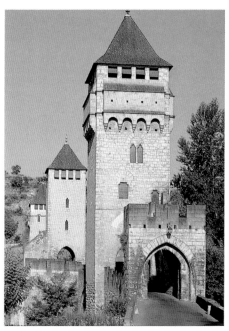

4. The 14th-century fortified bridge, the Pont Valentré, Cahors.

The pilgrimage 72-73   New worlds 268-269

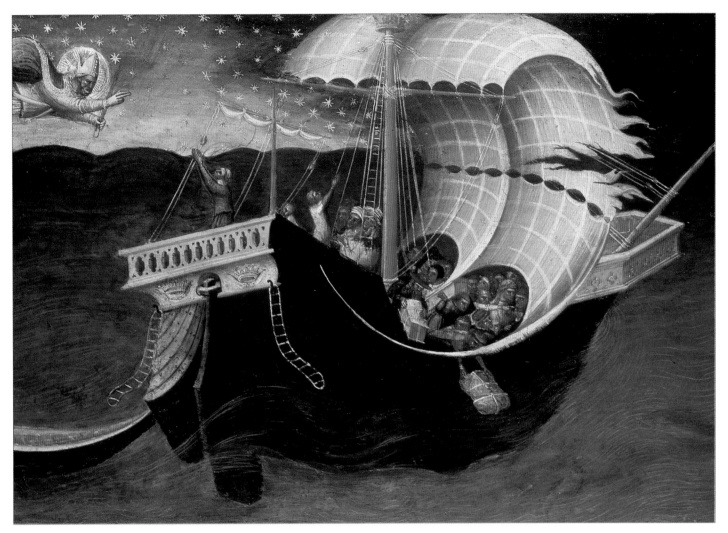

5. A sea-going ship of 1433 is portrayed in convincing detail in Bicci di Lorenzo's *St Nicholas Rebuking the Tempest*; Italian.

Travel by land and sea

The roads and rivers of medieval Europe were crowded with travellers: royal households on the move, government couriers on diplomatic missions, ecclesiastics going to Rome and back, pilgrims on journeys to Jerusalem or Compostela which could take months or even years. This in spite of the fact that maps were rudimentary, carriages uncomfortable (1, 3) and the dangers of robbery real. In the mid-13th century, Matthew Paris, a monk of St Albans, composed a pictorial itinerary to illustrate the route from London to Apulia (2). Towns are shown one day's journey apart. This detail, beginning at the bottom, takes us from Rochester via Canterbury to Dover. Sea voyages (5) were even more hazardous and were undertaken almost exclusively in the interests of trade.

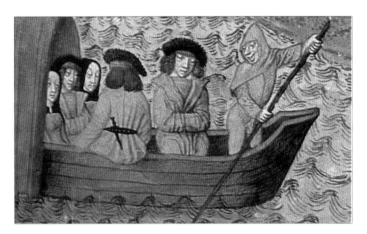

6. A party of pleasure, punting on a river; Flemish, 15th century.

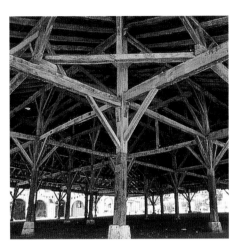

1. The covered hall of Beaumont-de-Lomagne (Tarn et Garonne), France, a typical structure for the weekly market.

2. Stalls in a covered market: shoes on the left, a cloth merchant with rolls of coloured cloth in the centre and dealers in gold plate and silverware on the right; French, 15th century.

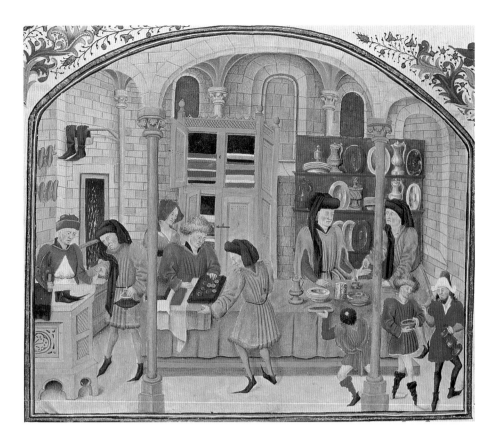

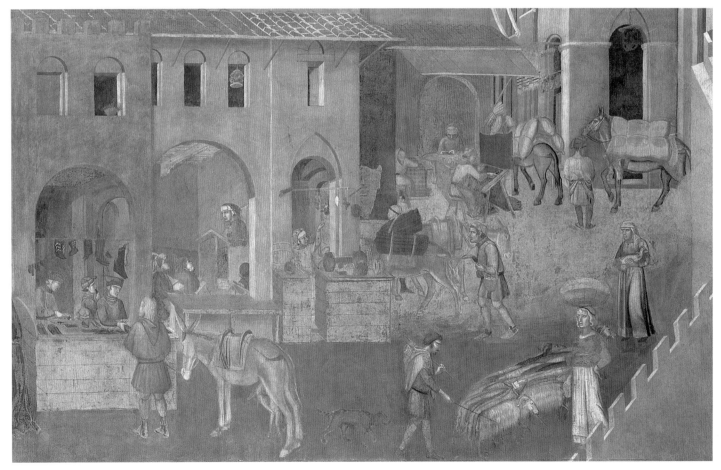

3. A Sienese street-scene, painted by Ambrogio Lorenzetti in 1337–39 as part of his ideal image of Good Government. In the street itself are laden asses, a goat-herd bringing his flock into town and two countrywomen with poultry and baskets. Behind them are a shoe-shop, a teacher with a class of children, a spice-dealer and a tailor cutting cloth on a sloping table.

Travel by land and sea
176-177

Cultural cross-currents
238-239

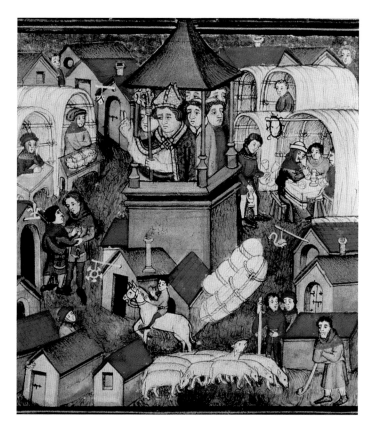

Patterns of trade

Trade crossed frontiers and was not easily controlled by either Church or state. Its extent, power and influence increased steadily throughout the Middle Ages. Because of the small size of most towns, buying and selling operated through weekly markets (1, 2) as much as permanent shops (3, 6). From these markets grew the great international fairs (4), held less frequently (once or twice a year) and lasting longer (sometimes several weeks). Here luxury goods from distant places, even outside Europe, could realize large profits, bringing wealth to individuals and to the combinations of merchants of which the Hanseatic League, based in north Germany, was the most important. Civic authorities made an income from licensing such fairs. Greatest of all were the fairs of Champagne, where international trade-routes met.

4. The fair of Lendit, near Paris, held annually in June. Here the Bishop of Paris blesses the fair; French, *c.* 1400.

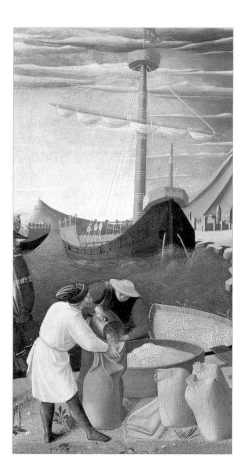

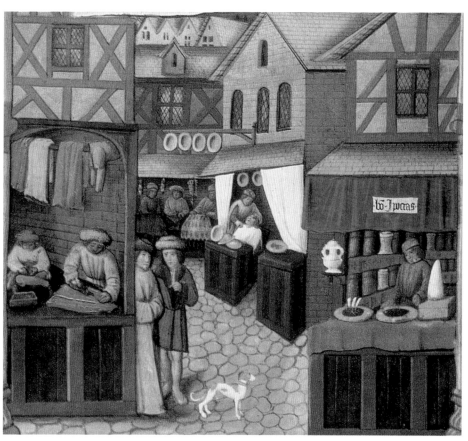

6. A cobbled street in France lined with shops – a tailor, furriers, barber and druggist; French, late 15th century.

5. Filling grain sacks at Bari, where a ship waits to export it; detail of a painting by Fra Angelico, mid-15th century.

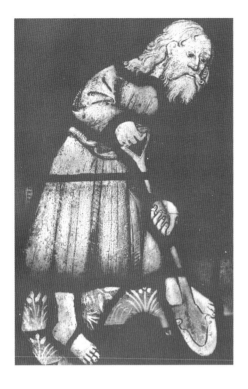

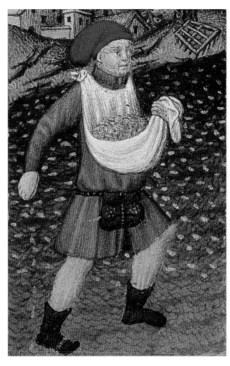

1. Adam digging. Stained glass from Mulbarton church, Norfolk; English, 15th century.

2. The sower. Miniature from a French Book of Hours; 15th century.

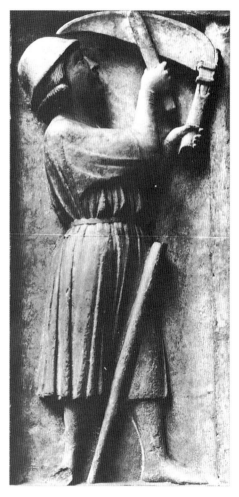

Tilling the soil

Medieval agriculture is profusely illustrated in painting and sculpture, but we must guard against taking these pictures literally. This was not art for peasants, but for rich patrons who did not want to be reminded of the (by modern standards) almost unendurably harsh condition of real life on the land. Work, after all, was God's punishment of Adam (**1**), but the sowers (**2**), reapers (**3**), shepherds (**8**), fishermen (**9**), threshers (**5**), poultry keepers (**6**) and ploughmen (**4**) whom we see are invariably happy and uncomplaining. The only agricultural process that was mechanized was the grinding of corn, for which the forces of wind and water were harnessed from a very early period. Physical survivals of medieval farming are rare (**7**).

3. Reaper sharpening his scythe. Sculpture from the façade of Notre Dame, Paris; 13th century.

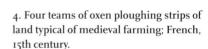

4. Four teams of oxen ploughing strips of land typical of medieval farming; French, 15th century.

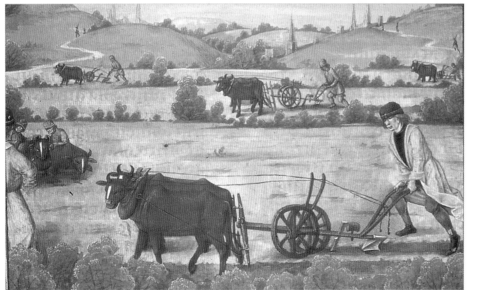

The three estates 100-101

The Labours of the Months 182-183

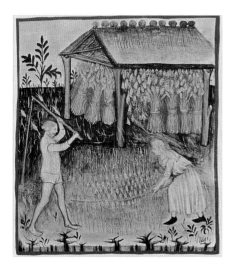

5. Threshing and storing sheaves in a covered shed; *Tacuinum Sanitatis*; North Italian, 14th century.

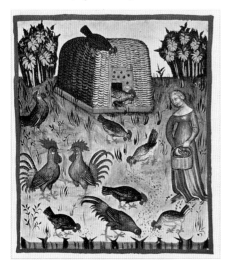

6. A hen-yard. Two cocks prepare for a fight; *Tacuinum Sanitatis*, 14th century.

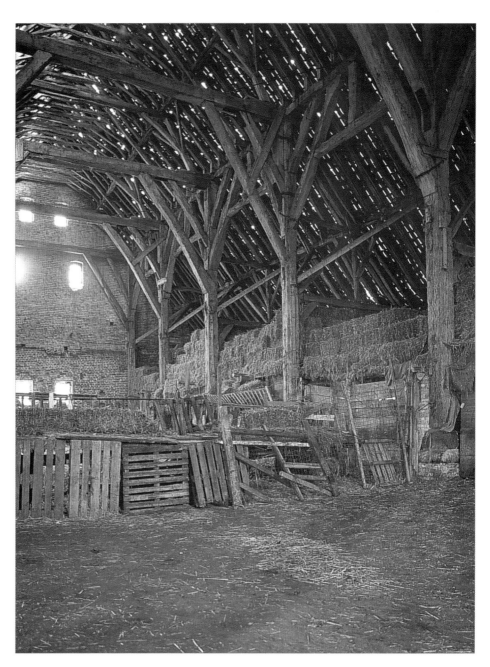

7. Tithe-barn at the monastery of Ter Doest, Belgium; 15th century.

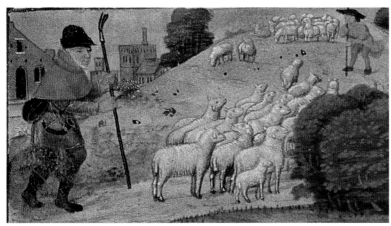

8. Sheep and shepherds; English, late 15th century.

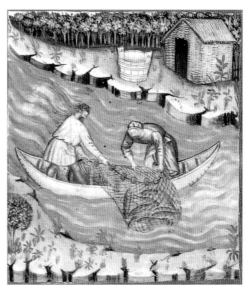

9. Fisherman from *Tacuinum Sanitatis*, 14th century.

The Labours of the Months

Nothing shows more clearly how secular and spiritual life were intermingled than the way in which the agricultural year is so prominently featured in religious art. Signs of the Zodiac correlated with personifications of the months go back to ancient Rome. By the 8th century they were joined by pictures of the labours associated with each month, forming a standardized series executed as sculptural reliefs or stained-glass windows in many Romanesque and Gothic cathedrals. They probably reflected the idea of the passage of time on earth between the Creation and the Last Judgment. Later they were incorporated into the Calendar pages of Books of Hours, bringing together the working year with the saints' days and festivals of the Church. The roundels on this page are from the south rose window of Lausanne Cathedral, Switzerland, *c.* 1170. The set has not survived complete. February and December are modern replacements.

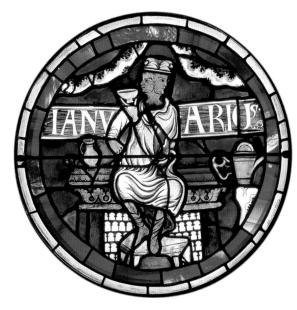

1. January: looking both ways.

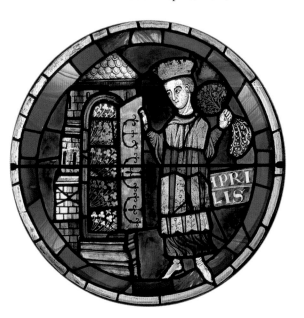

4. April: gathering flowers.

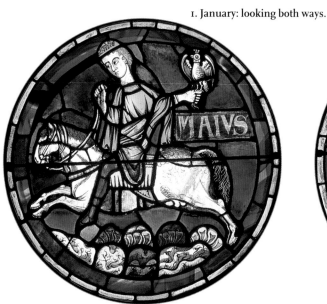

5. May: hawking.

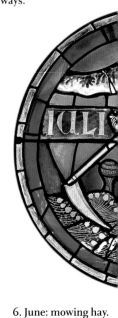

6. June: mowing hay.

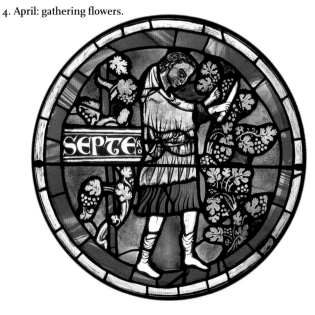

9. September: gathering grapes.

10. October: feeding pigs.

Tilling the soil 180-181   The Zodiac 200-201

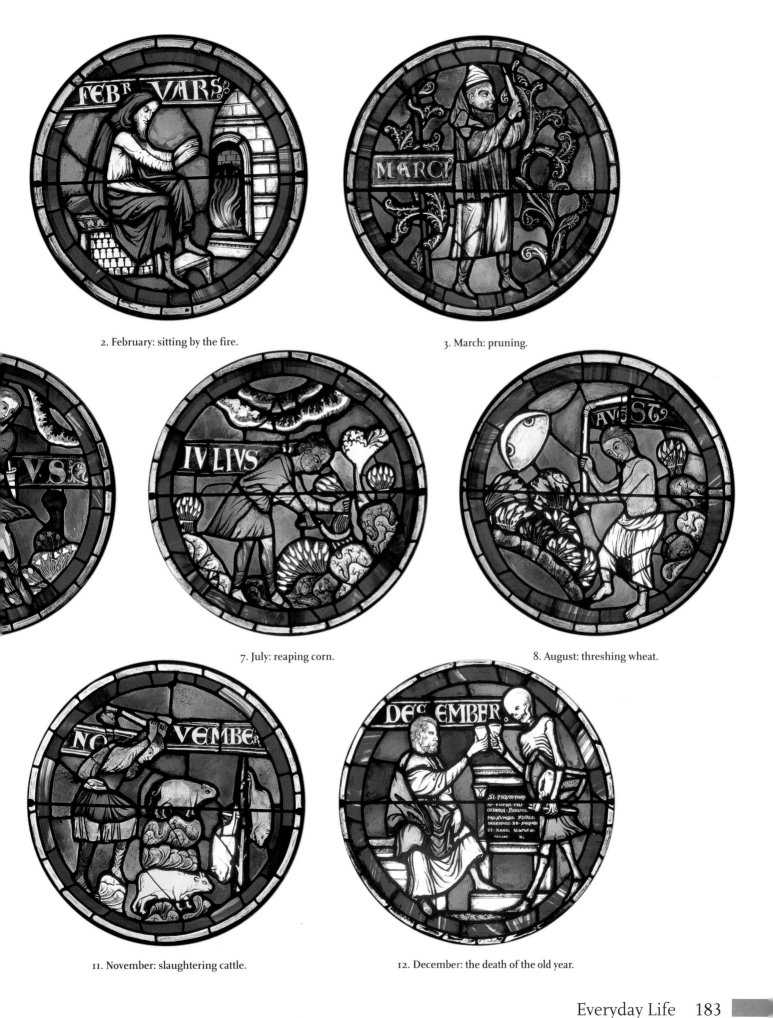

2. February: sitting by the fire.

3. March: pruning.

7. July: reaping corn.

8. August: threshing wheat.

11. November: slaughtering cattle.

12. December: the death of the old year.

Everyday Life   183

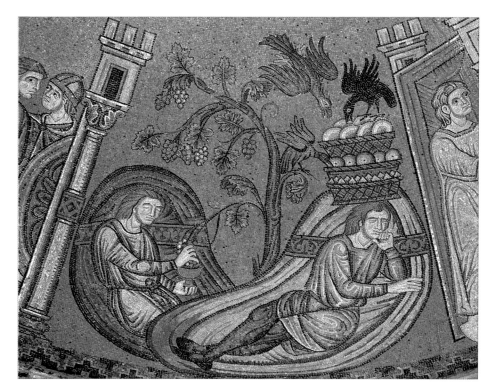

1. Bread and wine in the Old Testament: the dreams of Pharaoh's butler and baker. Mosaic in St Mark's, Venice; 13th century.

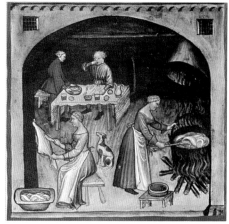

2. Tripe and chitterlings, the poor man's meat – preparation, cooking and eating; Italian, 14th century.

Pleasures of the table

For most of the population meals were fairly monotonous. There were vegetables as they came into season – peas, beans and onions and a few root-crops (though not potatoes) – but the main source of carbohydrate was bread (3), made of wheat, barley or rye. Protein came in the form of eggs and milk. Meat (2, 9) was a luxury, enjoyed in any quantity only by the rich. The well-known medieval cookery-books, such as the 14th-century *Menagier de Paris* in which meat figures prominently, give a misleading impression in this respect. Ways of preserving food for the winter were limited to drying, smoking and salting.

In practice, whatever was available would probably be combined together into 'pottage' (8), a thick soup or stew cooked in a large pot over a fire, and made tasty by herbs (4) or spices. Medieval ale, made from barley, was also a source of nourishment and its alcohol content was probably low. Wine was plentiful in France, Germany and Italy (7). The fullest records of medieval diet that survive relate to the monasteries which tended towards the upper end of the social scale. Monks in a wealthy monastery like Westminster could expect to eat fish fairly often, and had meat once or twice a week.

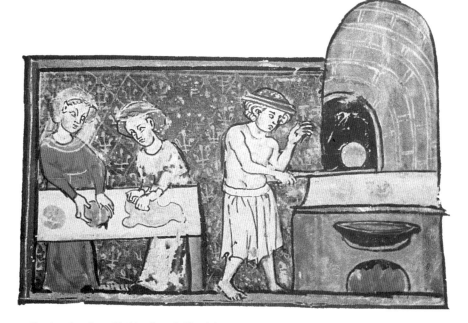

3. Shaping dough and baking bread; Flemish, 1320–30.

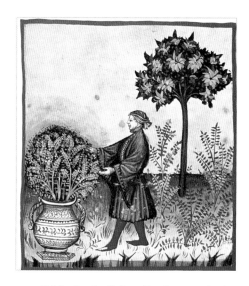

4. Cultivating basil; from *Tacuinum Sanitatis*.

The feast 122-123   Tilling the soil 180-181

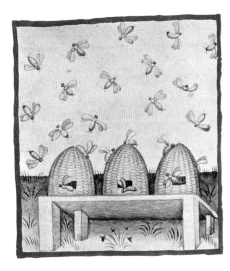

5, 6. Two miniatures from the 14th-century Italian *Tacuinum Sanitatis*: bee-hives for the production of honey and gathering roasting chestnuts.

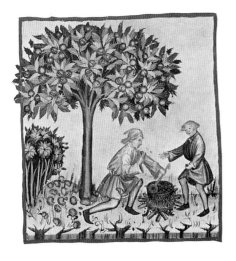

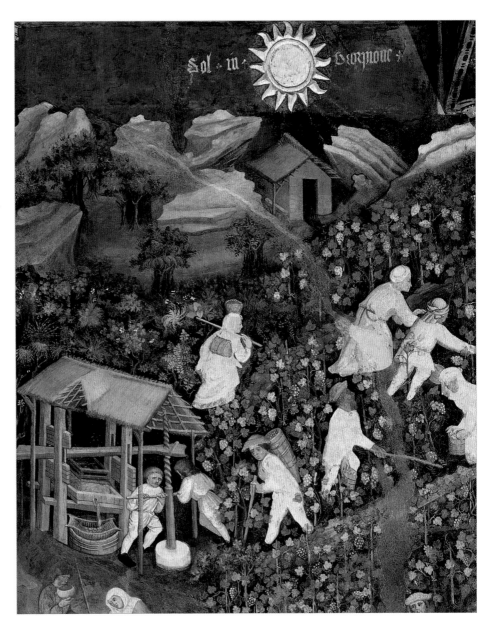

7. Gathering and treading the grapes; wall-painting, Italian, 14th century.

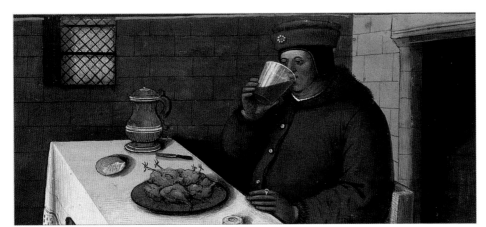

9. To illustrate the month of January, a French calendar attributed to Jean Bourdichon shows a comfortable bourgeois sitting down to a meal of small birds roasted whole. He has a knife but no fork.

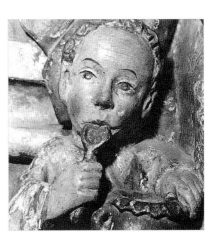

8. A child licks a wooden spoon after eating soup from a clay pot: detail from a carved and painted reredos showing the family of St Anne; Finnish, *c.* 1500.

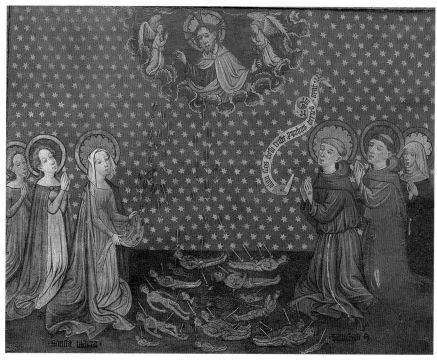

1. The plague as divine punishment: Christ sends a rain of arrows on the victims; German, 1424.

2. One of the miniatures in the *Très Riches Heures* represents a 6th-century procession to pray for the cessation of the plague; French, 1488–90.

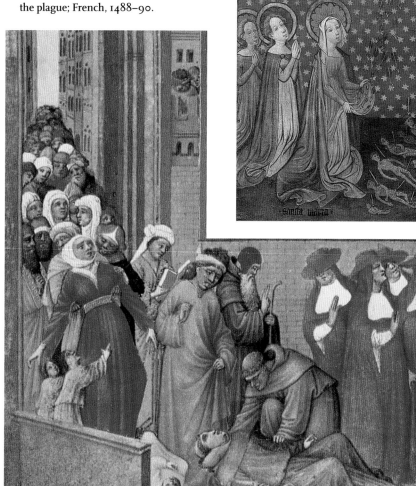

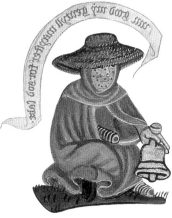

3. Lepers not in hospitals were obliged to ring a bell to warn people of their approach: 'Sum good, my gentyll mayster, for god sake'; English, 14th century.

In sickness

Sickness had two dimensions. As a physical affliction it had a physical cause to be cured by medical attention. As a spiritual affliction it had a spiritual cause to be cured by divine mercy. Epidemics like the plague were the consequences of God's anger (1), to be assuaged only by penitence, self-punishment and ritual observance (2). But at the same time doctors with medical training, possibly at a university, treated their patients according to the best empirical knowledge available (7), and hospitals, financed by private charity and often staffed by men and women in religious orders (5, 6), did their best to alleviate suffering. Many were small establishments sheltering a dozen or so patients, but some were on a grand scale (5), with open wards like churches with chapels at one end. People suffering from leprosy (3), the most feared medieval disease, were usually kept isolated. In Venice they had a separate island in the Lido.

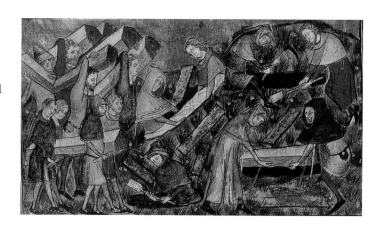

4. The Black Death of 1348–49 was Europe's worst plague epidemic. Here the dead of Tournai, then northern France, are buried.

The doctor's skill 206-207   Learning from Islam 240-241

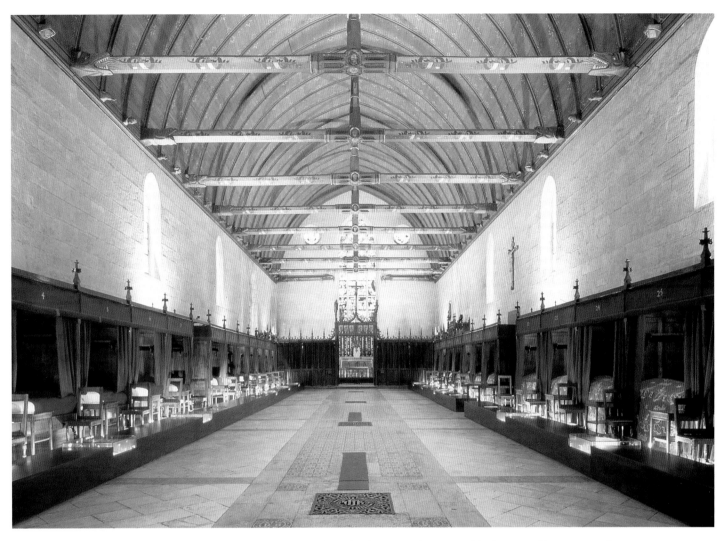

5. The main ward of the hospital at Beaune, France. Founded in the mid-15th century, this is one of the largest and best preserved of medieval hospitals, but there would originally have been simply rows of beds without canopies.

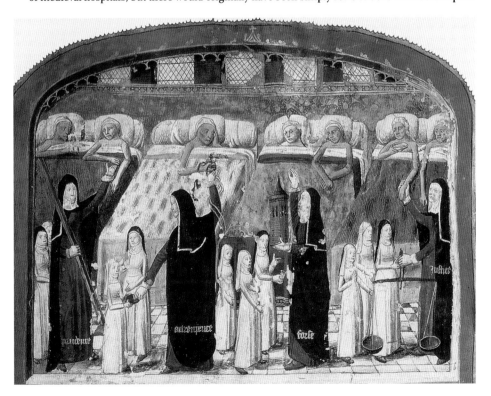

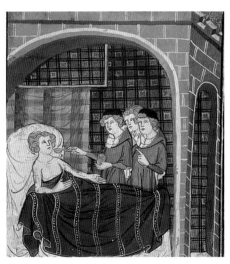

7. Doctors administering medicine to a bedridden patient; French, early 14th century.

6. Patients and nursing nuns at the Hôtel Dieu of Paris; 15th century.

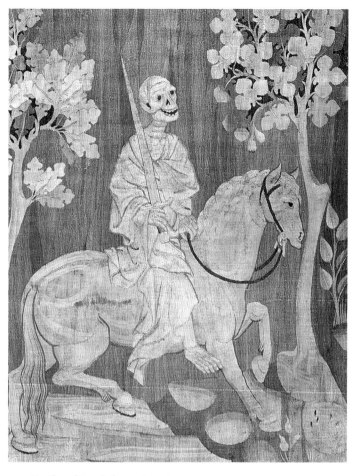

1. Death on his pale horse; tapestry, *c.* 1379.

2. Funerary mass for the soul of the dead man, which indeed is thereby released from Purgatory and received by angels at the moment of the elevation of the Host; French, *c.* 1460.

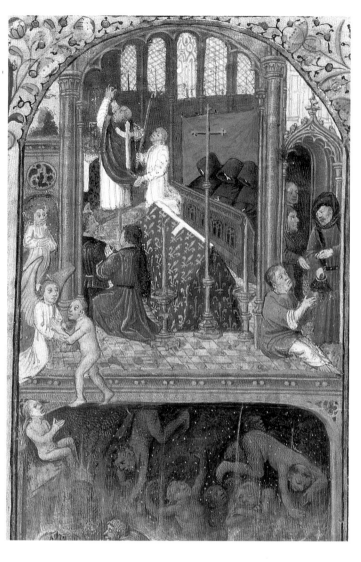

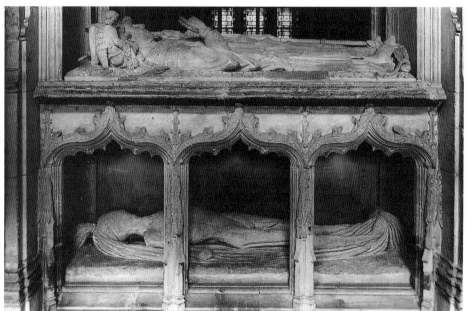

3. The tomb of Bishop Richard Fleming, in Lincoln Cathedral (1431), shows him above in his full ecclesiastical vestments, beneath as a naked corpse.

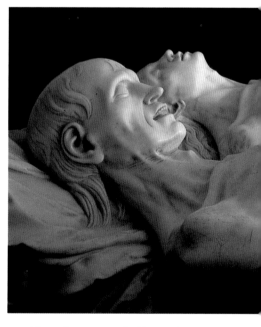

4. The cadaverous tomb effigies of King Louis XII of France and his queen Anne of Brittany, in the Abbey of Saint-Denis near Paris; after 1515.

After death 190-191

The battle for the soul 212-213

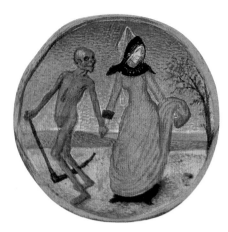

5. Death comes for the lady; French, 15th century.

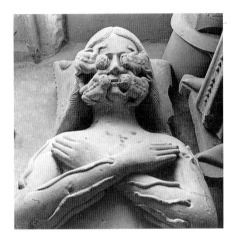

6. The tomb effigy of François de Sarrà shows his body being eaten by frogs and worms; La Sarraz, Switzerland, *c.* 1400.

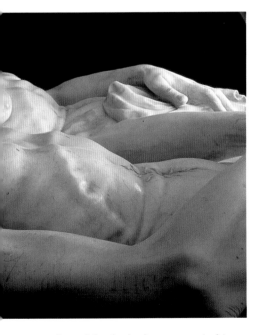

7. Above right: the dead man commits his soul to God, rescued from a devil by St Michael in the nick of time; the *Rohan Hours*, 1415–16.

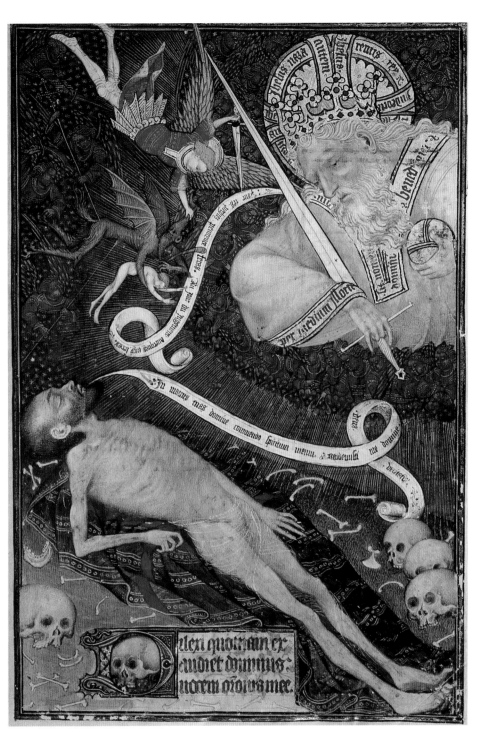

A good death

Death was constantly in the thoughts of medieval men and women. But this was not – as it too easily seems to the modern sensibility – merely a morbid preoccupation. Skulls, skeletons (1), the ghastly images of decaying corpses (3, 4, 6), cycles of the dance of death (5) – these were all warnings which, if heeded, would lead to eternal happiness. The care and expense lavished on funerals and the provision of prayers for the souls in Purgatory (2) were all dedicated to the same end. There were manuals on how to die well. The moment of death was crucial (7). A quick death was not desired; there should be time for repentances and absolution.

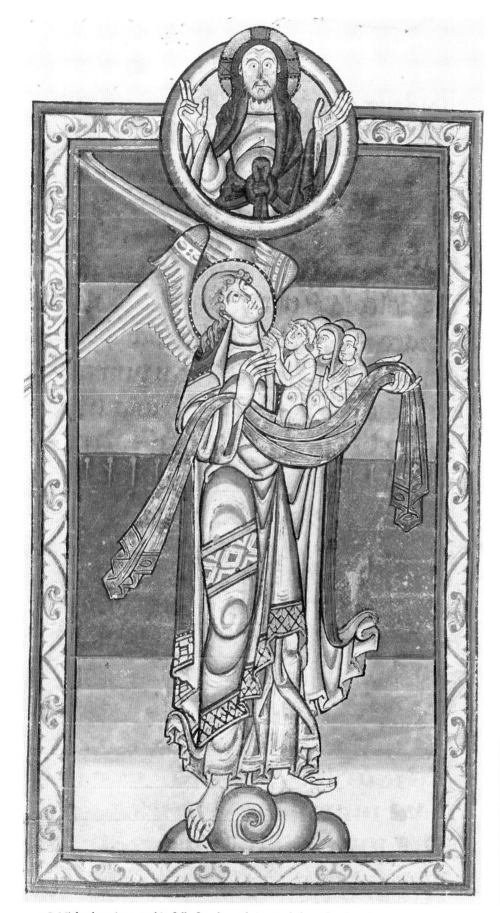

1. St Michael carries a napkin full of souls to Christ; English, mid-12th century.

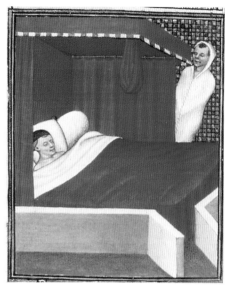

2. The ghost of a drowned man appearing to a sleeper, from a French version of Boccaccio; 15th century.

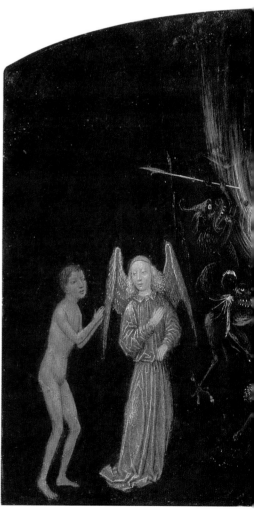

3. Miniature from a manuscript of *The Visions of the Knight Tondal*, attributed to Simon

Angels of light 78-79

The powers of darkness 80-81

4. The soul of St Bertin is called into the sky over the roof of the abbey church dedicated to him at St Omer, France; panel from an altarpiece by Simon Marmion, *c.* 1480.

After death

A good life and a good death led to eternal bliss. But what exactly happened to the soul at death? The doctrine of Purgatory grew up to account for those who were not good enough to go straight to Heaven or bad enough to go to Hell. This doctrine is not always reflected in iconography, where the soul is often shown being received by angels and taken to God (1, 4), or suffering the pains of Hell. *The Visions of the Knight Tondal* (3) is the narrative of a dream experienced by Tondal while seriously ill. An angel takes him on a tour of Hell, showing what would be the consequence of his dying without repenting. Originally written in Latin in about 1150, it was translated into French in 1475. Ghosts posed a problem in theology, but they were widely believed in (2) and even priests and monks reported dreams in which dead men returned.

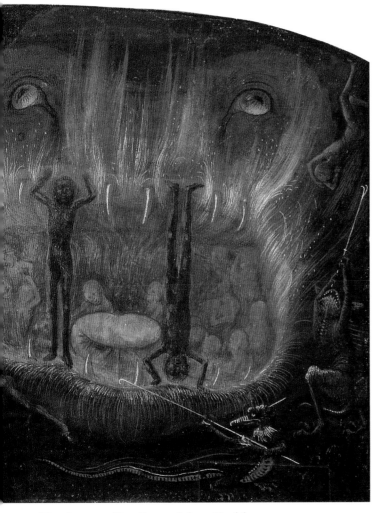

Marmion, 1475. Here the angel shows Tondal the Beast of Acheron, devourer of the avaricious.

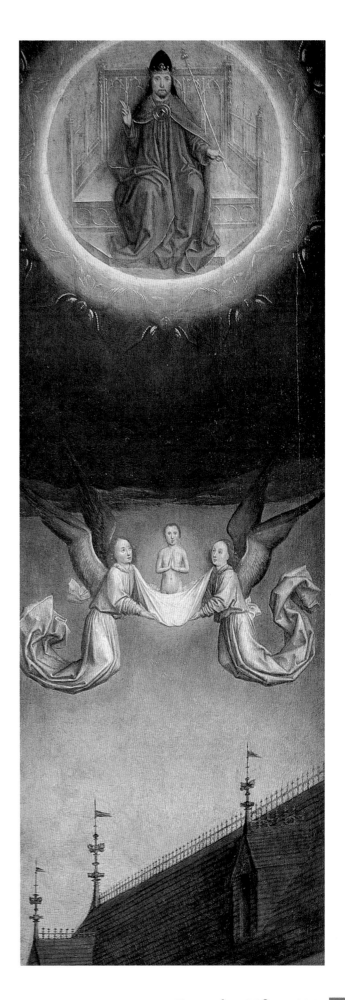

6

The Life
of the Mind

All knowledge – to be true – must conform to Christian revelation. History began with the Creation and would end with the Last Judgment. A superb 11th-century tapestry of the Creation at Gerona Cathedral, Spain, sets out the beginning of 'Genesis' in pictorial terms. In the centre is God the Father, creator of the Universe. The upper half of the circle illustrates the events of the First Day: the Earth waste and void (a circle of blackness); darkness covers the abyss (an angel); the spirit of God moves over the water (a bird in a circle); God says 'Let there be light' (an angel); God divides the waters below the firmament from those above it (figures of the sun and moon). The lower half skips to Chapter II of 'Genesis': Adam names the animals, birds and fishes, and finally God creates Eve from Adam's side.

I N THE EARLY MIDDLE AGES learning and scholarship were centred in the monasteries. Only there could one find even modest collections of books and the scribes able to copy and multiply them. If the monks did not transmit a work, it disappeared. Latin education was tied very closely to the needs of the Church. Monks were trained to chant the Psalms, the more talented of them could study the Bible in depth, while some became well acquainted with the Latin Fathers or even the authors of pre-Christian Rome. Monastic culture often produced impressive results, especially in theology and history, but tended to be turned inward, to a local community of monks or, at the widest, to monks in general.

However, even in the early Middle Ages monastic learning was not the only kind. In the cathedrals and other secular (i.e. non-monastic) churches a tradition of education was maintained, sometimes with difficulty, that was more open to the wider world. In the course of time this tradition slowly strengthened and eventually gave birth to an entirely new kind of educational institution and a new style of intellectual life. It was this path that led to the vibrant schools of the eleventh and twelfth centuries and then to the first universities, which gradually developed from them in the period 1150–1250. The most important were Paris, with a special reputation for philosophy and theology, and Bologna, the great centre of legal studies, but other, smaller universities arose in Italy, France, Spain and England. By the mid-thirteenth century the university had a clear institutional form and the distinguishing features had emerged that can still be recognized today: lectures, exams, degrees, students, academics, personal rivalries, intellectual fads and fashions. In the later medieval period, starting with the foundation of Prague in 1348, the princes and prelates of central and northern Europe sponsored the creation of a new wave of universities, designed to produce graduates to serve in their administrations. Sometimes they produced something rather different: Luther was a graduate of Erfurt, one of these newer universities.

The scheme of thought that developed in the schools and universities of the twelfth and thirteenth centuries is dubbed 'scholasticism' – the doctrine and method of the schools. Its foundation was the careful logical analysis of authoritative texts: the Bible, of course, the Church Fathers, but also other texts on more diverse subjects, such as the newly translated philosophical and scientific works of Aristotle or the scholars of the Islamic world. Thomas Aquinas (d. 1274), the best known of the scholastic thinkers, created in his *Outline of Theology* (*Summa Theologiae*) a vast and comprehensive survey, starting with a discussion of the nature of theology, then ranging through the existence and nature of God, created beings including angels, demons and human beings, good and evil, the passions, law and morality, to the saving work of Christ, the sacraments and the end of the world. Every issue is analysed with clarity and subtlety. Every effort is made to harmonize the teachings of scripture and philosophy.

The culture and learning of the Middle Ages was bookish and technology had only a limited scope and prestige, but this did not mean that practical men could not make innovations of all kinds. The windmill, as mentioned in Chapter 5, is first recorded in the twelfth century. Improvements in shipping continued throughout the period. Around the year 1300 two important new devices emerge

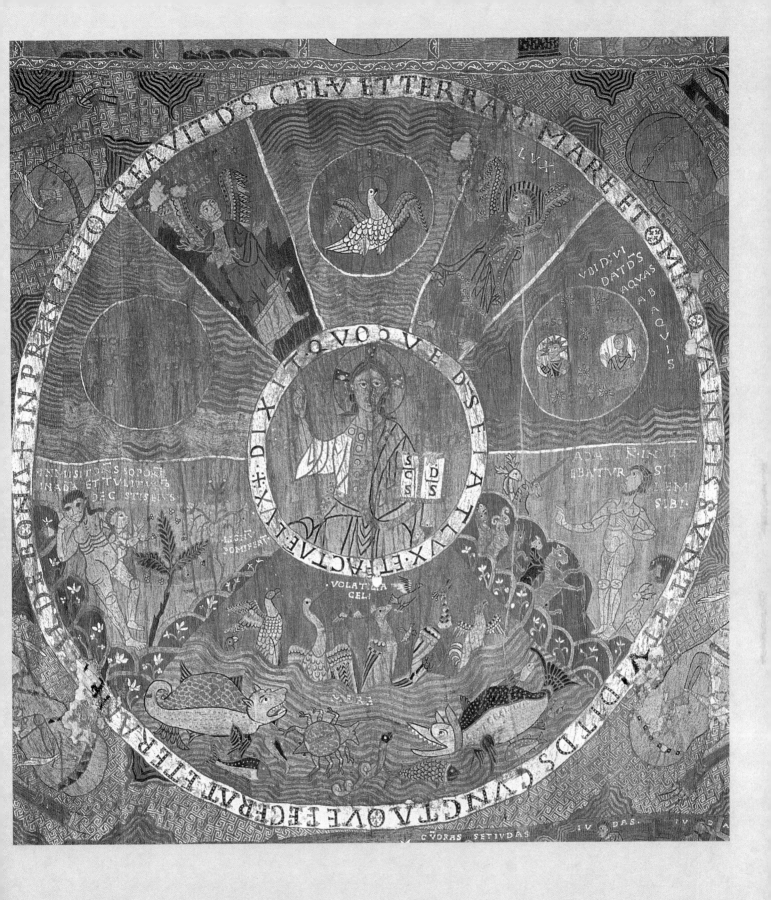

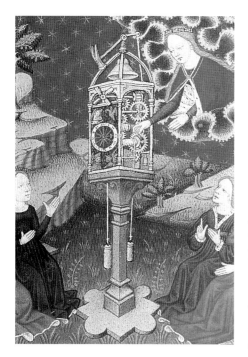

Mechanical clocks were a major innovation, revolutionizing the way time could be used. In Christine de Pisan's 'Epistre Othéa' of 1454, the personification of Temperance reaches down to adjust a pendulum clock in the presence of the four Cardinal Virtues.

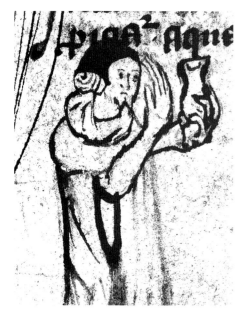

The classically derived theory of the body, with its elements, humours and temperaments, was of limited use in actual medical practice. Here a doctor holds what became almost a symbol of the profession, a urine flask. English, 14th century.

into record – spectacles and mechanical clocks. The former brought a new clarity to the long-sighted and enabled the elderly to extend their reading lives; Petrarch (1304–74) complained about having to wear glasses, but without them he would have had to give up reading. The clock provided a new measure of time, uniform and public. Cities and princes vied with each other in the grandeur of their public clocks and the fourteenth-century historian and poet Jean Froissart even wrote a love poem to the clock, praising it as 'a very beautiful and remarkable instrument'. Although the 'mechanical arts' were seen as inferior to the 'liberal arts' that were studied in the universities, they were pursued and with striking results.

The picture of the physical universe that educated people held in the Middle Ages was shaped partly by the Bible and partly by the learning inherited from the Greek and Roman world. God had created the universe in six days and he had created it and everything in it for man: 'The sun does not shine for itself but for man.' The cosmos consisted of a series of concentric spheres with the globe of the earth at the centre, then the seven planets (the Moon, Mercury, Venus, the Sun, Mars, Jupiter and Saturn), then the sphere of the fixed stars. Medieval astronomers, following their ancient predecessors, could quite easily fit their own detailed and precise observations into the framework of this system. Much more controversial was the extent to which the stars might influence or even govern human life. Astrology was both praised and condemned. Aquinas' teacher, the great German philosopher and scientific thinker Albertus Magnus, recognized that the stars had some effect on the physical behaviour of things on the earth. The seasons and the tides alone showed that. What was more difficult for a Christian was the idea that the stars might influence human action – what then became of free will and moral responsibility? Albertus sought to avoid this difficulty by distinguishing the way that the heavens might create a predisposition to behave in a certain manner from their absolutely determining a particular course of action. People born under a certain conjunction of the stars might be inclined to be angry, but whether they actually lost their temper was their choice.

Albertus Magnus compared the science of astrology with that of medicine: both looked for signs, although neither could always make exact predictions. The parallel between the body and the world was emphasized by the fact that both were composed of the same four elements – earth, air, fire and water. These in turn were the result of a combination of four qualities: earth was cold and dry, air hot and wet, fire hot and dry, water cold and wet. Each of these had its equivalent in the 'humours' of the human body and the dominating humour shaped the personality: those with an excess of the hot, dry humour choler tended to be hot-tempered, or 'choleric'. The small universe (microcosm) of the human being thus mirrored the large universe (macrocosm) around.

While it was well known to people in the Middle Ages that the earth was a huge sphere, their actual acquaintance with the globe was limited. The arctic and equatorial regions were deemed uninhabitable and the southern temperate zone was thought to be habitable but in fact uninhabited. After the abandonment of the fleeting Viking colony in Newfoundland there was no contact with or notion of the New World of the Americas. Hence in the eyes of the learned men of Catholic Europe the inhabited world consisted of the three adjacent continents of Europe, Asia and Africa. Their knowledge grew hazier and more improbably embroidered with distance from their home countries. The Muslim world was

194

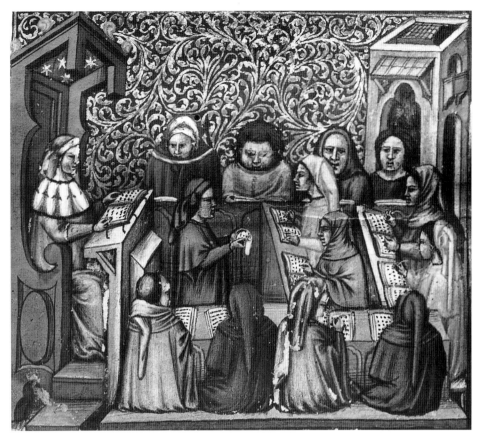

In the 12th century a new kind of educational institution evolved that was outside the monastic schools – the universities, which could explore new areas of secular learning: medicine, mathematics, law and philosophy. Here a leading Italian jurist, Johannes Andreae, lectures to a roomful of students.

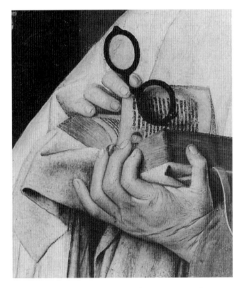

Jan Van Eyck's portrait of Canon Van der Paele (1436) is the earliest representation in art of spectacles with concave lenses for the short-sighted. Convex, long-sighted spectacles go back to the previous century.

a large and threatening neighbour, even if barely understood, sub-Saharan Africa an exotic mystery, while the Far East was populated in the mind's eye by cannibals, dog-headed men and other monstrosities. The large world maps of the thirteenth century, such as the Hereford Mappamundi and the Ebstorf map, present a schematic image of the world, with Jerusalem at its centre and the three continents arranged around it. The cities of Europe are usually positioned fairly accurately but the imagination has a freer range in the other continents, where one can actually locate the Earthly Paradise and Jason's Golden Fleece. When Asia was opened up to Europeans after the establishment of the Mongol Empire, friars and merchants, like the family of Marco Polo, travelled to Central Asia, India and China. They were astounded at the size and diversity of this unknown world, but also a little disconcerted at the absence of dog-headed men.

A similar interplay between the familiar and the fantastic can be found in medieval views of the animal world. While the farmers and hunters of the Middle Ages would have had a deep practical knowledge of some kinds of animals, book learning treated the natural world as a reservoir of symbols and lessons. The elaborate illustrated bestiaries of the period depict the unattested unicorn, griffin and phoenix alongside the prosaic pig, goat and crow and the less tame lion, tiger and bear, giving to each of them a moral point: lions do not get angry unless wounded, and 'people ought to pay attention to this, for men do get angry when they are not wounded'; crows look after their young carefully, 'hence let men learn to love their children from the example of the crows'. A more scientific approach to the natural world was not unknown and Albertus Magnus, inspired by the newly translated works of Aristotle, wrote a long study, *On Animals*, but there was a deeper habit of thought that saw the universe not only as created for human beings but also as bearing messages for them: 'every creature in the world is like a book or picture or mirror for us'.

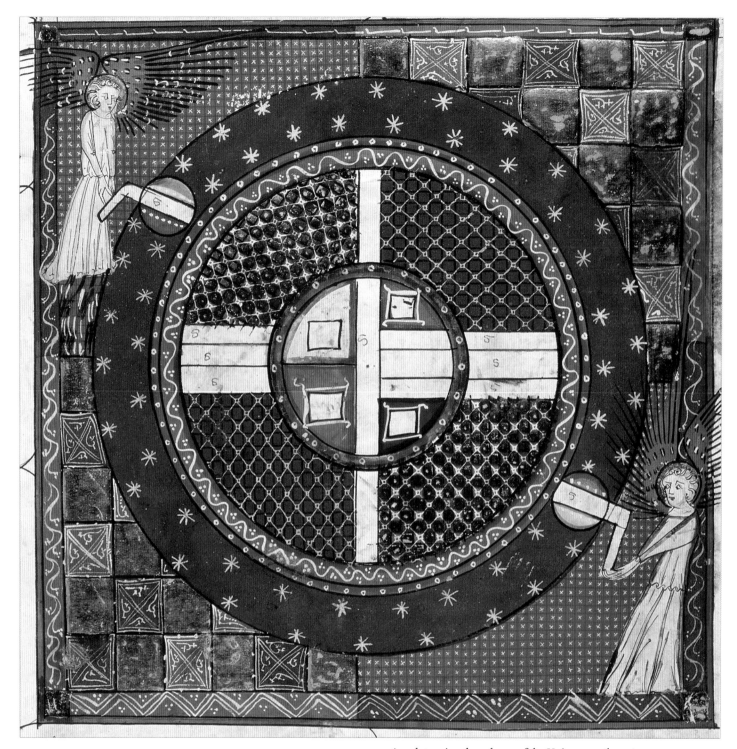

1. Angels turning the spheres of the Universe; 14th century.

2. The medieval universe; from a 13th-century French manuscript.

The Christian cosmos

No one in the Middle Ages found the universe a mystery or a puzzle. It had been created by God, the First Cause, the Unmoved Mover, as the setting for mankind's trial and judgment, and was kept in being by the continuous power of his will. That concept is conveyed with splendid naïveté in a 14th-century manuscript (1) showing angels – the agents of God's will – literally turning the celestial spheres with giant handles. The cosmos itself (2) was essentially that expounded by the Greek astronomer Ptolemy. The Earth was known to be

a sphere, and it was firmly the centre of everything. Round it revolved crystal spheres which held the Sun, the Moon and the Planets, which all turned round the Earth at different speeds. The outermost sphere held the fixed stars, which revolved every twenty-four hours. In the centre of the Earth is Hell, symbolized by Satan's inverted head, while above the spheres is Heaven, represented by God enthroned. In the corners are the symbols of the Evangelists, the source of all necessary revealed knowledge.

Astronomy: mapping the heavens 198-199

Picturing the world 208-209

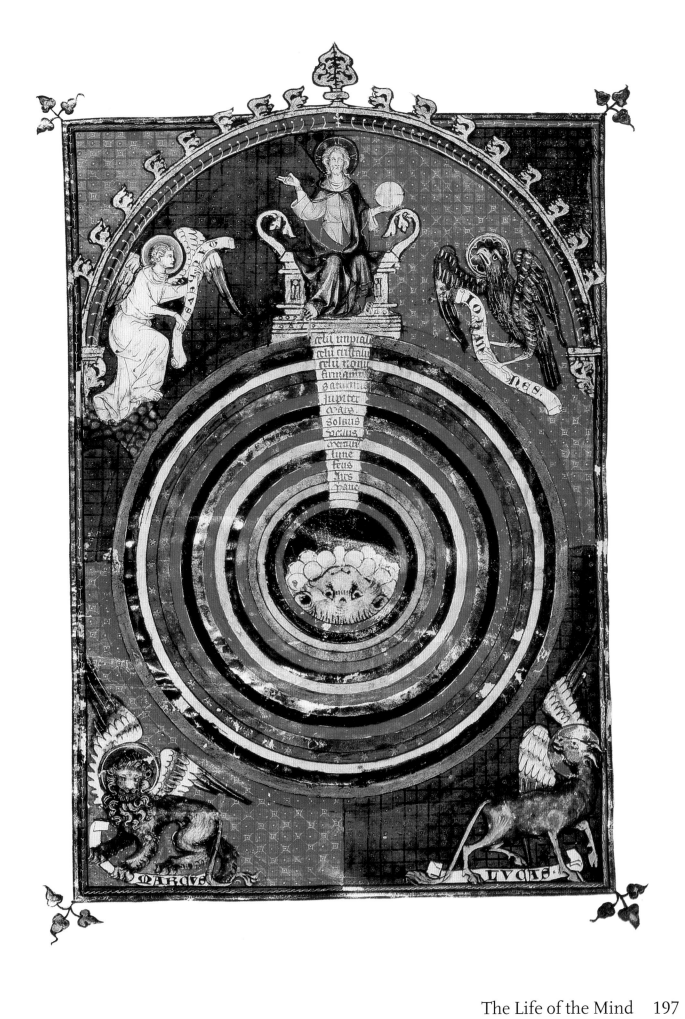

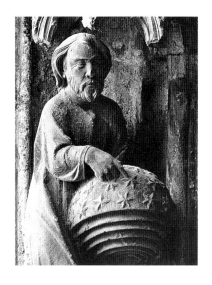

1. God creating the Universe, with the planetary spheres inside, covered by the sphere of the fixed stars; from Freiburg Cathedral, 13th century.

2. Saxon sundial from Yorkshire, c. 1060. The upright gnomon is missing.

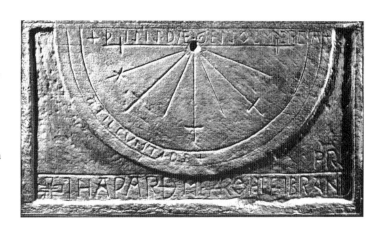

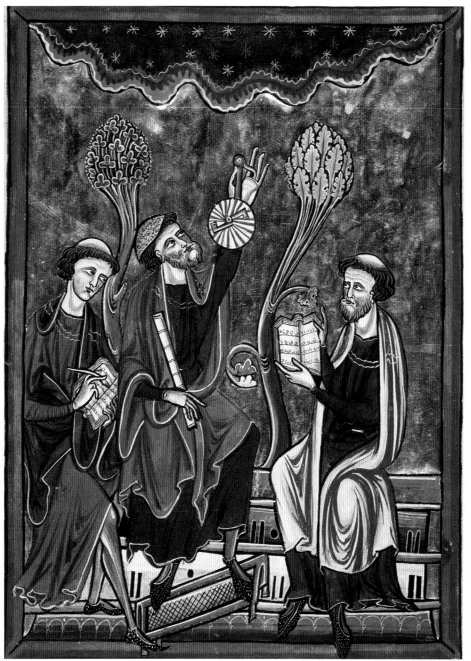

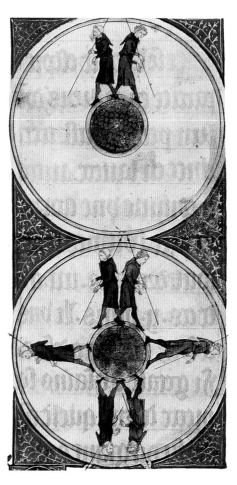

4. 'If of two men, from the same place, one set off towards the rising sun and the other towards the setting sun, they would certainly meet at the other end of the Earth' – Brunetto Latini, 13th century.

3. An astronomer (centre), with a clerk and mathematician, using an astrolabe; French, 13th century.

Picturing the world
208-209

Learning from Islam
240-241

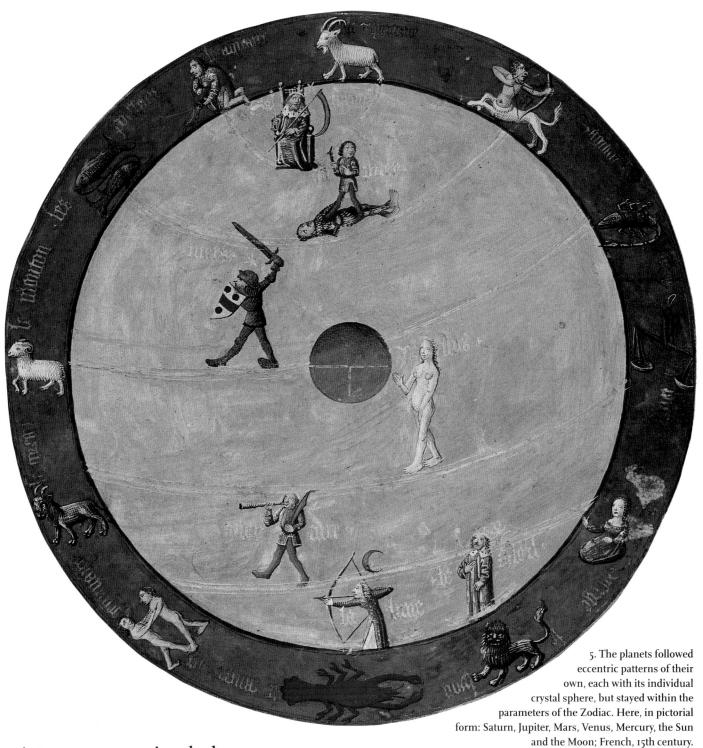

5. The planets followed eccentric patterns of their own, each with its individual crystal sphere, but stayed within the parameters of the Zodiac. Here, in pictorial form: Saturn, Jupiter, Mars, Venus, Mercury, the Sun and the Moon; French, 15th century.

Astronomy: mapping the heavens

Up to the 12th century astronomical knowledge was virtually at a standstill in Europe. The means of observation were primitive; for centuries the measurement of time depended on the sundial (2). Even when, after 1200, a more scientific approach evolves, it is not easy to disentangle medieval astronomy from astrology, since the former was pursued largely for the sake of the latter. There were, however, some serious advances. The invention (or adoption) of the astrolabe (3) made it possible to establish latitude with fair accuracy; the exact length of the year was fixed; a reliable chronological system was introduced, and the

compilation of astronomical tables plotting planetary motion provided the groundwork from which the later science of astronomy would grow. But until the advent of Copernicus, all this knowledge had to be made to fit into the framework of the Ptolemaic model (1, 5), which became increasingly top-heavy with data that it could no longer explain. Much of the new knowledge came from Arabic sources. One of the turning points of European astronomy was the publication of the Alphonsine Tables in Toledo in 1252.

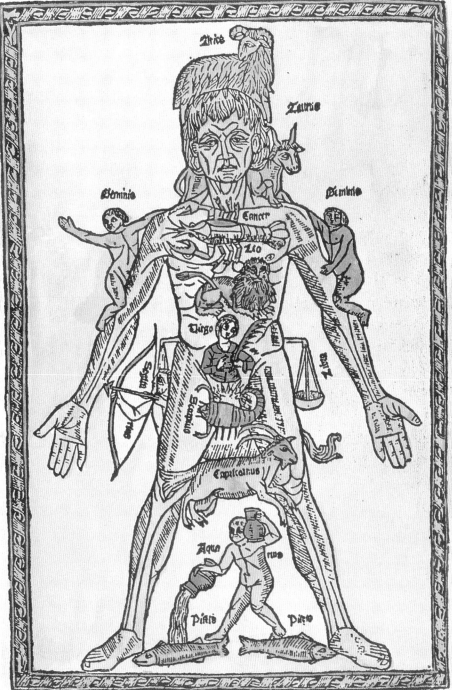

1. Diagram showing the areas of the human body subject to astral influences. Many versions exist; this one is an early woodcut, mass-produced for cheap distribution; early 16th century.

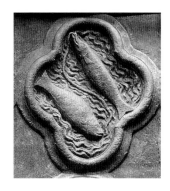

2, 3. The Sign of the Fish soon became conventionally two fishes facing opposite ways. Above: Amiens Cathedral, *c.* 1260. Below: a 14th-century Provençal manuscript.

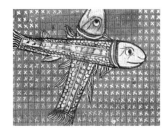

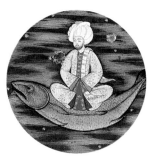

4. Above: Islamic Zodiac Signs offer interesting variants. Here the Fish has become an interpreter of mysterious messages; Turkish, 16th century.

5. Opposite: an early medieval chart of the Zodiac, based on classical models; the central figure is the Sun. From the top, going anti-clockwise, the signs are: Aquarius (water carrier), Pisces (fish), Aries (ram), Taurus (bull), Gemini (twins), Cancer (crab), Leo (lion), Virgo (virgin), Libra (scales), Scorpio (scorpion), Sagittarius (archer) and Capricorn (goat). In the corners are the four seasons.

The Zodiac

In order to codify and define the mass of the fixed stars into an ordered system the ancient astronomers grouped them into constellations (patterns of stars as seen from the Earth; they have no real existence), and drew imaginary lines between them to make pictures. The planets move in a relatively narrow belt across the sky (their orbits, as is now known, being arranged in a disk-like formation round the sun) and twelve constellations lie along this belt. These twelve constitute the Zodiac (5), and the way in which planets enter and leave them is the basis of astrology. The pictures made up from these constellations are extremely ancient. They can be traced back to the Babylonians of the 7th century BC and were adopted by the Greeks and Romans, descending thence to Islam (4) and to medieval Europe (2, 3). As a sort of parallel to the doctrine of the humours, they became incorporated into a pseudo-medical theory, each Sign governing a particular part of the body (1) – an example of 'correspondence', the human body (microcosm) reflecting the Universe (macrocosm).

The Labours of the Months
182-183

Astronomy: mapping the
heavens 198-199

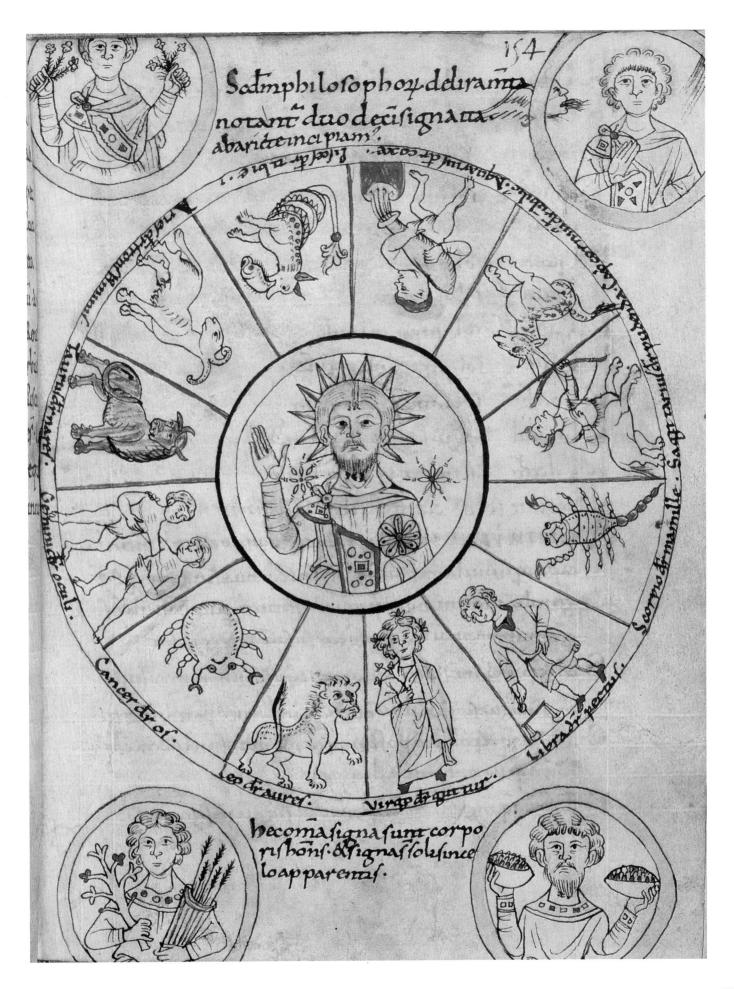

Alchemy, magic and witchcraft

The motive for alchemical experiment was not mere greed, nor, given the assumptions of medieval philosophy, was it beyond the bounds of possibility. All things – mineral, vegetable, animal and human – occupied places on a scale whose apex was perfection. As men and women could strive towards spiritual perfection, which was union with God, so the components of the earth could strive towards material perfection, which was gold (because of its splendour and value, and the fact that it was incorruptible). The world was full of transformations at every level (water into ice, sinner into saint). And since all things were linked through correspondences between microcosm and macrocosm, the quest for gold was also a moral quest, a process of greater and greater refinement, of purging away dross to leave pure essence. It was the knowledge of these correspondences – mystical, esoteric, even (according to the Church) forbidden – that gave the alchemist his power. Such an approach, now dismissed as 'magical' (from *magus*, a wise man), was not seen as opposed to the natural, but as in harmony with it, as indeed it partly was. Alchemists were the first physicists and chemists. 'Science' and 'magic' were the same thing (1, 2, 3, 4). The perversion of such knowledge was witchcraft, a practice that involved contact with the devil and was universally condemned (5, 6, 7, 8).

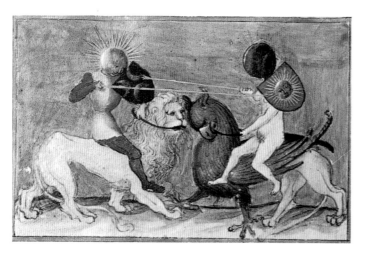

1. Four great alchemists (Geber, Arnold, Rhasis and Hermes Trismegistus) preside over workers who are carrying out various alchemical processes; English, 15th century.

2. The Sun and the Moon (also standing for sulphur and mercury and male and female) do battle; but the emblems on the shields show that they also contain their own opposites; late 14th century.

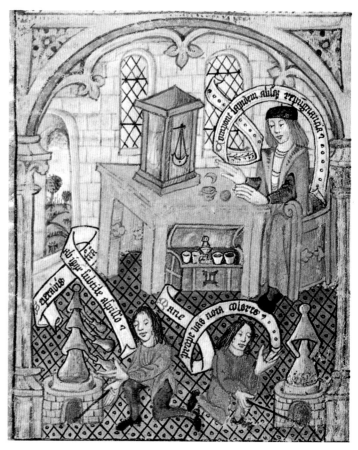

3. Master and two apprentices engaged in alchemical experiment; English, 15th century.

A unity of thought: the Elements and the Humours 204-205

Learning from Islam 240-241

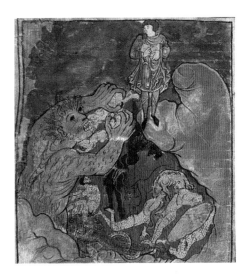

4. In an Anglo-Saxon manuscript (early 11th century) illustrating an apocryphal Biblical story, a magician is threatened by the monsters he has called up.

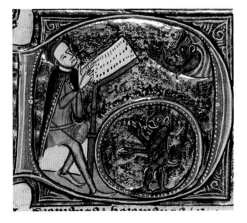

5. Magician invoking devils and endangering his immortal soul; English, 14th century.

6. Right: magic at its most banal. A young witch has used her powers to cast a love-spell on the youth who enters at the back; Flemish, 15th century.

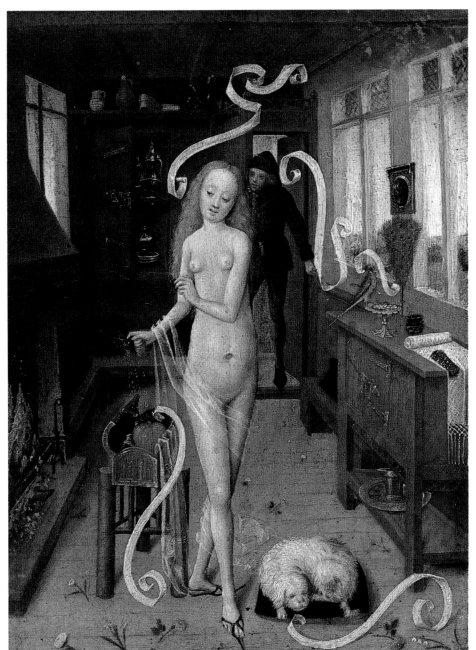

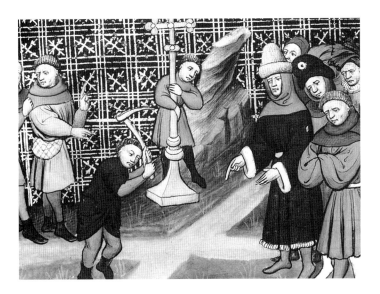

7. Left: the discovery of witches' implements and evidence of sorcery at a crossroads; French, 14th century.

8. Right: one of the stock beliefs about witches was that they could travel through the sky on broomsticks; marginal illustration to a French manuscript of 1451.

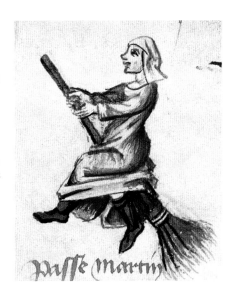

The Life of the Mind   203

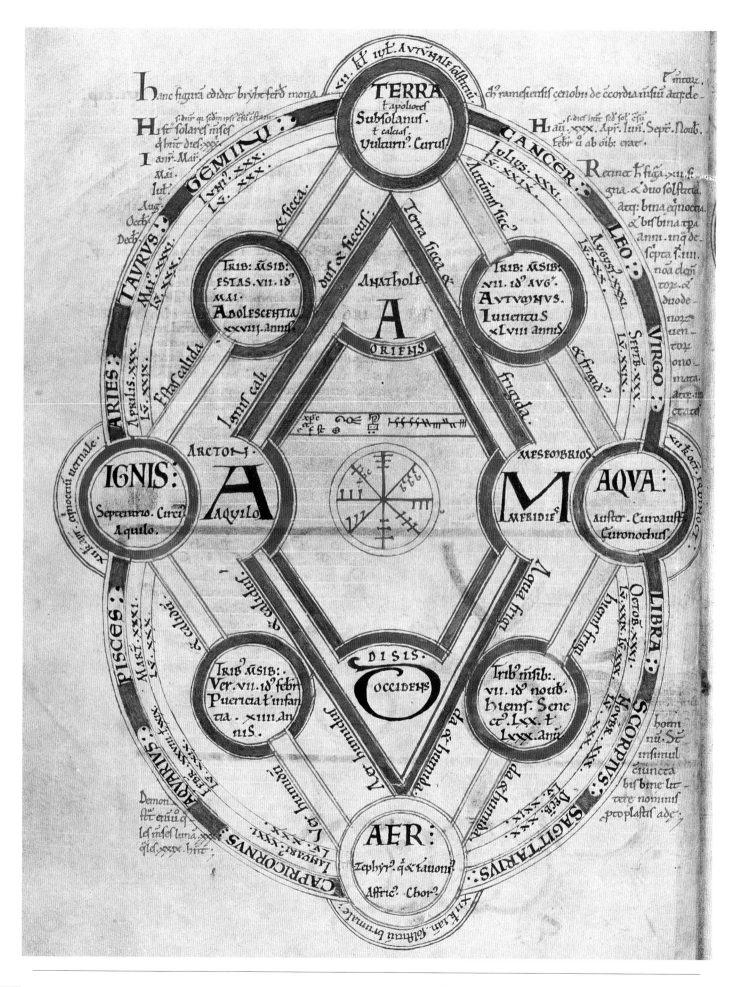

1. Schematic diagram linking the Elements, the directions, the seasons and the Zodiac. From the top clockwise: Earth (East), Water (South), Air (West), Fire (North). English, *c.* 1080/90.

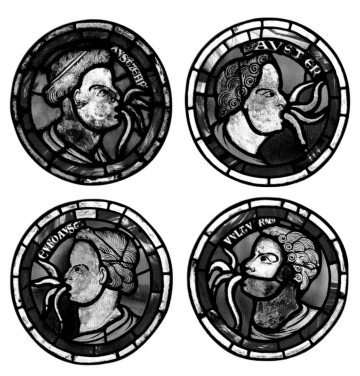

2. In the rose-window of Lausanne Cathedral, the four winds are extended to eight, but only five are preserved. Shown here are south-west, south, north-east and south-east; *c.* 1170.

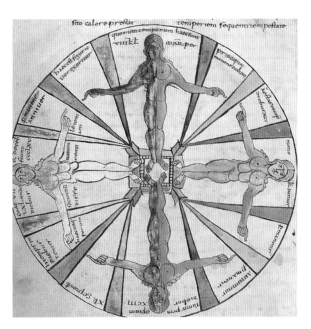

3. The seasons correlated with the Elements and the Humours. Autumn = black bile = melancholic = Earth. Summer = yellow bile = choleric = Fire. Spring = blood = sanguine = Air. Winter = phlegm = phlegmatic = water. From a manuscript of Isidore of Seville's *De Natura Rerum*, 9th century.

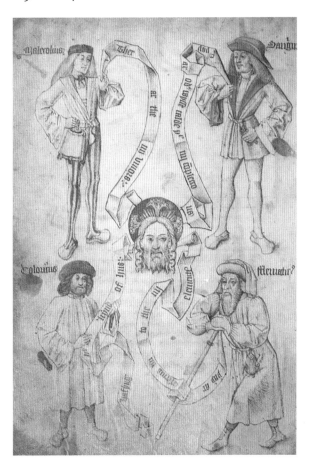

4. Nearly a thousand years after Isidore of Seville, the same scheme of the Humours linked to the seasons (and now the Ages of Man) is illustrated in a medical textbook; English, 15th century.

A unity of thought: the Elements and the Humours

Medieval thinking was dominated by the theory of 'correspondences', derived not from Christian revelation but from the idea, Greek in origin, that an explanation, to be part of the divine plan, had to be economical, symmetrical and aesthetically satisfying. What it ignored was the Greeks' readiness to test a hypothesis by observation and experiment. Everything in the Universe consisted of the four Elements – Earth, Fire, Water and Air. In the human body these 'corresponded' to the four fluids – blood, yellow bile, phlegm and black bile – which in turn, according to the proportions in which they were mixed, produced four Humours – sanguine, choleric, phlegmatic and melancholic (**3, 4**). The fact that there were also four cardinal directions, four winds (**2**), four seasons (and indeed four Gospels) only confirmed the theory. Put into diagrammatic form (**1**), the whole scheme was perfectly symmetrical, convincing evidence that it must be true.

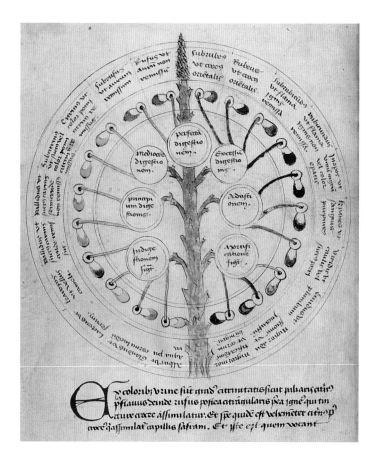

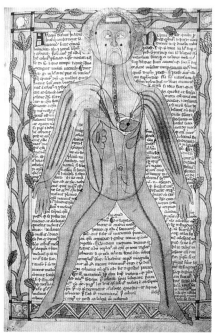

The doctor's skill

The doctrine of the four humours was neat and intellectually satisfying but of little practical use. The only area in which it actually determined medical treatment was that of illnesses thought to be caused by an excess of blood (the sanguine temperament) which could be alleviated by bleeding (4). In practice doctors worked by observation, for instance, the examination of urine (1), experience and trial and error. Anatomical research was rudimentary, largely because the Church forbade the dissection of dead bodies (3). How the organs functioned was barely understood (2), but some advances were made in the application of drugs (6, 7) and simple surgical operations (5). The new knowledge was Arabic, partly based on later Greek authorities (Galen, 2nd century AD). From the 10th century, the leading medical school in Europe was at Salerno, Italy (5). Medicine was also taught at Montpellier, Bologna, Padua and Paris.

1. Diagram illustrating the colours of urine, from a medical treatise of the 15th century.

2. Illustration of Galen's theory of the blood, in which the veins and arteries were thought to be quite separate; *c.* 1292.

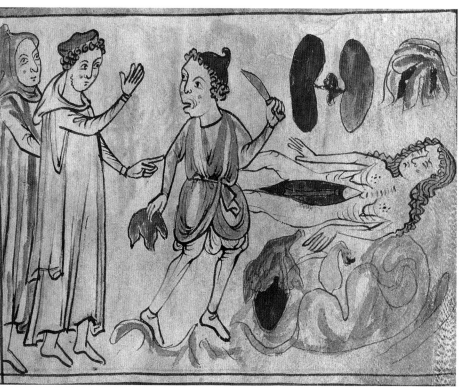

3. Physician dissecting a corpse (the lungs, heart and intestines are displayed above), but is rebuked by another doctor and a monk; English, *c.* 1300.

In sickness 186-187

Learning from Islam 240-241

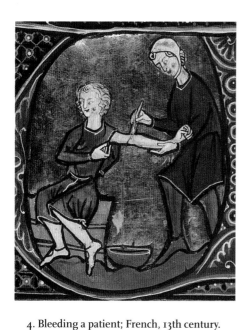

4. Bleeding a patient; French, 13th century.

5. The treatment of various wounds, from a treatise on surgery by Roger of Salerno; Italian, c. 1300.

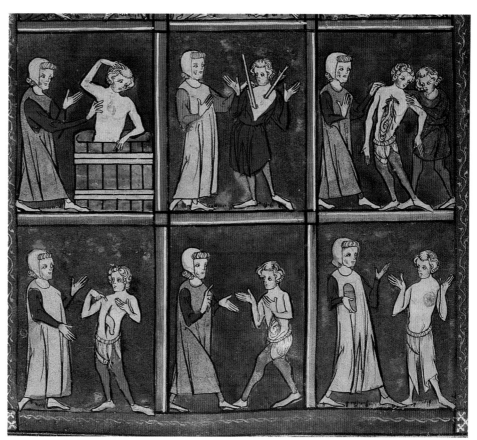

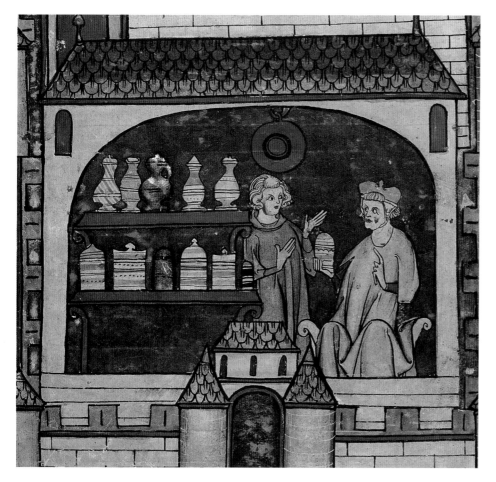

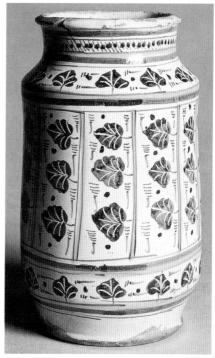

7. Italian drug-jar, 15th century.

6. A pharmacy with shelves holding drug-jars; Italian, c. 1300.

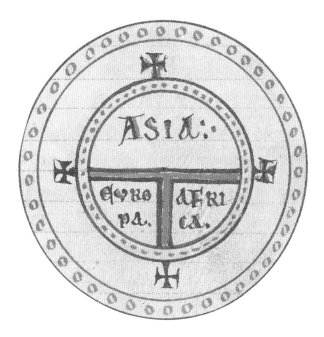

1. Schematic world-map: Asia, Europe and Africa, from Isidore of Seville's *Etymologia*, 12th century.

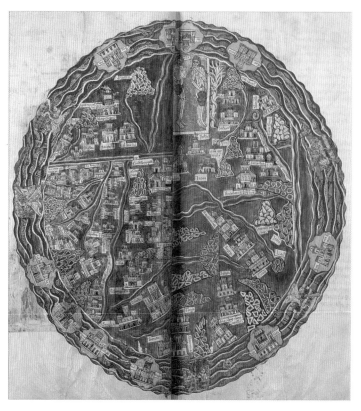

3. Mappamundi from a manuscript of Beatus' Commentary on the Apocalypse; Spanish, early 13th century.

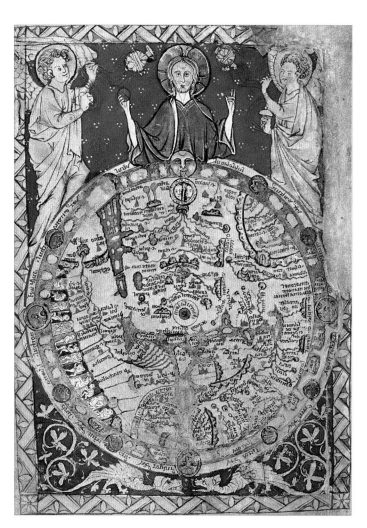

2. English world-map with Jerusalem in the centre; 13th century.

Picturing the world

Medieval world-maps reflected less the state of geographical knowledge (what *is*) than a schema of divine order (what *must be*). For practical purposes, to aid travellers and sailors, there were reasonably accurate maps, but the *idea* of the world was something different. Sometimes they become unambiguously diagrams (1). The great pictorial maps are equally schematic but with more anecdotal detail. The two shown here are roughly contemporary (1200–1300), but the Beatus mappamundi (3) goes back to a much earlier model. East is at the top, with the Garden of Eden and Adam and Eve. Europe is bottom left. Islands are arbitrarily grouped in the surrounding Ocean. The Hereford mappamundi (4) keeps the traditional Ocean. Again, the Garden of Eden is at the top – a circular island surrounded by flames – and Jerusalem now in the exact centre. The Red Sea (really red) and the Mediterranean occupy its lower half; Crete and its Labyrinth is prominent. Europe is again bottom left; Paris and Rome are both named and Britain is a long island in the sea. But this is essentially a symbolic world, conveying the truths of history and theology above those of geography.

Travel by land and sea 176-177

New worlds 268-269

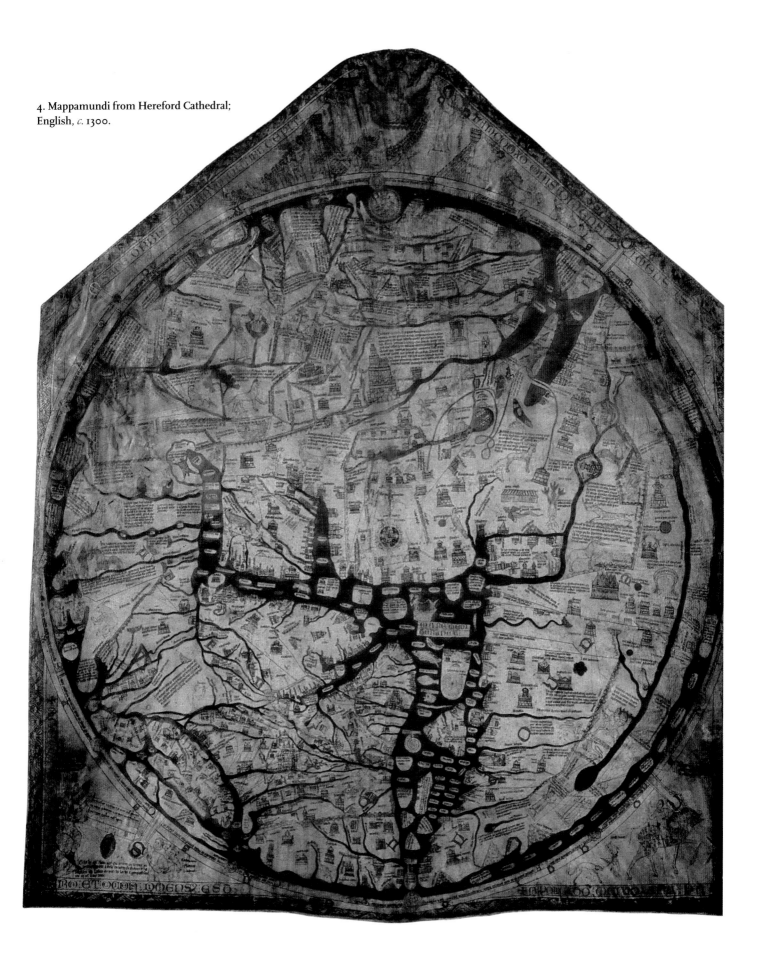

4. Mappamundi from Hereford Cathedral; English, *c.* 1300.

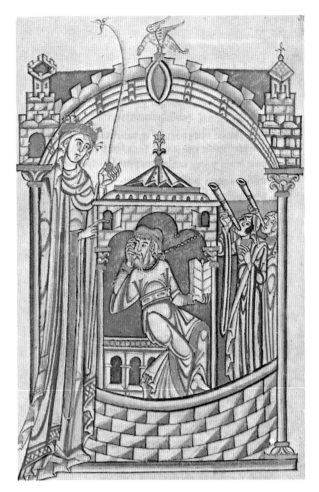

1. The Lady Philosophy visits Boethius in prison, from *De Consolatione Philosophiae*; **English, late 12th century.**

The categories of knowledge

Medieval educational theory divided the curriculum into the Seven Liberal Arts: Arithmetic, Geometry, Astronomy, Music, Dialectic (Logic), Rhetoric and Grammar. The first four (the Quadrivium) led to knowledge, the last three (the Trivium) to eloquence. These categories go back to the classical world and St Augustine, and reached their final form in Carolingian times. The Liberal Arts were frequently represented as allegorical females. One elaborate version is that of Andrea da Firenze in the Spanish Chapel of S. Maria Novella in Florence, painted in the late 14th century (**2**). The men seated in the front are those who were supposed to have invented the arts. Having mastered the Quadrivium and the Trivium, the student progressed to the Lady Philosophy who encompassed all (secular) knowledge. She achieved a sort of apotheosis in the work of Boethius, an official at the court of Theodoric the Ostrogoth, by whom he was imprisoned and executed. Philosophy, personifying wisdom, consoled him in his suffering (**1**). Above even Philosophy stood Theology, which supplemented knowledge acquired through reason with knowledge acquired through faith. This whole scheme, hallowed as it was by tradition, failed however to include two important areas of study: law and medicine.

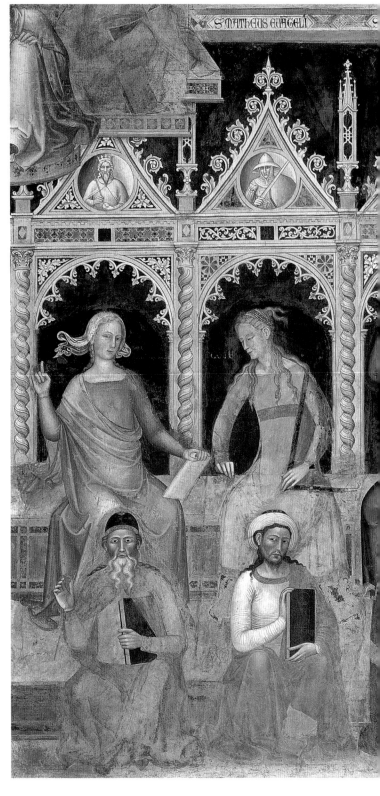

ARITHMETIC	GEOMETRY
Pythagoras	**Euclid**
Greek philosopher and mathematician, 6th century BC.	Greek mathematician, 3rd century BC; his textbook was used for 2000 years.

2. **Andrea da Firenze: detail from** *The Triumph of St Thomas Aquinas*; **Italian, late 14th century.**

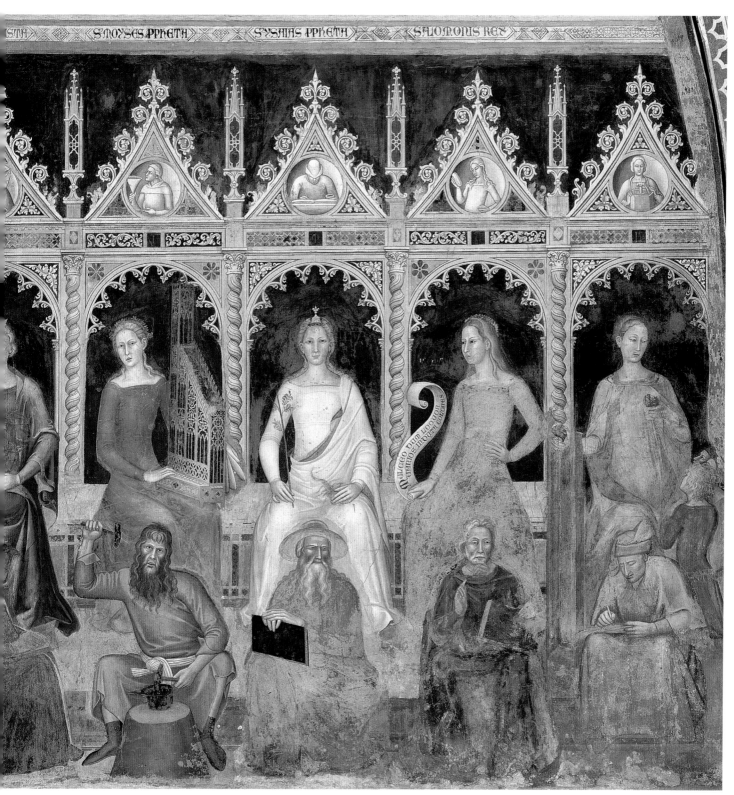

ASTRONOMY	MUSIC	DIALECTIC	RHETORIC	GRAMMAR
lemy	**Tubal-cain**	**Aristotle**	**Cicero**	**Priscian**
ek astronomer,	Metalworker, mentioned in	Greek philosopher,	Roman lawyer, orator and	Latin grammarian who lived
d century AD,	Genesis, identified with	4th century BC, who invented	statesman, 1st century BC.	in the 6th century AD.
ose system	music possibly through a	formal logic.		
vailed until	misunderstanding by			
ernicus.	Isidore of Seville.			

The Life of the Mind   211

The battle for the soul

In the neatly balanced world of medieval 'correspondences', it is unsurprising to find the cosmological (the seven planets) and the aesthetic (the seven Liberal Arts) mirrored by the moral (the seven cardinal virtues and deadly sins). To represent the moral life as a battle between good and evil is an idea that goes back to the 4th-century Latin poet Prudentius. His *Psychomachia* dramatizing the struggle between the Virtues and the Vices became a favourite vehicle for medieval exhortation. The seven Vices were Pride, Wrath, Envy, Lust, Gluttony, Avarice and Sloth, symbolized by hideous monsters (**2**) or caricatured human types (**1, 3, 4**). The Virtues – Faith, Hope, Charity, Justice, Fortitude, Prudence and Temperance – could also be anthropomorphized (**7, 8**) or represented as doves (**2**) or symbolized in other ingenious ways (**5**). In the Flemish miniature of Gluttony versus Temperance (**6**) the sedate, well-bred banquet at the back is contrasted with the boorish gathering in the foreground.

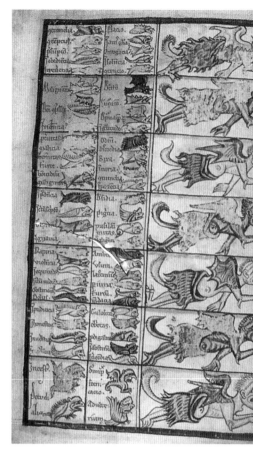

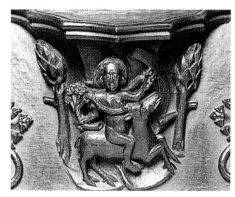

3. Lust, a naked woman on a stag. Misericord from the church of Stratford-on-Avon, 15th century.

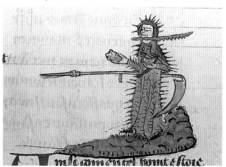

4. Personification of Wrath; French, *c.* 1400.

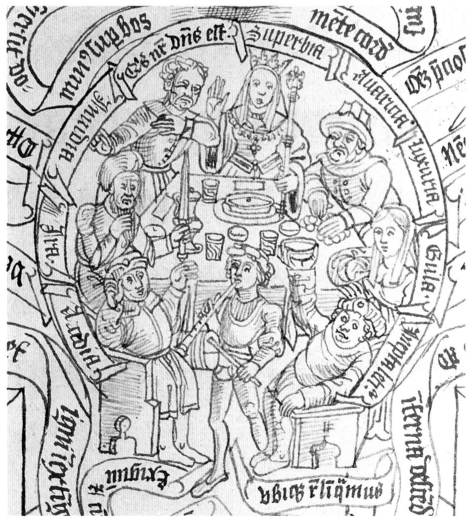

1. The seven deadly sins; Flemish, 1538.

The powers of darkness 80-81

After death 190-191

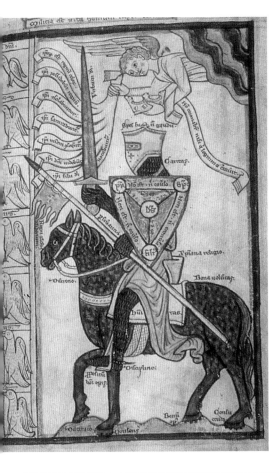

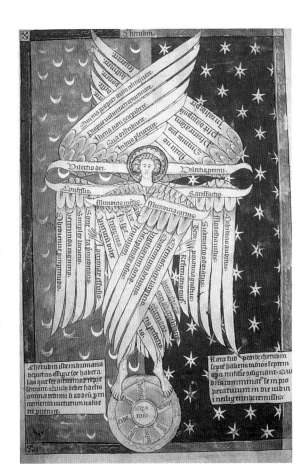

2. The Vices versus the Virtues (doves), who are supported by a Christian knight whose shield bears the emblem of the Trinity; German, 12th century.

5. The cherub of virtue; each of its six wings represents a virtue, and each feather an aspect of virtue. From an English 14th-century Psalter.

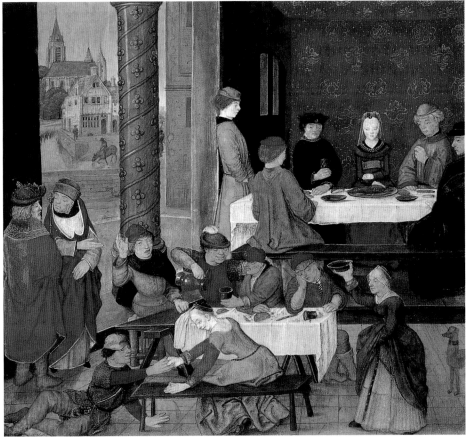

6. The Temperate and the Intemperate, by the Master of the Dresden Prayer Book, *c.* 1475–80.

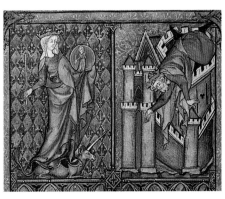

7. 'Humility', standing on a unicorn, is contrasted with Pride having a fall; 13th century.

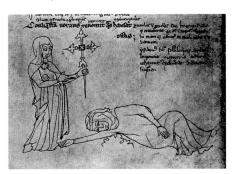

8. 'Sobrietas', or Temperance, kills Lust and harangues her corpse. A French illustration of Prudentius, 1298.

The Life of the Mind   213

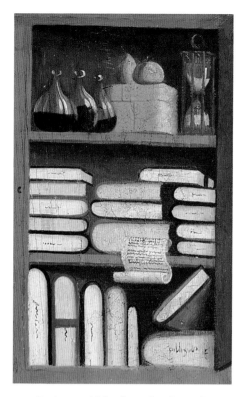

1. Bookcase with bottles and an hour-glass, part of the background to a portrait of St Ambrose by the Master of Mondsee, 1497.

2. Vincent of Beauvais at work in his study. He sits at a swivel desk: the weighted straps hanging over the top keep his book open. On the shelf behind him his other books lie flat. Flemish, late 15th century.

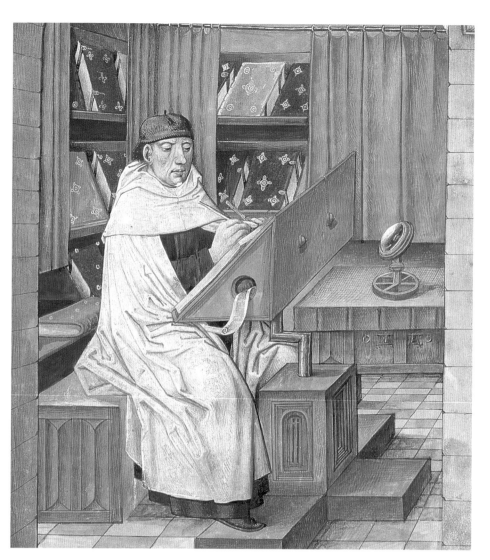

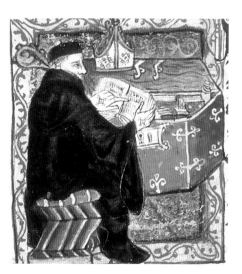

3. Simon, Abbot of St Albans, with his book-chest. He founded the abbey library. English, 14th century.

4. Amaury de Bène (died 1206) lecturing at the University of Paris. He ran into trouble over his teaching, was accused of heresy and forced to recant. French, early 14th century.

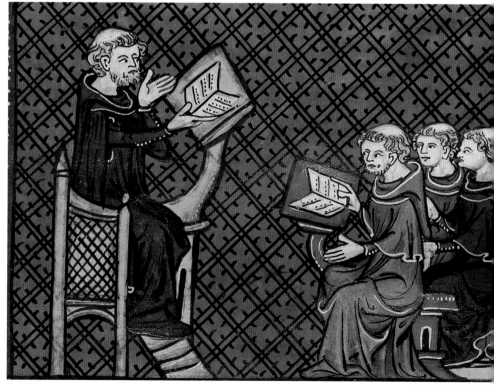

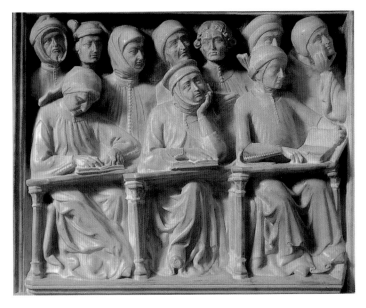

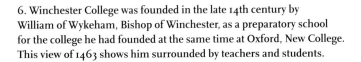

5. Law students at the University of Bologna listen to a lecture by the famous jurist Giovanni da Legnano; Italian *c.* 1385.

6. Winchester College was founded in the late 14th century by William of Wykeham, Bishop of Winchester, as a preparatory school for the college he had founded at the same time at Oxford, New College. This view of 1463 shows him surrounded by teachers and students.

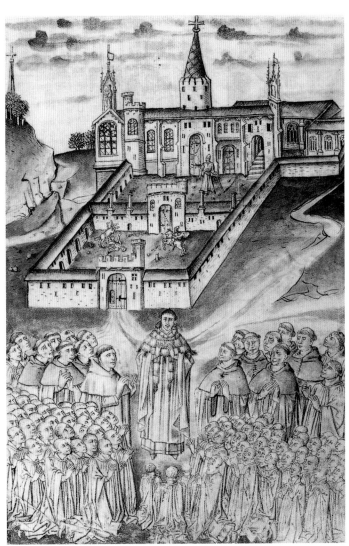

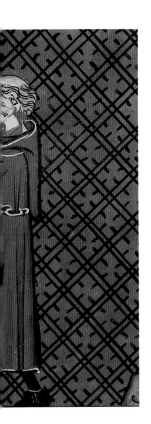

The scholar's world

In the early Middle Ages it had been the monasteries that kept literacy alive, but by the 13th century, in most European countries, groups of teachers had organized themselves into guilds, which grew into universities (7). These remained the main centres of learning, often having to struggle to assert their independence from ecclesiastical control. Mathematics, literature (the Latin classics), science (especially astronomy), medicine and law were all taught, but for most students a university training was the preliminary to a career in the Church, and theology took precedence over everything else. The great achievement of medieval learning was scholasticism, essentially the reconciliation, through tight formal argument, of Aristotelian logic with Christian revelation. Its culmination was St Thomas Aquinas's *Summa Theologica*, an authority which other scholars, such as William of Ockham, challenged at their peril. Universities flourished on the reputation of their teachers (2, 4, 5), men such as Peter Abelard and Albertus Magnus drawing students from all over Europe. At a lower level, most – but not all – primary and secondary education (6) was in the hands of the Church. The enormous cost of books meant that teaching was mostly oral.

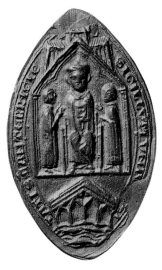

7. The first seal of Cambridge University, 1261, founded in 1209. The chancellor sits between two proctors; below, a bridge over the river Cam.

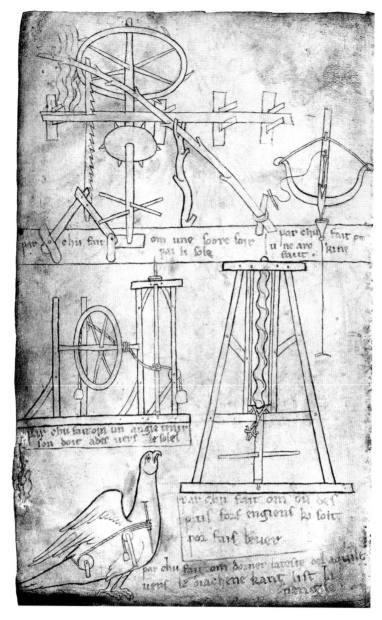

1. Page from the sketch book of Villard de Honnecourt; French, *c.* 1235.

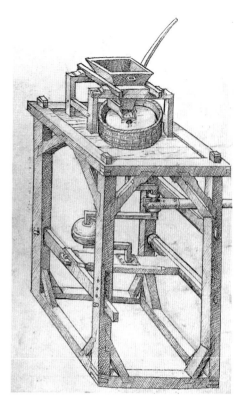

3. Powder-mill containing an ingenious set of gears worked by hand; German, 15th century.

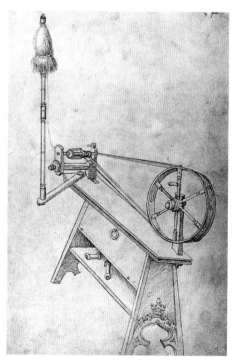

4. Spinning-wheel; German, 15th century.

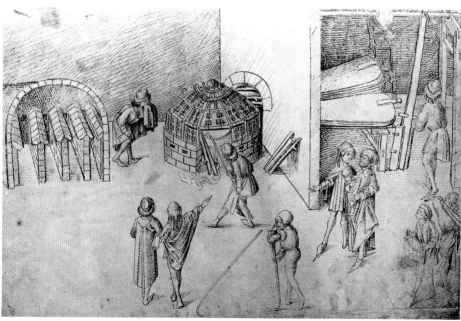

2. Smelting, with a brick-built furnace heated with the aid of two large bellows; German, 15th century.

Tilling the soil 180-181

Printing: the intellectual revolution 270-271

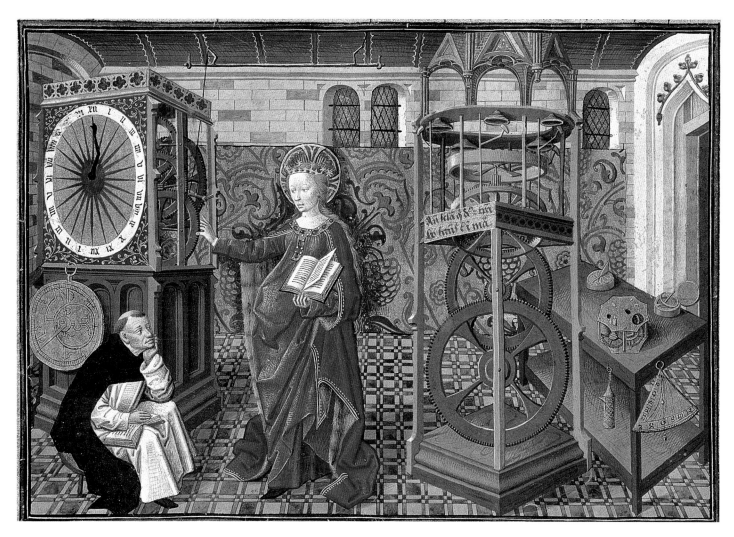

Medieval technology

From the 12th century to the Industrial Revolution there was a steady improvement in mechanical techniques, but no radical breakthrough. This could not happen until new sources of power were discovered. As long as man had to rely on his own strength, on that of animals and on the harnessing of wind and water, opportunities for progress were limited. The single most impressive advance was arguably that in clock-making (5). The earliest weight-driven clocks – highly elaborate machines affordable only by great churches – date from the 14th century. Windmills first appeared in England and France in the 12th century and for 700 years were among the most prominent features of any European landscape, eventually achieving unsurpassed feats of sophisticated carpentry. Streams were channelled into conduits for numerous mills worked by water (6). At a domestic level, thousands of individual spinning-wheels (4) supported the cloth industry before the days of factories. A surprising amount of ingenuity was devoted to what we should call toys. The 13th-century architect Villard de Honnecourt designed an eagle that could 'turn its head to the deacon during the reading of the Gospels' (1, bottom). On the same page he showed a saw worked by water-power, a cross-bow, a machine to make a statue point to the sun and another for lifting heavy weights.

5. An exhibition of 14th-century clocks from a book aimed at 'wakening the torpid from careless sleep to watchful virtue'. The two characters are the Dominican author, Heinrich Suso, and Lady Wisdom. The clocks, from left to right, are: an astrolabe, a clock which chimes the hour by pulling a rope running through the ceiling, a large mechanical clock with five bells and four smaller clocks on a table; French, *c.* 1334.

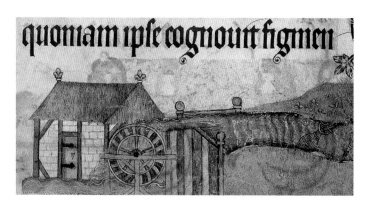

6. Watermill, from the Luttrell Psalter; English, 1370.

The natural world

The idea, once widespread, that it was only with the coming of the Renaissance that men began to enjoy the beauties of nature is demonstrably false. The borders of manuscripts (6), the sketchbooks of artists and the foliage carvings of great churches (4) are full of closely observed animals, birds and plants. Things are complicated, however, by the strong medieval tendency to construct a *schema* for every iconographic motif, and once this was established artists simply copied from each other, sometimes so naturalistically that one can hardly suspect that the picture is not made from life (1). An exception is Matthew Paris's drawing of an elephant (2) which he saw himself after it had been given to Henry III in 1255. Villard de Honnecourt is equally anxious to convince us that he had seen a real lion: 'Here is a lion seen from the front. Please remember that he was drawn from life' (3). But do we believe him? Drawings and carvings of plants (4, 5) are much more likely to have been observed from nature, since their symbolic or heraldic use was minimal.

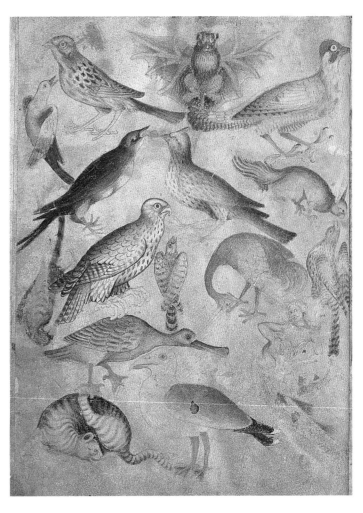

1. Page from an artist's sketchbook of about 1380–1400, showing birds to be used as models in the workshop.

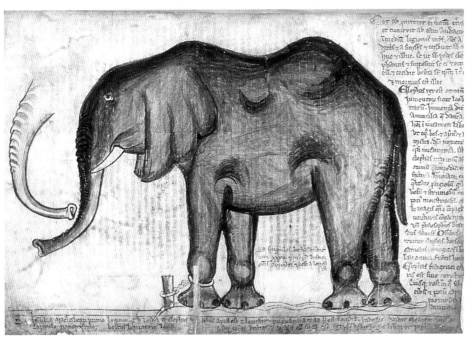

2. Matthew Paris's drawing of an elephant; English, mid-13th century.

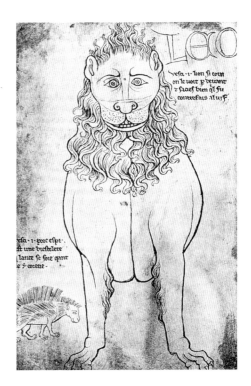

3. 'LEO', from the sketchbook of Villard de Honnecourt; French, *c.* 1235.

Marginal art 156-157   The Bestiaries 220-221

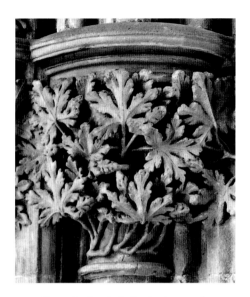

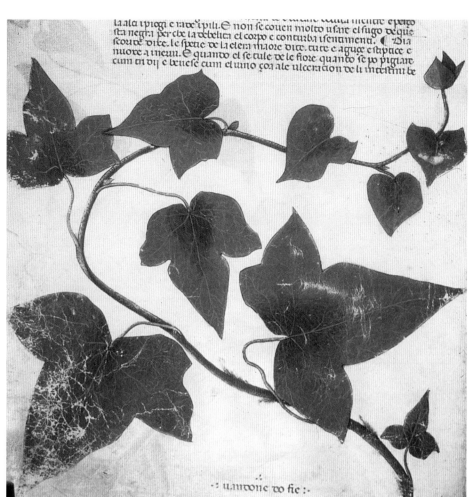

4. Above: leaf capital, chapter-house of Southwell Minster, England, *c.* 1300.

5. Right: Ivy, from an Italian *herborium*, late 14th century.

6. Below: realistic flowers from the hedgerows decorate pages from the Hastings Hours that illustrate the flight of the Holy Family into Egypt; *c.* 1480.

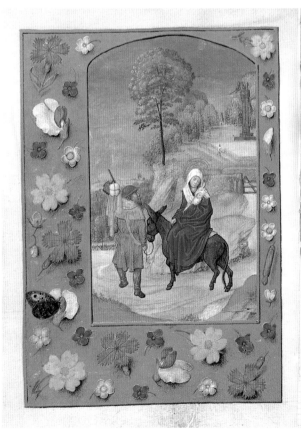

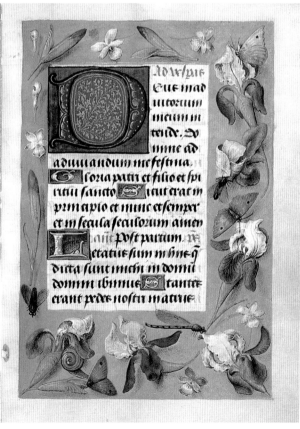

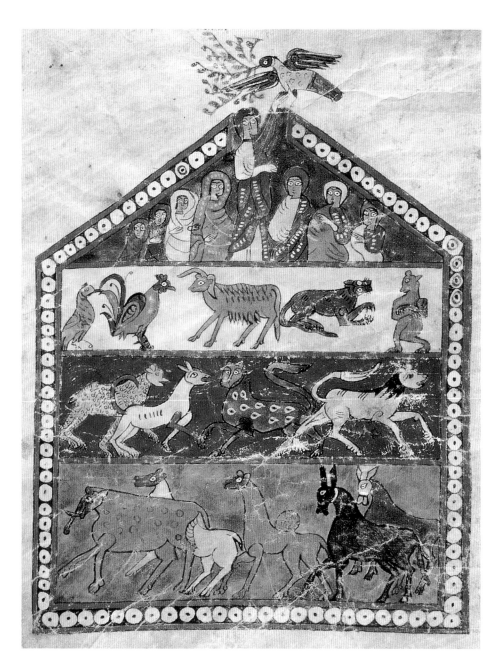

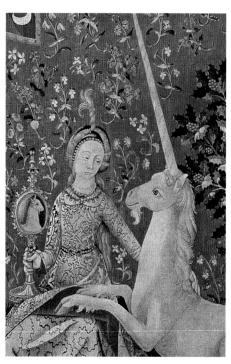

3. 'Our Lord Jesus Christ is the unicorn.' He is betrayed and killed by putting his head in a virgin's lap (the incarnation and crucifixion); French tapestry, 15th century.

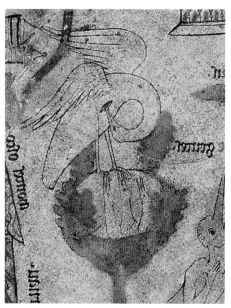

4. The pelican opening its breast to feed its young: an image of Christ. From the Hereford Mappamundi; English, *c.* 1300.

1. One of the earliest mentions of animals and birds in the Bible, Noah's Ark, shows a concern for their survival and endows one of them with its first symbolic associations: the dove of peace. Illustration from Beatus' Commentary on the Apocalypse; Spanish, 970.

2. The phoenix immolated itself on a pyre but rose from its ashes after three days. 'The phoenix signifies Jesus, who had the power to die of his own will, and from death came to life.' North German, 1504.

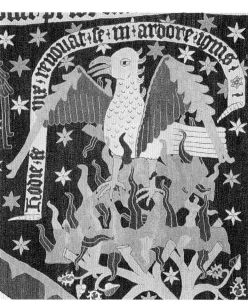

The natural world 218-219

Beyond the known world 256-257

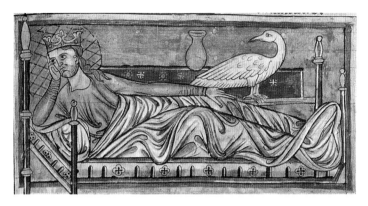

5. The caladrius is a strange bird used to prognosticate the course of an illness. 'If it looks towards the patient he will get well; if it looks away he will die. It lives in kings' houses.' 'Caladrius is like Our Saviour. Our Lord from heaven turns his face from the Jews because of their unbelief, but turns towards the people of our own sort, bearing our infirmities and taking away our sins.' English, 13th century.

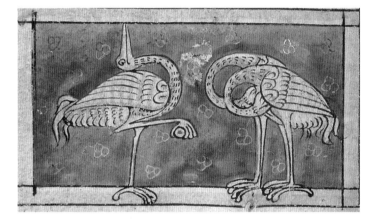

6. Cranes on sentry duty keep themselves awake by holding a stone in their claw; if they fall asleep the stone drops. The bird on the right is asleep with its head buried in its feathers; English, 13th century.

The Bestiaries

Books describing the behaviour of animals had been popular since Antiquity, Aesop's *Fables* being the best known. Medieval writers often gave these stories a new and wholly characteristic twist by bringing animals into the moral world and finding in them God's lessons for the salvation of mankind. Everything must have a meaning. Sometimes the behaviour that suggests such interpretations is observed from nature – e.g. the coot stays in one place and does not wander, just as the faithful 'always keep together and rest in the Catholic church' – and to that extent the Bestiaries are genuine works of natural history; but at others it is wholly fabulous – e.g. the pelican (4), which was supposed to restore its young to life with its own blood, a parallel to Christ's sacrifice. The first Bestiaries were compiled in Greek between the 2nd and 5th centuries AD by an anonymous writer who was given the name of Physiologus. Throughout the Middle Ages it was copied and expanded. Over forty copies exist, most of them illustrated.

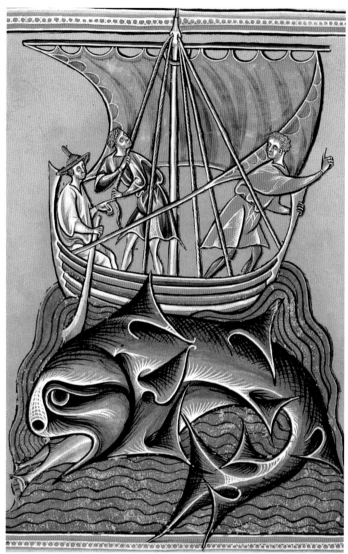

7. The whale floats on its back and unsuspecting sailors, mistaking it for an island, land on it, and it then plunges down with them into the sea. 'So people ignorant of the wiles of the Devil anchor themselves to him and down they go into the fires of Hell.' English, *c.* 1210.

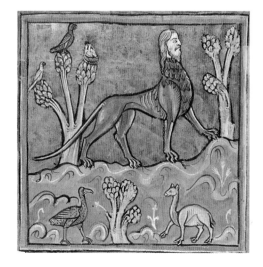

8. 'The manticora has the face of a man and a lion's body. It hankers after human flesh most ravenously.' English, *c.* 1230.

A new literature

Although the Latin classics were still studied, admired and enjoyed, the literature that arose in the new vernacular languages owed surprisingly little to their example. The first to produce a work of significance was English. The date of *Beowulf* is disputed, but seems likely to be before the 10th century, and *Beowulf* was not alone. The Norman Conquest was a setback, but by the 14th century English could boast a galaxy of talents including Langland, the *Gawain* poet and Chaucer (6). French came of age with the *Chanson de Roland* (c. 1100), Spanish with *El Cid* (c. 1140) and German with the *Nibelungenlied* (late 12th century). Italy was slower to find an individual voice, but in Dante's *Divine Comedy* (4) of the early 14th century it produced the supreme masterpiece of medieval civilization, uniting cosmology with religion, politics and human character in poetry of mystical beauty. These centuries also saw the beginning of a whole range of literary genres that were to be developed in the Renaissance and later – lyric poetry, often written to be sung (3), the short story (5), the exemplary narrative and the romance. Women were not excluded (1), though much depended on social position and patronage (2).

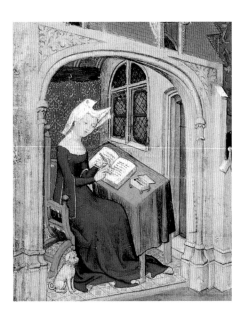

1. Christine de Pisan, a prolific writer of proto-feminist polemic; French, 1410–15.

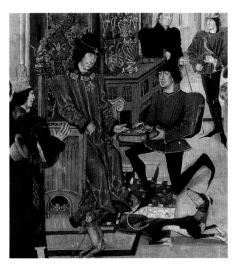

2. Vasco de Lucera presenting a book to Charles the Bold, Duke of Burgundy; French, 15th century.

3. Lyrics to be sung to the music of Guillaume Machaut; French, 14th century.

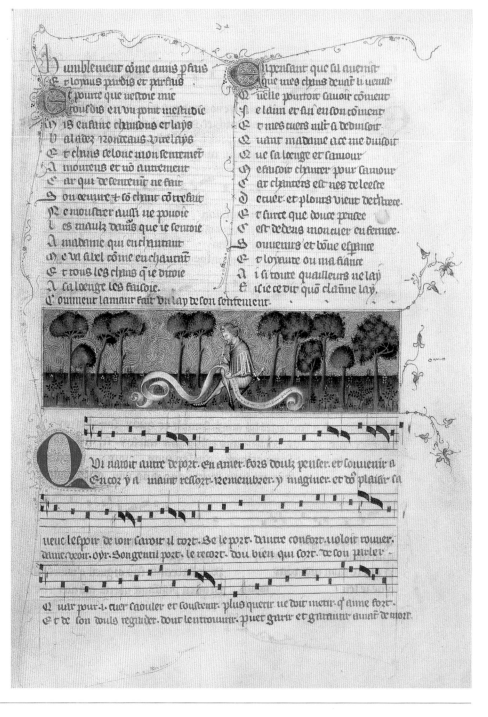

222

Reading the classics 34-35   Arthurian romance 226-227

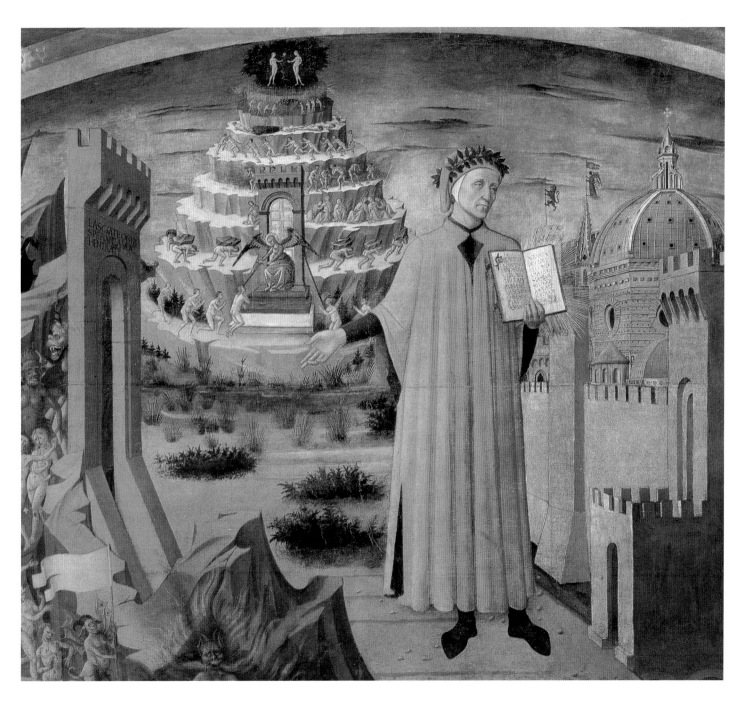

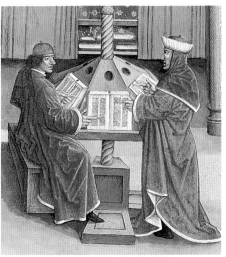

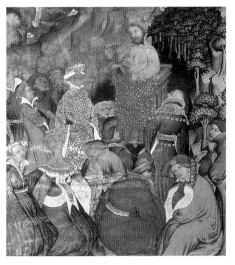

4. Dante Alighieri holding a book in which the opening lines of the *Divine Comedy* are written. To the left is the descent into Hell, the mountain of Purgatory, with, at the top, Paradise – the three books of the poem. On the right Dante's native city of Florence. Fresco in Florence Cathedral, 1465.

5. Petrarch and Boccaccio, masters of the Italian lyric and the short story, together in a study; Flemish, 15th century.

6. Geoffrey Chaucer reading to a noble audience: frontispiece to his long, psychologically probing poem of love, jealousy and betrayal, *Troilus and Criseyde*; English, 15th century.

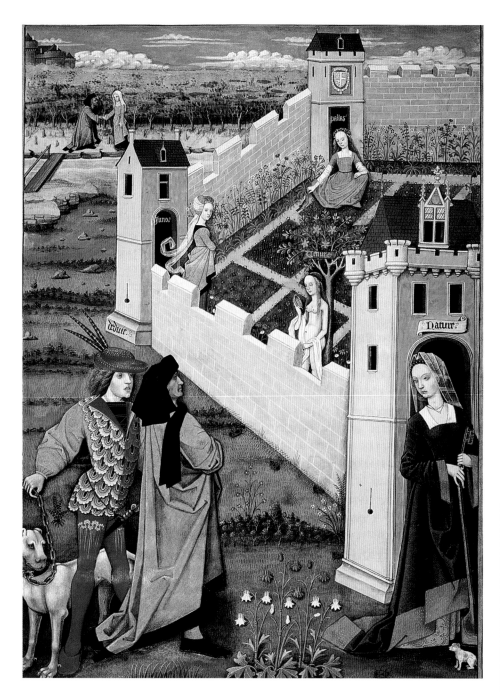

1. The Garden kept by Nature, inhabited by the three goddesses Venus, Juno and Pallas Athene. From the French poem *Les Echecs Amoureux*, 15th century.

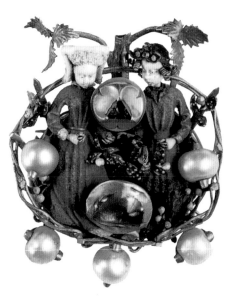

2. Lover's brooch; Burgundian, first half of the 15th century.

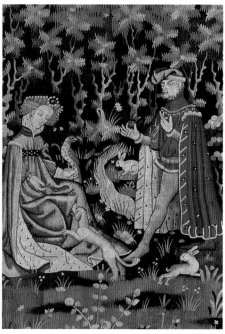

3. The lover offers his heart to the lady; French or Flemish tapestry, *c.* 1400.

Courtly love: sex and sublimation

The idea of courtly love, in which woman becomes an 'ideal', inspiring the lover to virtue, chivalry and courage (5), can be seen as a sort of secular equivalent of the cult of the Virgin. It was essentially a literary and poetic convention, though there are instances of its being acted out in real life, and its apogee is reached in the figure of Dante's Beatrice, a real woman, but transformed by the poet into a semi-divine intercessor (7). The element of sexual attraction is never absent, but the lover's aspiration is service, not possession. In stylized poetry and romance, this quest assumes a variety of allegorical forms featuring hearts (3), castles (6), jousts and enclosed gardens (1).

The order of knighthood 108-109

Tournaments: playing at war 116-117

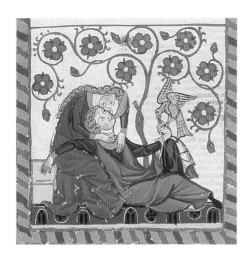

4. Lovers in a garden, from the German Manesse Codex, *c.* 1300.

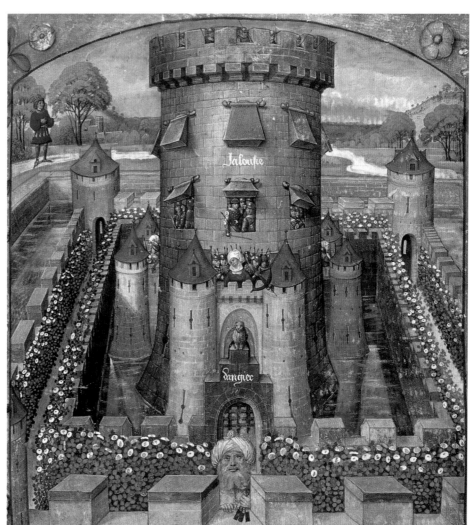

6. The Castle of Jealousy, from the *Roman de la Rose*; Bruges, *c.* 1490.

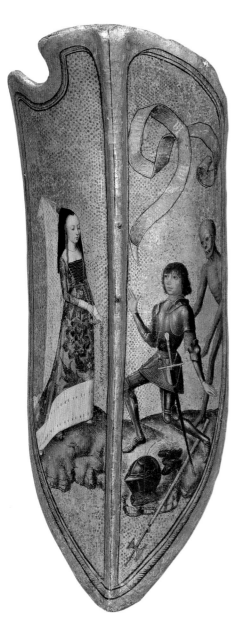

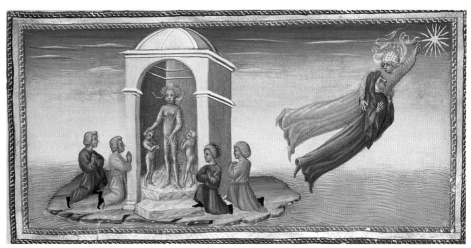

7. Giovanni di Paolo: illustration to Dante's 'Paradiso', Canto VIII, *c.* 1445. On the right Beatrice leads Dante to the next circle of Paradise; on the left is Venus, whom men once worshipped 'in their ancient error'.

5. A parade shield, with the knight kneeling before his lady and a skeleton behind him and the motto 'You or death'; Burgundian, 15th century.

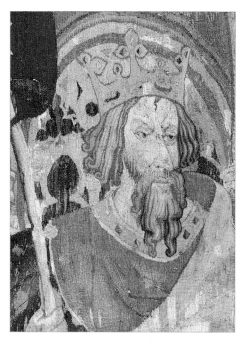

1. King Arthur, portrayed (along with Charlemagne and Godfrey of Bouillon) as one of the Nine Worthies in a French tapestry of about 1385.

Arthurian romance

The code of courtly love found its literary vehicle in the romance, a form invented and perfected in the Middle Ages. The romance in its turn found its perfect vehicle in the myth of King Arthur. Arthur himself had some historical foundation, but his legendary court became a means of expressing many facets of medieval idealism – ideals of kingship (1), ideals of knighthood (2), ideals of mystical Christianity, ideals of the relations between the sexes. After the late 12th century it became a highly elaborate, virtually self-contained world of its own, made up of contributions by many authors – largely anonymous – in many countries, including Geoffrey of Monmouth, Chrétien de Troyes, Robert de Boron, Wolfram von Eschenbach, Sir Thomas Malory . . . and Edmund Spenser. At a popular level the Arthurian cycle could be read as an adventure story involving love (4), infidelity, betrayal and death (6); at another it was a Christian allegory, the Grail being Christ's body in the Eucharist and the Round Table the Last Supper (5).

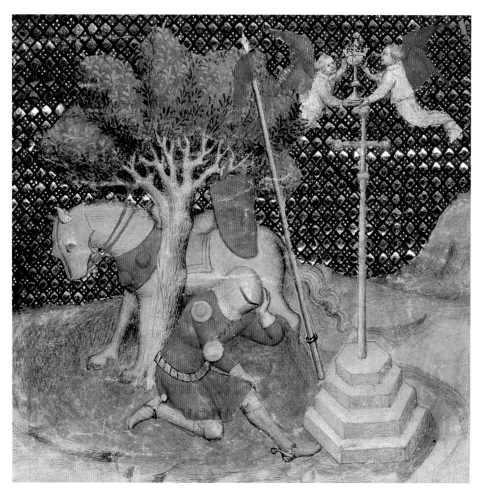

2. Lancelot dedicated himself to the quest for the Holy Grail, held before him in a vision by angels, but was diverted from it by his love for Guinevere; French, 15th century.

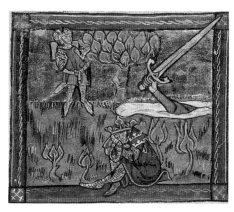

3. Arthur's sword Excalibur is received back by the mysterious hand rising from the waters of the lake. Arthur sits dying on the bank. French, 14th century.

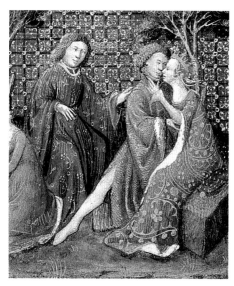

4. Lancelot's first guilty assignation with Arthur's unfaithful queen Guinevere; French, c. 1405.

The order of knighthood
108-109

Courtly love: sex and
sublimation 224-225

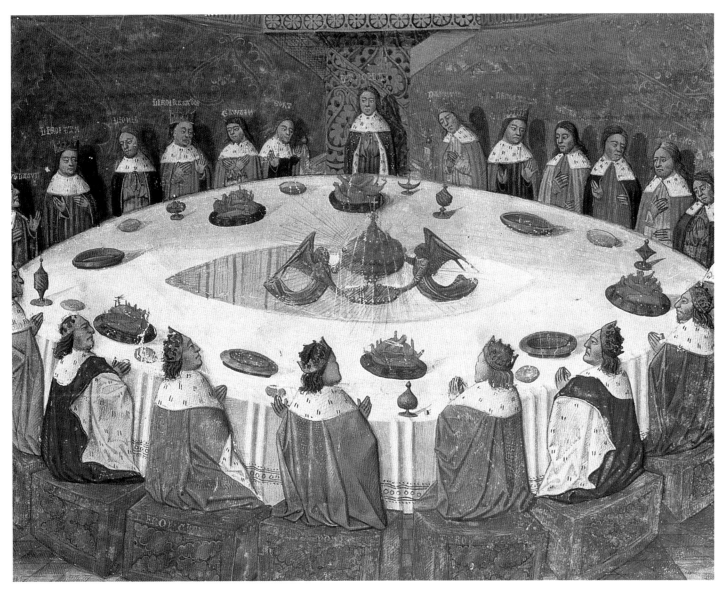

5. The Round Table and the vision of the Holy Grail on Whit Sunday. The names of the knights are inscribed above them or on their chairs. Here Lancelot presides instead of the king. The table recalls both the table of the Last Supper and the Cosmos itself. French, 15th century.

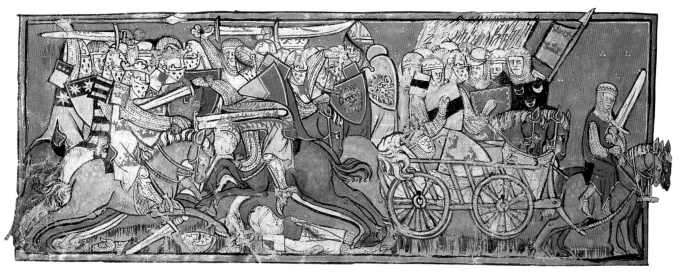

6. The battle between Arthur and the traitor Mordred, Arthur's illegitimate and incestuously conceived son. On the battlefield of Salisbury Plain both are killed. Here the dying Arthur is borne away on a cart. Flemish, 14th century.

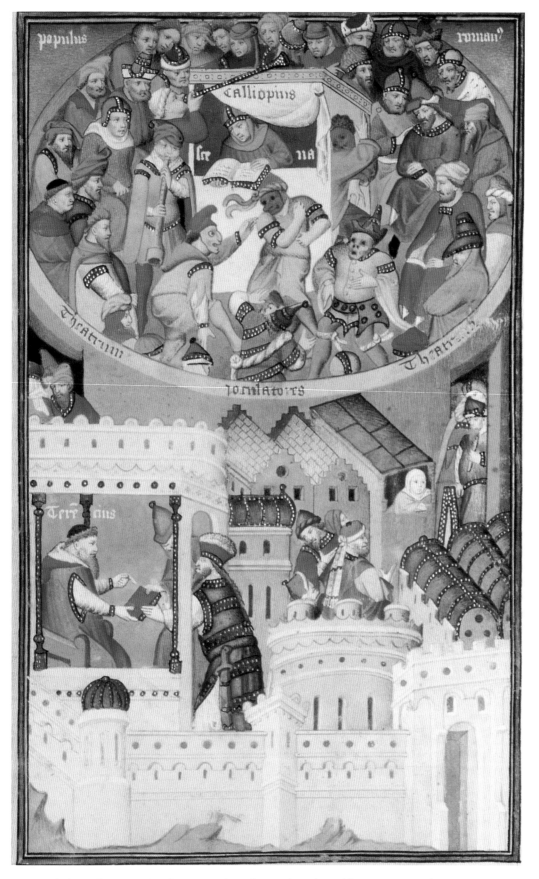

1. Frontispiece of a manuscript of Terence's plays, showing how the Middle Ages imagined classical drama. Within an amphitheatre masked actors mime the action while 'Calliopius' reads the script from a booth labelled 'scena'. The audience, 'Populus Romanus' is at the back. In the foreground Terence is being presented with – or presenting – a book. French, *c.* 1400.

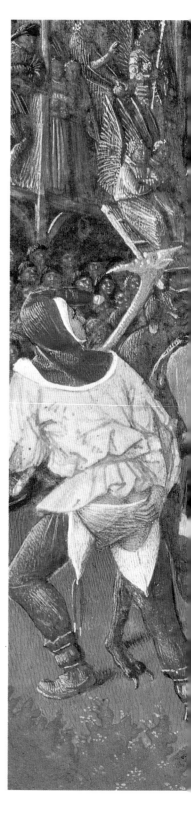

Medieval theatre

2. *The Martyrdom of St Apollonia* by Jean Fouquet, *c.* 1460.

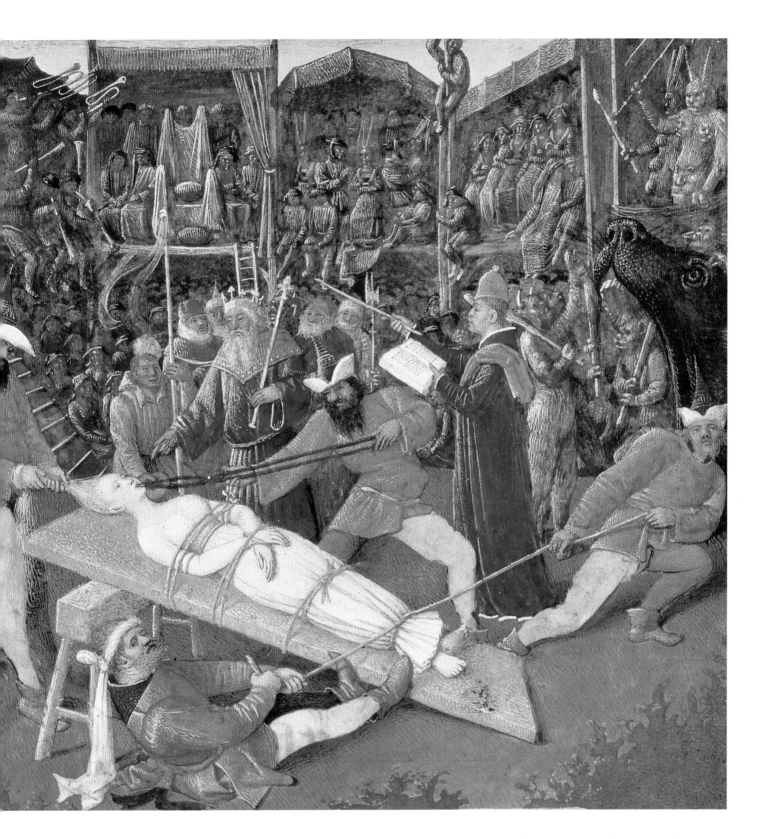

Drama was another art-form that had to be re-invented. Classical Latin plays by Seneca, Plautus and Terence were read during the Middle Ages, but the tradition of performance was lost (1). The new drama began in churches, where the episode of the Three Marys coming to the sepulchre was acted. This gradually expanded to cycles of short plays in the vernacular telling the whole Biblical story performed on Corpus Christi day by the trade guilds, and later to plays based on saints' lives. Our most detailed record is of the 15th-century *Martyrdom of St Apollonia* (2). The main action is the torture of the saint in the centre, directed by a crowned emperor (Decius): the man with the book and wand is the producer. At the back are six scaffolds holding, from left to right: Heaven, with God enthroned with angels; an orchestra of musicians; an empty throne (from which the emperor has descended); upper-class spectators; bourgeois spectators; and Satan with Hell-mouth.

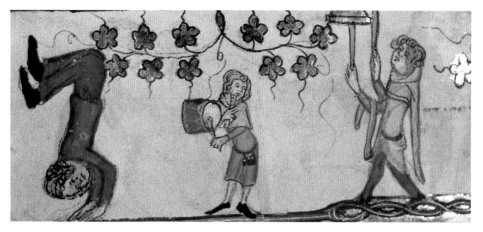

1. Dancers wearing traditional fools' costume; Flemish, c. 1340.

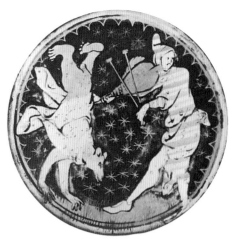

2. Musician with a dancing bear; a painting on glass from the abbey of Jumièges. French, c. 1350.

Mimes, minstrels and jongleurs

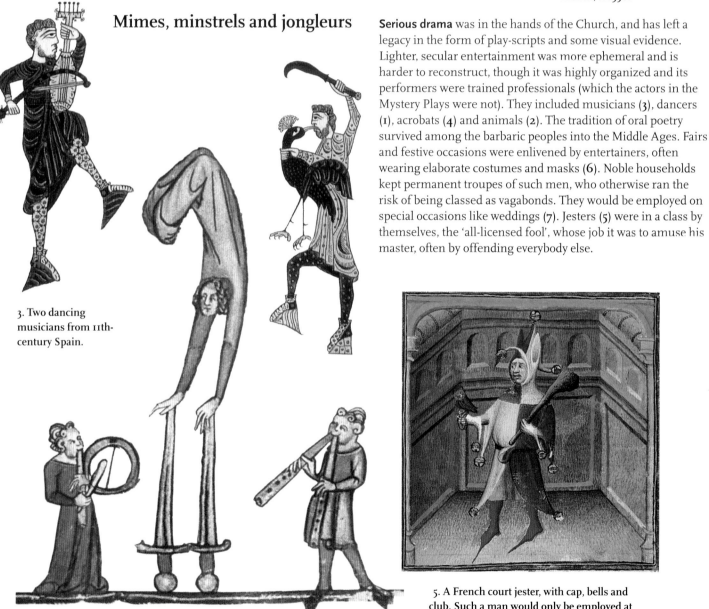

3. Two dancing musicians from 11th-century Spain.

4. An acrobat performing what seems a particularly risky routine, a handstand on the points of two swords; English, 14th century.

Serious drama was in the hands of the Church, and has left a legacy in the form of play-scripts and some visual evidence. Lighter, secular entertainment was more ephemeral and is harder to reconstruct, though it was highly organized and its performers were trained professionals (which the actors in the Mystery Plays were not). They included musicians (**3**), dancers (**1**), acrobats (**4**) and animals (**2**). The tradition of oral poetry survived among the barbaric peoples into the Middle Ages. Fairs and festive occasions were enlivened by entertainers, often wearing elaborate costumes and masks (**6**). Noble households kept permanent troupes of such men, who otherwise ran the risk of being classed as vagabonds. They would be employed on special occasions like weddings (**7**). Jesters (**5**) were in a class by themselves, the 'all-licensed fool', whose job it was to amuse his master, often by offending everybody else.

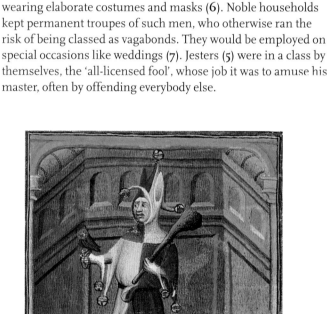

5. A French court jester, with cap, bells and club. Such a man would only be employed at a royal or noble court. French, 1411.

Tournaments: playing at war 116-117

Medieval theatre 228-229

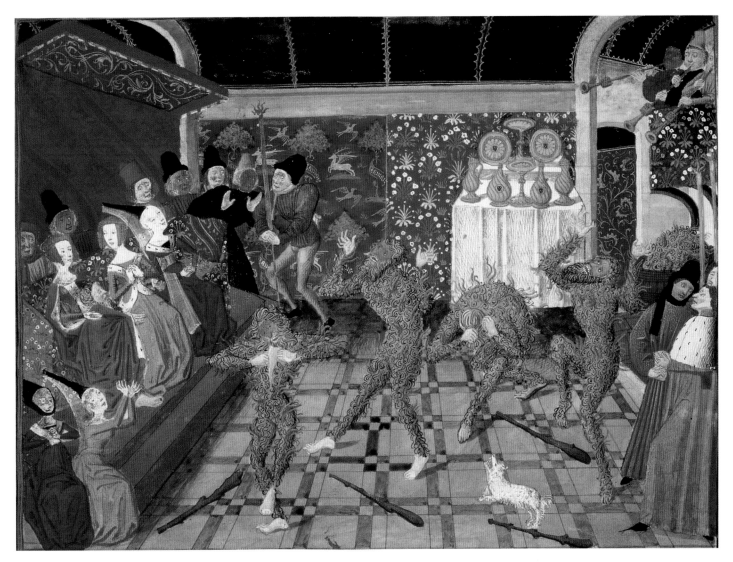

6. French court entertainment in the 15th century. A company of actors play wild men or 'woodwoses' before a distinguished audience of lords and ladies, but to the consternation of the little dog.

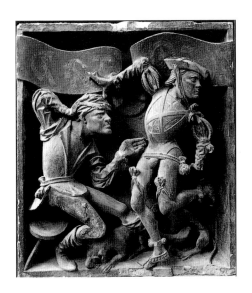

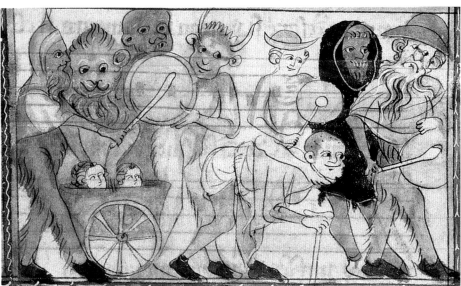

8. 'Charivaris' were boisterous entertainments involving dance, disguise, fantastic costumes, masks and general buffoonery, which sometimes got out of hand. French, 14th century.

7. A series of reliefs survive at Innsbruck commemorating the festivities at the wedding of the Emperor Maximilian I to Bianca Maria Sforza in 1494. The 'Marushka', being performed here, was a fashionable dance from Moorish Spain.

7

Christians and Non-Christians

THE CATHOLIC CHRISTIANS of Western and Central Europe were bordered not only by the Orthodox Christians of Byzantium and Eastern Europe but also by non-Christians. There were pagans in the Baltic region until the conversion of Lithuania in 1386, while in the Mediterranean basin Christians encountered the world of Islam – huge, rich, sophisticated and learned. The violent extension of the Christian frontier with Islam and the simultaneous borrowing by the Christians of Arabic scholarship are two of the most important themes of medieval history.

It was in the Iberian peninsula that Christian and Muslim were most deeply entwined. After their invasion of 711 the Muslims occupied most of the peninsula, leaving a tiny foothold to the Christians in the north. From the eighth century to the eleventh Muslim Spain was dominated by the Caliphate (originally Emirate) of Cordoba, an independent state that was wealthier and more refined than any of its Christian neighbours; its capital, Cordoba, was the largest city in Western Europe. Even after the collapse of the Caliphate in the eleventh century, Muslim Spain continued to be a society of great cultural creativity. Both Averroes (Ibn Rushd) (1126–98), one of the most important of medieval Islamic philosophers, and his slightly younger contemporary, Maimonides (Moses ben Maimon) (1135–1204), arguably the most important medieval Jewish philosopher, were born in Cordoba.

In the years following the disintegration of the Caliphate, the Iberian peninsula was politically fragmented. In the south and east were many small Muslim states, while the north was divided between the Christian kingdoms of Leon, Castile, Navarre and Aragon, along with the various counties that made up Catalonia. Alliances, hostilities and temporary unions succeeded each other in confusing complexity. Muslims fought Muslims and Christians Christians just as often as the adherents of the two rival religions clashed. El Cid (Rodrigo Díaz de Vivar, d. 1099), Spain's most famous medieval epic hero, was actually in the service of the Muslim king of Zaragoza for many years. Slowly, however, patterns of confrontation hardened. The Christian kings began to annex Muslim territory. In 1085 one of the most important cities of central Spain, Toledo, was conquered by Alfonso VI of Castile and Leon. He had difficulty holding onto it but he did.

In the four centuries between the fall of Toledo and the conquest of Granada in 1492 by the 'Catholic Kings' (Ferdinand of Aragon and Isabella of Castile), the Christians gradually extended their political control over the whole of the Iberian peninsula. The process was not swift or simple. Revivalist Islamic movements, the Almoravids (Murabids) and Almohads (Muwahhids) of the eleventh and twelfth centuries, swept into Spain from Morocco, re-establishing Islamic political unity and fervour for holy war. Yet slowly the frontier moved southwards. Zaragoza fell to the Christians in 1118, Lisbon in 1147. The victory of Las Navas de Tolosa in 1212 opened a particularly dramatic period of Christian reconquest, with the big cities of the south, like Valencia, Cordoba and Seville, coming under Christian rule. By the 1260s only the far south of Spain, around Granada, remained in Muslim hands.

As a consequence of the Reconquest the Iberian peninsula was one of the few parts of Catholic Europe where large numbers of people of different religions – Muslims, Christians and also Jews – lived in close proximity. It was a society

In spite of the ideological divide, medieval Spain and Portugal could not help being deeply influenced by Moorish culture. This 15th-century earthenware bowl is clearly in the Islamic tradition, the design perfectly adapted to the shape and the material. The boat, however, bears the arms of Portugal on the sail.

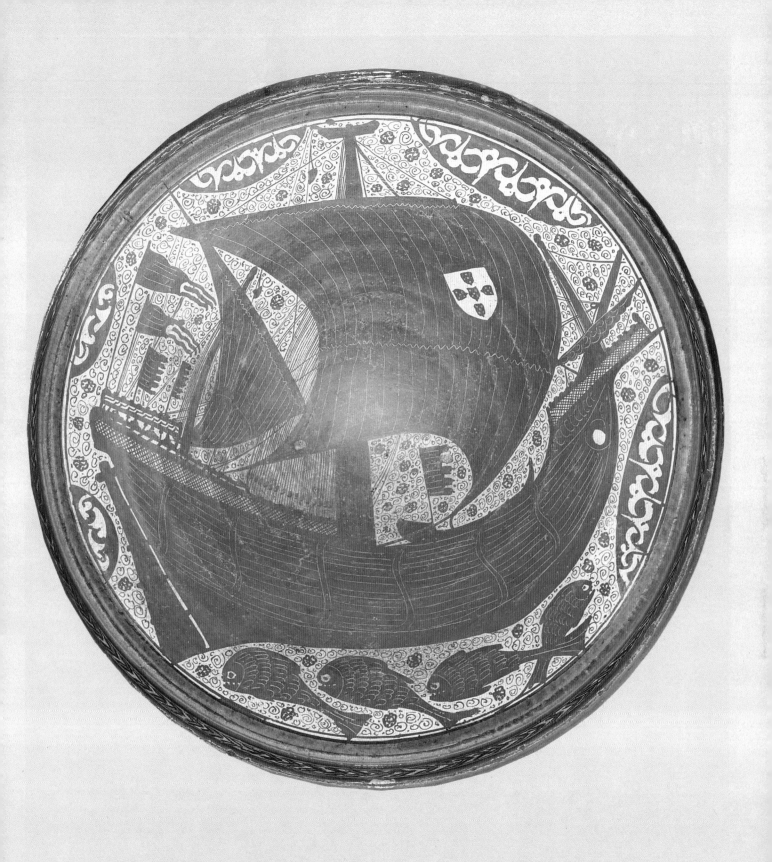

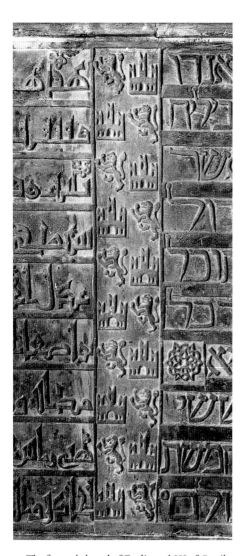

The funeral chapel of Ferdinand III of Castile in Seville Cathedral bears inscriptions not only in Latin and Castilian but also (seen here) in Arabic and Hebrew (separated by a band of lions and castles, standing for León and Castile): an expressive symbol of a multi-cultural society.

dominated by Christians – all the main mosques were converted into churches and the non-Christian population suffered various kinds of discrimination – but the long-term co-existence of followers of Islam and Christianity was assumed. Mutual linguistic and artistic influence took place, making the culture, cuisine and costume of Spain and Portugal distinctive in Western Europe. It is symbolic that the tomb of Ferdinand III of Castile, conqueror of Cordoba and Seville, bears inscriptions not only in Latin and Castilian but also in Hebrew and Arabic.

While the first stages of the Reconquest were taking place in the Iberian peninsula, another, much more unexpected, Christian conquest at the expense of Islam occurred. In 1096–99 several huge armies of Western knights and foot-soldiers marched, via Constantinople and Antioch, to the Holy Land, storming Jerusalem on 15 July 1099. The impulse to this astonishing expedition was a speech made by Pope Urban II on 27 November 1095, in a field near Clermont in France. Here he called on the knights of France to 'take the road to the Holy Sepulchre' with the sign of the cross on their chests. Stirring them up with stories of the atrocities committed by Muslims against Christians, he also promised that those who participated in the expedition would be freed from the burden of their sins. The response was spectacular. Enthusiasm for the enterprise swept across Western Europe and sustained the first crusaders through drought, disease and warfare until they attained their goal.

Many of the participants in the First Crusade returned home at its conclusion but others stayed, creating a series of states along the eastern Mediterranean coast. These territories, ruled by Catholics but with a majority population of eastern Christians, Muslims or Jews, survived precariously for almost 200 years and their defence was viewed as the common duty of Christendom. Western rulers, like Richard the Lionheart of England and St Louis of France, spent years in the East, trying to secure the defence of this vulnerable Christian bridgehead against Muslim counter-attacks. A colonial society grew up, with immigrants coming from Western Europe settling among the native populations. The towns were dominated by an aristocracy of French descent and by Italian merchants from the great trading cities of Venice, Genoa and Pisa. The city of Jerusalem itself was recaptured by the Muslim leader Saladin (Salah al-Din) in 1187 and was thereafter never more than briefly in Christian hands, but the sea-port of Acre served as the main city and capital of the Kingdom of Jerusalem until its end in 1291.

The crusading movement had an important impact not only on the Middle East but also in Western Europe, where it had first ignited. The harnessing of resources to support 'Outremer', the 'land across the sea', left its mark. Income tax was invented as a crusade tax. Successive generations of aristocrats went out to die in the East. New institutions arose, notably the Crusading Orders, chief among them the Hospitallers and Templars, who combined the celibacy and poverty of monks with the bellicosity of knights. Their cutting edge was in the Holy Land, but they had a vast root system of property and patrons throughout Western Europe. Moreover, crusades, once invented, proved a versatile tool. The wars between Christian and Muslim in the Iberian peninsula, already in progress long before 1095, were redefined as crusades. One of the Crusading Orders, the Teutonic Knights, launched holy war against the pagans of the Baltic region and created a major state in Prussia and Livonia (modern Latvia and Estonia) that lasted until the Reformation. Crusades could be turned against heretics, political opponents of the papacy or rebellious peasants.

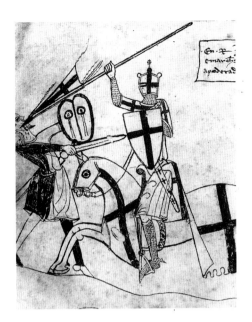

Crusader versus Saracen, a Spanish drawing of the 13th century. Outside Spain, the Crusades represented the major point of contact between the Christian and Islamic worlds.

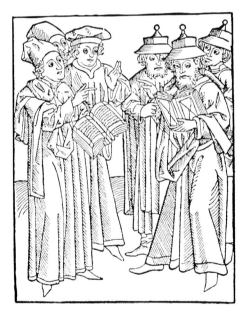

There was a genuine desire among many Christians to understand the Jewish point of view and by such understanding to convert them to Christianity. But medieval 'disputations' between Christians and Jews produced no tangible results, mainly because it was the Christians who made the rules.

In the very same centuries that the crusading movement brought an increased ferocity to Christian-Muslim relations, the scholars of the Catholic world became fascinated by Arabic learning and sought to incorporate it into their own culture. In science, mathematics and medicine Islamic scholarship was far superior to that of the West, partly because the Muslims had access to many writings of the ancient Greeks, which the West did not, partly because there was a long indigenous tradition of learning, with famous centres from Persia to Spain. In the eleventh, twelfth and thirteenth centuries, large numbers of Arabic scholarly works and Greek works in Arabic versions were translated into Latin, making them accessible to Westerners. By the middle of the thirteenth century the standard arts syllabus at European universities consisted largely of these newly translated texts. Traces of this debt to the Muslim world can be found in our reference to 'Arabic numerals' and to the tell-tale scientific words beginning with the Arabic word 'al' ('the'): algebra, alkaline, alchemy, alcohol and star names such as Aldebaran.

Muslims were not the only non-Christians whom Catholics encountered. Since the birth of the Church, from a Jewish womb, Jews and Christians had negotiated an uneasy relationship. In most parts of Europe Jews were the only legally tolerated religious minority. They had synagogues in the important towns, and in some regions, like the south of France, might be relatively numerous. Their situation was, however, precarious. The series of papal injunctions issued against mistreatment of the Jews makes this clear. There was to be no compulsory baptism of Jews, no extra-judicial violence against them and no extra-judicial deprivation of property; they should not be forced to change their approved customs; there were to be no attacks on them with sticks and stones during their holy days; they were not to be subject to forced labour; their cemeteries should not be desecrated; no one should dig up their dead to look for money. When rules of this kind are necessary, plainly someone is doing the forbidden things.

Popes and leading churchmen held that Jews were wrong-headed and should be subject to Christians but that they should be tolerated and their worship allowed. Kings and princes were normally willing to protect them for a price. Anti-semitism was, however, widespread in medieval society and seems to have become more violent over the course of time. The First Crusade of 1095–99 stimulated a series of pogroms in the Rhineland towns and subsequent crusades usually resulted in similar outbursts. In the twelfth and thirteenth centuries new slanders were born: Jews sacrificed a Christian child at Passover, they stole the consecrated host and stabbed it with knives. In the following century the Jews were blamed for the outbreak of the Black Death. Pogroms and expulsions continued periodically. In 1492 all Jews were expelled from Spain, where they had formed one of the largest, wealthiest and most learned communities in Europe. Medieval Europe had not begun as a tolerant society and it seems to have become less so.

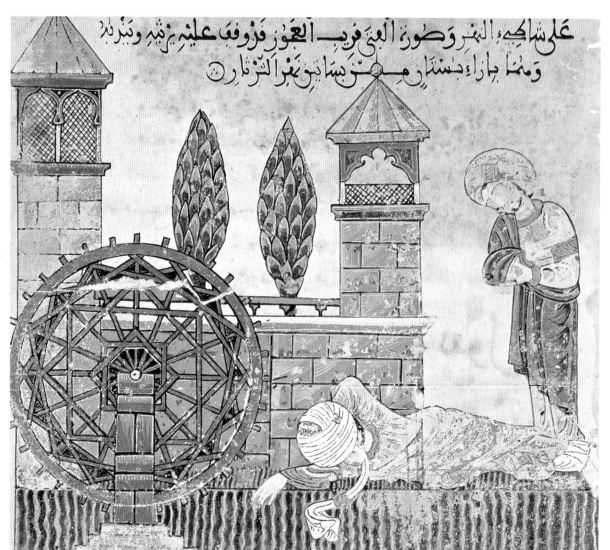

على شاطيء النهر وصورة البني فريه العبور فروقف عليه زنته وتبيرده
ومما باراء بستار من بستاين نفر الزنار

1. An episode from the tragic love-story of Bayad and Riyad. The lover faints on hearing bad news; Spanish or Moroccan, 13th century.

The vanished world of Moorish Spain

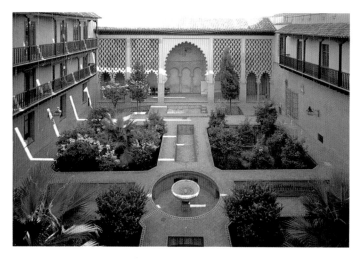

2. A 12th-century Moorish garden in Seville, the Crucero. The raised paths, sunken beds and arcaded galleries are typical of the gardens of Islam.

In Spain, medieval Christendom came into close contact with a civilization that was ideologically anathema but culturally could only be admired. Unlike Christendom, also, it was exceptionally tolerant, virtually the only place in the world where Christians, Muslims and Jews could (normally) live peacefully together without fear. Even the Muslim population was mixed. Arabs were in a minority; most of the population were Berbers from North Africa. It was always, therefore, an unusually diverse society, in many ways untypical of the rest of the Muslim world, from which, indeed, it became increasingly cut off. Politically, too, its history is one of disunity and internal conflict. All the more remarkable, therefore, is its cultural consistency. Here ideas were exchanged and discussed, art, poetry (1) and music cultivated and an architectural setting evolved which brought gardens (2) and buildings into a unity unimagined in the North. Later ages would look back on it as a lost paradise. The Alhambra (3) in Granada, was the last – and is still most perfect – of Moorish palaces, built when the rest of the country was already in Christian hands. Spain never truly renounced its medieval Moorish heritage, whether in architecture, in music, in dance or in cookery.

The rise of Islam 48-49

Reconquest: the end of Muslim Spain 242-243

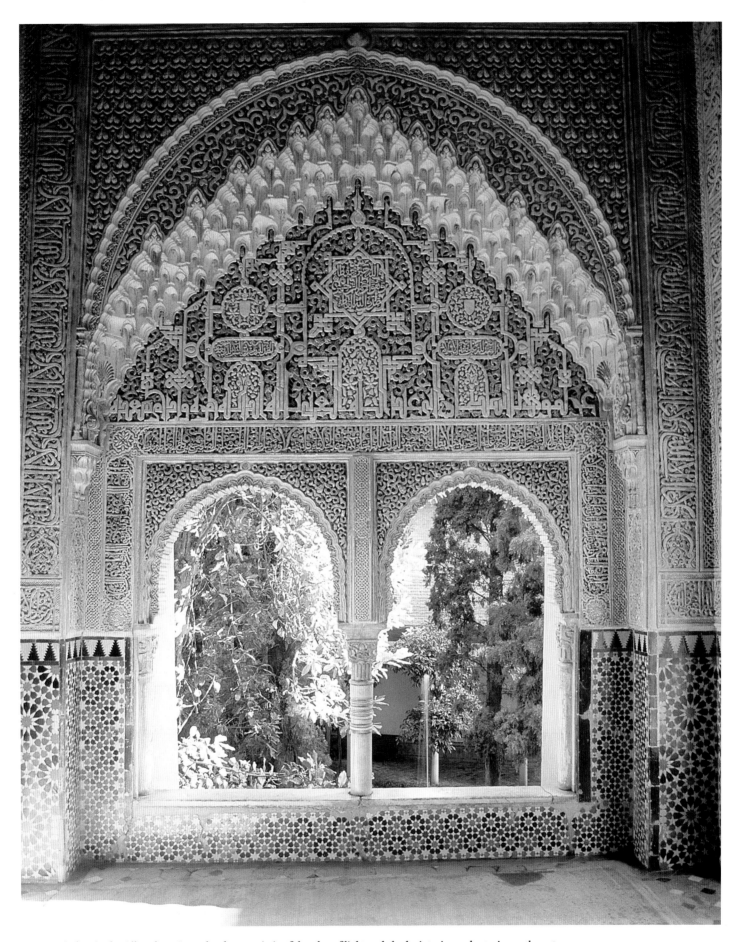

3. A window in the Alhambra, Granada, characteristic of the play of light and shade, interior and exterior; 14th century.

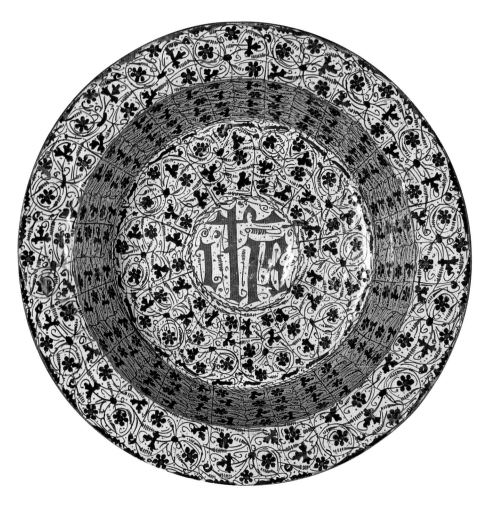

1. Lustre-ware dish made in the Hispano-Moresque style, probably by Moorish craftsmen but with the monogram of Christ, IHS, in the centre; mid-15th century.

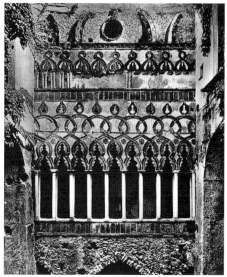

2. Ravello, Italy: the Moorish courtyard of the Villa Rufolo, 11th century.

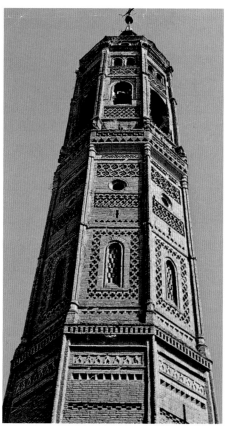

3. The ornate brick tower of S. Andres, Calatayud, Spain, built by Moorish workmen or by Christians trained in that tradition.

Cultural cross-currents

During the long centuries of Muslim occupation the Christians of Spain could not avoid learning from their more advanced neighbours. Their intellectual debt is examined overleaf. More vivid is the Islamic influence that comes across in architecture and decoration. This continued even after the Reconquest, when Moorish workmen created works of Muslim art for Christians (the Alcazar at Seville) and Jews (the Synagogue of Toledo). The style also made its way into French and Italian Romanesque (2) and to that great meeting-place of cultures, Palermo, Sicily (5). In the case of Christians absorbing aspects of Islamic art (Mozarabic) the motifs are isolated, e.g. the horseshoe arch (4), but men and animals are still represented, something prohibited by Islamic law. In the case of Moorish artists working for Christians (Mudéjar) the result is purely abstract (1, 3, 8). Influence in the opposite direction is inevitably rare, but the decoration of the Alhambra included illustrations of Christian tales of chivalry.

The vanished world of Moorish Spain 236-237

Learning from Islam 240-241

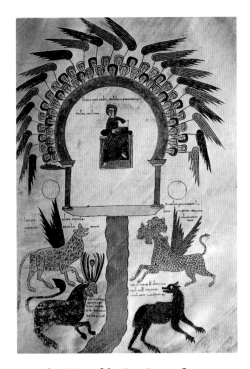

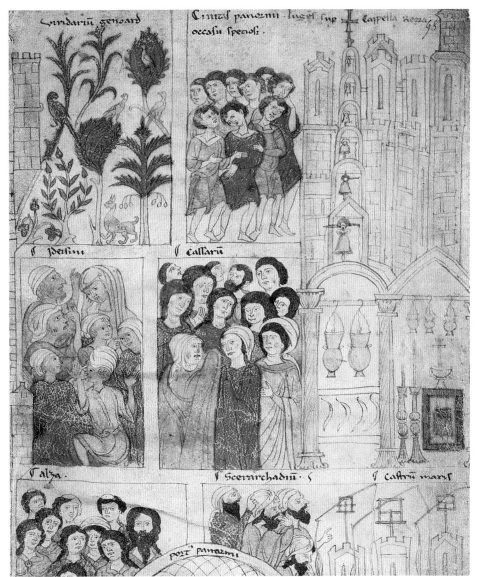

4. The Vision of the Four Beasts, from a manuscript of Beatus' Commentary on the Apocalypse. Totally Christian in inspiration, its horseshoe arch is evidence of Muslim influence; Spanish, 11th century.

5. The imperial court at Palermo, showing the Palatine chapel and the various peoples who lived in different quarters of the city; Italian, 1195.

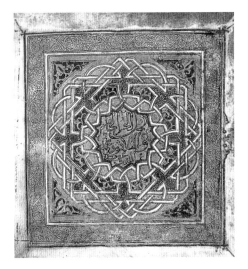

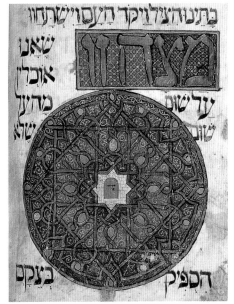

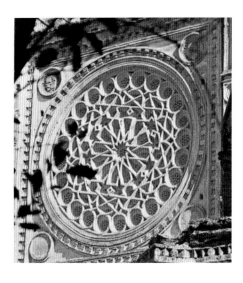

6, 7, 8. Islamic interlace patterns cross cultural boundaries. Above: page from a Muslim Koran, 10th century. Centre: a Jewish Haggadah, 1320. Right: rose window of the monastery of Guadeloupe in Spain, mid-14th century.

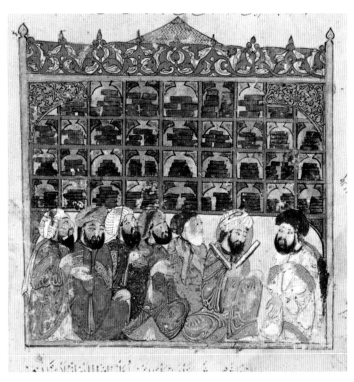

1. The Royal Library of Baghdad, a centre for Arabic translation. Books are laid flat on the shelves behind. From al-Hariri's *Maqamat*, Baghdad, 13th century.

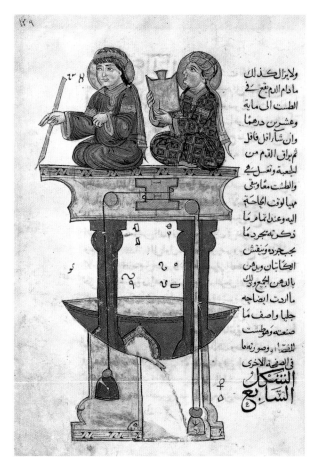

2. Two scribes sit on top of an elaborate machine for measuring the blood taken from a patient, which has been collected in the basin below. From the Book of Automata, 13th century.

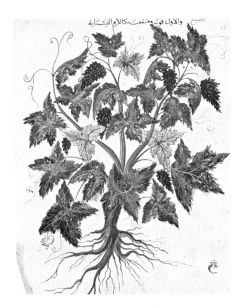

3. Grapevine from Diosconides, painted in Iraq or Syria, 13th century, and imported into the West.

4. Diagram of the nervous system from Avicenna's *Canon of Medicine*, 13th century. Based on Galen and Hippocrates, the book was translated into Latin in the 12th century and remained an authority for centuries.

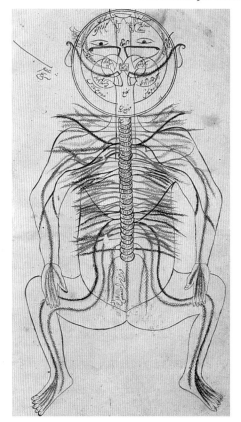

5. A treatise on surgical instruments by the 10th-century physician Albucasis was translated into Latin in the 12th century and into Italian in the 13th.

Astronomy: mapping the heavens 198-199

The scholar's world 214-215

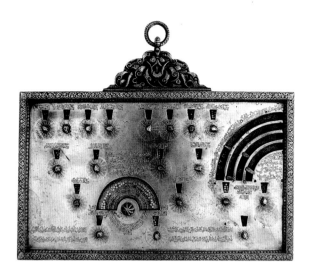

6. Instrument for astrological prognostication, from Mosul, 1241.

Learning from Islam

It is one of the paradoxes of medieval history that at a time when Christians were engaged in the most bitter ideological warfare against Muslims they were learning most from them intellectually. In mathematics, it was the introduction of 'Arabic' numerals in place of the cumbersome Roman numerals that made any advance possible. The Arabic source of algebra is betrayed (like that of alchemy and other words) by its prefix 'al-'. In philosophy, biology, astronomy and technology, the Arabs had the advantage of being able to read Greek texts that were inaccessible to Latin Christians (**1, 2**), and it was through translations from the Arabic that many eventually reached the West (**6**). Arab medicine was also in advance of European (**4, 5**) though it was based on the same theory of the four humours (**2**). Technologically, the most significant import was probably the astrolabe (**7, 9**), an instrument for calculating time and latitude by measuring the altitude of the sun or stars.

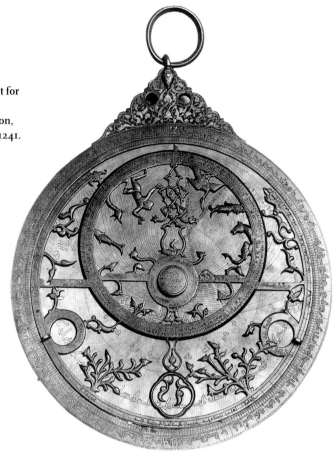

7. Brass astrolabe inlaid with copper and silver, made in Cairo in 1216.

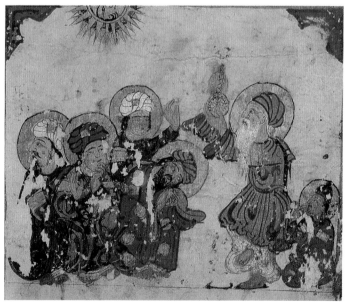

9. An astronomer using an astrolabe by measuring the altitude of the sun. From al-Hariri's *Maqamat*, Baghdad, 13th century.

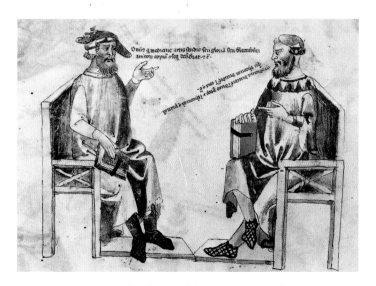

8. The Italian artist who illustrated this Latin version of Hippocrates and Galen shows their Arabic translators in contemporary European dress. From the mouth of Hunain ibn Ishaq on the right comes the first sentence of Galen. Italian, 13th century.

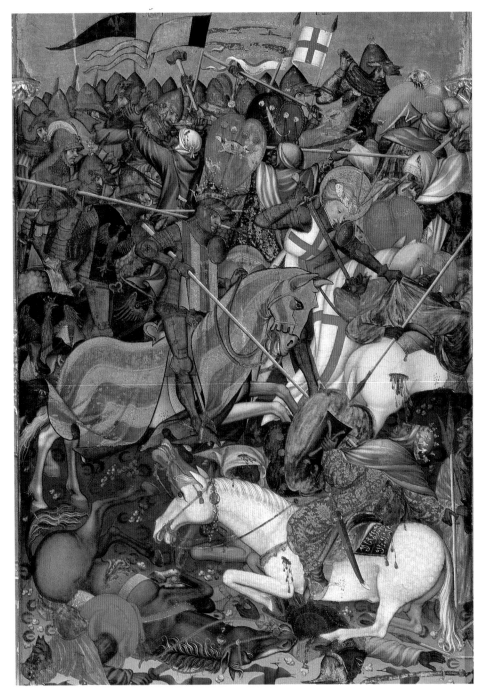

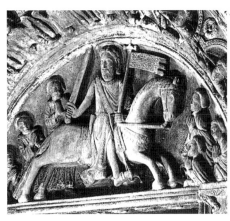

2. Saint James 'the Moor-slayer', the patron saint of the Reconquest: the tympanum of a doorway in the Cathedral of Santiago de Compostela; late 12th century.

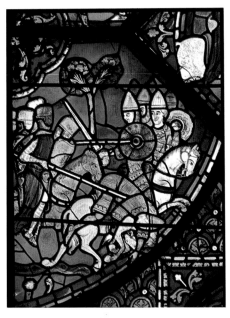

3. A detail from the Charlemagne window of Chartres Cathedral. The battle between Christians (left) and Moors (right). French, 13th century.

1. A Christian army under James I of Aragon defeats the Moors at the Battle of Puig, October, 1237. Supernatural help is provided in the shape of St James, the figure with the halo. Spanish, c. 1420.

4. The castle of Coca, built about 1400 for Alonso de Fonseca, Archbishop of Seville, probably by Moorish workmen. Its elaborate brick decoration is a sign that the serious fighting was now over.

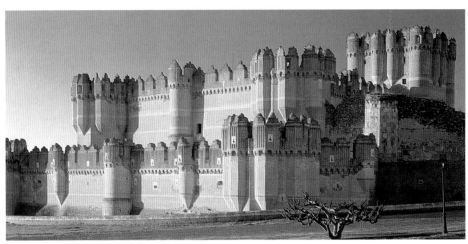

Charlemagne: Rome reborn
52-53

The vanished world of
Moorish Spain 236-237

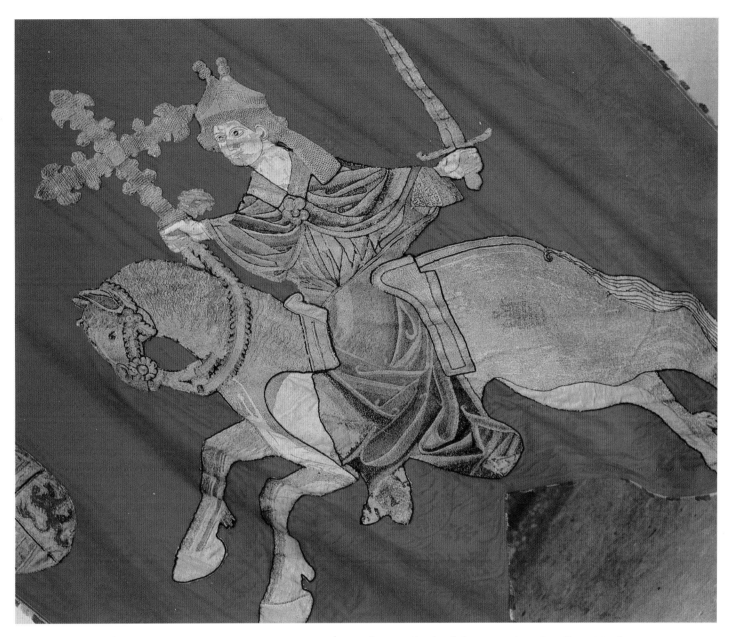

5. The miraculous banner of Baeza, which helped to bring victory to Spanish arms. This detail shows St Isidore of Seville, a Visigothic bishop more renowned for his scholarship than for his military prowess. Spanish, 13th century.

Reconquest: the end of Muslim Spain

However closely Christians and Muslims might approach each other at an intellectual level, it was clear that the religious gulf would always mean war. The movement to reconquer the peninsula began within a few years of the Muslim invasion. It features prominently in the life of Charlemagne (3) and is the main theme of the *Chanson de Roland*. For the Christians this was a holy war (1), fought under the banner of the Apostle James (Santiago), whose bones had been opportunely discovered at Compostela in the 9th century (2). Apocalyptic books were widely read and interpreted as prophecies of Spain's destiny, with Spanish saints as the leaders in the battle against the forces of evil (5). Although the Christians were no more politically united than were the Muslims, their advance was inexorable. By the end of the 10th century, they had reached Burgos, León and Barcelona; by the mid-11th century they held Salamanca and Avila, and by the 12th Toledo. By 1260 the whole of Spain was Christian except for the small area round Granada. Two effects of this 500-year war were to make Spain a land of castles (4) and to give Spanish Catholicism a particularly fervent edge. But for a certain time something of the old Muslim tolerance remained under the Christians. Not until after the fall of Granada in 1492 did attitudes harden and both Muslims and Jews were forbidden to practise their religion and forced to choose between apostasy and exile.

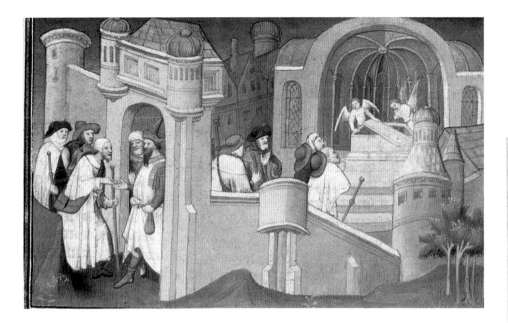

1. Pilgrims arriving at the Church of the Holy Sepulchre: after the Crusades, as before, they were obliged to buy permission from the Muslim rulers to visit this most sacred of shrines; French, 15th century.

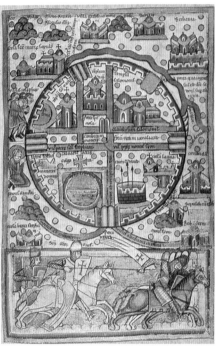

3. A highly formalized plan of Jerusalem, showing the various sites visited by pilgrims, including the Temple of Solomon (upper right) and Golgotha (lower left) within circular walls; French, *c.* 1170.

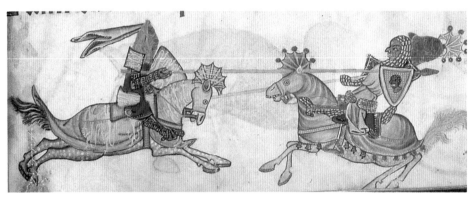

2. A fantasy of Crusader wish-fulfilment: Richard the Lionheart unhorses Saladin in battle; English, *c.* 1340.

The Crusades: the Christian Holy War

The Crusades have always been one of the most puzzling episodes of the Middle Ages. What could have induced thousands of men, led by kings (**7**) and members of the nobility, to cross the whole of Europe and Asia Minor, endure appalling hardships and fight bloody battles (**5**) to conquer a land whose only value was spiritual and symbolic? Marxist historians have sought an economic explanation, and the profit-motive was perhaps one factor, especially when in later Crusades the dispossessed were themselves Christians (e.g. the Venetians and Franks in Greece). But religious fervour must have been the primal cause, the belief, passionately preached by Pope Urban II in 1095 and passionately held by the Crusaders, that for the sacred sites of Christ's Passion to be in the hands of non-believers was unendurable. Jerusalem itself (**3**) was almost as much an idea as a real place, but after years of suffering and an orgy of bloodshed (**5**) in 1099 the Crusaders could kneel at the very sepulchre of Christ.

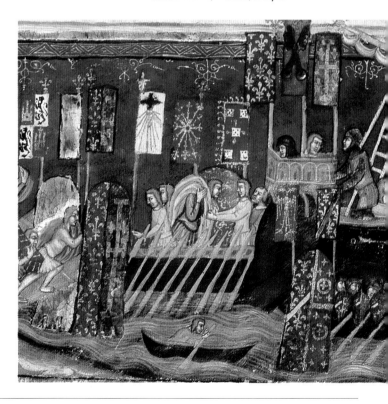

The kingdom 'beyond the sea': Outremer 246–247

Military monks: Hospitallers, Templars and Teutonic Knights 248–249

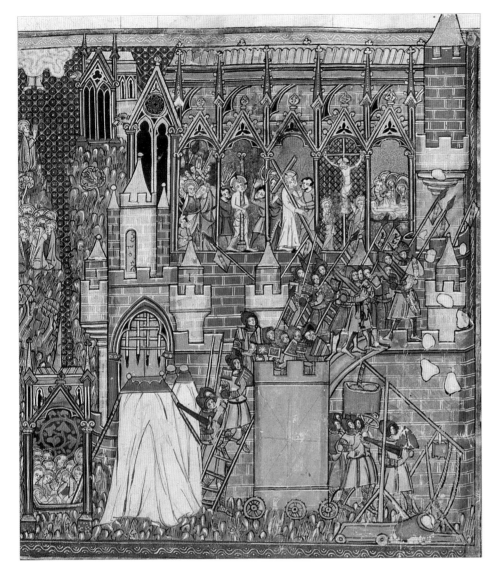

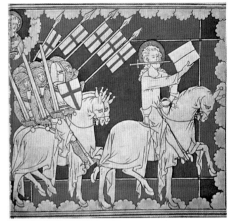

6. Christ himself leading the Crusaders to Jerusalem, from an English Apocalypse, 14th century.

5. The capture of Jerusalem in July 1099, a retrospective illustration from two hundred years later. In the foreground the battle is at its height, with armoured knights scaling ladders. In the background the Passion of Christ is revealed in the Betrayal, Flagellation, Carrying of the Cross, Crucifixion and Entombment; early 14th century.

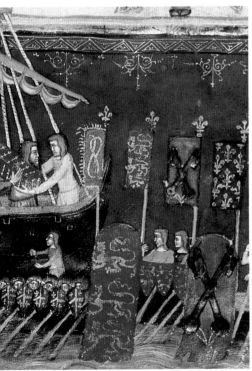

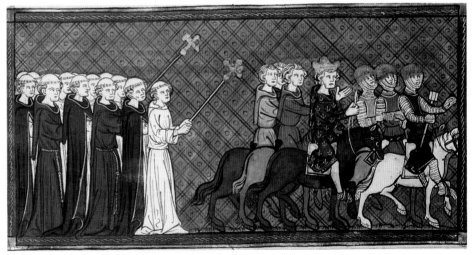

7. St Louis, King of France, sets off on the Seventh Crusade in 1248; French, 14th century.

4. Left: Crusaders embark for the voyage to the Holy Land; French, 14th century.

2. Head of St Peter, part of a capital from the destroyed church of the Annunciation in Nazareth, typical of French Romanesque sculpture of the late 12th century.

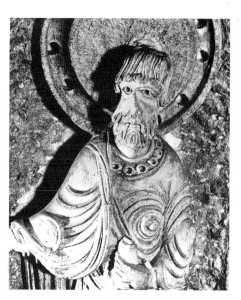

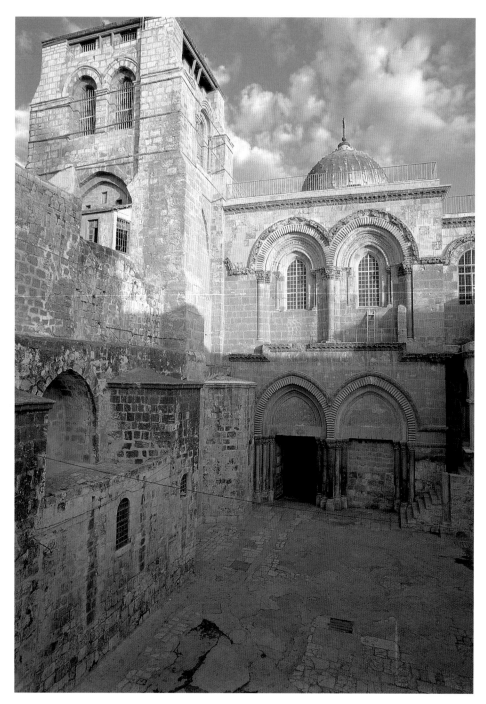

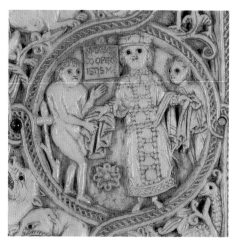

3. Detail of the mid-12th-century ivory cover of the Melisend Psalter, a unique work made in the Crusader Kingdom, showing one of the Seven Acts of Mercy, Clothing the Naked. Melisend was the daughter of King Baldwin II.

1. The church of the Holy Sepulchre had been built by Constantine in the 4th century, and it was he who founded the rotunda that contained the tomb of Christ. The Crusaders restored and enlarged it between 1100 and 1140, and the entrance, seen here, is their work. Godfrey of Bouillon and his brother Baldwin I are buried here. French, 15th century.

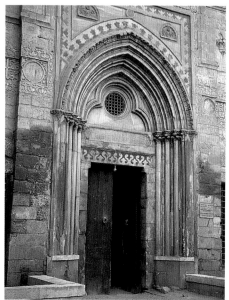

4. The Gothic doorway of the church of St John at Acre was plundered after 1291, taken to Cairo and incorporated in a mosque, a rare example of cultural interchange from West to East.

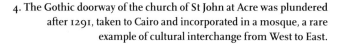

The Crusades: the Christian Holy War 244-245

Military monks: Hospitallers, Templars and Teutonic Knights 248-249

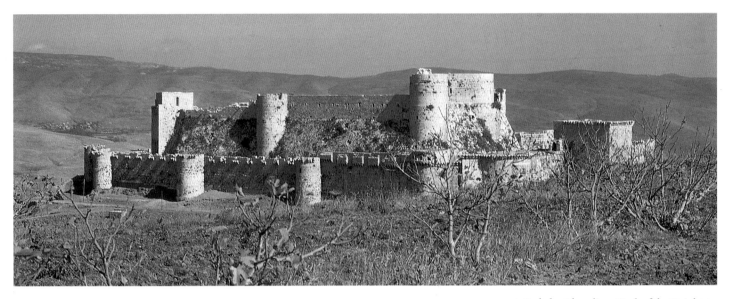

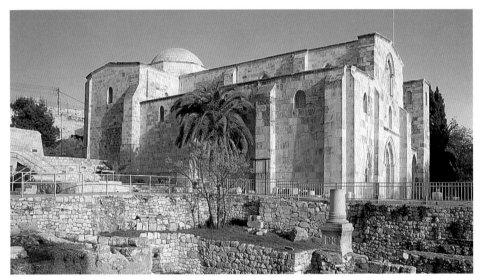

5. Krak des Chevaliers (Krak of the Knights) was built by the Hospitallers in the years after 1144, across a strategic route north of Jerusalem. It is the biggest and best preserved of all medieval castles.

6. The church of St Anne, built by the Crusaders soon after the capture of Jerusalem, close to the Pool of Bethesda.

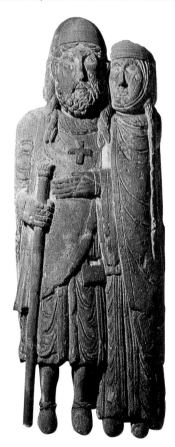

7. A moving image of an old Crusader who has returned from the Holy Land and is being greeted by his wife; the tomb of Count Hugues de Vaudemont, Nancy, early 12th century.

The kingdom 'beyond the sea': Outremer

In order to keep Jerusalem in Christian hands the Crusaders made it into an independent kingdom and elected Godfrey of Bouillon as its ruler. It and three other fiefdoms – Antioch, Edessa and Tripoli – formed a closely-knit coalition which constituted 'Outremer'. Surrounded as it was by Muslim peoples bitterly hostile to its existence, the story of Outremer is one of constant war. But it was supported by six further crusades, some led in person by the kings of France, England and Germany, and defended by the new military orders of Templars and Hospitallers (5), and a precarious stability was established. Jerusalem and other cities took on the aspect of European, more specifically French, towns, with Gothic churches (1, 4, 6) and a flourishing cultural life (2, 3). But after less than a century the forces massed against them were proving too much for the Franks. In 1187 the brilliant new commander of the Islamic armies, Saladin, reconquered Jerusalem. Subsequent counter-offensives failed (the Fourth Crusade was scandalously diverted from the Holy Land to Constantinople, to the benefit of the Venetians, who had financed it), and in 1291 the last stronghold of the Crusaders, the port of Acre, fell to the Mamluks.

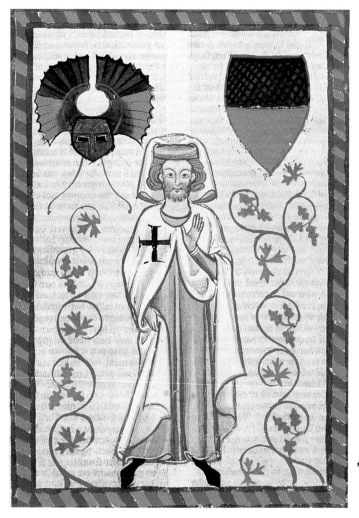

1. A Teutonic Knight with black cross and elaborate helmet; German, *c.* 1304.

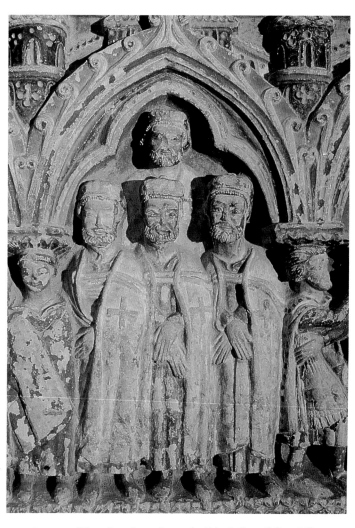

2. A group of Templars, from the tomb of the Infante Felipe, Villasorga, Spain; 13th century.

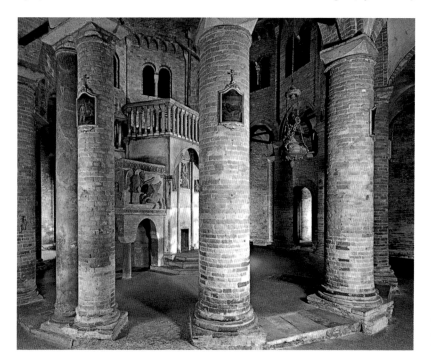

3. The 12th-century church of Santo Stefano, in Bologna, is a deliberate evocation of the Holy Sepulchre in Jerusalem.

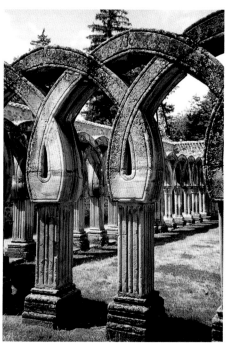

4. Cloister of the Romanesque Templar church at Soria, Spain.

The Crusades: the Christian Holy War 244-245

The kingdom 'beyond the sea': Outremer 246-247

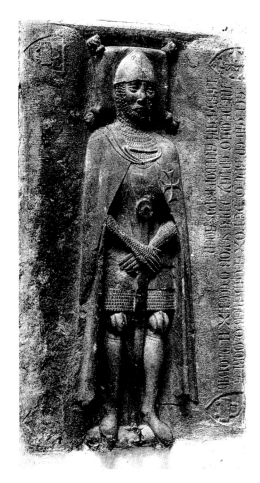

5. Tomb of a Knight Hospitaller, Bernard de Faixa (died 1382), at Faixa, Gerona, Spain.

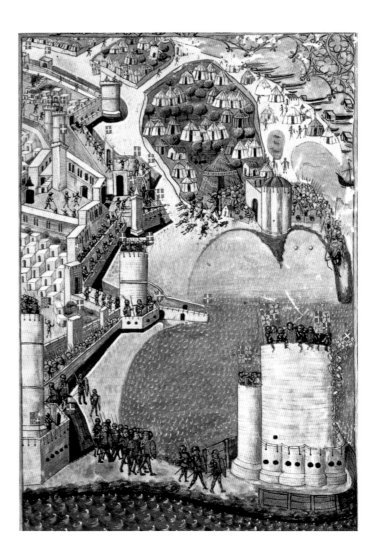

6. In 1308 the Hospitallers installed themselves on Rhodes, where they were besieged by the Turks, 1480. They held out until 1522, when they were forced to retreat to Malta. French, 15th century.

Military monks: Hospitallers, Templars and Teutonic Knights

The Crusades gave new scope for the monastic ideal – men living in a closed community dedicated to God's service. The 12th century saw the foundation of three new orders in the Holy Land – the Knights of the Temple (Templars) (2) around 1120, the Knights of St John (Hospitallers) (5) and the Teutonic Knights (1) later in the century. All took monastic vows but were organized on military lines with a Grand Master as commander-in-chief. Most of the campaigning in Outremer depended on these Orders, though they could not always be trusted not to abuse their power. After the fall of Acre in 1291 they suffered very different fates. The Teutonic Knights moved their headquarters to Prussia. In 1525 the Grand Master accepted the Reformation, secularized the Order and became a duke. The Hospitallers retreated first to Cyprus, then to Rhodes (6) and finally to Malta where they remained until they were dissolved in 1798. The Templars met with spectacular disaster. They were now extremely rich, with houses all over Europe (4), and had attracted powerful enemies. In 1307, Philip IV of France, crediting or pretending to credit horrendous accusations of homosexuality, heresy, blasphemy and witchcraft, arrested the whole Order and confiscated their property. The leaders were tried, tortured and executed and the Order was suppressed by the Pope (7).

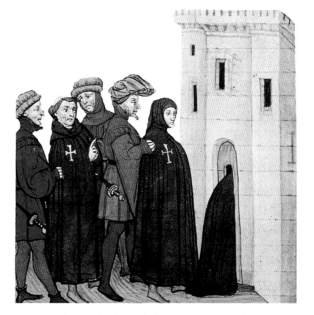

7. Templar Knights being led away into prison after their condemnation, on very dubious evidence, by Pope Clement V and Philip IV of France in 1311.

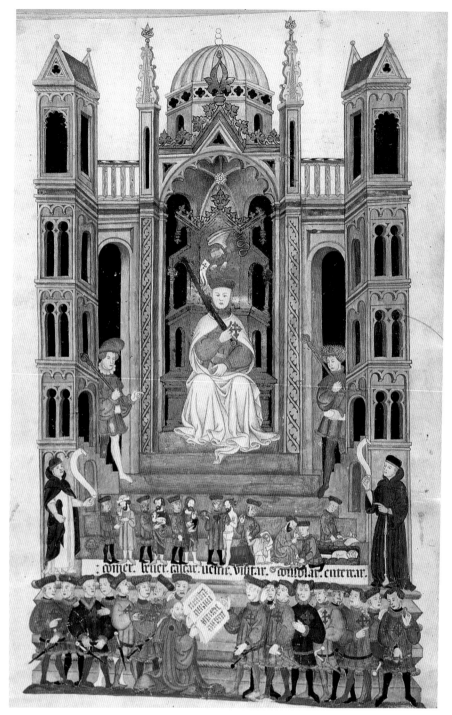

1. Page from the Alba Bible, probably painted by Christians under Rabbinic supervision; Spanish, 1422–30.

4. Detail from a German 13th-century law-code, the *Sachsenspiegel*, in which the Jew is confirmed as legally equal to the Christian. Again he wears the characteristic pointed hat; a 14th-century copy.

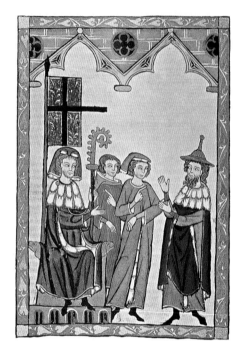

2. The Jewish Minnesinger (troubadour) Süsskind von Trit, distinguished by his pointed Jewish hat; German, 1304.

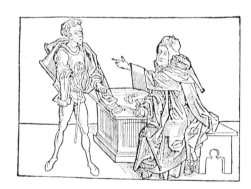

3. Christian borrowing money from a Jew; German, 1490.

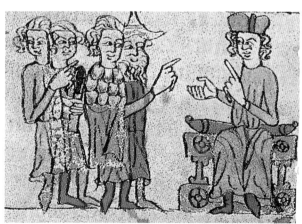

The Jews: precarious toleration 252-253

The Church in a new age 264-265

6. The oldest surviving synagogue in Europe is the so-called Old-New Synagogue in Prague, built in the 13th century.

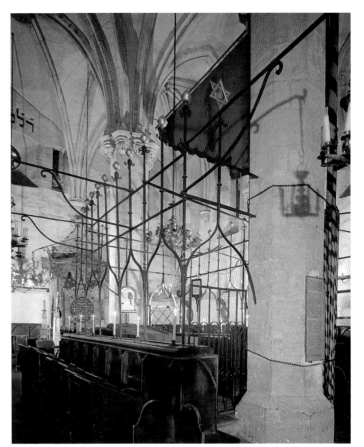

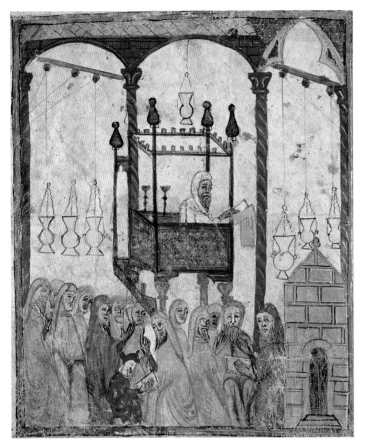

5. Scene in a Spanish synagogue, with a rabbi reading the sermon; Spanish, 14th century.

The Jews: strangers in the midst

The position of the Jews in medieval Europe was full of anomalies. Officially they were tolerated by both Church and state and allowed to practise their religion (5, 6). In several countries (2, 7) they contributed notably to national culture, especially as experts in Hebrew studies. One of the major monuments of such collaboration is the Alba Bible, commissioned by a Spanish nobleman from a team of Jewish advisers under Rabbi Moses. On the page illustrated (1), Don Luis, the patron, sits enthroned. Below him, beneath the towers, are two theologians who worked with the Jews on the translation. At the bottom, Rabbi Moses presents the finished book to Don Luis. But as non-Christians the Jews could never become integrated into their host society, and this was also their own choice. Forbidden to own land or to engage in many crafts and professions, they became specialists in money-lending (3), a necessary activity prohibited to Christians by canon law.

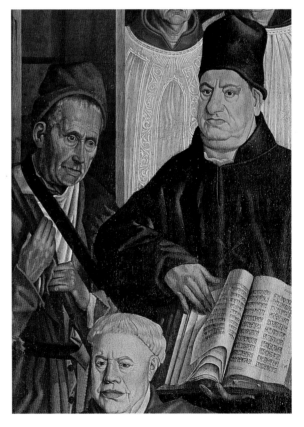

7. In 1465 the judicial head of Portuguese Jewry, here seen holding a Hebrew book, was a valued member of the court of Henry the Navigator in Lisbon; detail from the St Vincent Altarpiece by Nuño Goncalves.

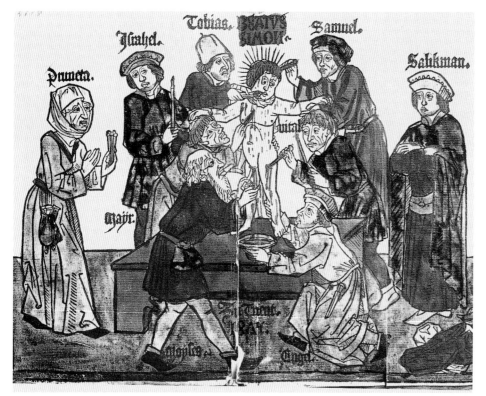

1. A woodcut made at Trento, Italy, in 1475, shows the supposed torture of a Christian child by Jews. The story had hideous consequences for the whole local Jewish community.

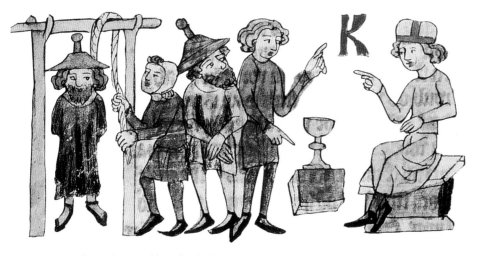

2. In Gothic art, Synagogue (i.e. Judaism) was conventionally represented as a beautiful woman blindfolded, so that she could not see Christ's truth, losing her crown and with a broken staff – the end of the Old Covenant. Rheims Cathedral, 13th century.

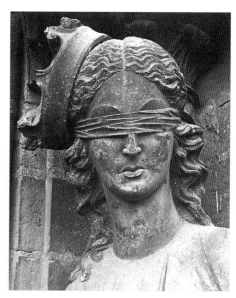

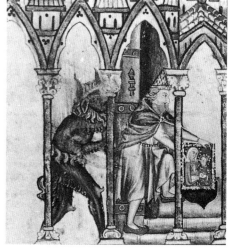

4. Part of a pictorial sequence from 13th-century Spain showing a Jew who had stolen a picture of the Virgin and Child being seized by a devil as he is about to throw it down a well.

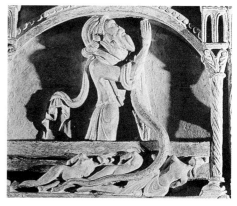

3. A Jew caught stealing a Bible and a chalice containing the host is hanged, a familiar anti-Jewish libel featured in the 13th-century *Sachsenspiegel*.

5. The repentant Jew: detail of a 13th-century tomb of three holy martyrs at Avila, Spain. The Jew attempted to desecrate the tomb but was miraculously prevented, converted to Christianity, and endowed a church.

The Jews: strangers in the midst 250-251

The Church in a new age 264-265

The Jews: precarious toleration

As the people of God's first Covenant, of the Old Testament prophets and the ancestors of Jesus, the Jews were always accorded a certain veneration. But they were also (a view vigorously promoted by the Gospel writers) the people responsible for Christ's death. They had, after all, deliberately rejected his message, a sign of spiritual blindness (2, 7). The fact that they were an easily identifiable minority (6), combined with their exclusiveness, their strange, rigid laws and their reputation for sharp financial dealing, made them obvious scapegoats in times of trouble. Grotesque anti-Jewish stories, all turning on the idea that they were the implacable enemies of Christianity, were ineradicable – stealing and burning the consecrated host (3) and holy images (4) and torturing children (1). These 'blood-libels' led to riots and persecution that could flare up at any time and cost the lives of thousands of innocent men and women.

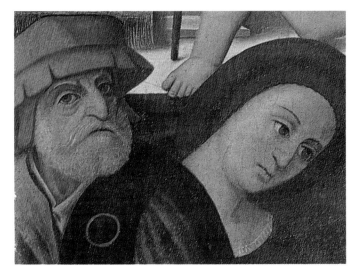

6. Jews were obliged to wear a coloured badge, featured in this portrait of the Mantuan banker Daniele Norsa; 15th century.

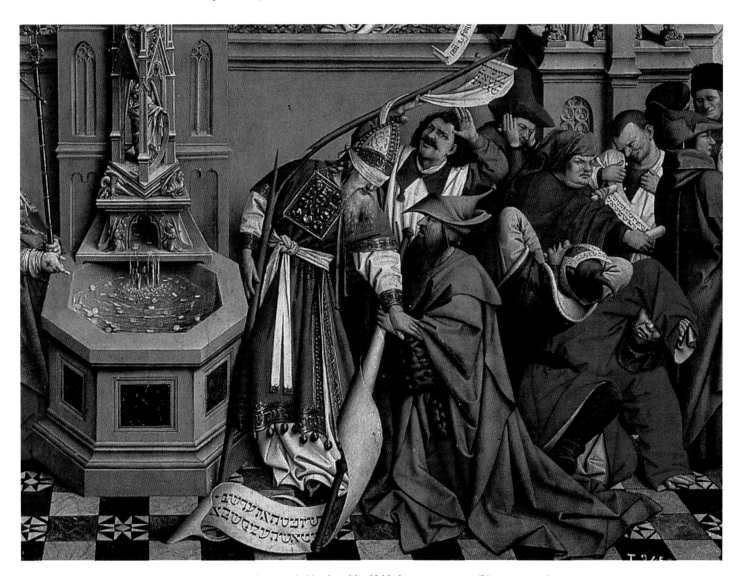

7. Faced with the living fountain of God's grace, the Jews, led by their blindfolded Synagogue, recoil in consternation. (The whole picture is shown on p. 145.) Flemish, *c.* 1450.

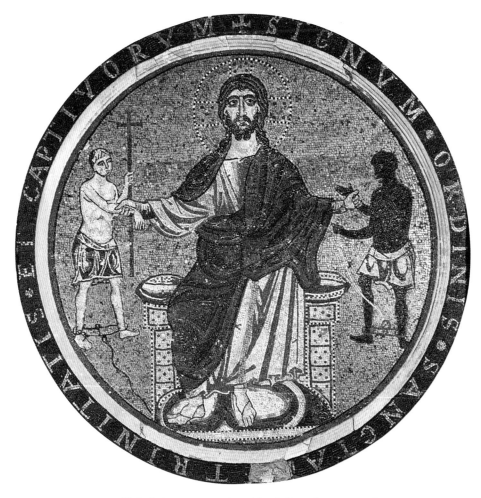

1. Christ between two captives. Mosaic from the convent of
S. Tommaso in Formis, Rome, about 1212.

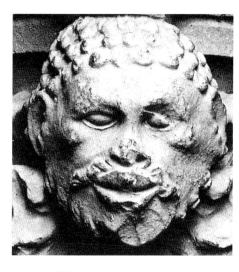

3. Detail from a Romanesque capital at
Troia, Italy, *c.* 1212–20, showing one of four
heads representing the peoples of the world.

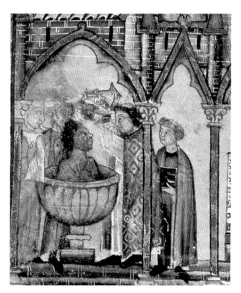

4. Baptism of a black man, from a Spanish
manuscript of about 1260–80.

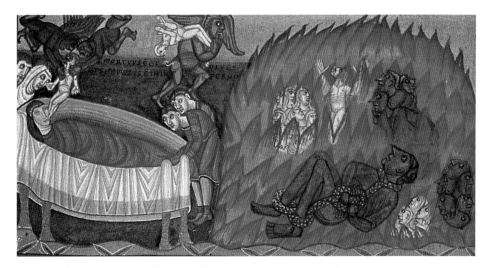

2. Detail from the parable of Dives and Lazarus. The rich Dives' soul
is carried off by devils to dwell with Satan. Codex Aureus, 1043–44.

5. One of the torturers beating Christ, from Giotto's *Flagellation*,
in the Arena Chapel, Padua, Italy, 1300–1310.

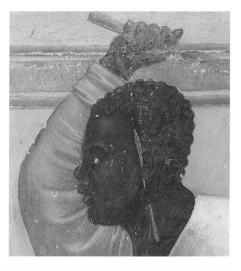

The powers of darkness
80-81

The vanished world of
Moorish Spain 236-237

The black in medieval society

Anti-black racism in the modern sense was unknown in the Middle Ages. There were not enough black people in Europe for whites to feel in any way under threat. Blacks were simply part of the human race (3), suffering, sinning and needing redemption like everyone else (1, 4). In the later Middle Ages there were even black saints (6), and one of the Magi was conventionally shown as black (7). On the other hand the colour black was the commonest way of signalling evil, and was very often associated with Satan (2), which, if it did not exactly demonize real black people, must have put them at some initial disadvantage. Executioners and torturers were often shown as black for this reason (5).

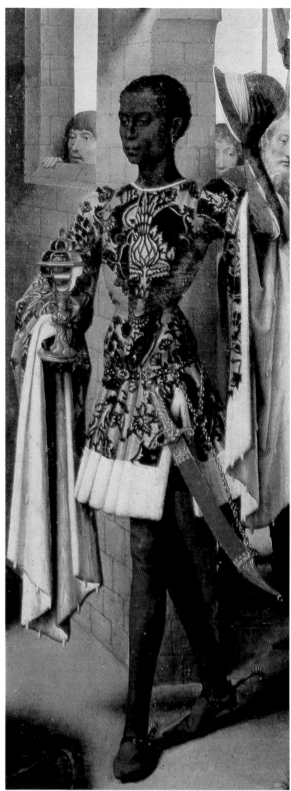

7. One of the three kings, from Hans Memling's *Adoration of the Magi, c.* 1470.

6. St Maurice was the leader of the Theban Legion, said to have been martyred in Switzerland in the 3rd century AD. In the 13th century, because of his supposed African origins, it became common to represent him as a black man. Magdeburg Cathedral, Germany, *c.* 1240–50.

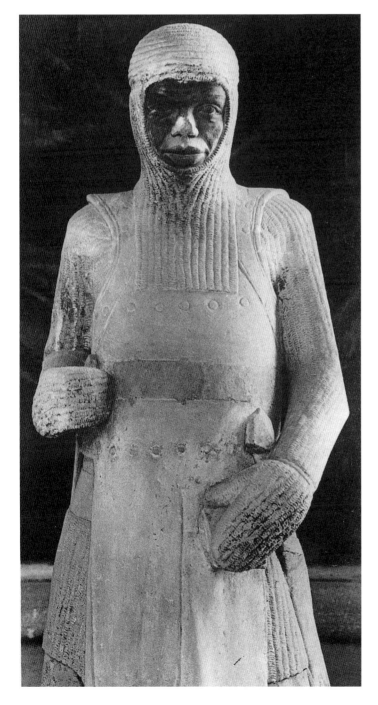

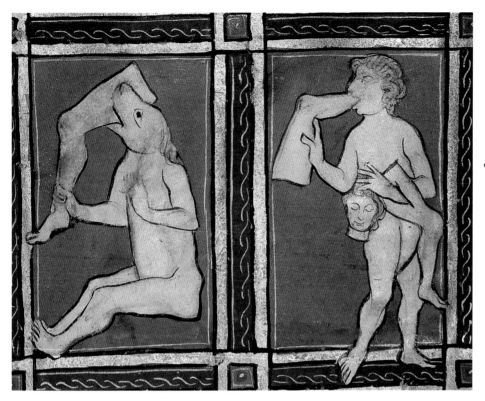

1. The horrors of cannibalism: human and half-human monsters – Cinomologus and Anthropophagus – from a manuscript of the *Marvels of the World*, after 1277.

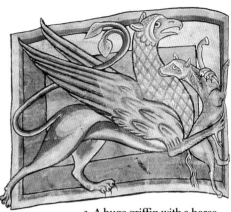

3. A huge griffin with a horse in its talons; 12th century.

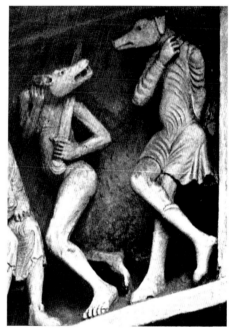

4. Dog-headed men from the tympanum of the church of Vézelay, France, 12th century. These strange creatures (see also opposite below) were examples of the remote peoples of the world to whom the Apostles were bidden to preach the Word of God.

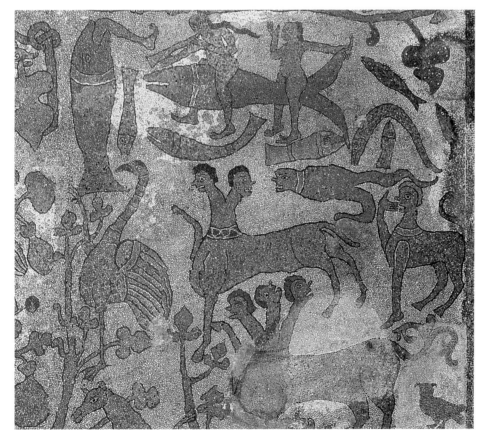

2. Part of the mosaic pavement of the Cathedral of Otranto, Italy, 1165, an extraordinary anthology of fables and romances, including multi-headed centaurs.

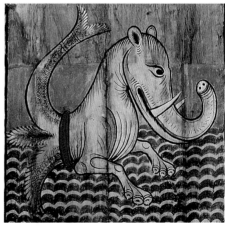

5. Fabulous beast from the ceiling of the church of St Martin, Zillis, Switzerland, early 12th century.

Picturing the world
208-209

New worlds 268-269

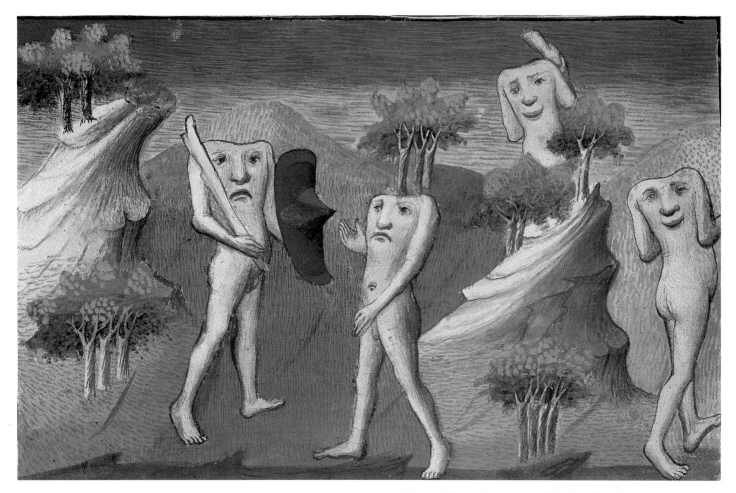

6. Mandeville described men with heads in their chests, and even – according to this imaginative illustrator – in their backs. From the *Livre des Merveilles*, French, 15th century.

Beyond the known world

Medieval Europe was a fairly closed society. Much was known of the Islamic world, if only through the distorting lens of religious prejudice. Jews were familiar and black people not mysterious. A few travellers had visited Persia, Central Asia and even China if we believe Marco Polo. But knowledge of the remote parts of the world consisted of fable more than fact, much of it going back to classical sources derived from Alexander's conquests in the East. These were elaborated in medieval texts such as the *Livre des Merveilles*, and taken still further by straightforward liars such as Sir John Mandeville, who pretended to have gone to Asia and Africa in the 14th century. Did educated men and women really believe these fantastic stories? Surely they did, since they appear in contexts like learned *mappamundi* and the imagery of churches (2, 4, 7). There was, after all, no way of checking. In the case of the animals one can see how dragons, griffins (3) and fishy elephants (5) might have originated through misunderstood verbal descriptions of real creatures. Human monsters are harder to account for. Among the most extraordinary are sciapods, men with one big foot, centaurs, some with two and three heads (2), people with big ears (7), men 'whose heads to grow beneath their shoulders' (6), whom Othello claimed to have seen, and dog-headed men, *cynocephali* (4), who communicated by barking.

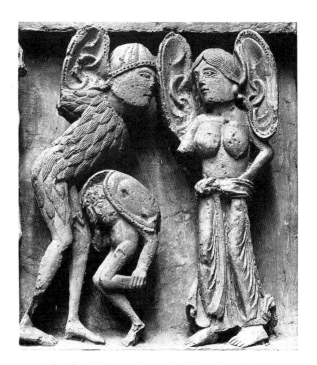

7. A family – father, mother and child – of people with very large ears, another detail from the tympanum of Vézelay, France; 12th century.

Christians and Non-Christians   257

8

Epilogue:
The End of the Middle Ages

A HISTORICAL PERIOD like the Middle Ages is a convenience created by scholars, and it is possible to place its beginning and end at various points. The fall of Constantinople to the Ottoman Turks in 1453 meant the final extinction of a state that claimed an ancestry going back to the Caesars and it used to be a common termination for the medieval period. Other critical dates include 1492, when, within one year, the Jews were expelled from Spain, the last Muslim state in the Iberian peninsula was conquered and Columbus sailed from the Old World to the New. National histories have their own turning-points: the establishment of the Tudor dynasty in England in 1485, the beginning of the French invasions of Italy in 1494. All these dates have their uses, but it would be fruitless to argue about them.

It is nevertheless clear that a series of major developments in the late fifteenth and early sixteenth centuries – the invention of printing, the beginnings of European expansion across the globe and the great crisis of the Reformation – resulted in a European society of 1550 that was very different from that of 1450. The fact that these tremendous transformations had roots in the medieval past should not disguise their novelty. In a sense, Renaissance humanism – the contemporary cultural innovation that blew its own trumpet most successfully – was the least important of all these major changes. The new face of the globe, the new medium of communication and the new schism in Christendom dwarf the fact that a classicizing Latin and artistic style came into fashion.

It is an easy enough matter, when discussing movements of reformist upheaval, like the Reformation, to amass a vast display case of 'abuses' that characterized the previous system and made the reforms expedient if not inevitable (histories of the French and Russian Revolutions usually do the same). It is certainly possible to do this in the case of the late medieval Church. It is worth pointing out two things, however: first that the 'abuses' were very often of great antiquity and might even be seen as unavoidable permanent features of any system that sought to combine authority and property with the message of the Gospel. Second, there is no doubt that many Church leaders thought that 'reform' was vital and undertook great pains in pursuing it. Pressure for change was not only from below. The gesture that ignited the Reformation – Luther's critique of the sale of indulgences (pardons for sin) in 1517 – was by no means an isolated or unusual protest against the condition of the contemporary Church. Throughout the later Middle Ages voices were raised in favour of ecclesiastical reform.

One of the most important ecclesiastical issues of the later Middle Ages was the fate of the monarchical papacy that had developed over the preceding centuries. After reaching great heights in both its political victories and its ideological pretensions in the thirteenth century, the papacy came crashing down in crisis at the very beginning of the fourteenth. Boniface VIII (1294–1303), who claimed that 'it is altogether necessary to salvation for every human creature to be subject to the bishop of Rome', clashed with the most powerful secular ruler of his time, Philip IV of France. Philip's agents kidnapped him and he died soon after his release. Clement V (1305–14) then moved the seat of the papacy to Avignon, initiating a long period of French domination. Clement and his six immediate successors all came from the south of France and it began to look as

The discovery of America – almost literally a 'New World' – coinciding as it did with momentous changes in cultural and religious life, was a potent symbol of the end of an era. At the same time the full extent of Africa and Asia began to be realized. The old images of a self-contained Europe and a universal Church were gone for ever. The first globe to incorporate America – 'Novus Mundus' – dates from about 1510 and is now in the University of Cracow, Poland. Only a few inches in diameter, it was based on a Spanish map of about 1500.

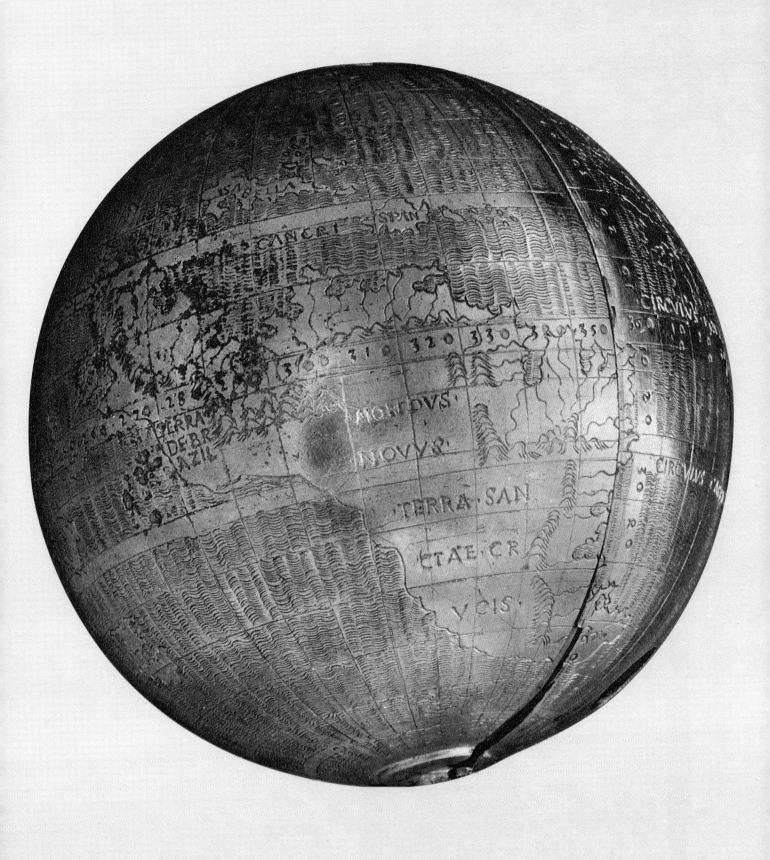

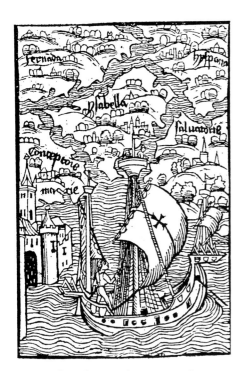

A woodcut of 1494, only two years after Columbus's first voyage, illustrates the Caribbean islands that he was able to explore. It was not immediately understood that these were only a part of an entirely unknown continent.

if the papacy would be permanently based in France and subservient to the French king. When an attempt was made to return the papacy to Rome, this simply resulted in a split in the Church, the so-called Great Schism of 1378 to 1417, with one line of popes in Rome and another in Avignon.

In an attempt to resolve this public scandal, many ecclesiastical leaders and thinkers turned to the idea that a General Council of the Church, composed of delegates from the whole of the Catholic world, was the proper instrument of reform. A series of Councils met in the first half of the fifteenth century (Pisa 1409, Constance 1414–18, Basel 1431–49), seeking to resolve the schism and reform ecclesiastical institutions. The Council of Constance asserted that it was 'a General Council and represents the Catholic Church and has authority directly from Christ, and everybody, including the pope, is bound to obey this council'. Its goals, in its own words, were 'the union and reformation of the Church of God'. Eventually, after many tortuous developments, including a period when there were three rather than merely two popes, the unity of the papacy was re-established and a single line of popes ruled again from Rome. Reform, however, was a less successful story. No fundamental changes were made and the papacy of the post-Conciliar period was just as monarchical and even more worldly than that of Avignon.

While the Church was grappling with, and failing to meet, the challenge of reform, secular states were amassing greater resources and flexing their muscles in wider arenas. Armies grew progressively larger and the taxes to pay for them progressively heavier. Successful kings were able to tame their aristocracies and harness them to their own desires. In some countries strong national feeling could be yoked to the traditional dynastic ambitions of monarchs. Moreover, tentatively in the fifteenth century, but more significantly in the following centuries, European states began to extend their dominion over other continents. The Portuguese edged their way down the west coast of Africa in pursuit of gold and slaves, conquering Ceuta in Morocco in 1415, rounding the Cape of Good Hope in 1488 and establishing a direct sea route from Europe to India in 1498. Columbus' voyage of 1492 started from the Canary Islands, a kind of laboratory of European colonialism, and led within a few years to the first trans-oceanic empires.

These unparalleled changes in the pattern of world politics coincided with a revolution in the primary medium of communication – writing. Literacy had been expanding in Europe ever since the tenth or eleventh centuries. More books were produced, they became smaller and more useable, while a cursive developed to enable scribes to work faster. Full-time professional scribes could be found in any major town. The numerous scrappy and dog-eared volumes dating from the fifteenth century are a witness to the penetration of habits of reading and writing to a degree far beyond that of the early medieval period, when books were rare treasures. Printing represented a quantum leap in the techniques of reproducing script but was also a logical next step in the late medieval world of proliferating texts.

The first surviving printed book is the famous Gutenberg Bible, produced at Mainz in 1455 by Johnannes Gutenberg. Printing then spread quickly throughout Europe. It reached Spain, Italy and France by 1470, England, the Low Countries and Eastern Europe by 1480, and most of the rest of Europe in the next few decades. It has been calculated that by 1500 some six million books had been printed – a number that dwarfs the manuscript production of the entire Middle

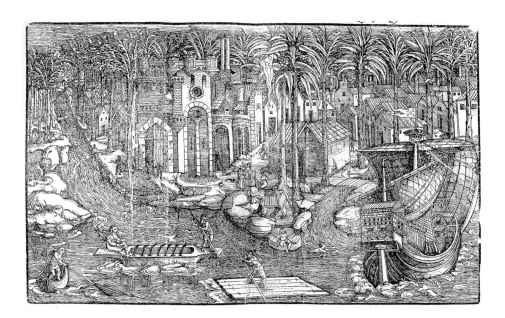

The tip of Africa had been passed in 1488, and in 1498 the Portuguese navigator Vasco da Gama landed at Calicut in India: a German woodcut of 1527.

Ages. The subversive possibilities of print were not at first apparent – in 1476 printing was hailed not only as 'the mother of all branches of knowledge' but also as 'the helper of the Church' – but millions of books meant something quite different from hundreds or even thousands of books. The words of the Bible, itself a text with great revolutionary potential, could now be pondered by any literate person. Diverse opinions, satire and political and religious controversies suddenly had an audience multiplied beyond any expectation.

If Luther's critique of the institutions of the Church was in origin entirely conventional and traditional, its results were not, and one of the main reasons for that success was that the new medium of printing took his writings, including his influential German translation of the Bible, into the homes of lay people of every class. Earlier movements of religious dissent, like the Cathars of the twelfth and thirteenth centuries and the Hussites of the fifteenth, had been crushed or turned aside, but Protestantism proved more lasting. Printing was not the only reason. Many of the powerful princely regimes of Northern Europe saw in the Reformation the path to new forms of sovereignty as well as rich pickings from the Church. Within 40 years of Luther's protest of 1517 half the princes of Germany and the monarchs of England and Scandinavia had established state churches of their own and confiscated the wealth of the monasteries and much other ecclesiastical property.

In many ways European society of the sixteenth, seventeenth and eighteenth centuries continued to resemble that of the medieval period. It was only the twin processes of industrialization and the growth of democracy in the years 1750 to 1900 that effected fundamental transformations, placing a kind of barrier of understanding between us and the pre-industrial and hierarchical past. Yet the changes that took place around the year 1500, even if not so epochal, were of significance in shaping the modern world: a global world, a culturally and religiously fragmented world, a world in which mass media were to be crucial in forming views and transmitting knowledge. The European Middle Ages, with its geographically circumscribed boundaries, its aspiration to Christian unity and its elite scribal culture, was gone forever.

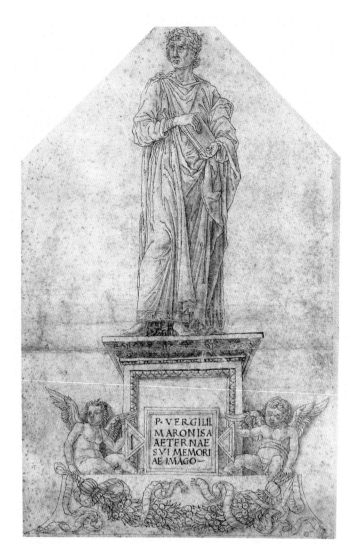

1. Mantegna: drawing for a proposed statue to Virgil; late 15th century.

Classicism reborn

As we reach the end of the 15th century it is revealing to look back at the three elements which at the beginning of this book were postulated as having 'made' the Middle Ages. The first was the classical civilization of the Roman Empire. This was on the brink of enjoying a Renaissance that would put all previous 'renaissances' in the shade. The Roman world would become a model not only for literature and art but also for philosophy, law and political theory. And whereas the Middle Ages had necessarily seen that world in medieval terms, the generation of humanists would try to see authentically (1, 4). Texts were studied with a new scholarship and a new impartiality, no longer tortured to yield a Christian meaning. Architecture no longer adopted isolated motifs but attempted to conform to strict Roman, Vitruvian, standards, at first fancifully (3) but after the advent of Alberti with growing confidence (2). It was this meeting of minds across the centuries that led people to see the intervening thousand years as a 'middle' age which merely interrupted the progress of history and which the Renaissance could afford to ignore.

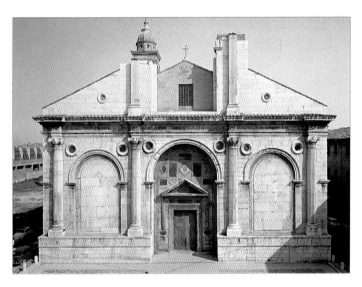

2. Alberti: unfinished façade of the Tempio Malatestiano, Rimini; c. 1450.

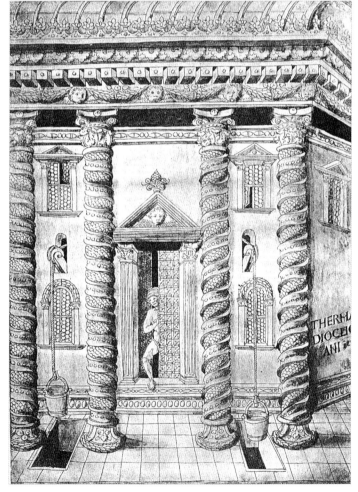

3. Giovanni Marcanova: reconstruction of the Baths of Diocletian, Rome; c. 1440.

Reading the classics 34-35   Classical revivals 36-37

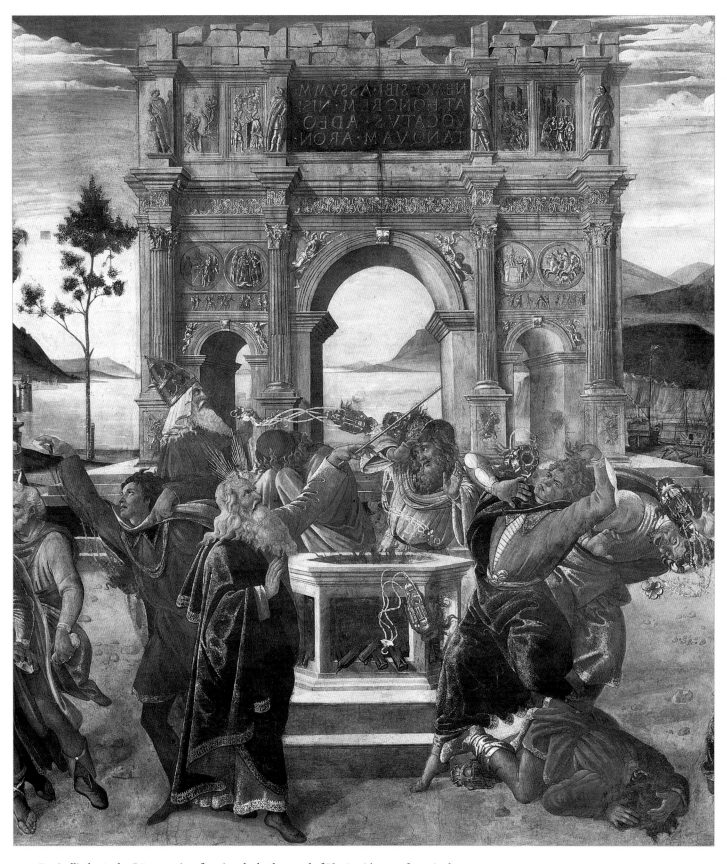

4. Botticelli: the Arch of Constantine, forming the background of *The Punishment of Cora* in the Sistine Chapel, Rome; 1482–83.

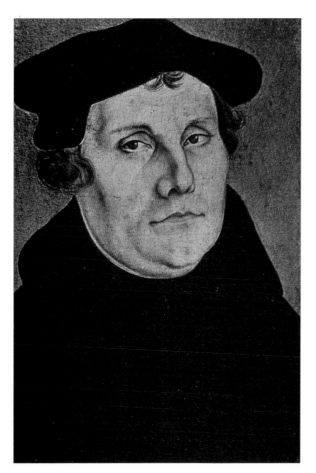

1. Lucas Cranach the Elder: portrait of Martin Luther, 1525.

The Church in a new age

Christianity was the second of the forces that 'made' the Middle Ages, and it had triumphed to a degree that its first adherents could hardly have dreamed of. As almost every page of this book has shown, the Church was for centuries the dominant intellectual and moral authority throughout Europe. Particular doctrines and particular practices had been disputed. There had never been any lack of voices calling for reform and sometimes these movements (as with the Hussites) had led to open secession. But on the whole reform meant reform from within. Except for the Cathars, there was never any idea of questioning the central beliefs of Christianity. Luther (**1**) saw himself in this sense as a reformer from within, and many shared both his disgust at indulgences (**2**) and his outrage at the contrast between Christ's poverty and the pope's wealth (**3**). The Church, however, rejected his calls. Unity was forever lost. Henceforth there could be no infallible voice, no final authority, no *summa theologica*. The end of these absolutes is a fitting point to define the end of the Middle Ages.

4. Opposite: *Protestant Church*, a coloured woodcut of about 1545, summarizing the tenets of Luther's reform. In the pulpit, he preaches his message, invoking God the Father, Christ and the Lamb. Opposite him are the only two sacraments recognized by the Lutheran Church – baptism and Communion (taken by the laity 'in both kinds', the bread and the wine). In the foreground Luther's patron, the Elector John Frederick, piously bears the cross.

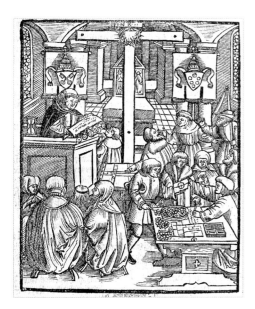

2. The selling of indulgences, which guaranteed the forgiveness of sins for money, was one of the scandals that sparked Luther's revolt. This woodcut is from one of his pamphlets, 1520.

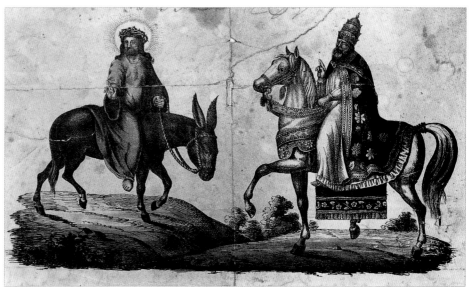

3. A satirical print contrasting the poverty of Christ with the luxurious wealth of the pope; German, *c.* 1540.

The hierarchy of the Church 60-61   Empire and Papacy 96-97

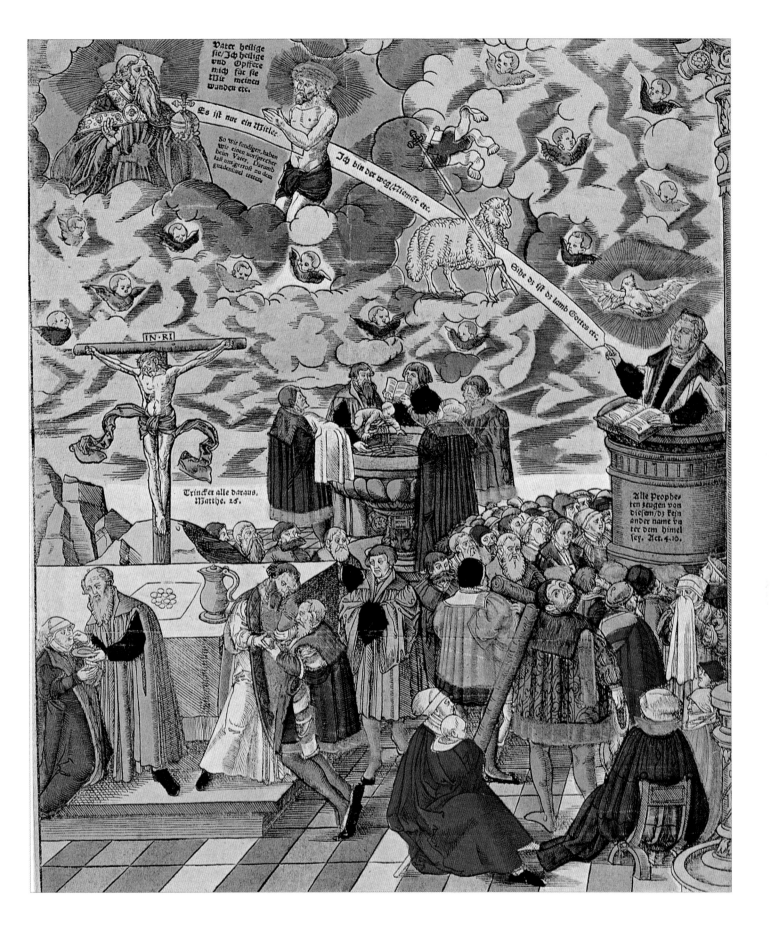

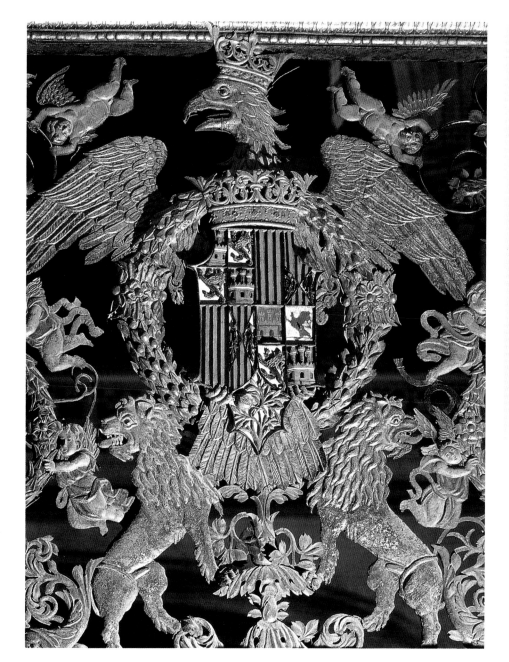

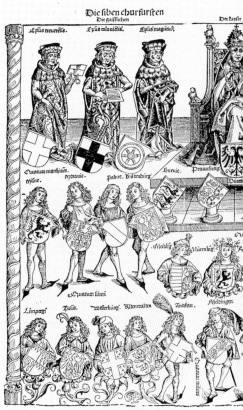

2. Germany, politically fragmented, was culturally united under the Holy Roman Emperor. A woodcut from the Nuremberg Chronicle of 1493 displays the coats-of-arms of the Electors (at the top), kings, dukes and free cities.

1. Spain became a single nation with the marriage of Ferdinand and Isabella, uniting Aragon, León and Castile in 1469. Their tomb in Granada Cathedral quarters the vertical stripes of Aragon with the lion and castle of León and Castile; Spanish, 1518.

From barbarians to nation-states

The third element in our notional 'making' of the Middle Ages was the invasion of the Germanic tribes from the east. After a long period of confusion and unrest, these wandering peoples had by around the years 800–1000 settled in the territories that they would henceforth occupy. Some of the Germanic barbarians, such as the Anglo-Saxons and the Franks, established hereditary monarchies, from which later states and nations developed. By the 10th and 11th centuries there were kings 'of the English' and poets wrote about 'sweet France'. There was also an awareness of how language, whether of Germanic or Latin descent, served as a mark of identity. In this way there arose many of the characteristics of nationhood.

How far ordinary people thought in these terms cannot be known. Faced with English aggression under Edward I, the Scots and Welsh certainly saw themselves as nations and actually used the word. But did the participants of the Hundred Years' War do so? When it began (1337) probably not. The quarrel was dynastic. Whether an English or a French family ruled was of small account. When it ended (1453) the two sides had moved closer to the national idea. A main factor was language. French had ceased to be the official court language of England. And even without political unity, German-speakers saw themselves as German and Italian-speakers as Italian. By 1500 the foundations of modern nationalism had been laid.

Germanic invaders 38-39   The assault on Christian Europe 54-55

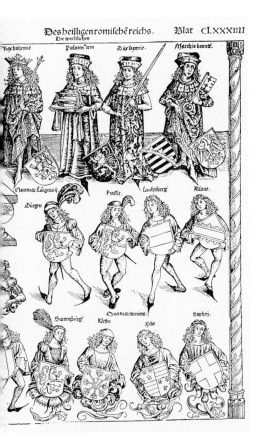

Des heiligen romischē reichs. Blat CLXXXIII
Die weltlichen

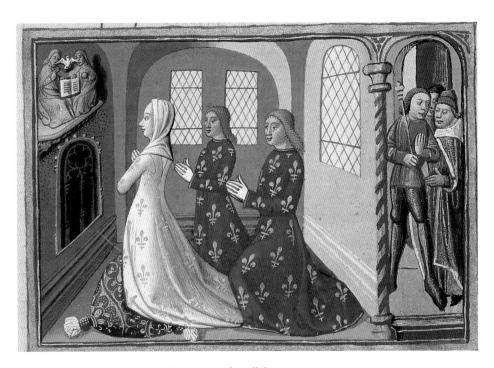

4. France at the same time was drawing together all the territories where French was spoken. In a miniature from the end of the 15th century, the nation is personified as a woman worshipping the Trinity. She and her attendants are arrayed in the fleur-de-lis.

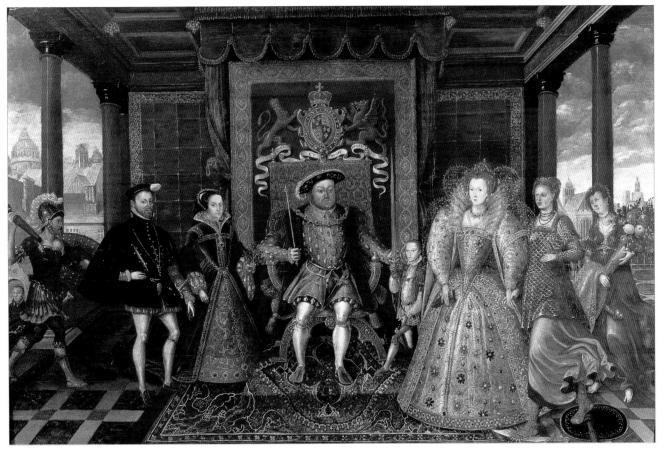

3. England was given a self-conscious national identity under the Tudors, who made a deliberate policy of appealing both to the reconciliation of factions and English historic tradition (Henry VII christened his eldest son Arthur). Here Henry VIII, surrounded by his family, sits beneath the national coat-of-arms.

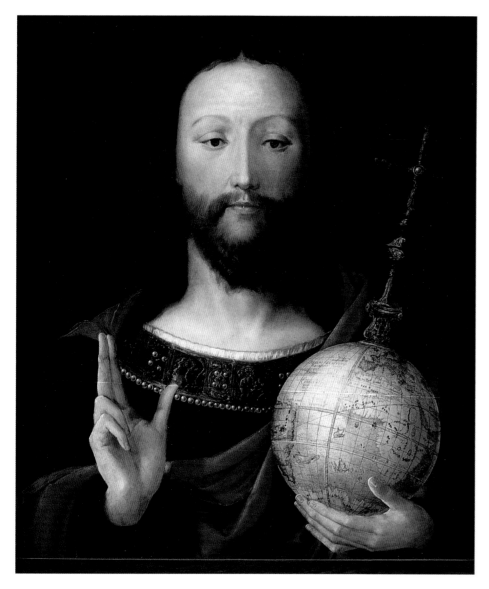

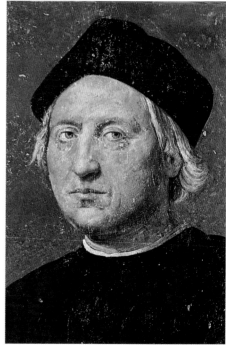

1. Christ holds an up-to-date globe: faith embraces the new knowledge; a painting by Oronce Finé, French, 1530.

2. Portrait of Christopher Columbus attributed to Ridolfo Ghirlandaio, *c.* 1525.

New worlds

At the very time when society and religion were facing such momentous challenges, the old medieval world-picture was shattered by the discovery that Europe was a much smaller and less important place than it once seemed. In 1488 Bartholomew Diaz rounded the Cape of Good Hope, revealing the extent of Africa. Ten years later Vasco da Gama reached India by sea. In 1492 Chistopher Columbus set foot in the New World, though it took some time to realize that this was a whole unknown continent (4). By 1521 the world had been circumnavigated by the ships of Ferdinand Magellan. Soon America was being conquered (5) and exploited for gain. Although the new discoveries prompted searching questions about much that had seemed self-evident, this was, nevertheless, still an 'age of faith' (1, 3), a faith as fanatical, if not as single-minded, as the days of the Crusades. It would be another century before science and secularism began to erode the Christian world-view.

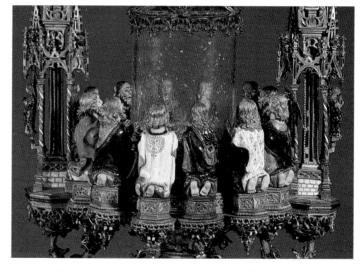

3. Detail of a monstrance made from the first gold brought back from America; Portuguese, 1506.

Travel by land and sea 176-177

Picturing the world 208-209

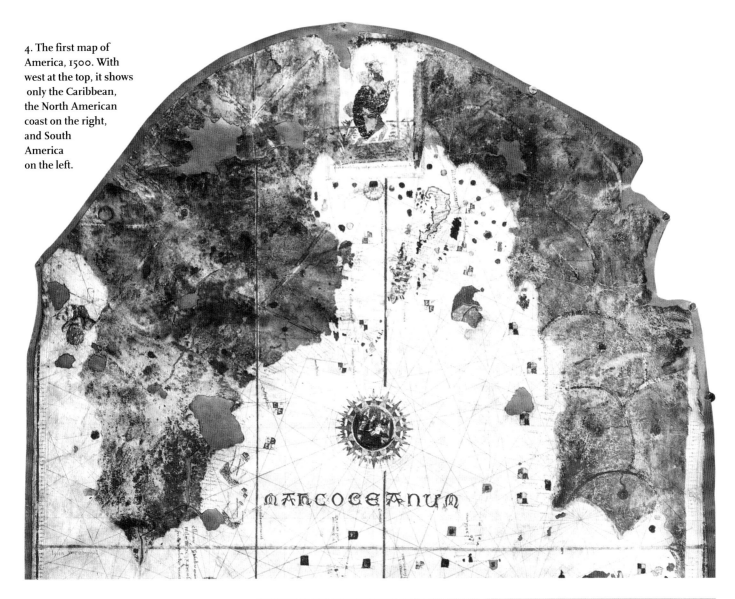

4. The first map of America, 1500. With west at the top, it shows only the Caribbean, the North American coast on the right, and South America on the left.

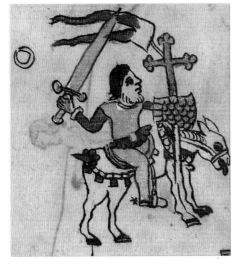

5. Hernán Cortes conquering Mexico, an Aztec drawing of about 1519.

6. Detail from Alejo Fernandes' *Virgin of the Navigators*, showing early 16th-century ocean-going ships; Spanish, 1531–36.

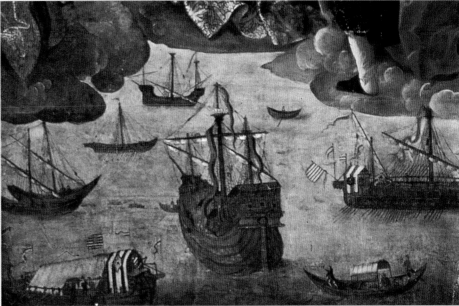

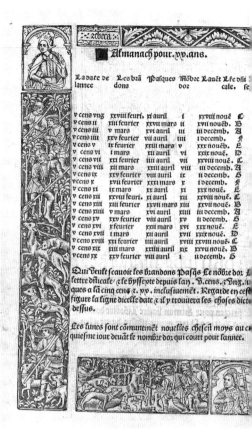

1. Calendar printed as a whole-page woodcut by Johann von Gmünd; *c.* 1440.

2. Printed Book of Hours, including a Zodiacal Man; French, 1500–01.

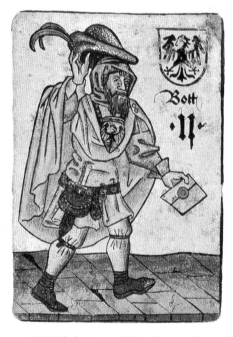

3. Printed playing-card featuring a postman; German, late 15th century.

Printing: the intellectual revolution

In the midst of these developments came the invention of printing, an event that signalled most unequivocally of all the transition from one age to the next. At a single stroke it completely transformed the dissemination of knowledge and ideas. Education could now escape the control of church and state; dissent could no longer be easily suppressed; and politically it meant the end of an elite which had monopolized the arts of communication. As an idea it was not completely new. Mass-produced block-books, pages combining text and pictures, were already common for such items as calendars (1), books of hours (2) and playing-cards (3). It was the composition of whole books in moveable type, the laborious putting together of separate letters, that was revolutionary. At first they imitated manuscripts as closely as possible, as Gutenberg's Bible does (5).

In the scriptorium 84   A new literature 222–223

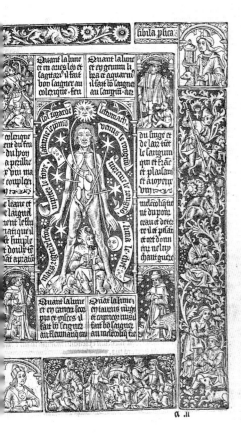

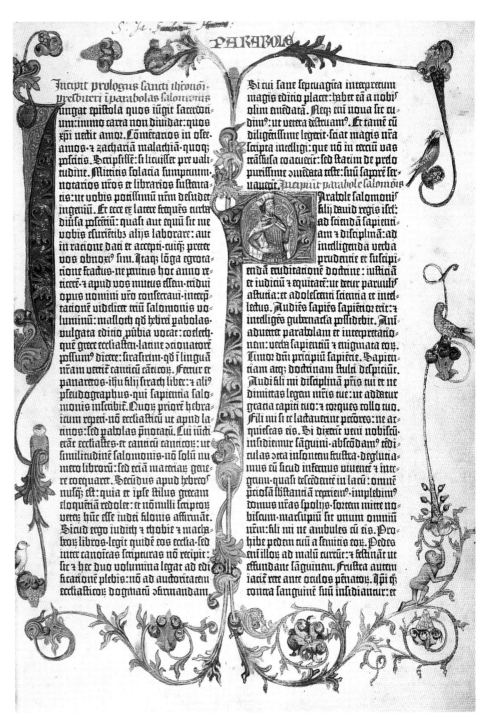

5. Right: page of Gutenberg's 42-line Bible with decoration added by hand; 1452–55.

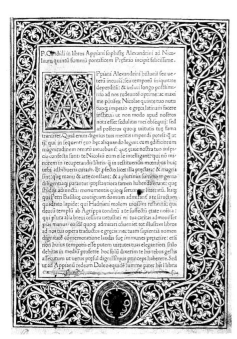

4. An early classical text printed in Venice: Appian's History, 1477.

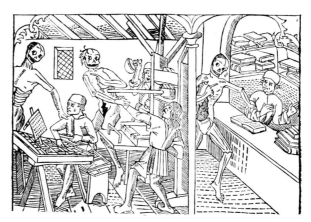

6. The earliest representation of a printing-house, showing a compositor, printing press and bookseller, is from a French Danse Macabre of 1499.

The End of the Middle Ages   271

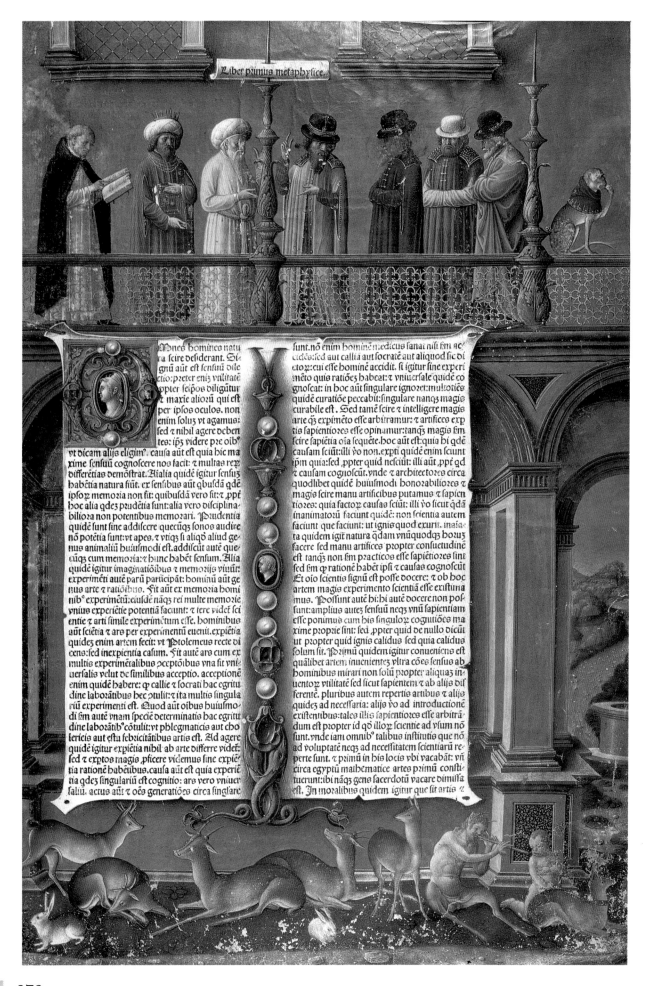

Reference

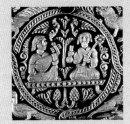

Biographical Dictionary • Timelines
Gazetteer • Maps • Glossary
Bibliography • List of Illustrations
Index

The first page of Aristotle's *Metaphysics* in Latin, published in Venice
in 1483. Only the columns of text are printed. The rest is a painted
scene of scholars standing on a balcony, from which a large parchment
is represented as hanging, with deer and a satyr in the foreground.
All this was intended to make the printed book look as much like
an illuminated manuscript as possible.

Biographical Dictionary

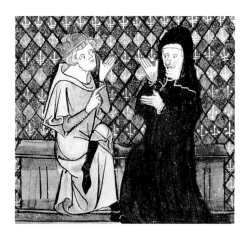

Miniature showing imaginary portraits of Abelard and Héloise, from a 14th-century manuscript of the 'Roman de la Rose'.

Abelard, Peter, *c.* 1079–1142. A charismatic teacher and a brilliant, self-confident intellectual, he played a significant role in creating Paris's reputation as a centre of learning. Born at Le Pallet, near Nantes, Abelard renounced his rights of inheritance and 'withdrew from the court of Mars in order to sit at the feet of Minerva'. He studied under the leading masters of the day and taught philosophy at Melun, Corbeil and Paris. Fulbert, a canon of Notre Dame, engaged Abelard to tutor his niece, HÉLOISE. The two fell in love and married secretly. Fulbert reacted by having Abelard castrated. Following this public humiliation, Abelard retired to the Benedictine monastery of Saint-Denis, Paris. His teachings on the nature of the Trinity led to his condemnation as a heretic at the Council of Soissons, 1122, where he was forced to burn his books. His unorthodoxy was again condemned in 1140 at the Council of Sens. BERNARD OF CLAIRVAUX, who saw him as a danger to the Church, was among his chief opponents. Abelard believed that reason could clarify matters of faith, and his *Sic et Non* employed dialectic to draw attention to apparent contradictions within Christian teaching. He was distinguished for his penetrating glosses on Aristotle and participated in the great debate on the nature of universals. Other major works include the *Theologia, Ethica* (*Know Thyself*) and the autobiographical *Historia Calamitatum*. He retired to Cluny and died at Saint Marcel in 1142.

Aethelred the Unready (Unraed), King of England 978–1016. Ruler of a beleaguered country, Aethelred was unable to defend England against persistent invasions from the North. Born *c.* 968, the son of King Edgar, he succeeded his half-brother Edward the Martyr, though many suspected him of complicity in the latter's murder. To cope with constant Danish and Norse invasions, Aethelred resorted to purchasing peace. In 1013 the Danish king Sweyn I received the submission of N. England and London, and Aethelred fled to Normandy. He returned, however, in 1014 and continued to rule until his death, whereupon his kingdom was divided up between his son Edmund Ironside and CANUTE.

Ailly, Peter D' (Petrus de Aliaco/ Cameracensis), *c.* 1350–1420. A leading French academic and fervent advocate of Church reform, D'Ailly's contemporaries called him 'the eagle of France and the indefatigable hammer of heretics'. Born at Compiègne, the son of an affluent butcher, he was educated at the College of Navarre in Paris. His commentaries on PETER LOMBARD's *Sentences* helped advance the cause of Nominalism in Paris. D'Ailly was Rector at the College of Navarre in 1384 and Chancellor of Paris in 1389, and later acted as Almoner and Confessor to Charles VI of France. He was elevated to the sees of Le Puy and Cambrai, served as cardinal papal legate, and played an active role in the Councils of Pisa and Constance; the latter terminated the Schism through the election of Martin V as pope. D'Ailly served as the latter's legate and remained at Avignon until his death. D'Ailly believed that bishops and priests did not hold their authority from the pope but from Christ, and argued that neither the pope nor council was infallible. He was greatly influenced by BACON and WILLIAM OF OCKHAM, and wrote in various genres on a wide range of subjects. Most of his works were concerned with ecclesiastical reform and the Great Schism. His *Image of the World*, which endorses the hypothesis that the world is round, was known to Christopher Columbus.

Alan of Lille (Alanus ab Insulis), *c.* 1128–*c.* 1203. One of the most learned figures of the twelfth century, he was a leading master at Paris and participated in the Third Lateran Council of 1179. Alan was a rationalist and also an innovator who fashioned new words and forms of expression. He was concerned with the care of souls and helped oppose Catharist heresy in S. France. Alan wrote on a wide range of subjects, and his two most popular works, *De Planctu Naturae*, a combination of prose and verse, and *Anticlaudianus*, an allegorical poem, espouse his belief in Nature as a mediator between Man and God. Towards the end of his life and in preparation for his death, Alan entered the Cistercian house of Cîteaux.

Albertus Magnus (Albert of Cologne), *c.* 1190–1280. Albertus contributed to philosophy, theology and the history of science, and appears amongst the lovers of wisdom in DANTE's *Divine Comedy*. Born in Lauingen, Germany, the son of a knight, he attended the University of Padua and pursued his studies at Paris. Albertus joined the Dominicans in 1223 and was appointed head of the Order in Germany in 1254. Elected to the bishopric of Regensburg in 1260, he resigned two years later and retired to Cologne to devote himself to scholarly works but left there in 1263 to preach the Eighth Crusade in German-speaking lands. Albertus paraphrased the entire corpus of Aristotle's works and his chief writings include the *Summa de Creaturis* and the incomplete *Summa Theologica*. He defended the doctrines of his pupil, THOMAS AQUINAS, at Paris in 1277, and was beatified in 1622 and canonized in 1931.

Alexander III, Pope 1159–81. He stands at the head of the line of lawyer popes, and his decretals made a greater contribution to the body of canon law than those of any other pope. Born Rolando Bandinelli in Siena, *c.* 1105, he trained as a lawyer at Bologna and earned renown as a canonist. He rose in papal service and was elected to the papacy by the majority of cardinals in 1159. A minority of the cardinals had voted for Cardinal Octavian and, supported by FREDERICK BARBAROSSA, they established him as the antipope, Victor IV, thereby inaugurating a seventeen-year schism. Alexander was forced to flee to France, where he resided for the most part until 1177, when the Peace of Venice forced Frederick to submit. Alessandria, founded on the Lombard plains, was named after Alexander in acknowledgement of his support for the Lombard communities against Barbarossa. During his papacy Alexander was also involved in BECKET's conflict with HENRY II. Alexander was a reformer and strengthened ecclesiastical administration. He summoned and presided over the Third Lateran Council of 1179, which was the highpoint of his papacy. Scholarly works attributed to him include a commentary on GRATIAN's *Decretum* and the *Sententiae Rolandi*.

Alexander of Hales, *c.* 1186–1245. *Doctor Irrefragabilis*, he was a great theologian, a prominent churchman, and effectively launched the Golden Age of scholasticism. Born in Hales, Shropshire, he studied philosophy and theology at Paris where he was a master from *c.* 1220. He represented the university at the Roman Curia. Alexander held several livings and was actively engaged in church affairs. He was involved in negotiations between HENRY III and LOUIS IX in 1235, and participated in the General Council of Lyons in 1245. Upon joining the Franciscans in 1236 he renounced his worldly possessions but retained his chair at the university. He is considered the founder of the Franciscan school of theology. He distinguished philosophy from theology and was influenced by Aristotle and Augustine. SALIMBENE refers to Alexander's many writings. His main work, the *Summa Universae Theologiae*, was begun *c.* 1231 but was unfinished at the time of his death. He also contributed to an exposition of the *Rule of St Francis*, and his glosses on PETER LOMBARD's *Sentences* launched this as a textbook for theologians.

Alfonso VI (the Brave), King of León and Castile 1065–1109. He sought to reconcile the kingdoms of Castile, León and Galicia, and whilst his reign is often remembered for political failures, he also initiated significant cultural changes, including the introduction of the Carolingian script and the Roman liturgy. Born *c.* 1042, Alfonso inherited the kingdom of León from his father in 1065, but faced opposition from his jealous brother, Sancho II of Castile, who twice defeated him and ordered his exile. However, following Sancho's death in 1072 Alfonso recovered León and inherited Castile. Within Spain he supported the Cluniacs. He also helped develop a safe pilgrim route to the shrine of St James of Compostela. By 1077 he had proclaimed himself Emperor of Spain. In 1085, after a long siege against the Muslims, he conquered Toledo. However, oppression of his new vassals – he exacted heavy tribute – led to the Almoravid invasion of Spain in 1086 and to the king's defeat. He had little military success thereafter and lost his only son in the fighting of 1108. He died the following year, without an heir, and civil war ensued.

Alfonso X (the Learned), King of León and Castile 1252–84. Though generally dismissed as a failure on account of his

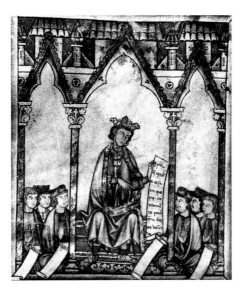

Alfonso X, King of León and Castile, from a manuscript of his 'Cantigas'; 13th century.

disastrous policies and domestic strife, Alfonso is nonetheless often hailed for his patronage of the arts and the promotion of his court as a centre for compilation and translation. He was born in 1221 and succeeded Fernando III in 1252. Alfonso lay claim to Gascony on the pretext that his grandmother was the daughter of HENRY II, but abandoned this with a treaty in 1254. From 1256 to 1275 he spent vast sums in pursuit of becoming Holy Roman Emperor – a ruinously expensive and futile campaign that provoked domestic unrest. Family dissension also dogged his reign. Two of his brothers rose against him and a third was executed; on the death of his eldest son, Fernando, his second son, Sancho, engaged the support of the nobles and rebelled. Alfonso was stripped of his powers and died amidst civil war with the succession in doubt. His cultural legacies include an extensive collection of translations and adaptations of Arabic scientific works, the largest collection of Marian poetry in the vernacular, encyclopaedic vernacular legal codes, a universal history and a history of Spain. However, Alfonso's cultural ventures were not always successful: the main law code was not actually promulgated during his reign and the two histories were incomplete. *See pp. 126-27*

Anselm of Bec, Archbishop of Canterbury 1093–1109. This 'philosopher-saint' was guided by the rational. 'I believe in order that I may understand.' Born in 1033 to a nobleman of Aosta, Lombardy, Anselm became a monk at Bec, Normandy, in 1060. He was appointed prior in 1063 and abbot in 1078, and rather reluctantly accepted the archbishopric of Canterbury in 1093. However, a series of disputes with the Crown resulted in his exile from 1097 to 1100 and

1103 to 1107. He quarrelled with William Rufus over the Canterbury knights and recognition of the pope. His disagreement with Henry I centred on the king's investiture of prelates with the symbols of office. He was a prolific writer and many of his letters and writings survive. His chief theological treatises include the *Monologion*, 'an example about meditating on the substance of faith', which is a soliloquy on the qualities of God; the *Proslogion*, a dialogue with God which contains the ontological proof of God's existence; the *Cur Deus Homo*, a study of the Atonement. The *De Grammatico* is his only non-spiritual work. Details of Anselm's public and private life are known from biographical works compiled by Eadmer, a monk of Canterbury and Anselm's constant companion from 1093. The saint's cult was slow to develop. BECKET requested his canonization in 1163 and while no formal record survives, his feasts are mentioned in a Canterbury calendar of *c.* 1165. He appears in the Roman Martyrology in 1586 and was made a Doctor of the Church in 1720.

Aquinas, Thomas, 1225–74. One of the greatest medieval theologians, he believed it possible to reconcile Aristotle with Christian theological tenets. Thomas was born into the minor nobility at Rocca, S. Italy, and presented as a child oblate to the monks of Monte Cassino. He completed his education at Naples and joined the Dominican Order in 1244, against the wishes of his family. At Paris he studied under ALBERTUS MAGNUS, who introduced him to Aristotle. Thomas spent the remainder of his years teaching in Paris and Italy, and died aged forty-nine. He was primarily a theologian but stressed that the study of philosophy should precede the study of theology. He was greatly influenced by Aristotle's metaphysical works. His teachings clearly distinguish faith from reason, and his works include the *Summa Contra Gentiles* (1259–64) and the *Summa Theologica*, begun in 1266 but incomplete at the time of his death. Thomas was greatly esteemed by LOUIS IX, consulted by the University of Paris, and his teachings were officially imposed on the Dominican Order in 1278. However the Franciscans forbade their members to study his works and his views were rejected by others including JOHN DUNS SCOTUS. The universities generally divided into Thomists and Scotists according to their loyalty. Thomas was canonized in 1323. *See pp. 210-11*

Averroes (Ibn Rushd), 1126–1198. The greatest Islamic philosopher in the West, Averroes was the author of numerous influential treatises and commentaries.

Born in Cordoba, he came under the patronage of Caliph Yusuf, who, impressed by the young scholar's learning, helped him to obtain a number of significant posts, including that of judge. Briefly interned in 1195, when the climate became hostile towards speculative studies, Averroes was then summoned to Morocco, where he died. His writings – many of which survive in manuscript – include works on medicine, jurisprudence, grammar, astronomy, philosophy, logic and religion. He is principally known, however, for his commentaries on Aristotle. Reconciling Islamic and Greek thought, Averroes' interpretations were to have a profound influence on later Jewish and Christian writers.

Avicenna (Ibn Sina), 980–1037. A brilliant scientist, scholar and philosopher, Avicenna was one of the chief Islamic interpreters of Aristotle and the Neoplatonists. After the Turkish conquest of 999 he left his native Bukhara and wandered throughout Persia, eventually becoming court physician and vizier to Shams ad-Dawlah in Hamadan. Renowned for his learning and medical skill, Avicenna wrote over 100 works on science, language, religion and philosophy, the most influential of which was his *Canon of Medicine*, still a standard text six hundred years after his death. He spent his last years in Isfahan. *See p. 240*

Bacon, Roger, *c.* 1214–*c.* 1292. *Doctor mirabilis*, he was an experimentalist who urged the need for observation in science, and believed that intellectual comprehension came from God alone. Born in Ilchester, Somerset, to a knightly family, he probably studied at Oxford and pursued his studies at Paris where he was one of the first to lecture on Aristotle's natural philosophy, which had hitherto been banned. He entered the Franciscans in *c.* 1256, but his opinions were seemingly denounced by the Master General of the Order in *c.* 1277. Bacon insisted that theology was the mistress of other sciences, and considered scientific study a tool for illuminating theological truths. He fervently believed in the unity of knowledge and maintained that an understanding of the Scriptures and Nature would lead to comprehension of God, that wisdom of the heavens would lead to knowledge of earth, and that the study of language was essential to an understanding of the Scriptures. Inspired by Augustine's *City of God*, he conceived of a Christian world united by one faith. Bacon wrote a variety of works in a number of genres including treatises on medicine, commentaries, polemic and scientific explanation. In the latter, he was heavily influenced by ROBERT GROSSETESTE. In 1266 Clement IV instructed him to present a summary of his thoughts; he responded by writing the seven-part encyclopaedic *Opus Maius*, followed by the *Opus Minus* and *Opus Tertium*. It was the Elizabethans who 'rediscovered' Bacon and fostered the image of him as a scientist.

Baldus de Ubaldis (Baldo degli Ubaldi da Perugia), *c.* 1320–1400. An energetic canonist and civil lawyer, he is particularly renowned for his commentary on feudal law, the *Usus Feudorum*. Born to a prominent Perugian family, he was probably educated at the University of Perugia and seems to have taught at Bologna, Perugia and Pavia. He also held public offices and served as vicar-general to the bishop of Todi, and acted as judge, legate and counsellor of Perugia. One of the greatest commentators on Roman law, Baldus also wrote extensively on canon, civil and feudal law. He was respected as a practising lawyer and Urban VI engaged his help against Clement VII.

Becket, Thomas, Archbishop of Canterbury 1162–70. Brutally murdered in Christ Church Cathedral, Thomas Becket was to become one of the most important saints of the Middle Ages. Born in *c.* 1120, the son of a London merchant, Becket received his early education at the Augustinian priory at Merton, Surrey, and pursued his studies at Paris, Bologna and Auxerre. He served in the household of Theobald, Archbishop of Canterbury, and in 1155 was appointed Chancellor to HENRY II, with whom he became great friends. Thomas succeeded Theobald as Archbishop of Canterbury and was consecrated in June 1162. This marked a turning-point in relations between Becket and the king. The flamboyant courtier now threw himself into the role of archbishop and opposed the king's infringements on ecclesiastical liberties: 'putting off the secular man, he now put on Jesus Christ'. Thomas and Henry clashed in particular over the matter of criminous clerks and whether these offenders should be tried in their own courts or by seculars. This led to Becket's flight to France in 1164, following the Council of Northampton, and his subsequent exile, along with some four hundred companions. During this time he sought refuge with the monks of Pontigny and Sens. Despite a brief reconciliation, relations remained sour. Henry's anger ultimately incited four of his knights to murder the archbishop in his own cathedral on 29 December 1170. Becket's martyrdom stunned the West and Henry, who was blamed for the act, was forced to do public penance. Miracles were reported at the tomb and Becket was canonized in 1173. Canterbury became a celebrated centre of pilgrimage. Phials containing water speckled with the martyr's blood were worn around the neck by pilgrims to his shrine.
See pp. 68, 152

Bernard of Clairvaux, *c.* 1090–1153. A charismatic leader and an energetic preacher, he participated in contemporary affairs of the Church and State. Born into the Burgundian nobility, Bernard was trained for a clerical career by the canons of Châtillon. However, when twenty years old, he chose to follow the austere life of the Cistercians and joined the monks of Cîteaux, *c.* 1112. In 1115 he was sent to found Clairvaux, the third daughter house of Cîteaux, which flourished under his leadership and became one of the chief Cistercian centres. Bernard was actively involved in current affairs. He obtained recognition for the Templars' rules in 1129, and in 1140 played a leading part in the condemnation of ABELARD's works at Sens. Furthermore he travelled extensively with

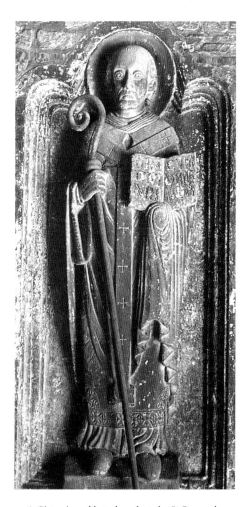

A Cistercian abbot, thought to be St Bernard of Clairvaux, at the church of St Mary at Maastricht; 12th century.

and on behalf of Innocent II, and was appointed to preach the Second Crusade in 1146 by his former pupil, Eugenius III. Bernard is also renowned for his extensive literary output. His writings include sermons, some five hundred letters, a *Life* of Malachy of Ireland, and theological tracts, including *The steps of humility and pride*, c. 1125. Bernard was formally canonized in 1174, although his cult began unofficially during his life.

Bernard Silvester (Silvestris; Bernard of Tours), *c*. 1100–*c*. 1170. Primarily celebrated as a poet, he was particularly interested in the universe and man's place therein, and was intrigued with questions of destiny and free will. Little is known of Bernard although he probably spent most of his life in Tours, where he taught at the cathedral school. He was seemingly connected with Chartres and his *Cosmographia*, an allegorical account of Creation, is dedicated to Thierry, who was Chancellor of Chartres in 1141. The *Cosmographia*, which was read before Pope Eugenius III in 1147, alternates a chapter of verse with a chapter of prose, after the fashion of Boethius' *De Consolatione Philosophiae*. It was extremely popular and accepted as a school textbook by the mid-thirteenth century. Other works include a long poem on destiny, the *Mathematicus*.

Bernardino of Siena, 1380–1444. A popular preacher, he initiated moral reform in the Italian city states through lively and emotive sermons, enhanced with examples from daily life. The son of a Sienese noble but orphaned at birth, Bernardino joined an aristocratic flagellant confraternity when he was eighteen. He entered the Franciscan Order in 1402, and the following year joined the branch of the Observants. He lived as a wandering preacher and drew large crowds as he travelled on foot through Italy, denouncing gambling, usury and witchcraft, and advocating voluntary poverty and penance. In 1437 Bernardino was appointed vicar-general of the Observant Franciscans, whom he encouraged to take a more active role as teachers and preachers. He attempted to heal the rift between the Observants and Conventuals, and was concerned that the former's zeal should not transgress the bounds of orthodoxy. Bernardino resigned from office in 1443 and resumed preaching, though with his health failing he now travelled by donkey. He was canonized in 1450.

Boccaccio, Giovanni, 1313–75. Founder of Italian prose literature, he is chiefly remembered for his secular epic, the *Decameron*, a human comedy comprising one hundred lively and often bawdy tales. Giovanni Boccaccio was born, illegitimate, in Tuscany,

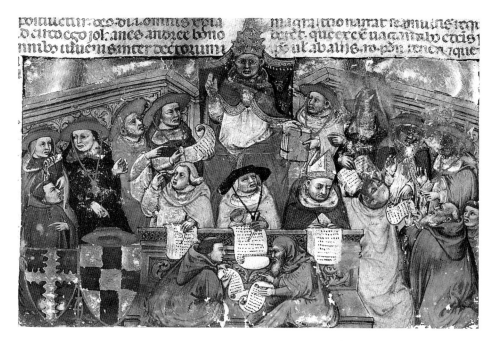

Pope Boniface VIII with the College of Cardinals; an early 14th-century manuscript of 'The Decretals of Boniface'.

but spent much of his youth in Naples. He returned to his native city after 1340 and became involved in Florentine politics, holding several civic offices. In addition to menial administrative duties he was involved in negotiations with the papacy and other foreign powers. However, Boccaccio is primarily celebrated for his contribution to vernacular literature, and his *Decameron*, ostensibly written to relieve women in love, was copied and admired by scholars and poets from CHAUCER to the sixteenth century. However, Boccaccio later regretted its lack of *gravitas* (seriousness). Other works include *La Caccia di Diana*, *De Mulieribus*, and his Latin encyclopaedia, *De Genealogia Deorum Gentilium*. Boccaccio, like PETRARCH, contributed to the revival of Greek studies. Indeed, he claimed that he had brought Homer to Florence, for he invited a Calabrian Greek, Leontius Pilatus, to stay with him whilst completing a translation of Homer. Boccaccio was accorded great honour in 1373 when he was asked to give the first lectures on DANTE's *Divine Comedy*.
See pp. 190, 223

Bonaventure, *c*. 1218–1274. A mystical theologian, he was devoted to the reformation of the Franciscans and is often considered their second founder. Born at Bagnoreggio, near Orvieto, the son of a physician, he joined the Franciscan Order in *c*. 1243, studied at Paris under ALEXANDER OF HALES, and was elected minister-general of the Order in 1257. He was appointed cardinal-bishop of Albano in 1273 and took a leading role in the Council of Lyons in 1274. He died in the same year and was buried at Lyons. During his lifetime he advocated an emotional sympathy with the Divine Mysteries. His most popular mystical work, *Itinerarium Mentis ad Deum*, was compiled after his pilgrimage to Alverna, where Francis had received the stigmata. Other works include the *Breviloquium*, the *Soliloquium*, and a fine commentary on PETER LOMBARD's *Sentences*. He also completed the official *Life* of ST FRANCIS and wrote an exposition of Francis' *Rule*. He was canonized in 1482.

Boniface VIII, Pope 1294–1303. A self-confident and hard-headed intellect, his firm beliefs in papal theocratic supremacy led to conflict with the leading rulers. Born Benedict Caetani in Anagni, Italy, *c*. 1234, he trained as a canon lawyer at Bologna and made a significant contribution with his *Liber Sextus*, a compilation of canon law from 1234 to 1298. He rose quickly in papal service and was made pope in 1294, following Celestine V's resignation. Like his predecessors, GREGORY VII and INNOCENT III, Boniface was a firm believer in the absolute power of the papacy. He enhanced his popularity in 1300 when he proclaimed the first Holy Year and promised indulgences to all who visited Rome on pilgrimage. However, he quarrelled with the kings of England and France over clerical taxation, and in a bull of 1296 forbade secular taxation of the clergy without papal approval. He was later forced to yield but continued his struggle with PHILIP IV of France, which was exacerbated by the papal bull, *Unam Sanctam* (1302), an extreme declaration of the papacy's theocratic precedence in spiritual and lay affairs. This culminated in Boniface's three-day imprisonment at Anagni by Philip in 1303. The elderly pope died shortly thereafter.

Bracton, Henry, d. 1268. Lawyer and royal judge, his fame rests primarily on the attribution of the *De legibus et consuetudinibus Angliae* to him. However, it is most likely that the treatise was the work of several persons, partly updated *c.* 1230–*c.* 1250, and that Bracton was the last author to insert his additions. Bracton served on the king's bench and from 1245 was a royal judge. He was part of the 1267 commission which heard the complaints of the disinherited following the DE MONTFORT rebellion. Bracton held various livings and died as Chancellor of Exeter Cathedral. The *De legibus*, the fullest medieval exposition of English law, is the most important common law treatise of the Middle Ages. It seeks to explain English law in terms of the *ius commune*, a composition of canon law and Roman law taught in the universities. The treatise draws on the *Decretum*, *Decretals*, the writings of the canonist, Tadeo, and the lawyer, Azo of Bologne. It incorporates the author's experiences as judge and introduces case law, recording some 450 studies.

Bradwardine, Thomas, *c.* 1295–1349. Scholastic and Archbishop of Canterbury, he was particularly renowned for his contribution to mathematics and theology, and believed that mathematics could provide the key to understanding Nature. Thomas was probably born at Hartfield, Sussex, and studied at Oxford where he was a fellow of Balliol and Merton. He was twice elected Proctor of the university. He was also Canon of Lincoln, chaplain to the bishop of Durham (1335), Chancellor of St Paul's Cathedral, London (1337) and confessor to EDWARD III He was consecrated to the archbishopric of Canterbury in July 1349 but died of the plague a month later. On account of the depth of his learning, he was accorded the title *Doctor Profundus*. Apart from the Bible his main sources were Augustine, ANSELM and AQUINAS: he was particularly influenced by the ontological argument first elaborated by Anselm. His works include the *De proportionibus velocitatum in motibus*, which was extremely influential in Europe, the *De causa Dei contra Pelagium et de virtute causarum*, his leading work in theology, and the *De insolubilibus*, an important treatise on logic.

Bridget (Birgitta) of Sweden, 1303–73. Visionary, foundress of the Bridgettine Order, and patron saint of Sweden, she was the daughter of one of the wealthiest landholders in the country. Bridget entered royal service in 1335 as chief lady-in-waiting to Magnus II's queen, Blanche of Namur. At this time she received her first visions. Following the death of her husband in 1343

she lived as a penitent for three years at the Cistercian house of Alvastra. She founded the Bridgettine Order at Vadstena in *c.* 1346. The community comprised sixty nuns and twenty-five monks, and the abbess had supreme authority. Three years later Bridget visited Rome and secured papal approval for the Order. Thereafter she completed several pilgrimages and lived a life of austerity, tending the sick. She was canonized in 1391.

Bruni, Leonardo, *c.* 1370–1444. A prominent Italian humanist, he played a significant role in the revival of classical learning in Italy, and was actively involved in civic affairs. Born in Arezzo, Tuscany, to humble parents, he studied at Florence and earned fame as a writer. He wrote propaganda to stimulate patriotic support for Florence against the Visconti of Milan. He was engaged in papal service from 1405 and acted as apostolic secretary to Gregory XII and Alexander V, and secretary to the anti-pope, John XXIII, with whom he fled to the Council of Constance in 1414. The following year he returned to Florence and began his chief work, the *Historia florentini populi*, a Latin history of Florence which celebrates the greatness of the city and her people. This was extremely influential and became the archetype for history-writing in Italy. His other works include translations of Aristotle and lives of DANTE and PETRARCH in Italian. In recognition of Bruni's achievement, Florence conferred upon him rights of citizenship and exempted him from taxation. By 1427 he had emerged as the most prominent man of letters in Florence and was appointed Chancellor. Bruni's funeral was conducted in great ceremony at the city's expense, in the presence of various dignitaries, testimony to his high renown. He was buried in the cemetery of Santa Croce.

Buridan, John, *c.* 1295–*c.* 1358. A renowned natural philosopher at the University of Paris, he is primarily remembered for his views on the earth's rotation and for his investigation of the possibility that the earth might rotate daily on its axis from the west to the east. Buridan was born in Arras and studied at Paris under WILLIAM OF OCKHAM; he was Rector of the university in 1328 and 1340. Buridan was an extreme Nominalist and sceptical of free will. He believed that knowledge of the world was attainable and sought to explore and thereby comprehend the physical world through experience, intellect and the use of 'Ockham's Razor', a theory which favours simplicity. Buridan was one of the few philosophers of the Middle Ages who was not a theologian. His works include the *Compendium Logicae*, *Summulae de Dialectica* and commentaries on Aristotle's

thought and logic. The number of surviving manuscripts is testimony to the popularity of his writings.

Canute (Knut), King of England and Denmark 1016–35. An ambitious and capable ruler, he was the first Viking king accepted amongst the circle of Christian monarchs, and by the time of his death he was the most powerful ruler in Western Europe. Born *c.* 995, the son of Sweyn Forkbeard, leader of the Viking army in English pay, he participated in his father's defeat of the Anglo-Saxon king, AETHELRED THE UNREADY, in 1013. Upon Aethelred's death he successfully subdued his son, Edmund Ironside, and on the latter's death was acknowledged King of the English. Following his marriage to Aethelred's widow, Emma of Normandy, in 1017, Canute was less hostile to the native English. He established a stable government that was able to support his heavy taxation – the heregeld – to maintain mercenaries and fleets. In 1019 he became king of Denmark and in 1028 ruler of Norway. Canute was a fine warrior and statesman, and presented himself as a great patron of the Church. He founded monasteries, gave generous benefactions and completed a pilgrimage to Rome in 1027. He also promoted trade and effectively saved England from further invasion.

Catherine of Siena, 1347–80. Mystic, virgin and saint, she rejected marriage and devoted herself to a life of prayer, penance and good works. Catherine, the daughter of a Sienese dyer, joined the Tertiary Order of the Dominicans and travelled around Italy with her followers, preaching repentance and reform of the Church. She was particularly concerned that the papacy be restored to Rome and urged Gregory XI to return from Avignon. During the Great Schism in 1378 she supported Urban VI against his Avignonese rival and died in his service at Rome in 1380. Catherine never learnt to write but dictated her compositions. Her literary works include the *Book of Divine Doctrine*, which was later considered one of the most important mystical works of the fourteenth century. Catherine was an influential spiritual leader and had a profound effect on her confessor and biographer, Raymond of Capua, who became minister-general of the Dominicans in 1380. His *Life* of Catherine was pivotal in securing her canonization in 1461. *See p. 89*

Caxton, William, *c.* 1422–91. English printer and translator whose texts promoted a standard form of printed English and were invaluable for the widespread dissemination of literary works. Born in Kent, Caxton was apprenticed to a London cloth merchant but left for Bruges in 1445 to complete his training. By 1464 he was governor of English merchants in the Low Countries. During a visit to Cologne in 1474 he learnt the art of printing and was responsible for the first English printed book, the *Recuyell of the Historyes of Troye*. In 1476 he returned to England and set up a press at Westminster where he printed, amongst other works, CHAUCER's *Canterbury Tales*, Gower's *Confessio amantis* and MALORY's *Morte d'Arthur*. He was succeeded by his assistant Wynkyn de Worde.

Charlemagne (Charles the Great), King of the Franks 768–814, Emperor 800–814. An historical and legendary figure, his reign is often portrayed as a Golden Age and a model for later generations of rulers. Charlemagne was born *c.* 742, the elder son of Pepin the Short and Bertrada. Following his father's death in 768 Charlemagne and his brother ruled the kingdom of the Franks; after his brother's death in 771 Charlemagne reigned alone. He was proclaimed emperor in Rome on 25 December 800, and was depicted as the Western equivalent of Byzantium's emperor. Charlemagne expanded the frontiers of the kingdom, spread Frankish influence, fostered reforms in administration and education,

and supported the Carolingian renaissance. He assumed authority over most of the Christian West, and led successful and profitable campaigns against the pagan Saxons, the Avars of the Danube and the Muslims in Spain. However, the final years of his reign saw a decline in many of his reforms. Furthermore the Franks were now occupied with defending their kingdom rather than launching lucrative wars of offence. *See pp. 52-53, 110, 152, 242*

Charles IV, Holy Roman Emperor 1355–78. He established his power base in Bohemia, founded the University of Prague in 1348, and built a bridge over the River Vltava. Born in 1316, a member of the Luxembourg family and grandson of Emperor HENRY VII, Charles succeeded his father, John of Bohemia, in 1346, and was crowned in 1347. He was elected anti-king to Louis of Bavaria and was crowned emperor in 1355. He preserved order through liberal bribes, maintained a solid system of government, and an alliance with the Avignon popes in 1365 enabled him to control Burgundy. Before his death, Charles secured the throne for his eldest son, Wenceslas – an unprecedented achievement. Charles is also remembered for the Golden Bull of 1356, which outlined the format for imperial elections. He wrote an auto-biography and was a patron of PETRARCH.

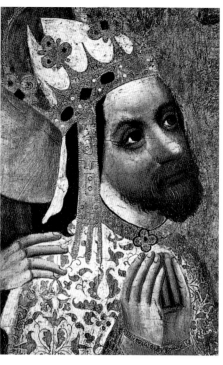

The Emperor Charles IV, a portrait by his court painter, Master Theodoric, c. 1370.

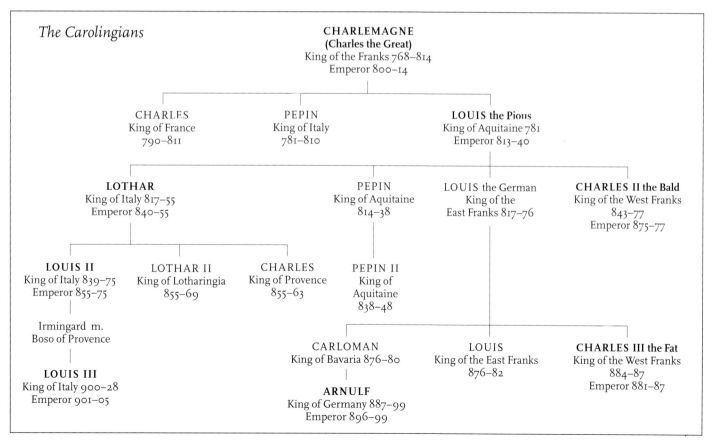

The Carolingians

CHARLEMAGNE
(Charles the Great)
King of the Franks 768–814
Emperor 800–14

CHARLES
King of France
790–811

PEPIN
King of Italy
781–810

LOUIS the Pious
King of Aquitaine 781
Emperor 813–40

LOTHAR
King of Italy 817–55
Emperor 840–55

PEPIN
King of Aquitaine
814–38

LOUIS the German
King of the
East Franks 817–76

CHARLES II the Bald
King of the West Franks
843–77
Emperor 875–77

LOUIS II
King of Italy 839–75
Emperor 855–75

LOTHAR II
King of Lotharingia
855–69

CHARLES
King of Provence
855–63

PEPIN II
King of
Aquitaine
838–48

Irmingard m.
Boso of Provence

CARLOMAN
King of Bavaria 876–80

LOUIS
King of the East Franks
876–82

CHARLES III the Fat
King of the West Franks
884–87
Emperor 881–87

LOUIS III
King of Italy 900–28
Emperor 901–05

ARNULF
King of Germany 887–99
Emperor 896–99

Charles of Anjou, King of Sicily and Naples 1266–84. An able soldier and ruler, he established an important French state in S. Italy. Charles was born in 1226, the youngest brother of LOUIS IX of France. Pope Clement IV, who hoped to establish a dependent state in the South that would support and not threaten the papacy, encouraged him to supplant FREDERICK II's son, Manfred, from Sicily. Charles responded enthusiastically and killed Manfred at Benevento in 1266. He suppressed a counter-invasion from Germany, led by Frederick's grandson, Conradin, whom he executed. He participated in both Louis IX's crusades against Egypt in 1248 and against Tunis in 1270. Throughout Charles' reign, his over-centralized system of government led to problems and further attempts to spread his influence in Italy provoked enmity. The Sicilian Vespers of 1282, a popular uprising supported by Charles' enemies, was a reaction to his oppressive rule, and forced the king to leave the island of Sicily to the Aragonese. He died in 1284, while planning a counter-offensive.

Charles the Bold (Charles the Rash), Duke of Burgundy 1467–77. An aggressive and impatient ruler, he sought independence from France and strove to extend his territories as far as the Rhine, but over-stretched himself. Born in 1433, the son of Philip the Good, Charles effectively exercised ducal powers from 1465, during his father's lifetime. His ambitions to make Burgundy independent of France led to a life-long struggle with LOUIS XI of France. Charles was initially successful. He was supported by the League of the Public Weal and King Louis' younger brother, Charles, and characteristically 'bought' the rebels' support through liberal bribes. However, the last three years of his reign were disastrous. In 1475 Louis forced the Treaty of Picquigny, which considerably undermined Burgundian power, and Charles' ambitions in Switzerland led to three defeats and his death at Nancy in 1477. His mutilated body was found half-buried in ice several days after his death. *See pp. 94, 222*

Chastellain, George, *c.* 1410–75. Chastellain was the official chronicler of the Burgundian dukes and a poet who experimented with versification. He was born in Flanders, studied in Louvain, travelled in England and France, and died at Valenciennes. He was a member of the *rhétoriqueurs*, a group of French writers who were court dependants. Chastellain was attached to the Burgundian ducal court and in 1473 CHARLES THE RASH made him Knight of the Golden Fleece and historiographer of the Order.

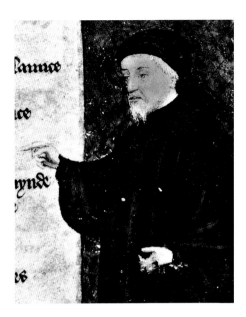

Geoffrey Chaucer, from Thomas Hocleve's 'De Regimine Principum'; early 15th century.

Chaucer, Geoffrey, *c.* 1342–1400. One of England's leading poets, Chaucer was also engaged in administrative life. The son of a vintner, he was active around court and enjoyed the patronage of John of Gaunt, later Duke of Lancaster. Chaucer travelled extensively in the 1370s, particularly in Italy where he may have met BOCCACCIO and PETRARCH. He officiated as knight of the shire and Justice of the Peace for Kent, and served in the 'Wonderful Parliament' of 1386. He is, however, primarily remembered for his *Canterbury Tales* (1386–1400), a selection of stories recounted by a group of pilgrims on their journey from Southwark to THOMAS BECKET's shrine at Canterbury. The pilgrims represent a cross-section of fourteenth-century society and their stories offer an interesting insight to social attitudes at this time. Other important works include *The Book of the Duchess, Troilus and Criseyde,* and translations of the *Roman de la Rose* and Boethius' *De Consolatione Philosophiae.* Chaucer was buried in Westminster Abbey on 25 October 1400. His tomb – the first of those comprising Poet's Corner – was erected by an admirer in the fifteenth century. *See p. 223*

Chrétien de Troyes, d. *c.* 1183. Pioneer of courtly romance, Chrétien effectively created Arthurian literature as it is today, for he was the first to speak of Guinevere's affair with Lancelot and write of the Holy Grail. Chrétien is something of an enigma and little is known of his life. He was probably a native of E. Champagne who spent most of his active career at Marie de Champagne's court, and indeed the romance, *Lancelot*, is dedicated to her. He may have visited HENRY II's court in England earlier in his career.

Chrétien wrote in the vernacular and drew his material from itinerant Breton minstrels. His romances, *Erec, Cliges, Yvain, Lancelot* and *Perceval*, describe the knight-errant's search for adventure, which is also a journey of self-discovery.

Christine de Pisan, *c.* 1364–*c.* 1430. The first known female professional writer, her works advocate the merits of women. Born in Venice to an Italian scholar and statesman who became court physician and astrologer to Charles V of France, she married the king's notary and secretary, Etienne du Castel. Christine was widowed only ten years later at the age of twenty-five, and with three young children to support she established herself as a writer. She began by composing love poems but then progressed to moral and historical themes. Her work was held in high regard and she enjoyed the patronage of the French kings and the dukes of Burgundy. Christine had a productive literary career and many of her writings survive. Her works include the *Avision-Christine* (1405), an account of her life, a history of Charles V, *The Treasure of the City of Ladies, The Book of the City of Ladies,* and a poem on Joan of Arc (1429). Christine spent the last years of her life in a convent and died after 1429, probably before 1434. *See pp. 194, 222*

Cimabue (Cenni di Pepi), *c.* 1240–*c.* 1302. A native of Florence, he is the legendary founder of Italian painting who influenced GIOTTO, Donatello, Masaccio and Michelangelo. DANTE maintains that he was the leading painter of his generation, but was later surpassed by Giotto. There is much dispute as to the identity of many of his surviving works. His earliest known work is the large Crucifix panel in S. Domenico, Arezzo, *c.* 1275. Other works include frescoes in the Basilica of St Francis, Assisi, the apse mosaic of Pisa Cathedral and a massive crucifix in S. Croce Museum, Florence, *c.* 1285.

Clare of Assisi, 1194–1253. Contemplative, foundress and saint, she was born at Assisi, but little is known of her early life. Inspired by FRANCIS' example Clare renounced her possessions in 1214 and joined him at the Portiuncula, where she took the nun's habit. Francis installed Clare and her companions in a house by the church of S. Damiano, and the Order of the Poor Clares was formed *c.* 1215. Clare remained in the convent where she devoted herself to contemplation and austerity, and prayed for Assisi in times of trouble. Indeed, it was alleged that on one occasion when the city was threatened by FREDERICK II's armies Clare was carried to the walls of the city with a pyx containing the Blessed Sacrament, causing the invaders to disappear. Clare was canonized in 1255, only two years after her death. *See p. 87*

Commynes (Comines), Philip de, *c.* 1447–1511. Biographer, historian and statesman, he introduced a political consciousness to his works and was particularly celebrated for his *Mémoires* of Louis XI of France. Philip was born near Lille. His father served the duke of Burgundy as the chief bailiff of Flanders, and Philip grew up in the Burgundian court as the godson of Duke Philip the Good. In *c.* 1464 he became squire to Charles the Rash, later Duke of Burgundy, and swiftly rose to positions of authority. Indeed he was one of the twenty-five Burgundian knights chosen to joust in honour of the duke's marriage in July 1468. Philip went on diplomatic missions on Charles' behalf, but in 1472 switched his loyalties to King Louis XI and was handsomely rewarded for his services. Philip's fortunes fluctuated thereafter. Following the king's death in 1483 he was deprived of his position and wealth, and imprisoned on the charge of treason. He was later released and became a prominent contributor to Louis XII's Italian policy. Philip dictated the first six books of his *Mémoires* between spring 1489 and spring 1491, at the request of Archbishop Cato of Vienna, who required information to write a Latin history of Louis XI. Philip portrays the brutality of war and describes betrayals and deceptions. He admits that he was not an eyewitness to the events, but claims that he records the truth.

Dafydd ap Guilym, *c.* 1320–80. The greatest Welsh poet of the Middle Ages, 'the nightingale of Dyfed' was both innovative and conservative. He described himself as 'Ovid's man'. Dafydd was born of Welsh nobility (*Uchelwyr*) in Cardiganshire, but little is known of his early life. He lived, for a time, in Glamorganshire with his patron, Hoe Hael, to whom several of his poems are addressed. His work was to some extent influenced by his predecessors – the court poets of the twelfth and thirteenth centuries – but he preferred to write of love and nature than elegy and praise. He writes of physical rather than spiritual love, and his poetry is often earthy and humorous. According to tradition he was buried at the Cistercian abbey of Strata Florida.

Damian, Peter, *c.* 1007–72. Prelate, theologian and saint, he was a prominent figure in Church reform and an influential writer who taught through anecdotes. Born in Ravenna to humble parents, he studied at Parma, Modena and Faenza. At the age of twenty-five, he sought seclusion and retired to the austere Camaldolese monastery at Fonte Avellana, Umbria, where he lectured to his fellow monks and neighbouring communities, and wrote a *Life* of St Romuald. He became prior of the community in *c.* 1043 and urged moderation of the *Rule of St Benedict*. In *c.* 1057 he finally yielded to Pope Stephen IX's decision to make him cardinal bishop of Ostia, and he became renowned as a zealous reformer, particularly opposed to clerical simony and the luxury of the Church. Peter was also a committed papalist and supported Alexander against the anti-pope and acted as papal ambassador. Indeed, it was on his return from Ravenna in 1072, where he had been sent to reconcile the people to the pope, that he died of a fever. While Peter was never formally canonized, several local cults developed after his death, for instance at Cluny, Monte Cassino and Faenza. Peter was concerned that philosophy should be subordinated to religion, and that secular writings remain subservient to spiritual works. A number of his writings have survived, including some fifty-three sermons, seven *Lives*, and around 180 letters. The latter reveal his skills in rhetoric. His major works are the *Liber Gratissimus* and the *Liber Gomorrhianus*. In art he is often depicted as a cardinal holding a discipline, or as a pilgrim with a papal bull in his hand.

Dante Alighieri, 1265–1321. The son of a Florentine lawyer, Dante is celebrated as one of the greatest poets of the Middle Ages. In his early years he endeavoured to render Occitan romance more suitable for the Florentine bourgeois. His poetry was inspired by his childhood love, Beatrice, and he was deeply affected by her death in 1290. *La Vita Nuova* (1292–93), a combination of poetry and prose in the vernacular, was written in her memory. It is a record of Dante's development as an artist and his celebration of Beatrice as a miracle, and is thus indicative of the close relationship between his life and poetry. Dante also became extensively involved with Florentine politics and was a prominent member of the White Guelphs. When the Black Guelphs assumed power he was banished from Florence and sought refuge in Verona. His works at this time include the *Convivio*, commentaries on canzoni, and the *Monarchia*, a statement of the political ideas of his maturity. His principal work, *The Divine Comedy*, was written in Ravenna. It comprises three sections – *Inferno*, *Purgatorio*, *Paradiso* – and describes man's spiritual and intellectual journey from darkness to understanding, with Dante himself as the protagonist who meets or observes contemporary and historical figures. It fuses allegory with realism, and incorporates numerology, astrology, philosophy and contemporary history. *See pp. 32, 90, 223, 225*

David I, King of Scots 1124–53. One of the greatest kings of Scotland, he refashioned the country along Anglo-Norman lines by erecting castles and extending feudal tenure; he also issued the first Scottish coinage. Born *c.* 1084, the youngest son of Malcolm Canmore and Margaret, he grew up in Henry I's court in England. Following his marriage to Earl Waltheof's daughter and heiress, Matilda, David emerged as the greatest baron in England. He was renowned as a pious king and established monastic centres in Scotland, including Melrose and Holyrood. However, he could be ruthless, and in 1130 initiated the brutal slaughter of the men of Moray and their king, Angus, to establish his power there. Despite his strong links with England, David sought independence for Scotland. The succession dispute in England, upon Henry I's death, enabled him to take Carlisle and Newcastle. While he was defeated at the Battle of the Standard in 1138, Stephen, who needed David's goodwill, gave Northumbria to his son, Henry. David died a year after the death of his only heir and was succeeded by his grandson, Malcolm IV.

Diarmait Mac Múrchada (Dermot MacMurrough), 1110–71. King of Leinster, he enlisted Henry II's support to retaliate against the High King, Rory O'Connor of Connacht, who had effected his defeat and exile, and thereby inaugurated the Anglo-Norman invasion of Ireland. Having been driven from Ireland in 1166, Diarmait received permission to seek recruits amongst Henry's Anglo-Norman vassals and he made terms with Richard 'Strongbow', Earl of Pembroke. In return for invading Ireland Diarmait promised the earl succession to the throne of Leinster and the hand of his daughter, Aoifa. Diarmait returned to Ireland with a small troop in 1167, the main fleet arrived in 1169 and 'Strongbow' landed in 1170. Richard took much of E. Ireland, including Dublin and Waterford, and married Aoifa. Diarmait died the following year. He was also patron of the Book of Leinster.

Dominic, *c.* 1170–1221. Founder of the Dominican Order, Dominic was born in Castile and joined the Austin Canons of Osma Cathedral, where he served as a priest for seven years and became prior in 1201. Following his encounter with Albigensian heretics at Toulouse in 1204, Dominic

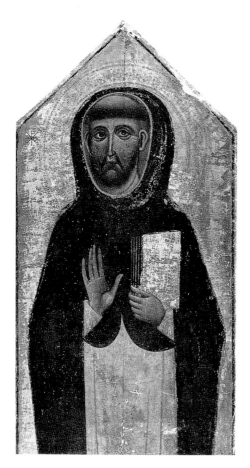

St Dominic, a portrait probably by Guido da Siena; 13th century.

endeavoured to reconcile them to the Church through peaceful means. He refused a bishopric three times and devoted himself to founding the Friars Preachers, a project which occupied him until his death. He secured papal approval for the Order in 1216 and the first Chapter General met at Bologna in 1220. The friars followed the *Rule of St Augustine* supplemented by Dominic's *Constitutions*. Dominic envisaged that the communities be centres of learning as well as prayer, and that the brothers should be mobile and devoted to preaching and teaching. They were the first Order officially to abandon manual labour. Dominic died in 1221 and was canonized in 1234.

Du Guescelin, Bertrand, *c.* 1320–79. A Breton military commander, his abilities enabled Charles V of France to instigate a French revival in the Hundred Years' War. He was constable of France in 1372.

Duccio di Buoninsegna, *c.* 1255–1319. 'Father of Sienese painting', and 'the Last of the Greeks', he was primarily influenced by the Byzantine tradition. His works, which combine great richness of colour, include the *Rucellai Madonna*, which is now in the Uffizi, and is considered by some to be his masterpiece. His main commission was the reredos for the High Altar (the *Maestà*) in Siena Cathedral, 1311. On the day of its installation the shops were shut and bells rung as the panel was escorted to the cathedral in a candle-lit procession.

Dufay, Guillaume, *c.* 1400–74. Burgundian composer attached to the court of Philip the Good, his works incorporated English, French and Italian influences. Dufay contributed to secular and religious music, and his compositions include some eight masses, two *Magnificats*, numerous hymns and notets, and over seventy *chansons*. He was also a singer at the papal court in Italy and the ducal court in Savoy. Dufay died at Cambrai.

Duns Scotus, John, *c.* 1265–1308. Eminent philosopher and theologian, he considered philosophy a vehicle for theology and was noted for his subtlety of thought. Born in Maxton, near Roxburgh, Scotland, he received his early education from the Franciscans at Dumfries and pursued his studies at Oxford. He lectured there and at Cambridge, held the Franciscan chair at Paris until 1307, and thereafter held a chair in theology at Cologne where he lectured until his death. His teachings utilize Aristotle and Augustine and introduce important philosophical concepts. His proof of the existence of God as an infinite being is both complex and ambitious. In moral philosophy he emphasized the primacy of love and the will over knowledge and reason. Duns Scotus was one of the first great thinkers to defend the doctrine of the Immaculate Conception. His works include commentaries on Aristotle and on PETER LOMBARD's *Sentences*. By the mid-fourteenth century the Scotist school of thought was extremely influential, especially amongst the Franciscans for whom it formed the basis of their doctrine. Duns Scotus was beatified in 1993.

Eckhart, Meister, *c.* 1260–*c.* 1327. Dominican mystic and master preacher and teacher, he has been hailed as the forerunner of Luther's teachings on faith, Hegel's Pantheism and Kant's Critical Idealism. Eckhart was born to an aristocratic family in Hochheim, Thuringia, but little is known of his early life. Records reveal that he was a member of the Dominicans and a student at Paris in 1277. He was elected provincial for the Dominicans in Saxony in 1303, vicar-general of Bohemia in 1307 and head of the Dominican *Studium Generale* in 1322. Eckhart, who preached and taught in both Latin and the German vernacular, was highly esteemed by his contemporaries. His corpus of German works comprises some fifty-nine authenticated sermons, and his Latin works include the *Opus Expositionum*. Cologne was his chief centre for preaching and it was here that mysticism entered his teaching. Eckhart approached a pantheistic interpretation of the Trinity which led to his conviction of heresy at Cologne in 1326. Although JOHN XXII condemned twenty-eight of his *Sentences* as heretical or dangerous, Eckhart's teachings remained influential.

Edward I, King of England 1272–1307. A ruthless, energetic ruler and an able warrior, he insisted upon the rights of kingship, but was less respectful of the rights of others. Edward, nicknamed 'Longshanks', was born at Westminster in June 1239, declared king in November 1272, and crowned in 1274. In 1277 he began campaigning in Wales and achieved great military victory. He reinforced conquest with the Statute of Rhuddlan (1284) and a series of great stone castles around Snowdonia, and declared his son Prince of Wales in 1301. Edward's military successes in Scotland earned him the title 'hammer of the Scots'. However, he failed to keep the country conquered and died on campaign on 7 July 1307. Edward, the 'English Justinian', is also remembered for his contribution to legal and constitutional developments, for instance, the Statutes of Westminster (1275, 1285), the Statute of Gloucester (1278), the *Quo Warranto* and *Quia Emptores* (1290). He did not promote the will of the prince as having the force of law but firmly believed that 'what touched all should be approved by all' and summoned representatives from local communities to parliament. Edward was greatly devoted to his wife, Eleanor of Castile, and upon her death in 1290 he erected twelve crosses from Lincoln to Westminster, to mark the halting places of her coffin. One of these stood at Charing Cross, London. *See pp. 102-103*

Edward III, King of England 1327–77. An ardent warrior and devotee of chivalry, his is the first English royal autograph to survive. Born at Windsor Castle on 13 November 1312, Edward succeeded to the throne at fourteen, following the deposition of his father, Edward II. His mother, Isabella of France, along with her lover, Roger Mortimer, effectively ruled until 1330. Edward achieved remarkable military victories in Scotland and was initially successful in France during the Hundred Years' War, notably at Crécy in 1346. In 1360 he secured total sovereignty over Aquitaine, Calais and Ponthieu with the Treaty of Brétigny, but was unable to sustain these successes when fighting resumed in 1369. During his reign the English parliament

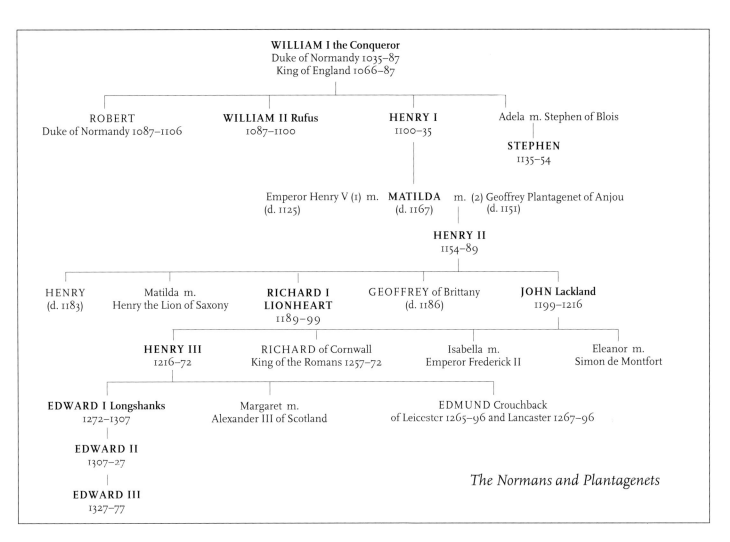

WILLIAM I the Conqueror
Duke of Normandy 1035–87
King of England 1066–87

ROBERT
Duke of Normandy 1087–1106

WILLIAM II Rufus
1087–1100

HENRY I
1100–35

Adela m. Stephen of Blois

STEPHEN
1135–54

Emperor Henry V (1) m. **MATILDA** m. (2) Geoffrey Plantagenet of Anjou
(d. 1125) (d. 1167) (d. 1151)

HENRY II
1154–89

HENRY
(d. 1183)

Matilda m.
Henry the Lion of Saxony

RICHARD I
LIONHEART
1189–99

GEOFFREY of Brittany
(d. 1186)

JOHN Lackland
1199–1216

HENRY III
1216–72

RICHARD of Cornwall
King of the Romans 1257–72

Isabella m.
Emperor Frederick II

Eleanor m.
Simon de Montfort

EDWARD I Longshanks
1272–1307

Margaret m.
Alexander III of Scotland

EDMUND Crouchback
of Leicester 1265–96 and Lancaster 1267–96

EDWARD II
1307–27

EDWARD III
1327–77

The Normans and Plantagenets

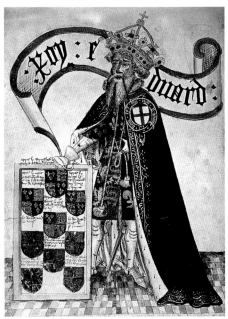

King Edward III of England wearing the robes of the Order of the Garter; 15th century.

became a regular institution and assumed considerable powers, for Edward was prepared to make substantial political concessions in return for resources required to finance the wars. While the king's relations with the nobility were generally good, there was disharmony in the last few years of his reign. Furthermore, high taxation for the renewal of a futile war led to complaints. In the Good Parliament of 1376, the Commons attacked financial incompetence and corruption of the court clique, impeached the leading offenders and implemented temporary measures to supervise the king. Edward's reign was also affected by the Black Death of 1348–50 which killed some forty per cent of the population. Edward's love of chivalry led him to institute the Order of the Garter, a brotherhood of twenty-six knights fronted by the king, whose motto was 'Evil be to him who evil thinks'.

Edward, the Black Prince, Prince of Wales 1359–76. He was hailed by his contemporaries as the epitome of knighthood and presented as a model of the successful military commander. The heir apparent to Edward III, he was born at Woodstock in 1330 and endowed with titles from an early age. Acclaimed for his military successes, his greatest victory was at Poitiers in 1356. He was made Prince of Aquitaine in 1362 and was completely responsible for the defence and administration of the province. One of the original Knights of the Garter, the prince was famed for his chivalry and pageantry. His black armour with bit, visor and ostrich plume was legendary, and his shield and armour hung above his effigy in Christ Church Cathedral, Canterbury; the replicas can still be seen. Edward's motto was *Humout, ich dene* (High Spirit, I serve). While his rule was cut short in 1376, when he contracted dysentery in Spain and died, his premature death perhaps preserved his reputation. *See p. 108*

El Cid, *c.* 1043–99. Born Rodrigo Díaz de Vivar, the son of a minor Castilian nobleman, he is celebrated as one of the greatest medieval heroes. In 1060 he was knighted by Sancho II of Castile, and became the king's standard-bearer and commander-in-chief of the armies. After Sancho's assassination in 1072 Rodrigo was removed from the centre of power and exiled following an unauthorized raid on the Muslim kingdom of Toledo in *c.* 1081. He then successfully commanded the amir of Saragossa's army and was accorded the title *Syyid* (lord), hispanicized as *Cid*. Although briefly reconciled with Alfonso in 1087, Rodrigo was banished again in 1089. He took possession of Valencia after a two-year siege and from 1094 was effectively sovereign of the city. Whereas Arabic historians portray him as a cruel oppressor, the *Historia Roderici* and legends of the monastery of S. Pedro de Cardeña, where Rodrigo is buried, present him as a lay saint. The *Poem of the Cid* (*c.* 1207) depicts him as a brave and astute ruler who was concerned about his soldiers' welfare.

Eleanor of Aquitaine, *c.* 1122–1204. A colourful and passionate lady, she was described by the monastic chronicler, Richard of Devizes, as 'beautiful, yet gentle, humble, yet keen-witted'. In 1137 Eleanor succeeded her father, William X of Aquitaine, and married the future Louis VII. The marriage was a disaster and annulled in 1152 on the grounds of consanguinity. Only two months later Eleanor married Henry, Duke of Normandy, later HENRY II of England, and their union brought Aquitaine within the Plantagenets' sphere of power, where it remained for the next three centuries. Eleanor led an eventful life. She accompanied her first husband on crusade, 1147–49, and there were rumours of an affair with her uncle, Raymond of Antioch. She was patron of the troubadours and courtly literature, and played an active role in political matters. However, Eleanor was imprisoned by Henry from 1174 to 1183, after supporting her sons' rebellion against their father, 1173–74. She was later released and shared Richard's government of Aquitaine, but was never completely free until Henry's death in 1189. Thereafter she asserted considerable political influence and provided crucial support for both Richard and John when they held the throne. Eleanor retired to Fontevrault in 1202 until her death in 1204.

Elizabeth of Thuringia, 1207–31. Celebrated for her great charity and devotion to the poor, she died when only twenty-four years of age and was canonized four years later. Born at Pressburg (Bratislava), the daughter of Andrew II of Hungary, she married Louis IV of Thuringia in 1221 and had three children. Elizabeth contributed great sums to almsgiving, hospitals and orphans, and was influenced by the Franciscans who had recently arrived in Thuringia. Louis' death in 1227 was a watershed. Elizabeth was driven

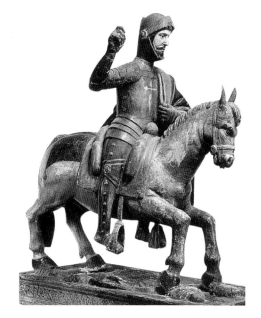

Ferdinand III, King of León and Castile; a later, 15th-century sculpture portraying him as a mounted knight.

from the court by her brother-in-law, who claimed that her enormous expenditure on charitable deeds was crippling the state finances. She renounced the world, settled at Marburg and joined the Franciscans as a Tertiary member. Elizabeth devoted the remainder of her short life to menial duties such as spinning, fishing and caring for the poor. Elizabethskirche was erected in Marburg to house her relics and remained a popular pilgrimage site until the relics were removed in 1539.

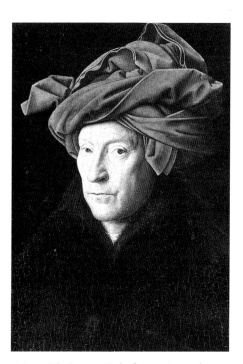

Portrait by Jan van Eyck of a man in a turban, now believed to be the painter himself.

Eyck, Jan van, *c.* 1390–1441. Leading painter of the early Flemish school, he served as court painter to John of Bavaria, Count of Holland, and Philip the Good, Duke of Burgundy, and travelled on diplomatic missions. Between *c.* 1429–32 he undertook the completion of the Ghent Altarpiece of the Lamb, a work of great detail and complex iconography. Other works include *A Portrait of a Man in a Red Turban* (1433). Van Eyck introduced a brilliance of colour into his works and often masked symbolism in everyday objects. His favourite theme was the glorification of the Virgin and Child.

Ferdinand III, King of León and Castile 1217–52. He was engaged in continual warfare against the Muslims and initiated the first major advance in the Reconquest for 150 years; by the time of his death the Muslims only held Granada and Alicante. Born in 1198 at Salamanca, Ferdinand succeeded to the kingdom of Castile in 1217 and inherited the kingdom of León from his father, Alfonso IX, in 1230. Throughout his reign he sought to establish justice and was concerned that his people should not be overburdened with heavy taxation. He also played a prominent role in founding the university at Salamanca. He joined the Franciscans as a member of the Third Order and strove to liberate Spain from the Muslims and spread the faith. The conquests of Cordoba in 1236 and Seville in 1248 were the highpoints of his reign. Whilst on campaign he lived as a religious. He died in Seville and was buried at the cathedral in the Franciscan habit. Miracles were reported at his tomb and Clement X proclaimed his canonization in 1671. *See p. 234*

Fibonacci (Leonardo of Pisa), fl. early 13th century. A mathematician heavily influenced by Islamic science, he introduced Arabic numerals to the West. He is best known for the 'Fibonacci series', a number sequence generated by adding the two previous numbers together (1, 1, 2, 3, 5, 8, 13, 21 ...), which explains many natural phenomena – the spirals on snail shells, the horn configuration of deer and the reproductive patterns of certain animals. In the nineteenth century it was discovered that the Fibonacci series was also linked to other mathematical problems such as the Golden Section and *Pi*. His *Liber Abaci* dates from 1202, the *Pratica Geometria* from 1220.

Francis of Assisi, *c.* 1181–1226. Founder of the Franciscans. The son of a wealthy cloth-merchant from Assisi, Francis renounced the knightly life and abandoned hopes of military glory to lead a life of voluntary poverty. To symbolise the beginning of this

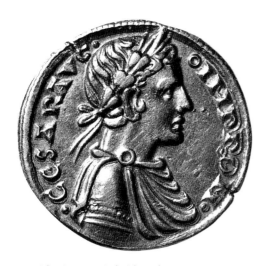

The Emperor Frederick II, shown as a Roman emperor on a coin of the mid-13th century.

new existence he dramatically stripped off his clothes before the bishop of Assisi. Francis lived alone for several years, wandering, begging and tending lepers, but was later joined at the Portiuncula, Assisi, by seven disciples. In 1210, when the community numbered twelve, they travelled to Rome and received papal approval for the Friars Minor. Unlike similar groups the Friars acted under the Church authorities. Their success necessitated change and practical administrative measures were now needed to deal with the growth in numbers. Francis composed the *Regula Bullata* in 1221, but gradually withdrew to a more contemplative existence. At this time he composed the *Canticle of the Sun* and received the stigmata, but his health was failing and he died on 3 October 1226. Less than two years later he was canonized, and a splendid basilica was erected at Assisi to accommodate his remains. *See pp. 86–87, 89*

Frederick I Barbarossa, Holy Roman Emperor 1152–90. Committed to restoring the Empire to its former glory, he was the first to systematically adopt the title 'Holy Roman Emperor'. He was born *c.* 1123 into the Hohenstaufen dynasty and related to the rival Welfs (Guelphs) through his mother; it was hoped that Frederick's election as king of Germany and the Romans in 1152 would terminate strife. Frederick sought an imperial coronation in Rome and achieved his ambition on 18 June 1155. He then returned to Germany and restored peace, but his territorial plans were disrupted with the schism following Pope Adrian's death in 1159. Frederick supported various anti-popes against ALEXANDER III but made peace with the pope in 1177, abandoned his plans for direct lordship in Italy and looked instead to feudal suzerainty in Germany. Frederick

drowned in the River Saleph in June 1190, on his way to fight the crusade against SALADIN. *See p. 96*

Frederick II, Holy Roman Emperor 1220–50. Frederick, who attempted to revive the imperial ideal and consolidate the Empire, was a remarkable and colourful figure, who often shocked his contemporaries. He was described by MATTHEW PARIS as the *stupor mundi* (the amazement of the world) and by SALIMBENE as the Antichrist. He was born at Jesi on 26 December 1194 and named after his grandfathers, the Holy Roman Emperor, FREDERICK BARBAROSSA, and ROGER II of Sicily. The union of the Holy Roman Empire and the Kingdom of Sicily was broken upon the death of Emperor Henry VI, for Frederick was only three years old. Anarchy erupted in Sicily and the German throne was contested. Otto IV of Brunswick secured power in Germany in 1208, but in 1212 a group of German princes, with papal support, offered the throne to Frederick. He was crowned at Aachen in 1214 and in 1220 was crowned emperor at Rome. On both occasions he vowed to go on crusade. In 1229 he temporarily recovered Jerusalem from the Muslims by treaty. His court was a cultural centre which fostered the composition of vernacular poetry and translations from Arabic and Greek. He himself composed a treatise on hunting with falcons, spoke a number of languages,

befriended the leading scholars and founded the first state university at Naples in 1224. He managed to consolidate his position in Germany, securing the election of his son, Henry, as German king, and sought to strengthen his hold over Sicily. However, his ambitions in the N. Italian communes caused a break in papal/imperial relations, which led to his excommunication by GREGORY IX; in 1245 he was deposed and excommunicated by Innocent IV at the Council of Lyons. He died in Apulia in 1250. *See p. 120*

Froissart, Jean, *c.* 1334–*c.* 1405. One of the finest medieval chroniclers, he was a great observer of warfare and a fine raconteur. Froissart was born at Valenciennes, and later served the counts of Hainault. In 1361 he visited the English court, where he enjoyed the patronage of EDWARD III's queen, Philippa. His later benefactors included Wenceslas of Luxembourg, the Duke of Brabant, and Guy, Count of Blois. He entered holy orders in 1373, and was rector of Les Estinnes, near Mons, from 1373 to 1382, and a canon of Chimay from 1383 until his death. He visited Europe to collect material for his works and gained success as a writer. His most notable work, the *Chroniques*, is a four-volume description of the major European countries from 1325 to 1400. While often inaccurate, it is a vivid and dramatic account. Although Froissart is generally associated

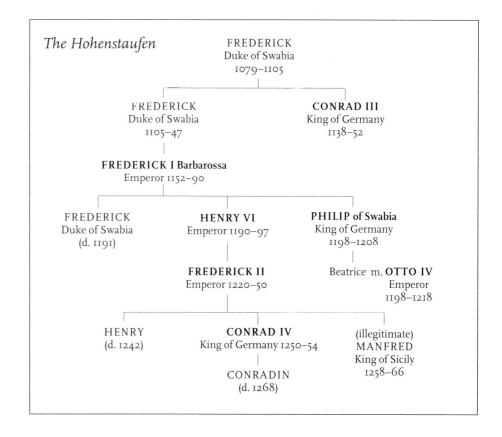

The Hohenstaufen

FREDERICK
Duke of Swabia
1079–1105

FREDERICK
Duke of Swabia
1105–47

CONRAD III
King of Germany
1138–52

FREDERICK I Barbarossa
Emperor 1152–90

FREDERICK
Duke of Swabia
(d. 1191)

HENRY VI
Emperor 1190–97

PHILIP of Swabia
King of Germany
1198–1208

FREDERICK II
Emperor 1220–50

Beatrice m. **OTTO IV**
Emperor
1198–1218

HENRY
(d. 1242)

CONRAD IV
King of Germany 1250–54

(illegitimate)
MANFRED
King of Sicily
1258–66

CONRADIN
(d. 1268)

with his work on warfare, he also wrote lyrical and narrative poetry, mostly in celebration of courtly love. *See p. 116*

Geoffrey de Vinsauf (Gaufridus de Vinosalua, Gaufridus Anglicus), fl. *c.* 1200. Poet and teacher of rhetoric in late twelfth- and early thirteenth-century England, he is most celebrated for his influential verse treatise on the art of poetry, the *Poetria Nova* (*c.* 1210), which he dedicated to INNOCENT III. This rather heavy-going work uses classical and contemporary writings. It describes how poetry should be taught and discusses the poet's practical training, including his choice of subject matter and words, the arrangement of his work, and the need for clarity. The *Poetria Nova* was widely disseminated and indeed around two hundred manuscripts survive from the thirteenth to fifteenth centuries. Geoffrey's other works include the *Documentum de modo et arte dictandi et versificandi*, a prose treatise which teaches the art of rhetoric. Some twenty manuscripts are extant.

Geoffrey of Monmouth (Galfridus Monemutensis), *c.* 1100–54. Renowned for his *Historia Regum Britanniae*, an extremely popular and widely circulated work of largely fictitious history, he was the first to develop fully the Arthurian legend. Geoffrey, a secular clerk, was elevated to the see of St Asaph in 1152, though he probably died before actually entering the diocese. His first work, the *Prophetiae (Libellus) Merlini*, commissioned by his superior, Alexander, Bishop of Lincoln, was written as an independent work but was later incorporated in the *Historia Regum*. It was translated into Welsh and Icelandic. The *Historia Regum*, completed shortly after Henry I's death in 1135, was a medieval bestseller. Geoffrey claimed it was a translation of a Breton manuscript given to him by Walter, Archdeacon of Oxford. It records the deeds of all the kings of Britain from Brutus to Cadwallader and, whilst highly influential, his contemporaries recognized that it was historically dubious. The Augustinian chronicler, William of Newburgh, dismissed it as a 'figment of the imagination'. Nevertheless, it enjoyed instant success and was immediately translated into French by the poet Gaimar and thereafter by the Norman, Wace.

Gerald of Wales (Giraldus Cambrensis; Gerald de Barri), *c.* 1146–*c.* 1223. A highly proficient Latinist, he was left embittered after his failure to secure the bishopric of St David's, which he wished to make an independent see. Gerald was born at Manorbier Castle, Pembrokeshire, of mixed

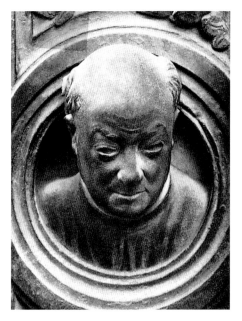

Lorenzo Ghiberti, a self-portrait from the second pair of doors that he made for the Florentine Baptistery, 1425–52.

ancestry. His father, William de Barri, was a Norman, his grandmother, Nesta, a Welsh princess. Gerald was educated at St Peter's Abbey, Gloucester, and continued his studies at Paris. In 1174 he held several livings in England and Wales and from 1175 to 1203 served as archdeacon of Brecon. He was rejected as a candidate for the see of St David's on two occasions. In 1176 he was nominated by the cathedral chapter, but refused by HENRY II, and thereafter remained hostile to the king. Twenty-two years later he was unanimously elected to the see, but opposed by Hubert Walter, Archbishop of Canterbury. From 1184 to 1194 Gerald served in the courts of Henry II and RICHARD I, and in 1188 he accompanied Baldwin, Archbishop of Canterbury, to preach the Third Crusade in Wales. On several occasions Gerald himself addressed the people, whom he claims were moved to tears. His *Journey through Wales* records their experiences on this tour. Seventeen of his works are extant. They record his own acute and at times acrid observations and include topographies of Ireland and Wales, the *Speculum Ecclesiae* and the *Instruction of Princes*.

Gerson, John, 1363–1429. Leading theologian and spiritual writer, he was actively involved in French attempts to heal the Great Schism. Gerson was born in the Ardennes and studied at Paris from 1377. He became Chancellor of Notre-Dame Cathedral and the University of Paris in 1395. He had a prominent role in the Council of Constance,

1414–18, which secured church unity in 1417 through the election of Martin V. He was involved in the council's attempts to obliterate heresy and participated in the condemnation of JOHN HUS. However, his belief that institutional reform was futile without personal reform differed from the opinions of those at Constance. As a prominent theologian and spiritual writer Gerson sought to initiate an intensification of the spiritual life in all sectors of society. His writings, which were greatly valued by Luther, include *De Consolatione Theologiae* (1418), modelled on Boethius, *Perfection of the Heart*, *Mystical Theology*, and *The Mountain of Contemplation* (1397), his greatest work. Gerson returned to Paris in 1419 and sought seclusion at Lyons until his death.

Ghiberti, Lorenzo, 1378–1455. Outstanding Italian sculptor whose masterworks are two celebrated sets of bronze doors for the baptistery of Florence Cathedral. In 1401 Ghiberti entered a competition, in which Brunelleschi amongst others participated, and won the commission for the north doors (1403–24). They portray, in International Gothic style, scenes from the Life of Christ. The east doors (1425–52), known as the 'Gates of Paradise' and constructed in a Renaissance style, depict subject matter from the Old Testament. Many renowned sculptors, including Donatello, Filarete and Uccello, trained in Ghiberti's studio. His other work includes three bronze statues for the Or San Michele in Florence and relief panels for the Siena Baptistery font. In his later years he wrote three *Commentarii* – treatises on art history and theory – one of which includes his autobiography.

Giles of Rome (Aegidius Romanus, Egidius Colonna), *c.* 1247–1316. This Augustinian philosopher was a fervent defender of the papacy and promoted the lordship of the Church over temporal matters. Born in Rome, he became an Augustinian hermit at an early age. He was noted for his intellect at Paris, where he studied theology and may have attended AQUINAS's lectures. He was expelled from Paris in 1277 for his condemnation of heterodox Aristotelianism; before his reinstatement by the pope he probably spent some time in Bayeux and his native Rome. He was appointed vicar-general of the Augustinians in 1285, prior-general in 1292, and in 1295 he was elevated to the see of Bourges and accorded the first Augustinian chair in theology. Giles served as tutor to Philip III's son, the future PHILIP IV of France, for whom he composed his most popular work, the *De regimine principum*. In 1287 Augustinian schools were prescribed to follow his teachings. In contrast to Aquinas, Giles asserted the primacy of the will over reason. In philosophy he is noted for his doctrine on the real distinction between essence and existence. Giles was a prodigious writer and wrote treatises on angels and Original Sin, and commentaries on PETER LOMBARD's *Sentences* and Aristotle. His *De Ecclesiastica Potestate* was fundamental to BONIFACE VIII's infamous bull, the *Unam Sanctam*. He also wrote on time and other basic scientific issues. Giles was also active as a preacher, and some seventy-six of his sermons are extant.

Giotto di Bondone, *c.* 1267/76–1337. Generally regarded as the forerunner of the Italian Renaissance, Giotto fused the study of Italo-Byzantine painting with Tuscan Gothic architecture, and is noted for the solidity of his figures. The few surviving documents relating to the artist's life testify to his widespread influence. For instance, he entered the service of Robert of Naples in 1330 and was named chief architect of Florence Cathedral in 1334. He was acknowledged by his contemporaries as a leading artist; Michaelangelo was greatly impressed with his frescoes in the Peruzzi chapel, S. Croce, Florence, and he is the only contemporary artist praised in DANTE's *Divine Comedy*. The precise chronology and development of Giotto's work is uncertain and there is some dispute as to which works should be attributed to him. Included amongst the works accepted as his are *The Life of Christ* in the Arena Chapel, Padua, his greatest fresco cycle, completed in 1306; *The Madonna*, a large-scale panel for the church of Ognissanti, Florence, *c.* 1305; *The Crucifixion*, *c.* 1290–1300. English scholars generally reject attribution of *The Life of St Francis* at Assisi to him. One of his last commissions was the Campanile of Florence Cathedral, *c.* 1334. *See p. 254*

Gottfried von Strassburg. Through his writings the German vernacular gained acceptance as an appropriate medium for great poetic works. Nothing is known of Gottfried's life. He composed a number of works in the courtly love tradition of the twelfth and thirteenth centuries, and is the author of the incomplete romance, *Tristan and Isolde*, *c.* 1200–10, written in the vernacular.

Gratian, fl. *c.* 1150. An ecclesiastical lawyer, he is remembered for his *Decretum Gratiani*, a textbook of Church law completed *c.* 1139–40, which fused new learning based on Roman law with contemporary dialectic methods. While little can be established of his early life, it seems he was a

Camaldonensian monk and trained in Bologna, where he probably taught law *c.* 1130–40. His *Decretum* comprises extracts from the Church Fathers, papal and imperial decretals and conciliar decrees, including pronouncements from the 1139 Lateran Council. It provides a systematic arrangement of canon law from its beginning until the twelfth century and was soon recognised as the standard textbook for European law-schools. It became the first part of the *Corpus Iuris Canonici* and remained one of the basic texts of canon law until 1917. Gratian had died by the 1160s and appears in Paradise in DANTE's *Divine Comedy*. *See pp. 96, 169*

Gregory VII, Pope 1073–85. One of the greatest popes of the Middle Ages, he initiated a programme of reform which included clerical celibacy, the abolition of simony, and the higher clergy's independence from secular authorities. Born 'Hildebrand', in Tuscany, *c.* 1020, he rose to prominence in the service of Gregory VI (1045–46), the first reforming pope, and was a chief advisor to Alexander II (1061–73), whom he succeeded in 1073. He asserted the supremacy of the pope as Vicar of St Peter and often quoted the text, 'I am not custom but truth'. His beliefs are defined in the *Dictatus Papae* of March 1075. However, Gregory's attitude, which undermined imperial authority, led to conflict with HENRY IV of Germany from 1075 to 1077, and culminated in Henry's deposition of Gregory. In response Gregory deposed and excommunicated Henry, who was forced to humiliate himself and seek papal absolution at Canossa. Henry later regained support and besieged Rome, necessitating Gregory's withdrawal to Salerno where he died in 1085, complaining, 'I have loved *justitia*, therefore I die in exile'.

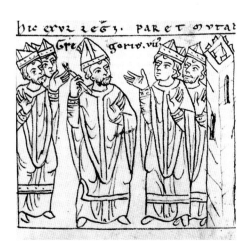

Pope Gregory VII, a miniature from the 'Weltchronik' of Otto of Freising, 1170.

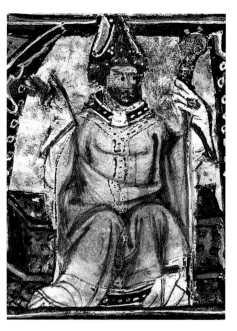

Robert Grosseteste, a portrait initial from a manuscript of his works; late 14th century.

Gregory IX, Pope 1227–41. A great supporter of the Dominicans and Franciscans, and a particular admirer of ST FRANCIS, his papacy was dogged by conflict with FREDERICK II. Born Ugolino dei Conti, *c.* 1148, he was the nephew of INNOCENT III. He studied at Paris and Bologna, and before his elevation to the papacy in 1227 served as cardinal-bishop and papal legate. Gregory continued his predecessors' struggle against the Holy Roman Emperors and greatly increased the church's resources to finance his ambitions. He excommunicated Frederick II in 1227, as he claimed the emperor had neglected his vows to go on crusade, and again in 1239 when Frederick threatened the Papal States. Gregory also acted against heresy and effectively inaugurated the Inquisition in 1231.

Grosseteste, Robert, *c.* 1168–1253. Scholar and ecclesiastic, he is chiefly remembered for his scientific works and commentaries on Aristotle, and as the first of the Oxford school of scientists. Born in Suffolk of humble parentage, Robert served as a cleric in the households of the bishops of Lincoln and Hereford. He may have studied at Oxford or Paris. By the early 1220s he was teaching in the faculty of theology at Oxford and may well have been the first chancellor of the university. He was elected to the see of Lincoln in 1235 and was an ardent reformer, deeply committed to his pastoral duties.

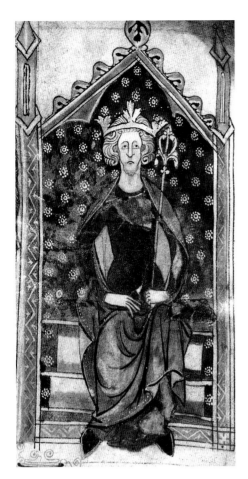

King Henry II of England; a 13th-century manuscript.

His early writings include didactic works in Latin, as well as in the English and French vernaculars, essentially for the laity. He also composed poems and treatises on household management and courtly etiquette. He wrote more scholarly works during his time at the universities, including the *Hexaëmeron,* written in the early 1220s, and a number of short theological treatises.

Gutenberg, Johannes, *c.* 1400–*c.* 1468. Pioneer in printing whose technique was standard in the West for some 350 years. He was born to a patrician family in Mainz, trained as a goldsmith and was in Strasbourg *c.* 1430–*c.* 1449, where he mastered the technique of printing from moveable type cast in individual copper letters. With the financial backing of the banker, Johann Fust, Gutenberg produced the partly printed *Letters of Indulgence* and the Gutenberg Bible (1453–55), the first printed book. The latter contained forty-two lines per page and with lead-type font, hand-cut in Gothic script, it could match handwritten script in elegance. Two hundred vellum and paper copies were printed. Once the partnership had been dissolved Gutenberg continued alone and his projects included the thirty-six-line Bible. *See p. 271*

Héloise, 1101–64. Celebrated lover of ABELARD, she was esteemed by her contemporaries for her learning. She received her early education at the nunnery of Argenteuil, and was later tutored by Abelard. The two became lovers; she bore his child, Astrolabe, and they married in secret. Héloise's uncle and guardian, Fulbert, a canon of Notre-Dame Cathedral, sought to uphold the family honour and ordered Abelard's castration. Abelard then retired to Saint-Denis and Héloise took the habit at Argenteuil in 1118, where she later became abbess. The nuns were dispersed in 1129 and moved to Abelard's oratory at the Paraclete, some sixty miles south-east of Paris, where Héloise was installed as prioress and then abbess; Abelard acted as *magister* (master). The foundation charter is dated 28 November 1131. Héloise was responsible for sixty nuns, as well as dependencies and new houses. She continued to correspond with Abelard and her letters show great passion and devotion. However, she also sought more practical advice and Abelard responded to her request for a letter of guidance. On her death she was buried beside him at the Paraclete. *See p. 274*

Henry IV, Holy Roman Emperor 1056–1106. Proud and suspicious, with a great sense of his royal dignity, Henry's ongoing struggles with the Church weakened the imperial position over the papacy. Born in 1050, Henry succeeded his father when only six years old, but was manipulated by ambitious clerics during his minority. On attaining his majority in 1065 Henry attempted to recover royal rights, crush Saxon independence and revive royal influence in Italy. His ambitions provoked a massive uprising of Saxon nobility and free peasantry in 1073. Henry also clashed with the Reforming Church. He opposed GREGORY VII's reform programme, which undermined imperial influence in the church and deposed the pope at Worms in 1076. Gregory, in return, deposed and excommunicated Henry who was forced to submit and seek papal absolution at Canossa. Henry was excommunicated for a second time in 1080, but in 1084 had himself crowned emperor by Clement III, the anti-pope. URBAN II renewed resistance in 1089, but was forced to withdraw. While Henry began to regain power in 1103, the following year he faced civil war in Germany led by his sons, and was forced to abdicate. He managed to escape from his captors but died before any conclusive fighting. *See p. 96*

Henry VII, Holy Roman Emperor 1308–13. Henry established the Luxembourg dynasty and his was the first serious attempt, since FREDERICK II, to re-launch the empire. Born

in 1269, Henry was elected as the anti-Habsburg candidate in 1308. He secured his power in Bohemia, which he won for his son, and entered Italy in 1310. Pisa initially supported Henry, but the Florentines successfully persuaded the other cities to join against him and thus thwarted his ambitions. Henry died of malaria shortly thereafter, but his efforts demonstrated that the imperial ideal had not been extinguished.

Henry II, King of England 1154–89. The first Plantagenet king, he was a magnetic but fiery character who ruled England energetically for thirty-five years. Born in 1133 at Le Mans, Maine, Henry became Duke of Normandy in 1150, and the following year succeeded his father as Count of Anjou and Maine. His marriage to ELEANOR OF AQUITAINE in 1152, only two months after the annulment of her marriage to Louis VII of France, brought him considerable control over the lands in S.W. France. King Stephen recognised Henry as his heir in the Treaty of Winchester in November 1153, and he was crowned king of England at Westminster Abbey on 19 December 1154. Henry is generally noted for his constitutional and legal developments, namely, the development of administration with the creation of the justiciarship, the use of assizes, the formulation of the English Common Law. He is also remembered for the martyrdom of his one-time friend and ally, THOMAS BECKET, in 1170. Henry's relationship with Thomas soured soon after Becket's elevation to the see of Canterbury, and disagreement culminated in the archbishop's murder in Christ Church Cathedral, Canterbury, by four of the king's knights. Henry, who was blamed, did public penance in 1174 and was scourged by all of the priory's seventy monks. His reign ended amidst rebellion from his sons, RICHARD and JOHN. He died at Chinon in 1189 and was buried at Fontevrault.

Henry III, King of England 1216–72. Assigned to Purgatory with the negligent rulers in DANTE's *Divine Comedy* and described by the monastic chronicler, MATTHEW PARIS, as a 'king with a heart of wax', his was the first royal minority since the Norman Conquest. Born in 1207, he succeeded his father, KING JOHN, when only nine years of age, and inherited a country divided by civil war with the future Louis VIII of France in control of E. England and London. However, the regent, William Marshal, Earl of Pembroke, who was legendary for his chivalric deeds, swiftly dealt with the French threat. While Henry declared himself of age in 1227 his personal rule effectively began in 1234. His reliance

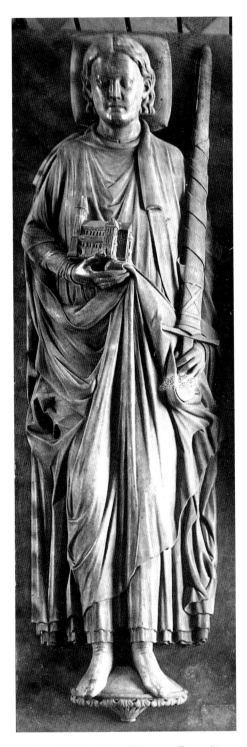

Henry the Lion, Duke of Saxony; effigy on his tomb in Brunswick Cathedral.

on the counsel of foreigners, whom he raised to positions of authority, provoked great resentment. Henry's foreign policy was also unsuccessful. His ambition to have his son crowned king of Sicily was particularly costly and futile. In pursuit of this goal he inflicted high taxation on his subjects and incurred a reputation for simplicity. Dissatisfaction at home and failure abroad led to the baronial revolt and the Provisions of Oxford, 1258;

Henry's failure to abide by the terms prompted three years of civil war. He was a pious king and despite his failings at home and abroad he contributed to cultural developments in England. He heard mass four times a day, fed the poor and instigated the rebuilding of Westminster Abbey, which was consecrated in 1269. Henry was buried there in 1272.

Henry V, King of England 1413–22. A determined and ambitious ruler, he is celebrated as a brilliant military leader, and particularly remembered for his triumph at Agincourt on 25 October 1415. Henry was born in 1387. He was exceptionally well-educated and a competent musician. On his succession to the throne in 1413 he quelled internal revolts and was especially severe in his suppression of Lollardy. Henry was primarily concerned to re-assert royal authority and present himself as an ideal king, the Vicar of God. He dedicated himself to expanding his territories and is renowned for his great successes in France. Henry instigated a new stage in the Hundred Years' War, and virtually conquered all of Normandy by 1419 through siege warfare. An alliance with the Burgundians forced the Treaty of Troyes, 1420, which accorded him the hand of Charles VI's daughter, Catherine, and recognised him as heir to the French throne. However, Henry died on campaign, just two months before the death of Charles VI. *See p. 169*

Henry the Lion of Saxony, 1129–95. Duke of Saxony 1142–80 and Duke of Bavaria 1156–80, he aimed to establish a unified dominion, but was overthrown and exiled in 1180 by his cousin, Emperor FREDERICK I. The Danish chronicler, SAXO GRAMMATICUS, gives a hostile account of the duke whom he describes as greedy and ambitious. Indeed Henry was probably wealthier than Frederick. Henry had supported Frederick's campaigns in Italy and had helped to maintain internal peace when the emperor was engaged with foreign affairs, but their twenty-five years of co-operation ended in 1176 when the duke refused Frederick aid at Chiavenna. His failure to appear for trial on three occasions resulted in charges of treason (*Acht* and *Oberacht*), the seizure of his duchies and his exile. For Frederick, this removed the threat of an over-mighty subject, but it also meant the division of Bavaria and Saxony and the disappearance of the last tribal duchies. Henry sought refuge at the court of his father-in-law, HENRY II, who petitioned for his return. Henry returned to Germany in 1185, but failed to restore his position. His deeds inspired poets, and legends soon developed.

Henry the Navigator of Portugal, 1394–1460. He is primarily remembered for his contribution to maritime exploration, for he was effectively the first to put nautical investigation on a scientific footing. The son of John I of Portugal, Henry won his knightly spurs in 1415 for his participation in the capture of Ceuta, Morocco, a natural continuation of the Reconquest of the Iberian peninsula. Thereafter, as Grand Master of the Military Order of Christ, he devoted himself to conducting war against the Infidel, and his ships bore a red cross on their sails. This crusading ideal was the impetus behind his exploration of Africa, though he was also driven by desire for knowledge and trade. Henry was concerned that his men should have access to the best nautical information. He employed an expert map- and instrument-maker, prescribed the study of ancient maps, and thereby contributed to the development of cartography and the improvement of navigational instruments. While Henry died in great debt, he had essentially 'joined East to West'. He prepared the way for Vasco da Gama's discovery of the route to India, 1497–98. His motto was *Taleant de bien faire* (the desire to do well).

Hermann von Salza, 1180–1239. Hermann revitalized the Teutonic Order, of which he was the Fourth Grand Master (*c.* 1210–39), and worked fervently for the recovery of the Holy Land. He led the Order to victory in 1219 with the capture of Damietta, although the city was afterwards lost. Hermann's close relationship with the emperor and popes secured great favours for the Order, and rulers invited the knights to undertake military duties. For example *c.* 1225 Duke Conrad of Masovia urged Hermann to overthrow the Prussians and Lithuanians, the last heathen tribes in Europe.

Hildegard of Bingen, 1098–1179. Visionary, abbess, theologian and poet, she was also renowned as a healer and physician. Born of noble parents in Bermersheim, Mainz, she was educated by an anchoress, Jutta, from the age of eight. She assumed the habit when fifteen and, on Jutta's death in 1136, became abbess of Diessenberg. The community grew to such an extent that they moved to Rupertsberg, near Bingen, in 1147. Hildegard wrote on a number of subjects. Her first major theological work, the *Scivias*, was written in Latin prose during the 1140s and received papal approval. It details the contents of her visions and revelations in twenty-six allegorical and symbolic sections. Her other writings include poems, hymns, medical works, commentaries on the Gospels and the *Rule of St Benedict*.

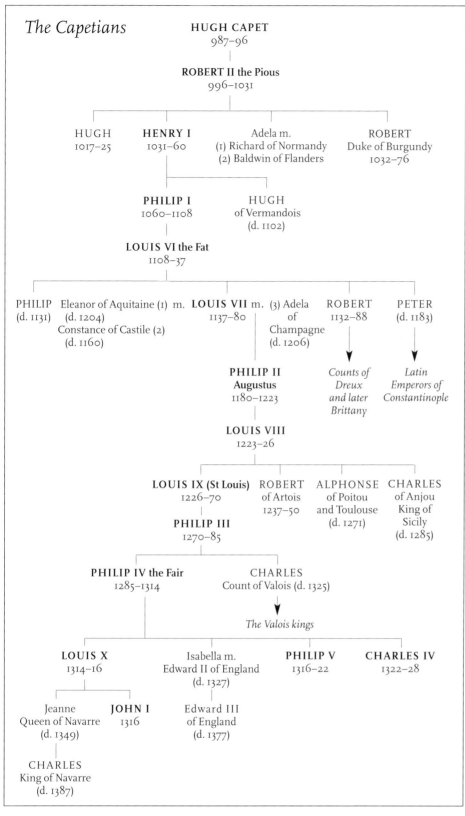

The Capetians

HUGH CAPET
987–96

ROBERT II the Pious
996–1031

HUGH
1017–25

HENRY I
1031–60

Adela m.
(1) Richard of Normandy
(2) Baldwin of Flanders

ROBERT
Duke of Burgundy
1032–76

PHILIP I
1060–1108

HUGH
of Vermandois
(d. 1102)

LOUIS VI the Fat
1108–37

PHILIP
(d. 1131)

Eleanor of Aquitaine (1) m.
(d. 1204)
Constance of Castile (2)
(d. 1160)

LOUIS VII m.
1137–80

(3) Adela
of
Champagne
(d. 1206)

ROBERT
1132–88

PETER
(d. 1183)

PHILIP II
Augustus
1180–1223

*Counts of
Dreux
and later
Brittany*

*Latin
Emperors of
Constantinople*

LOUIS VIII
1223–26

LOUIS IX (St Louis)
1226–70

ROBERT
of Artois
1237–50

ALPHONSE
of Poitou
and Toulouse
(d. 1271)

CHARLES
of Anjou
King of
Sicily
(d. 1285)

PHILIP III
1270–85

PHILIP IV the Fair
1285–1314

CHARLES
Count of Valois (d. 1325)

The Valois kings

LOUIS X
1314–16

Isabella m.
Edward II of England
(d. 1327)

PHILIP V
1316–22

CHARLES IV
1322–28

Jeanne
Queen of Navarre
(d. 1349)

JOHN I
1316

Edward III
of England
(d. 1377)

CHARLES
King of Navarre
(d. 1387)

---

the Carolingian King Lothar and, in 987, was elected heir to Lothar's successor, Louis V. In 991 he imprisoned the hereditary Carolingian claimant, Charles of Lorraine, and forced the new archbishop, Arnulf, to resign for plotting against him. Though he faced continued opposition, Hugh crowned his own son during his lifetime, thus ensuring the line of succession.

Hugh of St Victor, *c.* 1096–1141. An exceptional scholar and mystical theologian, he made a significant contribution to Scholasticism and established the school of St Victor in Paris as a leading intellectual centre. Born in Saxony to the family of the counts of Blankenburg, he was educated at the monastery of St Pancras, Hamerleve, and took the habit of the Augustinian canons. He entered the monastery of St Victor, Paris, *c.* 1115, and became head of the school in 1133. While Hugh was a prominent philosopher and scholastic theologian, he was also an outstanding teacher and the school flourished under his leadership. He believed that everything should be subordinated to the contemplative life and considered personal experience the highest form of knowledge. He was greatly influenced by the Platonic tradition as espoused by Augustine, and was the first to arrange the teachings of the patristic writers into a complete body of doctrine. He wrote on the arts, biblical studies and theology .

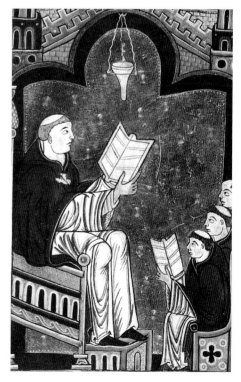

Hugh of St Victor, from an early 13th-century manuscript of his 'De arca morale'.

Hildegard died when she was eighty. Miracles were reported during her life and following her death and, while attempts to secure her canonization in the thirteenth and fourteenth centuries were unsuccessful, her cult was approved in Germany in the fifteenth century and her name entered in the Roman martyrology. *See pp. 88-89*

Hugh Capet, King of France 987–96. Founder of the Capetian line; Hugh's distinctive cloak or *capa* gave rise to the name by which the dynasty is known. He was born *c.* 938, the son of Hugh the Great, Duke of the Franks, and succeeded his father in 956. Encouraged by Archbishop Adalberon of Rheims, he intrigued against

His best-known work is the *Didascalion*, a guide for students seeking divine wisdom. Other writings include the *De Sacramentis Christianae Fidei*, his main theological work, and the *Summa Sententiarum*. He also completed commentaries and homilies.

Huss, John, *c*. 1373–1415. An inspirational teacher and preacher, his death as a heretic instigated the Hussite wars in Bohemia. Huss was born to a peasant family in Husinec, Bohemia, and educated at the University of Prague, where his promotion of anti-German feeling culminated in a German exodus from the university in 1409. He preached in Czech at the Bethlehem Chapel in Prague, espousing moral reforms of the Church and urging a return to the original ideals of poverty and piety. In 1410 Huss was condemned for heresy and excommunicated. Two years later he objected to the archbishop's burning of WYCLIFFE's books and was forced to leave Prague. In 1414 he was summoned to the Council of Constance to defend his beliefs and, although he had been given safe conduct by King Sigismund, he was arrested, condemned and burned on 6 July 1415. Huss's writings include homilies and letters, as well as polemical and scholastic works. His greatest work, *De Ecclesia*, was composed in 1412, following his departure from Prague. Huss was influenced by Wycliffe and translated around forty-five of his works. *See p. 91*

Innocent III, Pope 1198–1216. An ardent reformer, a skilled canonist and a shrewd diplomat, he called the Fourth Crusade and presided over the largest Lateran Council in 1215. Born *c*. 1160 of noble parents, he was educated at Paris and Bologna and elected pope in 1198, when only thirty-seven years old. Innocent strongly believed in the supremacy of the papacy and cultivated the theory of papal power (*plenitudo potestatis*). He was the first to assume the title Vicar of Christ, and saw himself as the judge of all men but judged by none. Innocent was a formidable character and sought to re-invigorate the papacy spiritually and politically. He strove to re-exert papal influence in S. Italy and Sicily, and challenged the greatest European powers. He excommunicated KING JOHN and placed England under interdict, following John's refusal of the papal nominee for the see of Canterbury. He also deposed Otto IV and forced PHILIP AUGUSTUS of France to take back his estranged wife, Ingebourg of Denmark. Innocent recognized the potential value of the Dominicans and Franciscans, and reconciled various heretical groups including the Humiliati. He wrote over six

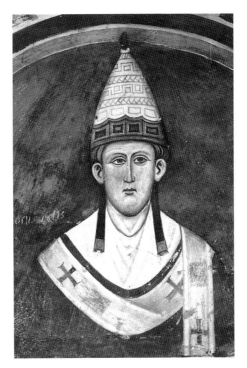

Pope Innocent III, a fresco in the lower church of Subiaco, Italy; 13th century.

thousand letters, some 3,700 of which are contained in the surviving six volumes of his Registers.

Jacques de Vitry, *c*. 1160–*c*. 1245. Celebrated as an historian and a fervent preacher of the Crusades, he was also known for his obstinacy and temper. Born at Vitry-sur-Seine, near Paris, he was educated at the University of Paris and took the habit of the Canons Regular. His devotion to preaching the Albigensian Crusade, 1210–13, secured his election to the see of Acre. In 1229 Jacques was created cardinal and bishop of Tusculum, and thereafter served as legate in Germany and France. However, he refused the Patriarchate of Jerusalem. His historical writings show great observation and detail. His main work, the *Historia Orientalis seu Hierosolymitana*, a history of Jerusalem and the East, discusses the history of the kingdom of Jerusalem, the geography of Palestine and the Crusades. Other works include sermon-models for preachers and letters to Pope Honorius, especially regarding the Egyptian Crusade; indeed he himself was present at the fall of Damietta in 1219.

James I, King of Scotland 1406–37. Born in Dunfermline in 1394, the son of Robert III, he was imprisoned by Henry IV of England in 1405 and remained at the English court for eighteen years. His crippled father died of shock on hearing of his son's capture, and the Scottish parliament of 1406 recognized James as King of the Scots. He was an

honoured prisoner in England and received a good education. He was athletic, a skilful musician and an able poet. He later composed the famous poem, *The King's Quair*. Upon his release in 1424, for a ransom of £40,000, James was crowned at Scone. He then set about restoring royal authority and controlling baronial anarchy. He strengthened government, doubled the revenue from customs and trebled income from royal lands. He established a central law-court, the Court of Session, and forbade private law. Further developments include his standardization and regulation of weights, the prohibition of football, and the construction of a fine palace at Linlithgow. James was murdered by rebellious Highlanders in 1437. He was buried at the Carthusian monastery in Perth.

James I (James the Conqueror), King of Aragon 1213–76. A great and able warrior, he resumed the re-conquest of Spain from the Muslims. Born in 1208, James succeeded to the throne of Aragon as a minor and was brought up in the custody of the Templars at Munzón, while his uncle supervised his reign. He achieved success in his crusade against the Muslims: Majorca fell on 31 December 1229, and Valencia was captured in 1236. However, his ventures in S. France were less decisive, and an overseas crusade in 1269 was a failure. Within the kingdom James promoted urban life and inaugurated significant administrative and institutional developments. The royal court now began to keep a register of administrative correspondence. The *Book of Deeds* recounts his own successes and those of his people. James died at Valencia on 29 July 1276.

Jean de Joinville, *c*. 1224–1319. A member of the noble family of Joinvilles of Champagne, he is particularly celebrated for his *History of Saint Louis*, a colourful and lively account of a friend, that includes his personal remembrances. Joinville inherited his father's position as seneschal of Champagne and the family castle on the River Marne. In 1248 he took the Cross and at his own expense joined the Seventh Crusade, 'the Egyptian disaster'. Joinville met LOUIS IX in Cyprus and was taken into the king's pay. When he returned to France in 1254 it was as a royal friend. He resumed his duties as seneschal and refused to take the Cross again in 1270 for the crusade to Tunis. He later gave evidence for Louis' canonization in 1282, witnessed the exhumation of the body in 1297 and, following a dream in which Louis appeared to him, he erected an altar to the saint in his chapel of St Laurent, Joinville. His *Life of Saint Louis*, completed *c*. 1309, was written at the request of PHILIP

IV's wife, Jeanne of Navarre. It comprises two parts and is often repetitious. The first part recounts Louis's administration and relationship with the Church. The second part, written when Joinville was about eighty years old, is concerned with Louis's prowess and tells of his crusading achievements. The work is fused with Joinville's own reminiscences delivered in an informal style, and successfully captures the spirit of the man and his times.

Jean de Meun (Meung), d. 1305. Scholar and poet, he is particularly remembered for his continuation of the *Roman de Rou*, *c.* 1270. Jean Chopinel (Clopinel) was born in Meung-sur-Loire, S.W. of Orléans, and graduated from the University of Paris. His works are rational, satirical and scholastic, and include his *Testamenta, Codicil,* and translations of Boethius' *De Consolatione Philosophiae*, GERALD OF WALES' *Wonders of Ireland,* Aelred of Rievaulx's *Spiritual Friendship*, and the *Life and Letters of Abelard and Héloïse*.

Joachim of Fiore, *c.* 1135–1202. This great, though rather controversial, mystic influenced several leading rulers, and was particularly renowned for his Trinitarian view of history. Little is known of Joachim's early life. He was abbot of the Cistercian house at Corazzo in 1177, but left to lead a more contemplative life and was living in the Cistercian house of Casamari in S. Italy by 1184. He then moved to Fiore in Calabria, where he founded the first house of the Florensian. The Order received papal approval in 1196. Joachim divided history into three periods, namely, the Old Testament, the New Testament, and the Third Age, beginning *c.* 1260, when the religious orders would convert the world. This Trinitarianism is espoused in his three main works, *Liber Concordiae Novi ac Veteris Testamenti, Expositio in Apocalypsim,* and *Psalterium Decem Cordarum*. There was a rather confused reaction to Joachim's writings. While the Fourth Lateran Council of 1215 condemned his criticism of PETER LOMBARD's Trinitarian doctrine, it underlined his essential orthodoxy. DANTE's *Paradiso* describes him as 'endowed with the prophetic spirit'.

Joan of Arc, *c.* 1412–1431. French patriotic leader and virgin, she was burned as a heretic and became a national heroine in the nineteenth century. Joan was born in Domrémy to a farming family. From the age of thirteen she heard voices, whom she identified as Sts Michael, Catherine and Margaret, guiding her to save France from the English and help the dauphin, Charles,

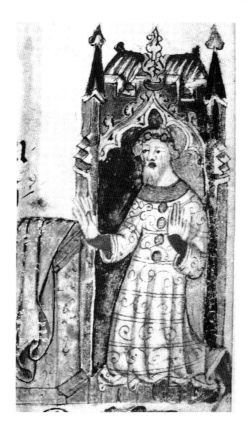

John of Gaunt, a portrait in the margin of the Book of Benefactors of St Alban's Abbey; c. 1380.

to be crowned. Dressed in white armour, Joan accompanied the French to victory at Orléans in 1429; Charles was crowned in her presence at Rheims on 17 July 1429. Thereafter the nineteen-year-old Maid of Orléans participated in several military ventures, but was taken prisoner by the Burgundians at Compiègne, May 1430, and sold to the English, who tried her at Rouen for heresy and witchcraft. A full record of the trial exists. Joan was given no counsel or representation and was charged with twenty-four counts of heresy, idolatry, blasphemy and immodest behaviour. She recanted and was sentenced to life imprisonment, but subsequently relapsed and was burned at the stake on 30 May 1431. She died with her eyes fixed on an image of the Cross, repeating the words 'Jesus, Mary, God'. King Charles opened a posthumous investigation in 1449 and Calixtus III annulled her sentence in 1456. Joan's cult grew rapidly. She was beatified in 1909 and canonized in 1920. *See p. 18*

John of Gaunt, Duke of Lancaster 1362–99. English prince and fourth son of EDWARD III, John of Gaunt was one of the richest and most powerful men in England. Born in 1340 in Ghent (hence his name), he married his cousin Blanche, daughter of Henry, first Duke of Lancaster, in 1359. On her death ten years later he married Constance of Castile and assumed kingship of Castile and León.

He incurred deep unpopularity by reversing the proceedings of the Good Parliament of 1376 and supporting the reformer JOHN WYCLIFFE, though disagreeing with the latter's religious and political views. The duke also helped to suppress the Peasants' Revolt of 1381. After suffering military defeats when posted to Scotland, he set sail for Spain to fight for his Spanish throne but, defeated again, surrendered his claims to his daughter, who was to marry the heir to Juan, King of Castile. Edward III's successor, RICHARD II, made John duke of Aquitaine and he managed to negotiate a truce with France. In 1396, two years after the death of his second wife, he married his mistress, Catherine Swynford, and Richard legitimated their sons under the name of Beaufort. One son, Henry (later Henry IV), was exiled in 1398 and the following year John died and was buried in St Paul's Cathedral.

John 'Lackland', King of England 1199–1216. While John is traditionally regarded as a bad king who suffered military defeat, quarrelled

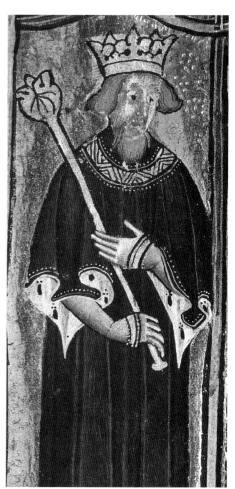

King John, portrait in an illuminated initial of an English manuscript; 13th century.

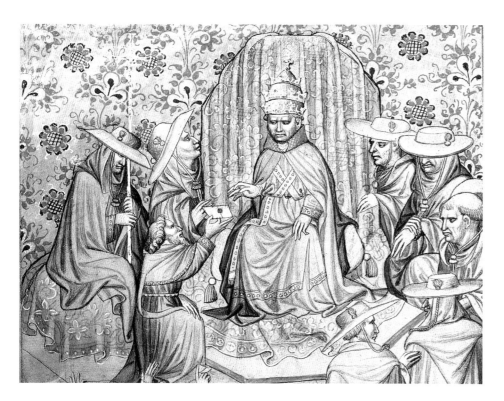

Pope John XXII receiving delegates of the Eastern Church in the presence of cardinals; 15th century.

with the papacy and argued with his nobles, he also implemented important administrative and judicial developments and had extensive knowledge of the geography of his country. John 'Lackland', the fifth and youngest son of HENRY II, was born on 24 December 1167, and succeeded his brother, RICHARD I, in 1199. Shortly after his succession John annulled his marriage to Isabella of Gloucester and married Isabella of Angoulême. This greatly angered Hugh le Brun, to whom Isabella had been engaged, and he complained to PHILIP II of France, John's overlord. John was called to trial at Paris in 1201, but ignored this summons and war ensued. John incurred great military defeats: he lost Anjou and Maine in 1203, Château Gaillard and Normandy in 1204, Brittany in 1206, and was finally defeated at Bouvines in 1214. Dissatisfaction at home was compounded with heavy taxation. John also clashed with the papacy. His rejection of the papal nominee for the see of Canterbury in 1205 prompted INNOCENT III to excommunicate him and place England under interdict. This was only lifted when John surrendered England as a papal fief. Discord with his barons led to the issue of Magna Carta in 1215 which placed John beneath the law, but his failure to uphold the terms provoked civil war. John died amidst fighting, leaving his nine-year-old son to succeed him. He was buried at Worcester Cathedral near the tomb of St Wulfstan.
See pp. 11, 120

John XXII, Pope 1316–34. A shrewd and forceful character, he revived and reorganized ecclesiastical administration and was actively involved in secular affairs. Born Jacques d'Euse at Cahors, 1249, he studied law at Montpellier and Paris. He was raised to the bishoprics of Fréjus (1300) and Avignon (1310), and was made cardinal-bishop of Porto in 1312. Four years later, he was elected to the papacy and crowned at Lyons. At this time the papal residence was at Avignon, where it remained for the eighteen years of his pontificate; John never entered Italy during his papacy. Despite his advanced age, John was an energetic administrator of papal affairs. He increased papal taxation, centralized ecclesiastical administration, helped restore peace to England and aided the king of Majorca against the Muslims. John was also embroiled in religious, political and theological conflicts. His intervention in a dispute amongst the Franciscans, regarding the nature of poverty, culminated in his dissolving the extreme branch of the friars – the Spirituals – in 1317. John was later involved in the imperial election dispute. This resulted in his feuding with Louis of Bavaria, whom he denounced as a heretic in 1324. Louis installed an anti-pope in Rome. Their conflict aroused a literary feud which led to MARSILIUS OF PADUA's anti-papal treatise, *Defensor Pacis*. The last years of John's pontificate were marred by a theological dispute regarding the Beatific Vision. Many masters of Paris denounced his assertion that the soul only beheld God after the Last Judgment, and condemned this as a heresy. Shortly before his death in 1334, John retracted this belief.

John of Salisbury, *c.* 1115–80. A fine Latinist and an outstanding scholar, especially in the fields of grammar and rhetoric, John was also an acute observer of contemporary society. Born in Old Sarum, Wiltshire, he studied at Paris and Chartres under the leading masters, including ABELARD. John then entered ecclesiastical administration and served in the papal court, where his experiences later inspired him to write the *Historia Pontificalis*. On BERNARD OF CLAIRVAUX's recommendation, John entered the household of Theobald, Archbishop of Canterbury, *c.* 1148, and it was here that he met THOMAS BECKET, a fellow member of the archbishop's household. John later supported Becket against HENRY II and accompanied the archbishop in exile, 1163–70. He was actively involved in working for Thomas's return to England and later, for his canonization. John was appointed to the see of Chartres in 1176, where he remained until his death. He was celebrated for his scholastic works, in particular the *Metalogicon* and the *Policraticus*, which he composed during his time in Theobald's household. The former, dedicated to Chancellor Becket, promotes the study of logic and metaphysics and argues the need to study grammar. For John, logic was a tool but not the solution to philosophical problems. With the *Metalogicon* he was the first to utilize all of Aristotle's logical writings, the *Organon*. The *Policraticus*, a discussion of the state, castigates Henry II's court, and the copy John presented to Becket survives in Christ Church. John was also renowned as a great – perhaps the greatest – letter-writer of the Middle Ages.

Kasimir III (Casimir the Great), King of Poland 1333–70. The only king of Poland accorded the title 'the Great', he implemented successful domestic and foreign policies, and is still celebrated as an ideal ruler. Born in 1310, the son of Ladislas I, Kasimir inherited a rather unsettled Poland, but transformed the country within thirty years. He realized the value of diplomacy and established peaceful relations with the Empire, Bohemia and the Teutonic Order. By 1366 he had extended the frontiers of the Polish state, and his success abroad raised his reputation in E. Europe. Within Poland Kasimir protected the peasants from tyrannical landlords and introduced military reforms, chiefly the erection of some fifty fortresses. In addition he revised the law, reformed the currency and supported the building of new churches. He also exploited the country's mineral resources, in particular the salt mines. In 1364 he founded the University of Cracow, the first university in Poland, which emphasised the study of

Roman law. He defended the rights of Jews in Poland and encouraged further immigration. He died in a hunting accident at the age of sixty, leaving no direct heir.

Kempe, Margery, *c.* 1373–*c.* 1438. Mystic and autobiographer, she was a rather controversial figure during her life, and notorious for her 'divinely-inspired' wails. The daughter of a prosperous townsman of Lynn, Norfolk, Margery married John Kempe, a merchant of Lynn, with whom she had fourteen children. She at one time served as miller and principal brewer, but interpreted her business failures as Divine disapproval. This, in part, induced her to lead a more pious life, and upon receiving a vision Margery devoted herself to prayer, fasting and vigils. In 1413 her husband finally agreed that they should live a chaste life. Margery completed several pilgrimages, visiting the Holy Land and Santiago de Compostela. Following the death of her husband in 1431 she dictated her memoirs, which were only discovered in 1934 and are thought to be the first English autobiography. While Margery was not always appreciated by her contemporaries, in 1438 she was received as a member of the guild of Holy Trinity in Lynn.

Langton, Stephen, *c.* 1150–1228. One of the greatest archbishops of Canterbury in the Middle Ages, he was also a renowned theologian and commentator on the Bible. Born in England, he studied in Paris under PETER LOMBARD, and was one of the leading theologians at the university. Langton was created cardinal-priest of St Chrysogonus in 1206. He was appointed to the see of Canterbury in 1207, but was compelled to stay with the Cistercian monks of Pontigny until 1213 when KING JOHN, who had refused to recognize him as primate, submitted to the pope. Stephen received the kiss of peace from John in July 1213. Stephen was an effective administrator of ecclesiastical affairs and a vigorous proponent of the primacy. In 1222 he promulgated special constitutions for the English Church, including laws ordering Jews to wear particular badges. He successfully advanced the archbishop of Canterbury's right to act as *legatus natus* and rebuilt the archbishop's palace at Canterbury. Stephen was also prominent in political events. His sympathy for the baronial opposition to John led to his suspension from office from 1215 to 1218, for he had refused to impose papal excommunication on the rebels. However during HENRY III's minority he supported the royalist party against baronial and papal threats.

Leo IX, Pope 1048–54. Committed to reform, he was dubbed 'the Apostolic Pilgrim', for he spent most of his time on the move holding synods to eradicate abuse. He was born Bruno of Egisheim, of noble descent, in 1002. In 1026 he commanded an army on Emperor Conrad II's behalf to suppress revolts in Lombardy. The following year, at only twenty-four years of age, Bruno was elevated to the see of Toul, where he embarked on a programme of reform throughout his diocese. He was elevated to the papacy in 1048 and devoted himself to matters of reform. He was especially concerned to eradicate simony and enforce clerical chastity, and travelled through Italy, France and Germany to hold reforming councils. In so doing he promoted the visibility of the pope, which in turn enhanced the prestige of the papacy. At Rome Leo gathered around him a group of advisors from which the College of Cardinals originated. In 1053 he led an army to drive out the Normans from S. Italy, but was defeated, captured and imprisoned for nine months. His involvement in military affairs was criticized and PETER DAMIAN condemned his behaviour as inappropriate to his papal standing. Furthermore Leo's interference in S. Italy and his promotion of papal prerogatives provoked hostility from Michael I Cerularius of Constantinople, and opened the way for the E. Schism. Leo died in 1054. Cures were said to have been effected at his tomb and he was venerated as a saint.

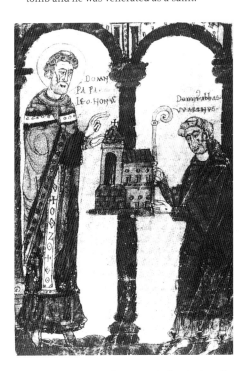

Pope Leo IX blesses the monastic foundation of St Arnulf at Metz, offered by Abbot Warinus; second half of the 11th century.

Llywelyn ab Iorwerth (the Great), 1173–1240. Prince of North Wales, he sought to establish a solid Welsh feudal state, and ruled by fear and favour, fostering peace, prosperity and cultural creativity. On attaining his majority in the 1190s Llywelyn pursued his claims to Gwynedd and Powys. In 1194 he engaged the help of various family members to expel his uncle, Dafydd, who had established himself as ruler of Gwynedd. Thereafter he secured supremacy over rival Welsh chiefs. His relationship with KING JOHN, who was also his father-in-law, was stormy and fluctuated between friendship and enmity. During HENRY III's minority the regent, William Marshal, sought to appease Llywelyn through concessions, and peace was secured at Worcester in 1218. Llywelyn formally paid homage to Henry and was granted custodianship of the royal castles at Cardigan and Carmarthen, which he was to hold during Henry's minority but lost to the Marshal in 1223. In S. Wales Llywelyn had to contend with the ambitions of the chief justiciar, Hubert de Burgh, but successfully undermined the latter's attempts to dominate this area and contributed to his downfall. In his mid-sixties Llywelyn suffered a stroke and died. He was buried at the Cistercian abbey at Aberconway, which he had founded.

Llywelyn ap Gruffudd (the Last), *c.* 1246–82. The grandson of LLYWELYN AB IORWERTH, the greatest of all Welsh rulers, he was the last to champion Welsh liberty and, like his grandfather, he was a capable soldier and astute diplomat. Llywelyn succeeded his uncle, Dafydd II, as Prince of N.W. Wales, and in 1247 did homage to HENRY III. At this time Llywelyn shared power with his brother, Owain, who launched an unsuccessful attempt to overthrow him in 1255. However, Owain's failure worked to Llywelyn's advantage and was effectively the turning-point which set Llywelyn on the path to becoming the leading ruler in Wales. Indeed, the treaty of Montgomery, 1267, recognized Llywelyn as Prince of Wales, an unprecedented honour which meant that he was now overlord of all the Welsh princes and the only tenant-in-chief of the English crown. Following EDWARD I's succession in 1272 Llywelyn withheld certain annual payments to England, refused to do homage to the king and failed to attend the coronation. He quarrelled with his brother, Dafydd III, and Gruffydd ab Gwenwynwyn, Lord of Upper Powys. In 1277 Edward led an attack which ended Welsh independence and forced Llywelyn to surrender with the Treaty of Conway. While Edward's disregard for Welsh customs incited Llywelyn and his brother, Dafydd, to submerge their hostilities and join in rebellion, Edward proved a formidable opponent and Llywelyn was killed at Radnorshire in 1282. His head was crowned with ivy and set on London Bridge, thereby fulfilling the prophecy that he would one day wear his crown in London.

Louis VI (the Fat), King of France 1108–37. His reign initiated the Capetians' efforts to recover royal power; he consolidated the Crown's position in the Ile-de-France and re-established royal control in the government. Born in 1081, Louis was educated at the royal abbey of Saint-Denis, Paris, and knighted in 1098. He survived his stepmother's attempts to prevent his succession. Like his father, Louis was corpulent and, according to one contemporary chronicler, his stomach was his god. Nevertheless, he was an energetic ruler and constantly engaged in military campaigns. During his reign he supported the growth of towns in France and sought amicable relations with the Church. He was a close friend of Suger, Abbot of Saint-Denis, and the Cistercian leader, Bernard of Clairvaux. Louis lived just long enough to see the fruition of his negotiations in arranging the marriage of his son, the future Louis VII, to Eleanor of Aquitaine.

Louis IX (St Louis), King of France, 1226–70. Renowned for his piety and acknowledged as an impartial judge, Louis regarded the Crown as the foundation of justice. Born in 1214 at Poissy, he succeeded to the throne when only twelve years of age with his mother, Blanche of Castile, as regent. Louis created French royal absolutism but recognised papal supremacy. He was dedicated to ruling his people well and greatly improved the quality of royal administration. He constructed the Sainte-Chapelle of Paris (1245–48) to house the relics of the Passion which he had acquired from Baldwin II. Louis was particularly severe in his treatment of heretics, and dealt harshly with blasphemers, whose lips and nose were branded. He cared for widows, orphans and the sick, and founded a hospital for the poor and blind. Louis favoured arbitration in his dealings with foreign leaders, signing, for instance, the Treaty of Corbeil with Aragon in 1258 and the Treaty of Paris with Henry III in 1259. His enthusiasm for crusading was almost obsessive, and he was devastated by the failure of his crusade against the Muslims in 1248. Nevertheless, Louis took the Cross for a second time in 1267, but died outside Tunis in 1270. Miracles were reported soon after his death, and he was canonized in 1297. *See p. 245*

Louis XI, King of France 1461–83. Known as the 'spider king', Louis was a suspicious and

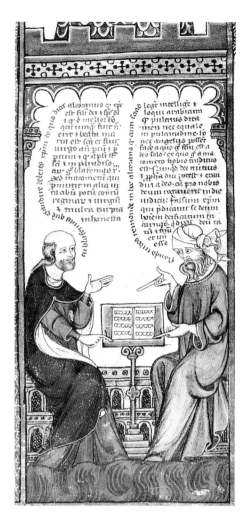

Ramon Lull (on the left) is taught Arabic by a Muslim slave; illustration in a contemporary Life of Lull.

at times ruthless ruler who employed trickery, bribery and intrigue, but brought stability and wealth to France and won Anjou, Provence and Maine for the French Crown. Born in 1423, he succeeded his father, Charles VII, against whom he had rebelled in 1440. He inherited sound military and fiscal structures and raised taxation, which enabled him to administer an effective and efficient policy. Louis sought closer relations with the papacy and in 1472 he signed an agreement with Sixtus IV, which acknowledged the pope's right, upon the king's recommendation, to appoint all major benefices. Louis was devoted to the hunt and loved dogs. He was also faithful to his wife. Philip de Commynes' remarks suggest that this was no mean feat, for he claims that although the queen was an excellent princess in other respects, 'she was not a person in whom a man could take any great delight'. While Louis was a harsh ruler and meted out severe punishment, Commynes maintains that 'he never did a person a mischief who had not offended him first'. *See p. 108*

Lull, Ramon (Raymond the Blessed), *c.* 1232–1316. Poet, mystic, philosopher and autobiographer, he was deeply interested in Islam and devoted to the conversion of the Muslims. Ramon was born into a wealthy family. His parents had participated in James I of Aragon's conquest of Majorca in 1229, and he became seneschal to Prince James, later James II of Majorca. He pursued his studies at Majorca, *c.* 1265–74, and learnt Arabic, Latin grammar, Christian philosophy and theology. Following his 'divine illumination' on Mount Randa, Majorca, in *c.* 1274, he composed the *Ars compendiosa inveniendi veritatem*. In 1275 his books were examined and approved by a Franciscan theologian at Montpellier and Ramon was permitted to teach in public. Some 250 of his 290 works survive. Amongst his best-known writings are the *Ars brevis et Ars generalis ultima*, his autobiography, the *Vida Coaetanea* and his masterpiece, the *Book of the Lover and the Beloved*. Ramon reasoned that as the Muslims began with belief in God's Unity and Divine Attributes, the logical conclusion was their conversion to Christianity. He presented several petitions for missions to Islam at the papal court, and persuaded Prince James to found a Franciscan monastery at Miramar, Majorca, where thirteen Franciscans would study Arabic and prepare for a mission; this received papal approval on 17 October 1270. Ramon died in Majorca in 1316. He was regarded as a saint from the sixteenth century, but attempts for his canonization failed. Pius IX beatified him in 1858.

Maimonides (Moses ben Maimon; Rambam), 1135–1204. The foremost intellectual figure of medieval Judaism, Maimonides was born in Cordoba but left Spain when the position became intolerable for the Jews. He eventually settled in Egypt, where he became head of the Jewish community, physician to the sultan, Saladin, and widely recognized as the greatest Rabbinic authority of his time. One of Maimonides' greatest achievements is *The Guide for the Perplexed* (1190), a work of religious philosophy in which he sought to reconcile Rabbinic Judaism with Aristotelianism. His other works, mainly written in Arabic, include rabbinical letters on contemporary problems and treatises on logic, mathematics, medicine, law and theology.

Malory, Sir Thomas, fl. 1470. This great English translator and writer is chiefly remembered for his classic *Morte d'Arthur*, printed by William Caxton in 1485. Malory's prose epic – the first in the English language – consists of Arthurian romances, chiefly

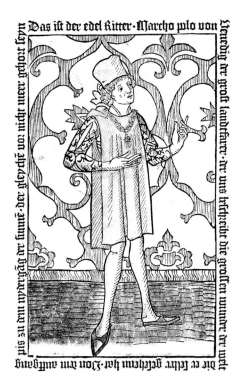

Marco Polo: his 'Travels' were translated into German in 1477 with this portrait on the title page.

translated from French sources, and written in a simple, idiomatic, yet graceful style. Little is known of Malory's life, though he may be identified with a knight and member of parliament who, after quarrelling with nearby monks, was arrested and died in 1471.

Marcabru, *c.* 1129–50. Provençal troubadour, he was a candid and often crude critic of the mores of his time, and attributed the ills of contemporary society to the promiscuity of the aristocracy. He was particularly censorious of male and female adulterers, and was concerned to distinguish true love from false love. Whereas the former might bring happiness and stability, the latter resulted in disorder. A remarkable forty-two of Marcabru's poems are extant, four with melodies. His work – an early phase of accomplished vernacular lyrical poetry – shows great originality of style. It incorporates unusual rhymes and words, and is permeated with natural imagery.

Marco Polo, *c.* 1253–1324. Merchant and explorer, his *Travels* (*Divisament dou Monde*) stimulated contemporary interest in the East and remains one of the greatest travel books. Born in Venice, his merchant father was one of the first Europeans to visit the court of the Mongol Great Khan Khublai in China. In 1271 the seventeen-year-old Marco accompanied his father and uncle on their return journey and made extensive notes on his voyage. After his arrival in 1275 he

remained in the Khan's service where his duties included governing a Chinese town for three years and accompanying the Khan's daughter to Persia, where she was to marry. On his return to Venice in 1295 Marco served in the Venetian naval forces, but was captured by the Genoese the following year. During this imprisonment he dictated his *Travels,* a practical guide to the trade routes and commodities of Asia, and a catalogue of bizarre customs, great treasures and fantastic creatures. On his release in 1299 he returned to Venice where he later died.

Margaret, Queen of Denmark, Norway and Sweden *c.* 1388–1412. An effective ruler of Scandinavia, she united the thrones of Denmark, Norway and Sweden. Born in 1353 to Waldemar IV of Denmark, she became queen of Norway and Sweden upon her marriage to Haakon of Norway. Following the death of her husband in 1380 and the sudden death of her son, Olaf, in 1387, Margaret established herself as the 'authorized lady and husband and guardian of all of the realm of Denmark', until a new king was elected with her approval; she achieved similar recognition in Norway and Sweden. In 1397 she effected the unification of the three kingdoms with the Union of Kalmar and the coronation of her great-nephew, Eric of Pomerania, as king of Denmark, Norway and Sweden. Nevertheless, Margaret herself acted as regent. She secured peace, stabilized the economy and recovered many of the Crown's alienated estates. She reportedly died of the plague while on board her ship.

Margaret of Scotland, *c.* 1045–93. A royal Anglo-Saxon exile, she was celebrated for her piety and canonized in 1249. The grand-daughter of Edmund Ironside, King of England, 1016–17, and the sister of Edgar Atheling, she fled to Scotland with other Saxon refugees after the Norman Conquest of 1066, and was married to Malcolm Canmore, King of the Scots, no later than 1071. She reputedly reformed the church in Scotland and anglicized and refined the Scottish court. She was devoted to prayer, reading, almsgiving, and ecclesiastical needlework; one of her favourite books of devotion is now in the Bodleian library. She introduced the use of the Roman Church in Scotland and restored the abbey at Iona, as well as initiating the construction of Dunfermline as a burial place for royals, akin to Westminster Abbey. She was especially noted for her devotion to lepers. The *Life* of Margaret, written by her chaplain, Turgot, emphasises the queen's public and private achievements. She died within a few days of her husband, Malcolm, who was slain while

raiding England. She was canonized in 1249 and a year later her body was translated to a new shrine at Dunfermline, following a papal inquiry into her life and miracles. She was named patron saint of Scotland in 1673.

Marsilius of Padua (Marsiglio dei Mainardini), *c.* 1280–1343. A political philosopher, he was an advocate of the autonomous state and sought to free Italy from the civil strife which, he claimed, was caused by papal appropriation of secular jurisdiction. The son of a notary, Marsilius was educated at the University of Padua and completed his studies at Paris, where he devoted himself to medicine. He was Rector of the university in 1313. His main work, the *Defensor Pacis*, was written in Paris in 1324, and is influenced by Aristotle's ideal of the State. Marsilius argued that authority should reside in a secular ruler empowered by the people; the Church should remain subservient to this secular power. When authorship of this anti-papal treatise became known in 1326 Marsilius fled the city and sought refuge with Louis of Bavaria, whom JOHN XXII had excommunicated. In 1327 John XXII selected five statutes of Marsilius' work which he denounced as heretical and from this point Marsilius devoted himself to defence of the Empire. His *Defensor Minor*, *c.* 1340, argued that the pope had usurped the temporal and spiritual power of the emperor. Marsilius may also have helped to draft a decree to depose John XXII.

Martini, Simone (Simone de Martino, Simone Memmi), *c.* 1284–1344. Sienese painter, his interest in the effects of light, colour and texture influenced later Tuscan artists. Simone was probably a pupil of DUCCIO, but his work was also affected by GIOTTO, and he fused these two contrasting styles to create his own personal approach. Simone was an official painter to the commune of Siena and later served in the papal court at Avignon, where he may have met PETRARCH. Little else is known about him. His wall-paintings are highly decorative with vibrant colours and free-flowing figures. The *Annunciation* triptych, the most influential of his works, is the first extant altar-painting in the West dedicated to this subject. His greatest fresco cycle, which is in the Church of St Francis, Assisi, depicts scenes from the *Life of St Martin. See pp. 66, 76, 111, 115*

Matthias Corvinus (Matthias I Hunyadi), King of Hungary and Bohemia 1458–90. Fine orator, soldier, statesman and patron of the arts. He was born in 1440, the son of János Hunyadi, commander-in-chief and treasurer of Ladislav V, King of Hungary.

Passionate about the arts and scholarship, he was essentially responsible for introducing the Renaissance into Hungary. He was famed for the brilliance of his international court at Buda and engaged in much large-scale building, most notably his summer palace at Visegrád, the university at Pozsony, and the library (Corvina), which he filled with manuscripts of classical texts. He secured his country against the Turks, conquered large parts of Austria and established a Central European empire.

Medici family. An affluent Florentine family, they rose to prosperity and standing through banking. In 1434 Cosimo the Elder, son of the wealthiest banker in Florence, attained (unofficial) lordship of Florence. His family consolidated and contributed to the powerbase he had established and in 1570 Cosimo de Medici (d. 1574) was crowned Grand Duke of Tuscany by the pope in Rome. Family members continued to rule in this capacity until 1737.

Michael Scot, *c.* 1200–*c.* 1235. Translator, writer and magician, Michael began his career as a translator in Toledo, Spain. He supervised a fresh translation of Aristotle as well as commentaries from Arabic to Latin. He later lived in Sicily and during his final years received the patronage of FREDERICK II and allegedly served as his court astrologer. His *Liber introductorius, Liber particularis,* and *De secretis naturae* are dedicated to Frederick. The latter includes astrology, astronomy, physiognomy and human reproduction. While ALBERTUS MAGNUS and ROGER BACON were dismissive of Michael's translations, the survival of some two hundred of his manuscripts from the thirteenth and fourteenth centuries is testimony to his popularity.

Nicholas of Cusa (Nicholas Kebs, Kryfts), 1401–64. German cardinal, he contributed to philosophy, theology, political theory and science, but is most celebrated for his metaphysical thought and as a collector of Greek and Latin manuscripts. His library at Cusa, on the River Moselle, can still be visited today and houses about three hundred manuscripts, some of which are in Nicholas' hand. Nicholas was educated at Heidelberg, Padua and Cologne, and received his doctorate of canon law. He was ordained in 1430 and undertook various ecclesiastical offices, including service as papal legate. Nicholas was greatly concerned with the idea of synthesis, by reconciling opposites and uniting discord. He sought to reconcile discontented parties and helped effect concord amongst religious groups and warring princes. He was also an ardent

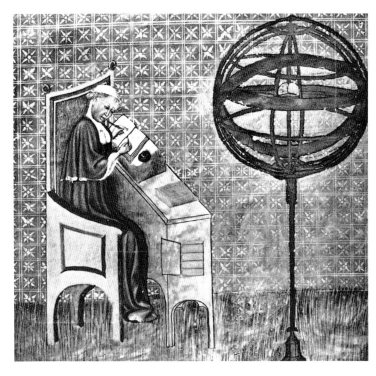

Nicole Oresme with his armillary sphere, a three-dimensional model of the Ptolemaic universe, from his translation of Aristotle's 'De coelo et mundo'; 14th century.

reformer, though his path was often rough; his *De Concordantia Catholica* sketched a programme for reforming the Church and Empire. While he initially favoured the Conciliar Movement, he later emerged as an advocate of the papacy. The *Docta Ignorantia* is perhaps the best-known of Nicholas' writings. It discusses the limitations of man's knowledge and the need to recognize one's own ignorance for knowledge, he argued, was effectively learned ignorance. While knowledge of God's existence was possible, all knowledge of his nature was unattainable and discussion of God was necessarily metaphorical. In *c.* 1452–58, Nicholas founded a hospital at Cues, which he endowed with his own library. The hospital was intended for the care of thirty-three old men, in memory of the number of years Christ lived on this earth, and still retains this original function. Nicholas is buried at the altar.

Olivi, Peter John, *c.* 1248–98. Leader of the Spiritual Franciscans, he was a vehement reformer and advocate of poverty, but his orthodoxy was repeatedly called into question. Born in Sérignan, Hérault (Languedoc), Olivi entered the Franciscan Order when twelve years old. He studied at Paris and perhaps also at Oxford. In 1279 Pope Nicholas III sought his opinion on Franciscan poverty, but in 1282, at the General Chapter of Strasbourg, Olivi was accused of heresy and his works were confiscated. Nevertheless, his orthodoxy was reconfirmed by the General Chapter of Montpellier in 1287 and he served in several convents until his death at Narbonne. There were mixed reactions to Olivi's works

following his death. Whereas the Spiritual Franciscans accorded him a tomb and honoured him as a saint, in 1299 the General Chapter at Lyons declared him heretical and ordered that his writings be burned. The friars destroyed his tomb in 1318 and he was severely condemned by JOHN XXII in 1326, for Louis of Bavaria had used his opinions in the *Appeal of Sachsenhausen* against the pope. Olivi saw himself primarily as a theologian. He wrote speculative and exegetical works, as well as biblical commentaries and works on the observance of the Franciscan Rule. His views on man's cognition and volition were influential and later adopted by WILLIAM OF OCKHAM and others. However, his theory of virtual extension, which defied traditional scholarly thought, was rejected by the Franciscans.

Oresme, Nicole, *c.* 1325–82. Celebrated as an economist, mathematician and physician, he is considered a leading founder of modern science who paved the way for Copernicus, Galileo and Descartes. Oresme studied theology at Paris, probably under BURIDAN, and was master of the College of Navarre in 1356. He occupied several ecclesiastical positions and was elevated to the see of Lisieux in 1377. Oresme was committed to the pursuit of scientific knowledge, but morally condemned magic and astrology. He maintained that apparently marvellous phenomena had natural causes, and argued that scientific theories were only hypotheses. After all, he reasoned, one could not prove by observation alone that the earth remained still while the heavens rotated. He wrote a number of philosophical and scientific works

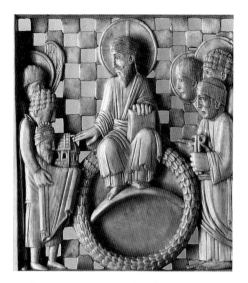

The Emperor Otto I (on the left) offering a model of Magdeburg Cathedral to Christ; ivory plaque, c. 970.

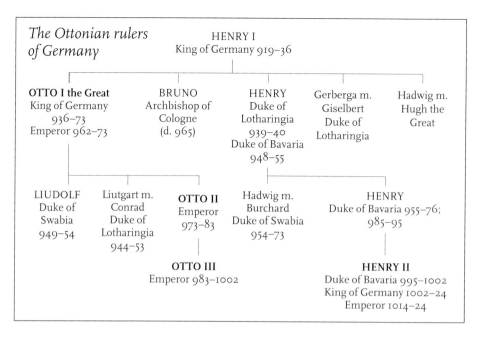

The Ottonian rulers of Germany

HENRY I
King of Germany 919–36

OTTO I the Great
King of Germany 936–73
Emperor 962–73

BRUNO
Archbishop of Cologne
(d. 965)

HENRY
Duke of Lotharingia 939–40
Duke of Bavaria 948–55

Gerberga m. Giselbert
Duke of Lotharingia

Hadwig m. Hugh the Great

LIUDOLF
Duke of Swabia 949–54

Liutgart m. Conrad
Duke of Lotharingia 944–53

OTTO II
Emperor 973–83

Hadwig m. Burchard
Duke of Swabia 954–73

HENRY
Duke of Bavaria 955–76; 985–95

OTTO III
Emperor 983–1002

HENRY II
Duke of Bavaria 995–1002
King of Germany 1002–24
Emperor 1014–24

in Latin and French. They include commentaries on Aristotle, a treatise on coins, and the *De Causis Mirabilium*, which considers the physiology and psychology of sensation.

Otto I, King of Germany 936–73. He brought Germany and most of Italy into one empire and established it as the greatest power in Europe. Born in 912, the son of Henry I (919–36), Otto was crowned emperor at Rome in 962 and was the only medieval German king accorded the title 'the Great'. He suppressed internal ducal rebellions and thereafter limited ducal power, and relied on bishops acting as royal agents. He initiated the Ottonian renaissance, a cultural revival of architecture, sculpture and the pictorial arts. Like his father, Otto successfully dealt with the threat of raiding pagan Hungarians: he extended Henry's fortifications and defeated the Magyars in 955 on the River Lech. In the West, Otto arbitrated in French conflict and intervened in Italy to discourage Italian sympathy for German malcontents. Indeed, he took considerable measures to stabilise his position in Italy and by the end of his reign effectively controlled N. and C. Italy.

Otto III, Holy Roman Emperor 983–1002. He was the first German emperor to establish Rome as his effective capital. Born in 980, the grandson of OTTO THE GREAT, he succeeded his father, Otto II, when only three years old and was crowned at Aachen on 25 December 983. He reached his majority in 994 and was crowned in 996 at Rome. Otto was greatly influenced by his teacher, Gerbert of Aurillac, later Pope SYLVESTER II, who encouraged him in his

duty, as emperor, to convert the pagans of E. Europe. As part of his programme to renew the Roman Empire – *Renovatio imperii Romanorum* – Otto built a palace on the Aventine and revived the imperial court offices. Pope Sylvester II helped him with this project and the two worked alongside one another in an imperial-papal alliance, with Otto as the 'servant of Christ'. However, Otto's policies were criticised by his contemporaries and by the time of his death Rome was in open rebellion. *See pp. 33, 43, 97*

Otto of Freising, *c.* 1112–58. While he is primarily celebrated as an historian, Otto was also one of the first theologians to acquaint Germany with the new works of Aristotle. The son of Leopold III of Austria and grandson of Emperor HENRY IV, he studied at Paris and was probably taught by ABELARD and HUGH OF ST VICTOR. Seeking a more ascetic way of life he entered the Cistercian abbey of Morimond, Champagne, in 1132, where he became abbot in 1136. He was elevated to the see of Freising two years later. He reformed his diocese and led a group of pilgrims on the Second Crusade from 1147 to 1149. He died en route to a Cistercian General Chapter, wearing the habit of his Order. A leading historian of the mid-twelfth century, his main work, *Chronicon seu Historia de Duabus Civitatibus*, modifies Augustine's concept of the heavenly and earthly cities. It presents the history of the world as the history of salvation, from the time of Creation until the Last Judgment, and advocates the need to study history to learn of God's ways. A later work, the *Gesta Friderici*, uses original documents to detail the first part of FREDERICK I's reign.

Owain Glun Dwr (Glendower), *c.* 1359–*c.* 1416. Regarded by the Welsh as a national hero but by others as a failed rebel, he was the last sovereign prince of Wales and briefly re-established Welsh independence. Owain was the son of a prosperous landowner and a descendent of the princes of Powys, N.E. Wales. He studied law at Westminster and inherited his father's estates in N. Wales. Following a quarrel with Lord Reginald Grey of Ruthin, who in 1400 accused Owain of seizing his lands, Owain and his men ravaged the nobleman's estates, withdrew to the mountains and effectively instigated a national uprising. Henry IV of England sought to pacify the area while Owain and his men lived as outlaws. Owain managed to avoid major battles and evade capture. By 1402 he held most Welsh castles and had established a shadow government; the rebel had turned ruler. However by 1408 Prince Henry, the future HENRY V, had re-imposed English rule. In 1415, as King of England, Henry sought reconciliation with Owain but received no response. The end of Owain's life remains shrouded in enigma. Commenting on the events of 1415 one Welsh chronicler remarks, 'very many say that he died; the seers maintain that he did not'.

Paris, Matthew, *c.* 1200–59. A candid and lively monastic chronicler, his wide-ranging works provide extensive information regarding domestic and international affairs in the thirteenth century. Matthew entered the Benedictine abbey of St Albans in 1217, where he remained for the rest of his life. The house received a number of royal visitors, foreigners and pilgrims, and was well-placed to hear of events at home and abroad. Matthew often recorded what he himself had seen or heard. Indeed he attended the translation of BECKET's body in 1220 and witnessed the marriage of HENRY III and Eleanor in 1236. In 1236 Matthew took over the St Albans' scriptorium, a position which he held until his death. He was an accomplished annalist and scribe and wrote numerous works including hagiography, a history of the abbots of St Albans, and his greatest achievement, the *Chronica Majora*. The latter – a history of the world from Creation to 1259 – was the first illustrated chronicle of contemporary affairs with sketches of elephants, camels and cannibal Tartars. Matthew's accounts are largely based on his personal observations and express his own, at times strong, opinions. He was particularly hostile to foreigners and the mendicant orders, and critical of the king, pope and itinerant judges. *See pp. 176, 218*

Peter Lombard, *c.* 1095–1160. 'Master of the *Sentences*', he is remembered for his *Liber Sententiarum*, which was the standard textbook for theology from the thirteenth to the sixteenth centuries. Born in Novara, Lombardy, he studied law in N. Italy and theology at Paris, where he taught for almost twenty years. In 1159, shortly before his death, he was elevated to the see of Paris. His early works include commentaries on the Pauline Epistles and Psalms, but his masterpiece was the work generally referred to as the *Sentences*. This clear exposition of Christian doctrine is arranged in four books and is effectively a work of compilation. It is steeped in quotations from patristic writers, especially Augustine, but also includes contemporary figures such as ABELARD, HUGH OF ST VICTOR, and GRATIAN. While the *Sentences* was criticized during Peter's life, and there were attempts to have the work censured after his death, it survived attack and its orthodoxy was confirmed by the Fourth Lateran Council in 1215. By the mid-thirteenth century the *Sentences* were central to university education. BONAVENTURA, WILLIAM OF OCKHAM, AQUINAS and DUNS SCOTUS, amongst others, wrote commentaries on the work.

Petrarch, Francesco, 1304–74. One of Italy's foremost poets and one of the first great representatives of Italian Renaissance humanism, he is celebrated as a creator of Italian literary language based on his native Tuscan dialect. Petrarch was born in Arezzo but largely raised at Avignon for, like DANTE, his father had been exiled from his native Florence for political reasons. Petrarch studied law at Montpellier and Bologna, and it was here that he wrote his first poems.

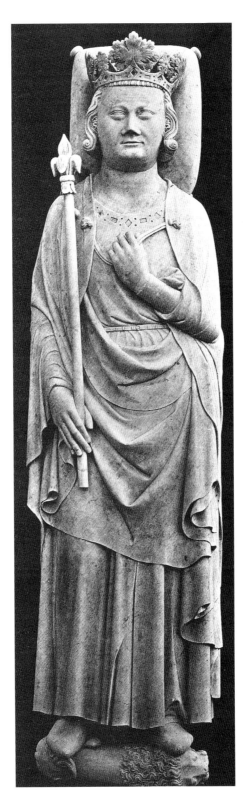

Philip IV (the Fair), King of France; his tomb in Saint-Denis.

Upon his father's death in 1326 he returned to Avignon and took minor orders in *c.* 1330. He served as chaplain to Cardinal Giovanni Colonna, held canonries in Lombez, Parma and Padua, and acted as papal emissary. Petrarch's recovery of classical texts, in particular Cicero's letters to Atticus in 1345,

has deservedly earned him the title 'Father' of the humanistic movement. He was convinced that Antiquity could offer contemporary society exactly what it lacked through the four Cardinal virtues and the realisation that man must react with his fellow men as well as God, i.e. 'to feel rightly about God and to act rightly among men'. Petrarch is primarily renowned for his love sonnets, especially his poems to Laura, his unrequited love. He also wrote scholarly poetry, prose, letters and historical works, which include *Africa*, *De viris illustribus* and *Rerum memorandarum libri*. He was crowned *magnus poeta et historicus* at Rome on Easter Day 1341 and died on 17 July, 1374, the eve of his seventieth birthday, whilst reading Virgil. *See p. 223*

Philip II (Augustus), King of France 1180–1223. An efficient and effective ruler of the Capetian dynasty, he firmly established French royal power and consciously developed Paris as a great centre. Born on 21 August 1165 in Paris, the long-awaited son of Louis VII, he was crowned co-regent at Rheims in 1179, while his father was still alive. Philip joined RICHARD I of England on Crusade to the Holy Land in 1190, after the fall of Jerusalem to the Muslims in 1187, and they successfully captured Acre in 1191. Philip centred administration in Paris, expanded the judiciary and reorganised the financial system by creating a central accounting bureau. He made territorial gains from the kings of England, acquiring Normandy in 1204 and driving them south of the Loire in 1206. These acquisitions were sealed by the Battle of Bouvines in 1214. Philip died on 14 July 1223 and was buried at the royal abbey of Saint-Denis, Paris. *See p. 223*

Philip IV (the Fair), King of France 1285–1314. A capable but harsh ruler, who was physically striking, he exercised more power in France than any other medieval French king. Born *c.* 1268, he succeeded his father, Philip III, who died on crusade. Philip nurtured a powerful administrative centre in Paris, but his ambitions to fully exploit French royal power brought him into conflict with his two most powerful vassals, the king of England and the count of Flanders. His annexation of Gascony in 1294 provoked war with England, and although he successfully conquered most of Gascony, he was driven out by rebellion in 1302 and made peace with England, restoring Gascony. He continued fighting Flanders but did not achieve a decisive victory. These wars were a considerable expense and Philip imposed heavy taxation to finance the fighting. His reign was also dogged by a series of disputes with the Church over taxation of the clergy

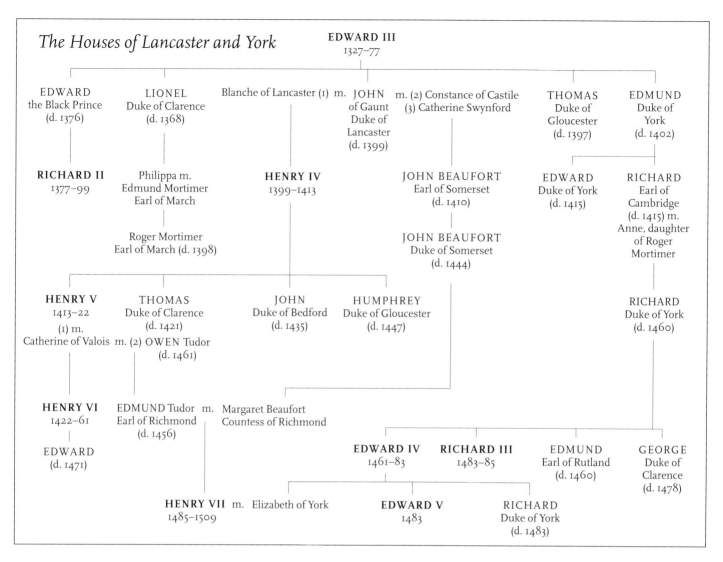

The Houses of Lancaster and York

EDWARD III
1327–77

EDWARD
the Black Prince
(d. 1376)

LIONEL
Duke of Clarence
(d. 1368)

Blanche of Lancaster (1) m. JOHN
of Gaunt
Duke of
Lancaster
(d. 1399)

m. (2) Constance of Castile
(3) Catherine Swynford

THOMAS
Duke of
Gloucester
(d. 1397)

EDMUND
Duke of
York
(d. 1402)

RICHARD II
1377–99

Philippa m.
Edmund Mortimer
Earl of March

HENRY IV
1399–1413

JOHN BEAUFORT
Earl of Somerset
(d. 1410)

EDWARD
Duke of York
(d. 1415)

RICHARD
Earl of
Cambridge
(d. 1415) m.
Anne, daughter
of Roger
Mortimer

Roger Mortimer
Earl of March (d. 1398)

JOHN BEAUFORT
Duke of Somerset
(d. 1444)

HENRY V
1413–22
(1) m.
Catherine of Valois m. (2) OWEN Tudor
(d. 1461)

THOMAS
Duke of Clarence
(d. 1421)

JOHN
Duke of Bedford
(d. 1435)

HUMPHREY
Duke of Gloucester
(d. 1447)

RICHARD
Duke of York
(d. 1460)

HENRY VI
1422–61

EDMUND Tudor m. Margaret Beaufort
Earl of Richmond   Countess of Richmond
(d. 1456)

EDWARD
(d. 1471)

EDWARD IV
1461–83

RICHARD III
1483–85

EDMUND
Earl of Rutland
(d. 1460)

GEORGE
Duke of
Clarence
(d. 1478)

HENRY VII m. Elizabeth of York
1485–1509

EDWARD V
1483

RICHARD
Duke of York
(d. 1483)

---

and their judicial immunity. He humiliated his chief opponent, BONIFACE VIII, whom he arrested at Anagni in 1303 and tried in a French court; the aged pope died several days later. Philip faced unexpected opposition at the end of his reign when many of the nobility and townsmen formed leagues to object to his policies. *See p. 102*

Pisano, Nicola *c.* 1220–78/84. Italian sculptor whose works show marked influence from Roman art. Particularly renowned for his hexagonal marble pulpit in the baptistery at Pisa, his other works include the octagonal pulpit at Siena Cathedral, designs for the Church of St Domenico in Bologna and sculptural decorations for the fountain at Perugia. His son **Giovanni** (*c.* 1250–after 1314) is regarded as the founder of Italian Gothic sculpture. He was responsible for the pulpit of Pisa Cathedral and statues on the façade of Siena Cathedral. *See p. 37*

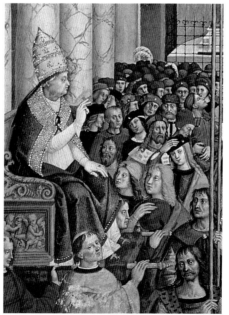

Pope Pius II; detail of a fresco by Pinturicchio in the Library of Siena, 1502.

Pius II, Pope 1458–64. He exercised great missionary zeal and was one of the leading humanists of the fifteenth century, but has received mixed opinions regarding his personality and actions. Born Aeneas Sylvius Piccolomini in Corsignano, near Siena, he was educated at the universities of Siena and Florence and earned renown for his literary works. Indeed Frederick III made him poet laureate in 1442 and, like PETRARCH, he was crowned on the Capitol. Aeneas was engaged in imperial service, and in 1447 he worked alongside NICHOLAS OF CUSA for the reconciliation of pope and emperor. Thereafter he was elevated to the see of Trieste. In 1450 he was translated to the bishopric of Siena, in 1456 he was made a cardinal and in 1458 he was elevated to the papacy. He continued his writings and compiled the *Commentaries*, an account of his own career. He endeavoured to unite Europe and reaffirm papal prerogatives; his bull, *Execrabilis*, rejected the notion that the pope was inferior to councils. He also devoted himself to war against the Turks.

In an attempt to convert the Muslims through argument he wrote a futile letter to the Sultan urging him to embrace Christianity: 'Thus you will be legitimately Emperor of the East.' Pius declared Holy War in 1463 and took the Cross in 1464, but died at Ancona, aged fifty-eight.

Porete, Marguerite, d. 1310. Belgian mystic, her *Mirror of the Simple Soul* – a dialogue between Love, Reason and the Soul – describes the seven states of grace through which the soul passes. It was condemned for its mystical pantheism in 1306, and Marguerite was burned as a heretic in the main square in Paris, June 1310.

Raymond of Pennaforte, *c*. 1180–1275. Spanish canonist and co-founder of the Order of Mercedarians, his contributions to canon law and Dominican legislation remained in effect until the twentieth century. Raymond taught logic and rhetoric at the University of Barcelona and studied law at Bologna, where he wrote a treatise on ecclesiastical legislation that is now in the Vatican library. Inspired by the preaching of the Dominican prior, Reginald of Bologna, he joined the Dominicans at Barcelona in 1223. Raymond served in the papal household and was named as GREGORY IX's confessor in 1230. He later officiated as papal chaplain and Grand Penitentiary, and was thus responsible for rewriting and condensing church canons. His edition of the decretals was completed in 1234 and prevailed as the authorized version until 1917. He was appointed General of the Dominicans in 1238 and his edition of the *Constitutions* remained in force until 1924. In 1240 he resigned as General to devote himself to the conversion of Jews and Muslims. He founded schools of Hebrew and Arabic and it was supposedly at his suggestion that AQUINAS wrote the *Summa contra Gentiles*. His own most notable work, the *Summa de poenitentia*, or *Summa casuum*, was written at the request of his superiors. It is a guide for confessors and the hundreds of extant manuscripts are testimony to its influence. Raymond was highly esteemed by his contemporaries and, following his death in 1275, there were constant requests for his canonization. He was eventually canonized by Clement III in 1601.

Richard I (Coeur de Lion), King of England 1189–99. A courageous warrior, he is popularly remembered for his valour and crusading feats. Born on 8 September 1157, in Oxford, the eldest surviving son of HENRY II, Richard grew up in Poitou and ruled Aquitaine from 1170. He revolted against his father, 1173–74, and in 1188–89 joined ranks

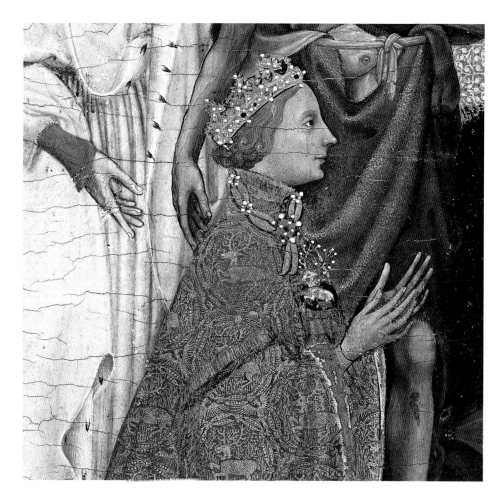

King Richard II of England, from the anonymous 'Wilton Diptych', c. 1400.

with PHILIP AUGUSTUS and forced Henry to make humiliating concessions. Richard succeeded to the throne in 1189, following his father's death, but immediately prepared to leave on the Third Crusade and was essentially an absentee ruler. He participated in the defeat of the Muslim leader, SALADIN, and the capture of Messina, Cyprus and Acre, but failed to re-take Jerusalem. A conspiracy by his brother, JOHN, necessitated Richard's return in 1192, but he was captured en route and imprisoned in Germany. His subjects raised the enormous ransom of 100,000 marks for Richard's release in 1194, and on his arrival in England he was crowned for a second time at Winchester Cathedral. However, he soon left England and spent the rest of his reign defending his French possessions. He died in 1199 from an infected arrow-wound to his left shoulder, and was buried at Fontevrault; his heart was interred at Rouen Cathedral.

Richard II, King of England 1377–99. Though a physically inspiring figure and a patron of the arts, a turbulent minority, his lofty ideal of kingship and ineffectual administration led to Richard's deposition and death. Born in Bordeaux on 6 January

1367, the younger son of EDWARD, THE BLACK PRINCE, he succeeded to a country afflicted by the financial burden of EDWARD III's wars in France, and aggravated further by the regency council's continuation of Edward's policies. This, and the imposition of a high poll tax, precipitated the Peasants' Revolt of 1381, a popular uprising led by WAT TYLER. Later in Richard's minority, discontent with royal indulgence and the young king's determination to choose his own counsellors culminated in the Commons dismissal and impeachment of the chancellor and royal favourite, Michael de la Pole. A council of eleven lords, the 'Appellants', was established to monitor and constrain royal power. Two years later the Merciless Parliament condemned a number of the king's intimates and supporters for treason; many were executed and Richard was threatened with deposition. He attained his majority in 1389 and vigorously asserted his royal prerogatives, effectively establishing a one-man rule: he used his own seal rather than the Great Seal and had a standing army. Moreover, he had not forgotten the events of 1388 and in 1397 he arrested and condemned the lords Appellant. However, Richard's policies raised alarm and in 1399 Henry, Earl of Hereford, usurped the throne and was crowned Henry IV. Richard was imprisoned in Pontefract Castle, where he died, or was murdered.

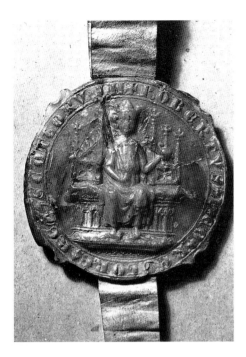

Great seal of Robert Bruce, 'Rex Scottorum'.

Richard III, King of England, 1483–85. Traditionally regarded as a murderous villain who usurped the throne, but recent attempts to redress this view argue that much of Richard's reputation is based on Lancastrian propaganda, and that he was perhaps driven as much by self-preservation as ambition. Richard was born in 1452, the youngest child of Richard, Duke of York, and was a loyal brother to King Edward IV, whom he accompanied in exile (1470) and to victory (1471). When Edward IV died, his elder son, Edward, Prince of Wales, was only twelve and Richard named himself protector. Faced with the growing threat of the young king's mother, Elizabeth Woodville, and her powerful and ambitious relatives, Richard overthrew his rivals and assumed the Crown. The young king and his brother were imprisoned in the Tower, and had most probably been murdered by October 1483. Richard then crushed the rebellion of his former supporter, the Duke of Buckingham. Richard's enemies turned to Henry Tudor, the Lancastrian claimant in exile, who landed in Wales in 1485. Richard was defeated and killed at the Battle of Bosworth on 22 August 1485. Despite his poor reputation, he was a patron of the arts, encouraged trade and founded a college for priests at All Hallows, Barking.

Richard fitzGilbert de Clare ('Strongbow'), d. 1176. Welsh Marcher baron and Earl of Pembroke, he played a prominent role in the Anglo-Norman invasion of Ireland. Following an agreement with DIARMAIT MAC MÚRCHADA, King of Leinster, Richard led a sizeable troop to Ireland to overthrow 'the traitors' who had expelled Diarmait from his kingdom. In return for his help Richard was promised succession to Leinster and the hand of Diarmait's daughter, Aoifa. Armed with some two hundred knights and a thousand troops the earl arrived in Ireland in 1170, took Waterford and married Aoifa. He advanced on Dublin in September 1170 and successfully withstood the siege launched by Rory O'Connor, the High King. Upon Diarmait's death in 1171 Richard was forced to campaign for his right to succession and successfully secured his claim. Shortly thereafter he allayed HENRY II's fears that he had become an over-mighty subject and pledged Dublin, Waterford, Wexford and Wicklow to the king as his feudal lord. Henry's overlordship was officially recognized when he visited Ireland in 1171.

Robert Bruce, King of Scotland, 1306–29. Leader of the anti-English nationalists, he led the Scots to a spectacular victory at Bannockburn in 1314. Born on 11 July 1274, to the Anglo-Norman Bruce family, his father was lord of Annandale, warden of Carrick Castle. Robert inherited his grandfather's claim to the Scottish throne and his mother's earldom of Carrick. Although he fought in EDWARD's army which invaded Scotland in 1296, the following year he joined WALLACE and rebelled against the English king, but he was forced to submit. After his father's death in 1304, Robert became head of the Bruce family, and two years later had emerged as leader of the anti-English nationalists. He murdered his only rival, John Comyn, and was consequently excommunicated by Pope Clement V and outlawed by EDWARD I. Robert then had himself crowned king of the Scots upon the stone of Scone on 25 March 1306. His title was recognised by the pope in 1323. While Robert initially had little support he gained power from 1307 and led the Scots to victory at Bannockburn in 1314, and Berwick in 1318; England recognised Scotland's independence in 1328, through the Treaty of Northampton and peace was sealed by the marriage of EDWARD III's sister, Joan, and Robert's son and successor, David, later DAVID I of Scotland. Robert died of leprosy in 1329, and was buried at Dunfermline; his heart was interred at Melrose. In 1370 John Barbour, archdeacon of Aberdeen, composed *The Bruce*, a poem which recounts Robert's struggles and successes.

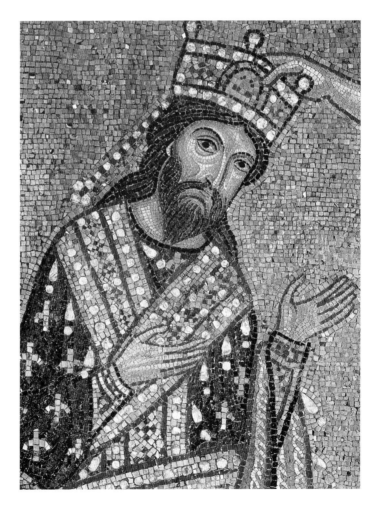

Roger II, King of Sicily; mosaic in the church of the Martorana, Palermo; 12th century.

Robert Guiscard, d. 1085. The son of a lesser Norman landholder, Tancred of Hauteville, he emerged as the strongest Norman leader in S. Italy and established his family as a ruling dynasty of consequence in Europe. Robert defeated LEO IX's army at the Battle of Civitate, 1053, but by the end of the 1050s was acting as defender of papal interests; at the pope's request he opposed HENRY IV. By the Treaty of Melfi, 1059, Robert was recognised as the feudal duke of Apulia and the potential ruler of Sicily. He dominated Italian politics in the 1060s and 1070s, and in 1071 successfully removed the last Byzantine stronghold from Bari. From this time Robert referred to himself as duke of Apulia.

Roger II (Roger the Great), King of Sicily 1130–54. Roger launched Sicily as a major power, and was noted for the racial and cultural integration of his court and for his patronage of the arts, sciences and philosophy. Born in 1095 to Count Roger I of Sicily, he successfully defeated the papal forces at Benevento and was invested as duke of Apulia on 23 August 1128. Roger introduced a new code of law in Sicily and established a strong centralized government, which was based on Western practices, but during the Schism, which began in 1130, Roger supported the anti-pope, Anacletus, over INNOCENT III. Anacletus crowned him king of Sicily, Apulia and Calabria at Palermo in 1130. This incited opposition from BERNARD OF CLAIRVAUX and Innocent II, and provoked rebellion at home. Upon Anacletus' death in 1139, Innocent, having suffered defeat, recognised Roger as king of Sicily, duke of Apulia and prince of Capua in the Treaty of Migano. Roger then concentrated his efforts on subduing Naples and Capua, and founded a short-lived empire in Tunisia.

Rogier van der Weyden, *see* **Weyden, Rogier van der**

Rudolf I of Habsburg, King of Germany 1273–91. His reign terminated the Interregnum and inaugurated Habsburg rule in Austria. Born in 1218, Rudolf succeeded his father as head of the family in 1239 and by 1273 was the most powerful man in S.W. Germany. In the same year he was elected and crowned king of the Germans, and successfully countered opposition from rivals. He occupied Austria and Styria, and conquered Ottokar II of Bohemia; these duchies were enfeoffed to his sons in 1282. Rudolf continued to expand his lands in S.W. Germany, a policy continued by his son and successor, Albrecht, and brought the lower nobility to prominence in his reorganization of imperial rule. Rudolf failed to secure the election of his son as his successor.

Ruysbroeck, Jan van, 1293–1381. Mystic and founder of a small Augustinian community at Groenendael, where he was prior, Jan was born in Ruysbroeck, near Brussels, and ordained as priest in 1317. His teachings were extremely influential and, whilst he respected the authority of the Church, he criticized corruption of the religious life. All Jan's works were in Flemish, although some were later translated into Latin. His most important prose work, *The Adornment of the Spiritual Marriage*, was composed *c.* 1350.

Saladin, 1138–93. Widely considered the greatest Muslim leader of all time, Saladin is credited with uniting the discordant East and stemming the tide of Western conquest in Eastern lands. His military career began with the conquest of Egypt (1164–74), and he was appointed vizier in 1169. In 1174 he won a series of victories in Syria, and was made sultan of Egypt and Syria. When the Franks broke a four-year truce in 1187, Saladin united troops from the Muslim territories of Syria, N. Mesopotamia, Palestine and Egypt, and routed the Christians at the battle of Hattin. The Muslims went on to capture numerous towns, including Acre, Nazareth, Ascalon and, most importantly, Jerusalem. RICHARD I's Third Crusade followed, but the treaty accorded was a triumph for Saladin and the death knell for the Latin kingdom. Saladin retired to Damascus in 1192, where he died a hero the following year.

Salimbene, 1220–*c.* 1288. Franciscan chronicler, he combines his own history with that of his Order and contemporary society. Salimbene d'Adam was born in Parma to landed parents and, like ST FRANCIS, renounced a comfortable lifestyle for a life of mendicancy. In 1238 he joined the Franciscans. His strong personality pervades his chronicle. Much is based on his personal observations and includes poetry, psalms, songs, remarks on the weather, as well as comments on momentous events that he witnessed, for instance, the Great Hallelujah of 1233, the flagellant movement of 1260, and FREDERICK II riding an elephant through Parma, accompanied by his menagerie. Salimbene emerges as a staunch defender of the Franciscans and his native Parma. He dismissed the Florentines as tricksters and was critical of new orders and sects whom he claimed were unskilled and untrained, though attractive as novelties.

Savonarola, Fra Girolamo, 1452–98. Italian monk and theologian whose rejection of papal authority and attacks on corruption, decadence and abuse of power led to his execution. In 1475, he left his native Ferrara and entered the monastery of St Domenico

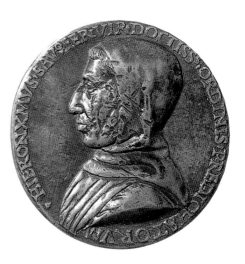

Fra Girolamo Savonarola; a medal of 1495.

at Bologna. He later became prior of the Florentine convent of St Mark's and was well known for his preaching. An outspoken critic of the Medici and the Florentine republic, he encouraged 'bonfires of the vanities' – public burnings of carnival masks, books, paintings, musical instruments and other items of luxury. Savonarola's attacks were also directed at the Church, he was excommunicated by Pope Alexander VI but continued to preach. Having made enemies of both the Florentine government and the papal authorities, he was imprisoned and tortured. In 1498, found guilty of heresy, he was hanged and burned in Florence.

Saxo Grammaticus, *c.* 1150–1208. Danish historian and skilful Latinist, his *Gesta Danorum*, a history of Denmark from mythical times to 1187, was intended to 'glorify the fatherland'. Little is known of his life, though he refers to himself as 'the humblest' of Absalon, Archbishop of Lund's men, at whose request he compiled his history. The *Gesta* covers a vast timespan. It draws on a wide range of sources including vernacular narrative poems, oral testimony, Runic inscriptions and other information collected by Icelanders. It also includes Saxo's own interpretations of legends. However, his accuracy as an historian needs to be treated with caution. The Latin of the *Gesta* is elegant but complex and causes difficulties for the reader.

Siger of Brabant (Siger the Great), *c.* 1240–*c.* 1284. Averroist philosopher, he opposed attempts to reconcile Christian and philosophic teachings, and thus crossed swords with AQUINAS and ALBERTUS MAGNUS; his principal work, *Tractatus de Anima Intellectiva*, called forth Aquinas' treatise on the unity of the intellect. Siger's other writings include *De Aeternitate Mundi*

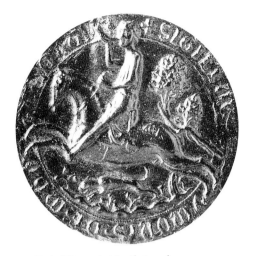

Seal of Simon de Montfort, 1258.

and commentaries on Aristotle's writings. He argued that where faith and philosophy conflicted, the former should be followed. He also held that while one could attain some knowledge of God, it was impossible to experience direct understanding of God on earth. While DANTE places Siger in *Paradise*, his writings were controversial. He was attacked by the bishop of Paris in 1270 and again in 1277, and was called to appear before the French Inquisition on charges of heresy, although he was never actually found guilty and was later acquitted by Pope Nicholas III. Siger was reputedly murdered by his insane secretary at Orvieto.

Simon de Montfort (the Younger),

c. 1208–65. A paradoxical figure, he has been celebrated as a martyr and denounced as a rebel and self-seeking adventurer. The son of Simon de Montfort the Elder, who led a crusade against the Albigensians in

Toulouse, he arrived in England in 1230 and successfully advanced his claim to the earldom of Leicester. Simon rose in royal favour and indeed married HENRY III's sister in 1238. However, from 1239 his relationship with the king soured and when Simon was called to trial in 1252, to account for his ruthless rule in Gascony, Henry denounced him as a traitor; Simon branded Henry a liar. Despite their rather stormy relationship Simon did not really take a prominent stand against the king until 1258, when he joined the rebel barons in England. In 1263 he emerged as their leader and the following year led them to victory at Lewes. Richard, Earl of Cornwall, and Prince Edward, the future EDWARD I, were imprisoned and the Mise of Lewes was implemented to contain the king. However Simon's success was short-lived and in August 1265 Edward led the royalists to triumph at Evesham. Simon was killed in the battle and his mutilated remains were buried at Evesham Abbey. Miracles were soon reported and his shrine became a place of popular pilgrimage, although the fervour of the 1260s and 1270s subsided.

Simon of Faversham (Simon Anglicus),

c. 1250–1306. Noted as a philosopher and commentator on Aristotelian writings, Simon was born at Faversham and studied at Oxford, where he later taught. He was ordained in 1289 and occupied various livings. In *c.* 1304 he was Chancellor of Oxford and the following year served briefly as archdeacon of Canterbury. His works include the *Quaestiones super libro Elenchorum* and the *Quaestiones super librum Physicorum.*

Snorri Sturluson, *c.* 1179–1241. Icelandic chieftain of the prominent clan of Sturlungar, he is regarded as one of the greatest saga writers. Snorri's most important work, *Heimskringla*, details the history of the kings of Norway of the Ynglinga dynasty, dating from mythological times. The *Prose Edda* is a mythological and poetical handbook. Snorri was raised and educated at Oddi, a renowned centre of teaching (especially in historical subjects) and culture. Snorri was sharp-minded, knowledgeable in the law and extremely ambitious, and acquired the necessary wealth to establish himself as a chieftain. His life as one of Iceland's leading chieftains is described in the *Islendinga saga*, composed by his nephew in the thirteenth century. Snorri received great honours from the royal court of Norway following his visit there, but was later embroiled in the feud between King Hákon of Norway and his former regent, Jarl Skulí. This led to his murder in 1241, when he was hacked to death in his bath on the orders of King Hákon, allegedly for treason, but effectively for his tacit refusal to further the Norwegian ruler's interests in Iceland.

Suger, Abbot of Saint-Denis, 1122–51. French scholar, abbot and patron of the arts, he participated in political and religious affairs. Born *c.* 1081 of humble parents, probably in Argenteuil, near Paris, Suger was given as a child oblate to Saint-Denis where he was educated. He completed his studies in one of the schools along the Loire. Suger may have met Prince Louis, the future LOUIS VI, at Saint-Denis. The two became good friends and Suger later served the king as a chief advisor, ambassador, companion and biographer. The abbey of Saint-Denis flourished during Suger's abbacy. He scoured the archives and reasserted various rights and claims that had lapsed, and implemented reform to address laxity at the house. His measures were praised by BERNARD OF CLAIRVAUX. Suger is perhaps best remembered for his reconstruction of the abbey church which was dedicated in 1147. It was the first great Gothic church and a model for Europe. Suger believed that the outward splendour of the building would elevate the mind to comprehending God's Majesty.

Suso, Heinrich, *c.* 1300–66. German Dominican mystic, 'the minnesinger of mysticism', his emotional mysticism was more accessible than ECKHART's intellectual mysticism. Born *c.* 1300 to a knight of the Van Berg family, he grew up at Lake Constance. A rather frail child, he preferred religion to knightly pursuits, and when thirteen or fourteen years old joined the

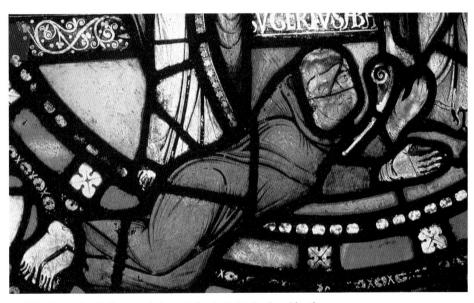

Abbot Suger, detail of a stained-glass window in Saint-Denis; mid-12th century.

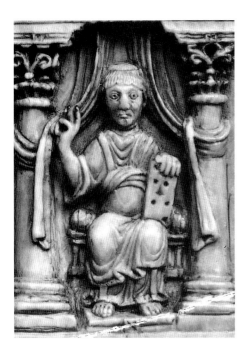

Pope Sylvester II; detail from an ivory situla of about 1000.

Dominicans. Following a profound religious experience when he was eighteen, Suso withdrew to lead a solitary and ascetic life of self-mortification. Some ten years later he re-entered the world and studied at the Dominican *studium generale* in Cologne, where he probably met his 'beloved Master', Eckhart. Suso then returned to Constance to teach the Dominican novices and conduct pastoral work. He became prior *c.* 1344, but resigned in 1348, when a woman who had visited for advice accused him of fathering her child. Suso retired to Ulm where he died in 1366. His works are both lyrical and poetic, and combine knightly imagery and religious symbolism. They were amongst the most popular in the late Middle Ages and include *The Little Book of Truth*, a dialogue between Truth and the Disciple, *The Little Book of Eternal Wisdom*, and *The Clock of Wisdom*, his only Latin work. *See p. 217*

Sylvester II (Gerbert of Aurillac), Pope 999–1003. An astute scholar and statesman, he was the first Frenchman to hold the papacy and is often presented as the model of papal-imperial partnership. Born of humble parents in the Auvergne, *c.* 940, Gerbert was educated at the Benedictine monastery of Aurillac. From *c.* 972 he pursued his studies at Rheims where he gained repute as a teacher and was particularly noted for his brilliance in mathematics. He was summoned to OTTO III's court in 997, and the following year he was promoted to the archbishopric of Ravenna. Upon his elevation to the papacy in 999 Sylvester encouraged Otto's vision of a restored Roman empire, and advocated

reforms within the Church, especially the need for clerical celibacy and the prohibition of simony. Gerbert also collected ancient manuscripts and was renowned as a scholar. He was particularly esteemed in the fields of mathematics, astronomy, logic and philosophy, and pioneered the abacus, organ, terrestrial and celestial globes. *See p. 96*

Thomas a Kempis (Thomas Hemerken), *c.* 1380–1472. An ascetical writer and a member of the spiritual movement known as the 'Modern Devotion', he is generally regarded as the author of the *De Imitatione Christi*, an accessible and anti-scholastic text, probably the most popular work on the spiritual life. Born of humble parents at Kempen, near Cologne, Thomas took the habit of the Canons Regular at the priory of St Agnietenberg, near Zollen, where his brother was prior. He was ordained in 1414 and spent most of his adult life at the priory transcribing and writing. His works are imbued with the devotional spirit and include homilies, meditations, poetry and biographies.

Tyler, Wat, d. 1381. One of the principal leaders of the Peasants' Revolt of 1381, Wat Tyler led the rebels in protest against the intolerable exploitation of England's peasantry. Rioting resulted in the murder of Archbishop Sudbury on Tower Hill and the burning of JOHN OF GAUNT's Savoy palace. At Smithfield, on 14 June, Tyler presented RICHARD II with demands for the abolition of serfdom, removal of restrictions upon freedom of labour and trade, and amnesty for rebels. The following day, when the

crowd assembled again to present fresh demands, Tyler was killed by William Walworth, Lord Mayor of London.

Urban II, Pope 1088–99. Reforming pope, who launched the crusading movement, he died just before news of the capture of Jerusalem. Born Odo of Lagery in *c.* 1042, he served as canon and archdeacon before entering Cluny, *c.* 1070, where he became prior. He was called to Rome by GREGORY VII, who made him cardinal bishop of Ostia in 1078, and ten years later he was elected to the papacy. Urban followed his predecessor's reforming policies, though with greater moderation. The highpoint of his pontificate was in 1095, at the Council of Clermont, where the whole question of reform was concentrated on investiture, and he preached the First Crusade. Urban died in 1099 and his cult was sanctioned in 1881. While his registers are not extant, many of his letters survive.

Urban V, Pope 1362–70. A scrupulous canon lawyer, a diligent reformer and a patron of scholars, he restored the papacy to Rome, albeit briefly. Born Guillaume de Grimoard in Languedoc, 1306, he took the Benedictine habit at Chirac, studied at Paris and Avignon and taught canon law at universities in France. He held abbatial office at St-Germain-d'Auxerre and St-Victor, Marseilles, and was elevated to the papacy in 1362. Urban refused to appear in public at his enthronement for he shunned pomp and ceremony, and considered the papacy exiled while away from Rome. During his papacy he pursued his predecessor's policy of

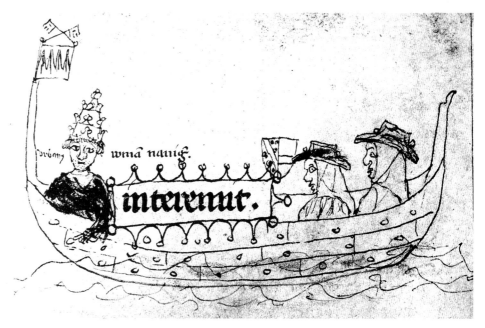

Pope Urban V shown returning from Avignon to Rome; 14th century.

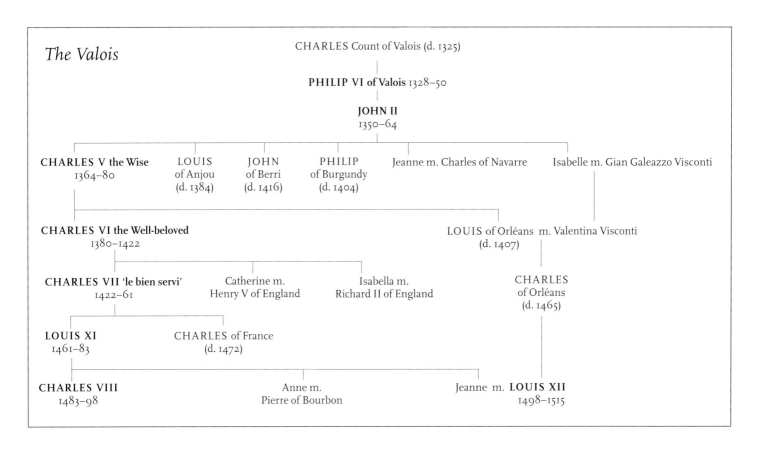

The Valois

CHARLES Count of Valois (d. 1325)

PHILIP VI of Valois 1328–50

JOHN II
1350–64

CHARLES V the Wise 1364–80 | LOUIS of Anjou (d. 1384) | JOHN of Berri (d. 1416) | PHILIP of Burgundy (d. 1404) | Jeanne m. Charles of Navarre | Isabelle m. Gian Galeazzo Visconti

CHARLES VI the Well-beloved 1380–1422 | LOUIS of Orléans m. Valentina Visconti (d. 1407)

CHARLES VII 'le bien servi' 1422–61 | Catherine m. Henry V of England | Isabella m. Richard II of England | CHARLES of Orléans (d. 1465)

LOUIS XI 1461–83 | CHARLES of France (d. 1472)

CHARLES VIII 1483–98 | Anne m. Pierre of Bourbon | Jeanne m. **LOUIS XII** 1498–1515

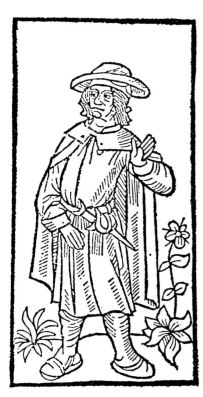

François Villon; a woodcut from his 'Grand Testament' of 1489.

centralization. He continued to erect a wall around Avignon and made improvements to the papal palace, adding a garden for peace and tranquillity. However, his plans for a crusade against the Turks failed through lack of support. In 1367, with England and France at peace, it was possible for Urban to transfer the papacy to Rome. Nevertheless, an administrative centre was maintained at Avignon. Urban was rapturously received at Rome and embarked on a programme of reform to re-establish discipline in the city. However, in 1369 England and France were once again at war. Urban decided to return to Avignon, a more central location for mediation and, as prophesied by BRIDGET OF SWEDEN, he died shortly thereafter. A cult developed at Urban's tomb and King Waldemar of Denmark requested his canonization, on account of his posthumous miracles. Gregory XI refused but Urban was beatified in 1870.

Villani, Giovanni, *c.* 1275/80–1348. Florentine historian, his expansive chronicle is an accurate historical record of Florence and incorporates his own lively observations. Born to a respectable mercantile family he was a member of the Black Guelphs and was actively involved in civic affairs. Villani held several important offices and helped guide Florence through the famine of 1320. Villani's chronicle covers a vast time-scale, but while he sketches world history, he focuses on Florence and provides

considerable detail of his native city. He is a balanced and analytical reporter, and includes a striking amount of statistical information, including the number of churches, monasteries, wool shops, and baptized children. Villani was a victim of the Black Death in 1348. His brother, Matteo, continued the chronicle until 1367, when he too died of the plague.

Villon, François, *c.* 1431–after 1463. An intensely autobiographical poet, his notoriety for crime led to his eventual exile from Paris. Villon led a colourful and rather turbulent life. Born into poverty, he was adopted by a Parisian canon, received minor orders and a university education at Paris, but was deprived of a profession or a clerical benefice. He was later charged with theft and the murder of a priest, which led to his imprisonment. However, following his release he was received at Charles of Orléans' court. Villon's poetry dwells on the passing of time, the imminence of death and the transience of beauty, fame and happiness. While his work is deeply personal and reflects his intense feelings and extreme remorse, it also describes fifteenth-century Paris. Villon has left some three thousand verses and is best known for his *ballades*, *rondeaux* and his *Grand Testament* (1461).

Waldes, Peter, d. *c.* 1216. A rich merchant of Lyons, he renounced his wealth to lead the Apostolic life as a wandering preacher, but was ultimately condemned as a heretic for preaching the Gospel without the sanction of the Church. Waldes underwent a radical conversion *c.* 1173, after hearing a minstrel sing of St Alexis. Deeply moved and concerned for the welfare of his soul, he gave up his riches and position, and was soon joined by a number of followers. Two by two, barefoot, clad in wool, 'naked following the naked Christ', the 'Poor men of Lyons' preached the Gospel and were dependent on begging. In 1179, Waldes and his followers travelled to the Third Lateran Council to receive papal authorization. While ALEXANDER III approved their way of life he did not permit them to preach. They continued to do so and were thus condemned as heretics in the papal bull, *Ad Abolendam*, of 1184.

Wallace, William, *c.* 1270–1305. Scottish soldier who led the Scots in their fight for independence, he is celebrated for his victory against the English at the Battle of Stirling Bridge, 1297. The son of a small land-holder, he was probably born near Paisley, Renfrewshire. In 1297 Wallace emerged as a leader of the Scottish resistance to EDWARD I's army. The Scots slaughtered the English as they crossed the Forth River near Stirling and then captured Stirling Castle. Wallace was knighted for his achievements and accorded the title 'Guardian of Scotland'. However, the Scots' triumph was short-lived, for on Edward's return from France he invaded Scotland and led the English to victory at Falkirk on 22 July 1298. Little is known of Wallace's activities from 1299 until 1305, when he was arrested near Glasgow

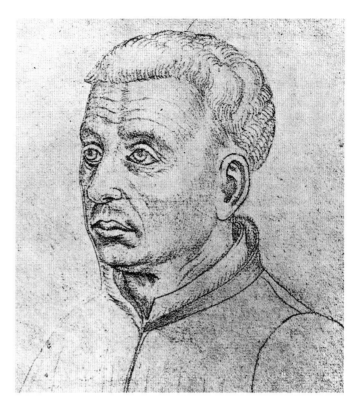

Rogier van der Weyden, a portrait drawing probably not made from life.

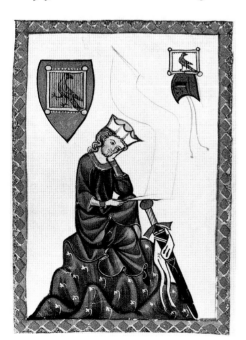

Walter von der Vogelweide, a miniature of 1308.

and taken to London. He was brought to trial at Westminster Hall on 23 August 1305, and condemned as a traitor. He was hanged and quartered at Tyburn and his head impaled on London Bridge, as an example to others.

Walter von der Vogelweide, *c.* 1170–*c.* 1230. The finest medieval German singer and composer, he compared himself to a nightingale, and sang of love, politics and morality. The little that is known of Walter is learnt from his songs. He acquired his skills as a minstrel in Austria and, whilst it is often thought that he was a knight, he was probably of humbler standing. Walter's songs are subjective, at times humorous, at times didactic. He advocated harmony, and urged the avoidance of vices, such as deceit and hypocrisy, and the practice of virtues, including love and self-control. He was scathing of the papacy and composed a sequence of diatribes against INNOCENT III. His best-known song, 'I sang upon a stone', is a lament.

Weyden, Rogier van der (Roger de la Pasture), *c.* 1399–1465. Renowned Flemish painter, he was noted for the excellence of his portraiture and for his altarpieces. Rogier was born in Tournai and, after a five-year apprenticeship to Robert Campin, became master in the painter's guild there in 1432. He was a 'city painter' in Brussels from 1435 and remained there for the rest of his life. His masterpieces include the *Deposition from the Cross* for the chapel of Crossbowmen's

Guild, in Notre-Dame hor ville, Louvain. *See p. 143*

William I (the Conqueror), King of England 1066–87. A forceful and charismatic leader, his triumph at Hastings in 1066 changed the course of English history, and meant that England was no longer an island state. Born *c.* 1028, the illegitimate son of Robert I of Normandy, he became Duke of Normandy in 1035, when still a child. In the 1060s William embarked on territorial expansion. He took Maine, campaigned on the Breton frontier, and pursued his claim to the English throne. The latter resulted in a Norman victory at Hastings, and William's coronation as king of England at Westminster Abbey on Christmas Day, 1066. In commemoration of his achievement at Hastings, and to atone for the loss of life involved, William founded Battle Abbey on the site of the battlefield, and set the High Altar on the spot where Harold, King of England, had met his death. In the precarious years following Hastings, William consolidated his conquest. He erected a number of defensive castles, which dominated the landscape and subdued the natives, and swiftly repressed internal revolts and dealt with external threats. The 'Harrying of the North' was particularly severe, but necessary, given that this was a focal point for rival claims. Most English landholders were replaced by Normans who were

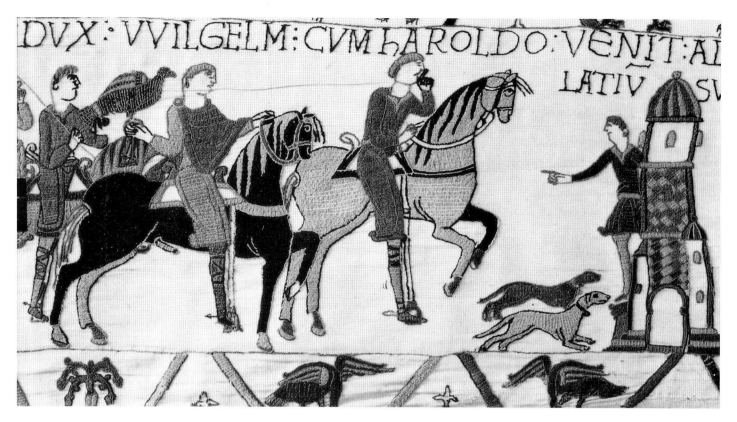

'Duke William [the Conqueror] with Harold comes to his palace', from the Bayeux Tapestry, late 11th century. William, holding the falcon, rides behind Harold.

personally bound to the king by oath and owed military obligations. When church offices fell vacant they were generally filled by Normans. Some twenty years after Hastings, William initiated the great Domesday Survey. This rigorous and comprehensive land survey notes every plough, pig, tenant and piece of productive land, county by county. William died on campaign in France and was buried at his own foundation of St Etienne, Caen. *See p. 122*

William of Auvergne (William of Paris), *c.* 1180–1249. Scholastic philosopher and theologian, he argued that God was the Mirror and Light that brought knowledge to the intellect. William taught theology at Paris and was a canon of Notre-Dame. In 1228 he was raised to the see of Paris and was influential at the court of Louis IX. He admired Aristotle, criticized Avicenna and fervently opposed superstition. His considerable corpus of writings includes a vast philosophico-theological encyclopaedia, the *Magisterium Divinale ac Sapientale*.

William of Moerbeke, *c.* 1215–86. Flemish Dominican, he edited and translated a number of Greek philosophical and scientific works, and his translation of Aristotle's *Politics* stimulated his contemporaries to reassess the role of the state. William was a Dominican in Greece and a penitentiary of the Apostolic See during the papacies of Clement IV (1265–68) and Gregory IX (1271–76). He participated in the Second Council of Lyons (1274) and was elevated to the see of Corinth four years later, but had returned to the papal court in Rome by 1283 where he probably remained until his death. William was a personal friend of Thomas Aquinas although the nature and extent of their relationship is a matter of contention. It was at Thomas' request that William undertook a new and extremely literal translation of Aristotle's Greek texts, and this became one of the most important translations of Aristotle into Latin.

William of Ockham, *c.* 1285–*c.* 1349. One of the greatest medieval philosophers, 'the invincible doctor' was the principal nominalist of the fourteenth century. Born at Ockham, Surrey, he joined the Franciscans before he was fourteen and was thus an exceptionally young recruit. He was ordained sub-deacon at Southwark in 1306 and pursued his theological studies at Oxford where he later taught, 1317–19. These were fruitful years when he composed a number of works. William completely undermined Aquinas' synthesis of reason and faith. He is best known for his principle of 'Ockham's Razor', which states that 'entities are not to be multiplied without necessity'. His opinions were controversial, for he regarded the existence of God as a probability rather than a certainty, argued that the bread and wine did not actually proceed from the body and blood of Christ but succeeded them, and denied the pope any temporal power. He came under investigation in 1324 at Avignon, but fled to Tuscany in May 1328. Under the protection of the pope's enemy, Louis of Bavaria, William travelled to Munich, where he remained at the Franciscan convent and wrote powerful political tracts, many against

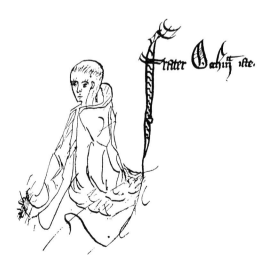

William of Ockham, a sketch in the margin of a contemporary copy of one of his works.

JOHN XXII and his successors, whom he accused of heresy. William's works include the *Quodlibeta Septem* and a commentary on PETER LOMBARD's *Sentences*. He died in Munich in 1347, probably of the Black Death, and was buried in the choir of the Franciscan church.

Wolfram von Eschenbach, *c*. 1170–after 1220. The most celebrated German poet of the Middle Ages, his *Parzifal* – partly based on earlier romance sources, including CHRÉTIEN DE TROYES' work – is considered one of the greatest narrative poems. Wolfram was born into the lesser Bavarian nobility, probably near Nuremberg. He was probably a knight and it seems he served several Franconian lords. Noted for his lyrical and epic poems, he was a prolific writer. The number of extant manuscripts testifies to his popularity. *See p. 118*

Wycliffe, John, *c*. 1330–84. Leading scholar and one of the most renowned theologians, he was hailed as 'the morning star of the Reformation' by sixteenth-century Protestants. Wycliffe was probably a Yorkshireman. He had graduated from Oxford by 1356, was Master of Balliol in 1360, and renowned as a teacher of philosophy in the 1360s. He embarked on theological studies in the 1370s, entered the political arena in 1371, and while he accumulated various livings from 1362, was mostly resident in Oxford from 1356 to 1381. Wycliffe was a prolific writer. He wrote on philosophical, theological and ecclesiastical matters, and was well informed on canon law. He vehemently denied the divine origin of papal authority, rejected the doctrine of transubstantiation, and argued that Christian doctrine should be based exclusively on the Scriptures. His views became increasingly worrying to the Church and a papal bull of 1377 condemned his doctrines as heretical. However, attempts at his arrest in England were futile, largely on

account of his protection by RICHARD II's mother. In 1380 a commission at Oxford deemed Wycliffe's teachings on the Eucharist heretical, and in 1382 the Earthquake Council denounced twenty-four of Wycliffe's conclusions as heretical or erroneous. JOHN OF GAUNT, the Duke of Lancaster, who had initially supported him, then had him retire to his rectory, where he died on 31 December 1384, still communicate. His body was exhumed and burned in 1428. Wycliffe believed that the Bible should be accessible to all, and the production of the 'Wycliffite Bible' in English by his followers was perhaps the most significant outcome of his activities. His doctrines also inspired a popular medieval heretical movement, Lollardy.

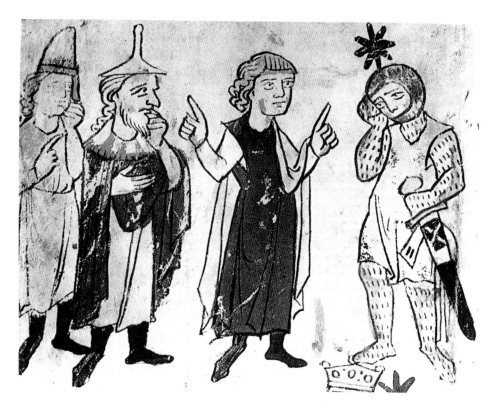

Illustration from a 13th-century manuscript of Wolfram von Eschenbach's 'Willehalm', showing the poet himself reconciling a Muslim, a Jew and a Crusader.

Timelines

	POPES, EMPERORS AND MONARCHS	HISTORY, POLITICS AND RELIGION	ART, ARCHITECTURE AND LITERATURE
800	**Charlemagne**, King of the Franks (768–814), Emperor (800–14)	Norsemen sack monastery of Iona (806)	Book of Kells (*c.* 800) Palatine Chapel at Aachen (*c.* 805)
810	**Michael I Rhangabe**, Byzantine Emperor (811–13) **Louis the Pious**, Emperor (814–40) **Pope Stephen V (IV)** (816–17) **Pope Paschal I** (817–24)	Second wave of iconoclasm in Byzantium (815–43)	**Abbot Gosbert** develops library and scriptorium at St Gallen (816–37)
820	**Pope Eugene II** (824–27) **Pope Gregory IV** (827–44) **Theophilus**, Byzantine Emperor (829–42)	Arab conquest of Crete (826) Arab conquest of Sicily and Sardinia begins (827) St Mark's, Venice, founded (828)	*Heliand* epic (*c.* 820) Utrecht Psalter (*c.* 825)
830	**Ethelwulf**, King of Wessex (839–58)	Viking raids on England begin (835)	
840	**Lothar I**, Emperor (840–55) **Lewis the German**, King of the East Franks (843–76) **Charles the Bald**, King of the West Franks (843–77)	Treaty of Verdun; Carolingian Empire split up (843) End of iconoclasm in Byzantine Empire (843) Arabs plunder St Peter's, Rome (846)	
850	**Louis II**, Emperor (855–75) **Kenneth MacAlpin**, first king of united Scotland (d. 858) **Pope Nicholas I** (858–67) **Photius**, Patriarch of Constantinople (858–67, 877–86)	Danes sack Canterbury (851)	*Ascension of Christ* frescoes, Lower Church of St Clement, Rome (855)
860	**Pope Hadrian II** (867–72) **Basil I**, Byzantine Emperor (867–86)	Vikings discover Iceland (*c.* 860) Schism between eastern and western churches (863–79) Mission of **Cyril** and **Methodius** to Slavs (*c.* 863–85)	
870	**Alfred the Great**, King of Wessex (871–99) **Pope John VIII** (872–82) **Louis II the Stammerer**, King of France (877–79)	**Alfred** defeats the Danes at Edington (878)	**Johannes Scotus Erigena** compiles encyclopaedia on nature (870)
880	**Charles the Fat**, Emperor (881–87) **Pope Marinus I** (882–84) **Pope Hadrian III** (884–85) **Pope Stephen VI (V)** (885–91) **Odo**, Count of Paris, King of the West Franks (888–98)	**Emperor Basil** reconquers S. Italy from the Arabs (880) Vikings besiege Paris (885–86)	
890	**Pope Formosus** (891–96) **Pope Stephen VII (VI)** (896–97) **Arnulf**, Emperor (896–99) **Pope Romanus** (897–98) **Pope John IX** (898–900)		Anglo-Saxon Chronicle begun (*c.* 892)

	POPES, EMPERORS AND MONARCHS	HISTORY, POLITICS AND RELIGION	ART, ARCHITECTURE AND LITERATURE
900	Pope Benedict IV (900–03) **Louis the Child**, last Carolingian king of Germany (900–11) **Pope Leo** (903) **Pope Sergius III** (904–11)	County of Navarre made a kingdom (905) Magyars destroy Moravian Empire (907) **Duke William the Pious of Aquitaine** founds Cluny (909)	Regino's *Chronicles* (*c.* 908)
910	Pope Anastasius III (911–13) **Abd al-Rahman III of Cordoba** (912–61) **Pope Lando** (913–14) **Pope John X** (914–28) Henry I, King of Germany (919–36)	Vikings settle in Normandy (911)	
920	Athelstan, King of England (925–39) Pope Leo VI (928) **Pope Stephen VIII (VII)** (928–31)	**Hugh the Great**, Duke of France (923–56) **St Odo** made Abbot of Cluny (927) **St Wenceslas**, Duke and patron saint of Bohemia, killed (929) Caliphate established at Cordoba (929)	
930	Pope Leo VII (936–39) **Otto I the Great**, King of Germany and Emperor (936–73) **Pope Stephen IX (VIII)** (939–42) Edmund I, King of England (939–46)		
940	Pope Marinus II (942–46) Pope Agapitus II (946–55)		
950	Pope John XII (955–64) **Edgar the Peaceable**, King of England (959–75)	**Otto I** defeats Magyars at the Lechfeld (955)	
960	Pope Leo VIII (963–65) Pope Benedict V (964) Pope John XIII (965–72)	**Otto I** crowned Emperor (962) Poland converts to Christianity (966)	**Hroswitha of Gandersheim**, nun and poet, active (960s)
970	Pope Benedict VI (973–74) Otto II, Emperor (973–83) Pope Benedict VII (974–83) **Aethelred the Unready (Unraed)**, King of England (978–1016)		
980	Otto III, Emperor (983–1002) Louis V, last Carolingian king of France (986–87) **Hugh Capet**, first Capetian king of France (987–96)	Beginning of Peace of God movement (989)	
990	Pope Gregory V (996–99) **Robert II the Pious**, King of France (996–1031) **Pope Sylvester II** (Gerbert of Aurillac) (999–1003)	**St Odilo** made Abbot of Cluny (994) **St Adalbert** martyred in Prussia (997)	**Aelfric**'s Homilies and Lives of the Saints (990s)

	POPES, EMPERORS AND MONARCHS	HISTORY, POLITICS AND RELIGION	ART, ARCHITECTURE AND LITERATURE
1000	**Sancho III the Great**, King of Navarre (1000–35) **Stephen I**, King of Hungary (1001–38) **Henry II**, Emperor (1002–24) **Pope John XVIII** (1003–09) **Pope Sergius IV** (1009–12)	Short-lived Viking settlement in N. America (*c.* 1000)	Gospels of **Otto III** (*c.* 1000) **Berno**, Abbot of Reichenau (1008–48), writes works on musical theory
1010	**Pope Benedict VIII** (1012–24) **St Olaf II Haraldsson**, King of Norway (1016–30) **Canute (Knut)**, King of England (1016–35) and Denmark (1019–35)	Danish conquest of England (1016)	Doors and bronze column of Hildesheim (1015–22)
1020	**Pope John XIX** (1024–32) **Conrad II**, Emperor (1024–39)		Construction of crypt, Chartres Cathedral (1020) **Burchard of Worms**, *Decretum* (*c.* 1020)
1030	**Henry I**, King of France (1031–60) **Pope Benedict IX** (1032–44; 1045; 1047–48) **Henry III**, King of Germany, Emperor (1039–56)		Speyer Cathedral begun (*c.* 1030) **Guy of Arezzo** develops systematic musical notation (*c.* 1030) Death of **Avicenna**, Muslim philosopher (1037)
1040	**Edward the Confessor**, King of England (1042–66) **Pope Sylvester III** (1045) **Pope Gregory VI** (1045–46) **Pope Clement II** (1046–47) **Pope Leo IX** (1049–54)	Synod of Sutri; beginning of Church Reform (1046)	
1050	**Pope Victor II** (1055–57) **Henry IV**, Emperor (1056–1106) **Pope Stephen X (IX)** (1057–58) **Isaac I Comnenus**, Byzantine Emperor (1057–59) **Pope Nicholas II** (1058–61)		**Edward the Confessor** begins Westminster Abbey (1052)
1060	**Alfonso VI the Brave**, King of León and Castile (1065–1109) **Harold II Godwinson**, King of England (1066) **William I the Conqueror**, King of England (1066–87)	Battle of Hastings (1066)	Remodelling of Pisa Cathedral begins (1064)
1070	**Pope Gregory VII** (1073–85)	Battle of Manzikert (1071) Death of **St Peter Damian** (1072) Investiture Dispute (1075–1122)	St Sernin, Toulouse, begun (*c.* 1070) Santiago de Compostela Cathedral begun (1075) **Anselm**'s *Monologion* and *Proslogion* (*c.* 1075–78)
1080	**Alexius I Comnenus**, Byzantine Emperor (1081–1118) **Pope Victor III** (1086–87) **William II Rufus**, King of England (1087–1100) **Pope Urban II** (1088–99)	**St Bruno of Cologne** founds Carthusian Order (1084) **Alfonso VI of Castile and León** conquers Toledo (1085) **William I** initiates Domesday Book (1085)	St Paul's, London, burns down and is rebuilt (1087) Third church of Cluny begun (1088)
1090	**Pope Paschal II** (1099–1118)	First Crusade (1095–99); fall of Jerusalem (1099) Foundation of the Cistercians at Cîteaux (1098) Death of **El Cid** (Rodrigo Díaz de Vivar) (1099)	Durham Cathedral begun (1093)

	POPES, EMPERORS AND MONARCHS	HISTORY, POLITICS AND RELIGION	ART, ARCHITECTURE AND LITERATURE
1100	Henry I, King of England (1100–35) Henry V, Emperor (1106–25) Louis VI the Fat, King of France (1108–37)		*The Song of Roland*, French heroic poem (*c.* 1100) Cloister of Moissac (*c.* 1100–25)
1110	Pope Gelasius II (1118–19) John II Comnenus, Byzantine Emperor (1118–43) Pope Callixtus II (1119–24)	Knights of the Temple (Templars) founded (*c.* 1118)	Earliest record of miracle play, England (1110)
1120	Pope Honorius II (1124–30) David, King of Scots (1124–53) Lothar III, Emperor (1125–37)		*The Last Judgment*, Church of Ste Foy, Conques (*c.* 1125) Death of **William IX of Aquitaine**, 'first of the troubadours' (1127) Campanile of S. Ambrogio, Milan (1128)
1130	Pope Innocent II (1130–43) Roger II, King of Sicily (1130–54) Stephen of Blois, King of England (1135–54) Louis VII, King of France (1137–80) Conrad III, King of Germany (1138–52)		**Gislebertus**, sculptures at Autun (*c.* 1130) **Geoffrey of Monmouth**, *Historia regum Britanniae* (1136) **Abbot Suger** begins Saint-Denis (1137) **Gratian**'s *Decretum* (1139–40)
1140	Pope Celestine II (1143–44) Manuel I, Byzantine Emperor (1143–80) Pope Lucius II (1144–45) Pope Eugene III (1145–53)	Second Crusade (1147–49)	Sens Cathedral begun (1142) Death of **Peter Abelard**, philosopher and theologian (1142) **Otto of Freising**'s *Chronicle* (1143–46)
1150	Frederick I Barbarossa, Holy Roman Emperor (1152–90) Henry II Plantagenet, King of England (1154–89) Pope Alexander III (1159–81)	Marriage of **Henry of Anjou** (later Henry II) and **Eleanor of Aquitaine** (1152) Death of **St Bernard of Clairvaux** (1153)	First privilege for students at Bologna (1158)
1160	William II, King of Sicily (1166–89)	Formation of Lombard League (1167)	Laon Cathedral begun (1160) Winchester Bible (1160–75) Notre-Dame, Paris, begun (1163)
1170		**Thomas Becket**, Archbishop of Canterbury, murdered (1170) Order of Knights of Santiago founded (1170) Downfall of Fatimid caliphate in Cairo (1171) Battle of Legnano (1176)	Leaning Tower of Pisa begun (1174) Canterbury Cathedral east end begun (1175) Death of Hildegard of Bingen (1179)
1180	Philip II Augustus, King of France (1180–1223) Isaac II Angelus, Byzantine Emperor (1185–95, 1203–04) Pope Clement III (1187–91) Richard I Coeur de Lion, King of England (1189–99)	**Henry the Lion**, Duke of Saxony and Bavaria, exiled (1181) Battle of Hattin; **Saladin** captures Jerusalem (1187) Third Crusade (1189–92)	**Chrétien de Troyes'** *Perceval* (*c.* 1180) **Nicholas of Verdun** metalwork (1180–90)
1190	Henry VI, Emperor (1190–97) Pope Celestine III (1191–98) Pope Innocent III (1198–1216) Otto IV, Emperor (1198–1218) John 'Lackland', King of England (1199–1216)	**Henry VI** conquers Sicily (1194) Teutonic Knights founded (1198)	Wells Cathedral (1192–1235) Rebuilding of Chartres Cathedral in Gothic style begins (1194) Bourges Cathedral begun (1195)

	POPES, EMPERORS AND MONARCHS	HISTORY, POLITICS AND RELIGION	ART, ARCHITECTURE AND LITERATURE
1200	**Alexius IV Angelus**, Byzantine Emperor (1203–04) **Alexius V Murtzuphlus**, Byzantine Emperor (1204) **Theodore I Lascaris**, Emperor of Nicaea (1205–22)	Fourth Crusade (1202–04) Conquest of Normandy by **Philip II of France** (1204) Crusade against the Cathars begins (1209)	**Wolfram von Eschenbach's** *Parzifal* (*c.* 1200–10) Death of **Maimonides**, philosopher (1204)
1210	**Frederick II**, Emperor (1212–50) **Pope Honorius III** (1216–27) **Henry III**, King of England (1216–72) **Ferdinand III**, King of León and Castile (1217–52)	Franciscan Order founded (1210) Battle of Las Navas de Tolosa (1212) Magna Carta (1215) Fourth Lateran Council (1215) Dominican Order founded (1216)	Rheims Cathedral begun (1210) **Gottfried von Strassburg's** *Tristan* (*c.* 1210) Earliest statutes of University of Paris (1215)
1220	**Louis VIII**, King of France (1223–26) **St Louis**, King Louis IX of France (1226–70) **Pope Gregory IX** (1227–41)	Death of **St Francis** (1226) Death of **Genghis Khan** (1227) Church of San Francesco, Assisi, begun (1228)	Salisbury Cathedral begun (1220) Amiens Cathedral begun (1220) Foundation of Padua University (1222) Beauvais Cathedral begun (1227)
1230		Teutonic Knights begin conquest of Prussia (1230) Capture of Cordoba by **Ferdinand III** (1236) Battle of Cortenuova (1237)	First part of Roman de la Rose (*c.* 1237) Alhambra, Granada, begun (1238)
1240	**Pope Celestine IV** (1241) **Pope Innocent IV** (1243–54) **Llywelyn ap Gruffydd the Last**, Prince of Wales (1246–82)	Mongol invasion of C. Europe (1241) Jerusalem falls to the Muslims (1244) Capture of Seville by **Ferdinand III** (1248) Crusade of **St Louis** (1248–54)	Death of **Snorri Sturluson**, author of *Heimskringla* and *Prose Edda* (1241) Sainte Chapelle, Paris (1243–48) Naumburg sculptures (*c.* 1245–50) Cologne Cathedral begun (1248)
1250	**Conrad IV**, last Hohenstaufen king of Germany (1250–54) **Alfonso X the Learned**, King of León and Castile (1252–84) **Manfred**, King of Sicily (1258–66)	Mamluk dynasty supersedes Abbasids in Egypt (1250) **Bonaventure**, minister-general of Franciscans (1257–74) Peace of Paris (1259)	León Cathedral begun (1255) **Nicola Pisano's** pulpit in Pisa Baptistery (1259) Death of **Matthew Paris**, historian and artist (1259)
1260	**Kublai Khan**, Mongol Emperor (1260–94) **Pope Urban IV** (1261–64) **Pope Clement IV** (1265–68) **Charles I of Anjou**, King of Sicily (1266–85)	First Corpus Christi (Feast Day of the Eucharist) (1264) Battle of Benevento (1266) Battle of Tagliacozzo (1268)	Major works of **Roger Bacon** (1260s) **Thomas Aquinas** begins his *Summa Theologica* (1266)
1270	**Philip III**, King of France (1270–85) **Pope Gregory X** (1271–76) **Edward I**, King of England (1272–1307) **Rudolf I of Habsburg**, Emperor (1273–91) **Pope Nicholas III** (1277–80)	**Marco Polo** enters the service of **Kublai Khan** (1271)	
1280	**Pope Martin IV** (1281–85) **Pope Honorius IV** (1285–87) **Philip IV the Fair**, King of France (1285–1314) **Pope Nicholas IV** (1288–92)	Sicilian Vespers (1282) **Edward I** conquers Wales (1282–83)	Roman de la Rose completed (*c.* 1280) Death of **Albertus Magnus**, scholar and theologian (1280) Caernarvon Castle (1283–1323) *Lohengrin*, epic poem (1285)
1290	**John Balliol**, King of Scotland (1292–96) **Pope Celestine V** (1294) **Pope Boniface VIII** (1294–1303)	End of Kingdom of Jerusalem (1291)	

	POPES, EMPERORS AND MONARCHS	HISTORY, POLITICS AND RELIGION	ART, ARCHITECTURE AND LITERATURE
1300	Pope Benedict XI (1303–04) Pope Clement V (1305–14) Robert I Bruce, King of Scotland (1306–29) Edward II, King of England (1307–27)	Execution of **William Wallace** (1305) **Duns Scotus** teaching (d. 1308) Papacy at Avignon (1309–77)	Syon Cope (*c.* 1300) Giotto, frescoes in Arena Chapel, Padua (1303–06) Dante, *Divine Comedy* (*c.* 1308–21) First public clock in Europe, in Milan (1309)
1310	Alfonso XI, King of León and Castile (1312–50) Louis X, King of France (1314–16) John I, King of France (1316) Philip V, King of France (1316–22) Pope John XXII (1316–34)	Council of Vienne (1311–12) **Pope Clement V** suppresses the Templars (1312) Battle of Bannockburn (1314) The Great Famine (1315–17)	**Duccio**'s *Maestà* (1311) **Pietro Lorenzetti**, frescoes, San Francesco, Assisi (1316–19)
1320	Charles IV, King of France (1322–28) Edward III, King of England (1327–77) Philip VI of Valois, first Valois king of France (1328–50)		Marsilius of Padua's *Defensor pacis* (1324) Tomb of **Edward II**, Gloucester (*c.* 1328) Octagon of Ely Cathedral (1328–47)
1330	Pope Benedict XII (1334–42) Peter IV, King of Aragon (1336–87)	Hundred Years War (1337–1453)	**Simone Martini**, *Annunciation* triptych (1333) Palace of the Popes, Avignon, begun (1335) Remodelling of Gloucester Cathedral choir begins (1337)
1340	Pope Clement VI (1342–52) Charles IV, Emperor (1347–78)	Edward, the Black Prince, Prince of Wales (1343–76) Battle of Crécy (1346) First wave of the Black Death (1347–50)	Luttrell Psalter (*c.* 1340) Death of **William of Ockham**, philosopher and theologian (1347) Foundation of Prague University (1348) **Boccaccio**'s *Decameron* (1349–51)
1350	John II, King of France (1350–64) Peter I, King of León and Castile (1350–69) Pope Innocent VI (1352–62)	Battle of Poitiers (1356) Peasant rebellion (Jacquérie), France (1358)	Rebuilding of Doge's Palace, Venice (1350s) **Peter Parler** takes over Prague Cathedral (1356)
1360	Pope Urban V (1362–70) Charles V the Wise, King of France (1364–80) Henry of Trastamara, King of León and Castile (1369–79)	Second wave of plague (1361)	**Froissart**'s *Chronicles* (1361–*c.* 1410) *Piers Plowman* ascribed to **William Langland** (1362) Foundation of Cracow University (1364) **Mandeville**'s *Travels* (*c.* 1366)
1370	Pope Gregory XI (1370–78) Tamberlaine, Mongol khan (1370–1405) Richard II, King of England (1377–99) Pope Urban VI (1378–89) John I, King of León and Castile (1379–90)	Death of **St Birgitta of Sweden** (1373) Great Schism in the Catholic Church (1378–1417)	Death of **Petrarch**, poet (1374) Angers's *Apocalypse* tapestry (1376–81)
1380	Charles VI the Well-beloved, King of France (1380–1422) Margaret, Queen of Norway, Denmark and Sweden (1387/9–1412) Pope Boniface IX (1389–1404)	Peasant uprising, England (1381) Death of **Jan van Ruysbroeck**, mystic (1381) Death of **John Wycliffe**, theologian (1384) Lithuania converts to Christianity (1386)	**Geoffrey Chaucer**, *Troilus and Criseyde* (*c.* 1382) **Geoffrey Chaucer**, *The Canterbury Tales* (1386–1400) Milan Cathedral begun (1387)
1390	Henry III, King of León and Castile (1390–1406) Martin I, King of Aragon (1395–1410) Henry IV, King of England (1399–1413)	Death of **John of Gaunt** (1399)	Hammerbeam roof, Westminster Hall, London (1394) *Wilton Diptych* (*c.* 1395)

	POPES, EMPERORS AND MONARCHS	HISTORY, POLITICS AND RELIGION	ART, ARCHITECTURE AND LITERATURE
1400	**Rupert of Wittelsbach**, King of Germany (1400–10) **Pope Innocent VII** (1404–06) **Pope Gregory XII** (1406–15) **John II**, King of León and Castile (1406–54)	Council of Pisa (1409)	**Ghiberti** begins Florentine Baptistery doors (1401) **Christine de Pisan**, *Book of the City of Ladies* (1405)
1410	**Sigismund of Luxembourg**, Emperor (1410–37) **Ferdinand I**, King of Aragon (1412–16) **Henry V**, King of England (1413–22) **Alfonso V**, King of Aragon (1416–58) **Pope Martin V** (1417–31)	Battle of Tannenburg (1410) Council of Constance (1414–18) **John Huss** burnt at the stake (1415) Battle of Agincourt (1415) End of Great Schism (1417)	Foundation of St Andrews University (1411) *Très Riches Heures* (c. 1412) **Brunelleschi**'s dome, Florence Cathedral, begun (1419)
1420	**Charles VII** ('le bien servi'), King of France (1422–61) **Henry VI**, King of England (1422–61)	**Leonardo Bruni** appointed Chancellor of Florence (1427)	**Masaccio**'s frescoes in the Brancacci Chapel, Florence (1425–28)
1430	**Pope Eugene IV** (1431–47) **Albert II**, Emperor (1438–39)	Dukes of Burgundy found the Order of the Golden Fleece (1430) **Joan of Arc** burnt at the stake (1431) Council of Basle (1431–49) Treaty of Arras (1435)	**Jan van Eyck**, *Ghent Altarpiece* (1432) **Donatello**, *David* (c. 1433) **Rogier van der Weyden**, *Descent from the Cross* (c. 1435)
1440	**Frederick III**, Emperor (1440–93) **Pope Nicholas V** (1447–55)		King's College Chapel, Cambridge (1446–1515)
1450	**Henry IV**, King of León and Castile (1454–74) **Pope Callixtus III** (1455–58) **Pope Pius II** (1458–64) **John II**, King of Aragon (1458–79) **Matthias Corvinus**, King of Hungary (1458–90)	Fall of Constantinople to Ottoman Turks (1453) Wars of the Roses (1455–85)	Gutenberg Bible printed at Mainz (1455) Façade of **Alberti**'s S. Maria Novella, Florence, begun (1458) Palazzo Pitti, Florence, begun (1458)
1460	**Edward IV**, King of England (1461–83) **Louis XI**, King of France (1461–83) **Pope Paul II** (1464–71) **Charles the Bold**, Duke of Burgundy (1467–77)	Marriage of **Ferdinand of Aragon** and **Isabella of Castile** (1469) **Lorenzo the Magnificent of Florence** (1469–92)	**François Villon**'s *Testament* (1461) Death of **Nicholas of Cusa**, ecclesiast and philosopher (1464)
1470	**Pope Sixtus IV** (1471–84) **Isabella**, Queen of León and Castile (1474–1504) **Ferdinand II**, King of Aragon (1479–1516)	Establishment of Spanish Inquisition (1478)	**William Caxton**'s printing press (1476) **Botticelli**, *Primavera* (1478)
1480	**Edward V**, King of England (1483) **Richard III**, King of England (1483–85) **Charles VIII**, King of France (1483–98) **Pope Innocent VIII** (1484–92) **Henry VII**, King of England (1485–1509)	Battle of Bosworth (1485) Portuguese round Cape of Good Hope (1487)	**Botticelli**, *The Birth of Venus* (1485)
1490	**Pope Alexander VI** (1492–1503) **Maximilian I of Habsburg**, Emperor (1493–1519) **Louis XII**, King of France (1498–1515)	Christian conquest of Granada (1492) **Christopher Columbus** discovers New World (1492) **Cabot**'s first voyage (1497) **Vasco da Gama** reaches India (1498) Execution of **Savonarola** (1498)	**Bramante**'s S. Marie delle Grazie, Milan, begun (1492) Death of Neoplatonist **Pico della Mirandola** (1494) **Leonardo da Vinci**, *Last Supper* (1497) **Michelangelo**, *Pietà* (1498) **Commynes**' *Memoirs* completed (1498)

Gazetteer

Most medieval works of art are in one of three places – a church, a museum or a library. Churches with sculpture and stained glass are generally accessible, though one needs a detailed guidebook to know exactly what to look for. Museums also hold some outstanding medieval sculpture, as well as representative furniture, altarpieces and metalwork. Library holdings of medieval manuscripts are not usually accessible to the public except for certain pages displayed in showcases. Of medieval architecture it has not been thought practicable or helpful to attempt a selection.

AUSTRIA

For small-scale works of art, the **Kunsthistorischesmuseum**, Vienna. For manuscripts, the **Österreichische National Bibliothek**, Vienna.

BELGIUM

Specially notable for manuscripts is the **Bibliothèque Royale de Belgique**, Brussels.

DENMARK

The **Medieval Centre**, Nykøbing, is a "living history" institution, with staff acting out scenes of daily life in period dress; reconstructions of medieval buildings; displays of military weapons and tournaments; and an authentic banquet hall in which food, ale and wine made to original recipes are served.

FRANCE

For stained glass, **Chartres**, **Bourges** and **Le Mans** Cathedrals, with the **Sainte Chapelle**, Paris, are essential.

For Romanesque sculpture, the churches of **Conques**, **Vézelay**, **Autun** and the exhibition at **Cluny**; for Gothic, **Chartres**, **Amiens**, **Rheims** and **Bourges**; for late Gothic, **Brou**.

The **Louvre**, Paris, is the greatest treasure-house of sculpture and precious objects. The **Musée de Cluny**, Paris, also has outstanding sculpture and small works of art. For many fine works of art, including the Isenheim retable, visit the **Musée d'Unterlinden**, Colmar.
Outside Paris, the **Musée de Dijon** with the nearby **Chartreuse de Champmol**, and the **Musée des Augustins**, Toulouse, must be visited for sculpture.

For royal tombs, visit **Saint-Denis**.

The **Bibliothèque Nationale**, Paris, has probably the greatest concentration of medieval manuscripts in the world. Also notable are the **Bibliothèque de l'Arsenal**, Paris, and the **Musée Condé** at Chantilly (which holds the *Très Riches Heures*).

GERMANY

Some of the finest early glass is at **Augsburg Cathedral**. Many German churches contain major sculpture and furnishings, notably **Aachen**, **Naumburg**, **Bamberg** and **St Lorenz, Nuremberg**.

The most important museums for medieval objects are the **Germanisches Nationalmuseum**, Nuremberg, and the **Staatliche Museen**, Berlin.

The **Wallraf-Richartz Museum**, Cologne, holds fine late medieval paintings, especially Rhineland altarpieces.

The **Bayerisches Staatsbibliothek**, Munich, has rich holdings of manuscripts.

GREAT BRITAIN AND IRELAND

Canterbury Cathedral has by far the best collection of early medieval stained glass in the country. **Fairford Church** in Gloucestershire and **King's College**, Cambridge, are notable for the later period.

Westminster Abbey is unique in the possession of royal tombs.

The **British Museum** and the **Victoria & Albert Museum**, London, have valuable items of small-scale sculpture, metalwork, ivories and textiles.

The **British Library**, London, has the largest collection of medieval manuscripts. The Libraries of **Oxford** (Bodleian) and **Cambridge Universities**, and those of individual colleges, are also rich in this respect.

The **Fitzwilliam Museum**, Cambridge, has a good collection of early medieval coins and medals.

A large collection of stringed, woodwind, brass and percussion instruments is displayed at the **Edinburgh University Collection of Historic Musical Instruments**.

The **Hunt Museum**, Limerick, has a varied collection of medieval artefacts, including statues, crucifixes, panel paintings, metalwork, jewelry, enamels, ceramics and crystal.

ITALY

Sculpture, stained glass, mosaic and frescoes are to be seen at the Cathedrals of **Siena** and **Orvieto** and **S. Francesco**, Assisi.

The **Museo Nazionale** (Bargello) in Florence has notable works of sculpture.

The greatest repository of manuscripts is the **Biblioteca Apostolica**, Vatican.

Archaeological material from excavations and collections of artefacts from the fourth to the thirteenth centuries are held at the **Early Middle Ages Museum**, Rome.

SPAIN

For stained glass, the Cathedral of **León** is outstanding.

For sculpture, visit **Santiago de Compostela** and the cloister of **Silos**.

The monastery of **Las Huelgas**, near Burgos, has a unique collection of medieval textiles.

For works of medieval art, see the **Museo Arqueologico Nacional**, Madrid, and the **Museo Nacional d'Art de Catalunya**, Barcelona.

The **Alhambra** and **Palacio de Generalife**, Granada, are incomparable for examples of medieval Islamic decorative art.

USA

For sculpture, metalwork and painting, the **Cloisters**, New York, is as rich as any European museum. The **Metropolitan Museum**, New York, also has important holdings.

For manuscripts, the major collections are the **Pierpont Morgan Library**, New York, the **Huntington Library**, San Marino, and the **Getty Museum**, Los Angeles.

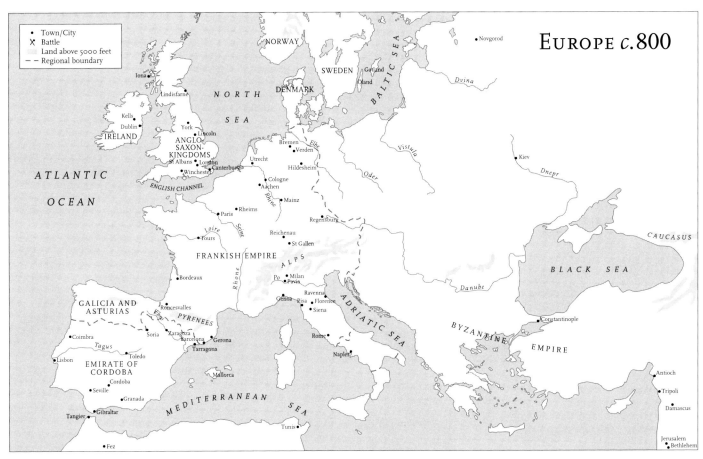

EUROPE c. 800

- Town/City
- ✕ Battle
- Land above 5000 feet
- – – Regional boundary

Ionia • Lindisfarne • Kells • Dublin • York • Lincoln • St Albans • London • Canterbury • Winchester • Paris • Rheims • Tours • Bordeaux • Roncesvalles • Soria • Zaragoza • Barcelona • Gerona • Tarragona • Coimbra • Toledo • Lisbon • Cordoba • Seville • Granada • Tangier • Gibraltar • Fez • Mallorca • Tunis • Bremen • Verden • Utrecht • Hildesheim • Cologne • Aachen • Mainz • Regensburg • Reichenau • St Gallen • Po • Milan • Pavia • Genoa • Pisa • Ravenna • Florence • Siena • Rome • Naples • Constantinople • Antioch • Tripoli • Damascus • Jerusalem • Bethlehem • Novgorod • Kiev

NORWAY · SWEDEN · DENMARK · Gotland · Oland · BALTIC SEA · NORTH SEA · ANGLO-SAXON KINGDOMS · IRELAND · ATLANTIC OCEAN · ENGLISH CHANNEL · Loire · Seine · Rhine · Rhone · Elbe · Oder · Vistula · Dvina · Dnepr · Danube · FRANKISH EMPIRE · ALPS · GALICIA AND ASTURIAS · Ebro · PYRENEES · Tagus · EMIRATE OF CORDOBA · MEDITERRANEAN SEA · ADRIATIC SEA · BYZANTINE EMPIRE · BLACK SEA · CAUCASUS

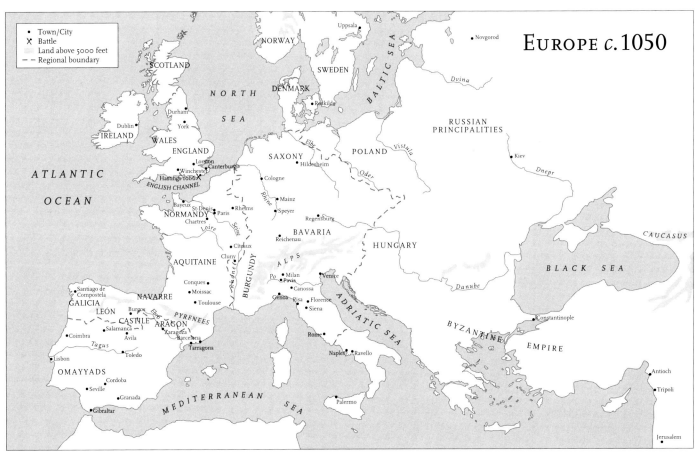

EUROPE c. 1050

- Town/City
- ✕ Battle
- Land above 5000 feet
- – – Regional boundary

Uppsala • Novgorod • Durham • Dublin • York • London • Canterbury • Winchester • Hastings 1066 ✕ • Bayeux • St-Denis • Paris • Rheims • Chartres • Cologne • Mainz • Speyer • Regensburg • Hildesheim • Cîteaux • Cluny • Reichenau • Po • Milan • Pavia • Canossa • Venice • Genoa • Pisa • Florence • Siena • Rome • Naples • Ravello • Palermo • Santiago de Compostela • Conques • Moissac • Toulouse • Burgos • Salamanca • Avila • Zaragoza • Barcelona • Tarragona • Coimbra • Toledo • Lisbon • Cordoba • Seville • Granada • Gibraltar • Roskilde • Kiev • Constantinople • Antioch • Tripoli • Jerusalem

NORWAY · SWEDEN · DENMARK · SCOTLAND · WALES · ENGLAND · IRELAND · NORTH SEA · BALTIC SEA · ATLANTIC OCEAN · ENGLISH CHANNEL · NORMANDY · AQUITAINE · BURGUNDY · SAXONY · BAVARIA · POLAND · HUNGARY · RUSSIAN PRINCIPALITIES · NAVARRE · GALICIA · LEÓN · CASTILE · ARAGON · OMAYYADS · PYRENEES · Ebro · Tagus · Loire · Seine · Rhine · Rhone · Elbe · Oder · Vistula · Dvina · Dnepr · Danube · ALPS · MEDITERRANEAN SEA · ADRIATIC SEA · BYZANTINE EMPIRE · BLACK SEA · CAUCASUS

318   Maps

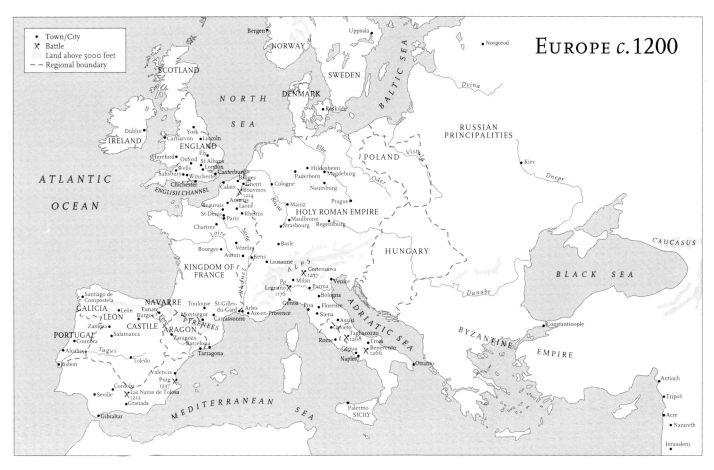

EUROPE c.1200

- Town/City
- ✕ Battle
- Land above 5000 feet
- Regional boundary

NORWAY
SWEDEN
DENMARK
BALTIC SEA
Bergen
Uppsala
Novgorod
Roskilde
RUSSIAN PRINCIPALITIES
POLAND
Kiev
Dvina
Dnepr
NORTH SEA
SCOTLAND
IRELAND
Dublin
York
Carnarvon
Lincoln
ENGLAND
Hereford
Ely
Oxford
St Albans
Wells
London
Salisbury
Canterbury
Chichester
Winchester
Bruges
Ghent
Calais
Cologne
Paderborn
Hildesheim
Magdeburg
Naumburg
Prague
ENGLISH CHANNEL
Bouvines 1214
Amiens
Laon
Beauvais
Rheims
Mainz
St-Denis
Paris
HOLY ROMAN EMPIRE
Maulbronn
Regensburg
Strasbourg
ATLANTIC OCEAN
Chartres
Loire
Rhine
Seine
Bourges
Vézelay
Basle
Autun
Sens
Lausanne
KINGDOM OF FRANCE
ALPS
Cortenuova 1237
HUNGARY
CAUCASUS
BLACK SEA
Milan
Venice
Legnano 1176
Po
Parma
Bologna
Santiago de Compostela
GALICIA
NAVARRE
Toulouse
St-Gilles-du-Gard
Arles
Genoa
Pisa
Florence
León
Eunate
Burgos
Montségur
Carcassonne
Aix-en-Provence
Siena
Assisi
LEÓN
PYRENEES
Ebro
Orvieto
ADRIATIC SEA
PORTUGAL
CASTILE
ARAGON
Zaragoza
Rome
Tagliacozzo 1268
Tarragona
Capua 1266
Benevento
Trani
BYZANTINE EMPIRE
Constantinople
Zamora
Salamanca
Barcelona
Coimbra
Tagus
Alcobaça
Lisbon
Toledo
Valencia
Puig 1237
Naples
Otranto
Seville
Cordoba
Las Navas de Tolosa 1212
Granada
Gibraltar
MEDITERRANEAN SEA
Palermo
SICILY
Antioch
Tripoli
Acre
Nazareth
Jerusalem

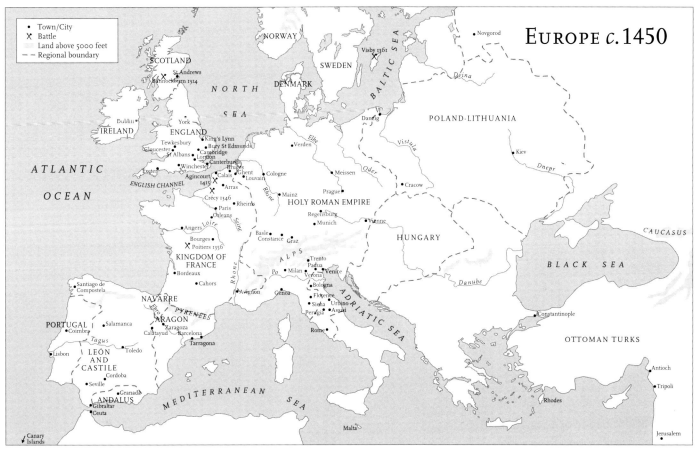

EUROPE c.1450

- Town/City
- ✕ Battle
- Land above 5000 feet
- Regional boundary

NORWAY
SWEDEN
DENMARK
BALTIC SEA
Novgorod
Visby 1361
Danzig
POLAND-LITHUANIA
Dvina
Kiev
Dnepr
NORTH SEA
SCOTLAND
St Andrews
Bannockburn 1314
IRELAND
Dublin
York
ENGLAND
King's Lynn
Tewkesbury
Bury St Edmunds
Gloucester
Cambridge
St Albans
London
Exeter
Winchester
Canterbury
Bruges
Ghent
Cologne
Verden
Meissen
Louvain
ENGLISH CHANNEL
Agincourt 1415
Calais
Arras
Rhine
Mainz
Prague
Cracow
Crécy 1346
Rheims
HOLY ROMAN EMPIRE
ATLANTIC OCEAN
Paris
Orléans
Regensburg
Loire
Seine
Vienna
Munich
Angers
Basle
Constance
Graz
HUNGARY
CAUCASUS
BLACK SEA
Bourges
Poitiers 1356
KINGDOM OF FRANCE
ALPS
Trento
Padua
Bordeaux
Rhone
Po
Milan
Verona
Venice
Cahors
Avignon
Genoa
Bologna
Florence
Constantinople
Santiago de Compostela
NAVARRE
PYRENEES
Ebro
Siena
Urbino
Perugia
Assisi
ADRIATIC SEA
PORTUGAL
Salamanca
ARAGON
Zaragoza
Calatayud
Barcelona
Rome
OTTOMAN TURKS
Coimbra
Tagus
Tarragona
Lisbon
LEÓN AND CASTILE
Toledo
Cordoba
Seville
Granada
ANDALUS
Gibraltar
Ceuta
Antioch
MEDITERRANEAN SEA
Tripoli
Rhodes
Malta
Canary Islands
Jerusalem

Glossary

*An asterisk * refers to another entry*

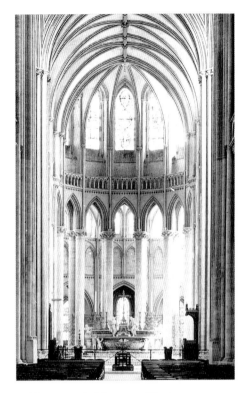

The east end of the apse of Coutances Cathedral, France.

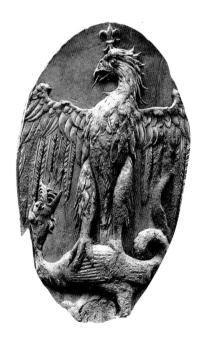

Stone relief in Florence showing the Guelph emblem.

altarpiece a painting standing on an altar and forming its back

apse semicircular or polygonal recess, especially at the east end of a church

Annunciation the announcement by Gabriel to the Virgin Mary that she was to become the mother of Jesus

Anti-Pope a pope not ultimately recognized as legitimate. From 1378 to 1417 (the so-called Great Schism) two rival factions within the Catholic Church each elected a pope who claimed to be the only authentic one. Seven of the claimants were declared unauthorized and are thus known as 'Anti-Popes'

Assumption the miracle by which the Virgin Mary was 'assumed' or taken up into heaven

baptistery part of a church, or a separate building, containing the font, where baptisms are carried out

campo literally, 'field'; an open space, or (as an abbreviation of *campo santo*) a cemetery

canonization the process by which the Catholic Church enrols a man or woman in the 'canon' or list of saints

capital the carved feature forming the top of a column, in classical architecture one of the main distinguishing elements of the order

chancel the part of the church, usually the east end, containing the altar and choir-stalls; the most sacred space of a church

chivalry a set of ideals and conventions about how knights should behave to each other and to ladies, pertaining to bravery, gallantry, honour and courtesy

clearstorey row of windows above the arcade of a basilican church

Corpus Christi literally, 'Christ's body'; a festival instituted in 1264 to celebrate the Real Presence of Christ in the Eucharist, according to the doctrine of *transubstantiation. By the 15th century this had become a major Church festival, involving a procession carrying the *host through the streets

diptych painting, generally an *altarpiece, in two parts

façade the front of a building

feudalism a term coined in the 19th century to describe the medieval hierarchy of power, by which every rank of society had legal obligations to the one above it, culminating in the king. Later historians have questioned whether the system was ever so clear-cut or universal as was once assumed

fresco literally, 'fresh'; a painting applied to a wall while the plaster is still wet, so that it becomes part of the surface

Guelphs (Guelfs) and Ghibellines supporters, respectively, of the Church and the Holy Roman Emperors. The conflict between the two parties dominated political life in Italy in the 13th and 14th centuries

guild a professional organization of craftsmen and merchants, analogous to a trade union, which governed conditions of entry and of work, and which operated as a monopoly. Guilds also performed charitable and social functions

host consecrated bread or wafer in the communion service

icon a picture or image which is the object of veneration

liturgy the prescribed order of a church service, comprising words and actions, especially the service used in the celebration and administration of the Eucharist

Lollard the name given to an English follower of John Wycliffe's popular heretical movement

Magna Carta charter of rights and feudal law issued by King John in June 1215, under compulsion from his barons

Marxism a theory, expounded by Karl Marx, that historical events can be explained in economic terms as the result of class conflicts, since the class that controls the means of production and distribution will exploit other classes and set the legal and moral codes of a society

mendicant literally, 'beggar'; a monastic order which in theory owns nothing and depends on charity

misericord bracket on a turn-up seat in a choir-stall, allowing worshippers some support when standing during long services

missal a book containing the complete service for mass throughout the year

nave the main body of a church, west of the *chancel, holding the congregation

nominalism a scholastic theory in which 'universals', i.e. abstract nouns like 'goodness' or 'beauty', are not real entities but only 'names'. The contrary theory is 'realism', which maintains the real existence of universals

oligarchy government by a small exclusive class

ontology the name given to the branch of philosophy that deals with the nature of being, i.e. reality in the abstract

Orthodox the Byzantine, later the Greek and the Russian branch of the Christian Church, which split from the Roman Church in 1054

paten communion plate or chalice-cover

Pietà the Virgin Mary with the dead Christ lying on her lap

pilaster square column that is partly built into, and partly projecting from, a wall

polyptych a painting, usually an *altarpiece, in several sections, often hinged so that the sections can be opened and closed

quatrefoil a shape with four lobes or cusps

relief sculpture which projects from the surface but is not fully three-dimensional

reliquary a container, usually of some precious metal, for the display of the relic of a saint or of Christ

reredos ornamental screen of stone or wood, built up or forming a facing to the wall behind a church altar. Reredoses are often decorated with scenes of the Passion or niches containing statues of saints

Resurrection Christ's return to life on the third day after his Crucifixion

sacrament ritual involving divine endorsement and therefore requiring the presence of a priest

sarcophagus stone coffin functioning as a tomb

scholasticism the characteristic intellectual method of medieval thinkers. Its foundation is logic, and its purpose the exposition and reconciliation of the Bible, the writings of the Church Fathers and classical philosophical texts, especially Aristotle, to create a unified system

transept part of a church at right angles to the *nave

Transfiguration on the top of a mountain Jesus appeared to his disciples with shining face and garments and with the prophets Moses and Elias at his side

transubstantiation the doctrine that the bread and wine of the Eucharist is changed by the priest's act of consecration into the body and blood of Christ; also called the Real Presence

Trinitarians a religious order founded in 1198 by St John of Matha and St Felix of Valois for the liberation of Christian prisoners and slaves from captivity under the Moors and Saracens

troubadour a poet and musician, especially in Southern France, who provided court entertainment and was influential in promoting the idea of courtly love

tympanum space between a lintel and an arch above it

vault a stone roof; either continuous (tunnel vault) or divided into bays or sections (groined or ribbed vault)

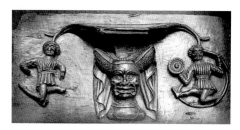

Misericord *from the stalls of St Lawrence, Ludlow, England: boys mocking an ugly lady.*

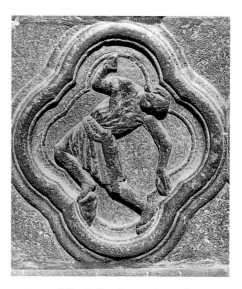

Quatrefoil *relief on the west front of Amiens Cathedral, France: the sin of despair.*

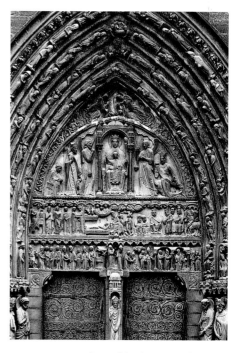

Tympanum *of one of the doorways of the Cathedral of Notre-Dame, Paris.*

Glossary 321

Bibliography

General

Aston, Margaret, *The Fifteenth Century*, London, 1968
Barber, Malcolm, *The Two Cities: Medieval Europe 1050–1320*, London, 1992
Bartlett, Robert, *The Making of Europe: Conquest, Colonization and Cultural Change 950–1350*, Harmondsworth, 1993
Bloch, Marc, *Feudal Society*, Eng. tr., Chicago, 1961
Brooke, Christopher, *Europe in the Central Middle Ages*, London, 1964
Evans, Joan (ed.), *The Flowering of the Middle Ages*, London, 1969
Hay, Denys, *Europe in the Fourteenth and Fifteenth Centuries*, London, 1966
Holmes, George (ed.), *The Oxford Illustrated History of Medieval Europe*, Oxford, 1988
Huizinga, Johan, *Autumn of the Middle Ages*, Eng. tr., Chicago, 1996
Le Goff, Jacques, *Medieval Civilization 400–1500*, Eng. tr., Oxford, 1989
Loyn, H. R. (ed.), *The Middle Ages: A Concise Encyclopedia*, London, 1991
Mundy, John, *Europe in the High Middle Ages*, 2nd ed., London, 1973
The New Cambridge Medieval History, Cambridge, 1995
Southern, Richard W., *The Making of the Middle Ages*, London and New Haven, 1953

1. Prologue: What Made the Middle Ages?

Brown, Peter, *The Rise of Western Christendom*, Oxford, 1996
———, *The World of Late Antiquity*, London, 1971
Bullough, Donald A., *The Age of Charlemagne*, 2nd ed., London, 1973
Campbell, James (ed.), *The Anglo-Saxons*, Oxford, 1982
Curtius, Ernst Robert, *European Literature and the Latin Middle Ages*, Eng. tr., London, 1953
Folz, Robert, *The Concept of Empire in Western Europe from the Fifth to the Fourteenth Century*, Eng. tr., London, 1969
Gibson, Margaret (ed.), *Boethius: His Life, Thought and Influence*, Oxford, 1981
Herrin, Judith, *The Formation of Christendom*, Princeton, 1987
McKitterick, Rosamond (ed.), *Carolingian Culture: Emulation and Innovation*, Cambridge, 1994
Sawyer, P. H., *The Age of the Vikings*, 2nd ed., London, 1971
——— (ed.), *The Oxford Illustrated History of the Vikings*, Oxford, 1997

Wallace-Hadrill, J. M., *The Barbarian West 400–1000*, London, 1952, rev. 1967
———, *Early Germanic Kingship in England and on the Continent*, Oxford, 1971
Whittow, Mark, *The Making of Orthodox Byzantium, 600–1025*, Basingstoke, 1996

2. Salvation of the Soul

Barlow, Frank, *Thomas Becket*, London, 1986
Barraclough, Geoffrey, *The Medieval Papacy*, London, 1968
Brooke, Rosalind and Christopher, *Popular Religion in the Middle Ages*, London, 1984
Bynum, Caroline Walker, *Holy Feast and Holy Fast: The Religious Significance of Food to Medieval Women*, Berkeley, 1986
———, *The Resurrection of the Body in Western Christianity*, New York, 1994
Constable, Giles, *The Reformation of the Twelfth Century*, Cambridge, 1996
Finucane, Ronald C., *Miracles and Pilgrims: Popular Beliefs in Medieval England*, London, 1977
Geary, Patrick, *Living with the Dead in the Middle Ages*, Ithaca, 1994
Hamilton, Bernard, *The Medieval Inquisition*, London, 1981
———, *Religion in the Medieval West*, London, 1986
Knowles, David, *The Monastic Order in England*, Cambridge, 1940, rev. ed.
Lambert, Malcolm, *Medieval Heresy*, 2nd ed., Oxford, 1992
Maxwell-Stuart, P. G., *Chronicle of the Popes*, London, 1997
Moore, R. I., *The Formation of a Persecuting Society: Power and Deviance in Western Europe, 950–1250*, Oxford, 1987
Moorman, J. R. H., *A History of the Franciscan Order*, Oxford, 1968
Morris, Colin, *The Papal Monarchy: The Western Church from 1050 to 1250*, Oxford, 1989
Pelikan, Jaroslav, *The Christian Tradition: A History of the Development of Doctrine*, 5 vols., Chicago, 1971–89
Robinson, Ian S., *The Papacy 1073–1198: Continuity and Innovation*, Cambridge, 1990
Southern, Richard W., *Western Society and the Church in the Middle Ages*, Harmondsworth, 1970
Sumption, Jonathan, *Pilgrimage: An Image of Medieval Religion*, London, 1975
Vauchez, André, *Sainthood in the Late Middle Ages*, Eng. tr., Cambridge, 1997
Ward, Benedicta, *Miracles and the Medieval Mind: Theory, Record and Event 1000–1215*, Aldershot and Philadelphia, 1982

3. Earthly Powers

Abulafia, David, *Frederick II: A Medieval Emperor*, London, 1988
Allmand, C. T., *The Hundred Years War: England and France at War, c.1300–c.1450*, Cambridge, 1988
Arnold, Benjamin, *German Knighthood 1050–1300*, Oxford, 1985
Baldwin, John W., *The Government of Philip Augustus*, Berkeley and Los Angeles, 1986
Barrow, Geoffrey, *Kingship and Unity: Scotland 1000–1306*, London, 1981
Bartlett, Robert, *England under the Norman and Angevin Kings 1075–1225*, Oxford, 2000
Bisson, T. N., *The Medieval Crown of Aragon: A Short History*, Oxford, 1986
Clanchy, Michael, *England and Its Rulers 1066–1272*, London, 1983
Contamine, Philippe, *War in the Middle Ages*, Eng. tr., Oxford, 1984
Davies, Rees, *Domination and Conquest: The Experience of Ireland, Scotland and Wales 1100–1300*, Cambridge, 1990
Duby, Georges, *The Chivalrous Society*, London and Berkeley, 1977
Dunbabin, Jean, *Charles I of Anjou: Power, Kingship and State-making in Thirteenth-Century Europe*, London, 1998
Duncan, A. A. M., *Scotland: The Making of the Kingdom*, Edinburgh, 1975
Frame, Robin, *The Political Development of the British Isles 1100–1400*, Oxford, 1990
Gillingham, John, *The Angevin Empire*, London, 1984
Guenée, Bernard, *States and Rulers in Later Medieval Europe*, Eng. tr., Oxford, 1985
Hallam, E. M., *Capetian France*, London, 1980
Holt, J. C., *Magna Carta*, 2nd ed., Cambridge, 1992
Kantorowicz, Ernst, *Frederick II, 1194–1250*, Eng. tr., London, 1931
Keen, Maurice, *Chivalry*, New Haven and London, 1984
Larner, John, *Italy in the Age of Dante and Petrarch 1216–1380*, London, 1980
Le Patourel, John, *The Norman Empire*, Oxford, 1976
Matthew, Donald, *The Norman Kingdom of Sicily*, Cambridge, 1992
Miller, William, *Bloodtaking and Peacemaking: Feud, Law and Society in Saga Iceland*, Chicago, 1990
Prestwich, Michael, *The Three Edwards: War and State in England, 1272–1377*, London, 1980
Reuter, Timothy, *Germany in the Early Middle Ages, 800–1056*, London, 1991

Reynolds, Susan, *Kingdoms and Communities in Western Europe, 900–1300*, 2nd ed., Oxford, 1997
Strayer, Joseph R., *On the Medieval Origins of the Modern State*, Princeton, 1970
Waley, Daniel, *The Italian City Republics*, London, 1969

4. The Legacy of Medieval Art

Baur, Julius, *German Cathedrals*, London, 1956
Beckwith, John, *Early Medieval Art*, London, 1983
Binski, Paul, *Westminster Abbey and the Plantagenets: Kingship and the Representation of Power, 1200–1400*, London, 1995
Bony, Jean, *French Cathedrals*, London, 1951
——, *French Gothic Architecture of the 12th and 13th Centuries*, Berkeley, 1983
Branner, Robert, *Chartres Cathedral*, London, 1969
Busch, Harald, *Deutsche Gotik*, Vienna, 1969
——, *Germania Romanica*, Vienna, 1967
Camille, Michael, *Gothic Art: Visions and Revelations of the Medieval World*, London, 1996
——, *The Gothic Idol: Ideology and Image-making in Medieval Art*, Cambridge, 1989
——, *Image on the Edge: The Margins of Medieval Art*, London, 1992
Conant, Kenneth, *Carolingian and Romanesque Architecture, 800 to 1200*, 4th ed., Harmondsworth, 1992
Decker, H., *Italie Gothique*, Paris, 1964
——, *Romanesque Art in Italy*, London, 1960
Dodwell, C. R., *The Pictorial Arts of the West 800–1200*, London, 1993
Erlande-Brandenburg, Alain, *Cathedral Builders of the Middle Ages*, London, 1995
Gantner, J. and M. Pobé, *Romanesque Art in France*, London, 1956
Gimpel, Jean, *The Cathedral Builders*, London, 1983
Hurlimann, Martin, *English Cathedrals*, London, 1961
Kahn, Walter, *Romanesque Bible Illumination*, Ithaca, NY, 1983
Lasko, Peter, *Ars Sacra, 800–1200*, Harmondsworth, 1972
Mâle, Emile, *The Gothic Image*, London, 1910
Martindale, Andrew, *Gothic Art*, London, 1967
Mentré, Mireille, *Illuminated Manuscripts of Medieval Spain*, London, 1996
Nussbaum, Norbert, *German Gothic Church Architecture*, London, 2000
Salzman, L. F., *Building in England down to 1540*, London, 1952

Sauerländer, Willibald, *Gothic Sculpture in France, 1140–1270*, London, 1972
Saul, Nigel (ed.), *Age of Chivalry: Art and Society in Late Medieval England*, London, 1992
Stalley, Roger, *Early Medieval Architecture*, Oxford, 1999
White, John, *Art and Architecture in Italy, 1250–1400*, London, 1993
Williamson, Paul, *Gothic Sculpture 1140–1300*, London, 1995
Wilson, Christopher, *The Gothic Cathedral: The Architecture of the Great Church, 1130–1530*, London, 1990
Zarnecki, George, *Romanesque Art*, London, 1971

5. Everyday Life

Brundage, James, *Law, Sex and Christian Society in Medieval Europe*, Chicago, 1987
Dobson, R. B. (ed.), *The Peasants' Revolt of 1381*, London, 1970
Dollinger, Philippe, *The German Hansa*, Eng. tr., London, 1970
Duby, Georges, *Rural Economy and Country Life in the Medieval West*, Eng. tr., London, 1968
Dyer, Christopher, *Standards of Living in the Later Middle Ages: Social Change in England c. 1200–1520*, Cambridge, 1989
Hanawalt, Barbara A., *The Ties that Bound: Peasant Families in Medieval England*, New York, 1986
Herlihy, David, and Christiane Klapisch-Zuber, *Tuscans and their Families: a Study of the Florentine Catasto of 1427*, London, 1985
Homans, G. C., *English Villagers of the Thirteenth Century*, Cambridge, Mass., 1941, repr. NY
Jewell, Helen, *Women in Medieval England*, Manchester, 1996
Lennard, Reginald, *Rural England, 1086–1135: A Study of Social and Agrarian Conditions*, Oxford, 1959
Lopez, Robert S., *The Commercial Revolution of the Middle Ages, 950–1350*, rev. ed., Cambridge, 1976
Mackenney, Richard, *Tradesmen and Traders: The World of the Guilds in Venice and Europe c. 1250–c. 1650*, London, 1987
Maitland, Frederic W., *Domesday Book and Beyond*, Cambridge, 1897, repr. 1988
Postan, M. M. (ed.), *The Cambridge Economic History of Europe 1: The Agrarian Life of the Middle Ages*, 2nd ed., Cambridge, 1966
——, and Edward Miller (eds), *The Cambridge Economic History of Europe 2: Trade and Industry in the Middle Ages*, 2nd ed., Cambridge, 1987
Reynolds, Susan, *An Introduction to the*

History of English Medieval Towns, Oxford, 1970

Siraisi, Nancy G., *Medieval and Early Renaissance Medicine*, Chicago, 1990

Spufford, Peter, *Money and its Use in Medieval Europe*, Cambridge, 1988

Ziegler, Philip, *The Black Death*, 2nd ed., Harmondsworth, 1998

6. The Life of the Mind

Baldwin, John W., *The Scholastic Culture of the Middle Ages, 1000–1300*, Lexington, 1971

Benson, Robert, and Giles Constable (eds), *Renaissance and Renewal in the Twelfth Century*, Cambridge, Mass. and Oxford, 1982

Burns, J. H. (ed.), *The Cambridge History of Medieval Political Thought*, Cambridge, 1988

Burrow, J. A., *Medieval Writers and Their Work : Middle English Literature and Its Background 1100–1500*, Oxford, 1982

Clanchy, Michael, *Abelard: A Medieval Life*, Oxford, 1997

——, *From Memory to Written Record: England 1066–1307*, 2nd ed., Oxford and Cambridge, Mass., 1993

Copleston, F. C., *Aquinas*, Harmondsworth, 1955

Dronke, Peter, *The Medieval Lyric*, 2nd ed., Cambridge, 1977

——, *Women Writers of the Middle Ages*, Cambridge and New York, 1984

—— (ed.), *History of Twelfth-century Western Philosophy*, Cambridge, 1988

Gaunt, Simon, and Sarah Kay (eds), *The Troubadours: An Introduction*, Cambridge, 1999

Haskins, Charles Homer, *The Renaissance of the Twelfth Century*, Cambridge, Mass., 1927

Hassig, Debra , *Medieval Bestiaries: Text, Image, Ideology*, Cambridge, 1995

Jaeger, C. Stephen, *The Origins of Courtliness: Civilizing Trends and the Formation of Courtly Ideals, 939–1210*, Philadelphia, 1985

Kenny, Anthony, *Aquinas*, Oxford, 1980

Kretzmann, Norman, Anthony Kenny and Jan Pinborg (eds), *Cambridge History of Later Medieval Philosophy*, Cambridge, 1982

Lewis, C. S., *The Discarded Image*, Cambridge, 1964

Murray, Alexander, *Reason and Society in the Middle Ages*, Oxford, 1978

Smalley, Beryl, *Historians in the Middle Ages*, London, 1974

——, *The Study of the Bible in the Middle Ages*, 3rd ed., Oxford, 1983

Southern, Richard W., *Medieval Humanism and Other Studies*, Oxford, 1970

7. Christians and Non-Christians

Barber, Malcolm, *The New Knighthood: A History of the Order of the Temple*, Cambridge, 1994

Burns, Robert I., *The Crusader Kingdom of Valencia: Reconstruction on a Thirteenth-Century Frontier*, 2 vols., Cambridge, Mass., 1967

Chazan, Robert, *European Jewry and the First Crusade*, Berkeley, 1987

Christiansen, Eric, *The Northern Crusades*, London, 1980

Ellenblum, Ronnie, *Frankish Rural Settlement in the Latin Kingdom of Jerusalem*, Cambridge, 1998

Fletcher, Richard, *The Conversion of Europe: From Paganism to Christianity 371–1386*, London, 1997

——, *The Quest for El Cid*, London, 1989

Hamilton, Bernard, *The Crusades*, Stroud, 1998

Jordan, William C., *The French Monarchy and the Jews: From Philip Augustus to the Last Capetians*, Philadelphia, 1989

Kennedy, Hugh, *Muslim Spain and Portugal: a Political History of Al-Andalus*, London, 1996

Lomax, Derek W., *The Reconquest of Spain*, London, 1978

MacKay, Angus, *Spain in the Middle Ages: From Frontier to Empire, 1000–1500*, London, 1977

Mayer, Hans Eberhard, *The Crusades*, Eng. tr., 2nd ed., Oxford, 1988

Prawer, Joshua, *The Latin Kingdom of Jerusalem: European Colonialism in the Middle Ages*, London, 1972

Pryor, John H., *Geography, Technology and War: Studies in the Maritime History of the Mediterranean, 649–1571*, Cambridge, 1988

Richard, Jean, *The Crusades*, Eng. tr., Cambridge, 1999

——, *The Latin Kingdom of Jerusalem*, 2 vols., Eng. tr., Amsterdam, etc., 1979

Richardson, H. G., *The English Jewry under Angevin Kings*, London, 1960

Riley-Smith, Jonathan (ed.), *Atlas of the Crusades*, London, 1991

——, *The Crusades: A Short History*, New Haven, 1987

—— (ed.) *The Oxford Illustrated History of the Crusades*, Oxford, 1995

Runciman, Steven, *A History of the Crusades*, 3 vols., Cambridge, 1951–54

Setton, Kenneth M. (ed.), *A History of the Crusades*, Philadelphia and Madison, 6 vols., 1955–89

Smail, R. C., *Crusading Warfare, 1097–1193*, Cambridge, 1956

Spiegel, Gabrielle, *Romancing the Past: The Rise of Vernacular Prose Historiography in Thirteenth-century France*, Berkeley, 1993

Southern, Richard W., *Western Views of Islam in the Middle Ages*, Cambridge, Mass., 1962

Stow, Kenneth R., *Alienated Minority: The Jews of Medieval Latin Europe*, Cambridge, Mass., 1992

8. Epilogue: The End of the Middle Ages

Elliot, John , *The Old World and the New, 1492–1650*, Cambridge, 1970

Febvre, Lucien, *The Coming of the Book: The Impact of Printing, 1450–1800*, Eng. tr., London, 1076

Goodman, Anthony, and Angus MacKay (eds), *The Impact of Humanism on Western Europe*, London, 1990

Hale, J. R., *Renaissance Europe 1480–1520*, London, 1971

Mandrou, Robert, *From Humanism to Science, 1480–1700*, Eng. tr., Harmondsworth, 1978

Ozment, Steven, *The Age of Reform, 1250–1550*, New Haven, 1980

Phillips, J. R. S., *The Medieval Expansion of Europe*, Oxford, 1988

Thomas, Keith, *Religion and the Decline of Magic*, London, 1971

Websites

There are a vast number of World Wide Websites dedicated to the Middle Ages. Every aspect of the period is covered, from iron and steel production, through courtly love and kingship, to costume and recipes. Below is a listing of some of the most useful and interesting sites. The publishers can take no responsibility for the sites' contents, nor does the listing serve as a company endorsement.

http://argos.evansville.edu/
Argos: Ancient World Database
Outstanding search engine devoted to sites containing information on ancient and medieval history

http://eawc.evansville.edu/mepage.htm
Exploring Ancient World Cultures: Medieval Europe Homepage
Site based at the University of Evansville, containing a thorough chronology of major cross-cultural events in medieval history

http://ebbs.english.vt.edu/medieval/medieval.ebbs.html
Privately maintained site containing useful, basic information about academic discussion lists, and links to other medieval resources: databases, archives, libraries and mailing lists, and texts from and about the period

http://encarta.msn.com/find/Concise.asp?z=1&pg=2&ti=06994000
Mine the Middle Ages (Encarta Encyclopedia)
General overview of the Middle Ages with articles on topics including 'The Carolingian world and its breakup', 'The Central Middle Ages: An Age of Growth' and 'The Late Middle Ages: Crisis and Renewal'

http://members.aol.com/McNelis/Medsci/hunting.html
Privately maintained website with comprehensive set of links to all websites containing information on medieval hunting and falconry, including a listing of museums with collections devoted to the history of hunting, falconry and/or fishing

http://orb.rhodes.edu/
ORB: On-Line Reference Book for Medieval Studies
Excellent online textbook for medieval studies produced by medieval scholars across the Internet
See also:
http://www.fordham.edu/halsall/sbook.html
(part of ORB) Internet Medieval Sourcebook
Based at Fordham University Center for Medieval Studies, New York, and specifically designed for teachers to use in teaching, this

invaluable collaborative collection of resources includes an index of a wide range of selected and excerpted texts on topics including governmental, legal, religious and economic concerns, as well as social, women's and gender history, and Islamic, Byzantine and Jewish history

http://scholar.chem.nyu.edu
The Medieval Technology Timeline
Hosted by New York University, this site offers a timeline of technological advances and population growth in the Middle Ages and includes detailed information about technologies

http://sunsite.berkeley.edu/OMACL/
The Online Medieval and Classical Library
Part of the Berkeley Digital Library, this site contains online versions of many medieval and classical texts

http://users.erols.com/zenithco/Intro13.html
Privately maintained site containing information on translators and promulgators of scientific knowledge in the Middle Ages

http://www.georgetown.edu/labyrinth/labyrinth-home.html
The Labyrinth
Based at Georgetown University, this superb site provides a comprehensive list of links to a variety of Internet resources for medieval studies, as well as bibliographies and online forums

http://www.godecookery.com/godeboke/godeboke.htm
'A Boke of Gode Cookery' is a privately maintained site offering tips on cooking authentic medieval dishes. Recipes in the original Middle English, with translations in modern English

http://www.harbrace.com/art/gardner/Med.html
Gateway to Art History, compiled for use with Gardner's Art Through the Ages
Harcourt College Publishers' Art History Resources on the Web
Early medieval art in the West, including the Book of Kells, treasures of Sutton Hoo and wooden stave church design

http://www.learner.org/exhibits/middleages/
Annenberg/CPB Exhibits Project
Information on daily life in the Middle Ages – feudalism, religion, homes, clothing, health, arts, entertainment and town life – plus a bibliography and links to related sites

http://www.millersv.edu/~english/homepage/duncan/medfem/medfem.html
Women Writers of the Middle Ages

Based at the English Department, Millersville University, this site contains information on writers such as Julian of Norwich, Hildegard of Bingen and Margery Kempe, as well as lesser-known figures

http://www.msu.edu/~georgem1/history/medieval.htm
The WWW Virtual Library
Excellent list of on-line references maintained by The Michigan State University Graduate Student Medieval and Renaissance Consortium, under the sponsorship of ORB, for The World Wide Web Virtual Library History Section: a history index of medieval Europe with links to hundreds of information sites, covering every aspect of the Middle Ages, from arms and armour to Gregorian chant

http://www.netserf.org/
NetSERF: The Internet Connection for Medieval Studies
Research centre plus links to sites relating to medieval archaeology, architecture, art, Arthuriana, civilizations, culture, drama, history, law, literature, music, people, philosophy, religion, science, technology and women

http://www.pbm.com/~lindahl/dance.html
SCA (Society for Creative Anachronism) Dance Homepage
Information on 15th-century dances, including step-by-step choreography

http://www.personal.utulsa.edu/~marc-carlson/shoe/SHOEHOME.HTM
Privately maintained comprehensive site on every aspect of medieval footwear

http://www.pitt.edu/~medart/
Privately maintained site aiming to promote education and research in medieval art and architecture

http://www.s-hamilton.k12.ia.us/antiqua/instrumt.html
Privately maintained site offering pictures, descriptions and recordings of musical instruments from the Middle Ages

http://www.ucalgary.ca/HIST/tutor/endmiddle/
The End of Europe's Middle Ages
'Tutorial' from the University of Calgary containing illustrated texts on topics including economy, feudal institutions, monarchy, the Holy Roman Empire, Italy's city-states, Eastern Europe, Ottoman Turks, the Church, literature, intellectual life, visual arts and music.

List of Illustrations

3. Earthly Powers

Index

Page numbers in *italic* refer to illustrations